Exploring Books
with Children

Iris M. Tiedt

Exploring Books with Children

96519

HOUGHTON MIFFLIN COMPANY   BOSTON

Atlanta   Dallas   Geneva, Ill.   Hopewell, N.J.   Palo Alto   London

Library of Congress Catalog Card Number: 78-69530

ISBN: 0-395-25498-1

Credits

Lloyd Alexander. Excerpt from *The Cat Who Wished to Be a Man* by Lloyd Alexander. Copyright © 1973 by Lloyd Alexander. Reprinted by permission of the publishers, E. P. Dutton.   **William H. Armstrong.** Excerpt from *Sounder* by William H. Armstrong. Text copyright © 1969 by William H. Armstrong. By permission of Harper & Row, Publishers, Inc.   **Joseph Auslander.** "A Blackbird Suddenly" from *Sunrise Trumpets* by Joseph Auslander. Copyright, 1924, by Harper & Row, Publishers, Inc. Renewed, 1952, by Joseph Auslander. By permission of Harper & Row, Publishers, Inc.   **Mary Austin.** "A Song of Greatness" from *The Children Sing in the Far West* by Mary Austin. Copyright 1928 by Mary Austin, renewed 1956 by Kenneth Chapman and Mary C. Wheelwright. Reprinted by permission of Houghton Mifflin Company.   **Natalie Babbitt.** Excerpt from *The Horn Book,* April, 1974. Reprinted by permission of The Hour Book, Inc.   **Rhoda Bacmeister.** "Galoshes" from *Stories to Begin On* by Rhoda Bacmeister. Copyright 1940 by E. P. Dutton & Co.; renewal © 1968 by Rhoda Bacmeister. Reprinted by permission of the publishers, E. P. Dutton & Co., Inc.   **Nina Bawden.** Excerpt from *The Peppermint Pig* by Nina Bawden. Copyright © 1975 by Nina Bawden. Reprinted by permission of J. B. Lippincott Company.   **Harry Behn.** Excerpt from *Faraway Lurs.* Reprinted by permission of the William Collins and World Publishing Co., from *The Faraway Lurs* by Harry Behn. Copyright © 1963 by Harry Behn.   **Hilaire Belloc.** "The Frog" from *Cautionary Verses,* by Hilaire Belloc. Published 1941 by Alfred A. Knopf, Inc.   **Rowena Bennett.** "Motor Cars" and "A Modern Dragon" from *Songs from Around a Toadstool Table* by Rowena Bennett. Copyright © 1967 by Rowena Bennett. Used by permission of Follett Publishing Company, a division of Follett Corporation. Excerpt from "The Witch of Willowby Wood," from *The Reading of Poetry,* Lyons et al., eds. Follett Publishing Company, 1963. Reprinted by permission of Kenneth C. Bennett, Jr.   **Evelyn Beyer.** "Jump or Jiggle" from *Another Here and Now Story Book* by Lucy Sprague Mitchell. Copyright 1937 by E. P. Dutton & Co.; renewal © 1965 by Lucy Sprague Mitchell. Reprinted by permission of the publishers, E. P. Dutton & Co., Inc.   **Gwendolyn Brooks Blakely.** "Rudolph Is Tired of the City" from *Bronzeville Boys and Girls* by Gwendolyn Brooks. Copyright © 1956 by Gwendolyn Brooks Blakely. By permission of Harper & Row, Publishers, Inc.   **Lucy Boston.** Excerpt from *The Children of Green Knowe.* Harcourt Brace Jovanovich, Inc., 1954.   **Franz Brandenberg.** Excerpt from *A Robber! A Robber!* Greenwillow Books, William Morrow & Company, 1976.   **Virginia Brasier.** "Wind Weather" in *Stories and Verses for Children,* comp. by Miriam Huber. Macmillan, 1955. Reprinted by permission of Virginia Brasier.   **Betsy Byars.** Excerpt from *The Summer of the Swans* by Betsy Byars. Copyright © 1970 by Betsy Byars. Reprinted by permission of The Viking Press.   **Bliss Carman.** Excerpt from "A Vagabond Song" from *Poems* by Bliss Carman. Reprinted by permission of Dodd, Mead & Company.   **Rosemary Carr and Stephen Vincent Benet.** Excerpts from "Abraham Lincoln" and "USA" in *Book of Americans,* Brandt & Brandt, 1952. Reprinted by permission of Brandt & Brandt.   **Guy Wetmore Carryl.** "The Embarrassing Episode of Little Miss Muffett" by Guy Wetmore Carryl. Reprinted by permission of Houghton Mifflin Company.   **Ann Nolan Clark.** Excerpt from *Circle of Seasons* by Ann Nolan Clark, illustrated by W. T. Mars, Copyright © 1970 by Ann Nolan Clark. Reprinted by permission of Farrar, Straus & Giroux, Inc.   **Vera and Bill Cleaver.** Excerpt from *Where the Lilies Bloom* by Vera and William J. Cleaver. Copyright © 1969 by Vera and William J. Cleaver. Reprinted by permission of J. B. Lippincott Company.   **Lucille Clifton.** "Monday Morning Good Morning" from *Some of the Days of Everett Anderson* by Lucille Clifton. Copyright © 1970 by Lucille Clifton. Reprinted by permission of Holt, Rinehart and Winston, Publishers.   **Elizabeth Coatsworth.** "Down the Rain Falls." Reprinted with permission of Macmillan Publishing Co., Inc., from *Five Bushel Farm* by Elizabeth Coatsworth. Copyright 1939 by Macmillan Publishing Co., Inc., renewed 1967 by Elizabeth Coatsworth Beston. "He Who Has Never Known Hunger." Reprinted with permission of Macmillan Publishing Co., Inc., from *The Fair American* by Elizabeth Coatsworth. Copyright 1940 by Macmillan Publishing Co., Inc., renewed 1968 by Elizabeth Coatsworth Beston. "Poem of Praise." Reprinted with permission of Macmillan Publishing Co., Inc., from *Away Goes Sally* by Elizabeth Coatsworth. Copyright 1934 by Macmillan Publishing Co., Inc., renewed 1962 by Elizabeth Coatsworth Beston.   **Hilda Conkling.** "Water," "Dandelion," and "Mouse" from *Poems by a Little Girl,*

Contents

Preface   xiii

1 ❦ *Who's There? Open the Door!*
EXPLORING CHILDREN'S BOOKS   2

Introduction to Children's Books 4 / *Old Favorites* / *Meeting Authors and Illustrators* / *Assessing New Books That Show Promise* / Children, Literature, and Adults 16 / *What Is Children's Literature?* / *Adults and Children's Books* / Planning Classroom Experiences 19 / *The Art of Reading Aloud* / *Aids to Planning Instruction* / *Games and Literature*

2 ❦ *When We Were Very Young*
EVERY CHILD'S LITERARY HERITAGE   30

Browsing in the Picture Book Section 33 / *Criteria for Illustration and Content* / *The Keys to the Kingdom: Nursery Rhymes* / *Alphabet Books* / *Counting Books* / *Books About Animals* / *Fanciful Fun in Picture Books* / *Illustrated Folktales* / *The Realities of Life* / *Search for Information* / Creating Books for Young Children 58 / *Outstanding Books* / *Introducing Authors and Illustrators* / Teaching with Picture Books 70 / *Stimulating Creativity* / *Wordless Books* / *Sharing Books* / *The Controversial Monsters* / *Avoiding the Stereotyped Image* / *Realism for Young Children*

3 ❦ *Roads Go Ever Ever On*
FANCIFUL TALES FOR CHILDREN   84

An Overview of Fantasy for Children 86 / *Characteristics of Outstanding Fantasy* / *Fanciful Tales About Animals* / *Fantasy About "Human Beans"* / Fantasy Worlds 116 / *Discovering Narnia* / *Visiting Middle Earth* / *Traveling to Prydain* / Science Fiction 123 / *Teaching Fantasy 129* / *Outstanding Fantasies* / *Contemporary Authors of Fantasy* / *Two Novels to Teach*

4 ❦ *What Is Real?*

REALISTIC PERSPECTIVES OF LIFE FOR CHILDREN   144

Children and Interpersonal Relations 148 / *Developing Self-Awareness* / *The Need for Family* / *Peer Relationships* / Understanding Others 168 / *American Women Today* / *The Aged Person* / *Native Americans* / *Mexican-Americans or Chicanos* / Realistic Perspectives for the Classroom 196 / *In Praise of Authors* / *Teaching a Novel* / *Breaking Down Stereotypes*

5 ❦ *The Sun Is a Golden Earring*

THE UNIVERSAL AND TRADITIONAL IN LITERATURE   214

The Fable 217 / Mirror, Mirror on the Wall 221 / *Discovering the Folktale* / *The Cumulative Tale* / *The Fairytale* / *Drolls: Realistic Tales* / *Folktales From Many Countries* / *The Folktales of Russia* / In the Land of the Gods 246 / *Pourquoi Tales* / *The Mythology of Greece* / *Norse Gods and Giants* / The Great Heroes 256 / *Robin Hood* / *King Arthur* / Storytelling 262 / *Choosing A Story* / *Telling the Story* / *Student Story Tellers*

6 ❦ *Be Like the Bird*

EXPLORING POETRY WITH CHILDREN   268

Exploring Poetry 271 / *What Is Poetry?* / *What Poetry Communicates* / *The Language of Poetry* / *Forms of Poetry* / *Poets Are People* / Poetry in Classrooms 307 / *Poetry Related to Themes* / *Speaking Poetry* / *Children Can Read Poems* / *Children Write Poetry*

7 ❦ *Come Read with Me*

TEACHING READING WITH TRADE BOOKS   324

Developing a Literature Program 326 / *Why Include Literature?* / *Teaching Literature and Reading* / *Placing Literature in the Curriculum* / *Planning a Scope and Sequence for Literature* / *Selecting Books for a Literature Program* / Inviting Children to Read 343 / *Oral Foundation for Reading* / *Developing a Reading Environment* / *Scheduling Time for Reading* / *Displaying Books*

8 ❦ *The Many Ways of Seeing*

READING FOR INFORMATION   374

Studying the English Language 377 / Selected Science Topics 382 / *Down to the Sea* / *Animal Life* / *Ecology: Struggle for Survival* / *The How-To Book* / Books for Special Days 399 / *Other Religious Holidays* / *Sources of General Information* / Creating a Learning Module 410 / *Living in the City*

9 ❦ *They Were Strong and Good*
LITERATURE FOR THE SOCIAL STUDIES 426

The Growth of Our Country 430 / *The American Revolution* / *The Mississippi River* / *Black Americans* / *Historical Novels* / Great Americans 445 / *Focusing on One Person* / *Focusing on a Theme* / Teaching the Social Studies with Trade Books 456 / *The Area Study* / *A Contemporary Problems Approach*

10 ❦ *Nobody is Perfick*
NEW AND OLD DIRECTIONS IN CHILDREN'S LITERATURE 466

Issues and Directions in Children's Literature 468 / *Realism in Children's Books* / *Adult Dominance of Children's Literature* / *Combating Stereotyping in Children's Books* / *Films and Recordings of Children's Literature* / Research in the Field of Children's Literature 478 / *Reading Interests* / *Language and Reading Abilities* / *Teaching Literature* / *Poetry in the Elementary School* / *Effect of Television* / *Selected Research References* / The Development of Children's Literature 490 / *Early Antecedents* / *Eighteenth-Century Developments* / *The Nineteenth Century* / *Children's Books in the Twentieth Century* / *What of the Future?*

Appendix 504

Awards Given to Children's Books / *The Caldecott Award* / *The Newbery Award* / *Directory of Sources* /

Index 535

Color Section following page 80

Preface

Books for children are meant to be enjoyed; they are meant to be shared. Nothing is more rewarding than sharing a book with a child—the colorful illustrations of Brian Wildsmith, the fantasy of Lloyd Alexander, the exciting realism of Norma Klein. Through books you can invite children to explore; you can "help children to wonder" as Rachel Carson urges us to do:

If I had influence with the good fairy who is supposed to preside over the christening of all children I should ask that her gift to each child be a sense of wonder so indestructible that it would last throughout life, an unfailing antidote against the boredom and disenchantments of later years, the sterile preoccupation with things that are artificial, the alienation from the sources of our strength.

Exploring Books with Children has been prepared for you—teacher, librarian, parent—who want to know more about books for children. This text is designed to meet the following objectives:

Provide an overview of children's literature and its development, emphasizing contemporary materials

Recognize current trends in education that affect what is published and how literature is used in the classroom.

Encourage students of children's literature not only to read *about* books, but also to read the books themselves

Present specific strategies and skills that will aid a teacher in using literature as an integral part of the elementary school curriculum

This balanced introduction to literature for children focuses on contemporary books and their place in elementary school classrooms. We all need information about content or "what" to teach, but we also need specific suggestions about "how" to bring literature and children together. In each chapter, therefore, you will find ideas for teaching—storytelling, reader's theater, literature games, learning centers, teaching modules, creative drama, and many more. Three chapters focus directly on literature in the elementary curriculum in the areas of reading, social studies, and other subjects such as science and the study of language.

In discussing various topics, it should be noted, there is no intent to organize this book by specific literary genres, so that you will find poetry and biography included in Chapter 4, "Realistic Perspectives of Life for Children," as a means of understanding people of different cultures, for realism is not limited to fiction. Biography, historical fiction, and nonfiction are also presented in Chapter 9, which suggests ways of using trade books to teach social science concepts. A form or genre approach to children's literature is not appropriate to working in elementary classrooms where we should integrate the breadth of literature available to us as we explore the world with children.

Outstanding features of this text that you will find especially helpful include the discussion of stereotyping, the problems facing American women, and teaching for liberation. A timely related topic that has yet to be thoroughly explored is the relationship of children to aged persons in our society and their learning to cope with such a concept as death. Throughout this book there is an emphasis also on the authors who write for children, because young readers should be familiar with their names and what each one has to offer. Stress is placed, too, on your reading as many books as possible as you consider how these books can be used with children in classrooms.

The development of the chapters on focused topics facilitates study of each subject independently. The objectives are clearly spelled out, followed by specific activities that encourage exploration, preparation of teaching aids, and experimentation. The final chapter presents a brief historical overview of the development of literature for children as well as information about related research and a discussion of contemporary issues in the field. This information is presented at the end of the book rather than the beginning so that you will know the literature and the issues involved before reading this summary.

Classroom time can be used in a number of ways. Your class may wish to try some of these activities:

Hear lectures on specific topics designed to enrich independent investigation

Have small group discussions of topics under study

Explore questions that arise from the group

Schedule individual conferences with the instructor to evaluate progress and to plan further investigation

The length of this text has been planned to permit an instructor to include other interesting readings and to allow students to use some of their time for reading the books discussed. You should have time also to construct materials described and to try suggested teaching ideas in your classroom.

Not an exhaustive study of books for children, *Exploring Books with Children* is intended to open doors. It invites you to explore a wide variety of books, to enjoy children's literature, and to share what you discover with the children in your life.

I.M.T.

*Exploring Books
with Children*

1

Who's There?
Open
the Door!

Exploring Children's Books

Title from *Who's There? Open the Door* by Bruno Munari (World, 1958). Illustration reproduced by permission of the publisher from *Henry Huggins* by Beverly Cleary. Illustrated by Louis Darling. Copyright 1950 by William Morrow & Company, Inc.

I have in these years, learned a great deal about the minds and imaginations of the young. I know that, if they have been nurtured and nourished by an early love of books, they have far finer and more sensitive minds and imaginations.

Mary Ellen Chase
Recipe for a Magic Childhood

Opening books for children opens doors to worlds as yet unseen, to experiences as yet untried, to people as yet unknown. As a teacher, you have the singular opportunity of introducing children to the beautiful illustrations in Brian Wildsmith's *Circus* or Marcia Brown's *Once a Mouse . . .* , and of sharing their laughter over the crazy antics of Henry Huggins, Homer Price, or Curious George. You can lead them to books that will feed the imagination as well as that "insatiable curtiosity," to use Rudyard Kipling's phrase from "How the Elephant Got a Long Trunk." Fiction, nonfiction, poetry—children's literature offers a vast treasure trove to be explored.

Think back to your own experiences with children's literature. Do you remember certain books with great pleasure? Consider also your relationship with children's literature today, as you answer the following questions:

1. List five books that you remember enjoying as a child.

2. Did adults—parents, teachers, friends—read aloud to you when you were a child?

3. Have you read a children's book during the past year?

4. Can you name five authors of children's books?

Chuck

5. Have you ever read or told a story to a child?

6. What is children's literature?

Discuss the answers to these questions with others in your group.

Then enjoy exploring the realm of children's literature. In this chapter you will be introduced to:

Books that have become old favorites with children

A few noted authors and illustrators

Some of the newer books that show promise

Suggestions for assessing new books

Selection aids to help you locate books

Teaching ideas that you can use immediately in the classroom

The intent of this introductory chapter is to entice you with a sampling of the wide variety of fine books for children, ranging from the picture book to the junior novel, from fantasy to realistic fiction and nonfiction, and from old favorites that have lasted over the years to the newest books that have just been published—to open the door to children's literature.

INTRODUCTION TO CHILDREN'S BOOKS

Only adults who are enthusiastic and knowledgeable about books for children will be able to project enthusiasm for reading to the young people with whom they come in contact. The first aim, therefore, in exploring books for children is to ensure that you are literally steeped in the wealth of literature available to children today.

One sure way to get "hooked" on children's books is to begin reading them yourself, for who can resist the charm of such characters as Pippi Longstocking or the beauty of illustrations by Ezra Jack Keats? In this section we will explore a number of books that have become favorites of children over the years, a few authors and illustrators who create books for children, and at the end of the section, a sampling of new books that show promise, with suggestions about assessing new titles as they appear.

OLD FAVORITES

Rediscover Pippi in Villa Villekula, visit the Borrowers in their tiny house, and meet Wilbur, the pig, and his friend Charlotte, the gray spider. These ageless fantasies lead the lists of books that children have enjoyed for many years. These books and the others discussed are outstanding, so why not begin reading the best?

Read the delightful story of the little people—Pod, Homily, and their daughter, Arrietty. *The Borrowers* (Harcourt Brace Jovanovich, 1953) is the first of a series by Mary Norton. You will be intrigued by the Clock family (they live under the grandfather clock) and their "borrowings" from the big people who live upstairs. Even the Boy is a frightening creature to these little beings, although he tries to be friends. Mary Norton describes his gift of a toy dresser from a doll house, an episode that was horrifying at the time.

He knelt down—but Homily did not flinch as the great face came slowly closer. She saw his under lip, pink and full—like an enormous exaggeration of Arrietty's —and she saw it wobble slightly. "But I've got something for you," he said.

Homily's expression did not change and Arrietty called out from her place in the doorway: "What is it?" The boy reached behind him and very gingerly, careful to keep it upright, he held a wooden object above their heads. "It's this," he said, and very carefully, his tongue out and breathing heavily, he lowered the object slowly into their hole: it was a doll's dresser, complete with plates. It had two drawers in it and a cupboard below; he adjusted its position at the foot of Homily's bed.

A favorite of boys and girls of many ages is *Pippi Longstocking* (Viking, 1950) by Astrid Lindgren. Pippi lives all alone in an old house in Villa Villekula; all alone, that is, except for her horse and pet monkey, Mr. Nilsen. She is a real treat for Tommy and Annika who live next door, and she'll be a treat for you as you follow her over the rooftop to elude a policeman who wants to take her to an orphanage to live, or to school where she proves to be the most unpredictable student a teacher ever met. The spirit of the book is reflected in the illustration of a tea party at Pippi's house.

Another book that has touched the heart of every reader, young or old, is *Charlotte's Web* (Harper, 1952) by E. B. White, a well-known writer for adults. Written with obvious delight and sensitivity, this book tells of Fern and the runt pig she saves from being killed. Wilbur lives a great life in the big barn with comically realistic Templeton the rat, the goose who gives him sage advice, and all the other animals. His best friend, however, is Charlotte, the spider who is not only intelligent but practical. Charlotte tries to save Wilbur from the fate of being slaughtered by creating a fantastic animal with magic powers. She does this by spinning significant words in her web above Wilbur.

From Pippi Longstocking *by Astrid Lindgren. Illustrated by Louis S. Glanzman. Copyright 1950 by The Viking Press, Inc. Reprinted by permission of the Viking Press.*

A truly outstanding picture book for primary grade children is *Make
Way for Ducklings* (Viking, 1941), written and illustrated more than thirty
years ago by Robert McCloskey. This charming story of a duck family
that lives in Boston continues to delight children. It is the illustration that makes the book truly outstanding, however, for McCloskey is
at his best with the black and white drawings that appear in this book, as
well as in the ones for older boys and girls such as *Homer Price* and *Lentil*.

Published forty years ago, *Madeline* (Viking, 1939) is a favorite picture
book. "In an old house in Paris that was covered with vines lived twelve
little girls in two straight lines." Thus begins the first book by Ludwig
Bemelmans about the audacious Madeline who says "pooh-pooh" to
lions and, in this book, gets appendicitis. Of course, Madeline has fun at
the hospital and lets the other girls admire her scar so that all of them
want to have appendicitis. *Madeline,* supported effectively by large illustrations, presents a strong, adventurous female character that both boys
and girls will enjoy knowing.

Representative of the fine nonfiction for young people is Alastair
Reid's *Ounce, Dice, Trice* (Little, Brown, 1955) illustrated by Ben Shahn.
This book is all about words—squishy words for wet days, words for
times of day, words for counting, odd words to be spoken out loud
for fun. The author writes: ". . . if you grow to love words for their
own sake, you will begin to collect words for yourself, and you will be
grateful, as I am, to all the people who collect odd words and edit odd
dictionaries, out of sheer astonishment and affection." An example of the
contents is the garland of ideas and definitions entitled "What Is a Hamburgler?"

WHAT IS A HAMBURGLER?

A *hamburgler* is a hamburger
which you creep downstairs
and eat in the middle of
the night when you
wake up hungry.
Mim people never
eat hamburglers.

WHAT ARE MIM PEOPLE?

Mim people are very proper
people who always sit with
their fingertips together and
their lips pursed tight, who
always do the right thing,
and who disapprove. Mim
people have *worgs* in
their gardens.

WHAT IS A WORG?

A *worg* is a plant which never
grows. There is practically always
one worg in a row of plants.
You can tell it by the *gnurr*
on its leaves.

WHAT IS GNURR?

**GNURR is the substance which
collects after periods of
time in the bottom of
pockets or in the cuffs of
trousers. Gnurr is a
smaller variety of *oosse*.**

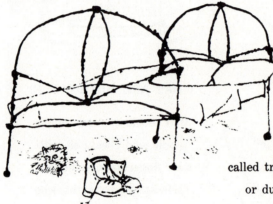

WHAT IS OOSSE?

OOSSE is the airy
furry stuff that
ultimately gathers
under beds and
gonomonies. It is also
called trilbies, kittens,
or dust-bunnies.

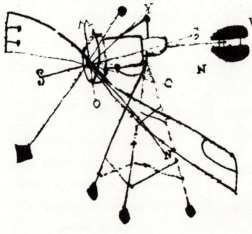

WHAT IS A GONOMONY?

A *gonomony* is any
strange object that is
difficult to name, that
is curiously unlike
anything else, and that
serves no useful
purpose. Gonomonies
abound in the
houses of *glots*.

WHAT IS A GLOT?

A *glot* is a person who cannot bear to waste anything, who stuffs his attic full of treasures which nobody else wants, and who always eats the last chocolate in the box. Glots can be recognized by the *poose* on their noses.

WHAT IS A POOSE?

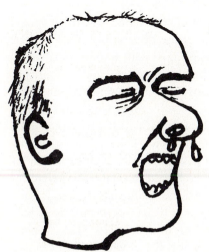

A *poose* is a drop which stays on the end of the nose and glistens. It happens to ordinary people when they have colds, or when they come out of the sea for a *chittering-bite.*

WHAT IS A CHITTERING-BITE?

A *chittering-bite* is a snack eaten after a cold
swim to keep the teeth from chattering. It may
consist of anything from an apple to a
piece of leftover *hamburgler.*

MEETING AUTHORS AND ILLUSTRATORS

No introduction to children's books would be complete without special
mention of the men and women who create these books. One of your
first objectives should be to become acquainted with authors and illustrators who write or paint successfully for the wonderful audience of children. Gradually you will come to know the work of many, but begin
with a few specific persons.

For example, take a look at books by Ezra Jack Keats, an author–illustrator who has made a significant contribution. He introduced the character of Peter, a small black boy who has numerous adventures with his
friends and his dog. The first book, which won the Caldecott award for
outstanding illustration, was *The Snowy Day* (Viking, 1963). In this book
for young children you will see examples of Keats' spectacular art, which
often incorporates collage. In the excellent film *Ezra Jack Keats* (Weston
Woods) about his work, Keats explains how he came to create Peter as a

main character. He also demonstrates how he makes the collages he uses as backgrounds, wall coverings, dress materials, and landscapes in his illustrations. Children will delight in making these collages, too, for they are simple but excitingly effective.

When you visit the library, look for these other books by Ezra Jack Keats:

Whistle for Willie

Peter's Chair

Goggles!

Hi, Cat!

Apt. 3

A Letter for Amy

In addition, you will find many of Keats' illustrations in works by other authors, for example, Lloyd Alexander's *The King's Fountain.* One of the most beautiful collections of illustrations is in *In a Spring Garden,* a selection of haiku compiled by Richard Lewis (see the color section).

An author who writes chiefly for older readers is Marguerite Henry, the creator of many fine horse stories. The best known is probably *King of the Wind,* which won the coveted Newbery award in 1948. Marguerite Henry obviously knows horses. Her books, carefully researched, present a variety of horses, from the wild ones on the island of Chincoteague in Virginia to the grand Lipizzaners in Vienna.

Read two or three of the following books to get the full flavor of Marguerite Henry's work:

Misty of Chincoteague

King of the Wind

Sea Star, Orphan of Chincoteague

Brighty of the Grand Canyon

Justin Morgan Had a Horse

Gaudenzia

White Stallion of Lipizza

This author loves to write. She comments on her love of writing as follows:

From age ten on, I was addicted . . . to the habit of writing. As early as that, I couldn't walk past a telegraph office in a railroad station. The inviting yellow tablet, carefully lined, the sharpened brown pencil chained to the counter were more irresistible than an opened box of divinity fudge. Compulsively, I stopped and wrote my telegram to the world.

Sometimes it was just a simple message, such as:

BE SURE TO END YOUR TELEGRAM WITH L-O-V-E.

Other times I'd do a quick sketch of a horse's head, adding my favorite quote beneath:

I look into your great brown eyes
And wonder where the difference lies
Between your soul and mine.

Furtively then I'd skip away, happy at this miniature outpouring.[1]

To guide your beginning explorations, here are a few additional names of people whose work will surely excite you. Sample the wonderful picture books for primary and preschool children by looking for the name of Uri Shulevitz, an author-illustrator whose work will be discussed in detail in the next chapter. Look also for the work of Mercer Mayer, who has produced delightful wordless stories as well as other fine books for young children. Investigate titles, too, by Charlotte Zolotow, charming, heartwarming stories on sensitive topics.

As you explore books for the middle school, sample the writing of Zilpha Keatley Snyder for intriguing tales that are of high interest. Another prolific and outstanding author is Jean Craighead George, who writes wonderful stories about people and animals. Just for fun read a humorous book by Keith Robertson. And then you must try Judy Blume, and Natalie Babbitt, and Scott O'Dell, and . . . many others whom you'll meet in the chapters that follow.

To explore further, consult *Books Are by People* (Citation, 1969), Lee Bennett Hopkins' compilation of interviews with authors and illustrators of children's books. In this volume are interviews, for example, with Dr. Seuss, Eve Merriam, Aileen Fisher, and others. A second volume, *More Books by More People* (Citation, 1974), includes additional interviews.

---

[1] Marguerite Henry, "A Weft of Truth and a Warp of Fiction," *Elementary English* 51 (October 1974): 921.

Each year thousands of new books for young people appear in the bookstores. The variety and quality of these books are amazing and exciting. Choosing among these titles, however, can prove perplexing as you try to identify new books that are worth recommending to students and books that should be purchased for the school library. To aid you in assessing new books that you are examining, take note of the reputation of the author and illustrator, the timeliness of the topic presented, reviews by a reliable periodical, and your own judgment.

New books by known authors and illustrators always deserve special attention. Any new book written by Marcia Brown, Judy Blume, or Robert McCloskey will be welcomed by an eager audience. The reputation of the author, therefore, and knowledge of other books they have written provide good indications of the worth of a new book by that same person.

Such a book is *Tin Lizzie* (Doubleday, 1975), written and illustrated by Peter Spier. As you open the oversized volume, you are immediately struck by the quantity and quality of the detailed drawings for which this Dutch illustrator is noted. His work in such books as *The Fox Went Out on a Chilly Night, The Erie Canal,* and *The Star-Spangled Banner* has been acclaimed. *Tin Lizzie,* which chronicles the life of a Model-T Ford

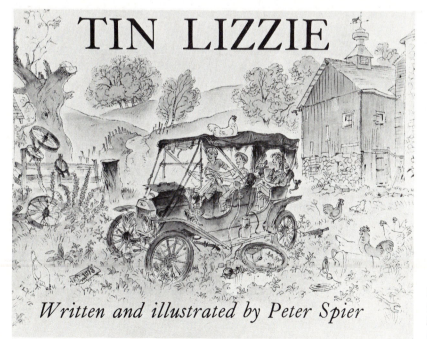

From Tin Lizzie, *copyright* © *1975 by Peter Spier. Reprinted by permission of Doubleday and Company, Inc.*

THE FRIENDLY WOLF

Paul and Dorothy Goble

*Copyright © 1974 by Paul and
Dorothy Goble. From the book*
The Friendly Wolf. *Published
by Bradbury Press, Inc., Scarsdale, New York. Reproduced by
permission of Macmillan London
Ltd.*

through a series of owners from 1909 to the present, exemplifies Peter Spier's high standards, an excellent book for middle grade and older students as well.

Clyde Robert Bulla is another noted author, whose book *Shoeshine Girl* (Thomas Y. Crowell, 1975) has much to recommend it. Eleven-year-old Sarah Ida can't get along with her mother, so she is sent to Aunt Claudia's house for the summer. She gets a job with Al, who has a shoeshine stand, and gradually gains confidence in her ability. When Al is hurt, she manages the shoeshine stand alone. The summer experience provides a time for growing that helps Sarah Ida face her problems. The story is well written and sensitively told.

Books on timely topics are worth looking at carefully. *The Friendly Wolf* (Bradbury, 1975) by Paul and Dorothy Goble helps fill the need for works on the American Indian. When Little Cloud and his sister Bright Eyes, are lost during a berry-picking excursion, a kindly wolf helps them find their way home. The Indians extend their friendship to the wolf in return. This story of the Plains Indians is handsomely illustrated, colorful but restrained and authentic.

Treating the same Indians is Shirley Glubok's *The Art of the Plains Indians* (Macmillan, 1975), nonfiction that features photography by Alfred Tamarin and is designed by Gerard Nook. Although she focuses on the arts and crafts of these tribes, the author also conveys much about the lives and history of the Plains Indians, creating a book that would be an excellent addition to a school library.

A third way of evaluating new books is to rely on a periodical that reviews books. One of the best available is the *Bulletin of the Center for Children's Books,* published monthly by the University of Chicago Press, edited by Zena Sutherland, a well-known name in the field of children's literature. (Available from The University of Chicago Press, 5801 Ellis Avenue, Chicago, Illinois 60637.)

This bulletin not only provides a lengthy annotation for each title, but also evaluates the quality of each book reviewed. A book that is recommended can be counted on to be outstanding, and those few that are marked with an asterisk for special distinction are especially worth searching out. (It should be noted that the reviewers do not hesitate to mark a book *Not Recommended,* when appropriate.) One book marked with an asterisk, for example, is *The Dollhouse Caper* (Thomas Y. Crowell, 1976) by Jean S. O'Connell. Illustrated by Erik Blegvad, this fantasy by a new author is recommended for the middle grades. A story of dolls that come to life is well told with a humorous touch and excellent characterization. The dolls, owned by three brothers, try to communicate to the humans about a robbery that is going to take place.

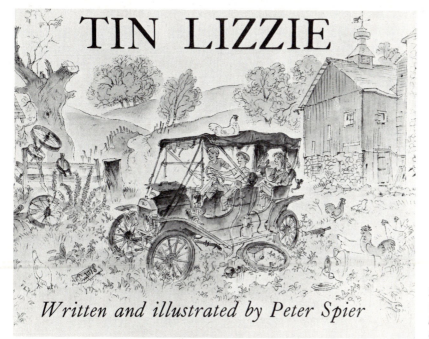

A second book considered outstanding by the *Bulletin* reviewers is *Letters to Horseface: Being the Story of Wolfgang Amadeus Mozart's Journey to Italy 1769–1770 When He Was a Boy of Fourteen* (Viking, 1975) by a respected author, Ferdinand N. Monjo. "The versatile Mr. Monjo moves to a new form with great success in this collection of . . . letters from the young Mozart to his sister." The reviewers see the letters as "ebullient, teasing, boyish" as well as "amusing and informative." This book should be valuable in providing biographical and historical information for upper elementary and junior high school students.

One final means of assessing the value of a new book is to trust your own judgment. You are the person who will use this book. Even if reviewers rate a new title as outstanding, you may not agree, or the book may not meet your specific needs. On the other hand, you may find something appealing about a book that has not been highly rated. Do assert your own tastes and knowledge as you develop a background for evaluating literature for children.

❦ *GETTING ACQUAINTED WITH BOOKS* Begin a Book File on 4″ × 6″ cards. Include the following information that will be useful to you later as you use these books in the classroom:

Author

Title

Publisher

Date of publication

Number of pages

Illustrator (if named)

Brief synopsis

Also jot down any ideas that occur to you as you read for using this book with children. Add other ideas later.

Choose one of these activities as a way of getting started on your exploration of children's books:

1. Spend two hours browsing in a large bookstore. Notice the kinds of children's books on display. Do you find a number of old familiar titles as well as books that bear a recent copyright date? Are children welcome in this bookstore?

2. <u>Go to the library in your community</u>. Find out where the picture books are shelved, the fiction for older readers, the nonfiction. Spend two hours browsing and reading a number of books. Explore books in each section. How does this library try to entice young readers?

CHILDREN, LITERATURE, AND ADULTS

Throughout this study of children's literature it is essential to keep constantly in mind the young people with whom this literature will be shared. Poetry, myths, and well-told stories are meaningful and beautiful in themselves, of course, and you will enjoy them personally, but your major concern is helping children to discover these treasures, to experience their literary heritage, to make it part of their lives.

Lucy Boston, author of *The Children of Green Knowe* (Harcourt Brace Jovanovich, 1955), expresses this idea, thus:

I would like to remind adults of joy, now considered obsolete, and would like to encourage children to use and trust their senses for themselves at first hand—their ears, eyes, and noses, their fingers and the soles of their feet, their skins and their breathing, their muscular joy and rhythms and heartbeats, their instinctive loves and pity and their awe of the unknown. This . . . is the primary material of thought. It is from direct stimulus that imagination is born.[2]

WHAT IS CHILDREN'S LITERATURE?

Children's literature can be defined in many ways. Is children's literature, for example, books written for children? Instantly there come to mind the many books written for adults that children have commandeered as their own. *Robinson Crusoe,* written by Daniel Defoe in 1719, and Jonathan Swift's *Gulliver's Travels,* which appeared in 1726, are two examples of books that were never intended for children; yet children in succeeding generations have continued to find them absorbing.

Can we, then, define children's literature as all the books that children read? Here, too, we run into difficulty for this definition is limited to books, and we know that children read things that cannot be labeled *books*. We know, furthermore, that children experience literature in many

---

[2] John Rowe Townsend, *A Sense of Story; Essays on Contemporary Writers for Children* (The Horn Book, 1971), p. 36.

ways that do not even involve the written symbol. Young people begin experiencing literature orally and aurally, and it is to be hoped that they would continue to have these vital literary experiences as they listen to stories being told, act out the tales from their own folklore, and even create literature themselves. The visual aspects of literature—fine illustrations in books themselves as well as the presentation of these same illustrations on film and the filming of literature in dramatic form—should not be ignored either.

What then is children's literature? Children's literature is *literature for children,* which has a strangely different connotation. As such, it includes a breadth of experience that many would not admit. Remembering that we always speak through a veil woven of our personal values, understandings, and experiences, I prefer this definition, which I have phrased here in the form of a poem:

Children's literature is . . .
   stories—exciting, well-loved, satisfying;
   pictures—joyful, interpretive, enhancing;
   films—animating, sensory, perceptive;
   recordings—voicing, hearing, reacting;
Children's literature is adventurous, informative, and poetic.

Literature for children is . . .
   feeling—hurting, laughing, hoping;
   experiencing—dramatizing, interacting, socializing;
   sharing—identifying, reaching, understanding;
   languaging—explaining, questioning, responding;
Literature for children is drama, song, and dance.

Literature is very much a part of every child's environment. It is not limited to the book nor is it only part of the school setting. It includes the jingles of childhood, the rope-jumping songs that children teach each other, the imaginary play that they invent. It includes stories recorded in books, on films or cassettes. As we consider the relationships of books, literature, and children, we need to remember this breadth of experience that is possible if we refrain from defining limitations.

ADULTS AND CHILDREN'S BOOKS

What role can an adult play in working with children and literature? There are many exciting and enjoyable possibilities. In all cases, however, we must be very much aware of ourselves as adults and as individuals in order to avoid some of the pitfalls that we might encounter. The roles we do not want to play, for example, are those of censor or the person who forces students to read because they "ought to" or because reading is "good for you." The following roles offer adults a responsible, reasonable opportunity to facilitate interaction between children and books.

ADULTS CAN PURCHASE BOOKS. As parents, teachers, and librarians, adults purchase the books that children read. This task offers a real opportunity, but it also carries a load of responsibility.

Select books with the child in mind. Will children enjoy the book? Consider these aspects of the books you look at:

1. Are the illustrations good art that fits the story?

2. Is the size of the book comfortable for the child to hold, appropriate to the type of book?

3. Is the print easily read and well placed on the page?

4. Are the characters believable?

5. Is the language natural and interesting?

6. Is the story or information presented worth reading?

ADULTS CAN SHARE BOOKS WITH CHILDREN. Sharing books is a highly pleasurable experience, but it does mean that we need to take time to participate. It is easy to become so busy that we never get around to sitting down with a child at home to read Mother Goose rhymes together or to share the exciting adventures in books such as *The Princess and Curdie* (Macmillan, 1954) by George MacDonald. As teachers, we may become too concerned about covering the textbook to take time to read with children, although studies show that reading aloud really does increase reading achievement.

ADULTS CAN PROVIDE POSITIVE REINFORCEMENT. We can encourage children to respond to books. We can show obvious interest when children want to talk about books. Our willingness just to listen is a positive factor, for children are often put aside by adults who are too busy. We can invite children to go with us to libraries and bookstores or to see films of stories that have been made of such books as *Mary Poppins* by Pamela Travers or Norton Juster's *The Phantom Tollbooth.*

ADULTS CAN KNOW CHILDREN'S BOOKS. It is most important that we know children's books if we are to share in and to encourage a love of literature in children. We need to explore actively and to examine reference books that will help us find out more about books for children. A course in children's literature is a good beginning although even that is not enough, for books are published at a rate of several thousand per year. Browsing in libraries and bookstores and reading reviews will help you keep in touch with new developments, as well as being an enjoyable pastime.

PLANNING CLASSROOM EXPERIENCES

Albert Einstein said, "It is the supreme art of the teacher to awaken joy in creative expression and knowledge." As you read books for children, you will naturally be thinking about using these books with young people. Literature lends itself to stimulating creative expression and to promoting joy in learning.

In this section the emphasis is on beginning skills that you can use immediately. Reading aloud, for example, is one of the simplest ways of presenting a book to any group, and you can learn certain skills that will improve this type of sharing. In addition, basic resources that any teacher will find helpful as well as gaming techniques related to literature will be discussed.

THE ART OF READING ALOUD

Why read aloud to children? It is important to have your objectives clearly in mind before you begin, because they will influence the selection of what you read. They may even influence the manner in which you read a book to a group. There are many reasons for reading aloud, for example:

1. Stimulation of thinking
2. Motivation to read independently
3. Amusement and sheer entertainment
4. Sharing of feelings and reassurance
5. Appreciation of an author's performance
6. Development of student language abilities

Any single experience of sharing a book may actually contribute to each objective as we select a book for reading, but obviously there are some books that are more amusing than others, some that do present the feelings of children, and others that are stylistically more outstanding.

The first rule in selecting a book to share with young people is to choose one that you really like, for your enthusiasm will carry over to the children through your voice. It is virtually impossible, on the other hand, to project enthusiasm when you don't feel it. If you select a book you like, this presupposes that you have read the book you are going to share. Avoid falling into the trap of picking up just any book at the last minute or of reading books children bring to school that you don't know. Taking time to read the book first is essential.

Sharing a book offers the opportunity to provide much incidental or planned learning. In order to take advantage of these opportunities, however, you need to be prepared. Planning this part of the curriculum is just as important as any other. Lucy Boston's *The Children of Green Knowe* (Harcourt Brace Jovanovich, 1954), for example, is set in Great Britain. Reading this excellent fantasy aloud could serve to introduce a fascinating comparison of British and American English as children discover the meaning of words like *windscreen* and *gum boots*.

Another important aspect of reading aloud is the follow-up. What happens after you finish a story or the chapter of a longer book? Discussion stimulated by your questions is a natural follow-up for most books. You may also, however, have more specific ideas in mind. After reading Dr. Seuss' *And to Think That I Saw It on Mulberry Street,* for instance, you might want the group to begin a colorful mural based on the parade that Marco imagined. Following the story, you could ask primary children to name all the interesting things Marco imagined—reindeer, a chariot, a big brass band. Then each child could choose something to paint in the parade—almost anything would be appropriate.

How can you improve your effectiveness as a reader? Like most skills, you will learn to read well by reading. Choose a book that you enjoy. In a room by yourself—the empty classroom or your own bedroom—read the story aloud before an imagined audience. Read with full voice, speaking clearly and stopping to show a picture or to explain a word occasionally as appropriate. Although you sometimes read a story to a very small group of children, it is more common in the classroom to be reading to the entire class. It is important, therefore, to consider the following aspects of reading aloud:

1. Can you be heard easily by all children?

2. Does your reading flow pleasantly?

3. Is the reading paced appropriately—not too fast?

4. Can you use expression (varied intonation) to add to the effect?

5. Do you feel at ease enough to really enjoy the experience of sharing a good book with children?

Listen to yourself as you read. You can actually hear yourself as you read aloud, and sometimes you will have the impression that you are really coming across well. That impression, of course, serves to increase your self-confidence, and you perform even more effectively. Another way of hearing yourself is to tape a portion of your reading on a cassette. You can note specific lines that you would like to read differently. Read the passage again as you consciously make the changes. When you read the story to a real audience, you will read much more effectively than if you had not practiced.

Short stories are excellent for reading aloud. Two collections you might enjoy are:

The Devil's Storybook by Natalie Babbitt. Farrar, Straus & Giroux, 1974.

A Book of Monsters by Ruth Manning-Sanders. Dutton, 1976.

AIDS TO PLANNING INSTRUCTION

As you work with children's literature in a classroom situation, there are many resources that will be helpful in developing plans for teaching. At this stage, we are going to discuss only a few that are outstanding and, therefore, will be most beneficial for beginning literature experiences. In addition to the *Bulletin of the Center for Children's Books* mentioned earlier, investigate the following resources:

Children's Catalog. Wilson, 1971. Annual supplements. This catalogue is up-to-date and comprehensive. Available as a reference tool in college and public libraries, it is also recommended for school libraries as it is well worth the investment. A teacher who is planning a unit of study, a learning center around a specific topic, or small group research of varied topics will find this reference invaluable. It can be used readily by upper elementary children as well as the teacher to prepare bibliographies or reading lists.

Both nonfiction and fiction are listed, with excerpts from reviews included that provide information about the contents of each book. Nonfiction is classified according to the Dewey decimal system so that you can easily find groupings of books on specific topics, for example, American Indians or Mexico. Fiction is listed alphabetically by author with special groupings of short stories and easy books.

Of particular help to the teacher is the subject index, which lists both fiction and nonfiction under topics of general interest. A sample page is included here to show you the organization under one topic. For more complete information about individual books, you need to refer to the detailed listing included in the first half of this reference.

Language Arts (formerly *Elementary English*). An official publication of the National Council of Teachers of English, 1111 Kenyon Rd., Urbana, Illinois 61801.
This journal is published from September through May with articles on all aspects of the language arts—reading, writing, speaking, and listening—as well as topics of general interest to elementary classroom teachers. Many articles focus on children's literature and include full-page pictures of authors. Articles range in variety from very practical ideas described by teachers across the country to reports of research related to instruction. At times children's writing is featured. Special columns present reviews of books for children, professional materials, and nonprint media.

A subscription to *Language Arts* is available with membership in NCTE. A special student rate is available, which also includes membership in NCTE and a newsletter published especially for interested students. Student memberships must be submitted by college professors in whose classes students are enrolled.

Children and Books by May Hill Arbuthnot and Zena Sutherland. 5th ed. Scott, Foresman, 1977.
This is the most comprehensive general reference on children's literature. Available in college and public libraries, it is also recommended for professional libraries in elementary schools. Extensive booklists are included as well as good commentaries on individual authors and their work.

Reading Ladders for Human Relations edited by Virginia M. Reid. 5th ed. National Council of Teachers of English, 1972.
This annotated bibliography is an excellent up-to-date source of fiction that would be useful in developing understandings at four levels: primary, elementary, junior high, senior high, and adult. Entries are grouped under the following categories:

Creating a Positive Self-Image

Bunche, Ralph
   See pages in the following book:
  Sechrist, E. H. It's time for brotherhood
    p245-50 (5-7)   **301.11**
Burchard, Marshall
  Sports hero: Bobby Orr (2-4)   **92**
Burchard, Sue
  (jt. auth.) Burchard, M. Sports hero:
    Bobby Orr   **92**
Burchardt, Nellie
  Reggie's no-good bird; excerpt
  In Association for Childhood Education
    International. Literature Commit-
    tee. Told under the city umbrella
    p173-93   **S C**
Buren, Nathalie van. See Van Buren,
  Nathalie
Buried treasure
        Fiction
  Cresswell, H. The Beachcombers (4-6)
                        Fic
Burma
    See pages in the following book:
  Poole, F. K. Southeast Asia p24-31 (5-7)
                    915.9
Burr, Dane
  (illus.) Abdul, R. ed. The magic of Black
    poetry   **808.81**
Burro. See Asses and mules
Burroway, Janet
  Lord, J. V. The giant jam sandwich **E**
Burundi
  Carpenter, A. Burundi (4-7)   **916.7**
Buses
        Fiction
  Young, M. If I drove a bus   **E**
Bushmen
    See pages in the following book:
  Carpenter, A. Botswana p23-25 (4-7)
                   916.8
Busoni, Rafaello
  (illus.) Simon, H. W. ed. A treasury of
    Christmas songs and carols   **783.6**
Butterflies
    See pages in the following book:
  Villiard, P. Insects as pets p64-83 (5-7)
                   595.7
The butterfly. Andersen, H. C.
  In Andersen, H. C. The complete fairy
    tales and stories p782-84   **S C**
The Butterfly that stamped. Kipling, R.
  In Kipling, R. Just so stories   **S C**
Butterworth, Oliver
  The narrow passage (4-6)   **Fic**
Byard, Carole
  (illus.) Phumla. Nomi and the magic fish
                   398.2
Byars, Betsy
  The 18th emergency (4-6)   **Fic**
Byrd, Richard Evelyn
    See pages in the following book:
  Ross, F. Historic plane models p145-50
    (5-7)   **629.133**
Byrd, Robert
  (illus.) Scheib, I. The first book of food
                   641.3

C

Cabinet work. See Woodwork
Cabot, John
  Kurtz, H. I. John and Sebastian Cabot
    (4-6)   **92**
Cabot, Sebastian
  Kurtz, H. I. John and Sebastian Cabot
    (4-6)   **92**
Cacao
    See pages in the following book:
  Hays, W. P. Foods the Indians gave us
    p52-55 (5-7)   **641.3**
Caddie Woodlawn. Brink, C. R.   **Fic**
Caines, Jeannette Franklin
  Abby   **E**
Cairo
    See pages in the following book:
  Lengyel, E. Modern Egypt p15-19 (5-7)
                   916.2
Cake
  Paul, A. Candies, cookies, cakes (3-6)
                   641.8
Caldecott Medal books
  Zemach, M. See Zemach, H. Duffy and
    the devil (1974)   **398.2**
Caldecott Medal books (as subject)
  Haviland, V. ed. Children and literature
    p416-31   **809**
  MacCann, D. The child's first books
    p115-20   **741.64**
Caldwell, John C.
  Let's visit China today (4-7)   **915.1**
Call me Heller, that's my name. Pevsner, S.
                   Fic
Camels
    See pages in the following book:
  Fenton, C. L. Animals that help us p83-
    92 (4-6)   **636**
Cameron, Eleanor
  The court of the stone children (5-7) **Fic**
Camp cooking. See Outdoor cookery
Camping
  Paul, A. Kids camping (4-6)   **796.54**
Can invertebrates learn? Ford, B. **156**
Canada
      Discovery and exploration
    See America—Discovery and explora-
  tion
        Farm life
    See Farm life—Canada
Canals
  Franchere, R. Westward by canal (5-7)
                   386
Cancer
  Silverstein, A. Cancer (4-7)   **616.9**
Candies, cookies, cakes. Paul, A. **641.8**
Candles
    See pages in the following book:
  Fisher, L. E. The homemakers p11-21 (4-
    6)   **680**
The candles. Andersen, H. C.
  In Andersen, H. C. The complete fairy
    tales and stories p992-94   **S C**

Living with Others

Appreciating Different Cultures

Coping with Change

The Children's Book Council (various publications). 175 Fifth Avenue, New York, New York 10010.
This organization publishes *The Calendar,* a periodical that lists concepts and events related to the seasons and their specific dates. Also included are suggested books that are appropriate for study on the topics featured. In addition, this council prepares excellent material for the purpose of publicizing Book Week in November each year. A streamer by Wallace Tripp, for example, was created in 1974. Send for a catalogue of their materials and a sample copy of *The Calendar.*

LIBRARY CHECKLIST Visit your college and local libraries to determine what kind of material is available to help you and to examine some of the items we've discussed. Locate the following aids. Examine them carefully to see what each one has to offer.

1. *The Children's Catalog* (ask the reference librarian)

2. Bound volumes of *Elementary English* or *Language Arts* and current issues (in the Periodical Room or Education Library)

3. The subject index of the card catalogue (what is listed under the heading *Children's Literature?* Ask a librarian to help you find any related entries.)

Find out if your library has the following:

1. A film collection

2. Recording and listening rooms

3. Picture collection

4. File of clippings and other ephemeral material

5. Collection of juvenile books

BOOKS FOR ALL REASONS

Streamer by Wallace Tripp for 1974 Children's Book Week sponsored by The Children's Book Council, Inc.

GAMES AND LITERATURE

Playing games has come into its own, and the study of literature can take advantage of this interest. Innumerable games that are exciting, yet serve to enhance learning, are presented throughout this textbook so that you will eventually have a rich store of ideas. Here are three good activities that you can use immediately.

ACROSTICS The acrostic is a special kind of puzzle that you can introduce to children of all ages. The unique feature of the acrostic is the spelling of a word vertically with the first letters of each line. In this example we have printed the key word in to help establish the theme of the puzzle, which is *titles and authors:*

	Title of Book
A _ _ _ _ _ _ _ _	*The Cat Who Wanted to Be a Man*
U _ _ _ _ _	*The Promised Year*
T _ _ _ _ _	*Anatole and the Thirty Thieves*
H _ _ _ _ _ _	*Paddle-to-the-Sea*
O _ _ _ _	*Island of the Blue Dolphins*
R _ _	*Curious George*

Answers

Alexander

Uchida

Titus

Holling

O'Dell

Rey

As you can see, this puzzle will send children to the library card catalogue or to reference books. An even more challenging activity for the able student is producing an original acrostic. After solving a sample acrostic like this one, students can create their own with which to challenge their classmates.

CHARADES Charades, an old game that uses silent language, can be played by students of all ages. It is adaptable to many aspects of literature; for example, an author's name, the title of a book, or the main character in a book. To facilitate this game, develop a set of cards on which you print characters, authors, or titles of books known to the group, like this:

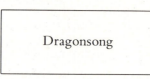

Dragonsong

Small groups of students can then choose a card and present a charade to the large group, which tries to guess the appropriate word or phrase. Give each group a few minutes to prepare for its presentation as it considers what elements of the information can be acted out or conveyed through the stylized signals traditionally used in playing charades. Discuss some of the following ideas, which the group can practice using as they become familiar with the game.

Signals for the Category Portrayed

Book: Open hands held out before you as though holding a book

Person: Hands over heart

Author: Writing motion on open hand

Character: Open hand over face (person playing a part)

Quotation: Hold up two fingers of each hand to signal quotation marks

Animal: Pose on all fours

Bird: Flap arms as wings

Place: Indicate circle with arms

Signals for Other Information

Number of words: Hold up appropriate number of fingers

Sequence of word being portrayed: Hold up appropriate number of fingers again

Length of word: Hands far apart for *long;* hands close together for *short*

No and Yes: Nod or shake head to provide feedback

Keep going; you're on the right track: Move both hands repeatedly from audience toward person presenting charade, beckoning, to encourage them to give you more along the same line

Let's start over: When things get hopelessly confused, move both hands sideways several times to clear away that effort

Rhymes with: Point to ear to indicate *sounds like*

Syllable: Cut across extended finger

As the group gains skill in working with charades, develop additional signals. Let them decide how to indicate some of the following helpful clues:

Synonym

Antonym

Compound word

Preposition

Pronouns: I, you, he, she, it, we, they

Prepare a set of charade cards for use with a class that you are working with. Play Charades with the group to see how it works. You play, too!

CATEGORIES Categories is an adaptable game that can be used with varied subject matter. To give this game a literary twist, focus on *characters*. The task is to fill in as many spaces as possible with the name of a character.

Any group of categories could be used; for example, you might use the word *literature* down the side with the categories *authors* and *characters* at

		Animals	Boys	Girls
	C	Charlotte	Charlie	
	H	Honk	Henry	Harriet
	A	Angus		
	R	Ribsy	Rufus	Ramona
	A	Anatole		
	C			
	T	Tico	Tom	
	E			Ellen
	R	Rascal		
	S			

the top. Another variation is the name of a character down the left, for example *Tom Sawyer,* with the categories *adjectives* and *verbs* at the top. Again, encourage students to construct their own versions of this game.

❦ *GETTING STARTED* You now have enough ideas to make a good beginning. Try each of the following activities.

1. Choose a book that you would like to share with a group of children. Go through the steps of preparing yourself to do a good job of presenting the book through reading aloud and select a follow-up activity. Share the book with a class and have them complete the activity that you have in mind.

2. Prepare a game that you can use in a classroom such as a version of Categories or try playing Charades with a group of children.

Carlson, Ruth Kearney. *Enrichment Ideas: Sparkling Fireflies*. 2nd ed. Literature for Children Series. Brown, 1976.

Egoff, Sheila et al. *Only Connect: Readings on Children's Literature*. Oxford University Press, 1969.

Huck, Charlotte and Doris Kuhn. *Children's Literature in the Elementary School*. 3rd ed. Holt, 1976.

Hunter, Mollie. *Talent Is Not Enough*. Harper, 1976.

Root, Shelton L., Jr. *Adventuring with Books: Twenty-four Hundred Titles for Preschool—Grade 8*. National Council of Teachers of English, 1973.

Sebesta, Sam and William Iverson. *Literature for Thursday's Child*. SRA, 1975.

Sutherland, Zena. *The Best in Children's Books: The University of Chicago Guide to Children's Literature, 1966–72*. The University of Chicago Press, 1973.

Tiedt, Iris M. and Sidney W. Tiedt. *Contemporary English in the Elementary School*. 2nd ed. Prentice-Hall, 1975.

Townsend, John Rowe. *A Sense of Story: Essays on Contemporary Writers for Children*. Lippincott, 1972.

2

When We Were
Very Young

Every Child's Literary Heritage

Title from *When We Were Very Young* by A. A. Milne (Dutton, 1924). Illustration from *Sam, Bangs & Moonshine* written and illustrated by Evaline Ness. Copyright © 1966 by Evaline Ness. Reproduced by permission of Holt, Rinehart & Winston, Publishers.

Everything must have a beginning, and I often think that my beginning must have begun in a very bright and happy childhood.

Howard Pyle
"When I Was a Little Boy"

"It took hundreds of years for grownups to realize that children have the right to be children," writes Kornei Chukovsky in *From Two to Five* (University of California, 1966, p. 111). Today the number of books published especially for young children is impressively large. The quality is also impressive.

The first experiences with books from the age of two, when parents share Mother Goose rhymes and the ABC books, through the initial use of books in school are crucial to a child's developing attitude toward books and learning. Growth within a rich language environment shapes the child's linguistic facility. This is the time, too, when children are first exposed to much of their literary heritage. Books should be an important part of these early years.

In order to understand the needs of young children the aims in exploring books for the very young should be:

1. To read a wide variety of books for young children.

2. To know excellent illustrators and authors of books for the young child.

3. To share books with children of different ages in different situations.

4. To encourage children's language and literature development through art, drama, and other learning experiences.

The chief aim of this chapter is to help you get acquainted with illustrated books for children. You will be asked to read a number of representative titles, for you need to know as many books as possible in order to be able to select the right book at the right time. We will examine collections of nursery rhymes, alphabet books, counting books, books about animals, books that offer fanciful fun, adaptations of folklore, and informational or realistic stories—a wide variety to get you started on your explorations. We will also devote attention to the authors and illustrators who create books for young children, as we discuss outstanding books, the work of a number of specific authors, and provide a sampling of the art from children's books in a special color section. In the last section of the chapter we focus on teaching with picture books—stimulating creativity, developing language abilities, and sharing books.

❦ See if you can answer these questions before beginning your study of books for young children.

1. Which two of these persons are well-known illustrators of children's books?

a. Alvin Goldsmith

b. Leo Politi

c. Lawrence Watson

d. Sylvia Tyrrell

e. Brian Wildsmith

2. What is the Caldecott Medal? _____

_____

3. Who wrote and illustrated *The Snowy Day, Whistle for Willie,* and *Goggles?* _____

4. Can you recite one of these three nursery rhymes?

   Simple Simon

   One, Two, Buckle My Shoe

   Hey, Diddle, Diddle

5. Can you name a book for young children that deals with death or the birth of a baby?

These questions give you some idea of the specific things that will be discussed in the following pages. Notice the questions you were unable to answer, because these questions indicate the kind of information you need to discover as you work through this chapter.

BROWSING IN THE PICTURE BOOK SECTION

The most effective way to become acquainted with these marvelous books for children is to go to the public library where you can look at the many books that we will be talking about. There is no substitute for seeing each book in its entirety.

On the other hand, since there are limits to your time and physical endurance, a guide to your investigation may be helpful. In this section are listed most of the names of the authors and illustrators who contribute to this wealth of literature, for it is important that you come to know authors and illustrators by name as well as the kind of work they do. There are a large number of books, too, that every teacher, librarian, or parent ought not to miss because they're just too good; every child should know such books as *Make Way for Ducklings* or *Madeline;* every child should be exposed to the art of Uri Shulevitz and Marcia Brown. From the fairly comprehensive coverage that is offered, of course, you must still make choices, sometimes depending on the realistic limitation of just which books are actually in your library.

In this section we will first discuss the qualities that make a picture book outstanding. Then we will explore various categories of books—nursery rhymes, alphabet and counting books, books about animals, folklore and fanciful tales, realism, and informational books.

CRITERIA FOR ILLUSTRATION AND CONTENT

As we examine these books for early childhood, it becomes clear that we are dealing with a wide range of content as well as differing approaches to illustration. Wordless books depict a story with no words at all; for example, Mercer Mayer's funny *Frog, Where Are You?* (Dial, 1969). Other authors tell a fairly complex story, as in *Joseph's Yard* (Watts, 1969) written and illustrated handsomely by Charles Keeping. The criteria for selecting outstanding books for young children become, therefore, complex because we need to consider both content and illustration as well as the interrelationship of these two elements of the book.

What makes a book such as John Steptoe's *Stevie* (Harper, 1969), Marcia Brown's *Once a Mouse* (Scribner's, 1961), or Brian Wildsmith's illustration of Robert Louis Stevenson's *A Child's Garden of Verses* stand out on the shelves of books for young children? It is the sensitive integration of pictures and content that incorporates most of the following criteria.

Effective illustrations in a book for children should:

1. Suit the content of the book

2. Be understood by children

3. Support or extend the story content

4. Represent excellent art in varied media

5. Avoid stereotyped approaches to art and the ideas portrayed

Effective content in children's books for the early years should:

1. Interest young children

2. Present original ideas

3. Depict characters realistically and honestly

4. Include appropriate emotions, but not sentimentality

5. Be comprehensible to young children

6. Incorporate a distinctive style that uses vivid imagery, exciting vocabulary, and appropriate idiom

As you explore books for young children, you will probably be amazed by the great variety of topics presented, the sheer beauty of many books, and the wealth of information that children are given. We need to be aware, however, that all children do not see the books you may examine during your exploration. It is important, therefore, to consider how we can bring children and books together, so that more children do benefit from this potential wealth.

Photograph Copyright © 1976 by Christopher G. Knight. From I Have Four Names for My Grandfather *by Kathryn Lasky, by permission of Little, Brown and Co.*

THE KEYS TO THE KINGDOM: NURSERY RHYMES

A part of every child's heritage are the nursery rhymes we commonly attribute to Mother Goose. Jack Sprat, Bobby Shaftoe, Little Bo Peep, Simple Simon—all these names should be familiar to children growing up today, but we adults must make the introduction.

Although the identity of Mother Goose lies hidden in history, the speculations are many. Boston claims that Dame Goose lies at rest in the Old Granary Burying Ground, a claim based only on legend. The name Mother Goose appears to have been used first in French, *Contes de Ma*

Mère l'Oye (*Mother Goose Tales*), by Charles Perrault when he published a collection of his first fairytales, which included *Sleeping Beauty*. One artist's conception of Mother Goose appears in Feodor Rojankovsky's *Tall Book of Mother Goose*.

Whatever their origin, these jingles have endured over a period of time and have consistently been favorites of young children. And we adults have an opportunity to enjoy the verses again as we share them with toddlers, as well as children in the primary and upper grades. What a rich source of language, imagery, and story content!

Here is a selected list of editions of nursery rhymes to examine:

Adams, Charles, illus. *The Charles Adams Mother Goose*. Harper, 1967.

Aliki, illus. *Hush Little Baby*. Prentice-Hall, 1968.

Anglund, Joan Walsh, illus. *A Mother Goose ABC; In a Pumpkin Shell*. Harcourt Brace Jovanovich, 1960.

Briggs, Raymond, illus. *The Mother Goose Treasury*. Coward-McCann, 1966.

———. *Ring-a Ring o' Roses*. Coward-McCann, 1962.

———. *The White Land*. Coward-McCann, 1963.

Brooke, Leslie, illus. *Ring O'Roses: A Nursery Rhyme Picture Book*. Warne, 1922.

Caldecott, Randolph, illus. *Hey Diddle Diddle Picture Book*. Warne, n.d.

Cooney, Barbara. *The Courtship, Merry Marriage, and Feast of Cock Robin and Jenny Wren, to which is added the Doleful Death of Cock Robin*. Scribner, 1965.

De Angeli, Marguerite, illus. *Marguerite de Angeli's Book of Nursery and Mother Goose Rhymes*. Doubleday, 1954.

Emberley, Ed, illus. *London Bridge Is Falling Down; The Song and Game*. Little, Brown, 1967.

Frasconi, Antonio, illus. *The House That Jack Built*. Harcourt Brace Jovanovich, 1958.

Galdone, Paul. *The History of Simple Simon*. McGraw-Hill, 1966.

———. *The House That Jack Built*. McGraw-Hill, 1960.

———. *Old Mother Hubbard and Her Dog*. McGraw-Hill, 1960.

———. *The Old Woman and Her Pig*. McGraw-Hill, 1960.

———. *Tom, Tom the Piper's Son*. McGraw-Hill, 1964.

"Mother Goose" from The Tall Book of Mother Goose *illustrated by Feodor Rojankovsky. Copyright 1942 by Western Publishing Company, Inc. Reprinted by permission.*

I had a little nut-tree, nothing would it bear
But a silver nutmeg and a golden pear;
The King of Spain's daughter came to visit me,
And all because of my little nut-tree.
I skipp'd over water, I danced over sea,
And all the birds in the air couldn't catch me.

There was a crooked man, and he went a
    crooked mile,
And found a crooked sixpence against a crooked
    stile;
He bought a crooked cat, which caught a
    crooked mouse.
And they all lived together in a little crooked
    house.

Simple Simon met a pieman
    Going to the fair;
Says Simple Simon to the pieman,
    "Let me taste your ware."

Says the pieman to Simple Simon,
    "Show me first your penny."
Says Simple Simon to the pieman,
    "Indeed I have not any."

Simple Simon went a-fishing
    For to catch a whale;
All the water he had got
    Was in his mother's pail!

Greenaway, Kate, illus. *Mother Goose; or, The Old Nursery Rhymes.* Warne, 1882.

Grover, Eulalie Osgood, ed. *Mother Goose; The Volland Edition.* Hubbard Press, 1971.

Jeffers, Susan. *Three Jovial Huntsmen.* Bradbury Press, 1973.

Kepes, Juliet. *Lady Bird, Quickly.* Little, Brown, 1964.

Lines, Kathleen, ed. *Lavender's Blue.* Illustrated by Harold Jones. F. Watts, 1964.

Montgomerie, Norah and William, comps. *A Book of Scottish Nursery Rhymes.* Illustrated by T. Ritchie and Norah Montgomerie. Oxford, 1965.

Montresor, Beni. *I Saw a Ship A-Sailing.* Knopf, 1967.

Mother Goose in Hieroglyphics. Houghton Mifflin, 1962. Originally published in Boston over a century ago.

Opie, Iona, ed. *Ditties for the Nursery.* Illustrated by Monica Walker. Walck, 1954.

Opie, Iona and Peter, comps. *A Family Book of Nursery Rhymes.* Illustrated by Pauline Baynes. Oxford, 1964.

————and————, comps. *The Oxford Nursery Rhyme Book.* Illustrated from old chapbooks with additional pictures by Joan Hassall. Walck, 1955.

Rackham, Arthur, illus. *Mother Goose; The Old Nursery Rhymes.* Watts, 1969.

Reed, Philip, illus. *Mother Goose and Nursery Rhymes.* Atheneum, 1963.

Reeves, James. *One's None; Old Rhymes for New Tongues.* Watts, 1968.

Sendak, Maurice, illus. *Hector Protector, and As I Went Over the Water.* Harper, 1965.

Spier, Peter, illus. *London Bridge Is Falling Down!* Doubleday, 1967.

Tenggren, Gustaf, illus. *The Tenggren Mother Goose.* Little, Brown, 1956.

Tucker, Nicholas, comp. *Mother Goose Lost.* Illustrated by Trevor Stubley. Thomas Y. Crowell, 1971.

Tudor, Tasha, illus. *Mother Goose.* Walck, 1944.

Wildsmith, Brian, illus. *Brian Wildsmith's Mother Goose.* Watts, 1965.

Wright, Blanche Fisher, illus. *The Real Mother Goose.* Rand, 1916.

We may often assume that everyone knows Mother Goose because the lines are so familiar as we read them. Can you supply the second line that follows each of these famous first lines?

A diller, a dollar . . .

Peter, Peter, pumpkin eater . . .

Diddle, diddle, dumpling, my son John . . .

Tom, Tom, the piper's son . . .

Hush-a-bye, baby, on the tree top . . .

Mary, Mary, quite contrary . . .

Georgie, Porgie, pudding and pie . . .

Higgledy, piggledy, my black hen . . .

Wee Willie Winkie runs through the town . . .

There was an old woman who lived in a shoe . . .

This is an interesting thing to do with children, too. Their answers will give you insight into their knowledge of Mother Goose rhymes.

Mother Goose rhymes offer an excellent source of delightful language activities for young children, for example, active games such as "London Bridge" or "Ring Around the Rosey." The hand motions to accompany "Peas Porridge Hot" provide a pleasantly intricate game that two young people can engage in while chanting the words of the rhyme, thus:

1	2	3		
Peas	Porridge	hot		
2	1	2		
Peas	Porridge	cold		
3	2	1		2
Peas	porridge	in	the	pot
3	2	1		
Nine	days	old,		
1	2	3		
Some	like	it	hot,	
2	1	2		
Some	like	it	cold,	
3	2	1		2
Some	like	it	in	the	pot,
3	2	1		
Nine	days	old		

1. Each person slaps his or her own knees.

2. Each person claps his or her hands together.

3. The players clap their hands against each others (palm to palm).

The trick, of course, is to say the lines as quickly as possible and still keep the motions correct. Try this activity with a child. It's fun!

Older children, too, will enjoy these verses if you can provide an acceptable reason for reading and saying them. You might, for example, focus on developing oral interpretation with middle school students, using these verses as the medium for working on intonation, enunciation, and pacing. Students will read many rhymes as they select the ones, for example, they will develop for presentation to a kindergarten class. Encourage them to act out the dramatic elements in such verses as "Little Miss Muffet." Visualize the action in this short poem as you read it.

Little Miss Muffet
Sat on a tuffet
Eating her curds and whey.

Along came a spider
And sat down beside her
And frightened Miss Muffet away!

The language in these verses is also intriguing. What are *curds* and *whey?* What is a *tuffet?*

A group of students will have fun speaking a poem that requires good timing and careful pronunciation of each word such as this tongue twister about Betty Botter:

Betty Botter bought some butter,
But, she said, the butter's bitter;
If I put it in my batter,
It will make my batter bitter,
But a bit of better butter,
Will make my batter even better.
So she bought a bit of better butter,
And she put it in her batter,
And the batter was not bitter.
So 'twas better Betty Botter
Bought a bit of better butter.

Mother Goose rhymes should be a part of every child's background. If the boy or girl in seventh grade has somehow missed knowing them, make sure these students meet Jack and Jill, Georgie Porgie, Little Boy Blue, and all the rest of this large family before leaving your classroom.

✿ *THE NURSERY RHYMES* Examine several editions of Mother Goose rhymes to familiarize yourself with the variety that is included. You may discover some verses that you never heard before. Then complete these activities:

1. See if you can find one example of each of these topics or categories:

Song	King
Story	Alphabet
Riddle	Proverb
Game	Superstition
Animal	Weather
Child	

2. Memorize at least three rhymes that you can share with children.

3. Try one of the activities described on the preceding pages. Work with either younger or older students.

ALPHABET BOOKS

Books based on the alphabet are now so numerous that they form a special category. Well-known illustrators have found the ABC books an appropriate framework for their art, and so we have *Brian Wildsmith's ABC* (Watts, 1963). Poets have also used this method of presenting concepts to children as in *All Around the Town* (Lippincott, 1948) by Phyllis McGinley and *Puptents and Pebbles* (Little, Brown, 1959) by William Jay Smith. Additional alphabet books you might find interesting include:

Alexander, Anne. *ABC of Cars and Trucks*. Illustrated by Ninon. Doubleday, 1956.

Baskin, Hosea, Tobias, and Lisa. Illustrated by Leonard Baskin. *Hosie's Alphabet*. Viking, 1972. (See the color section.)

Deers, Dorothy Sands. *ABC Alphabet Cookbook*. Illustrated by Denise Drag. Schmitt, Hall & McCreary, 1972.

Delaunay, Sonia. *Sonia Delaunay's Alphabet*. Thomas Y. Crowell, 1972.

Duvoisin, Roger. *A for the Ark*. Lothrop, 1952.

Eichenberg, Fritz. *Ape in a Cape*. Harcourt Brace Jovanovich, 1952.

Gág, Wanda. *The ABC Bunny*. Coward-McCann, 1933.

Garten, Jan. *The Alphabet Tale*. Illustrated by Muriel Batherman. Random House, 1964.

Grossbart, Francine. *A Big City*. Harper & Row, 1964.

Lear, Edward. *ABC*. McGraw-Hill, 1965.

Matthiesen, Thomas. *ABC An Alphabet Book*. Platt & Munk, 1966.

Morse, Samuel French. *All in a Suitcase*. Illustrated by Barbara Cooney. Little, Brown, 1966.

Munari, Bruno. *Bruno Munari's ABC*. World Publishing, 1960.

Piatti, Celestino. *Celestino Piatti's Animal ABC*. Atheneum, 1966.

Shuttlesworth, Dorothy. *ABC of Buses*. Illustrated by Leonard Shortall. Doubleday, 1965.

Tallow, Robert. *Zoophabets*. Bobbs-Merrill, 1971.

Tudor, Tasha. *A Is for Annabelle*. Walck, 1954.

Walters, Marguerite. *City-Country ABC*. Illustrated by Ib Ohlsson. Doubleday, 1966.

Zacks, Irene. *Space Alphabet*. Illustrated by Peter Plascencia. Prentice-Hall, 1964.

The alphabet book is obviously very popular. The books are attractive and they present interesting concepts and things to talk about. ABC books should not be misconceived as a means, however, to teach children the relationship of sound and symbol, because the selection of words presented is not linguistically sound. The fact that we have identified forty sounds in spoken English that are represented by only twenty-six letter symbols presents difficulty. Will *A* stand for *apple, ape, army,* or *Alice?* Few of the alphabet books will stand up to such rigorous analysis as books that help teach reading or spelling because they were never intended for that purpose.

The use of the alphabet as a framework for presenting ideas is largely a matter of convenience. The child's learning of alphabetical order or recognition of the letter symbols is purely incidental. If we examine ABC books from this viewpoint, we will then be concerned with the quality of the illustrations and the originality of the words and concepts selected. The books will be used as a pleasurable way of presenting varied information to a child, for example, the names of animals. These books are true picture books because there is no meaningful story. They are highly useful as prereading books if children are encouraged to talk about the tiger that Brian Wildsmith has painted or the big city ideas contributed by Francine Grossbart.

Alphabet books have something to offer older students, too, if you present them in the right light. Norma Farber's *I Found Them in the Yellow Pages* (Little, Brown, 1973), for example, might interest fourth grade students who are studying the community. Upper elementary or junior high schoolers would be intrigued by *Handtalk: An ABC of Finger Spelling & Sign Language* by Remy Charlip et al. (Parents, 1974), an attractive explanation of sign language. Another interesting collection of ideas is *The Mime Alphabet Book* by Nina and Cathy Gasiorowicz (Lerner, 1974), in which the mime figures enact words suggested by each letter, for example, *i—icky*.

COUNTING BOOKS

Counting books are similar to those based on the alphabet and are usually very short because they present only ten numbers. Again, Wildsmith has colorfully illustrated *Brian Wildsmith's 1, 2, 3's,* and Tasha Tudor's lovely illustrations can be enjoyed in *1 Is One.* Representative titles include:

Alain, pseud. (Emile Chartier). *One, Two, Three, Going to Sea.* Scott, 1964.

Carle, Eric. *The Rooster Who Set Out to See the World.* Watts, 1972.

Duvoisin, Roger. *Two Lonely Ducks.* Knopf, 1955.

Eichenberg, Fritz. *Dancing in the Moon.* Harcourt Brace Jovanovich, 1955.

Elkin, Benjamin. *Six Foolish Fisherman.* Illustrated by Katherine Evans. Childrens Press, 1957.

Françoise, pseud. (Françoise Seignobosc.) *Jeanne-Marie Counts Her Sheep.* Scribner, 1951.

Hoban, Russell C. *Ten What? A Mystery Counting Book.* Illustrated by Sylvie Selig. Scribner, 1975.

Ipcar, Dahlov. *Brown Cow Farm.* Doubleday, 1959.

———. *Ten Big Farms.* Knopf, 1958.

Kirn, Ann. *Nine in a Line.* Norton, 1966.

Kruss, James. *3 X 3 Three by Three.* Translated by Geoffrey Strachan. Illustrated by Johanna Rubin. Macmillan, 1965.

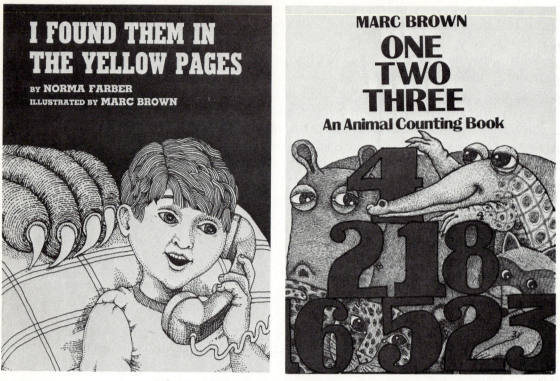

Left: Copyright © 1973 by Marc Brown. From I Found Them in the Yellow Pages *by Norma Faber, by permission of Little, Brown and Co.*

Right: Copyright © 1976 by Marc Brown. From One Two Three: An Animal Counting Book *by Marc Brown, by permission of Little, Brown and Co.*

Langstaff, John. *Over in the Meadow*. Illustrated by Feodor Rojankovsky. Harcourt Brace Jovanovich, 1957.

McLeod, Emilie W. *One Snail and Me: A Book of Numbers and Animals and a Bathtub*. Illustrated by Walter Lorraine. Little, Brown, 1961.

Moore, Lilian. *My First Counting Book*. Illustrated by Garth Williams. Golden Press, 1956.

Sendak, Maurice. *One Way Johnny*. Nutshell Library, vol. 3. Harper & Row, 1962.

Tudor, Tasha. *1 Is One*. Walck, 1956.

Wildsmith, Brian. *Brian Wildsmith's 1, 2, 3's*. Watts, 1965.

Zolotow, Charlotte. *One Step, Two . . .* Illustrated by Roger Duvoisin. Lothrop, 1955.

The counting books can be readily used for teaching children number concepts because there is no conflict between the concept and the symbol. Children who are fascinated by these new concepts pore over the attractive books as they count repeatedly the figures in each illustration. Encouraged by parents and their own sense of accomplishment, they learn naturally in this way.

❦ *ALPHABET AND COUNTING BOOKS*   Select two of these activities as you investigate ABC and counting books:

1. Examine at least three ABC books and three counting books. Make a card for each book you examine, noting your reaction especially to the illustrations and the vocabulary as well as other features that interest you.

2. Plan an original alphabet book or a counting book that you think would be interesting and informative for children. Prepare at least one full-size page for your book. Share your ideas with others in the class.

If you think you have a really good idea, you might wish to prepare several pages and send them to a publisher listed in *Writer's Market* or *Literary Marketplace*. (These reference books are available in your local public library.)

3. Choose one alphabet or counting book to present to a kindergarten or first grade class. Plan how you would present it and what follow-up activities would be appropriate—art, music, discussion, movement. Carry out this presentation as planned.

BOOKS ABOUT ANIMALS

Bears and beavers, tigers and tomcats, dogs and dinosaurs—all kinds of animals appear in books for young children. Animals consistently have a high appeal for children, even those they've never seen except in a zoo.

Some authors portray animals as almost human. The parent animals talk, worry, and solve the family problems. Such a story is Walter Steig's *Sylvester and the Magic Pebble* (Simon and Schuster), which was selected for the Caldecott award in 1970. Sylvester and his parents are donkeys. They walk erect and wear clothes (Mother even wears an apron!). Mother cries when she is worried about Sylvester, and is comforted by

Father. Indeed, this author has made the mother donkey so human that she represents a deplorable stereotype of a mother.

Beatrix Potter's *The Tale of Peter Rabbit* (1901) is a well-known animal story that depicts the animals wearing clothes and exemplifying human characteristics. Peter, for example, is the typical naughty little boy while his sisters are well-behaved, conforming little girls. Peter is put to bed by a concerned mother and given camomile tea to make him feel better.

Another charming story of animals with human characteristics is *A Robber! A Robber!* (Morrow, 1976), written by Franz Brandenberg and illustrated by Aliki Brandenberg. This book presents two rascally "cat-kids" named Elizabeth and Edward; only the illustrations reveal that these characters are cats. When they hear noises at night, they worry about the robbers stealing Edward's stamp collection or Elizabeth's seashells. Big-eyed, Edward peers from the covers:

"If I scream for help, the robber will wake up," thought Edward.

"He'll get angry and take the postcards Uncle Peter has sent me from all over the world." He didn't wiggle a toe.

Some other stories that present animals in a humanized fashion are:

Kesselman, Wendy. *Time for Jody.* Illustrated by Gerald Dumas. Harper, 1975. (*A young female groundhog gets a job.*)

Schecter, Ben. *Molly Patch and Her Animal Friends.* Harper, 1975. (*Molly loves all the animals and they love her.*)

Sharmat, Marjorie Weinman. *Burton and Dudley.* Illustrated by Barbara Cooney. Holiday, 1975. (*The story of two possum friends.*)

More commonly, authors portray animals behaving realistically—except that the animals do talk about their animal problems, which often involve humans.

Aileen Fisher tells a story in rhyme entitled *You Don't Look Like Your Mother* (Bowmar, 1973), beautifully illustrated by Ati Forberg. Part of a series, this book shows a robin that is perturbed because the baby animals she sees don't look like their mothers. When her eggs hatch, however, she has no trouble identifying the "naked, scrawny chicks" as her own, even if they don't look like their mother.

Robert McCloskey's award-winning book *Make Way for Ducklings* (Viking, 1941) presents ducks in a similar fashion. Mr. and Mrs. Mallard

2. Explore the work of one author who has written books about animals for children, for example, Beatrix Potter. To find out more about this particular author you might read *Nothing Is Impossible: The Story of Beatrix Potter* by Dorothy Aldis (Atheneum, 1969), a biography written for older students. And of course, examine her many small books that are just as entertaining as the familiar *Peter Rabbit.* Then plan how you could share this information with children through a poster, clay figures, an enlarged illustration, or an attractive bulletin board display.

3. Search for a number of books about one animal; for instance, several about bears are: *Little Bear* by Else Minarik (Harper, 1957); *Eddie's Bear* by Miska Miles (Little, Brown, 1970), or *The Biggest Bear* by Lynd Ward (Houghton Mifflin, 1952). There are a number of stories also about frogs, toads, ducks, whales, and of course, cats, dogs, and horses. Try to find nonfiction about animals as well as poetry. Plan how you could present a study of one animal: beginning with a story, discussing with primary children how the author portrays the animal, and moving on to nonfiction as you discover together.

FANCIFUL FUN IN PICTURE BOOKS

A large group of books for the very young are fanciful tales that usually are humorous. Many of the animal stories we have discussed in which animals talk and have marvelous adventures fall into this category, for example, *Anatole and the Cat* (McGraw-Hill, 1957), the story of a French mouse, by Eve Titus. *Jasmine* (Knopf, 1973) by Roger Duvoisin tells how Jasmine the cow finds a hat and admires her reflection in the pond as all her friends, Petunia and the other animals on Pumpkin Farm, watch.

One of the masters of such writing for children is Theodor Seuss Geisel (Dr. Seuss), whose first book, *And to Think That I Saw It on Mulberry Street,* appeared in 1937 (Vanguard). Bartholomew Cubbins is introduced in *The 500 Hats of Bartholomew Cubbins* (Vanguard, 1938) as the poor boy tries to honor the king by removing his hat. *McElligott's Pool* (Random House, 1947) is an imaginative tale of a boy who sits fishing in a farmer's pool even though the farmer calls him a fool. Imagining how the pool might connect underground with a river going to the ocean, he envisions all the wild and wonderful fish that might be attracted to his hook. The boy replies: "If I wait long enough, if I'm patient and cool, who knows what I'll catch in McElligott's Pool!" In 1957, this prolific author and illustrator produced a highly influential little book called *The Cat and the Hat* (Random House), a crazy story told in nonsense verse

Top left: Illustration by Garth Williams from Bedtime for Frances *by Russell Hoban. Pictures copyright © 1960 by Garth Williams. Reprinted by permission of Harper & Row, Publishers, Inc.*

Top right: From The Story of Babar, *illustrated by Jean De Brunhoff. Copyright 1933 and renewed 1961 by Random House, Inc. Reprinted by permission of the publisher.*

Bottom left: Illustration from Owl at Home *by Arnold Lobel. Copyright © 1975 by Arnold Lobel. Reprinted by permission of Harper & Row, Publishers, Inc.*

Bottom right: Lyle, Lyle Crocodile *by Bernard Waber, illustrated Copyright © 1965 by Bernard Waber. Reprinted by permission of Houghton Mifflin Publishers.*

Who's Who in the Animal World? *How many of the animal characters do you know in this Who's Who in the Animal World?*

molt as ducks are supposed to, but they also speak a combination of human language and "quackery." A typical dialogue occurs when Mr. Mallard decides to spend a week exploring the river:

"I'll meet you in a week, in the Public Garden," he quacked over his shoulder. "Take good care of the ducklings."

"Don't worry," said Mrs. Mallard. "I know all about bringing up children." And she did.

The Church Mice Spread Their Wings (Atheneum, 1975) by Graham Oakley includes such characters as Humphrey the Schoolmouse, who lectures to his mice friends about their struggle for survival "crushed by the Pressures of Modern Life." Aided by Sampson the church cat, who "had taken a solemn vow never to harm mice," they set off for a weekend in the country to cool their "fevered brows." Beautifully illustrated by the author, this picture book presents a sophisticated but hilarious story that will delight older readers. Other books in this series include *The Church Mouse, The Church Cat Abroad,* and *The Church Mice and the Moon.*

The most realistic treatment of animals is told in the third person by an observer of animal behavior. One of the best known books of this type for young children is *The Biggest Bear* (Houghton Mifflin, 1951) by Lynd Ward, which won the Caldecott Medal in 1952. This comic story tells of Johnny's efforts to capture a bear and then to raise the bear as it keeps on growing bigger and bigger.

Another realistic story is *Nobody's Cat* by Miska Miles (Little, Brown, 1969), who writes of an old alley cat that "knew many things about the city. He knew about trucks and dogs. And he knew about people. He knew when to run. And he knew when to walk without fear."

The Biggest Bear *by Lynd Ward. Copyright 1952 by Lynd Ward. Reprinted by permission of Houghton Mifflin Publishers.*

Donald Carrick tells of a deer that becomes so tame that it comes into the barn with the cows. Although it seems cruel, the farmer and the game warden finally have to teach the deer to be frightened of guns as hunting season approaches. *The Deer in the Pasture* (Morrow, 1976) is a simple story with attractive illustrations by the author.

A number of authors have written realistic books about animals that delight young children. Look for some of these favorites:

C. W. Anderson. *Billy and Blaze.* Macmillan, 1936. (*About a horse.*)

Mary Marsh Buff and Conrad Buff. *Dash and Dart.* Viking, 1942. (*About two deer.*)

Marjorie Flack. *The Story of Ping.* Viking, 1953. (*About a duck.*)

Wanda Gág. *Millions of Cats.* Coward, 1928.

Dorothy Lathrop. *Who Goes There?* Macmillan, 1935. (*About many small forest animals.*)

Philip Stong. *Honk: the Moose.* Dodd, 1935.

Books about animals continue to appeal to both child and adult, so we enjoy such books as Dr. Seuss' *Horton Hears a Who* and Michael Bond's tales of Paddington or Olga da Polga, a bear and a guinea pig, respectively, and move on to *The Wind in the Willows,* and still later, Richard Adams' *Watership Down.* As Margaret Blount concludes in her intriguing study, *Animal Land: The Creatures of Children's Fiction* (Morrow, 1975):

The animals in fact and fiction will not leave us alone. Perhaps that is well, we love them, and as in all good tales, want to be loved by them, and live with them happily for ever. They teach us about themselves—and ourselves—and can give us those amusing, thoughtful, bookish holidays that are as refreshing as the physical kind. Long may they continue to do so.

❦ *BOOKS ABOUT ANIMALS* Examine some of the representative titles presented in the discussion of animal books. Then choose two of the following activities as you explore these books in greater depth:

1. Read three books about animals written for preschool or primary children. Analyze the books to determine how the author portrays the animals and how each book meets the criteria listed on page 34.

that is easy to read. Thus began a whole series of such books for beginning readers.

A series of books that delight children are those about Georgie, a friendly ghost who is always getting into trouble. Robert Bright introduced this character in *Georgie* (Doubleday, 1944). Georgie lived with Mr. and Mrs. Whittaker in New England then, but he moves to other locations in such subsequent adventures as *Georgie to the Rescue* (Doubleday, 1956) and *Georgie Goes West* (Doubleday, 1973).

Edward Ardizzone has written a collection of books about Tim, a small boy who goes to sea as a stowaway in *Little Tim and the Brave Sea Captain* (Walck, 1955). He experiences a shipwreck in *Tim All Alone* (Walck, 1957) and *Tim's Last Voyage* (Walck, 1973). Ardizzone tells the stories as seriously as if they were fact, which entrances the reader, and he illustrates these popular books with color washes and high good humor.

Crockett Johnson writes about Harold, an imaginative young man who creates new worlds with a purple crayon, in *Harold and the Purple Crayon* (Harper, 1955) and *A Picture for Harold's Room; A Purple Crayon Adventure* (Harper, 1960). In the second book, he draws a picture and steps into it for a series of encounters with things he himself has created.

Illustration from Harold and the Purple Crayon *by Crockett Johnson. Copyright, 1955, by Crockett Johnson. Reprinted by permission of Harper & Row, Publishers, Inc.*

And then Harold made his bed.   **He got in it and he drew up the covers.**

Such books may be useful in stimulating children's artistic ability and appreciation of fantasy.

Other fanciful tales that you might investigate for sharing with young children include:

Crosby Bonsall. *The Case of the Cat's Meow.* Harper & Row, 1965. (*One of a series of easy-to-read mysteries.*)

Dahlov Ipcar. *The Biggest Fish in the Sea.* Viking, 1972. (*Tino catches the fish, but it swallows him and his family.*)

Peggy Parish. *Come Back, Amelia Bedelia.* Harper & Row, 1971. (*Tales of a funny housekeeper; look for other books about Amelia Bedelia.*)

Tomi Ungerer. *Moon Man.* Harper & Row, 1967. (*The man in the moon takes a trip to earth.*)

ILLUSTRATED FOLKTALES

Many author–illustrators have turned to folklore, which they may retell or simply interpret anew through artistic means. A beautiful example is Nonny Hogrogian's *One Fine Day* (Macmillan, 1971), an Armenian tale that develops in cumulative style. Gabriela Mistral, Chilean poet, presents a fable, *Crickets and Frogs,* bilingually, with the text in both Spanish and English (Atheneum, 1972). Gail E. Haley retells an African tale in *A Story, A Story* (Atheneum, 1970), and James Houston tells an Eskimo legend for young children *Kiviok's Magic Journey* (Atheneum, 1973). Here is just a sampling of the fine lore from around the world that is available for preschool and primary grades:

The Magician of Cracow by Krystyna Turska. Morrow, 1975. (*Poland*)

The Sultan's Bath by Victor G. Ambrus. Harcourt Brace Jovanovich, 1972. (*Hungary*)

The Boy, The Baker, The Miller and More by Harold Berson. Crown, 1974. (*France*)

Dance of the Animals by Pura Belpre, illustrated by Paul Galdone. Warne, 1972. (*Puerto Rico*)

Clever Kate adapted by Elizabeth Shub. Illustrated by Anita Lobel. Macmillan, 1973. (*Germany*)

The Clay Pot Boy adapted by Cynthia Jameson. Illustrated by Arnold Lobel. Coward-McCann, 1973. (*Russia*)

The Magic Tree adapted and illustrated by Gerald McDermott. Holt, 1973. *(Congo)*

Turnabout adapted and illustrated by William Wiesner. Seabury, 1972. *(Norway)*

The Cool Ride in the Sky told by Diane Wolkstein. Illustrated by Paul Galdone. Knopf, 1973. *(USA, black)*

At times modern authors and illustrators choose to emulate the folktale style as they create original stories. An outstanding example is *The King's Fountain* (Dutton, 1971) written by Lloyd Alexander and illustrated with stunning color by Ezra Jack Keats, a tale of a poor man who tried to persuade the king not to take the city's water to create a beautiful fountain for himself. Evaline Ness wrote *The Girl and the Goatherd; or, This and That and Thus and So* (Dutton, 1970) about a girl who became uglier and uglier so that no one would marry her. When she was granted beauty, however, she found that it did not ensure happiness. Jane Yolen also writes in folktale form in *The Bird of Time* (Thomas Y. Crowell, 1971), which is illustrated by Mercer Mayer (see the color section). Here is the traditional conflict between good and evil as Pieter, son of a poor miller, uses his gift to rescue the princess.

THE REALITIES OF LIFE

A surprising number of books for preschool and primary children deal with very real subjects—getting along with other people, coping with emotions and problems, understanding the feelings of others. Children today need help, even in the early years, with problems such as divorce, death, being different (too little, fat, black-skinned), and they need to be able to understand how other people feel about these problems, too.

One able author who writes with great sensitivity about such topics for young children is Charlotte Zolotow. Although not all her books focus on the feelings of children, she has made a distinctive contribution in this area. One of her early books, *Do You Know What I'll Do?* (Harper, 1958), tells a tender story of a little girl who plans the things she will do for her baby brother; for example, she will build him a snowman when it snows or blow away his nightmares. Another book that tells of sibling relationships is *Big Sister and Little Sister* (Harper & Row, 1966), in which two girls learn to appreciate each other. *A Father Like That* (Harper & Row, 1971) tells of a little boy's imagining what having a father would be like. *Janey* (Harper & Row, 1973) describes a child's feelings when her best friend has moved away. *William's Doll* (Harper & Row, 1972) brings

Illustration by Martha Alexander
from Big Sister and Little
Sister *by Charlotte Zolotow.*
Pictures copyright © 1966 by
Martha Alexander. Reprinted by
permission of Harper & Row,
Publishers, Inc.

mixed reactions to children and adults, for William's grandmother understands this little boy's desire for a doll, and she gives him one so he can learn to be a good father. *My Grandson Lew* (Harper & Row, 1974) presents a child's feelings when his grandfather just doesn't appear anymore, and no one thought to tell the little boy that Grandfather has died. When his mother realizes that Lew misses his grandfather, they share their feelings about missing him.

Joan Lexau is another author who writes effectively about realistic topics for very young children. *Me Day* (Dial, 1971) is a good example, for she relates a young black boy's feelings about his father after a divorce; Rafer wants his father to share his birthday, and he does! A familiar situation is described in *I Should Have Stayed in Bed* (Harper & Row, 1965); Sam, a young black boy, oversleeps, and after that everything goes wrong. *Emily and the Klunky Baby and the Next-door Dog* (Dial, 1972) tells of a lonely little girl's attempt to reach her father who has moved out.

An interesting collection of ten stories called *Families Are Like That!* (Thomas Y. Crowell, 1975) has been compiled by the Child Study Association of America. Included are stories by Joan Lexau, Janice Udry, Rose Blue, Emma Brock, Carolyn Haywood, Marion Holland, Doris Johnson, Patricia Miles Martin, and Ruth Sonneborn. This is good read-aloud material.

An excellent book about adoption is *I Am Adopted* (Bradbury Press, 1975) by Susan Lapsley. First published in England, this story presents a positive picture of adoption because Charles speaks naturally of being adopted and then goes on to the more important things in his life, such as his toy tractor.

The Quitting Deal (Viking, 1975) tells of the difficulty of giving up thumb-sucking or smoking or anything that is a strong habit. Jenny and her mother make a deal, but they find it very hard, even with moral support from the other person. Here is a contemporary family and a realistic view of personal problems.

An outstanding book about a child's experience with love and death is *Do You Love Me?* (Seabury, 1975), in which Walter handles a hummingbird too much and it dies. His sister gives him a puppy, which he can hug without hurting it.

There are many other recommended books that treat these kinds of topics. Some are mentioned elsewhere in this text, particularly in Chapter 4, which deals with realism in children's books. Additional titles you might like to investigate include:

Chihiro Iwasaki. *What's Fun without a Friend?* McGraw-Hill, 1975. (*Child misses her puppy.*)

Winfred Rosen. *Henrietta, The Wild Woman of Borneo.* Four Winds, 1975. (*Henrietta's family loves her even if she is messy.*)

Jannifer Bartoli. *Nonna.* Harvey House, 1975. (*Death of a grandparent seen from child's viewpoint.*)

June Jordan. *New Life: New Room.* Thomas Y. Crowell, 1975. (*Making room for a new baby.*)

Barbara Williams. *Kevin's Grandma.* Dutton, 1975. (*An up-to-date grandmother.*)

Ruth A. Sonneborn. *Friday Night Is Papa Night.* Viking, 1970. (*Papa works away from home, so Pedro's family celebrates Friday when he comes home.*)

SEARCH FOR INFORMATION

Why? Why? Why?—the young child is known for curiosity. Many non-fiction books provide information for children through detailed pictures or simple explanation. Much information can also be presented, how-ever, through a fictional story and sometimes poetic language.

Alvin Tresselt's *The Dead Tree* (Parents' Magazine Press, 1972) is an attractive book, illustrated by Charles Robinson. The language is factual but poetic; the author talks of the giant oak:

It stood tall in the forest.
For a hundred years or more the oak tree
had grown and spread its shade.
Birds nested in its shelter.
Squirrels made their homes in ragged bundles
of sticks and leaves held high in the branches.
And in the fall they garnered their winter food
from the rich rain of acorns that fell
from the tree.

Tresselt tells how, even as the tree grows, there are insects eating inside it until the tree finally dies. Even then, the great tree has not finished its usefulness, its role in the ecological relationship with the animals that live in the forest.

Gail E. Haley's *Jack Jouett's Ride* (Viking, 1973) is a story based on a real happening, a dramatic event in the development of the Revolution. Handsome linoleum block prints provide additional information about the clothing worn, the buildings of the times, and the uniforms of the soldiers.

Norma Klein provides a message about the career possibilities of women in a simple story entitled *Girls Can Be Anything* (Dutton, 1973). Marina rebels when her friend Adam won't let her be a pilot or a doctor. Her parents support her by telling her about her own aunt who is a sur-geon. She convinces Adam that "girls can be anything."

Smoke (Coward-McCann, 1972) is Ib Spang Olsen's story about the effects of pollution. Half fantasy, his writing has a clear statement none-theless, and children will learn that pollution is a problem that all of us must consider.

Historical facts, scientific background information, animal lore— much can be learned from carefully written fiction. In many ways this manner of presenting information is very effective, as learning is made highly palatable. In addition, of course, there is considerable nonfiction published for the young child.

An interesting series of books about careers for women is being devel-oped, for example, *What Can She Be? A Lawyer* (Lothrop, 1973) by

Gloria and Esther Goldreich. A kind of case study approach is used in this series with the life of one woman described. Other titles suggest different careers.

Science experiments for primary grades are presented in *Adventures with a Cardboard Tube* (Dutton, 1972) by Harry Milgrom, who does a good job of helping children explore the properties of the tube. A series of books published by Coward-McCann lead children to understand various environments, as in *The Desert: What Lives There* by Andrew Bronin. Knowledge about animals is the subject of many books for young children, for example, *Animal Homes* (Coward-McCann, 1973) by Sally Cartwright or *Twist, Wiggle and Squirm* (Thomas Y. Crowell, 1973) by Laurence Pringle, which is about earthworms.

The best way to find out what kinds of informational books are available is to check the *Children's Catalog,* which lists the books by subject and provides an indication of difficulty level.

❦ *BOOKS FOR YOUNG CHILDREN* Complete two of these activities as you get acquainted with more books for preschool and primary grades.

1. Develop a slide collection that you could use in the classroom by photographing illustrations from children's books. You might focus on such specific themes as:

   The work of one illustrator

   Telling a fairytale

   The folklore of one country

   Factual information about a topic: animals, trees

   Pictures to motivate creative writing

2. Read three folktales written for young children. Prepare one to tell to a group of children. See page 19 for help with storytelling. Arrange to tell the story in a classroom or library.

3. Prepare a bulletin board display based on the information presented in one book, for example: *A Book about Pandas* (Dial, 1973) by Ruth Belov, *Gorilla Gorilla* (Random House, 1973) by Carol Fenner, or *Bodies* (Dutton, 1973) by Barbara Brenner. Display the book you choose as well as any related fiction or nonfiction that children can investigate.

4. Create a model or diorama depicting a fanciful tale for young children. Make a papier mâché or clay figure for the main character, for example, the crocodile in *The Crocodile in the Tree* (Knopf, 1973) by Roger Duvoisin or Everett Mouse in *The Sugar Snow Spring* (Harper & Row, 1973) written and illustrated by Lillian Hoban. Prepare to tell the story as you share the model with children.

CREATING BOOKS FOR YOUNG CHILDREN

Who are the writers and illustrators who have created books for the youngest book lovers? Which books stand out as exceptionally good stories that will last for many generations? Which illustrators have made particular contributions to the field of children's literature? These are the questions we will discuss in this section.

OUTSTANDING BOOKS

One way of giving recognition to the work of authors and illustrators of books is through the presentation of awards for outstanding work. The number of such awards is steadily increasing in the field of children's literature. In general, however, these awards are given for story content rather than illustrations, which means that awards more commonly go to books for older readers. Awards for story content will be discussed, therefore, in the next chapter.

The most important award given for the illustration of children's books is the Caldecott Medal, named for an early illustrator of children's books, Randolph J. Caldecott (1846–1886). Established in 1937 by Frederic J. Melcher, an American editor and publisher, the Caldecott Medal honors the illustrator of one exceptionally fine book published in the United States each year. A varying number of Honor Books are also announced, for it is often difficult to choose only one in a year when many noteworthy books are published. The award is supervised by the American Library Association's Children's Services Division.

The list of award winners presents an assortment of excellent books for young children. It also includes most of the well-known illustrators. Perusing these titles, therefore, is a good way to become acquainted with some fine books published for the very young. At the same time we must be aware that tastes differ and that many excellent books may be eliminated from consideration by virtue of the limitations placed on the

The Association for Library Service to Children, a division of The American Library Association.

award; for example, books published in any country other than the United States are ineligible.

A complete list of awards and Honor Books is included in the Appendix. Here we will merely cite some of the outstanding works that appear on the Caldecott list. Only three illustrators, for example, have won the Caldecott Medal twice; namely, Robert McCloskey, whose illustrations in the following books were judged outstanding: *Make Way for Ducklings* (1942) and *Time of Wonder* (1958); Marcia Brown who won the award for *Cinderella* (1955) and *Once a Mouse* (1962); and Nonny Hogrogian who won the medal for one of her own books and another listed below. Books that have won the Caldecott award in the past include:

1965 *May I Bring a Friend?* by Beatrice Schenk de Regniers
Illustrator: Beni Montresor (Atheneum)

1966 *Always Room for One More* by Sorche Nic Leodhas
Illustrator: Nonny Hogrogian (Holt)

1967 *Sam, Bangs, and Moonshine* by Evaline Ness
Illustrator: Evaline Ness (Holt)

1968 *Drummer Hoff* by Barbara Emberley
Illustrator: Ed Emberley (Prentice-Hall)

1969 *The Fool of the World and the Flying Ship* by Arthur Ransome
Illustrator: Uri Shulevitz (Farrar, Straus)

1970 *Sylvester and the Magic Pebble* by William Steig
Illustrator: William Steig (Simon and Schuster)

1971 *A Story, A Story* by Gail E. Haley
Illustrator: Gail E. Haley (Atheneum)

1972 *One Fine Day* by Nonny Hogrogian
Illustrator: Nonny Hogrogian (Macmillan)

1973 *The Funny Little Woman* retold by Arlene Mosel
Illustrator: Blair Lent (Dutton)

1974 *Duffy and the Devil* by Harve Zemach
Illustrator: Margot Zemach (Farrar, Straus)

1975 *Arrow to the Sun* by Gerald McDermott
Illustrator: Gerald McDermott (Viking)

1976 *Why Mosquistoes Buzz in People's Ears* retold by Verna Aardema
Illustrators: Leo and Diane Dillon (Dial)

If you examine the complete list of awards and Honor Books in the Appendix, you will find many fine illustrators in addition to those above, listed repeatedly, for example:

Maurice Sendak	Marc Simont
Marie Hall Ets	Barbara Cooney
Leo Politi	Paul Galdone
Taro Tashima	Adrienne Adams
Leo Lionni	Arnold Lobel
Ezra Jack Keats	Tom Feelings
Leonard Weisgard	Dr. Seuss (Theodor Geisel)
Kurt Wiese	Lynd Ward
William Pène du Bois	James Daugherty
Clare Newberry	Wanda Gág
Robert Lawson	Berta and Elmer Hader
Ludwig Bemelmans	Maud and Miska Petersham
Elizabeth Orton Jones	Nicolás

You can find listings of the work of these illustrators in the *Children's Catalog,* which indicates the books that they have both written and illustrated as well as the ones they have just illustrated.

Only a few other awards are given for the artistry of children's books. The American Institute of Graphic Arts' Children's Books Show, held since 1941, displays books that are considered excellent in design. Fifty Books of the Year are selected by the American Institute of Graphic Arts, although these books are not all children's books. The New York *Times* has sponsored an annual award for the best illustrated children's books of the year since 1952. The Boston *Globe* and the *Horn Book* have united in giving an annual award to both an author and illustrator since 1967. Additional awards are described briefly in the Appendix.

An interesting collection of books for young children that is featured each year is the Children's Book Showcase, a juried selection conducted by the Children's Book Council. Initiated in 1972, this collection features books that exemplify the best in graphic design. Showcase catalogues available from the council include detailed information about book production and critiques of the books selected. Also available is a pamphlet describing ways of organizing displays of these books in local areas.

In addition to the books already discussed or listed in this chapter, many other books stand out as having something significant to offer. Here is another collection of picture books that are recommended for any library.

Crow Boy by Taro Yashima. Viking, 1955.
We never do know his name, but the children call him "Chibi," *little boy*. Silent, he sits in the classroom, an outsider. Finally a new teacher begins to talk to him, learning that he walks miles each day to school, that he knows much about the plants of the countryside, and that he knows how to imitate the many calls of the crows that fly above him. When he demonstrates this ability, the children give him the new name of Crow Boy, and he becomes an accepted member of the group. An outstanding combination of beautiful art and a good story, this book presents an important message without moralizing.

The Story of Ferdinand by Munro Leaf. Illustrated by Robert Lawson. Viking, 1939.
Peaceful Ferdinand preferred to smell the flowers rather than fight. He makes a great impression as a ferocious bull when a bee stings him, however. Here is a well-told story set in Spain illustrated with exceptionally fine black and white drawings by Robert Lawson.

From Crow Boy *by Taro Yashima. Copyright © 1955 by Mitsu and Taro Yashima. Reprinted by permission of The Viking Press.*

The Happy Owls by Celestino Piatti. Atheneum, 1963.
The owls sit calmly and wisely observing the squabbling in the poultry yard below. When asked why they are so happy, they enumerate all the good things they enjoy in each season of the year, the "secrets of their peace." The peacock and other fowl consider this nonsense and go on living as before. The legend is simply and effectively told and is supported by the strength of the bold poster art for which Piatti has won acclaim in Switzerland. The book has been filmed by Weston Woods.

Stevie by John Steptoe. Harper & Row, 1969.
Here is a young black author who portrays black children and their families realistically. The language is well handled, contemporary, and authentic, and the illustrations are spectacular—strong, colorful, and supportive of the story, which tells of Robert's resentment of Stevie until Stevie is gone and he realizes that he misses the child.

Swimmy by Leo Lionni. Pantheon, 1963.
This fish story tells how cooperation can result in a solution. The little fish are threatened by a huge fish, so they unite to form an even bigger fish that frightens their common enemy away. Leo Lionni's illustrations are delicately beautiful in his depictions of the underwater scenes.

Petronella by Jay Williams. Parents' Magazine Press, 1973.
In the tradition of all great fairy tales, there are three princes and the youngest prince always triumphs. King Peter and Queen Blossom are chagrined, therefore, when the third child turns out to be a girl! Petronella, as she is christened, has a mind of her own. When the older princes

set out to seek their fortunes, she appears with her bag packed determined to find a prince! She finds a prince, a very unsatisfactory prince, so she brings home an enchanter instead.

These books are ones that most children will enjoy. As you become better acquainted with books, and as new ones appear, you will make other choices, but the books described in this section will continue to have appeal for many generations.

❦ *OUTSTANDING BOOKS*   These activities are designed to help you organize your study of children's books.

1. You have already read a number of the Caldecott books. Check this list of award winners as well as the Honor Books in the Appendix. Note which ones you have read.

   Note also those that you would like to read. Perhaps some titles just sound appealing or maybe you've heard of others. Include the work of various illustrators and authors that you would like to know.

   Read at least ten books from this list. Make a card for each book. As you move into the last section of this chapter, you will be asked to prepare teaching materials for these books or others you have read.

2. Begin now to compile your own list of outstanding books. Some books you read, even if they won an award, won't appeal to you. Divide your list into sections now so that it will be more useful later, thus:

   Picture Books

   Easy to Read Books

   Books for Good Readers (grades 4–6 reading level)

   Books for Advanced Readers (junior high level up)

   You may also wish to separate fiction and nonfiction as your list grows.

INTRODUCING AUTHORS AND ILLUSTRATORS

Even very young children can become acquainted with the people who create their books. As we admire the bold illustrations in Feodor Rojankovsky's *Tall Book of Mother Goose,* we can tell children that the pictures were created by this man. We might also bring in other illustrations by the same artist. We can help them become sensitive to the art as well as the story presented by Marcia Brown in *Once a Mouse* or the humor of a story like *Just the Thing for Geraldine* that Ellen Conford wrote for them. In order to do this, of course, we need to know about the authors and illustrators of books for preschool and primary grade children. As we discuss these writers and illustrators we will find that they fall into three groupings: authors who concentrate on writing and do not illustrate; illustrators; and, probably the largest group, author-illustrators, who may illustrate other people's work but often create the story as well as the pictures.

Of the authors, we might begin with Margaret Wise Brown who wrote *The City Noisy Book* (Harper, 1939), and later one of the early attempts to talk about death with children, *The Dead Bird* (Scott, Foresman, 1958). Under the pseudonym Golden MacDonald, she wrote *The Little Island* (Doubleday, 1946), illustrated by Leonard Weisgard, which won a Caldecott Medal. Another outstanding author for young children is Joan Lexau who portrays the feelings of young children with great sensitivity in *Benjie* (Dial, 1964), *The Trouble with Terry* (Dial, 1962), *Striped Ice Cream* (Lippincott, 1968), and *Me Day* (Dial, 1971). Miska Miles, pseudonym of Patricia Miles Martin, writes animal stories such as *Eddie's Bear* (Little, Brown, 1970), *Fox and the Fire* (Little, Brown, 1966), and *Mississippi Possum* (Little, Brown, 1965). Other authors for the youngest readers include the following, for whom representative titles are listed:

Sesyle Joslin. *What Do You Say, Dear?* Illustrated by Maurice Sendak. Young Scott Books. Addison Wesley, 1958.

Ruth Krauss. *A Hole Is to Dig.* (See Illus. p. 67.) Illustrated by Maurice Sendak. Harper, 1952.

Beatrice Schenk de Regniers. *May I Bring a Friend?* Illustrated by Beni Montresor. Atheneum, 1964.

Eve Titus. *Anatole and the Cat.* Illustrated by Roger Duvoisin. McGraw-Hill, 1957. (*And many more tales of Anatole, the French mouse.*)

Alvin Tresselt. *White Snow, Bright Snow.* Illustrated by Roger Duvoisin. Lothrop, 1947.

Jane Yolen. *The Emperor and the Kite.* Illustrated by Ed Young. World, 1967.

Another interesting group of authors and illustrators are those who are married and work as a team. One writes the story, for example, Harve

Zemach, while the other, Margot Zemach, does the illustrations to produce *The Judge: An Untrue Tale* (Farrar, Straus & Giroux, 1969). Russell Hoban wrote *The Mole Family's Christmas* (Parents' Magazine Press, 1969) and Lillian Hoban illustrated it. This team has also done a whole series of tales about Frances the badger. Louise Fatio writes the stories for *The Happy Lion* (McGraw-Hill, 1954) series while husband Roger Duvoisin creates the illustrations, but he writes his own stories for the Petunia and Veronica books about a duck and a hippo respectively. Mary and Conrad Buff write beautiful animal stories such as *Hurry, Skurry, and Flurry* (Viking, 1954), a story of three baby squirrels pictured by Conrad Buff with exquisite detail. Barbara and Ed Emberly also combine their talents, as in *Drummer Hoff* (Prentice-Hall, 1967), which is illustrated boldly by Ed Emberly.

As we begin to consider the illustrators, the list becomes longer. We could begin, for example, with some of the earlier illustrators whose work is still available to young children today. Arthur Rackham illustrated *The Fairy Tales of Grimm* and *The Wind in the Willows*. Ernest H. Shepard illustrated *Winnie-the-Pooh* (see page 88), *The Wind in the Willows,* and *The Reluctant Dragon* (see page 103).

An impressive group of artists are illustrating the work of authors who write for young children. Feodor Rojankovsky stands out with his rich textured figures in *The Old Man Is Always Right* by Hans Christian Andersen and his entertaining illustration of *The Frog Went a-Courtin'* that

From the book Drummer Hoff *by Emberley & Emberley.* © *1967 by Edward R. Emberley and Barbara Emberley. Published by Prentice-Hall, Inc., Englewood Cliffs, New Jersey.*

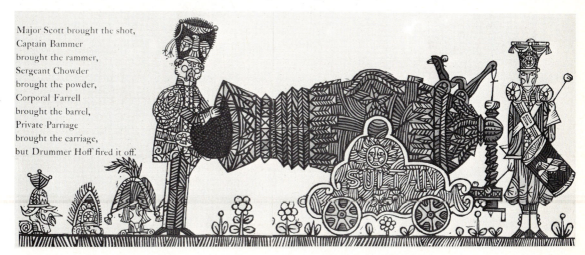

won a Caldecott Medal. Adrienne Adams creates delicate, detailed illustrations in *Thumbelina* (Scribner, 1961), another tale by Hans Christian Andersen, and *Painting the Moon* by Carl Withers. Blair Lent achieves a rare beauty that enhances the telling of *Tikki Tikki Tembo* by Arlene Mosel, which has been filmed by Weston Woods, and *The Angry Moon,* a Tlingit Indian legend told by William Sleator.

It is very difficult to separate illustrators from author-illustrators, because sooner or later most of the excellent illustrators create books of their own. Blair Lent, for example, wrote and illustrated *John Tabor's Ride* (Little, Brown, 1966), the story of a man's ride on the back of a whale across the oceans to Nantucket. Often illustrators turn to fairytales and folklore, as did Nancy Ekholm Burkert who created an outstanding version of *The Fir Tree* by Andersen, but her work also graces Roald Dahl's *James and the Giant Peach* (Knopf, 1961). The work of a number of author-illustrators is so outstanding that we will look at their work individually; namely, Maurice Sendak, Marcia Brown, Evaline Ness, Uri Shulevitz, and Barbara Cooney. Artists whose work lends itself to presentation in color will be presented in a special section included for that purpose.

Photograph of Marcia Brown is used with the permission of Charles Scribner's Sons.

MARCIA BROWN   The daughter of a minister, Marcia Brown was born in Rochester, New York, on July 13, 1918. She was a high school English and drama teacher, a librarian, and a teacher of puppetry before embarking on the career for which she was obviously intended, creating a wealth of books for young people.

Marcia Brown usually illustrates her own stories or those from folklore. Her translation and illustration of Charles Perrault's well-known story *Cinderella, or the Little Glass Slipper* (Scribner, 1954) won the Caldecott award in 1955. She won this award again in 1962 with *Once a Mouse . . .* (Scribner) (see page 220), a folktale from India that she illustrated with striking woodcuts. Perhaps one of the best known of her books, however, is *Stone Soup* (Scribner, 1947), which depicts French peasants who are fooled by a group of lighthearted soldiers into concocting a hearty soup with only a stone.

Marcia Brown's techniques vary widely as she suits the medium for the illustrations to the content of the tale—linoleum blocks in black and brown for *Dick Whittington and His Cat* (England), rich oriental rug tones for *The Flying Carpet* (Arabia), and watercolor and line drawing for *Puss in Boots* (France), a flamboyant figure (see the color section). Speaking of the illustrating of children's books, she states:

There is still among laymen a lack of comprehension of the discipline needed to pare a text to a basic line that looks simple. A picture book is as concise as poetry. Text and pictures combine to form an essence that expands in the child's mind.[1]

MAURICE SENDAK Born on June 10, 1928 in Brooklyn, Maurice Sendak has used his artistic talent to illustrate numerous books for children. His black and white illustrations portray funny little children that some editors don't like, in such books as *A Hole Is to Dig* by Ruth Krauss. A touch of color is added for Beatrice Schenk de Regniers' *What Can You Do with a Shoe?* (Harper, 1955), in which a mischievous boy sings:

You can put it on your ear
  On your beery-leery-ear.
You can put it on your ear, tra-la!

As Sendak says: "I am trying to draw the way children feel—or rather the way I know I felt as a child." He illustrated Else Minarik's Little Bear series as well as Sesyle Joslin's humorous books: *What Do You Say, Dear?* (Young Scott Books, Addison Wesley, 1958) and *What Do You Do, Dear?* (Young Scott Books, Addison Wesley, 1961) (see page 353). He has also illustrated books by Janet Udry (*The Moon Jumpers* and *Let's Be Enemies*), Meindert DeJong (*Along Came a Dog* and *Hurry Home, Candy*), and Randall Jarrell (*The Bat-Poet* and *The Animal Family*).

It was his own story, however, that won the Caldecott award for Maurice Sendak. *Where the Wild Things Are* (Harper, 1963) upset some people with its ugly, humorous, but never fearsome beasts. As Sendak commented in his acceptance speech, "Expurgated vision has no relation to the way real children live." As the Cleveland *Press* noted in a review: "Boys and girls may have to shield their parents from this book. Parents are very easily scared." An excellent film by Weston Woods presents Maurice Sendak in his New York apartment where he talks about his work. Sendak is one of the few Americans to receive the Hans Christian Andersen Award given by the International Board on Books for Young People.

Photograph of Maurice Sendak by Candid Lang.

---

[1] Marcia Brown, "One Wonders . . . ," in *Illustrators of Children's Books: 1957–1966,* Lee Kingman et al., comps. (Horn Book, 1968), p. 24.

*Photograph of Evaline Ness is
used with permission of Charles
Scribner's Sons.*

EVALINE NESS An able author and illustrator, Evaline Ness was born in Union City, Ohio, on April 24, 1911. She attended Ball State Teachers College, various art schools such as the Chicago Art Institute, and now lives in New York City.

Sam, Bangs & Moonshine, pictured at the beginning of this chapter. won the Caldecott Medal for Evaline Ness in 1967. A charming story of a little girl named Samantha, whose mother has died, and Bangs, her old black cat, it tells realistically of the child's loneliness and her tendency to fabricate "moonshine," which gets Sam in trouble. The illustrations are in ink with pale washes of mustard and grayish-green that seem especially appropriate to the setting along the seaside.

Other easy books for young children written by Evaline Ness include *Exactly Alike* (Scribner, 1964), the story of Elizabeth who had four freckled brothers who teased her constantly, especially since she couldn't tell them apart. *Josefina February* (Scribner, 1963), set in Haiti, tells of a little black burro, Cap; illustrations are woodcuts executed in muted tones ranging from orange, greenish-brown, and black against bands of lavender. *Pavo and the Princess* (Scribner, 1964), about a white peacock and the princess who teases him, is enhanced by ornately colorful illustrations. Her *Tomten and the Fox* (Coward-McCann, 1966) is beautiful in shades of the night, while *Do You Have the Time, Lydia?* (Dutton, 1971) is illustrated with ink drawings touched with pinks and yellows. You can find her work also in *Some of the Days of Everett Anderson* by Lucille Clifton and *The Woman of the Wood* (Holt, 1973) retold by Algernon Black.

This illustrator has been honored through recognition of her art that appears in books she has written as well as in the work of other authors. Named as Honor Books for the Caldecott Medal, for example, were *All in the Morning Early* by Sorche Nic Leodhas (Holt, 1963), *A Pocketful of Cricket* by Rebecca Caudill (Holt, 1964), and in 1966 her *Tom Tit Tot* (Scribner, 1965), an English folktale.

BARBARA COONEY Born on August 6, 1917 in Brooklyn, New York, Barbara Cooney was a Second Lieutenant in the Women's Army Corps during World War II. She attended Smith College for her bachelor's degree, married a doctor, and has four children. They live in Pepperell, Massachusetts. Barbara Cooney's way of working within this family setting is featured in the long film *The Lively Art of Picture Books* (Weston Woods).

Like Marcia Brown, Barbara Cooney enjoys stories that originate in legend and lore. The book that won a Caldecott Medal for her is *Chanticleer and the Fox* (Thomas Y. Crowell, 1958), adapted from "The Nun's Priest's Tale" in *The Canterbury Tales,* which she illustrated with striking

*Photograph of Barbara Cooney
by Bradford Bachrach.*

scratchboard art in strong basic reds, blues, and greens. Her work reflects the lengthy and careful research that sometimes takes her to other countries in preparation for a specific book.

Barbara Cooney has illustrated a number of old favorites for older children, such as Louisa May Alcott's *Little Women* (Thomas Y. Crowell) and *Bambi* (Simon & Schuster) by Felix Salten. Her favorites with young children will probably be the book by Lee Kingman, *Peter's Long Walk* (Doubleday, 1953), the story of a five-year-old's search for someone to play with, and Phyllis Krasilovsky's *The Man Who Didn't Wash His Dishes* (Doubleday, 1950). Others to look for include: *Christmas in the Barn* (Thomas Y. Crowell, 1952) by Margaret Wise Brown; *The Courtship, Merry Marriage, and Feast of Cock Robin and Jenny Wren . . .* (Scribner, 1965); and the beautiful edition of Walter de la Mare's volume of poetry, *Peacock Pie* (Knopf, 1961).

URI SHULEVITZ Born in Warsaw, Poland, on February 27, 1935, Uri Shulevitz attended a Teacher's College in Israel and served in the Israeli Army from 1956 to 1959. A master of ink, sometimes overlaid with washes, his rich colorful art enhances many books for young children, especially folktales. "Realizing the excess of words in our culture, I followed an Oriental tradition, trying to say more with fewer words," he states in *Contemporary Authors*. He works with the "purpose of awakening the child's imagination, leaving him free space to add to his own." Shulevitz intends his art to be suggestive, therefore, rather than descriptive.

Photograph of Uri Shulevitz by Donald Wallace. Reproduced with the permission of Farrar, Straus & Giroux, Inc.

This intent is carried out effectively in *Dawn* (Farrar, Straus & Giroux, 1974) with illustrations that change from the darkness of night to the blues of dawn until the yellow sun changes the blue water to green. The storyline is simple: two men sleep under a tree, awaken with the dawn, and go out on the water to fish. The poetic language is brief, but not limited, as in these lines:

The oars screak and rattle,
churning pools of foam.

An excellent example of Uri Shulevitz' more colorful art is found in *Soldier and Tsar in the Forest* (Farrar, Straus & Giroux, 1972), based on a Russian tale translated by Richard Lourie. Heavy black ink outlines brilliant illustrations depicting how a runaway soldier saves the life of the tsar, who is traveling incognito, and thereby saves himself (see the color section).

Waves billow and roll,
Rush, splash and surge,
Rage, roar and rise.

Reproduced with the permission of Farrar, Straus & Giroux, Inc. From Rain, Rain Rivers *words and pictures by Uri Shulevitz. Copyright © 1969 by Uri Shulevitz.*

Other works in which illustrations by Uri Shulevitz can be viewed include his adaptation of *The Magician* (Macmillan, 1973), a Yiddish tale of Elijah the Prophet's visit to a village the night before Passover. *One Monday Morning* (Scribner, 1967), a delightful fantasy, displays his remarkable ability to relate language and art. *Rain, Rain, Rivers* (Farrar, Straus & Giroux, 1969) is informational as well as artistic, for the rain that a little girl views in the city is followed from city puddles to brooks and streams, and then the rivers that finally join the roiling ocean.

Although Uri Shulevitz is at his best illustrating his own books, in which he skillfully plans the relationship between words and art, his work can also be found in books by other authors. Among these are Isaac Bashevis Singer's *The Fools of Chelm and Their History* (Farrar, Straus & Giroux, 1973), a satire for middle grade students, and Arthur Ransome's retelling of *The Fool of the World and The Flying Ship* (Farrar, Straus & Giroux, 1968), a Russian folktale, for which Shulevitz was awarded the Caldecott Medal.

TEACHING WITH PICTURE BOOKS

Illustrated books offer exciting material for use in the classroom. These books provide stimulating stories for children to listen to and to read themselves as soon as they have the desire and the beginning skills of decoding. Picture books offer much more than the enjoyment of a good story, however. In this section we will discuss varied ways that books can be used to stimulate creativity and many pleasurable ways of sharing books through reading aloud, art, films, and dramatization. We will also talk about the popular wordless books that are especially useful in developing language abilities. In addition, we will probe such controversial issues as (1) monsters for children, (2) stereotypes in picture books, and (3) realism for youngsters.

STIMULATING CREATIVITY

The child's world is the poet's world where dimensions differ only according to feeling, not fact, that place of the fourth dimension that eludes all but painters, poets, lunatics, and the players of musical instruments. And it even eludes those at times. That is why they remain children, eternally committed to chasing after it, clinging to the tatters of those clouds of glory with which we are all born and which only rationalisation can rip off.

Yehudi Menuhin
Preface to Tiger Flower

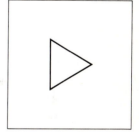

Beautiful illustrations are stimulating to a child's imagination, sensitivity, and response to beauty. Children need time to savor the artistry, the sheer wonder of some beautiful books. An outstanding example is *Tiger Flower* by Robert Vavara (Reynall, 1969), a beautiful book with illustrations consisting of exotic paintings by Fleur Cowles.

Books stimulate the child's creativity in varied ways. Cliff Robertson challenges children in *The Hole* (Watts, 1963) to notice common shapes that appear in the real world around us, for example, a crescent. "Can it be," the author asks, "a slice of watermelon or a bird's nest?" In each picture the crescent is a hole cut out of the paper.

It would be fun to follow this book with a drawing activity that stimulates children's creative perception. Give each child a sheet of paper from which a shape has been cut out, and then ask questions about the shapes.

Another imaginative book that presents funny definitions is *A Hole Is to Dig* by Ruth Krauss, illustrated by Maurice Sendak (Harper, 1952). "A face is so you can make faces"; or "A face is something to have on the front of your head." After sharing this book with children let them add their own definitions to those supplied by Ruth Krauss. Then talk about humorous definitions for objects around the room. Print these "daffyni-

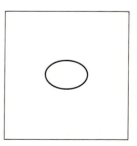

What kind of animal can you imagine that has this shape as part of its body? The triangle might be one wing of a butterfly, while the oval becomes the body of a fat rabbit.

tions" on the board as they are suggested by children. What a wonderful motivation for reading new words! Try some of these ideas:

A table is . . .

A cupboard is . . .

A drawer is . . .

A window is . . .

You can also enlarge Maurice Sendak's black and white line drawings by using an opaque projector. Trace one or two of the enlarged drawings with a black felt pen on paper to display in your classroom. Include the words to encourage children's reading.

A clever story that you might choose to tell a group of children is *The Tale of a Black Cat* (Holt, 1966) by Carl Withers, who tells the story of Tommy's adventures. As you tell this story, present chalkboard illustrations as developed by the author. The story begins as shown on the next page. The adventures continue until the denouement and the final picture. Can you see the T for Tommy with which the story began?

The Mean Mouse and Other Mean Stories (Harper, 1962) is a collection of funny short stories by Janice Udry. In each story the mean animals or people get "their just desserts." Children will be delighted by these stories that they can retell. They may also be motivated to write their own mean stories.

Additional teachable books for primary students include the following:

A Handful of Surprises by Anne Heathers and Esteban Francés. Harcourt Brace Jovanovich, 1961. (*A wonderful approach to puppetry; puppets are made of a garden glove with each character one finger puppet.*)

Mud Pies and Other Recipes by Marjorie Winslow. Macmillan, 1961. (*Easy to read; children can write other funny recipes.*)

Tell Me a Mitzi by Lore Segal. Farrar, Straus & Giroux, 1970. (*Good motivation for storytelling by children.*)

How the Sun Was Brought Back to the Sky by Mirra Ginsburg. Macmillan, 1975. (*Motivates the telling or writing of pourquoi tales, which explain why or how something happened.*)

The Parade by Adelaide Holl. Watts, 1975. (*Great for acting out; children can compose similar verses; also read* And to Think That I Saw It on Mulberry Street *to motivate painting of a mural.*)

Once there was a little boy named Tommy. And there's a T That stands for Tommy.

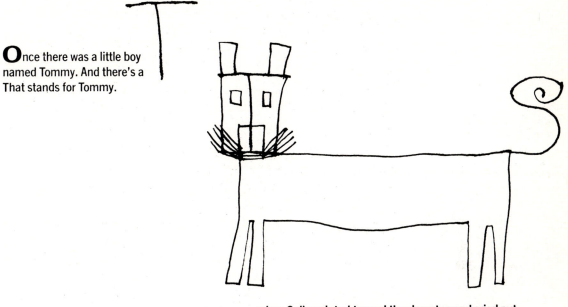

—when Sally pointed toward the doorstep and cried out,

"O-o-o-o-o-o-oh! SEE THAT big **Black Cat!**"

From The Tale of a Black Cat *adapted by Carl Withers. Illustrated by Alan Cober. Copyright © 1966 by Carl Withers. Copyright © 1966 by Alan Cober. Reproduced by permission of Holt, Rinehart & Winston, Publishers.*

WORDLESS BOOKS

A very special kind of book that is gaining popularity is the book without words. Any book of pictures, of course, is a wordless book, but those that are especially interesting tell a story through pictures. One of the earliest books of this type is Ruth Carroll's *What Whiskers Did* (Walck), first published in 1932 and reissued in 1965.

A marvelous series of wordless books has been created by Mercer Mayer. Beginning with *A Boy, A Dog and A Frog* (Dial, 1967), the author-illustrator portrays a series of hilarious events as a small boy and his dog attempt to catch a frog. The frog follows them home at last and they all end up in the bathtub. Other adventures are developed in *Frog, Where Are You?, A Boy, A Dog, A Frog and a Friend,* produced with Marianna Mayer, and *Frog on His Own.* Perhaps the funniest is *Frog Goes to Dinner* (Dial, 1974) in which the frog leaps into a musician's instrument, hides under the lettuce in a lady's salad, and peers at a gentleman from his champagne glass. Although the frog is bounced and the family is forced to leave the Fancy Restaurant, only the boy and his frog fully appreciate the situation.

Here is an annotated list of selected wordless books that you may find useful with young children.

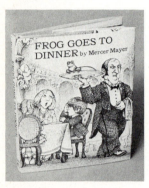

Martha Alexander. *Bobo's Dream.* Dial, 1970.
When Bobo, a Dachshund, loses his bone to a big dog, his owner retrieves the bone. Then Bobo dreams he returns his master's football when bigger boys take it.

Martha Alexander. *Out! Out! Out!* Dial, 1968.
A bird flies into the house through an open kitchen window. Neither mother, grocery man, nor custodian can chase it out. A little boy leads it back to the window with a trail of cereal.

José Aruego. *Look What I Can Do.* Scribner, 1971.
Two silly carabaos (water buffalo) play the "Anything you can do I can do better" game getting themselves into some funny predicaments. Suggested from an old Philippine proverb.

Byron Barton. *Elephant.* Seabury, 1971.
A little girl sees a toy elephant, a poster elephant, an elephant in a book and on TV. She then has a wild dream about elephants. When she awakens, her parents take her to the zoo where she sees the most wonderful elephant of all—a real one.

Willi Baum. *Birds of a Feather.* Addison-Wesley, 1969.
An inventive bird decides to leave the flock and improve his plumage with the feathers from a passing lady's hat. He's trapped by a bird catcher, caged, then released when his ruse is discovered.

Antonella Bollinger-Savelli. *The Knitted Cat.* Macmillan, 1971.
A little girl knits a cat, leaving its tail unfinished. That night a mouse unravels the tail. The cat walks around outside, and an owl ties up the unraveling tail. The next morning the girl finishes the tail.

Eric Carl. *Do You Want to Be My Friend?* Thomas Y. Crowell, 1971.
Little Mouse is looking for a friend. On each page he finds a tail, and as the page is turned the owner of the tail is revealed.

Ruth Carroll. *The Christmas Kitten.* Walck, 1970.
A little kitten, persistent in looking for a home, is finally allowed to stay with a family.

John Goodall. *The Adventures of Paddy Pork*. Harcourt Brace Jovanovich, 1968.
Paddy, a pig, leaves home to join the circus. After some frightening and unsuccessful experiences, he returns home. A sequel is *The Ballooning Adventures of Paddy Pork,* 1969. Both are depicted in detailed black and white drawings.

John Goodall. *Shrewbettina's Birthday*. Harcourt Brace Jovanovich, 1971.
Full color drawings show the eventful day—Shrewbettina gets robbed, does her shopping, cleans her house, has a party. The ingenious use of half pages gives more visual details in the Goodall books.

Elizabeth Goshorn. *Shoestrings*. Carolrhoda, 1975.
A humorous portrayal of a child's trying to tie her shoestrings and the strange things that happen.

Tina Hoban. *Look Again!* Macmillan, 1971.
No story is told, but this is one of the most fascinating of the textless picture books. A two-inch-square peephole allows the viewer to see only a portion of a black and white photograph. After guessing, turning the page usually unveils a surprise close-up photograph. A third page puts the object in perspective or proportion. The book points to the beauty of simple things and our usual disregard for detail.

Pat Hutchins. *Changes, Changes*. Macmillan, 1971.
Children's play blocks are used to tell a fast moving story. The figures build a house that catches fire. They build a fire engine that puts out the fire but causes a flood. So they move by boat, truck, and train to a new location and build another house.

Fernando Krahn. *A Flying Saucer Full of Spaghetti*. Dutton, 1970.
Small elf-like creatures entertain a rich little girl and fly her unwanted spaghetti across town to feed a hungry girl.

Fernando Krahn. *Journeys of Sebastian*. Delacorte, 1968.
An imaginative boy has three adventures: a fly becomes a space ship and he journeys into the center of a flower; he steps through his mirror and becomes a King; he races on a monster.

Renate Meyer. *Hide-and-Seek*. Bradbury, 1969.
Two children play a game of hide and seek. Through the yard, into the barn, into the house, out to the garden the girl in pink chases the boy in

blue. He is barely seen in the branches, behind the clothesline, under a chair, but he is finally caught.

Renate Meyer. *Vicki*. Atheneum, 1969.
Pictures not a sequence of events as much as a mood of friendlessness and loneliness.

Guillermo Mordillo. *The Damp and Daffy Doings of a Daring Pirate Ship*. Harlin Quist, 1971.
Daffy little characters build a sailing ship, launch it, become pirates. Their ship sinks from the weight of their booty, so they bravely try again. Fascinating, light-hearted pictures.

Eleanor Schick. *Making Friends*. Macmillan, 1969.
Tells of a shopping trip with Mother and all the things a young child can notice along the way, many of which Mother did not see because she didn't look. Simple, for the youngest child.

Peter Wezel. *The Good Bird*. Harper, 1964.
A bird sees an unhappy goldfish, catches a worm to share with the fish, and both are contented. Large, vivid pictures make it possible to use this book with large groups of children.[2]

What can you do with wordless books? Their chief value lies in language development, but those that present a story in sequence also help children become aware of plot, sequence, characterization—early literature learnings.

Encourage children to work in pairs or small groups of four or five as they tell and retell a story. They can take turns "reading" the story page by page. After children are familiar with a particular story, one child can "read" the whole thing to a small group. Children will also enjoy "reading" these stories to a tape recorder. Help children understand that each person will tell the story differently, just as storytellers did before books were invented.

SHARING BOOKS

One of the delights of the classroom is introducing children to books and sharing their enjoyment of stories that you have selected. Encourage chil-

---

[2] Adapted from Donald J. Bissett, "Literature in the Classroom," *Elementary English* 49 (November 1972): 1016–1019.

dren to take pleasure in the books presented and experienced in a variety of ways—reading aloud, filmed literature, art activities, and dramatization. In this section we suggest a number of ideas that you might like to explore.

READING ALOUD The classroom in which there is always a good story going exudes a warm camaraderie. Books are in evidence. Children are reading at different stages. There is frequent reference to humorous incidents or the words of familiar characters. The teacher who loves books conveys this love to children.

Reading a good book to the class as a whole is an activity that everyone can enjoy. A good story will sell itself, so the selection of the book to read is crucial. In addition to the discussion on reading aloud in Chapter 1, here are a few points to keep in mind.

1. Choose a book that you really like so that you can present it enthusiastically.

2. Sometimes read a book that is easy enough for the children to read themselves, because hearing the story will motivate their reading it.

3. Alternate easy books with more advanced books that few of the children could read themselves. A longer story with chapters offers continuity and excitement, a chance to become involved with a character.

ART Children will enjoy interpreting books they have read through varied art techniques. Painting scenes from favorite stories or a picture of the storybook person they like best provides incentive to look at books and to share them with others.

You can also develop specific activities after reading a book to children. For instance, follow up the reading of *McElligott's Pool* by developing a pool and underground river on a large bulletin board. Each child can then create an original kind of fish to place in the water. Children can make up names for their fish and describe them to their classmates.

Help the class create a story parade mural, with each person drawing or painting an animal or person from a book he or she really likes. Across the wall go Anatole, Thidwick the Kindhearted Moose, Custard the Dragon, Drummer Hoff, three Jovial Huntsmen, Curious George, the five Chinese brothers, Harold, Snoopy, Petunia, the Selfish Giant, Crow Boy, Cinderella, and many others.

DRAMATIZING Children's stories provide excellent ideas for dramatizing. These activities can involve the whole group. They can be simple movement activities, pantomime, monologue, dialogue. They can involve children in puppetry, role playing, or the creative interpretation of an author's story.

Children can waddle like the parade of ducklings in *Make Way for Ducklings,* or they can swim through the water to join Leo Lionni's Swimmy in his defiance of the big fish that ate all the little fish. They can move through fog after reading *Hide and Seek Fog* by Alvin Tresselt, or fly kites with Gilberto as in *Gilberto and the Wind* by Marie Hall Ets.

Children can play roles in the story of *Crow Boy* to experience the feelings of someone who is different. They can act out the stories in Lore Segal's *Tell Me a Mitzi* just for fun.

There are many exciting ways to work with dramatic techniques from puppetry to pantomime. Additional ideas are suggested in such books as:

Complo, Sr. Jannita Marie. *Dramakinetics in the Classroom; A Handbook of Creative Dramatics and Improvised Movement.* Plays, 1974.

Ehrlich, Harriet. *Creative Dramatics Handbook.* The School District of Philadelphia, 1974. (Available from the National Council of Teachers of English.)

Gillies, Emily. *Creative Dramatics for All Children.* Association for Childhood Education International, 1974.

Tiedt, Iris M., ed. *Drama in Your Classroom.* National Council of Teachers of English, 1974.

❦ Choose two of these activities as a way of culminating your study of books for young children.

1. Present a wordless book to a small group of children. Help them tell the story together collectively; then help them tell the story page by page with each one taking a turn.

2. Plan a creative activity based on one of the books you have read—art, discussion, drama, whatever appeals to you. Try this activity with a classroom of children.

3. Preview three films of books for children. Enter these films in your card file. Show one of the films to a class, followed by discussion.

Parents and teachers are especially concerned about the books that are placed in the hands of preschool and primary grade children. Certainly this is a justifiable concern because we should want and expect to have the very best books for children. When it comes, however, to the content of books, we run into differences of values and personal taste, and we may be confronted with efforts at censorship.

Attitudes and values are obviously changing within our society, and in a similar manner we find attitudes toward books changing from year to year. What was found offensive five years ago, therefore, is probably not a problem today. When Maurice Sendak's *Where the Wild Things Are* appeared in 1963, for example, many parents, teachers, and librarians were highly critical about this presentation of "monsters" to little children.

"Let the wild rumpus start!" shouts Max in *Where the Wild Things Are*. The publication of this popular book brought about much discussion of the desirability of monsters for children, and some teachers and librarians banned this book from the shelves. Children, however, seem to enjoy the delicious horror and the gentle spoofs of the wild things, as well as the creatures in other Sendak books that followed, such as *In the Night Kitchen* (Harper & Row, 1970).

Another author–illustrator who shares this interest in strange beings is Mercer Mayer, whose story *A Special Trick* (Dial, 1970) tells of Elroy's discovery of a magician's dictionary. Elroy accidentally calls forth a "galaplop" and other weird creatures. Mercer Mayer also created *There's a Nightmare in My Closet* (Dial, 1968).

A different kind of monster is Nessie, who lives at the bottom of a Scottish loch. Ted Hughes, an English poet-novelist, has created a female monster who "is sick with sorrow" because nobody thinks monsters exist anymore (Bobbs-Merrill, 1974).

Edward Gorey frequently features monsters, too. He writes of *The Wuggly Ump* (Lippincott, 1963) in poetry:

Sing twiddle-ear, sing twaddle-or,
The Wuggly Ump is at the door

Even after the Wuggly Ump gobbles them up, the three children sing undauntedly:

Sing glogalimp, sing gluggalump,
From deep inside the Wuggly Ump.

Illustration from In the Night
Kitchen *by Maurice Sendak.*
Copyright © 1963 by Maurice
Sendak. Reprinted by permission
of Harper & Row, Publishers,
Inc.

Presented in the humorous, tongue-in-cheek language of these skillful
authors, is it really likely that a healthy five- or six-year-old will take
these monsters seriously? Clearly they belong in the land of the dragons
and witches, the goblins and trolls. What is life without a little shiver or
two? As long as we adults keep such characters in proper perspective,
they will not trouble children.

AVOIDING THE STEREOTYPED IMAGE

Stereotyping is a particular problem in picture books for young children,
for stereotyped images can occur either through words or illustration.
Various studies have attempted to focus attention on this type of unrealistic portrayal of people of different races, roles, or sexes. Books that
have received the Caldecott award have been studied in detail for several
reasons: (1) they were selected as the outstanding books of their year; (2)

Joseph was happy.

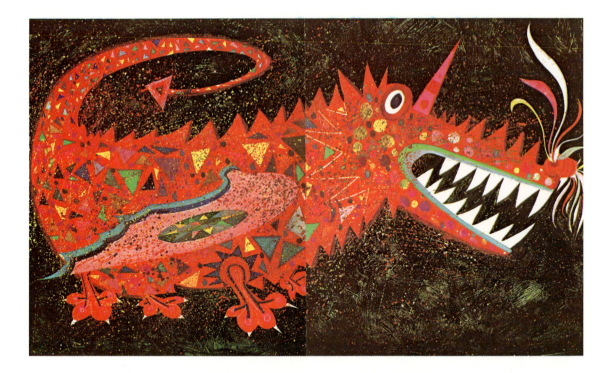

Above: Illustration by Brian
Wildsmith from his book,
Puzzles, copyright 1971 by
Brian Wildsmith. Used by permission of Franklin Watts, Inc.
and Oxford University Press
1970.

Right: Illustration by Janusz
Grabianski from his book, Gra-
bianski's Wild Animals, copy-
right 1969 by Carl Ueberreuter
Druck und Verlag. Used by per-
mission of Franklin Watts, Inc.
& Verlag Carl Ueberreuter,
Vienna, Austria.

Just simply alive,
Both of us, I
And the poppy.
                —Issa

Illustration from Thumbelina *by Adrienne Adams is reprinted with permission of Charles Scribner's Sons, Copyright © 1961 Adrienne Adams.*

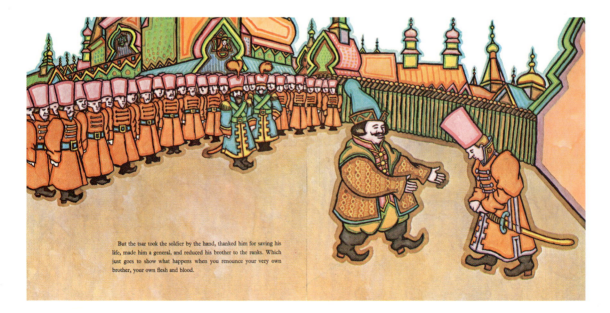

But the tsar took the soldier by the hand, thanked him for saving his
life, made him a general, and reduced his brother to the ranks. Which
just goes to show what happens when you renounce your very own
brother, your own flesh and blood.

Top left and right: Reprinted with permission of Macmillan Publishing Co., Inc. from One Fine Day *by Nonny Hogrogian. Copyright © 1971 by Nonny Hogrogian.*

Left: Reproduced with the permission of Farrar, Straus & Giroux, Inc. From The Soldier and the Tzar in the Forest: A Russian Tale *translated by Richard Lourie, Pictures by Uri Shulevitz, Copyright © 1972 by Uri Shulevitz. Translation copyright © 1972 by Farrar, Straus & Giroux, Inc.*

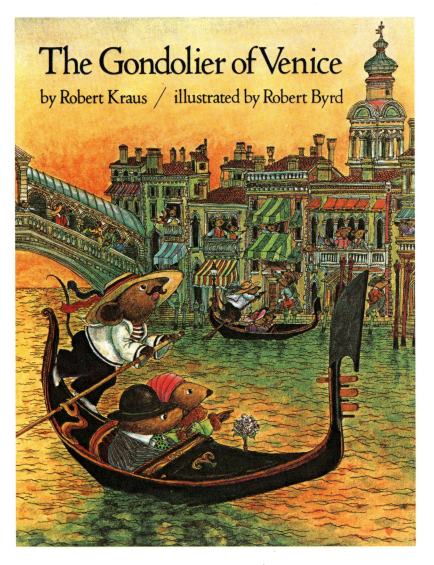

The Gondolier of Venice

by Robert Kraus / illustrated by Robert Byrd

the award has been given over a period of time (since 1922); and (3) they offer a reasonable number of items for a research project. The findings of such studies are enlightening, for example:

1. Omitting women or people of different ethnic groups creates a stereotype just as effectively as including members of these groups in a limited manner. The "invisible female," for example, gives children the impression that they live in a man's world, and young girls have few models to emulate.

   Weitzman, Lenore J. et al. "Sex Role Socialization in Picture Books for Pre-school Children." *American Journal of Sociology.* 77:1125–1150, 1972.

2. Behavior depicted as appropriate for girls and boys or men and women leads to unrealistic expectations. Books can be instrumental in promoting values and in socializing children so that they know at a very early age, for instance, that boys don't cry, but girls do or that boys protect girls who are weak and helpless, the Miss Muffett syndrome.

   Key, Mary Ritchie. "The Role of Male and Female in Children's Books—Dispelling All Doubt." *Wilson Library Bulletin.* 46:167–76, 1971.

3. Group differences in language use is also clear in children's books. Realistic dialects have appeared only recently, so that it is clear that the only "proper" language is a rather formal educated white English. Also implicit in the language of children's books is the differentiation of male and female language, an aspect of the sex role: Boys talk "rougher" than girls; girls are taught to be polite, "little ladies," who speak without forcefulness, always deferring to the male.

   Lakoff, Robin. "Language and Woman's Place," *Language in Society,* 2:45–80, 1973.

   Lee, Patrick G. and Nancy B. Gropper, "Sex-Role Culture and Educational Practice." *Harvard Educational Review.* 44:369–410, 1974.

4. Illustrations alone can depict a stereotype although the image does not occur in the content. In *Sylvester and the Magic Pebble,* a Caldecott award book, for example, William Steig, portrays the policemen as pigs. In many books the owl appears, and of course, an owl is *wise,* a kind of stereotype that occurs in many animal stories.[3]

   Gunderson points to a need for research related to sex differences in language and reading. Clearly there is reason to study in greater detail the

---

[3] Doris V. Gunderson, "Sex Differences in Language and Reading," *Language Arts* 52 (March 1976): 300–306.

effects of images and language in children's books. We should also consider the possible implications of stereotyping on children's learning to read. Stereotyping is discussed further in Chapter 10.

REALISM FOR YOUNG CHILDREN

As we have noted, books for young children tend to be more and more realistic. Books treat subjects today that would have been particularly avoided even five years ago—divorce, death, sex. Attitudes do change, however. For example, Margaret Wise Brown's *The Dead Bird* was controversial when it appeared in 1958, but it seems very mild and unobjectionable now that we have more realistic treatments of human death. The chief demand of those who select children's books is that realism be handled with sensitivity. A number of authors and illustrators, as we have pointed out, can present such topics as adoption, the death of a loved grandparent, or the child's missing a parent after a divorce in an effective realistic manner.

One topic that still arouses heated disagreement is sex education. Books that describe birth for young children have been available for some time, for example:

The Wonderful Story of How You Were Born by Sidonie Matsner Gruenberg. Doubleday, 1970.

A New Baby Comes by Julian May. Creative Education, 1970.

A Baby Starts to Grow by Paul Showers. Thomas Y. Crowell, 1969.

These earlier books include pictures of the embryo developing within the womb, although there is no attempt to portray conception. It should be noted, too, that most of the early books were written for older students.

Today we see books appearing that include more explicit information even for the youngest child. Margaret Sheffield's *Where Do Babies Come From?* (Knopf, 1973) is an example of a good treatment of birth from conception through the actual delivery as the infant leaves the mother's body. Used in the British primary school system, the book answers questions that children often ask. Nude figures are included, but the information is presented seriously and factually. The appropriate terminology is used, and throughout there is a respect for human life and for the human body.

A book that is not recommended is *Show Me!* by Helga Fleischhauer-Hardt (St. Martin's, 1975). Subtitled *A Picture Book of Sex for Children and*

Parents, the book is addressed to adults at least in part. The text and photographs treat homosexuality, masturbation, intercourse, and other adult sexual relations in a manner that seems too mature for young children. Although we certainly need an open attitude toward the human body and sensuality, the Sheffield book handles the presentation of such information more appropriately.

ADDITIONAL SOURCES TO INVESTIGATE

Blount, Margaret. *Animal Land: The Creatures of Children's Fiction.* Morrow, 1975.

Carlson, Ruth Kearney. *Speaking Aids through the Grades.* Teachers College Press, 1975.

Cianciolo, Patricia J., editor, and the NCTE Elementary Booklist Committee. *Picture Books for Children.* American Library Association, 1973. *(Graded and annotated; preschool through middle school.)*

Cianciolo, Patricia J. *Illustrations in Children's Books.* 2nd. ed. W. C. Brown, 1976.

Donovan, John, ed. "Editors Write About Authors." *Elementary English* 51 (September 1974): 767–805. *(Six articles.)*

Jones, Helen L. *Robert Lawson, Illustrator: A Selection of His Characteristic Illustrations.* Little, Brown, 1972.

Kingman, Lee et al. *Illustrators of Children's Books, 1957–1966.* Horn Book, 1968.

MacCann, Donnarae and Olga Richard. *The Child's First Books: A Critical Study of Pictures and Text.* Wilson, 1973.

Miller, Bertha Mahony and Elinor Whitney Field. *Caldecott Medal Books: 1938–1957.* Horn Book, 1957. *(Includes acceptance papers, biographical notes, and articles about illustrating children's books.)*

Ward, Martha E. and Dorothy A. Marquardt. *Illustrators of Books for Young People.* Scarecrow, 1970.

3

*Roads Go
Ever Ever On*

Fanciful Tales for Children

Where, oh where is fancy bred,
In the heart or in the head?

William Shakespeare

The excitement of fantasy is that the possibilities are limitless; anything can happen! Good fantasy must include, however, at least two character-istics—a sense of wonder and at the same time a feeling of familiarity similar to that of returning home. As we read the very best fantasy, we are stimulated to see old objects in a new light, to find fairies in a moonlit meadow, to encounter adventure at the end of any street. At any moment a wizard might tap you on the shoulder; a furry mongrel might speak to you with a twinkle in its eye.

Willingly we suspend our disbelief as we follow the lead of the master-ful storyteller. We accept the author's reality, whether it brings us to a new world, transports us to another time, or introduces us to a person who has unusual powers. An air of mystery, the unknown, suspense, in-trigue—fantasy for children has the universal appeal of a story well told. For years children have been delighted to meet such characters as Toad of Toad Hall, the children of Green Knowe, and Chester, the cricket who lives in Times Square. Eagerly they have followed the path through the wardrobe to Narnia or traveled to Prydain in another time and in another place.

As we explore fantasy for young people, it is helpful to have clear ob-jectives in mind, for example:

1. To become acquainted with a representative sample of good fantasies for children.

2. To know something about the authors who write fantasy for young people.

3. To explore methods of introducing fantasy to children and to incorporate fantasy in a literature program.

❦ Exploring fantasy will prove fascinating. This set of questions is designed to help you determine the baseline from which you begin.

1. Can you name the authors of the books on which two of these popular films were based: *Mary Poppins, Charlotte's Web, Alice in Wonderland?*

2. What is the Newbery Medal? Name one fantasy that was awarded this medal.

3. Can you name two authors who created fantasy lands as settings for a series of adventures?

4. Can you match these authors with the titles of the books they wrote?

Lloyd Alexander	____	a. *The Borrowers*
George Selden	____	b. *The High King*
Mary Norton	____	c. *The Light Princess*
George MacDonald	____	d. *The Twenty-One Balloons*
William Pène duBois	____	e. *The Cricket in Times Square*

5. How might you distinguish between science fiction and other fantasy?

AN OVERVIEW OF FANTASY FOR CHILDREN

Some of the finest writing for children is in the realm of fantasy. This fantasy ranges from semirealistic humorous stories such as Lucretia Hall's *The Peterkin Papers* to the fanciful tales of *Winnie the Pooh* or *Mrs. Frisby and the Rats of NIMH*. In this section we will first discuss the general characteristics of fantasy for children. Then we will examine selections from outstanding fantasies grouped under categories focusing on: (1) animals, (2) human beings, (3) fantasy worlds, and (4) science fiction.

What are we looking for in fantasies that we choose for children? In general the best fantasies stand out in these respects:

The plot is original and logically organized.

The pace is fast moving with few long descriptive passages.

Dialogue is realistic and adds to both the action and the characterization.

Characters are developed in depth through conversation and behavior.

Writing is sharp and fresh and demonstrates the skilled use of language.

These are the same criteria that we will use for realistic books for children. They are the same criteria that we would establish for adult literature. In addition, of course, the writer of fantasy must provide that sense of wonder whereby the familiar is enhanced and is viewed through a new perspective. Can any writer meet these demanding criteria? Of course they can, for some of the finest authors write fantasy for children.

One of the most famous of the early fantasies is *Alice's Adventures in Wonderland,* first published in 1865. Written by Charles Lutwidge Dodgson, a mathematician who became better known by his pseudonym Lewis Carroll, this popular tale was followed in 1871 by *Through the Looking Glass*. Charles Kingsley's *The Waterbabies,* published in 1863, is the tale of Tom, a chimney sweep captured by fairies who live under the water. A third nineteenth-century writer of fantasy for children was George MacDonald, whose *At the Back of the North Wind* published in 1871 has been acknowledged as influential in the writing of fantasies by later writers.[1] Other familiar books that you may know include *Peter Pan* by Sir James Barrie, available in an attractive edition illustrated by Nora Unwin (Scribner, 1950); *The Wizard of Oz,* written by L. Frank Baum at the turn of the century; *The Adventures of Pinocchio* by Carlo Collodi (pseudonym for Carlo Lorenzini); and Hugh Lofting's *The Story of Dr. Dolittle*. These books have all been read and reread and presented in motion pictures for children.

Although today books for children tend toward a higher degree of realism, fantasy is still a major form of literature for young people. Many outstanding contemporary authors are writing fantasy, so that we can see the humor of fantasies such as *Chitty-Chitty-Bang-Bang; The Magical Car* (Random House, 1964) by Ian Fleming contrasted to the fine writing of

---

[1] James Higgins, *Beyond Words,* Teachers College, 1973, pp. 8–10.

Susan Cooper in *The Dark Is Rising* (Atheneum, 1973). Fantasy has expanded, too, into the subgenre of science fiction, with books by such authors as Ursula LeGuin who wrote *The Tombs of Atuan* (Atheneum, 1971) and Anne McCaffrey who wrote *Dragonsong* (Atheneum, 1976).

FANCIFUL TALES ABOUT ANIMALS

Here is Edward Bear, coming downstairs now, bump, bump, bump, on the back of his head, behind Christopher Robin. It is, as far as he knows, the only way of coming downstairs, but sometimes he feels that there really is another way, if only he could stop bumping for a moment and think of it. And then he feels that perhaps there isn't. Anyhow, here he is at the bottom, and ready to be introduced to you.

The animals in this story, *Winnie-the-Pooh* (Dutton, 1926) by A. A. Milne, aren't meant to be real because they're toys, but they seem like real animals so we included the book in this section. Christopher Robin

From Winnie-the-Pooh *by A. A. Milne, illustrated by Ernest H. Shepherd. Copyright 1926 by E. P. Dutton; renewal 1954 by A. A. Milne. Reprinted by permission of the publishers, E. P. Dutton.*

and his friends—Pooh, Piglet, Rabbit, Owl, Kanga, Little Roo, and
Eeyore—live in a forest where they have many thrilling adventures. Illustrated by Ernest H. Shepard, the stories are told with sensitivity and
humor. Children of all ages delight in the adventures of Poo and the other
animals.

Another unusual family of beings that may be animals, but then again
they may not, are the Moomins. Created by the Finnish author Tove
Jansson, they appear in *Finn Family Moomintroll* (McKay, 1958). Jansson
received the Hans Christian Andersen International Medal for the Moo-
min books, which she also illustrated. A Moomin-Gallery describes the
whole lot with both words and pictures.

Michael Bond, an English writer, created the whimsical Paddington,
who appears in *A Bear Called Paddington* (Houghton Mifflin, 1958).
"Please look after this bear," reads the sign attached to Paddington's neck
as he sits on the platform of the London railway station. He's a rare bear
from darkest Peru, he explains to Mr. and Mrs. Brown who examine
him curiously. These kind people just can't leave him, so they take him
home, and thus Paddington's adventures begin. Jonathan and Judy are
just as delighted with this comical new friend as primary grade children
will be if you read the book to them. It's a delightful fantasy for sharing.
And of course, there are more books about Paddington.

Michael Bond also writes of Olga da Polga, a lovable guinea pig who
tells stories. Feisty and imaginative, she appears in *Olga Meets Her Match*
(Hastings House, 1975) in an encounter with Boris who says, "It seems
only yesterday that I used to sit on the steps outside my father's palace
listening to the balalaikas. Afterwards we would all go for long rides
through the snow on a horse-drawn sledge. I can still hear the sound of
the bells tinkling in the moonlight. We had a real moon in those days. A
great big one—not like that thing they've got up there now." The tales
of Olga are just as much fun as those about Paddington.

Perhaps one of the best known fantasies about animals is Kenneth Grahame's *The Wind in the Willows* (Scribner, 1908). An attractive recent edition is that by the Heritage Press, which includes an introduction by
A. A. Milne and is illustrated by Arthur Rackham (see the color section
for a reproduction of one of his illustrations). Grahame tells of the
timid Mole and an adventurous, wise Rat as well as the solitary gray
Badger and the blustering, swaggering Mr. Toad. Set in the Wild Wood
and nearby environs, the escapades of these friends center around rescu-
ing Toad from mishaps that culminate in his stealing a motorcar. As the
owner and his friends try to stop Toad, "Toad sent the car crashing
through the low hedge that ran along the roadside. One mighty bound, a
violent shock, and the wheels of the car were churning up the thick mud

of a horse-pond." His friends rescue him once again, but this time they insist that he turn over a new leaf. Later as the four friends stroll together on a summer evening, mothers tell their children:

"Look, baby! There goes the great Mr. Toad! And that's the gallant Water Rat, a terrible fighter, walking along o' him! And yonder comes the famous Mr. Mole, of whom you so often have heard your father tell!" But when their infants were fractious and quite beyond control, they would quiet them by telling how, if they didn't hush and not fret them, the terrible grey Badger would up and get them. This was a base libel on Badger, who, though he cared little about Society, was rather fond of children; but it never failed to have its full effect.

Although most of us know *The Wind in the Willows* as Kenneth Grahame's major contribution, he was best known at the time it was published as the author of *The Golden Age* (1895) and *Dream Days* (1898). The sketches that appear in these books are delightfully funny and would be good humorous material to share with children about ten or eleven years old.

Included in *Dream Days* is "The Reluctant Dragon," which has been published separately by Holiday House (1938) as a short book. This story is so entertaining that we are reprinting it here; it is the kind of tale that children and adults can enjoy sharing together.

THE RELUCTANT DRAGON
Kenneth Grahame

Long ago—might have been hundreds of years ago—in a cottage half-way between this village and yonder shoulder of the Downs up there, a shepherd lived with his wife and their little son. Now the shepherd spent his days—and at certain times of the year his nights too—up on the wide ocean-bosom of the Downs, with only the sun and the stars and the sheep for company, and the friendly chattering world of men and women far out of sight and hearing. But his little son, when he wasn't helping his father, and often when he was as well, spent much of his time buried in big volumes that he borrowed from the affable gentry and interested parsons of the country round about. And his parents were very fond of him, and rather proud of him too, though they didn't let on in his hearing, so he was left to go his own way and read as much as he liked; and instead of frequently getting a cuff on the side of the head, as might very well have happened to him, he was treated more or less as an equal by his parents, who sensibly thought it a very fair division of labour that they should supply the practical knowledge, and he the book-learning. They knew that book-learning often came in useful at a pinch, in spite of what their neighbours said. What the Boy chiefly dabbled in was natural history and fairy-tales, and he just took them as they came, in a sandwichy sort of way, without making any distinctions; and really his course of reading strikes one as rather sensible.

One evening the shepherd, who for some nights past had been disturbed and preoccupied, and off his usual mental balance, came home all of a tremble, and, sitting down at the table where his wife and son were peacefully employed, she with her seam, he in following out the adventures of the Giant with no Heart in his Body, exclaimed with much agitation:

"It's all up with me, Maria! Never no more can I go up on them there Downs, was it ever so!"

"Now don't take on like that," said his wife, who was a *very* sensible woman: "but tell us all about it first, whatever it is as has given you this shake-up, and then me and you and the son here, between us, we ought to be able to get to the bottom of it!"

"It began some nights ago," said the shepherd. "You know that cave up there —I never liked it, somehow, and the sheep never liked it neither, and when sheep don't like a thing there's generally some reason for it. Well, for some time past there's been faint noises coming from that cave—noises like heavy sighings, with grunts mixed up in them; and sometimes a snoring, far away down—*real* snoring, yet somehow not *honest* snoring, like you and me o'nights, you know!"

"*I* know," remarked the Boy quietly.

"Of course I was terrible frightened," the shepherd went on; "yet somehow I couldn't keep away. So this very evening, before I come down, I took a cast round by the cave, quietly. And there—O Lord! there I saw him at last, as plain as I see you!"

"Saw *who?*" said his wife, beginning to share in her husband's nervous terror.

"Why *him,* I'm a telling you!" said the shepherd. "He was sticking half-way out of the cave, and seemed to be enjoying of the cool of the evening in a poetical sort of way. He was as big as four cart-horses, and all covered with shiny scales— deep-blue scales at the top of him, shading off to a tender sort o' green below. As he breathed, there was a sort of flicker over his nostrils that you see over our chalk roads on a baking windless day in summer. He had his chin on his paws, and I should say he was meditating about things. Oh, yes, a peaceable sort o'beast enough, and not ramping or carrying on or doing anything but what was quite right and proper. I admit all that. And yet, what am I to do? Scales, you know, and claws, and a tail for certain, though I didn't see that end of him—ain't *used* to 'em, and I don't *hold* with 'em, and that's a fact!"

The Boy, who had apparently been absorbed in his book during his father's recital, now closed the volume, yawned, clasped his hands behind his head, and said sleepily:

"It's all right, father. Don't you worry. It's only a dragon."

"Only a dragon?" cried his father. "What do you mean, sitting there, you and your dragons? *Only* a dragon indeed! And what do *you* know about it?"

"'Cos it *is,* and 'cos I *do* know," replied the Boy quietly. "Look here, father, you know we've each of us got our line. *You* know about sheep, and weather, and things; *I* know about dragons. I always said, you know, that that cave up there was a dragon-cave. I always said it must have belonged to a dragon some time, and ought to belong to a dragon now, if rules count for anything. Well, now you tell me it *has* got a dragon, and so *that's* all right. I'm not half as much surprised as when you told me it *hadn't* got a dragon. Rules always come right if you wait quietly. Now, please, just leave this all to me. And I'll stroll up to-morrow morning—no, in the morning I can't, I've got a whole heap of things to do—well, perhaps in the evening, if I'm quite free, I'll go up and have a talk to him, and you'll find it'll be all right. Only please, don't you go worrying round there without me. You don't understand 'em a bit, and they're very sensitive, you know!"

"He's quite right, father," said the sensible mother. "As he says, dragons is his line and not ours. He's wonderful knowing about book-beasts, as every one allows. And to tell the truth, I'm not half happy in my own mind, thinking of that poor animal lying alone up there, without a bit o' hot supper or anyone to change the news with; and maybe we'll be able to do something for him; and if he ain't quite respectable our Boy'll find it out quick enough. He's got a pleasant sort o' way with him that makes everybody tell him everything."

Next day, after he'd had his tea, the Boy strolled up the chalky track that led to the summit of the Downs; and there, sure enough, he found the dragon, stretched lazily on the sward in front of his cave. The view from that point was a magnificent one. To the right and left, the bare and billowy leagues of Downs; in front, the vale, with its clustered homesteads, its threads of white roads running through orchards and well-tilled acreage, and, far away, a hint of grey old cities on the horizon. A cool breeze played over the surface of the grass, and the silver shoulder of a large moon was showing above distant junipers. No wonder the dragon seemed in a peaceful and contented mood; indeed, as the Boy approached he could hear the beast purring with a happy regularity. "Well, we live and learn!" he said to himself. "None of my books ever told me that dragons purred!"

"Hullo, dragon!" said the Boy quietly, when he had got up to him.

The dragon, on hearing the approaching footsteps, made the beginning of a courteous effort to rise. But when he saw it was a Boy, he set his eyebrows severely.

"Now don't you hit me," he said; "or bung stones, or squirt water, or anything. I won't have it, I tell you!"

"Not goin' to hit you," said the Boy wearily, dropping on the grass beside the beast: "and don't, for goodness' sake, keep on saying 'Don't'; I hear so much of it, and it's monotonous, and makes me tired. I've simply looked in to ask you how you were and all that sort of thing; but if I'm in the way I can easily clear out. I've lots of friends, and no one can say I'm in the habit of shoving myself in where I'm not wanted!"

"No, no, don't go off in a huff," said the dragon hastily; "fact is—I'm as happy up here as the day's long; never without an occupation, dear fellow, never without an occupation! And yet, between ourselves, it *is* a trifle dull at times."

The Boy bit off a stalk of grass and chewed it. "Going to make a long stay here?" he asked politely.

"Can't hardly say at present," replied the dragon. "It seems a nice place enough—but I've only been here a short time, and one must look about and reflect and consider before settling down. It's rather a serious thing, settling down. Besides—now I'm going to tell you something! You'd never guess it if you tried ever so!—fact is, I'm such a confoundedly lazy beggar!"

"You surprise me," said the Boy civilly.

"It's the sad truth," the dragon went on, settling down between his paws and evidently delighted to have found a listener at last: "and I fancy that's really how I came to be here. You see all the other fellows were so active and *earnest* and all that sort of thing—always rampaging, and skirmishing, and scouring the desert sands, and pacing the margin of the sea, and chasing knights all over the place, and devouring damsels, and going on generally—whereas I liked to get my meals regular and then to prop my back against a bit of rock and snooze a bit, and wake up and think of things going on and how they kept going on just the same, you know! So when it happened I got fairly caught."

"When *what* happened, please?" asked the Boy.

"That's just what I don't precisely know," said the dragon. "I suppose the earth sneezed, or shook itself, or the bottom dropped out of something. Anyhow there was a shake and a roar and a general stramash, and I found myself miles away underground and wedged in as tight as tight. Well, thank goodness, my wants are few, and at any rate I had peace and quietness and wasn't always being asked to come along and *do* something. And I've got such an active mind—always occupied, I assure you! But time went on, and there was a certain sameness about the life, and at last I began to think it would be fun to work my way upstairs and see what you other fellows were doing. So I scratched and burrowed, and worked this way and that way and at last I came out through this cave here. And I like the country, and the view, and the people—what I've seen of 'em—and on the whole I feel inclined to settle down here."

"What's your mind always occupied about?" asked the Boy. "That's what I want to know."

The dragon coloured slightly and looked away. Presently he said bashfully: "Did you ever—just for fun—try to make up poetry—verses, you know?"

"'Course I have," said the Boy. "Heaps of it. And some of it's quite good, I feel sure, only there's no one here cares about it. Mother's very kind and all that, when I read it to her, and so's father for that matter. But somehow they don't seem to—"

"Exactly," cried the dragon; "my own case exactly. They don't seem to, and you can't argue with 'em about it. Now you've got culture, you have, I could tell it on you at once, and I should just like your candid opinion about some little things I threw off lightly, when I was down there. I'm awfully pleased to have met you, and I'm hoping the other neighbours will be equally agreeable. There was a very nice old gentleman up here only last night, but he didn't seem to want to intrude."

"That was my father," said the Boy, "and he *is* a nice old gentleman, and I'll introduce you some day if you like."

"Can't you two come up here and dine or something tomorrow?" asked the dragon eagerly. "Only, of course, if you've got nothing better to do," he added politely.

"Thanks awfully," said the Boy, "but we don't go out anywhere without my mother, and, to tell you the truth, I'm afraid she mightn't quite approve of you. You see there's no getting over the hard fact that you're a dragon, is there? And when you talk of settling down, and the neighbours, and so on, I can't help feeling that you don't quite realise your position. You're an enemy of the human race, you see!"

"Haven't got an enemy in the world," said the dragon cheerfully. "Too lazy to make 'em, to begin with. And if I *do* read other fellows my poetry, I'm always ready to listen to theirs!"

"Oh, dear!" cried the Boy, "I wish you'd try and grasp the situation properly. When the other people find you out, they'll come after you with spears and swords and all sorts of things. You'll have to be exterminated, according to their way of looking at it! You're a scourge, and a pest, and a baneful monster!"

"Not a word of truth in it," said the dragon, wagging his head solemnly. "Character'll bear the strictest investigation. And now, there's a little sonnet-thing I was working on when you appeared on the scene—"

"Oh, if you *won't* be sensible," cried the Boy, getting up. "I'm going off home. No, I can't stop for sonnets; my mother's sitting up. I'll look you up to-morrow, sometime or other, and do for goodness' sake try and realise that you're a pestilential scourge, or you'll find yourself in a most awful fix. Good night!"

The Boy found it an easy matter to set the mind of his parents at ease about his new friend. They had always left that branch to him, and they took his word without a murmur. The shepherd was formally introduced and many compliments and kind inquiries were exchanged. His wife, however, though expressing her willingness to do anything she could—to mend things, or set the cave to rights, or cook a little something when the dragon had been poring over sonnets and forgotten his meals, as male things *will* do, could not be brought to recognise him formally. The fact that he was a dragon and "they didn't know who he was" seemed to count for everything with her. She made no objection, however, to her little son spending his evenings with the dragon quietly, so long as he was home by nine o'clock: and many a pleasant night they had, sitting on the sward, while the dragon told stories of old, old times, when dragons were quite plentiful and the world was a livelier place than it is now, and life was full of thrills and jumps and surprises.

What the Boy had feared, however, soon came to pass. The most modest and retiring dragon in the world, if he's as big as four cart-horses and covered with blue scales, cannot keep altogether out of the public view. And so in the village tavern of nights the fact that a real live dragon sat brooding in the cave on the Downs was naturally a subject for talk. Though the villagers were extremely frightened, they were rather proud as well. It was a distinction to have a dragon of your own, and it was felt to be a feather in the cap of the village. Still, all were agreed that this sort of thing couldn't be allowed to go on. The dreadful beast must be exterminated, the country-side must be freed from this pest, this terror, this destroying scourge. The fact that not even a hen-roost was the worse for the dragon's arrival wasn't allowed to have anything to do with it. He was a dragon, and he couldn't deny it, and if he didn't choose to behave as such that was his own look-out. But in spite of much valiant talk no hero was found willing to take sword and spear and free the suffering village and win deathless fame; and each night's heated discussion always ended in nothing. Meanwhile the dragon, a happy Bohemian, lolled on the turf, enjoyed the sunsets, told antediluvian anecdotes to the Boy, and polished his old verses while meditating on fresh ones.

One day the Boy, on walking into the village, found everything wearing a festal appearance which was not to be accounted for in the calendar. Carpets and gay-coloured stuffs were hung out of the windows, the church-bells clamoured noisily, the little street was flower-strewn, and the whole population jostled each other along either side of it, chattering, shoving, and ordering each other to stand back. The Boy saw a friend of his own age in the crowd and hailed him.

"What's up?" he cried. "Is it the players, or bears, or a circus, or what?"

"It's all right," his friend hailed back. "He's a-coming."

"*Who's* a-coming?" demanded the Boy, thrusting into the throng.

"Why, St. George, of course," replied his friend. "He's heard tell of our dragon, and he's comin' on purpose to slay the deadly beast, and free us from his horrid yoke. Oh my! won't there be a jolly fight!"

Here was news indeed! The Boy felt that he ought to make quite sure for himself, and he wriggled himself in between the legs of his good-natured elders, abusing them all the time for their unmannerly habit of shoving. Once in the front rank, he breathlessly awaited the arrival.

Presently from the far-away end of the line came the sound of cheering. Next, the measured tramp of a great war-horse made his heart beat quicker, and then he found himself cheering with the rest, as, amidst welcoming shouts, shrill cries of women, uplifting of babies, and waving of handkerchiefs, St. George paced slowly up the street. The Boy's heart stood still and he breathed with sobs, the beauty and the grace of the hero were so far beyond anything he had yet seen. His fluted armour was inlaid with gold, his plumed helmet hung at his saddle-bow, and his thick fair hair framed a face gracious and gentle beyond expression till you caught the sternness in his eyes. He drew rein in front of the little inn, and the villagers crowded round with greetings and thanks and voluble statements of their wrongs and grievances and oppressions. The Boy heard the grave gentle voice of the Saint, assuring them that all would be well now, and that he would stand by them and see them righted and free them from their foe; then he dismounted and passed through the doorway and the crowd poured in after him. But the Boy made off up the hill as fast as he could lay his legs to the ground.

"It's all up, dragon!" he shouted as soon as he was within sight of the beast. "He's coming! He's here now! You'll have to pull yourself together and *do* something at last!"

The dragon was licking his scales and rubbing them with a bit of house-flannel the Boy's mother had lent him, till he shone like a great turquoise.

"Don't be *violent,* Boy," he said without looking around. "Sit down and get your breath, and try and remember that the noun governs the verb, and then perhaps you'll be good enough to tell me *who's* coming?"

"That's right, take it coolly," said the Boy. "Hope you'll be half as cool when I've got through with my news. It's only St. George who's coming, that's all; he rode into the village half an hour ago. Of course you can lick him—a great big fellow like you! But I thought I'd warn you, 'cos he's sure to be round early, and he's got the longest, wickedest-looking spear you ever did see!" And the Boy got up and began to jump round in sheer delight at the prospect of the battle.

"Oh deary, deary me," moaned the dragon; "this is too awful. I won't see him, and that's flat. I don't want to know the fellow at all. I'm sure he's not nice. You must tell him to go away at once, please. Say he can write if he likes, but I can't give him an interview. I'm not seeing anybody at present."

"Now, dragon, dragon," said the Boy imploringly, "don't be perverse and wrong-headed. You've *got* to fight him some time or other, you know, 'cos he's St. George and you're the dragon. Better get it over and then we can go on with the sonnets. And you ought to consider other people a little, too. If it's been dull up here for you, think how dull it's been for me!"

"My dear little man," said the dragon solemnly, "just understand, once for all, that I can't fight and I won't fight. I've never fought in my life, and I'm not going to begin now, just to give you a Roman holiday. In old days I always let the other fellows—the *earnest* fellows—do all the fighting, and no doubt that's why I have the pleasure of being here now."

"But if you don't fight he'll cut your head off!" gasped the Boy, miserable at the prospect of losing both his fight and his friend.

"Oh, I think not," said the dragon in his lazy way. "You'll be able to arrange something. I've every confidence in you, you're such a *manager.* Just run down, there's a dear chap, and make it all right. I leave it entirely to you."

The Boy made his way back to the village in a state of great despondency. First of all, there wasn't going to be any fight; next, his dear and honoured friend the dragon hadn't shown up in quite such a heroic light as he would have liked; and lastly, whether the dragon was a hero at heart or not, it made no difference, for St. George would most undoubtedly cut his head off. "Arrange things indeed!" he said bitterly to himself. "The dragon treats the whole affair as if it was an invitation to tea and croquet."

The villagers were straggling homewards as he passed up the street, all of them in the highest spirits, and gleefully discussing the splendid fight that was in store. The Boy pursued his way to the inn, and passed into the principal chamber, where St. George now sat alone, musing over the chances of the fight, and the sad stories of rapine and of wrong that had so lately been poured into his sympathetic ears.

"May I come in, St. George?" said the Boy politely, as he paused at the door. "I want to talk to you about this little matter of the dragon, if you're not tired of it by this time."

"Yes, come in, Boy," said the Saint kindly. "Another tale of misery and wrong, I fear me. Is it a kind parent, then, of whom the tyrant has bereft you? Of some tender sister or brother? Well, it shall soon be avenged."

"Nothing of the sort," said the Boy. "There's a misunderstanding somewhere, and I want to put it right. The fact is, this is a *good* dragon."

"Exactly," said St. George, smiling pleasantly, "I quite understand. A good *dragon*. Believe me, I do not in the least regret that he is an adversary worthy of my steel, and no feeble specimen of his noxious tribe."

"But he's *not* a noxious tribe," cried the Boy distressedly. "Oh dear, oh dear, how *stupid* men are when they get an idea into their heads! I tell you he's a *good* dragon, and a friend of mine, and tells me the most beautiful stories you ever heard, all about old times and when he was little. And he's been so kind to mother, and mother'd do anything for him. And father likes him too, though father doesn't hold with art and poetry much, and always falls asleep when the dragon starts talking about *style*. But the fact is, nobody can help liking him when once they know him. He's so engaging and so trustful, and as simple as a child!"

"Sit down, and draw your chair up," said St. George. "I like a fellow who sticks up for his friends, and I'm sure the dragon has his good points, if he's got a friend like you. But that's not the question. All this evening I've been listening, with grief and anguish unspeakable, to tales of murder, theft, and wrong; rather too highly coloured, perhaps, not always quite convincing, but forming in the main a most serious roll of crime. History teaches us that the greatest rascals often possess all the domestic virtues; and I fear that your cultivated friend, in spite of the qualities which have won (and rightly) your regard, has got to be speedily exterminated."

"Oh, you've been taking in all the yarns those fellows have been telling you," said the Boy impatiently. "Why, our villagers are the biggest story-tellers in all the country round. It's a known fact. You're a stranger in these parts, or else you'd have heard it already. All they want is a *fight*. They're the most awful beggars for getting up fights—it's meat and drink to them. Dogs, bulls, dragons—anything so long as it's a fight. Why, they've got a poor innocent badger in the stable behind here, at this moment. They were going to have some fun with him to-day, but they're saving him up now till *your* little affair's over. And I've no doubt they've been telling you what a hero you were, and how you were bound to win, in the cause of right and justice, and so on; but let me tell you, I came down the street just now, and they were betting six to four on the dragon freely!"

"Six to four on the dragon!" murmured St. George sadly, resting his cheek on his hand. "This is an evil world, and sometimes I begin to think that all the wickedness in it is not entirely bottled up inside the dragons. And yet—may not this wily beast have misled you as to his real character, in order that your good report of him may serve as a cloak for his evil deeds? Nay, may there not be, at this very moment, some hapless Princess immured within yonder gloomy cavern?"

The moment he had spoken, St. George was sorry for what he had said, the Boy looked so genuinely distressed.

"I assure you, St. George," he said earnestly, "there's nothing of the sort in the cave at all. The dragon's a real gentleman, every inch of him, and I may say that no one would be more shocked and grieved than he would, at hearing you talk in that—that *loose* way about matters on which he has very strong views!"

"Well, perhaps I've been over-credulous," said St. George. "Perhaps I've misjudged the animal. But what are we to do? Here are the dragon and I, almost face to face, each supposed to be thirsting for each other's blood. I don't see any way out of it, exactly. What do you suggest? Can't you arrange things, somehow?"

"That's just what the dragon said," replied the Boy, rather nettled. "Really, the way you two seem to leave everything to me—I suppose you couldn't be persuaded to go away quietly, could you?"

"Impossible, I fear," said the Saint. "Quite against the rules. *You* know that as well as I do."

"Well, then, look here," said the Boy, "it's early yet—would you mind strolling up with me and seeing the dragon and talking it over? It's not far, and any friend of mine will be most welcome."

"Well, it's *irregular,*" said St. George, rising, "but really it seems about the most sensible thing to do. You're taking a lot of trouble on your friend's account," he added good-naturedly, as they passed out through the door together. "But cheer up! Perhaps there won't have to be any fight after all."

"Oh, but I hope there will, though!" replied the little fellow wistfully.

"I've brought a friend to see you, dragon," said the Boy rather loud.

The dragon woke up with a start. "I was just—er—thinking about things," he said in his simple way. "Very pleased to make your acquaintance, sir. Charming weather we're having!"

"This is St. George," said the Boy, shortly. "St. George, let me introduce you to the dragon. We've come up to talk things over quietly, dragon, and now for goodness' sake do let us have a little straight common sense, and come to some practical business-like arrangement, for I'm sick of views and theories of life and personal tendencies, and all that sort of thing. I may perhaps add that my mother's sitting up."

"So glad to meet you, St. George," began the dragon rather nervously, "because you've been a great traveller, I hear, and I've always been rather a stay-at-home. But I can show you many antiquities, many interesting features of our country-side, if you're stopping here any time——"

"I think," said St. George in his frank, pleasant way, "that we'd really better take the advice of our young friend here, and try to come to some understanding, on a business footing, about this little affair of ours. Now don't you think that after all the simplest plan would be just to fight it out, according to the rules, and let the best man win? They're betting on you, I may tell you, down in the village, but I don't mind that!"

"Oh, yes, *do,* dragon," said the Boy delightedly; "it'll save such a lot of bother!"

"My young friend, you shut up," said the dragon severely. "Believe me, St. George," he went on, "there's nobody in the world I'd sooner oblige than you and this young gentleman here. But the whole thing's nonsense, and conventionality, and popular thick-headedness. There's absolutely nothing to fight about, from beginning to end. And anyhow I'm not going to, so that settles it!"

"But supposing I make you?" said St. George, rather nettled.

"You can't," said the dragon triumphantly. "I should only go into my cave and retire for a time down the hole I came up. You'd soon get heartily sick of sitting outside and waiting for me to come out and fight you. And as soon as you'd really gone away, why, I'd come up again gaily, for I tell you frankly, I like this place, and I'm going to stay here!"

St. George gazed for a while on the fair landscape around them. "But this would be a beautiful place for a fight," he began again persuasively. "These great bare rolling Downs for the arena—and me in my golden armour showing up against your big blue scaly coils! Think what a picture it would make!"

"Now you're trying to get at me through my artistic sensibilities," said the dragon. "But it won't work. Not but what it would make a very pretty picture, as you say," he added, wavering a little.

"We seem to be getting rather nearer to *business,*" put in the Boy. "You must see, dragon, that there's got to be a fight of some sort, 'cos you can't want to have to go down that dirty old hole again and stop there till goodness knows when."

"It might be arranged," said St. George thoughtfully. "I *must* spear you somewhere, of course, but I'm not bound to hurt you very much. There's such a lot of you that there must be a few *spare* places somewhere. Here, for instance, just behind your foreleg. It couldn't hurt you much, just here!"

"Now you're tickling, George," said the dragon coyly. "No, that place won't do at all. Even if it didn't hurt—and I'm sure it would, awfully—it would make me laugh, and that would spoil everything."

"Let's try somewhere else, then" said St. George patiently. "Under your neck, for instance—all these folds of thick skin,—if I speared you here you'd never even know I'd done it!"

"Yes, but are you sure you can hit off the right place?" asked the dragon anxiously.

"Of course I am," said St. George, with confidence. "You leave that to me!"

"It's just because I've *got* to leave it to you that I'm asking," replied the dragon rather testily. "No doubt you would deeply regret any error you might make in the hurry of the moment; but you wouldn't regret it half as much as I should! However, I suppose we've got to trust somebody, as we go through life, and your plan seems, on the whole, as good a one as any."

"Look here, dragon," interrupted the Boy, a little jealous on behalf of his friend, who seemed to be getting all the worst of the bargain: "I don't quite see where *you* come in! There's to be a fight, apparently, and you're to be licked; and what I want to know is, what are *you* going to get out of it?"

"St. George," said the dragon, "just tell him, please—what will happen after I'm vanquished in the deadly combat?"

"Well, according to the rules I suppose I shall lead you in triumph down to the market-place or whatever answers to it," said St. George.

"Precisely," said the dragon. "And then—?"

"And then there'll be shoutings and speeches and things," continued St. George. "And I shall explain that you're converted, and see the error of your ways, and so on."

"Quite so," said the dragon. "And then—?"

"Oh, and then—" said St. George, "why, and then there will be the usual banquet, I suppose."

"Exactly," said the dragon; "and that's where *I* come in. Look here," he continued, addressing the Boy, "I'm bored to death up here, and no one really appreciates me. I'm going into Society, I am, through the kindly aid of our friend here, who's taking such a lot of trouble on my account; and you'll find I've got all the qualities to endear me to people who entertain! So now that's all settled, and if you don't mind—I'm an old-fashioned fellow—don't want to turn you out, but—"

"Remember, you'll have to do your proper share of the fighting, dragon!" said St. George, as he took the hint and rose to go; "I mean ramping, and breathing fire, and so on!"

"I can *ramp* all right," replied the dragon confidently; "as to breathing fire, it's surprising how easily one gets out of practice; but I'll do the best I can. Good night!"

They had descended the hill and were almost back in the village again, when St. George stopped short. "*Knew* I had forgotten something," he said. "There ought to be a Princess. Terror-stricken and chained to a rock, and all that sort of thing. Boy, can't you arrange a Princess?"

The Boy was in the middle of a tremendous yawn. "I'm tired to death," he wailed, "and I *can't* arrange a Princess, or anything more, at this time of night. And my mother's sitting up, and *do* stop asking me to arrange more things till tomorrow!"

Next morning the people began streaming up to the Downs at quite an early hour, in their Sunday clothes and carrying baskets with bottle-necks sticking out of them, every one intent on securing good places for the combat. This was not exactly a simple matter, for of course it was quite possible that the dragon might win, and in that case even those who had put their money on him felt they could hardly expect him to deal with his backers on a different footing to the rest. Places were chosen, therefore, with circumspection and with a view to a speedy retreat in case of emergency; and the front rank was mostly composed of boys who had escaped from parental control and now sprawled and rolled about on the grass, regardless of the shrill threats and warnings discharged at them by their anxious mothers behind.

The Boy had secured a good front place, well up towards the cave, and was feeling as anxious as a stage-manager on a first night. Could the dragon be depended upon? He might change his mind and vote the whole performance rot; or else, seeing that the affair had been so hastily planned without even a rehearsal, he might be too nervous to show up. The Boy looked narrowly at the cave, but it showed no sign of life or occupation. Could the dragon have made a moon-light flitting?

The higher portions of the ground were now black with sightseers, and presently a sound of cheering and a waving of handkerchiefs told that something was visible to them which the Boy, far up towards the dragon-end of the line as he was, could not yet see. A minute more and St. George's red plumes topped the hill, as the Saint rode slowly forth on the great level space which stretched up to the grim mouth of the cave. Very gallant and beautiful he looked on his tall war-horse, his golden armour glancing in the sun, his great spear held erect, the little white pennon, crimson-crossed, fluttering at its point. He drew rein and remained motionless. The lines of spectators began to give back a little, nervously; and even the boys in front stopped pulling hair and cuffing each other, and leaned forward expectant.

"Now then, dragon!" muttered the Boy impatiently, fidgeting where he sat. He need not have distressed himself, had he only known. The dramatic possibilities of the thing had tickled the dragon immensely, and he had been up from an early hour, preparing for his first public appearance with as much heartiness as if the years had run backwards, and he had been again a little dragonlet, playing with his sisters on the floor of their mother's cave, at the game of saints-and-dragons, in which the dragon was bound to win.

A low muttering, mingled with snorts, now made itself heard; rising to a bellowing roar that seemed to fill the plain. Then a cloud of smoke obscured the mouth of the cave, and out of the midst of it the dragon himself, shining, sea-blue, magnificent, pranced splendidly forth; and everybody said, "Oo-oo-oo!" as if he had been a mighty rocket! His scales were glittering, his long spiky tail lashed his sides, his claws tore up the turf and sent it flying high over his back, and smoke and fire incessantly jetted from his angry nostrils. "Oh, well done, dragon!" cried the Boy excitedly. "Didn't think he had it in him!" he added to himself.

St. George lowered his spear, bent his head, dug his heels into his horse's sides, and came thundering over the turf. The dragon charged with a roar and a squeal, —a great blue whirling combination of coils and snorts and clashing jaws and spikes and fire.

"Missed!" yelled the crowd. There was a moment's entanglement of golden armour and blue-green coils and spiky tail, and then the great horse, tearing at his bit, carried the Saint, his spear swung high in the air, almost up to the mouth of the cave.

The dragon sat down and barked viciously, while St. George with difficulty pulled his horse round into position.

"End of Round One!" thought the Boy. "How well they managed it! But I hope the Saint won't get excited. I can trust the dragon all right. What a regular play-actor the fellow is!"

St. George had at last prevailed on his horse to stand steady, and was looking round him as he wiped his brow. Catching sight of the Boy, he smiled and nodded, and held up three fingers for an instant.

"It seems to be all planned out," said the Boy to himself. "Round Three is to be the finishing one, evidently. Wish it could have lasted a bit longer. Whatever's that old fool of a dragon up to now?"

The dragon was employing the interval in giving a ramping performance for the benefit of the crowd. Ramping, it should be explained, consists in running round and round in a wide circle, and sending waves and ripples of movement along the whole length of your spine, from your pointed ears right down to the spike at the end of your long tail. When you are covered with blue scales, the effect is particularly pleasing; and the Boy recollected the dragon's recently expressed wish to become a social success.

St. George now gathered up his reins and began to move forward, dropping the point of his spear and settling himself firmly in the saddle.

"Time!" yelled everybody excitedly; and the dragon, leaving off his ramping, sat up on end, and began to leap from one side to the other with huge ungainly bounds, whooping like a Red Indian. This naturally disconcerted the horse, who swerved violently, the Saint only just saving himself by the mane; and as they shot past the dragon delivered a vicious snap at the horse's tail which sent the poor beast careering madly far over the Downs, so that the language of the Saint, who had lost a stirrup, was fortunately inaudible to the general assemblage.

Round Two evoked audible evidence of friendly feeling towards the dragon. The spectators were not slow to appreciate a combatant who could hold his own so well and clearly wanted to show good sport; and many encouraging remarks reached the ears of our friend as he strutted to and fro, his chest thrust out and his tail in the air, hugely enjoying his new popularity.

St. George had dismounted and was tightening his girths, and telling his horse, with quite an Oriental flow of imagery, exactly what he thought of him, and his relations, and his conduct on the present occasion; so the Boy made his way down to the Saint's end of the line, and held his spear for him.

"It's been a jolly fight, St. George!" he said, with a sigh. "Can't you let it last a bit longer?"

"Well, I think I'd better not," replied the Saint. "The fact is, your simple-minded old friend's getting conceited, now they've begun cheering him, and he'll forget all about the arrangement and take to playing the fool, and there's no telling where he would stop. I'll just finish him off this round."

He swung himself into the saddle and took his spear from the Boy. "Now don't you be afraid," he added kindly. "I've marked my spot exactly, and *he's* sure to give me all the assistance in his power, because he knows it's his only chance of being asked to the banquet!"

St. George now shortened his spear, bringing the butt well up under his arm; and, instead of galloping as before, he trotted smartly towards the dragon, who crouched at his approach, flicking his tail till it cracked in the air like a great cart-whip. The Saint wheeled as he neared his opponent and circled warily round him, keeping his eye on the spare place; while the dragon, adopting similar tactics, paced with caution round the same circle, occasionally feinting with his head. So the two sparred for an opening, while the spectators maintained a breathless silence.

Though the round lasted for some minutes, the end was so swift that all the Boy saw was a lightning movement of the Saint's arm, and then a whirl and a confusion of spines, claws, tail, and flying bits of turf. The dust cleared away, the

. . . *winked solemnly*

spectators whooped and ran in cheering, and the Boy made out that the dragon was down, pinned to the earth by the spear, while St. George had dismounted, and stood astride of him.

It all seemed so genuine that the Boy ran in breathlessly, hoping the dear old dragon wasn't really hurt. As he approached, the dragon lifted one large eyelid, winked solemnly, and collapsed again. He was held fast to earth by the neck, but the Saint had hit him in the spare place agreed upon, and it didn't even seem to tickle.

"Bain't you goin' to cut 'is 'ed orf, master?" asked one of the applauding crowd. He had backed the dragon, and naturally felt a trifle sore.

"Well, not *to-day*, I think," replied St. George pleasantly. "You see, that can be done at *any* time. There's no hurry at all. I think we'll all go down to the village first, and have some refreshment, and then I'll give him a good talking-to, and you'll find he'll be a very different dragon!"

At that magic word *refreshment* the whole crowd formed up in procession and silently awaited the signal to start. The time for talking and cheering and betting was past, the hour for action had arrived. St. George, hauling on his spear with both hands, released the dragon, who rose and shook himself and ran his eye over his spikes and scales and things, to see that they were all in order. Then the Saint mounted and led off the procession, the dragon following meekly in the company of the Boy, while the thirsty spectators kept at a respectful interval behind.

There were great doings when they got down to the village again, and had formed up in front of the inn. After refreshment St. George made a speech, in which he informed his audience that he had removed their direful scourge, at a great deal of trouble and inconvenience to himself, and now they weren't to go about grumbling and fancying they'd got grievances, because they hadn't. And they shouldn't be so fond of fights, because next time they might have to do the fighting themselves, which would not be the same thing at all. And there was a certain badger in the inn stables which had got to be released at once, and he'd come and see it done himself. Then he told them that the dragon had been thinking over things, and saw that there were two sides to every question, and he wasn't going to do it any more, and if they were good perhaps he'd stay and settle down there. So they must make friends, and not be prejudiced, and go about fancying they knew everything there was to be known, because they didn't, not by a long way. And he warned them against the sin of romancing, and making up stories and fancying other people would believe them just because they were plausible and highly-coloured. Then he sat down, amidst much repentant cheering, and the dragon nudged the Boy in the ribs and whispered that he couldn't have done it better himself. Then every one went off to get ready for the banquet.

Banquets are always pleasant things, consisting mostly, as they do, of eating and drinking; but the specially nice thing about a banquet is, that it comes when something's over, and there's nothing more to worry about, and to-morrow seems a long way off. St. George was happy because there had been a fight and he hadn't had to kill anybody; for he didn't really like killing, though he generally had to do it. The dragon was happy because there had been a fight, and so far from being hurt in it he had won popularity and a sure footing in Society. The Boy was happy because there had been a fight, and in spite of it all his two friends were on the best of terms. And all the others were happy because there had been a fight, and—well, they didn't require any other reasons for their happiness. The dragon exerted himself to say the right thing to everybody, and proved the life and soul of the evening; while the Saint and the Boy, as they looked on, felt that they were only assisting at a feast of which the honour and the glory were entirely the dragon's. But they didn't mind that, being good fellows, and the dragon was not in the least proud or forgetful. On the contrary, every ten minutes or so he leant over towards the Boy and said impressively: "Look here! you *will* see me home afterwards, won't you?" And the Boy always nodded, though he had promised his mother not to be out late.

At last the banquet was over, the guests had dropped away with many good nights and congratulations and invitations, and the dragon, who had seen the last of them off the premises, emerged into the street followed by the Boy, wiped his brow, sighed, sat down in the road and gazed at the stars. "Jolly night it's been!" he murmured. "Jolly stars! Jolly little place this! Think I shall just stop here. Don't feel like climbing up any beastly hill. Boy's promised to see me home. Boy had better do it then! No responsibility on my part. Responsibility all Boy's!" And his chin sank on his broad chest and he slumbered peacefully.

"Oh, *get* up, dragon," cried the Boy piteously. "You *know* my mother's sitting up, and I'm so tired, and you made me promise to see you home, and I never knew what it meant or I wouldn't have done it!" And the Boy sat down in the road by the side of the sleeping dragon, and cried.

The door behind them opened, a stream of light illumined the road, and St. George, who had come out for a stroll in the cool night-air, caught sight of the two figures sitting there—the great motionless dragon and the tearful little Boy.

"What's the matter, Boy?" he inquired kindly, stepping to his side.

"Oh, it's this great lumbering *pig* of a dragon!" sobbed the Boy. "First he makes me promise to see him home, and then he says I'd better do it, and goes to sleep! Might as well try to see a *haystack* home! And I'm so tired, and mother's—" Here he broke down again.

"Now don't take on," said St. George. "I'll stand by you, and we'll *both* see him home. Wake up, dragon!" he said sharply, shaking the beast by the elbow.

The dragon looked up sleepily. "What a night, George!" he murmured: "what a—"

"Now look here, dragon," said the Saint firmly. "Here's this little fellow waiting to see you home, and you *know* he ought to have been in bed these two hours, and what his mother'll say *I* don't know, and anybody but a selfish pig would have *made* him go to bed long ago—"

"And he *shall* go to bed!" cried the dragon, starting up. "Poor little chap, only fancy his being up at this hour! It's a shame, that's what it is, and I don't think, St. George, you've been very considerate—but come along at once, and don't let us have any more arguing or shilly-shallying. You give me hold of your hand, Boy—thank you, George, an arm up the hill is just what I wanted!"

So they set off up the hill arm-in-arm, the Saint, the Dragon, and the Boy. The lights in the little village began to go out; but there were stars, and a late moon, as they climbed to the Downs together. And, as they turned the last corner and disappeared from view, snatches of an old song were borne back on the night-breeze. I can't be certain which of them was singing, but I *think* it was the Dragon!

As you read fantasy for children, you will discover numerous titles about specific animals—cats, rabbits, dogs. Familiar animals featured in literature surprisingly often are mice and rats. It is difficult to explain this emphasis because in many respects mice and rats have been associated with negative feelings. These animals are presented, however, as lovable and often wise; many of them have humorous ways with words, certainly a great facility with language.

An unusual story of a jewel theft is *Dear Rat* by Julia Cunningham (Houghton Mifflin, 1961). This entertaining story begins as Andrew the rat arrives in France where "rat language is the same . . . as elsewhere."

A cricket, a mouse, and a cat are the main characters in the fantasy *The*

I AM A RAT. I'm tough and I'm tender. I know my way around, thanks to having been bounced off the hard surfaces of the world. I do okay in any company you care to name and that's saying a lot when you consider my great flaw. What I am on the edge of saying, right out in cold print, is dangerous and stupid. But the truth is — I'm honest.

Cricket in Times Square (Farrar, Straus & Giroux, 1960) by George Selden, illustrated by Garth Williams. Connecticut-born Chester the cricket is carried to New York City by accident in a picnic basket. He manages to scramble out of the basket only to land in a pile of litter in the subway station at Times Square, hardly an auspicious introduction to city life. He finds, however, three good friends—Mario Bellini, whose parents run the newsstand; Tucker, a mouse who makes his living by "scrounging"; and Harry the cat, Tucker's oldest friend, who lives with him in the drain pipe.

The three animals share many misadventures, but they also save the Bellini family from going broke. They discover that Chester is a great musician able to draw crowds who not only pay to hear his performances but also buy papers and magazines while they listen. Finally, however,

Chester is so homesick for Connecticut that Tucker and Harry help him get on the Late Local Express at Grand Central Station. Back in the drain pipe, they find it difficult to go to sleep.

Tucker Mouse changed his position. "Harry," he said.
  "Yes?" said Harry Cat.
  "Maybe next summer we could go to the country."
  "Maybe we can."
  "I mean—the country in Connecticut," said Tucker.
  "I know what you mean," said Harry Cat.

This would be an excellent selection to read aloud. (Ignore the Chinese dialect that the author unfortunately used for the man who provided the charming cricket cage.) A second fantasy by George Selden is the humorous *The Genie of Sutton Place,* which is discussed in detail on page 139.

A charming mouse is Miss Bianca, who "in her capacity as Perpetual Madam President of the Mouse Prisoners' Aid Society, had amongst other duties that of weighing the credentials of all candidates for the annual award of Tybalt Stars (bravery in face of cats)." Margery Sharp's *Miss Bianca in the Salt Mines* (Little, Brown, 1966) is illustrated by Garth Williams. Miss Bianca, an intelligent and efficient mouse, manages to free Teddy-Age-Eight from the salt mines where he has been imprisoned. There is also *Miss Bianca in the Orient* (Little, Brown, 1970).

Mrs. Frisby and the Rats of NIMH is an unusual book by Robert C. O'Brien (Atheneum, 1971). Winner of the Newbery Medal in 1972, this book tells the story of a mouse widow, Mrs. Frisby, and a band of rats who help her and her children. The rats had been imprisoned for years in a laboratory called NIMH (National Institute of Mental Health). Inoculations made them strangely wise, inventive, and long-lived. They even learned how to read! Imagine what happens when these superior beings escape from the laboratory!

Other delightful fantasies about mice and rats include both picture books (marked with an asterisk) and books for older children.

Anatole and the Cat by Eve Titus. McGraw-Hill, 1957. And other titles.

Ben and Me by Robert Lawson. Little, Brown, 1939.

The Orchestra Mice by Jacqueline Jackson. Reilly & Lee, 1970.

* *Walter the Lazy Mouse* By Marjorie Flack. Macmillan, 1932.

Feldman Fieldmouse by Nathaniel Benchley. Harper & Row, 1971.

Runaway Ralph by Beverly Cleary. Morrow, 1970. Also *The Mouse and the Motorcycle*.

*Frederick by Leo Lionni. Pantheon, 1967.

Maximilian's World by Mary Stolz. Harper & Row, 1966. Also *Belling the Tiger* and *The Great Rebellion*.

If you want still more fantasies that feature animals, try some of these:

Atwater, Richard and Florence. *Mr. Popper's Penguins*. Little, Brown, 1938.

*Ayme, Marcel. *The Wonderful Farm*. Harper, 1951.

* Bianco, Margery. *The Velveteen Rabbit*. Doubleday, 1926.

Brooks, Walter. *Freddy Goes to Florida*. Knopf, 1949. (*Followed by many more adventures of Freddy the pig.*)

Coatsworth, Elizabeth. *The Cat Who Went to Heaven*. Macmillan, 1930.

————. *Cricket and the Emperor's Son*. Norton, 1965.

Erwin, John. *Mrs. Fox*. Simon and Schuster, 1969.

Lawson, Robert. *Mr. Revere and I*. Little, Brown, (*About a horse.*)

————. *Rabbit Hill*. Viking, 1944.

Sleigh, Barbara. *Carbonel: The King of the Cats*. Bobbs-Merrill, 1957.

Stolz, Mary. *Pigeon Flight*. Harper, 1962.

❦ *ANIMAL FANTASIES* Choose one of the following activities as you explore popular fantasies about animals.

1. Develop a bulletin board display on the work of one author, such as George Selden, or on one book, such as *Wind in the Willows*. Include as much relevant information as you can, designed both to educate and to entertain, for example:

   A picture of the author

   Enlarged figures from the story or stories

   Facts about the author's life; quotations

   A book jacket

   The book(s) itself

Objects that fit the plot development (a map, toy animal, key)

2. See how many fantasies you can find about one particular animal, much as we have noted for mice and rats. You might find several that include a lion, a dog, or even rabbits, as in Lonzo Anderson's *Two Hundred Rabbits* (Viking, 1968)—the author himself turns out to be a rabbit! Outline a plan for developing a study of fantasy rabbits or other animals with children of a specified age. Let yourself go and have fun!

FANTASY ABOUT "HUMAN BEANS"

"Human beans are *for* Borrowers—like bread's for butter!" Arrietty explains to the boy who lives Upstairs and tries to tell her that "borrowing" is stealing. "But we are Borrowers," she explains, "like you're a-a human bean or whatever it's called. We're part of the house. You might as well say that the fire grate steals the coal from the coal scuttle."

The Borrowers (Harcourt Brace Jovanovich, 1952) by Mary Norton is one of the many excellent fantasies that focus on human beings. In this case the main characters are little people who live beneath the home of Great-aunt Sophy, and the story centers on their efforts to avoid being discovered by the big people who live upstairs. Fantasy about human beings ranges from that which is very near reality, as we know it, to that about characters who have unusual powers and fantastic adventures. We will examine the most realistic stories first and gradually move toward the more fanciful.

A book that hovers on the line between fantasy and realism is *Homer Price* (Viking, 1943) and its sequel *Centerburg Tales* (Viking, 1953) by Robert McCloskey. Homer is a boy who does zany but half-believable things, for example, catching some robbers single-handedly except for the help of his pet skunk Aroma. The other characters are humorous, eccentric, and improbable—Uncle Ulysses who concocts spoonerisms every time he gets excited, Miss Terwilliger who collects string, and the lady who loses her diamond bracelet in the doughnut batter. "The Doughnut Machine," a story from *Homer Price,* was made into a film by Weston Woods.

Published in 1911, a book that still appeals to contemporary readers is *The Secret Garden* (Lippincott) by Frances Hodgson Burnett, who blends realism and fantasy to create a strangely fascinating mystery. Although the characters are real, the atmosphere of the setting and the events that occur give this story an air of fantasy. "Mistress Mary, quite contrary" is anything but a likable character when she first arrives from India to live in England at Misselthwaite Manor, the home of her uncle, Archibald Craven. Ten-year-old Mary Lennox soon discovers that life is different in England, and she finds people who interest her despite her haughty coldness—Martha, the housemaid; Dickon, who makes friends with animals; and Colin Craven, whose mother died when he was born. Best of all, however, she discovers the garden that has been locked since Colin's mother died. With the help of Dickon and Ben Weatherstaff, the gardener, she makes the garden beautiful again. Mary's happiness spills over to Colin, who learns to walk, and to his father, who learns to love his son. This is an excellent book for reading aloud to a group of fourth or fifth graders, if you don't mind trying the Yorkshire dialect that appears occasionally.

Another early example of fantasy that has some realistic elements is *The Peterkin Papers,* which chronicles the humorous adventures of the Peterkins—Mrs. Peterkin, Mr. Peterkin, Agamemnon, Solomon John, Elizabeth Eliza, and the little boys with the India rubber boots. Written by Lucretia P. Hale, this engaging story first appeared in 1880. Somehow the Peterkins constantly get into extraordinary difficulties, only solved through great exertion. There was the time, for example, when Mrs. Peterkin put salt in her coffee by mistake. No one knew what to do, even the chemist with all his chemicals or the herbwoman with all her herbs. The amazing lady from Philadelphia, as usual, comes to the rescue. She listened attentively and then said, "Why doesn't your mother make a fresh cup of coffee?"

Elizabeth Eliza started with surprise. Solomon John shouted with joy; so did Agamemnon, who had just finished his sum; so did the little boys, who had followed on. "Why didn't we think of that?" asked Elizabeth Eliza; and they all went back to their mother, and she had her cup of coffee.

In a fantasy world anything is possible as we move farther away from realism. Imagine digging in a gravel pit all the way to Australia and hearing a voice say: "Let me alone!"

The children stood round the hole in a ring, looking at the creature they had found. It was worth looking at. Its eyes were on long horns like a snail's eyes, and it could move them in and out like telescopes; it had ears like a bat's ears, and its tubby body was shaped like a spider's and covered with thick soft fur; its legs and arms were furry too, and it had hands and feet like a monkey's.

The diggers—Jane, Cyril, Robert, and Anthea—should have known, of course, that they had found a Psammead, or Sand-fairy, and that Psammeads are to be treated with respect, for they can grant wishes. These characters are introduced in E. Nesbit's *Five Children and It* (Coward-McCann), which first appeared at the beginning of the century. Since the children have had no experience with wishes, they have trouble thinking of good ones, and every wish seems to get them in trouble. It does no good, for example, to wish yourself beautiful if the servants don't recognize you and won't let you come in the house for dinner. They forget, too, that the wishes expire at sundown, so they are left stranded on a church steeple after a pleasant day of flying. By the end of the book, they are happy to give up wishing. They meet the Psammead again in two books that follow—*The Phoenix and the Carpet* and *The Story of the Amulet*. E. Nesbit also wrote a series of fantasies about the Bastable Family, beginning with *The Treasure Seekers*.

Lucy Boston interweaves reality and fantasy with great skill. She has created an unusual setting for a series of outstanding fantasies. Green Knowe is a large, very old English country home in which Mrs. Oldknow lives with a few servants. In *The Children of Green Knowe* (Harcourt Brace Jovanovich, 1954) Toseland, who soon becomes known as Tolly, comes there to live with his great-grandmother. Their relationship is warm and intimate as they share the mysteries of the old house. They also share a friendship with the children who appear from the past, children who lived at Green Knowe in the seventeenth century—Toby and his pony Feste; Linnet; Alexander and his flute. Lucy Boston's masterful use of the English language is exemplified by this passage that describes Tolly's thoughts as he approaches Green Knowe on the train during a flood. He sits opposite two women who are knitting as the train lurches through the countryside:

"I wish it was *the* Flood," thought the boy, "and that I was going to the Ark. That would be fun! Like the circus. Perhaps Noah had a whip and made all the animals go round and round for exercise. What a noise there would be, with the lions roaring, elephants trumpeting, pigs squealing, donkeys braying, horses whinnying, bulls bellowing, and cocks and hens always thinking they were going to be trodden on but unable to fly up on to the roof where all the other birds were singing, screaming, twittering, squawking and cooing. What must it have sounded like, coming along on the tide? And did Mrs. Noah just knit, knit and take no notice?"

Tolly is also the main character in *Treasure of Green Knowe,* which followed this first book. In the next book, *The River at Green Knowe,* however, the author introduces three new characters—Ida, an English girl; Oskar, a Polish refugee; and Ping, a displaced boy from the Orient. Ida's aunt rents the house for the summer, bringing the children with her for a glorious few months of exploring and meeting such fantasy figures as an old hermit, winged horses, and an amiable giant.

Quite a different story is *A Stranger at Green Knowe,* in which Ping comes to live with Mrs. Oldknow. The stranger, however, is not Ping, but a huge gorilla named Hanno that Ping first viewed sympathetically in the London Zoo. This book begins in the tropical forest where Hanno was born. The author provides a good bit of information about the life style of this gorilla family headed by Old Man—their ways of communicating, physical interaction among members of the gorilla family, even the way they sleep. Then the hunters come; Old Man is killed; Hanno and his sister are captured. Thus, Hanno comes to the London Zoo, where he is seen by Ping. Coincidentally, when Ping goes to Green Knowe, however, the gorilla escapes and appears in Mrs. Oldknow's formal English garden where Ping tries to protect him. In contrast to other books set at Green Knowe, this story is realistic. It is interesting, but less effective than the fantasies.

Another British writer, Philippa Pearce, won the Carnegie Medal (an English award) for an intriguing fantasy, *Tom's Midnight Garden* (Lippincott, 1958). Tom Long has been anticipating a pleasant summer building a tree house with his brother Peter. Peter gets the measles, however, so Tom is sent instead to stay with his Aunt Gwen and Uncle Alan who live in a "poky flat" and have no children. Angry and disappointed, Tom is rude and unhappy until he hears the grandfather clock in the hall of the converted mansion strike thirteen! Thus begins an exciting adventure as Tom visits the secret garden where he meets Hatty in an earlier time. Hatty, as it turns out, is Harriet Bartholomew, the old woman who owns the house and whose dreams Tom has been sharing.

Another fantasy that focuses on human characters is *The Twenty-One Balloons* (Viking, 1947), a well-known fantasy by William Pène duBois. Although the story begins rather slowly, once Professor William Waterman Sherman begins telling about his trip around the world, the author carries readers along easily with clear descriptions of exciting events in a well-developed plot. Professor Sherman, a retired school teacher, escapes

From The Twenty-One Balloons *by William Pène du Bois.
Copyright 1947, © renewed
1975 by William Pène du Bois.
Reprinted by permission of The
Viking Press.*

a humdrum life by floating above the earth in a neat little basket home
suspended from a huge balloon. On the seventh day, however, a sea gull
jabs a hole in the top of the balloon, which the professor cannot reach.
Fortunately, he is able to land on a small island, Krakatoa, which he as-
sumes is uninhabited. Much to his amazement, however, twenty families
are living an idyllic life on the island funded by an enormous diamond
mine that they dare not reveal to the world. When a volcano erupts, they
all sail off just in time on a platform lifted by twenty-one balloons to
places where they can drop off by parachute. Finally only the professor is
left to bring the platform down in the Atlantic, where he is rescued and
tells the incredible tale of his journey.

Named as an Honor Book for the Newbery Award, *Fog Magic* (Viking, 1943) is Julia Sauer's enchanting fantasy of Greta's mysterious visits
to another time that exists only in the fog. Greta's father understands her

need to disappear into the fog as he had once done himself. He helps her understand that when she becomes twelve, she will no longer have this ability, but he adds, ". . . none of the things you think you've lost on the way are *really lost*. Every one of them is folded around you—close."

In *The Weirdstone of Brisingamen* (Walck, 1960), Alan Garner writes of Susan and Colin, two English children who anticipate an ordinary vacation in the countryside. The bracelet that Susan wears unexpectedly plunges them into a struggle begun many centuries ago between wizards, elves, and dwarves on one side and the forces of evil, represented by the Morrigan, a shape-changing witch, on the other. The seriousness of the contest and the portrayal of the forces of good and evil are the strongest elements of the book, for the characters derive from the rich British mythology. The story continues in *The Moon of Gomrath* (Walck, 1967) as Susan and Colin play an even more active role in containing the power of the Morrigan. Alan Garner's other books, *Elidor* (Walck, 1967) and *The Owl Service* (Walck, 1967), are also fantasies that demonstrate his interest in and knowledge of British mythology.

Jay Williams writes fantasy about people that at times leans toward science fiction. In *The People of the Ax* (Walck, 1974), he writes of the *crom*. "The *crom* were not human, but neither were they animals. They resembled people but were hairier, often bigger and with flat eyes like pieces of slate. They were strong and furtive and above all they were full of hate." Arne, a young boy from Strand, has just reached the time when he ceases to be an Unfinished Person with no soul and becomes fully Human:

He felt a smooth hand on his forehead, and fingers touched and tapped his skull as if whoever it was were making certain of the shape of it. The fingers tightened and pressed on the top of his head with such force that pain ran down on either side of his nose and exploded in his cheekbones. It seemed to him that fine threads of heat shot from the probing fingers into some spot behind his eyes, and then the fingers were withdrawn and the pain ceased. (p. 21)

Arne, encountering the crom again, finds that he can waken the soul in another being and that crom can be Human Beings. Jay Williams also wrote *The Hawkstone* and *The Hero from Otherwhere*. These books are quite different from the humorous Danny Dunn series he co-authored with Raymond Abrashkin.

Fantasies about people, usually children, are numerous. Often children appear in the fantasies that we have placed in the section about animals, and certainly they are in science fiction. In addition to those we have already discussed in some detail, there are others that you will want to know. Listed here are recommended works of authors that are not presented later in the chapter.

Babbitt, Natalie.
    Dick Foote and the Shark. Farrar, Straus & Giroux, 1967.
    Kneeknock Rise. Farrar, Straus & Giooux, 1970.
    The Search for Delicious. Farrar, Straus & Giroux, 1969.
    The Something. Farrar, Straus & Giroux, 1970.

Bond, Nancy.
    A String in the Harp. Atheneum, 1976.

Clarke, Pauline.
    The Return of the Twelves. Coward-McCann, 1964.

Coombs, Patricia.
    Lisa and the Grompet. Lothrop, 1970.

Cunningham, Julia.
    Dorp Dead. Pantheon, 1965.
    Viollet. Pantheon, 1966.

Dahl, Roald.
    Charlie and the Chocolate Factory. Knopf, 1964.
    James and the Giant Peach. Knopf, 1961.
    The Magic Finger. Harper, 1966.

Harris, Rosemary.
    The Moon in the Cloud. Macmillan, 1970.
    The Seal-Singing. Macmillan, 1971.
    The Shadow on the Sun. Macmillan, 1970.

Hunter, Mollie.
    The Kelpie's Pearls. Funk & Wagnalls, 1966.
    The Walking Stones. Harper & Row, 1970.
    A Stranger Came Ashore. Harper & Row, 1975.

Juster, Norton.
    The Phantom Tollbooth. Random House, 1961.

Stockton, Frank Richard.
    The Bee-Man of Orn. Holt, 1964.
    The Griffin and the Minor Canon. Holt, 1963.

Stolz, Mary.
    Cat in the Mirror. Harper & Row, 1975.

Travers, Pamela L.
Mary Poppins. Harcourt Brace Jovanovich, 1934.
Other Mary Poppins books.

✿ *HUMAN BEINGS IN FANTASY*   There is a wide range of fantasy that includes human characters. Try two of these activities.

1. Choose one scene from a fantasy such as *The Borrowers* or *Children of Green Knowe*. Construct a diorama or a peekbox display that you could share with children as a way of showing them how to make similar scenes from stories they choose.

2. Select one fantasy that you think is especially well written. Go through this book noting examples of interesting language that you might point out to children to help them appreciate the writing ability of the author. Look for unusual words, figurative language (personification, similes, metaphor), appeal to the senses (especially smell, taste, and touch), or stylistic devices that stand out, perhaps repetition of certain words or phrases, word play, noticeable variation of sentence length, and so on. Plan at least one lesson that you could develop based on one of these aspects of the author's language ability.

3. Contrast two fantasies written by one author or two fantasies that have some similarity. Outline the plot structure of each, the characters included, how the book begins, how it ends. Which book has a more powerful impact? Why?

FANTASY WORLDS

One of the special joys of writing fantasy is the creation of new worlds. As readers, we share the author's excitement of discovering a fantasy world's geography, its history, and its inhabitants. Children have the pleasure of exploring whole series of books about Narnia, Middle Earth, or Prydain, lands that may become as real and familiar to them as their own.

DISCOVERING NARNIA

Narnia is a country that children and adults discover anew each time they read C. S. Lewis's *The Lion, The Witch, and the Wardrobe* (Macmillan,

1970), the first volume in the chronicles of Narnia, and go through the door to Narnia with Peter, Susan, Edmund, and Lucy. The four children, on a vacation together, step into adventure when they accidentally find a passage into the mysterious Narnia, inhabited by Talking Beasts and Fauns. Here they meet Aslan, the King of the Beasts, and help free Narnia from the enchantment of the White Witch. When this adventure ends, they return to find no time has passed. The Professor who owns the wardrobe is remarkably unsurprised, merely advising them that it is no use trying that route again.

Indeed, don't *try* to get there at all. It'll happen when you're not looking for it. And don't talk too much about it even among yourselves. And don't mention it to anyone else unless you find that they've had adventures of the same sort themselves. What's that? How will you know? Oh, you'll *know* all right. Odd things, they say—even their looks—will let the secret out. Keep your eyes open. Bless me, what *do* they teach them at these schools? (p. 186)

"I wrote the books I should have liked to read," wrote Clive Staples Lewis, theologian and noted author. "That's always been my reason for writing. People won't write the books I want, so I have to do it myself." He believed, furthermore, that the proper reason for writing a children's story is that "a children's story is the best art form for something you have to say." C. S. Lewis created six more volumes about Narnia because, of course, readers of *The Lion, The Witch, and the Wardrobe* wanted to know more. This extensive conflict between good and evil is further developed in:

Prince Caspian

The Voyage of the "Dawn Treader"

The Silver Chair

The Horse and His Boy

The Magician's Nephew

The Last Battle

Although *The Lion, The Witch, and the Wardrobe* was the first book published in this series, *The Magician's Nephew* is the first in terms of the chronicle, for it tells of the creation of Narnia, of the power of Aslan, the coming of the White Witch, and how travel between our world and Narnia began. Digory and Polly, two children who lived next door to each other in London, were exploring secret passageways, when they discovered that Digory's Uncle Andrew was a magician. Unfortunately, Uncle Andrew knew just enough magic to cause trouble and not enough to be really sensible. He tricked Polly and Digory into another world, actually an in-between world, that was something like a woods in appearance, with pools scattered about that were also different worlds. In one world the children awaken an evil queen and accidentally bring her back with them to London. In an effort to get rid of the witch, they jump into a pool where at first they find nothing. Then they hear a voice singing.

Then two wonders happened at the same moment. One was that the voice was suddenly joined by other voices; more voices than you could possibly count. They were in harmony with it, but far higher up the scale: cold, tingling, silvery voices. The second wonder was that the blackness overhead, all at once was blazing with stars. They didn't come out gently one by one, as they do on a summer evening. One moment there had been nothing but darkness; next moment a thousand, thousand points of light leaped out—single stars, constellations, and planets, brighter and bigger than any in our world. There were no clouds. The new stars and the new voices began at exactly the same time. If you had seen and heard it, as Digory did, you would have felt quite certain that it was the stars themselves which were singing, and that it was the First Voice, the deep one, which had made them appear and made them sing. (pp. 93–94)

A lion was singing. He sang the grass to cover the world and the trees to spring up, and the animals to be born out of the earth. "Can you imagine a stretch of grassy land bubbling like water in a pot? For that is really the best description of what was happening. In all directions it was swelling into lumps. They were of different sizes, some no bigger than molehills, some as big as wheelbarrows, two the size of cottages. And the humps moved and swelled till they burst, and the crumbled earth poured out of them, and from each hump there came out an animal."

It's impossible to tell it all, of course, but if you had been there, you might have seen "a swift flash like fire (but it burnt nobody) either from the sky or from the Lion itself, and every drop of blood tingled in the children's bodies, and the deepest, wildest voice they had ever heard was saying: 'Narnia, Narnia, Narnia, awake. Love. Think. Speak. Be walking trees. Be talking beasts. Be divine waters.'"

If you follow this book to the end, you will find that Digory grows up to be the professor who appears in the first book of the series and that a seed from Narnia grew into the tree from which the wardrobe was made.

C. S. Lewis, author of the Narnia series, belonged to a group called the Inklings, whose members shared an interest in fantasy as well as theology; in this group was another famous writer of fantasy for both children and adults, J. R. R. Tolkien. Tolkien's book *The Hobbit* (Houghton Mifflin, 1938) is an introduction to Middle Earth, the inhabitants and the history thereof, and also to the larger events continued in *The Lord of the Rings* trilogy.

In *The Hobbit* we meet a most special hobbit named Bilbo Baggins:

I suppose hobbits need some description nowadays, since they have become rare and shy of the Big People, as they call us. They are (or were) a little people, about half our height, and smaller than the bearded Dwarves. Hobbits have no beards. There is little or no magic about them, except the ordinary sort which helps them to disappear quietly and quickly when large stupid folk like you and me come blundering along, making a noise like elephants which they can hear a mile off. They are inclined to be fat in the stomach; they dress in bright colours (chiefly green and yellow); wear no shoes, because their feet grow natural leathery soles and thick warm brown hair like the stuff on their heads (which is curly); have long clever brown fingers, good-natured faces, and laugh deep fruity laughs (especially after dinner, which they have twice a day when they can get it). Now you know enough to go on with. (p. 16)

Now Bilbo was a very well-to-do hobbit who lived comfortably in a hobbit-hole. The Baggins family had lived in this neighborhood since time out of mind and were considered very respectable because "they never had any adventures or did anything unexpected"—until Bilbo was almost fifty years old.

Actually it was Gandalf the Wizard's fault for involving Bilbo in the adventures. Knowing Bilbo, perhaps better than Bilbo did himself, he arranged for an expedition of dwarves to meet right in Bilbo's house, so it was only natural that he would get involved and agree to accompany them. Gandalf, furthermore, even recommended him as an excellent Burglar (an Experienced Treasure-Finder).

Bilbo and the Dwarves set out to kill the Dragon that had captured their mines and treasure hoard, a hard enough task without all the hazards of the journey. There were evil things abroad in the wild and even the help of the elves and the presence of Gandalf could barely save them from being eaten by trolls, captured by goblins, and pursued by wargs (wolves living at the Edge of the Wild). Poor Bilbo spent the entire journey half wishing he were home having breakfast with a teakettle singing

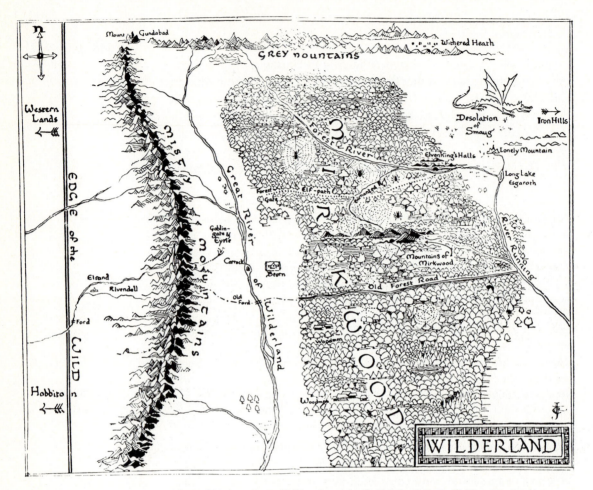

The following labels appear on the map:

n (compass)

Mount Gundabad · Withered Heath

GREY MOUNTAINS

Western Lands ← · Forest River · Desolation of Smaug · Iron Hills

MISTY · Elvenking's Halls · Lonely Mountain

EDGE of the · Great River · anduin · Forest Gate · Elf path · Long Lake Esgaroth

M I R K W O O D

Goblin-gate & Eyrie · Forest River

Carrock · Beorn · Mountains of Mirkwood · River Running

Elrond Rivendell · Old Ford · Old Forest Road

Ford · Mountains · Wilderland

WILD · Woodmen

Hobbiton ← · Woodmen

WILDERLAND

The Hobbit by J. R. R. Tolkien Copyright © 1966 by J. R. R. Tolkien. Reprinted by permission of Houghton Mifflin Company and George Allen & Unwin Ltd., London.

on the fire, and half caught up despite himself in the thrill of seeing new places and meeting new friends. By the time they reach the Lonely Mountain to confront Smaug, the dragon, Bilbo has become positively brave. All adventures must come to an end, however, and eventually Bilbo finds himself back in his own country, tired, but wealthier, wiser, and glad to be home. As he views his homeland, he stops to say:

Roads go ever ever on,
    Over rock and under tree,
By caves where never sun has shone,
    By streams that never find the sea;

Over snow by winter sown,
  And through the merry flowers of June,
Over grass and over stone,
  And under mountains in the moon.

Roads go ever ever on
  Under cloud and under star,
Yet feet that wandering have gone
  Turn at last to home afar.
Eyes that fire and sword have seen
  And horror in the halls of stone
Look at last on meadows green
  And trees and hills they long have known. (p. 284)

TRAVELING TO PRYDAIN

Lloyd Alexander, a modern American writer, follows the same tradition as did C. S. Lewis and J. R. R. Tolkien. Featuring the boy Taran, his series of fantasies take place in Prydain, a country recognizably inspired by Welsh mythology. Taran's story has the rich quality of a familiar legend retold. His adventures are described in writing that is laced with humor and sadness.

The first book of this series, *The Book of Three* (Holt, 1964), begins as Taran is chafing at the constraints of his job as assistant pig-keeper responsible for the oracular pig Hen Wen. Taran wants the glamor of swordplay and heroic deeds. When Hen Wen runs off, and he must rescue her, he learns that heroism isn't as glamorous as he had thought. First, he meets his idol, Prince Gwydion, who looks like a disreputable wanderer, completely unlike the boy's idea of a hero. From each of Taran's companions on his quest, he learns something new. We meet Fflewddur Fflam, the bard whose harp strings break with a twang whenever he stretches the truth; Eilonwy, a determined young woman who escapes from the enchantress Achren; and Gurgi, a creature whose ugliness belies his faithfulness.

When Taran finally returns home to the peaceful castle, he is considerably older than when he left and more appreciative of the worth of those around him. Lloyd Alexander shows this development in Taran's character with great sensitivity rather than didacticism. As the reader follows Taran in subsequent books, we see him battle the forces of Arawn, the Lord of the Dead, and face the riddle of his own parentage, until in the last book, *The High King,* Taran faces the gravest decision of his life. The Wizard Dallben then writes the concluding words in The Book of Three:

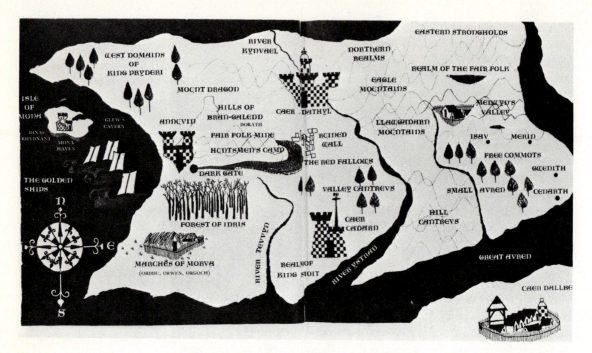

From The High King *by Lloyd Alexander. Map by Evaline Ness. Copyright © 1968 by Lloyd Alexander. Copyright © by Holt, Rinehart & Winston. Reproduced by permission of Holt, Rinehart & Winston, Publishers.*

"And thus did an Assistant Pig-Keeper become High King of Prydain." This concluding book of the series was awarded the Newbery Medal, but without doubt the award is due the whole fantasy set in Prydain: *The Book of Three; The Black Cauldron; The Castle of Llyr; Taran Wanderer,* and *The High King.*

❦ *FANTASY WORLDS*   The three series of books presented here are set in well-developed worlds. Complete one of these exploratory activities:

1. Read the full set of books about Narnia or Prydain just to know them and to become acquainted with the land developed. Consider how you might work with these books in a classroom.

2. Draw an enlarged map of one of the lands created so that you could use it in a classroom as you perhaps read one or more of the books aloud. Develop a game based on this poster or gameboard.

3. Imagine a fantasy world of your own. Give it a name. Describe the characters that inhabit it. Begin writing an adventure that might happen there.

SCIENCE FICTION

All science fiction is an extension of trends seen occurring in present day society. Until recently science fiction focused chiefly on future scientific developments. Today, however, we see many themes reflecting an author's concern for possible social changes. The author poses a kind of "What if?" situation and then builds a society around that possibility as if it were true.

The value of good science fiction is that it allows us to see ourselves more clearly. The skilled writer of science fiction enables us to contrast our society with other societies and other possibilities. Some of the outstanding authors who specialize in science fiction that older children can enjoy include Robert Heinlein and Andre Norton, whose work is discussed in the following pages. Another is Ursula LeGuin, whom we introduce in the section on contemporary authors of fantasy for children.

Robert Heinlein is an expert at weaving scientific details and futuristic scientific speculation into his stories of real human beings facing realistic problems. One such story is *Tunnel in the Sky* (Scribner, 1955), which tells of a high school student, Rod Walker, who faces his solo survival exam. He is to be left on an unknown planet, expected to survive on his own, a task even more difficult than it sounds.

☖ **PATRICK HENRY HIGH SCHOOL**

Department of Social Studies

SPECIAL NOTICE to all students Course 410
(elective senior seminar) *Advanced Survival,*
instructor Dr. Matson, 1712-A MWF

1. There will be no class Friday the 14th.

2. *Twenty-Four Hour Notice* is hereby given of final examination in Solo Survival. Students will present themselves for physical check at 0900 Saturday in the

dispensary of Templeton Gate and will start passing through the gate at 1000, using three-minute intervals by lot.

3. TEST CONDITIONS:
   a. ANY planet, ANY climate, ANY terrain;

   b. NO rules, ALL weapons, ANY equipment;

   c. TEAMING is PERMITTED but teams will not be allowed to pass through the gate in company;

   d. TEST DURATION is not less than forty-eight hours, not more than ten days.

4. Dr. Matson will be available for advice and consultation until 1700 Friday.

5. Test may be postponed only on recommendation of examining physician, but any student may withdraw from the course without administrative penalty until 1000 Saturday.

6. Good luck and long life to you all.

B. P. Matson, Sc.D.

Approved:

J. R. Roerich, *for the Board*   (pp. 7–8)

The impossible, of course, happens and the students are not picked up on time. Not knowing when or if they will be rescued, those who survive band together to organize a colony. They make mistakes, but their ingenuity and courage keep them alive.

Heinlein has written a number of other books that are suitable for young readers, for example, *Podkayne of Mars* (Putnam, 1963), which describes a sixteen-year-old girl's first trip to Venus. Unfortunately for her welfare and that of those around her, she is precocious and has an unerring nose for trouble. As background for this story, Heinlein provides detailed information about this society for the future—its people, customs, and scientific development. Other books by Robert Heinlein that you might like to investigate include: *Have Space Suit—Will Travel* (Scribner, 1958), *Rocket Ship Galileo* (Scribner, 1947), *Space Cadet* (Scribner, 1948).

Andre Norton (Alice Mary Norton) is one of the most prolific science fiction writers; yet she continues to produce inventive, absorbing books. *Star Born* (World, 1957) tells of a colony established on the planet Astra by refugees from an oppressive Earth government. As the book begins, the present generation of colonists know only vague stories of Earth and have established a partnership with the amphibian natives of Astra. Dalgard Nordis is on his man-journey to prove himself an adult, accompanied by Sssuri, an Astran native. They are unaware that an Earth-ship has landed in a once mighty city on the other side of the world to trade dangerous science information with the native inhabitants, who plan to use the information to obliterate the Earth colony and their Astran friends. When Raf Kurbi, a starship crew member, begins questioning the motives of the city's inhabitants, there is trouble for the new arrivals and the colony. *Star Born* is the sequel of *The Stars Are Ours* (World, 1955). Another favorite of Andre Norton's many titles is *Secret of the Lost Race* (World, 1959).

Often mentioned as an outstanding science fiction book for elementary school children is *A Wrinkle in Time* (Farrar, Straus & Giroux, 1962) by noted author Madeleine L'Engle. Winner of the 1963 Newbery Medal, this writer introduces the concept of a "tesseract," a "wrinkle in time" that shortens the distance between two points in time. Discovered by scientist Dr. Murry, who is lost in space, the tesseract is the means by which his children, Meg and Charles Wallace, are able to save him. Mrs. Whatsit explains the tesseract to the children thus:

"You see," Mrs. Whatsit said, "if a very small insect were to move from the section of skirt in Mrs. Who's right hand to that in her left, it would be quite a long walk for him if he had to walk straight across."

Swiftly Mrs. Who brought her hands, still holding the skirt, together.

"Now, you see," Mrs. Whatsit said, "he would *be* there, without that long trip. That is how we travel."

Charles Wallace accepted the explanation serenely. Even Calvin did not seem perturbed. "Oh, *dear,*" Meg sighed. "I guess I *am* a moron. I just don't get it."

"That is because you think of space only in three dimensions," Mrs. Whatsit told her. "We travel in the fifth dimension.

"And the fourth?"

"Well, I guess if you want to put it into mathematical terms you'd square the square. But you can't take a pencil and draw it the way you can the first three. I know it's got something to do with Einstein and time. I guess maybe you could call the fourth dimension Time."

"That's right," Charles said. "Good girl. Okay, then, for the fifth dimension you'd square the fourth, wouldn't you?"

"I guess so."

"Well, the fifth dimension's a tesseract. You add that to the other four dimensions and you can travel through space without having to go the long way around. In other words, to put it into Euclid, or old-fashioned plane geometry, a straight line is *not* the shortest distance between two points."[2]

Penelope Farmer also plays with moving through time in *Charlotte Sometimes* (Harcourt Brace Jovanovich, 1969). Charlotte Makepeace goes to boarding school, but she immediately finds her life complicated by unexpectedly alternating places in time with Clare Mary Moby who had attended the school forty years earlier. At one point Charlotte is caught in time and fears that she will never be able to return to her rightful place. In *The Summer Birds* (Harcourt Brace Jovanovich, 1962) and *Emma in Winter* (Harcourt Brace Jovanovich, 1968), Penelope Farmer also explores the relationships between the real and the imagined.

Nicholas Fisk writes for children because: "Books are innately superior things and children are innately superior humans." He has created an unusual story for middle grades in *Grinny* (Nelson, 1974), subtitled *A Novel of Science Fiction*. The story is told by Timothy Carpenter, who was eleven at the time that Great-Aunt Emma appeared much to everyone's surprise; no one seemed to know GAE, though she certainly knew everyone else. Based on Timothy's diary, the story is funny and intriguing. Older students will also enjoy this short, easily read novel.

Alan Nourse draws from a background of medical knowledge for such titles as *The Bladerunner* (McKay, 1974). Set in the twenty-first century, this tale of Billy Gimp, a bladerunner for Doc, a skilled surgeon, involves

---

[2] Madeleine L'Engle, *A Wrinkle in Time* (Farrar, Straus and Giroux, 1962), pp. 75–76, 78. Art reproduced with the permission of Farrar, Straus & Giroux, Inc. From *A Wrinkle in Time* by Madeleine L'Engle. Copyright © 1962 by Madeleine L'Engle Franklen.

the illegal procuring of medical supplies. Underground medical care is essential for the thousands who cannot qualify for legal medical aid, and Doc provides such aid illegally at night. An epidemic brings the illegal system out in the open. Look for other titles by this prolific author.

John Christopher has written many science fiction stories, including a trilogy: *The Prince in Waiting, Beyond the Burning Lands,* and *The Sword of the Spirits* (Macmillan, 1970, 1971, 1972). The setting for these stories is England, reduced to a feudal, anti-technological society. The main character, Luke, rules a city-state after civilization has been destroyed. A cache of inventions and machinery is hidden underground only to be brought back into use after a mutiny. Luke is amazed to see "machines that could do things more marvelous than anything that had been supposed to be done by the Spirits. Machines for seeing and listening at a distance, machines that could propel a carriage ten times faster than a team of horses could pull it, machines that could detect metal under earth, that could chill meat and keep its sweetness without salting throughout a summer, that could show strange beasts living inside the smallest drop of water . . . a score and more of wonders." Men have destroyed civilization and must work to bring it into being once more from the Sanctuaries where it has been hidden.

A similar theme is developed in Peter Dickinson's *The Weathermonger* (Little, Brown, 1969), and the setting is also the British Isles. The time appears to be the Middle Ages, for people have forgotten how to operate machinery. Geoffrey, however, has retained forbidden knowledge of things mechanical. Using a motorboat, he and his twelve-year-old sister Sally escape to France. A 1909 Rolls Royce, the Silver Ghost, is their means to bring about changes so that mechanical things can be accepted again. As Geoffrey notes, however, "the English air would soon be reeking with petrol fumes." This book is followed by *Heartsease* (Little, Brown 1969) and *The Devil's Children* (Little, Brown, 1970).

Ann Burden is the main character in an intriguing science fiction story of the aftermath of a nuclear war. *Z for Zachariah* (Atheneum, 1975) by Robert C. O'Brien tells of a strong young woman, who celebrates her sixteenth birthday with the only other human in the valley, John R. Loomis. She accepts her fate, first entirely alone, and later with John, with amazing fortitude, planning ahead for the growing of crops, raising a herd of cattle, and so forth. Finally, frightened by John's apparently insane attempts to kill her, Ann steals the radiation-proof suit and walks out of the valley to seek a new life.

Here are additional titles that will appeal to better readers in the upper elementary grades:

S Is for Space by Ray Bradbury. Doubleday, 1966. *(Many titles by Bradbury; Medicine for Melancholy, a collection of short stories, is good for reading aloud.)*

The Weathermakers by Benjamin Bova. Holt, 1967.

Sky Man on the Totem Pole by Christie Harris. Atheneum, 1975.

Doctor to the Galaxy by Alice M. Lightner. Norton, 1965.

Worlds to Come by Damon Knight, ed. Harper & Row, 1967. *(Short stories.)*

Journey between Two Worlds by Sylvia Engdahl. Atheneum, 1970.

The City under the Ground by Suzanne Martel. Viking, 1964.

The Calibrated Alligator; And Other Science Fiction Stories by Robert Silverberg. Holt, 1969.

Dolphin Island by Arthur C. Clarke. Holt, 1963.

Danny Dunn and the Smallifying Machine by Jay Williams and Raymond Abrashkin. McGraw-Hill, 1969. *(Other titles about Danny Dunn.)*

Science fiction stories are plentiful also for younger readers. Although they do not usually have the same qualities found in books for older readers, children do often enjoy these stories, which tend to be humorous rather than concerned with solid scientific backgrounds.

Space Ship under the Apple Tree by Louis Slobodkin. Macmillan, 1967.

Miss Pickerell Goes to Mars by Ellen MacGregor. McGraw-Hill, 1951.

Space Cat by Ruthven Todd. Scribner, 1952.

Freddy and the Men from Mars by Walter Brooks. Knopf, 1954.

Time at the Top by Edward Ormondroyd. Parnassus, 1963.

Wonderful Flight to the Mushroom Planet by Eleanor Cameron. Little, Brown, 1954.

❦ *SCIENCE FICTION* Science fiction opens up many possibilities before us. Select one of the following ways of exploring further:

1. List three problems that you see as very important in our society today. Choose one of these problems and outline how a science fiction writer might develop a plot focused on that problem. Would you set the story in the past or in the future?

2. Read three books by Robert Heinlein or Andre Norton. Compare the

books you read, noting how they are similar or different. How would you describe the characteristics of this author's work? What makes it distinctive? Would you like to read more books by this author?

3. Write a short science fiction story about something that interests you. Illustrate the story and share it with your classmates or a group of children you are working with.

TEACHING FANTASY

There are many excellent selections from fantasy that you might choose to teach. As you read books discussed in this chapter, note teachable elements as they occur. The kind of things you might find include:

Interesting use of language, for example, British English

Good examples of imagery, perhaps, sensory images

Content that relates to other subjects such as history or art

Illustrations that suggest art activities

Mythological backgrounds to be explored

These elements differ for individual books. Each teaching idea will suggest activities that can be used concurrently with the reading of the book or as a follow-up activity designed to extend understandings developed or to expand the student's enjoyment of the story. In this section we will discuss outstanding fantasies written for children by American and British authors. We will also focus on selected contemporary authors of fantasy and explore the possibilities for teaching two representative fantasies to demonstrate how literature can become an integral part of the curriculum.

OUTSTANDING FANTASIES

It is interesting to note which fantasies have been selected for awards given yearly to outstanding books. The major award given in the United States for the writing of a book for children is the Newbery Award, which was established in 1921 by Frederic G. Melcher, editor of R. R. Bowker Company. It was awarded for the first time in 1922 to Hendrik Willem van Loon for *The Story of Mankind,* the only nonfiction work that has received this medal. Like the Caldecott award, the Newbery award is supervised by the Children's Services Division of the American Library Association and is given to the author of "the most distinguished contribution to literature for children published in the United States during the preceding year." Because this award emphasizes story content rather than illustrations, it tends to be given to books for more advanced readers.

Although a complete list of books that have won the Newbery Medal is included in the Appendix, let us observe at this point those American fantasies that have been so honored. Winners of the Newberry Medal since 1921 include:

The Voyages of Doctor Dolittle by Hugh Lofting

Rabbit Hill by Robert Lawson

The Twenty-One Balloons by William Pène duBois

A Wrinkle in Time by Madeleine L'Engle

The High King by Lloyd Alexander

Mrs. Frisby and the Rats of NIMH by Robert C. O'Brien

The Grey Wolf by Susan Cooper

As we read the great fantasies written for children, we must acknowledge our debt to British writers, for many of the best fantasies have crossed the Atlantic to be enjoyed by American children. Both C. S. Lewis and John R. R. Tolkien are English, as were their predecessors Lewis Carroll, George MacDonald, and Kenneth Grahame. Lucy Boston, author of the Green Knowe series, is another British writer, as is Susan Cooper, an author we will discuss in the next section. Joan Aiken, Alan Garner, Peter Dickinson, and John Christopher are also English writers. These authors share a wealth of tradition—history, legend, mythology—that provides a rich background for their work.

It is interesting to contrast the list of American fantasies that have received awards with a similar list of similar British authors. The Carnegie Medal was first given in 1937 by the British Library Association. Among the fantasies honored since 1937 are:

The Borrowers by Mary Norton

The Last Battle by C. S. Lewis

Tom's Midnight Garden by Philippa Pearce

The Twelve and the Genii by Pauline Clarke

The Owl Service by Alan Garner

The Moon in the Cloud by Rosemary Harris

Watership Down by Richard Adams

The Stronghold by Mollie Hunter

Comparing the lists of winners of these top medals is enlightening because it does seem that fantasy has a stronger hold in British literature for children than it does in the United States. It is interesting to observe, too, that even American writers of fantasy often turn to these British traditions for their content, as did Lloyd Alexander for his Prydain series and Elizabeth Marie Pope for *The Perilous Gard,* a fine book that is discussed at the end of this chapter.

CONTEMPORARY AUTHORS OF FANTASY

Children should become acquainted with authors who write especially for them. Often we read a story aloud or assign books to be read with emphasis chiefly on the storyline. We forget to present books as the works of human beings who are sharing their ideas, their way of looking at life, their humor and warmth. Although we can't introduce each author who has written fantasy for young people, we will include brief biographical information, a picture, and something about the writing of several authors who have made distinctive contributions. In this way you will begin to know some of these authors yourself so that you can in turn introduce them to young people who are reading their books. The authors presented here are Susan Cooper, Ursula LeGuin, E. B. White, Joan Aiken, and Lloyd Alexander.

SUSAN COOPER   Author of *The Dark Is Rising* (Atheneum, 1973), Susan Cooper was born May 23, 1935 in Buckinghamshire, which is the setting for this outstanding book. She holds an M.A. from Oxford and was a reporter for the London *Sunday Times* for a number of years. She married an American, has two children, and now lives near Boston.

The Dark Is Rising is part of a series that began with *Over Sea, Under Stone* in which the author develops the conflict between the Light and the Dark. Will Stanton becomes aware on his eleventh birthday that he has a special gift and that he is the last of those called "The Old Ones," who have devoted their existences to combating the forces of evil. With other members of the group, Will can sense that "the dark is rising," and Merriman Lyon, the first of the Old Ones, who appears in the first book of the series, recites the charge:

*Photograph of Susan Cooper by
Zoe Dominick.*

When the Dark comes rising, six shall turn it back,
Three from the circle, three from the track;
Wood, bronze, iron; water, fire, stone;
Five will return, and one go alone.

Drawing from ancient Celtic mythology as well as English tradition and
the legends of Buckinghamshire, Susan Cooper is developing a powerful
series of fantasies for children. *The Grey Wolf* (Atheneum, 1976) won the
Newbery award for 1977. The last book of the series is *Silver on the Tree*.

URSULA LeGUIN Ursula Kroeber LeGuin was born on October 21,
1929 in Berkeley, California. She is the daughter of a well-known anthropologist, Alfred Kroeber, and Theodora Kroeber, who wrote the children's book *Ishi, Last of His Tribe* (Parnassus, 1964). A graduate of Rad-
cliffe with a master's degree from Columbia University, Ursula LeGuin
married a historian, has three children, and lives in Portland, Oregon. She
is a member of the Science Fiction Writers of America and has written
much adult fiction.

Ursula LeGuin's work for young people, more fantasy than science
fiction, is characterized by *The Farthest Shore* (Atheneum, 1972). Arren,
the young heir of the Principality of Morred, seeks help from the great
Archmage of Roke, Ged. As Arren tells Ged of the evil at work in his
homeland, he expresses his desire to serve the powerful wizard:

*Photograph of Ursula LeGuin
used by permission of Atheneum
Publishers.*

As he had made his act of submission he had forgotten himself, and now he saw
the Archmage: the greatest wizard of all Earthsea, the man who had capped the
Black Well of Fundaur and won the Ring of Erreth-Akbe from the Tombs of
Atuan and built the deep-founded sea wall of Nepp; the sailor who knew the seas
from Astowell to Selidor; the only living Dragonlord. There he knelt beside a
fountain, a short man and not young, a quiet-voiced man, with eyes as deep as
evening. (p. 9)

Arren and Ged travel to the farthest reaches of Earthsea, even to the
land of the Dead, and to the "last shore of the world" in Selidor. They are
saved by the great dragon, Orm Embar, and returned in safety to their
home by Kalessin:

In the days of high summer on the island of Ully a great dragon was seen flying
low, and later in Usidero and in the north of Ontuego. Though dragons are

dreaded in the West Reach, where people know them all too well, yet after this one had passed over and the villagers had come out of their hiding place, those who had seen it said, "The dragons are not all dead, as we thought. Maybe the wizards are not all dead, either. Surely there was a great splendor in that flight; maybe it was the Eldest." (p. 220)

Other books by Ursula LeGuin are *A Wizard of Earthsea* and *The Tombs of Atuan.*

E. B. WHITE Born July 11, 1899 in Mount Vernon, New York, Elwyn Brooks White has written three fantasies for children: *Stuart Little* (Harper, 1945), *Charlotte's Web* (Harper, 1952), and *The Trumpet of the Swan* (Harper, 1970). A graduate of Cornell University, he was on the staff of the *New Yorker* for many years, writing editorials, satirical essays, and poetry. He has lived on a farm in Brooklin, Maine, for many years.

Stuart Little is a charming fantasy of a mouse (another to add to the list) who, surprisingly, is born to Mrs. Frederick C. Little.

Photograph of E. B. White by Donald E. Johnson.

The doctor was delighted with Stuart and said that it was very unusual for an American family to have a mouse. He took Stuart's temperature and found that it was 98.6, which is normal for a mouse. He also examined Stuart's chest and heart and looked into his ears solemnly with a flashlight. (Not every doctor can look into a mouse's ear without laughing.) Everything seemed to be all right, and Mrs. Little was pleased to get such a good report. (p. 3)

The Littles also adopt a small bird, Margalo, who becomes Stuart's best friend. Stuart has many exciting adventures, not the least of which is his day as a substitute teacher; he is a great hit with the students who are remarkably well behaved with this unorthodox teacher. Garth Williams' illustrations add to the humor of this fantasy for the primary grades.

Garth Williams also illustrated *Charlotte's Web.* This fantasy of a pig, Wilbur, who makes friends with Charlotte, a wise gray spider, and Templeton, an avaricious but comical rat, has entranced middle grade children since its publication more than twenty years ago. A Newbery Honor Book, this fantasy was made into a film for children. E. B. White explains how the fantasy came to be written:

I like animals and my barn is a very pleasant place to be, at all hours. One day when I was on my way to feed the pig, I began feeling sorry for the pig because,

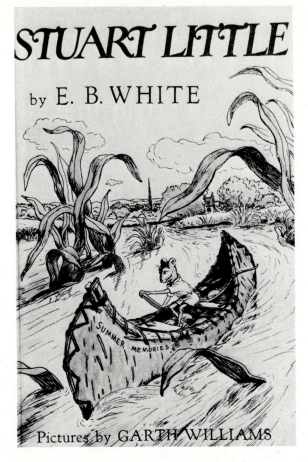

like most pigs, he was doomed to die. This made me sad. So I started thinking of ways to save a pig's life. I had been watching a big, grey spider at her work and was impressed by how clever she was at weaving. Gradually I worked the spider into the story, a story of friendship and salvation on a farm.

Acknowledging that his stories aren't true, he comments, "real life is only one kind of life—there is also the life of the imagination. And although my stories are imaginary, I like to think that there is some truth to them, too—truth about the way people and animals feel and think and act." It is this truth that permeates E. B. White's writing and makes his books stand out.

JOAN AIKEN   A noted author of fantasies, Joan Aiken was born September 4, 1924 in Sussex, England. The daughter of poet Conrad Aiken, she married and had two children. When at the age of thirty she was widowed, she began writing to please herself and to amuse her children. As she states in *Contemporary Authors* (Volume 9–10):

I always intended to be a writer; when I was five I went to the village store and spent two shillings (a huge sum then) on a large, thick writing-block in which to write poems, stories, and thoughts, as they occurred. It lasted for years (I still have it) and when it was finished I bought another and then another. I used to tell stories to my younger brother to beguile the boring parts of walks. My first work was published when I was 17—a story broadcast on the B.B.C. children's hour. In my children's books I write the sort of thing I should have liked to read myself when I was young, and am helped by comments and criticisms from my own children who read each work as it goes along. (p. 12)

Joan Aiken's first book, *The Wolves of Willoughby Chase* (Doubleday, 1963), is probably her best known. The story opens with Miss Bonnie bouncing eagerly in anticipation of the arrival of Sylvia, her cousin who is coming to live with the family of her uncle, Sir Willoughby. In the midst of this happiness, however, arrives Miss Slighcarp, the new governess, a bitter, conniving woman who fits her name. Because Bonnie's mother is ill, her parents leave soon on a trip for her health, leaving the two girls at home with Miss Slighcarp, who is also a distant cousin. Almost immediately it becomes clear that this woman intends to take over the estate by arranging for the convenient sinking of the ship on which the Willoughbys had sailed. The girls manage to escape with the help of a resourceful boy Simon and several loyal servants. The wolves serve as an element of evil lurking in the background throughout the story, but not proving to be any realistic threat. The true Wolves of Willoughby Chase are obviously Miss Slighcarp and her cohorts.

Photograph of Joan Aiken by Liz Brown.

Other books by this talented author are *Black Hearts of Battersea* (Doubleday, 1964), *Nightbirds on Nantucket* (Doubleday, 1966), *The Whispering Mountain* (Doubleday, 1969), and *Smoke from Cromwell's Time* (Doubleday, 1970). She has also published a book of poetry, *The Skin Spinners* (Viking, 1976).

LLOYD ALEXANDER Creator of Prydain and the series of stories set in that mythical land discussed earlier in this chapter, Lloyd Alexander was born on January 30, 1924 in Philadelphia. He married a French woman, Janine Denni, and wrote a book about her, *Janine Is French* (1958). He studied at the Sorbonne and has translated French writings. Alexander is also very much interested in music, in particular the violin, which explains in part *The Marvelous Misadventures of Sebastian* (Dutton, 1970), which he considers to be a very personal metaphor, explaining his conception of the creative process and the demands that it makes on the creator. Unlike some authors, Lloyd Alexander does not try out his writing on young people. About his writing he comments:

The day begins at 4:00 A.M., barring the occasional household disasters, naturally. It lasts until I have the impression that's about all that's going to happen for the day. I rework constantly and continually, until I'm more or less resigned to the fact that that's the best I can do at this particular moment. I don't try out my ideas on children. Story ideas seem to evolve from my own personal attitudes and ongoing explorations of life, from trying to understand where my head is.[3]

*Photograph of Lloyd Alexander
reprinted by permission.*

Another book completed after the Prydain series is *The Cat Who Wished to Be a Man* (Dutton, 1973), which children aged seven through ten would probably enjoy. Dedicated to "us, born human, to make the best of it," this story begins with a request by Lionel, a young orange-tawny cat: "Please, master, will you change me into a man?" Stephanus, the wizard, who had granted speech to the cat, replies:

"Be glad you are a cat!" Stephanus cried. "Let me tell you about men: Wolves are gentler. Geese are wiser. Jackasses have better sense. And You—I warn you, don't try my patience."

Despite Strephanus' exhortations, however, Lionel persuades him to grant the gift. Needless to say, Lionel has much to learn and is involved in many a humorous situation. He makes friends, however, with Gillian who questions the right of the wizard or anyone to own the life of another, whether it be cat or man. Although Gillian says she will become a cat in order to be with Lionel, this unprecedented act is unnecessary because Stephanus is unable to make Lionel into a cat again. So off goes Lionel, purring, with Gillian.

TWO NOVELS TO TEACH

In this section we are focusing on two fantasies that are recommended for teaching: *The Genie of Sutton Place* by George Selden and *The Perilous*

---

[3] Quoted in Lee Bennett Hopkins, *More Books by More People* (Citation, 1974), p. 17.

Gard by Elizabeth Marie Pope. Consider using these books and the activities described as part of a learning center on fantasy.

As you plan to teach a novel, or any literary work, there are a number of questions to consider, for example:

1. What goals and objectives will be met by this unit of study?

It is essential that you have clearly in mind the purpose for including any study in the curriculum. This purpose or goal, furthermore, needs to be made explicit to students.

As discussed in more detail in Chapter 7, goals and objectives are most meaningful if stated in terms of what the student will learn. The goals for teaching a novel will contribute to all of the six competencies discussed on page 335: valuing, describing, discriminating, generalizing, relating, and judging. Each activity planned should be designed to achieve a specific objective. For example, ask students to identify language that appeals to the different senses, sensory imagery.

2. How will you introduce the study and stimulate student involvement?

Students will certainly not be excited if you announce: "Today we are going to begin reading a book together." It is far more effective to introduce an interesting topic related to the content of the book to be read. Once student interest is aroused, moving to the book is a natural sequence of events. The topic can be introduced through various means, for example:

Asking a question to stimulate discussion:
"Have you ever wondered what would happen if animals could talk?" (Good idea for *The Genie of Sutton Place*.)

Displaying intriguing pictures, maps, information:
Prepare a bulletin board display several days before you plan to begin reading a novel. Give students a chance to examine the display. Then discuss the topic. (Display information about druids and fairy folk, a map of early England, pictures of castles to introduce *The Perilous Gard*.)

Playing music to set a mood:
Choose circus music to set the stage for *The Great Geppy* by William P. duBois. "In the Hall of the Mountain Kings" from *The Nutcracker Suite* would be great to introduce *Rip Van Winkle*.

3. How will the literature be presented?

Use varied methods of reading a novel. If the whole group is to study the same book, an excellent way to present a novel is for the teacher to read it aloud, one chapter each day, followed by one or two activities that involve speaking or writing. Don't think you aren't teaching reading through this kind of presentation, because students are hearing more so-phisticated language so they are learning new sentence structures, new concepts and vocabulary, and they are hearing "book language," a for-mal register that differs markedly from speech.

If you have multiple copies of a single title, students can read indepen-dently. A small group can study the same book together. You may have a learning station at which students complete tasks individually. Activi-ties are presented on large task cards that children use in turn.

4. What kinds of questions will promote learning?

Questions we ask about literature should quickly move from the literal level to inference and synthesis. The following question requires a re-sponse based on factual information presented in *The Genie of Sutton Place:*

Describe the genie as he appeared in the tapestry.
Based on the same book, this question requires greater thinking on the part of the student:

Have you ever thought about how people resemble animals?
Questions should lead students to relate literature to their own lives, to help them make inferences, and to question assumptions as they develop greater perception.

5. What specific activities can be developed around each work of litera-ture?

Response to literature should meet specific objectives and entail per-formance by the student that demonstrates learning. Activities should in-volve students in using varied language skills—listening, speaking, read-ing, and writing.

Each story or poem offers special content that you need to assess as you read it. Ask: "What does this book teach the reader?" Don't expect one novel to teach everything. Select those aspects of a book that are especially strong, for example:

Use of language—imagery, vocabulary, word play
Plot development—theme, character traits, humor

Emphasis should always be on reading for enjoyment. At least half of the reading in a classroom should not be "reported" on or followed up in any way other than talking about books or sharing ideas encountered. Don't overdo the formal study or analysis of literature. Literature can, however, serve to stimulate thinking and writing. It can provide models for student writing, and it certainly does feed the brains of young readers who are eagerly learning new concepts, picking up new vocabulary and ways of coping with life.

In this section we present two novels that can be studied in a classroom. For each we provide an introductory synopsis and a list of characters, as well as some information about the author. Included, too, are sample activities. If you decide to teach one of these novels, you will need to consider the five questions we have discussed. Obviously, you need to begin by reading the book in order to make these decisions. There is no single "right" way to approach such a study. The way you choose depends on your objectives for teaching as well as the specific needs of your students.

Notice that we do not use grade levels to indicate the reading difficulty of a book, for there is too wide a range of reading abilities in any classroom to make that a valid approach. Ages given reflect the interests of children at that age or the appropriateness of the content. Clearly the first book is easier to read than the second.

The Genie of Sutton Place by George Selden. Farrar, Straus & Giroux, 1973

This humorous novel appeals to students from about nine to fourteen. The characters are:

Tim Farr—a young boy who tells the story

Dooley—Abdullah, an Arabian genie

Aunt Lucy—Tim's father's sister

Madame Sosotris—Muriel Glicker, a medium, Tim's friend

Sam Bassinger—formerly Tim's dog Sam

Rose—Aunt Lucy's housekeeper

Mr. Watkins—Aunt Lucy's lawyer

SYNOPSIS

When Tim Farr's father dies, he is invited to live with Aunt Lucy. His rangy dog Sam, however, doesn't fit in the elegant Sutton Place apartment, so problems ensue. Finally, Tim is told to get rid of the dog. Just then, fortunately, he discovers Abdullah, the genie who has been locked in an ancient tapestry. The adventures that follow are hilarious. Dooley turns Sam into a man who has to learn to give up his doglike behavior. Funniest of all is Aunt Lucy's attraction to handsome Sam Bassinger.

THE AUTHOR

George Selden (Thompson) was born in Hartford, Connecticut, on May 14, 1929. Although he had always wanted to be a writer, it was not until almost 1960 that he wrote his first book for children, *The Dog That Could Swim under Water,* which was later published as *Oscar Lobster's Fair Exchange* (Harper & Row, 1966). One of his most popular books is *The Cricket in Times Square,* which was named as an Honor Book for the Newbery award in 1961.

SAMPLE LEARNING ACTIVITIES

1. Good authors make you see, hear, and feel the things described. They may even make you experience smells and tastes as you use all of your senses. On page 48, this author makes you use your sense of hearing:

   The guards were making their rounds, and every half hour or so I'd hear a man's step going *klomp klomp klomp* through the Renaissance rooms—much harder than the sloshing of the charwomen.

   See if you can find at least one example of imagery that plays on each of the five senses.

2. When Tim is packing his belongings to move to Aunt Lucy's, he includes two children's books that have been his favorites. Which ones does he choose? Which two would you choose? Why?

3. Draw a picture of the situation in this book that you think is the funniest of all. Tim describes one that Rose especially liked:

   The one Rose enjoyed most—but Aunt Lucy sure didn't—was when she'd left her bedroom door ajar and woken up to find Sam's head asleep beside her on the pillow. She'd screamed, "Sam!"—and he'd said, "Woof," and gone back to his box.

4. Make a collection of the funny things Felix the parakeet says about Sam. For example:

   "You ain't nothin' but a hound dog!" (p. 94)

   "A man's best friend is—!" (p. 96)

   Can you invent other funny things Felix might say to Sam Bassinger that refer to his former dog's life?

5. On page 86 Tim talks about the way people resemble certain animals:

I think inside of everybody, along with the humanity, there exists a possible animal . . . I mean like what that person might have been. For instance Aunt Lucy: there's a little nervous squirrel sitting up on its hind legs inside of her. And Dooley—he'd have been, perhaps not a bull or a bear, some thing big and dark and powerful. Rose has a panther inside her, but a quiet one, with its tail switched around its legs—only don't make her mad.

Have you ever thought about that? What animal would you imagine you might be? Why? Work with three classmates as you decide on animals for each other, as you see each person, and as they see you.

The Perilous Gard by Elizabeth Marie Pope. Houghton Mifflin, 1974.
Students from about eleven through fifteen will enjoy *The Perilous Gard*. The characters in this book include:

Kate Sutton—sixteen-year-old living in sixteenth-century England

Alicia Sutton—her beautiful sister

Sir Gregory—the man in whose care Kate is placed by Queen Mary

Christopher Heron—Sir Gregory's younger brother

Old Randal—minstrel bewitched by the fairy folk

Master John—manager of the estate for Sir Gregory

SYNOPSIS

Kate Sutton is exiled to Elvenwood Hall in the care of Sir Gregory Heron when she displeases the Queen. Here she learns of the Fairy Folk who inhabit the caves and carry out the old beliefs including human sacrifice on All Saints Eve. These people are portrayed sympathetically and realistically. Sir Gregory's small daughter Cecily is stolen by the Fairies who demand a man as substitute. Christopher thinks Cecily has been lost because of his carelessness, so he offers himself to obtain her release. Because she witnesses this transaction, Kate herself is taken into the caves where she gains favor with the Fairy Lady. Kate is strong enough to save Christopher and herself from the power of these folk just in time. Note that Fairies as described here are not the stereotyped tiny beings that we may envision.

Photograph of Elizabeth Marie Pope by Caroline Field. Courtesy of Houghton Mifflin.

THE AUTHOR

Elizabeth Marie Pope is an English professor at Mills College in Oakland, California. She graduated from Bryn Mawr College and received a doctorate from John Hopkins University. She specializes in Elizabethan England, which is evident in *The Perilous Gard*. This work was named as an Honor Book for the Newbery award. She also wrote *The Sherwood Ring*.

SAMPLE LEARNING ACTIVITIES

1. Write a description of Katherine Sutton. Jot down all the things the author tells you about her appearance, behavior, what she thinks about. Then summarize your impression of this young woman.

2. Select one passage from this book that you think is especially important. Prepare to read this passage aloud to other students as you explain why you chose the particular passage you did.

3. Draw a map of Elvenwood and the area around it as you envision it. Mark the location of significant events in the story; for example, the riverbank where Kate saved the child from drowning.

4. Can you tell the meaning of the underlined word in each of these sentences? Look at the paragraphs around each sentence if you wish.

   "Pilgrims?" she repeated *incredulously*. (p. 47)

   You're *smirking* like somebody with a sweet for a child . . . (p. 87)

   Kate looked from the *inexorable* face to the blazing lights, and back again. (p. 179)

   Are there other interesting words that you especially like?

5. What does Kate mean when she says:

   "I cannot tell," said Kate. "But he was named for a man who bore the whole weight of Our Lord once, on his own shoulders and His power was with him, even though he—" her voice suddenly wavered and broke, "*he* did not know it, either, and thought he was caring for a child." (p. 210)

   How does this fit into the story? Had there been any previous mention of this before in the book?

❦ *TEACHING FANTASY* Choose one fantasy that you particularly like. Plan to teach this fantasy. Outline the information much as we have for the two fantasies *The Genie of Sutton Place* and *The Perilous Gard:*

1. Write a synopsis and list of characters.

2. Note suggestions for presenting the book to students.

3. Take notes about teaching ideas that occur to you as you scan the book completely again. Construct five task cards based on your ideas. Make each card at least 8½ × 11 inches.

4. Learn something about the author. Most contemporary writers are listed in *Contemporary Authors,* which is available at public or college libraries.

ADDITIONAL SOURCES TO INVESTIGATE

Alexander, Lloyd. "Seeing with the Third Eye." *Elementary English* 51 (September 1974): 759–66.

Arbuthnot, May Hill and Zena Sutherland. "Modern Fantasy" in *Children and Books*. Scott, Foresman, 1977.

Cameron, Eleanor. *The Green and Burning Tree; On the Writing and Enjoyment of Children's Books*. Little, Brown, 1969.

Guiliano, Edward. *Lewis Carroll Observed*. Potter, 1976.

Lanes, Selma G. *Down the Rabbit Hole; Adventures and Misadventures in the Realm of Children's Literature*. Atheneum, 1971.

Lewis, C. S. *Of Other Worlds: Essays and Stories*. Harcourt Brace Jovanovich, 1966.

Lines, Kathleen, ed. *J. M. Barrie; Lucy Boston; Lewis Carroll; Kenneth Grahame; C. S. Lewis; Beatrix Potter*. Walck Monographs. Walck, varied dates.

4

What
Is Real?

Realistic Perspectives of Life for Children

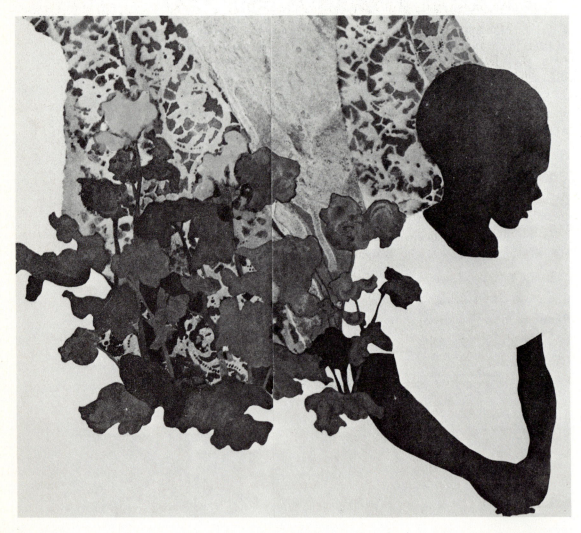

Illustration from *Sound of Sunshine, Sound of Rain* by Florence Parry Heide. Text copyright by Florence Parry Heide © 1970. Illustration copyright by Kenneth Longtemps © 1970. By permission of Parents Magazine Press.

Because writers have sovereignty over their own inventions, they appear to make an outrageous claim. They will tell you everything about the characters in their stories. This is a world, they say; and every stick of its furnishings—every gesture and grimace of the people who live among these furnishings—is true and revealed. But this is not what happens in life. In real life, we stammer, we dissimulate, we hide. In stories, we are privy to the secrets, the evasions, the visions of characters in a fashion which real life only permits us during periods of extraordinary sensibility, before habit has made us forget that the cries behind the locked doors are our own.

Paula Fox
Newbery Award Acceptance Speech, 1974

"What is real?" the curious Rabbit asks in *The Velveteen Rabbit* by Margery Williams (Doubleday, 1926). The old Skin Horse, whose brown coat is worn and who lost most of the hairs in his tail long ago, answers:

"Real isn't how you are made. . . . It's a thing that happens to you. When a child loves you for a long, long time, not just to play with, but REALLY loves you, then you become Real." (p. 17)

The Skin Horse explains that you become real gradually. He also admits that the process might hurt a little, but "when you are Real, you don't mind being hurt."

Children need books that present what is real. They need stories about people interacting with all the stress and emotion that accompanies human relations. They need to read about children like themselves who are coping with situations that are real to a child growing up. In *Good Times,* Lucille Clifton describes, for example, Doretha's feelings when her father suddenly dies and she observes the problems of her mother and older sister. In *Don't Feel Sorry for Paul,* an excellent photographic story, Bernard Wolf presents a realistic picture of a handicapped boy.

As children grow, they also need books that promote multicultural understandings. Books can provide the opportunity of getting inside a skin of a different color, of experiencing empathy for different values and ways of doing things based on another culture. Realistic, nonstereotyped portrayals of American Indians, black Americans, and other ethnic groups, as well as nationalities represented in our society will help all children to appreciate the rich pluralistic heritage from which we benefit. New images of women and aged persons must also be realistic. Such books as *Julie of the Wolves* by Jean Craighead George and Scott O'Dell's *Island of the Blue Dolphins* portray strong female characters who also represent specific ethnic groups. Tove Jansson depicts a humorous, realistic Finnish grandmother in *The Summer Book,* while Brenda Wilkinson describes a young black girl's life in *Ludell.*

Books that present what is real for children must be honest books written by sensitive authors who dare to treat controversial issues. These books must present nonstereotyped characters and situations that represent varied ethnic and national groups. Honest, realistic writing is not limited to fiction, for all forms of literature can contribute to a child's conception of reality. The objectives that we will keep in mind as we explore realism in children's literature need to be as open and flexible as we would hope children's attitudes would be. We will try to:

1. Increase our own awareness of self and books that will help increase the child's awareness of self

2. Identify books and materials that will increase effective interpersonal communication and help children deal with feelings

3. Know a number of books that treat various ethnic groups realistically and sympathetically

4. Learn how to cope with stereotypes that appear in published works

5. Discover a selection of well-written realistic books for young people

The books we choose for reading aloud or for purchase as part of the school library collection are instrumental in shaping the values and the understandings of children. Chosen wisely, realistic books may help children grow. We should expect these books for young people to provide the following:

An original plot that is logically developed

Representation of the broad spectrum of human life

Honest characterization that avoids stereotyping

Competent use of language that is stylistically interesting

Content that reflects real concerns of young people

Presentation of a worthwhile theme

Inclusion of humor as part of life

We will find many fine authors whose works meet these criteria. In this chapter we first examine books that treat interpersonal relations, moving from awareness of self to friendships and getting along with others. Included are such important topics as divorce and death. The second part of the chapter deals with intergroup relations. Here we explore books that provide realistic pictures of American women, the aged in our society, native Americans, and Americans who have Mexican heritage. The final section of the chapter suggests teaching strategies for the classroom that focus on outstanding authors, outstanding books, and ways of actively combating stereotypes.

❦ Study these questions as you begin your investigation of realistic writing to get some idea of the kinds of books we will examine.

1. Discuss three books that present positive images of women that seem realistic today. Why is it important to emphasize such books?

2. Name two books that include divorce as part of the setting or action. Why should we have such books in libraries for young people?

3. Name three books that you might suggest to a fifth grader who has ridiculed someone who is physically handicapped.

4. Who wrote *Julie of the Wolves, My Side of the Mountain,* and *Coyote in Manhattan?*

5. Can you name one book written by each of these authors?

a. Virginia Hamilton

b. Charlotte Zolotow

c. Paula Fox

d. Scott O'Dell

e. James Houston

6. Match the titles of these well-known books with the topic they feature.

a. *Tituba of Salem Village*   ____ death of a young boy

b. *The Cay*   ____ divorce

c. *A Taste of Blackberries*   ____ witchcraft

d. *It's Not the End of the World*   ____ mental retardation

e. *Me Too*   ____ relationahip of old man and boy

CHILDREN AND INTERPERSONAL RELATIONS

Children are real people. Just as much as adults, they have honest needs as they grope for positive self-concepts and struggle with interpersonal relationships.

Books have much to offer young people as a way of exploring themselves and learning to get along with others. The openness of children's books today permits young people to discover ways of coping with life. Without moralizing, contemporary authors present characters and situations with which modern young people can identify. In this section we will explore books related to the following topics: developing self-awareness, the need for family, peer relationships, and the handling of divorce and death.

DEVELOPING SELF-AWARENESS

When I am a man, then I shall be a hunter
When I am a man, then I shall be a harpooner
When I am a man, then I shall be a canoe-builder

When I am a man, then I shall be a carpenter
When I am a man, then I shall be an artisan

Oh father! ya ha ha ha

Kwakiutl Indian Chant[1]

This Indian chant begins the beautiful book *And I Must Hurry for the Sea Is Coming In* (Prentice-Hall, 1970), which combines George Mendoza's poetry and De Wayne Dalrymple's impressionistic photography. A young black boy is pictured as he fantasizes being the captain of a boat. Finally he is shown in reality playing with a tiny toy boat in the gutter of a city street. Any young person can identify with this kind of imagining.

Children need books about other young people like themselves. They need the opportunity to view other children who have problems similar to their own, who share the same desires and anxieties, who have trouble coping with interpersonal relationships. Books can help children grow.

One of the strong needs of the child is for love. Betty Miles shows love as a valid need of all people in a warmly exuberant book, *Around and Around Love* (Knopf, 1975). "When you feel it and know it, tell it and show it." Here is a book that stresses the importance of caring, a reassuring concept for people of all ages.

A child's unabashed expression of love permeates Paul Zindel's *I Love My Mother* (Harper & Row, 1975). Illustrated flamboyantly by John Melo, this brief story describes an open, warm relationship between a mother and her son, who says, "She has a nice nose and taught me judo." And he adds, "She tells me secrets like she's lonely." This very positive book shows children, too, a variation of what constitutes a family.

Very young children have special problems. In *Sam* (McGraw-Hill, 1967), Ann Scott tells, for example, of a little boy who always seems to get in trouble until at last Sam's family understands his need for feelings of success. They find jobs that Sam can accomplish successfully. Norma Simon portrays a young Puerto Rican girl with a similar problem in *What Can I Do?* (Whitman, 1969). This story, too, talks about the little child's need to feel capable. Acceptance of a new baby is another problem common to small children. *The Knee-Baby* (Farrar, Straus & Giroux, 1973) by Mary Jarrell tells of Alan's feelings as he waits for a turn at sitting in Mother's lap as he did before the baby came.

A child's name is perhaps the most personal thing he or she possesses. In a picture book *Ebbie* (Morrow, 1975), Eve Rice tells the story of Eddie

---

[1] From the book, *And I Must Hurry for the Sea Is Coming In,* by George Mendoza. Published by Prentice-Hall, Inc., Englewood Cliffs, New Jersey.

who couldn't pronounce his own name when he lost his two front teeth. His loving family begins to call him Ebbie, too, just as he pronounces it. They continue to do so, however, long after Eddie has new teeth and can say his name distinctly. Finally he is able to show his family that saying his name properly is important to him.

The Secret Name (Harcourt Brace Jovanovich, 1972), a book for middle graders, also focuses on the importance of a name. Barbara Williams writes of an eight-year-old Navaho girl who comes from a reservation to attend school in Salt Lake City. Betsy lives with the family of Laurie, who narrates the story, and comes to understand to some extent the Navaho girl's problems in adjusting to a strange new life and her reluctance to reveal her name. The author makes an effort to depict white prejudice and the feelings of a child entering a different culture; there are some problems in handling the Navaho child's speech.

Growing up presents both problems and pleasures. *Ludell* (Harper & Row, 1975) is a realistic story of a fifth grade black girl, written by Brenda Wilkinson. Ludell lives with her grandmother in Waycross, Georgia, in the 1950s and next door lives Ruthie Mae, Ludell's best friend. Life in Waycross is depicted realistically—poverty, segregation, racism, selfishness, but also love and friendship. The author develops the characters skillfully and presents southern black dialect that appears authentic throughout the book. Ludell, the child of an unwed mother and an unknown father, copes with experiences that may not enter the lives of many readers. She approaches life positively, however, a vital person with real strength who is just discovering her own potential.

Alice Bach writes of the problems of a boy who is in the middle, between two sisters. Ten-year-old Mike creates a fantasy world to spark up his dull life in *The Meat in the Sandwich* (Harper & Row, 1975). When superjock Kip moves next door, however, he bullies Mike into an active sports role. Character development of Mike is well handled as he learns to assert himself both with Kip and his own liberated family.

Lizzie Lies a Lot (Delacorte, 1976) by Elizabeth Levy is the heartwarming story of Lizzie who habitually embroiders the truth. For some time even her best friend believes her wild stories. At last, however, Lizzie gets so tangled up in the web of lies that she just has to tell the truth. Lizzie herself realizes that she lies "about a lot of things I want to be true, but they aren't." Her parents, too, gain insight into Lizzie's reasons for lying, and they agree to help her. Lizzie also discovers that her imaginative tales are applauded in school when she writes stories. Other books for the middle grades by Elizabeth Levy include: *Something Queer Is Going On, Something Queer at the Ball Park, Nice Little Girls,* and *The People Lobby: The SST Story.*

Nina Bawden brings tenderness and suspense together in *Carrie's War* (Lippincott, 1973), a book for older readers. "Carrie had often dreamed about coming back" to Druid's Grove, where the yew trees "were dark green and so old that they had grown twisted and lumpy like arthritic fingers." And Carrie does come back, thirty years after she lived in the little Welsh mining town during the war in 1939 when children were evacuated from London. With her this time are her own children, and she tells them the story of the bleak life she and her brother Nick shared in the home of Mr. Evans, a miserly shopkeeper, and his sister Lou, who was kind to them. Their lives were changed, however, when they went to Druid's Bottom, where Mr. Evans' sister Dilys lived, cared for by motherly Hepzibah Green, whose kitchen was a joyous place. Nina Bawden is an exceptionally fine author, whose work is presented on page 204.

Today we find in children's literature more books that feature strong female characters who defy sex role stereotypes. An excellent book for primary grades is *The Girl Who Would Rather Climb Trees* (Harcourt Brace Jovanovich, 1975) by Miriam Schlein, who portrays an independent six-year-old, Melissa. Although friends and relatives give her a doll and a doll carriage, Melissa much prefers to play with her baby cousin Phillip. Considerately, but not too realistically, Melissa spares adult feelings by saying the doll is asleep when she goes outdoors to climb trees.

Another Melissa is a contemporary eleven-year-old girl who wants to play baseball. In *The Glad Man* (Knopf, 1975) by Gloria Gonzalez we see Melissa's aspirations set in a rich plot that presents relationships among children, parents, teachers, and old people. Character development is honest and change is evident. Current issues are also included, such as the right of citizens to question the administration of the law.

In *Sing to the Dawn* (Lothrop, 1972) by Minfong Ho, we see a determined fourteen-year-old Thai girl, Dawan, who strives to become educated. The situation is complicated not only by traditional concepts of woman's role, but also by the competition of her younger brother for the same scholarship and ensuing family hostility. Only the support of her grandmother and a young flower girl, strong women who never had the chance to be educated, makes it possible for Dawan to persevere. She convinces her brother that he should help her, and justice does prevail.

A Mennonite family that has fled Czarist Russia is depicted in *Winter Wheat* (Putnam, 1975) by Jeanne Williams. A pioneering family living in a sod house on the Kansas prairie consists of mother, father, and five daughters. Seventeen-year-old Colbie is depicted as a strong young woman who is determined to see that the immigrant family succeeds in its undertaking. Religous persecution and a realistic background of native Americans add dimension to this historical novel.

Jacket illustration by Colleen Browning. From Carrie's War by Nina Bawden. Reproduced by permission of J. B. Lippincott Company.

Many books reflect the search for identity and the confused conflicts with which children struggle as they grow up. Here are additional titles to explore:

Bradbury, Bianca. *The Loner*. Houghton Mifflin, 1970.

Buck, Pearl. *Matthew, Mark, Luke and John*. John Day, 1967.

Bulla, Clyde Robert. *White Bird*. Thomas Y. Crowell, 1966.

*Caudill, Rebecca. *Did You Carry the Flag Today, Charley?* Holt, 1966.

Clymer, Eleanor. *My Brother Stevie*. Holt, 1967.

Cone, Molly. *Annie Annie*. Houghton Mifflin, 1969.

Farley, Carol. *Mystery of the Fog Man*. Watts, 1966.

Fox, Paula. *Blowfish Live in the Sea*. Bradbury, 1970.

Little, Jean. *Kate*. Harper & Row, 1971.

Means, Florence C. *Us Maltbys*. Houghton Mifflin, 1966.

Sachs, Marilyn. *Amy and Laura*. Doubleday, 1966.

*Turkle, Brinton. *The Adventures of Obadiah*. Viking, 1972.

*Zolotow, Charlotte S. *A Father Like That*. Harper & Row, 1971.

Wojciechowsha, Maia. *Shadow of a Bull*. Atheneum, 1964.

THE NEED FOR FAMILY

Akin to the development of self-awareness and a positive self-concept is the need for family, for a sense of belonging. Many books for children feature a family and the interactions of its members. Today children's books are helping children recognize that families differ. Families portrayed are not always the stereotyped mother, father, and two children living a white middle class suburban life. Children's books are presenting, too, families in which parents are divorced and children face problems. The treatment of death as a part of life that families inevitably face is also a major theme in many books for children today. These are the topics we will explore in this section.

FAMILIES DIFFER   In the preceding section we have already mentioned a number of books that depict families that differ from the stereotype. Zindel shows young children a boy living with his mother in *I Love My Mother*. *Ludell* is the story of an elementary school girl who lives with her grandmother and seldom sees her unwed mother, who works in the city

---

* For younger children.

and occasionally sends Ludell clothes. Ludell wonders about her father but knows better than to ask questions.

In *Jenny's Revenge* (Four Winds, 1974) by Anne Norris Baldwin we see a family that consists of a mother, a young daughter, and the baby sitter. Despite the fact that her divorced mother needs to work, young Jenny thinks her mother should stay home "as other mothers do," a norm that causes difficulties for many children. Jenny learns to get along with the baby sitter, Mrs. Cramie, when Mother sympathizes but goes to work anyway. We will see more examples of single parent families in books described in the section Divorce in the Family.

The stereotyped role of the mother as a housewife who services the family is also being actively combated in a number of books about families for children today. One example is *The Terrible Thing That Happened at Our House* (Parents' Magazine Press, 1975) written by Marge Blaine and illustrated by John C. Wallner. "My mother used to be a real mother," sighs a rather spoiled little girl. When her mother decides to return to teaching, the child misses the nice lunches Mother used to prepare and having Mother at home when she comes home from school. Not unexpectedly, life gets more complicated when Mother chooses to work outside the home. Instead of listening to the children, for example, Mother might say, "I need a few minutes to clear my head, kids—I've had a really tough day." At last the family talks things over and agrees on ways to meet the needs of each member of the family. The young girl concludes: "I guess they're a real mother and father after all." More books about appropriate sex roles for women are described later in this chapter and in Chapter 10.

Emily Cheney Neville introduces an alcoholic mother in a book for older children, *Garden of Broken Glass* (Delacorte, 1975). Thirteen-year-old Brian's father deserted the family so he lives with an older sister, a younger brother, and his mother on welfare. Gradually Brian learns to relate effectively with other people as well as his brother and sister. When his mother is hospitalized, black neighbors and friends are surprised that the children have no relatives that will come to their assistance. Here is a realistic picture of poverty and racism.

An unusual relationship between a mother and her daughter is described in the picture book *The Quitting Deal* (Viking, 1975). Tobi Tobias tells how Mother, who wants to stop smoking, and her seven-year-old daughter, who wants to stop sucking her thumb, try to help each other. They try various methods, concluding most realistically that breaking a habit isn't easy. The story ends with their decision to try a method of gradual withdrawal.

A theme that occurs in many books is the child's need for a parent. Alison Morgan writes of a boy's need for a father in *Pete* (Harper & Row,

1973). Adolescent Pete Jenkins seldom sees his father, who is a traveling construction worker. When Pete gets in trouble, he decides to travel across the British countryside to find his father. After many adventures, he reaches the construction site and does get to know his father, not as the figure he had romanticized, but as a real person.

This kind of need is part of Bill's life, too, in *Houseboat Summer* (Macmillan, 1942) by Elizabeth Coatsworth. Bill couldn't remember his father, who had died when he was very small. Brought up by his mother and grandmother, Bill was shyer and less outgoing than his younger sister Sandy, but he finds himself during his summer adventures while living on a houseboat with his aunt and uncle. "Maybe he didn't have a father to back him and understand what he was driving at. But he had an uncle, didn't he? An uncle's pretty nearly as good as a father—an uncle like Uncle Jim anyway." This theme is present in the books that treat divorce and death, which are discussed later in the chapter.

Need for a sense of family is expressed by Kate, an orphan who has lived with her Aunt Millicent until she is sent to live with Cousin Lawrence Chatteris with the words: "It's time your father's family took you on, and that Chatteris man's got a whole house to himself with not a soul to share it." A sense of mystery pervades *The Family Tree* (Nelson, 1973) by Margaret Storey as ten-year-old Kate discovers her family through their possessions and old photographs stored in the attic.

Robert Lawson's *They Were Strong and Good* (Viking, 1940) is an excellent presentation of the narrator's ancestors as ordinary people who were "strong and good." Children's self-concepts can benefit from this sense of pride in family and the family heritage.

If the lack of parents is a problem for some children, just getting along with them is a real problem for others. This poem, which expresses one child's reaction, appears in Karla Kuskin's *The Rose on My Cake* (Harper & Row, 1964).

I WOKE UP THIS MORNING

I woke Up This Morning
At quarter past seven.
I kicked up the covers
And stuck out my toe.
And ever since then
(That's a quarter past seven)
They haven't said anything
Other than "Please, dear,
Don't do what you're doing,"

Or "Lower your voice."
Whatever I've done
And however I've chosen,
I've done the wrong thing
And I've made the wrong choice.
I didn't wash well
And I didn't say thank you.
I didn't shake hands
And I didn't say please.
I didn't say sorry
When passing the candy.
I banged the box into
Miss Witelson's knees.
I didn't say sorry.
I didn't stand straighter.
I didn't speak louder
When asked what I'd said.
Well, I said
That tomorrow
At quarter past seven
They can
Come in and get me
I'm Staying in Bed.

Getting along with Father is a major theme in Emily Neville's *It's Like This, Cat* (Harper & Row, 1963), winner of the Newbery award. "My father is always talking about how a dog can be very educational for a boy. This is one reason I got a cat." Rebellion against the dominance of his father is woven through the plot as Dave struggles to gain independence. When his friend Tom needs help, however, Dave recommends his father, who comes through admirably. Pop also gains understanding of his son and later apologizes for laughing when Cat leaps out of the car in the middle of the freeway. "Then of all things, he picks up Cat himself. 'Come on. You're one of the family. Let's get on with this vacation.'" Characterization of the parents is perceptive as is that of adolescent Dave Mitchell.

Jessica's problem is just the opposite in *The Witches of Worm* (Atheneum, 1972) by Zilpha Keatley Snyder. Jessie's mother, Joy, is always saying, "I'm sorry, Jessie Baby," as she explains her latest plans:

If Jessica had waited, Joy would have said one, or all of a number of things. She would certainly have said she was sorry that, since Alan had asked her out to dinner, there would be a lonely TV dinner for Jessica again that night. Then she might have mentioned some other things she was usually sorry about: that her job kept her away from home until so late, and that they had to live in a city apartment rather than a real house. If she was feeling particularly dramatic, she might have gone on to say that she was sorry she was such a lousy mother, but she guessed she'd never been cut out for motherhood. Sometimes she even cried a little; Jessica knew that part by heart, too.

Twelve-year-old Jessica is independent, but lonely. No wonder she turns her attention to the strange cat, Worm, which seems to be making her do things against her will.

Additional pictures of contemporary family life are presented in such books as:

*Adoff, Arnold. *Black Is Brown Is Tan*. Harper & Row, 1973.

Blume, Judy. *Tales of a Fourth Grade Nothing*. Dutton, 1972.

Clymer, Eleanor. *How I Went Shopping and What I Got*. Holt, 1972.

Ellis, Ella Thorp. *Celebrate the Morning*. Atheneum, 1972.

Little, Jean. *One to Grow On*. Little, Brown, 1969.

Rabin, Gil. *Changes*. Harper & Row, 1973.

Sachs, Marilyn. *The Truth about Mary Rose*. Doubleday, 1973.

Smith, Doris B. *Tough Chauncey*. Morrow, 1974.

Terris, Susan. *The Drowning Boy*. Doubleday, 1972.

Walter, Mildred. *Lillie of Watts*. Ward Ritchie, 1969.

DIVORCE IN A FAMILY   Divorce is a serious problem that affects many children today. It is treated both directly and indirectly in many current children's books. Judy Blume, for example, describes twelve-year-old Karen's attempts to effect a reconciliation between her parents in *It's Not the End of the World* (Bradbury, 1972). When she finally realizes that a reconciliation is not possible, she accepts the reality of divorce and concludes that it isn't the end of the world, an important understanding for many young people to share.

A similar situation is presented in *A Month of Sundays* (Watts, 1972) by Rose Blue. A boy and his mother move to a big city where the boy expe-

---

* For younger children.

riences loneliness as a result of missing his father, the very real problems related to his mother's working, and the adjustment to a new environment.

In *I Know You, Al* (Viking, 1975) Constance Greene writes of Alexandra, whose divorced mother has a boyfriend. Al, afraid they may be considering marriage, tells her friend, "Suppose he asks me for her hand. . . . Suppose he asks me for my mother's hand in marriage. Seeing as I'm her daughter, maybe he'll ask me for my permission to marry my mother." A sequel to *A Girl Called Al* (Viking, 1969), this book continues the dialogue between preadolescent Al and her friend. Al's father appears after almost six years to ask Al to come to his wedding, and Al tells him she'll have to think about it.

"That was pretty nervy, telling your own father you'll have to think about going to his wedding," I said.

"Well, it was pretty nervy of him to do what he did," Al said angrily. "How would you like it if your father walked out on you when you were eight years old?"

"I wouldn't," I said.

When the Sad One Comes to Stay (Lippincott, 1975) by Florence Parry Heide is a realistic story of a contemporary divorced woman, Sally, and her daughter, Sara. Sally never talks of Sara's father and focuses all her attention on success and getting to know the right people. Sara meets an interesting old woman, Maisie Best, who encourages Sara to talk about the important things "you keep sewed inside yourself." In the end Sara weakly, but perhaps realistically, decides to accept Sally's way of life.

Last Night I Saw Andromeda (Walck, 1975), Charlotte Anker's first book, is exceptional. It is exciting and humorous, and it actively combats both sexism and racism. Eleven-year-old Jenny Berger is afraid that her father will discontinue his visits after her parents are divorced, because she thinks he is bored. She determines, therefore, to pursue interests that will entice her scientist father. A black boy, Toby, helps her collect fossils and shares his hobby, raising snakes, with Jenny. Both children and parents are depicted honestly.

It is most appropriate to have divorce play an important role in developing a plot in children's literature today, but as with death it must be handled sensitively. One of the first books that was written on this timely theme is *Where's Daddy?* (Beacon Press, 1969) by Beth Goff. The main character is a very small girl, Janey Dear, who misses her father.

This book focuses too directly, however, on the divorce and the fact that Daddy has moved out of the house. It is more appropriate for adults who are having problems talking about divorce with children than for the children themselves. *Me Day* (Dial, 1971) by Joan Lexau is a better book for primary grade children.

Other books that might be helpful to have available as good reading for any child include the following:

Barnwell, Robinson. *Shadow on the Water*. McKay, 1967.

Cleaver, Vera and Bill Cleaver. *Ellen Grae*. Lippincott, 1967.

Gardner, Richard. *The Boys and Girls Book about Divorce*. Aronson, 1970.

Sachs, Marilyn. *Veronica Ganz*. Doubleday, 1968.

DEATH AS PART OF LIFE A part of life that adults have not always been willing to deal with is death, especially where children are concerned. We have "protected" children from this experience only to shut them out in a way that may actually have increased their very real fears. As Stephen M. Joseph writes in *Children in Fear:*

When there were deaths in our family, of aunts, uncles, or grandparents, no one seemed to cry openly, or at least not in front of me. They mentioned these deaths, briefly and matter-of-factly, but no one ever discussed them with me. I was left to figure out for myself what death must be like.[2]

He comments further on the discomfort of adults when children ask questions about death. We are only now beginning to learn to handle death more openly; an open attitude is better for those who are dying as well as those who care about that person. This current trend should help children as well.

Authors who cautiously presented the death of animals as a major theme in children's books were heavily criticized. When Margaret Wise Brown wrote the first book on the subject, *The Dead Bird* (Scott, 1965), many teachers and librarians berated it, for death was not considered an appropriate subject for children to read about. Sandol Stoddard Warburg later wrote of the death of a dog in *Growing Time* (Houghton Mifflin,

[2] Stephen M. Joseph, *Children in Fear* (Holt, 1974), p. 139.

1969). Judith Viorst showed a child remembering the good things about a pet cat that died, in *The Tenth Good Thing about Barney* (Atheneum, 1971).

Today there are many books that discuss death openly as a realistic part of life. Death has often been mentioned peripherally, as in *Carrie's War,* in which one of Carrie's children thinks about their father who has recently died. Death occurs peripherally also in *Sounder, The Big Wave, Little Women, Shadow of a Bull,* and *Charlotte's Web.* In an increasing number of children's books, however, death is a major theme. This seems to reflect a maturity for children's literature that need not be morbid, albeit realistic, as in the following sampling of well-written books.

In *Nana Upstairs and Nana Downstairs* (Putnam, 1973) four-year-old Tommy visits his great-grandmother who is the Nana living downstairs. His relationship with this old woman is an important part of his life. Author Tomie De Paola also deals, however, with the inevitable death of the great-grandmother. Tommy's mother tells him of Nana's death and helps him handle his grief.

Doris Buchanan Smith writes of a boy's feelings when his friend dies of a bee sting in *A Taste of Blackberries* (Thomas Y. Crowell, 1973). The unnamed friend is disgusted with Jamie's behavior as he writhes on the ground after being stung, so he goes away. When he learns of his friend's death, he is of course stricken with remorse and guilt. Again, the reader shares his feelings and learning to cope with grief.

Alfred Slote develops a main character who is dying of leukemia in *Hang Tough, Paul Mather* (Lippincott, 1973). Paul, who knows of his terminal condition, loves to play baseball, but participating in this vigorous sport is soon too exhausting for him. As a result, he is hospitalized. The relationships of Paul with both his doctor and a younger brother are well handled.

"I miss Grandpa," said six-year-old Lewis one night, much to his mother's amazement. Charlotte Zolotow sensitively reveals a young child's feelings of loneliness in *My Grandson Lew* (Harper & Row, 1974), a small picture book. Lew's grandfather had died when Lew was only two, so his mother never thought of telling Lew. Not until four years later did she finally realize that Lew was waiting for his grandfather to come as he always had, irregularly, often unexpectedly, but always welcome. Lew and his mother talk about how they both miss Grandpa, a feeling they are now able to share. As Lew's mother says:

We will remember him together and neither of us will be so lonely as we would be if we had to remember him alone. (p. 32)

Pedro's mother dies when he is eleven in *Away Is So Far* (Four Winds, 1974) by Toby Talbot. Pedro's father cannot bear remaining in the house where his wife's long illness had taken place. Pedro sympathizes, for he too misses his mother terribly:

Pedro felt a deep ache for him. His father seemed so small and lonely and lost. Pedro walked over and reached out for his father's arm. As he touched the weathered corduroy jacket, he felt a quiver and then a yielding. (p. 82)

They leave the little Spanish village near Málaga and travel to Paris, making a living through playing the guitar. Finally, the father realizes that running away does not help, so they return home to live and to remember.

In *Good Times* (Random House, 1969) by Lucille Clifton we learn about Doretha through her diary, her "Doretha Book." Doretha's father dies in the midst of good times, when everyone is having fun at a picnic. Suddenly "the lemonade was warm, the chicken leg lay in the dust, and her daddy was dead." The mother expresses her grief realistically as well as her need for love.

Additional books that help children cope with the death of human beings in their lives include:

*Bartoli, Jennifer. *Nonna*. Harvey House, 1975.

Brooks, Jerome. *Uncle Mike's Boy*. Harper & Row, 1973.

Cleaver, Vera and Bill Cleaver. *Grover*. Lippincott, 1970.

————. *Where the Lilies Bloom*. Lippincott, 1969.

Dixon, Paige. *May I Cross Your Golden River?* Atheneum, 1975.

*Dobrin, Arnold. *Scat*. Four Winds, 1971.

Lee, Virginia. *The Magic Moth*. Seabury, 1972.

*Miles, Miska. *Annie and the Old One*. Little, Brown, 1971.

Orgel, Doris. *The Mulberry Music*. Harper & Row, 1971.

Rhodin, Eric. *The Good Greenwood*. Westminster, 1971.

Whitehead, Ruth. *The Mother Tree*. Seabury, 1971.

Zindel, Paul. *The Pigman*. Harper & Row, 1968.

————

* For younger children.

Nonfiction, too, deals with the biological, psychological, and sociological facts of death. Joan Fassler, for example, describes death factually for young children in *My Grandpa Died Today* (Behavioral Publication, 1971). *Why Did He Die?* (Lerner, 1965) written by Audrey Harris, is a mother's explanation to a young child. An excellent presentation is *Life and Death* (Morrow, 1970) by Herbert Zim and Sonia Bleeker, who treat the subject comprehensively and calmly, discussing death as a part of life. *Learning to Say Good-by* (Macmillan, 1976) by Eda Le Shan treats loss of a parent.

A guide to death education, *Discussing Death* (ETC, 1976) has been prepared by Gretchen Mills and others. This guide lists books that would be helpful at different age levels as well as suggesting concepts that can be presented.

It is interesting to note that there is no subject entry for divorce in the 1971 edition of the *Children's Catalog*. There is an entry for death although only one title, *Grover* by Vera and Bill Cleaver, is listed. Clearly, these topics have entered the field of children's literature very recently, although they have long been an important part of the lives of children.

PEER RELATIONSHIPS

Children of all ages spend much time with their friends, their peers. Nothing can cause more hurt than rejection by the gang or a falling out between two "best friends." Reading about such universal problems may help students cope with upsetting experiences that come their way as they realize that other people have the same kinds of feelings—grief, loneliness, frustration. It may aid them in gaining a new perspective of their own feelings.

THE NEED FOR FRIENDS "I like you/And I know why/I like you because/You are a good person/To like . . . When I think something is important/You think it's important too/When I say something funny/You laugh/I think I'm funny and/You think I'm funny too/Hah-hah . . ." The exuberant tone of this delightful small book, *I Like You* (Houghton Mifflin, 1965), by Sandol Stoddard Warburg can only be compared to *Hooray for Us* (Houghton Mifflin, 1970), which also extols friendship. "Hooray for us!/Hooray/I say/That's the message for today." The whimsy is enhanced by Jacqueline Chwast's illustrations.

A Friend Is Someone Who Likes You (Harcourt Brace Jovanovich, 1958) by Joan Anglund is another small book that extols friendship of all kinds —with a boy or girl, a dog, a white mouse, the wind. Everybody needs at least one friend.

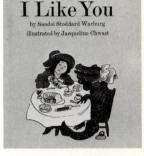

I Like You by Sandol Sloddard Warburg, illustrated by Jacqueline Chwast. Copyright © 1965 by Sandel S. Warburg, Copyright © 1965 by Jacqueline Chwast. Reprinted by permission of Houghton Mifflin Company.

I Need All the Friends I Can Get (Determined Productions, 1964), by Charles Schultz, presents important concepts for both adults and young people. "A friend is someone who sticks up for you for what you are." "A friend is someone who sticks up for you when you're not there." This book and others such as *Happiness Is a Warm Puppy* and *Happiness Is a Sad Song* are humorous, but real; they offer something to children that is direct and meaningful.

The need for friends is also the main theme in *The Noonday Friends* (Harper & Row, 1965) by Mary Stolz. Important in this book, too, is the family interaction and the relationship of eleven-year-old Franny and her younger brother Marshall. The Davis family is poor, and Franny is very much conscious of having only one pair of shoes and having to depend on getting a free lunch pass at school.

Many stories feature peer relationships and the problems involved in getting along with other young people. *Queenie Peavy* (Viking, 1966), for example, by Robert Burch is an unusually interesting character study of a girl living in rural Georgia. Here is a bright, strong, independent young woman in eighth grade who faces real problems, namely, that her father is in jail, and the kids taunt her. The story opens with Queenie in the principal's office being reprimanded for throwing rocks at the boiler room door (she hit the latchstring ten times out of ten). "Queenie Peavy was the only girl in Cotton Junction who could chew tobacco. She could also spit it—and with deadly aim." Robert Burch has written a number of stories about young people as they move into adolescence, for example, *D. J.'s Worst Enemy* (Viking, 1965), one of a collection of books about young boys who participate in farm life activities and manage to get into many humorous escapades along the way.

Billy's friends get him into an unusual situation in *How to Eat Fried Worms* (Watts, 1973), written by Thomas Rockwell. "Fifty dollars. That was a lot of money. How bad could a worm taste? He'd eaten fried liver, salmon loaf, mushrooms, tongue, pig's feet. . . . If he won fifty dollars, he could buy that minibike George Cunningham's brother had promised to sell him in September before he went away to college. Heck, he could gag *anything* down for fifty dollars, couldn't he?" After this reasoning, Billy agrees to the bet with his friend Alan. Billy not only wins the bet, but even grows to like worms! The story ends with his plaintive questions, "Do you think there's something the doctors don't know? Do you think I could be the first person who's ever been *hooked* on worms?"

A delightful, realistic tale of best friends, Tassie and Sooky, is told by Lucille Clifton in *The Times They Used to Be* (Holt, 1974). Illustrated by Susan Jeschke, this short book for upper elementary students, describes

the happenings in a single summer, the summer of 1948. That was the summer that Tassie and Sooky decide to run away because they fear that Tassie's grandma's dire predictions about sin and unclean bodies have come true. Then Mama tells them about "coming into your nature," and they learn about menstruation.

Fast Sam, Cool Clyde, and Stuff (Viking, 1975) is a moving novel by Walter Dean Myers about black and Puerto Rican friends. This book for older students includes the three boys in the title as well as several lively young women who join the boys in a game of basketball. They share their problems and support each other in the realistic struggle for survival on 116th Street.

Books that feature friendship and the importance of peer relationships will be a welcome part of any library collection. Other recommended titles include:

Young Children

Cohen, Miriam. *Will I Have a Friend?* Macmillan, 1967.

Cohen, Miriam. *Best Friends.* Macmillan, 1971.

Kantrowitz, Mildred. *I Wonder If Herbie's Home Yet.* Parents' Magazine Press, 1971.

Sherman, Ivan. *I Do Not Like It When My Friend Comes to Visit.* Harcourt Brace Jovanovich, 1973.

Zolotow, Charlotte. *Janey.* Harper, 1973.

Middle School

Coles, Robert. *Dead End School.* Little, Brown, 1968.

Corcoran, Barbara. *Sam.* Atheneum, 1967.

Fox, Paula. *Portrait of Ivan.* Bradbury, 1969.

Little, Jean. *One to Grow On.* Little, Brown, 1969.

Sachs, Marilyn. *Peter and Veronica.* Doubleday, 1969.

Sharmat, Marjorie Weinman. *Getting Something on Maggie Marmelstein.* Harper & Row, 1971.

Smith, Doris B. *Tough Chauncey.* Morrow, 1974.

Stolz, Mary S. *A Wonderful, Terrible Time.* Harper & Row, 1967.

Wallace, Barbara Brooks. *Victoria.* Follett, 1972.

SPECIAL CHILDREN Books can often serve to promote understanding of other children who are different in a special way, children who are handicapped because they are blind, deaf, or mentally retarded, for example. Lack of knowledge often permits children who are not handicapped to make fun of children they do not understand.

Young people, and adults too, would gain insight into the world of a blind person through the very beautiful book *Sound of Sunshine, Sound of Rain* (Parents' Magazine Press, 1970), written by Florence Parry Heide with fine artwork by Kenneth Longtemps. Not only is the boy in this story blind, but he is also "colored." His friend Abram, the ice cream man, tells him that there is no best color, that colors are just the same, but his sister feels the hurt of being referred to as "colored" and of being rejected.

"So we're colored," says my sister to me as she pulls me along. "So what else is new? I've heard it a million times. I guess I heard it before I was even born."

"Abram says color don't mean a thing," I say.

My sister drags me along. I can tell by her hand that she's mad. "What does he know? Is he black, your friend?" she asks.

"I don't know," I say.

"You don't even know if your friend is black or not," says my sister. "I wish everyone in the whole world was blind!" she cries.

The Blue Rose (Lawrence Hill, 1974) by Gerda Klein, with beautiful photographs by Norma Holt, is another sensitive portrayal of a child who is different. This is the story of Jenny, a lovely little girl with brown eyes and dark brown hair, but Jenny is like a bird with very short wings. Learning to fly is harder for Jenny; it takes "more strength, more effort, more time," for Jenny is mentally retarded.

An especially fine book that portrays a retarded child within a family setting is *The Summer of the Swans* (Viking, 1970) by Betsy Byars. Sara is fourteen years old and experiencing feelings of discontent with her physical appearance. "She could never be really sure of anything this summer. One moment she was happy, and the next, for no reason, she was miserable." When Sara's mentally retarded brother Charlie disappears, however, Sara is the one who finds him with the help of Joe Melby. Sara is ecstatic:

She thought for a minute she was going to faint, a thing she had never done before, not even when she broke her nose. She hadn't even believed people really did faint until this minute when she clung to the tree because her legs were as useless as rubber bands.

The characterization of both Charlie and Sara is outstanding. Black and white illustrations by Red Coconis are attractive additions to the text of this Newbery award winner. An easy book to read, this title is an excellent selection for slower adolescent readers.

The Story of Helen Keller (Grosset & Dunlap, 1958) by Lorena Hickok is inspirational to students who are touched by this courageous woman's achievements. Deaf, mute, and blind from the age of two, she manages to overcome her handicaps and to communicate to the world.

Don't Feel Sorry for Paul (Lippincott, 1974) is the straight-forward description of Paul's life in both words and pictures.

When Paul Jockimo was born, something was wrong. On his right hand, where there should have been five fingers, there was only the stump of a flexible wrist. On his right foot, where there should have been five toes, there was only the stump of a flexible heel. On his left hand, there was an enlarged thumb and a

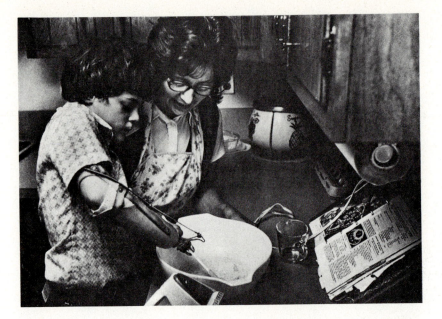

webbing-together of two fingers, and on his left foot, there was only the heel and
the big toe. What went wrong? Not even the medical experts can say. (p. 5)

Author-illustrator Bernard Wolf portrays Paul with sympathy, but no
sentimentality. Paul rides a horse; he wrestles with his father; he washes
the family car. The reader learns about each prosthesis and sees Paul
struggle to put them on himself. We can also understand why Paul occasionally doesn't want to go to school.

In *Me Too* (Lippincott, 1973) Vera and Bill Cleaver introduce Lydia
Birdsong and her identical twin, Lornie, who is severely retarded. When
Lornie is taken out of the special school she has attended, Lydia is certain
that she can succeed in "curing" her twin. She experiences many frustra-
tions and finally must admit that she cannot accomplish what experts
have been unable to do. Lornie returns happily to the special school, and
Lydia comes to understand the special nature of her sister's development.
Lydia is a strong vital person who grows perceptibly through introspec-
tion, learning to accept reality.

Glen, in *The Nothing Place* (Harper & Row, 1973) by Eleanor Spence,
becomes deaf as a result of illness. Afraid to tell people that he can't hear,
Glen tries to manage by lip-reading. Despite his intelligence, therefore,
he has difficulty with school and especially with the other children who
just do not understand his behavior.

Other books about special children who have specific problems that require understanding include:

Blume, Judy. *Deenie*. Bradbury, 1972. (*Wearing a brace*)

Crane, Caroline. *A Girl Like Tracy*. McKay, 1966. (*Retarded*)

De Angeli, Marguerite. *Door in the Wall*. Doubleday, 1949. (*Paralysis*)

De Gering, E. *Seeing Fingers: The Story of Louis Braille*. McKay, 1962.

Friis-Baastad, Babbis. *Don't Take Teddy*. Scribner, 1967. (*Retarded*)

Hunter, Edith Fisher. *Child of the Silent Night*. Houghton Mifflin, 1963. (*Story of Laura Dewey Bridgman who was blind and deaf.*)

Konigsburg, E. L. "Inviting Jason." In *Altogether, One at a Time*. Atheneum, 1971. (*Retarded*)

Little, Jean. *Take Wing*. Little, Brown, 1968. (*Retarded*)

Little, Jean. *From Anna*. Harper & Row, 1972. (*Eyes*)

Potter, Bronson. *Antonio*. Atheneum, 1968. (*Crippled hand*)

Putnam, Peter. *The Triumph of the Seeing Eye*. Harper, 1963.

Rinkoff, Barbara. *The Watchers*. Knopf, 1972. (*Physical handicap*)

Southall, Ivan. *Let the Balloon Go*. St. Martin's, 1968. (*Spastic*)

Weik, Mary Hays. *The Jazz Man*. Atheneum, 1966. (*Neurotic; lame*)

Wrightson, Patricia. *A Racecourse for Andy*. Harcourt Brace Jovanovich, 1968. (*Retarded*)

❦ *ACTIVITIES TO PROMOTE AWARENESS* Try three of these activities as you explore your own emotions and begin to share feelings with children you work with.

1. Make a list of twenty things you really like to do. Then before each item place a $ if this activity costs money. Put a + before each thing you have done in the past month. Put an A before those things you like to do alone. Read through your list. What does it tell you? Can you talk about the things you have listed with a friend?

2. Use the above technique with a class or group of students. Ask them to write only ten items. You might consider asking them to do some of these:

   Put M before the things you think your mother would enjoy too.

Put F before the things your father would enjoy.

Put the figure 20 before things you think you'll be doing twenty years from now.

Have the students discuss their lists on a volunteer basis.

3. Read one of the books listed in the preceding section. Plan how you could present it in a class that you work with. How would you follow it up?

4. Develop an annotated list of five books that explore sensitive topics that you feel might be helpful to include in a school library. Consider such topics as:

Being Afraid
Blume, Judy. *Otherwise Known as Sheila the Great.* Dutton, 1972.

Having a Younger Brother or Sister
Zolotow, Charlotte. *If It Weren't for You.* Harper & Row, 1966.

Being Overweight
Solot, Mary Lynn. *100 Hamburgers: The Getting Thin Book.* Lothrop, 1972.

Being Small
Bawden, Nina. *The Peppermint Pig.* Lippincott, 1975.

UNDERSTANDING OTHERS

In our pluralistic society it is essential that children gain real understanding of people who are different from themselves in some way—skin color, language used, modes of behavior, values, the food they eat. Literature offers one means for developing understanding and more accepting attitudes toward people who differ in some way. It is interesting to help children become aware that we all differ from each other because no two individuals are exactly alike. We differ in age, height, name, the color of our eyes and hair, voice, and so on. We also need to become aware that being different is not "bad."

As we explore books and other forms of literature that portray groups of people realistically, we need to realize how many different ways of grouping people there are. Often we consider only racial groups—black, Caucasian, Oriental. We can also notice, however, the obvious groupings by sex. In addition, there are groupings based on religious beliefs such as

Jews, Catholics, Amish; groupings based on national origins, for example, Irish, Chicanos, Japanese; or groupings by age, young people and old people.

As children read about different peoples, the literature presented will aid individual children in developing greater self-awareness as well as an understanding of the group of which they are members.

As we probe the possible materials for developing understanding about these many different groups, we have chosen, of necessity, to focus on the following representative groups in order to provide in-depth coverage of each topic:

American women today

The aged in our society

Native Americans

Mexican-Americans or Chicanos

The literature of black Americans is featured in Chapter 9.

As we strive to improve intergroup relations, we look for stories written realistically. We may also need, however, to delve into the lore, the poetry, the nonfiction, and even fantasy as we develop a realistic perspective, a feeling of empathy for others. It is not easy to break down stereotypes and the prejudice that has become almost institutionalized.

AMERICAN WOMEN TODAY

The facts are clear and indisputable. Women have usually been portrayed in children's literature wearing aprons in the kitchen, and girls help their mothers around the house. The contrasting roles of the active, adventurous boys and the passive, fearful girls is obvious. No wonder, as is often stated by educators, boys will not read books about girls while girls enjoy books about boys. No wonder, too, many girls wish they were boys.

What effect does this literature have on children? Do these images of women and girls serve to socialize young girls to be passive, spineless persons with low aspiration levels? These are the kinds of questions that have been asked. The conclusion is that we need to break down stereotypes of women just as we are trying to eliminate stereotypes based on race, for both racism and sexism are harmful to our total population.

Sexism can occur in illustrations. It can also show up in language, in attitudes expressed toward women and their achievements, and the way they are characterized. Sexism can even occur when women are ignored or omitted. As stated in the pamphlet *Improving the Image of Women in Textbooks,* which was prepared by the Sexism in Textbooks Committee of Women at Scott, Foresman:

> Sexism refers to all those attitudes and actions which relegate women to a secondary and inferior status in society. Textbooks are sexist if they omit the actions and achievements of women, if they demean women by using patronizing language, or if they show women only in stereotyped roles with less than the full range of human interests, traits, and capabilities.[3]

The problem of sexism is especially noticeable in picture books. The fact that an illustrator pictures the characters and the action presented in the story provides a second opportunity for sexism to creep in. This is not as likely in books for older children since they are often not illustrated. Illustrations, moreover, are immediately visible and have more direct impact than do the words. Another factor that makes sexism a special problem in picture books is that mothers play a more prominent role in books for young children than they do for children at later stages.

A number of studies have focused, therefore, on picture books and in particular on such notable books as the winners of the Caldecott award for illustrations. In surveying the eighty Caldecott winners and runners-up from 1950 to 1970, Alleen Pace Nilsen found, for example, that there was "a steady decline in the number of women and girls included in the illustrations. From 1951 to 1955 the percentage of females as compared to males was forty-six. From 1956 to 1960 the percentage of females was forty-one. Between 1961 and 1965 the percentage of females was down to thirty-five, while in the five year period, 1966 to 1970, twenty-six percent of the pictured characters were females."[4]

Not only is the actual number of women compared to men important, however; we need to look also at *how* women are portrayed. One of the best examples of a stereotyped image of a woman is the mother in *Sylvester and the Magic Pebble* (Simon and Schuster, 1969), a Caldecott winner written and illustrated by William Steig. The donkey mother wears an apron throughout the book and is depicted as a fearful female who needs

---

[3] Copies are available from Scott, Foresman, 1900 East Lake Avenue, Glenview, Illinois 60025.

[4] Alleen P. Nilsen, "Books a la Mode: A Reader's Digest," *Elementary English* (October 1973) 50:1030.

the support of a strong male, in this case, the donkey father. If published today, this book would undoubtedly be criticized.

Few would deny the existence of sexism in children's books. The major thrust today focuses, therefore, on ways to cope with stereotyped images of women. The Committee on the Role and Image of Women of the National Council of Teachers of English states in their guidelines: "If women are to be treated as full human beings, we must confront sexist bias in the same way we have begun to confront racist and religious bias: recognize its existence, look for its causes, and then, step by step, work toward elimination of the causes and the bias."[5] There are many ways to handle this problem as we function in our various roles as educators, and we do not suggest banning objectionable books. We can operate instead along these positive lines:

1. We can teach children to recognize stereotyping and to question stereotyped portrayals of anyone.

2. We can emphasize books that depict women more realistically and that acknowledge their achievements.

3. We can also examine our own attitudes and behaviors both in and out of the classroom.

Many fine books portray women and girls as strong, lively persons who are doing interesting things. Although it is true that more such books are being published today, some of the very best have been around a long time. Few modern heroines could match Pippi or Madeline as audacious, lovable girls that delight boys as well as girls; yet Ludwig Bemelmans' *Madeline* was published in 1939 and *Pippi Longstocking* by Astrid Lindgren appeared in 1950.

Many authors have presented strong female characters. A strong young woman is presented by the well-known poet Harry Behn in *The Faraway Lurs* (World, 1963), his first novel for adolescent readers. Heather, a maiden of the Bronze Age is expected to marry Blue Wing, a boy from her village of Forest People. Instead, however, she falls in love with Wolf Stone, child of the Sun People, who were fearsome invaders, a warring barbaric tribe. When Blue Wing kills Wolf Stone, and disaster strikes her people, young Heather knows that "the ancient way would be

---

[5] Free copies of guidelines such as, "Guidelines for Women's Studies, Grades 1–12" are available from this committee: 1111 Kenyon Rd., Urbana, Illinois 61801.

to offer a sacrifice of something treasured. Something . . . or someone!" When members of her tribe prepare for the sacrifice and dance toward her proffering a drink that smells "faintly of clover," Heather
knows and accepts the inevitable:

Heather felt a dark wind swooping down out of the sky. She shivered, and closed
her eyes. In a moment her fear was gone, swept away by the sunny stillness of the
forest, the timeless voice of peace. She opened her eyes and smiled as she thought
of Wolf Stone waiting for her in the glade only a little distance away. She drank
deeply.

Norma Klein is a contemporary author who particularly strives to picture women realistically. In *Girls Can Be Anything* (Dutton, 1973) she
directly addresses the problem of stereotyped roles for women. In this
book for primary grades, Marina wants to play being a doctor or a pilot,
not a nurse or stewardess. Adam, her friend, protests until they discover
that Marina's aunt is not only a real doctor, but a surgeon! After that
Adam and Marina take turns being President. In *Mom, The Wolf Man and
Me* (Avon, 1974) Norma Klein depicts an eleven-year-old girl who lives
with her unmarried mother. Brett isn't at all sure she wants her mother
to get married. Two eight-year-old girls are the main characters in *Confessions of an Only Child* (Pantheon, 1974).

Another feminist author and poet is Eve Merriam who wrote the first
picture book for primary children about working women. *Mommies at
Work* (Knopf, 1955) shows women doing varied kinds of jobs, including
loving their children. A second book shows children choosing careers
that are not bound by traditional sex stereotyping, *Boys and Girls; Girls
and Boys.* In *Independent Voices* Eve Merriam extols real persons who had
courage enough to be themselves. Included in this collection of biographical verse are Elizabeth Blackwell, Lucretia Mott, and Ida B. Wells. Eve
Merriam also edited a collection of women's autobiographies entitled
Growing Up Female in America; Ten Lives, which older students would
find fascinating. Nancy Larrick and Eve Merriam collected the writing of
young people about their own sex roles in *Male and Female Under 18*
(Avon, 1973).

Discussed elsewhere in this book are such outstanding young women
as Robert Burch's Queenie Peavy, who can outdo any boy (see page
167). This author also created Ann, the competent young heroine in a
science fiction story (see page 127). Vera and Bill Cleaver write of Ellen
Grae and Mary Call, both admirable young women; the work of these

authors is discussed on page 197. Betsy Byars tells of Sara's capable handling of problems in *Summer of the Swans,* described in the preceding section. Certainly, Karana who spent eighteen years alone on an island in *Island of the Blue Dolphins* by Scott O'Dell, is a self-sufficient young woman who could cope with life (see page 187).

For primary children, too, there are a number of books that depict girls who manage very well. The series of stories about Madeline (see page 6), which Ludwig Bemelmans created, stands out, and Paul Zindel's picture of a mother in *I Love My Mother* is warm and sympathetic (see page 149). The Feminist Press has developed a whole series of small paperbound books designed to combat sex stereotypes. *The Dragon and the Doctor* by Barbara Danish (1971) tells how a woman doctor and her nurse, the doctor's brother, cure a dragon. *Firegirl* by Rich Gibson (1973) is the story of a girl who works in the fire station.

One of the finest of more recently published books is *Julie of the Wolves* (Harper & Row, 1972) by Jean Craighead George, which won the Newbery award in 1973. Thirteen-year-old Julie, whose Eskimo name is Miyax, manages to survive on the Alaskan tundra through her close observation of the ways of the wolves. Using the training of her father, Kapugen, a famous Eskimo hunter, this young Eskimo girl is able to imitate wolf behavior so well that she is accepted by the pack that provides her with food. She later endeavors to help the wolves when hunters are shooting them. Julie's strength of character is shown when she faces an identity crisis between being Julie or Miyax. She evaluates her relationship with her father and concludes realistically, but sadly, that the ways of the wolves and the Eskimo are over.

Following is a list of additional books for both primary and middle school children that present strong female characters. Boys too will enjoy reading these stories because the action is lively and the characters have imagination and vitality.

Primary Grades

Edward Ardizzone. *Diana and Her Rhinoceros.* Walck, 1964. (*A young girl takes care of a sick rhino.*)

Cecily Brownstone. *All Kinds of Mothers.* McKay, 1969. (*Mothers love their children.*)

Ivor Cutler. *Meal One.* Watts, 1971. (*Helbert and his Mum enjoy each other.*)

Louann Gaeddert. *Noisy Nancy Norris.* Doubleday, 1965. (*Nancy is assertive and intelligent.*)

M. B. Goffstein. *Two Piano Tuners*. Farrar, Straus & Giroux, 1970. (*A young girl learns how to tune a piano.*)

Gloria Goldreich and Esther Goldreich. *What Can She Be?—A Lawyer*. Lothrop, 1973. (*Career choices. Nonfiction.*)

Lillian Hoban. *A Wolf of My Own*. Macmillan, 1969. (*A birthday puppy becomes a wolf friend.*)

Fred Phleger. *Ann Can Fly*. Beginner Books, 1959. (*Ann's father teaches her to fly.*)

Sam Reavin. *Hurray for Captain Jane!* Parents' Magazine Press, 1971. (*Jane has an imagination without limits.*)

Jane Thayer. *Quiet on Account of Dinosaur*. Morrow, 1964. (*A dinosaur is a girl's pet.*)

Miriam Young. *Jellybeans for Breakfast*. Parents' Magazine Press, 1968. (*Girls fantasize exploring the moon.*)

Upper Grades

Natalie Babbitt. *Phoebe's Revolt*. Farrar, Straus & Giroux, 1968. (*A sit-down strike against feminine frills.*)

Natalie Savage Carlson. *Ann Aurelia and Dorothy*. Harper & Row, 1968. (*Girls at a convent school.*)

Cora Cheney. *The Incredible Deborah*. Scribner, 1967. (*Story of a soldier during the Revolutionary War.*)

Eleanor Clymer. *My Brother Stevie*. Holt, 1970. (*Annie tries to help her brother.*)

Alberta Constant. *The Motoring Millers*. Thomas Y. Crowell, 1969. (*Story of a girl who races cars.*)

Louise Fitzhugh. *Harriet the Spy*. Harper & Row, 1964. (*Harriet spies on everyone and records notes.*)

Constance Greene. *A Girl Called Al*. Viking, 1969. (*Alexandra is plump, intelligent, and caustic.*)

Maria Gripe. *The Night Daddy*. Delacorte, 1971. (*A young male writer stays with Julia at night.*)

Lee Kingman. *Georgia and the Dragon*. Houghton Mifflin, 1972. (*Girl earns money to honor her suffragist great-grandmother.*)

Mildred Lee. *The Rock and the Willow*. Lothrop, 1963. (*Enie wants to get away from her joyless home.*)

Doris Orgel. *Next Door to Xanadu*. Knopf, 1969. (*Fat Patricia is looking for a friend.*)

Marilyn Sachs. *Veronica Ganz*. Doubleday, 1968. (*Tiny Peter "gets to" tall Veronica.*)

Zilpha K. Snyder. *The Changeling*. Atheneum, 1970. (*Imaginative Ivy insists she is a changeling.*)

Elizabeth Speare. *The Witch of Blackbird Pond*. Houghton Mifflin, 1959. (*Story of a girl accused of witchcraft.*)

Mary Stolz. *A Wonderful Terrible Time*. Harper & Row, 1967. (*Two black girls living in a racially mixed community.*)

Isabella Taves. *Not Bad for a Girl*. M. Evans, 1972. (*People are angry when Sharon plays on a Little League team.*)

Betty Underwood. *The Tamarack Tree*. Houghton Mifflin, 1971. (*Subservient role of women and prejudice against blacks.*)

Ursula Moray Williams. *The Cruise of the Happy-Go-Gay*. Meredith, 1968. (*Victorian Aunt Hegarty is an indomitable explorer.*)

The problems that women face today can be summarized by this letter written by a young girl in Stuart Hample's *Children's Letters to God* (Essandess Paperbacks, 1966):

Dear God:

    Are boys better than girls? I know you are one, but please try to be fair.

Love,
Sylvia

In addition to fiction, there are a number of nonfiction titles that should be in any library, for example:

Coolidge, Olivia E. *Women's Rights: The Suffrage Movement in America, 1848–1920*. Dutton, 1966.

De Crow, Karen. *Young Women's Guide to Liberation*. Bobbs-Merrill, 1971.

Ingraham, Claire R. and Leonard W. Ingraham. *An Album of Women in American History*. Watts, 1972.

Komisar, Lucy. *The New Feminism*. Watts, 1971.

Ross, Pat, ed. *Young and Female; Turning Points in the Lives of Eight American Women.* Random House, 1972.

Stevenson, Janet. *Women's Rights.* Watts, 1972.

Biographies of women provide another avenue toward understanding the problems women have faced, as well as recognizing their individual contributions. Representative titles follow:

Ida Tarbell

Fleming, Alice. *Ida Tarbell; First of the Muckrakers.* Thomas Y. Crowell, 1971.

Rachel Carson

Latham, Jean Lee. *Rachel Carson: Who Loved the Sea.* Garrard Publishing Co., 1973.

Laura Ingalls Wilder

Wilder, Laura Ingalls. *The First Four Years.* Harper & Row, 1971. (*Autobiography*)

Free to Be . . . You and Me, a multimedia collection of nonsexist materials for use with children, was developed by Marlo Thomas and others (McGraw-Hill, 1974). Fifteen recorded selections include songs, stories, poems, and a dialogue.

The problem of sexism in children's literature exists. The best way of combating sexism is to provide more realistic ways of looking at women, their roles, and their contributions. A touch of humor may help, too, as in this poem by Lee Bennett Hopkins:

GIRLS CAN TOO!

Tony said: "Boys are better!
  They can . . .
  whack a ball,
  ride a bike with one hand
  leap off a wall."
I just listened

and when he was through,
I laughed and said:
  "Oh, yeah! Well girls can, too!"
Then I leaped off the wall,
  and rode away
With his 200 baseball cards
  I won that day.

THE AGED PERSON

"Ageism," as much as sexism and racism, is an ideology that we need to confront in children's literature. Are children provided with realistic pictures of the aged person? This aspect of children's literature has not received much attention. The percentage of older persons in our society is steadily increasing. No longer, however, do the older aunts and uncles or grandparents commonly live with their children's families. Children today, therefore, may not know many older persons very well, thereby missing an enriching experience. This experience can be supplied to some extent through reading books that present warm, realistic relationships between children and old people. We need books for children that actively combat the stereotyped images of aged men and women in our society.

Books can serve, for example, to provide new images and counteract old stereotypes of grandparents. In *Granny's Fish Story* (Parents' Magazine Press, 1975) Phyllis La Farge presents a grandmother who wears blue jeans and knows all about animals. Primary grade children will enjoy and identify with Julie and Sarah's feelings as city children going to live in the country.

In *The House of Wings* (Viking, 1972) by Betsy C. Byars we meet a grandfather who also knows about animals. At first Sammy, who is dumped abruptly by his parents, resents being left behind even temporarily in a dilapidated old house with an old man whom he considers crazy. There are geese in the kitchen and an owl that flies freely through the house. It is the wounded crane, however, that gradually arouses Sammy's interest and opens the door to understanding between the boy and his grandfather.

One of the most delightful pictures of a relationship between a young person and an old one is *The Summer Book* (Pantheon, 1975), an adult book that older students would enjoy. Written by Finnish author Tove Jansson, the book was translated from the Swedish by Thomas Teal. Sophia and her grandmother may be seventy years apart in age, but in spirit they are much alike. They talk about such important subjects as Hell,

God, and Heaven. Sophia asks her grandmother, "When are you going to die?" and her grandmother replies brusquely, "Soon. But that is not the least concern of yours." Throughout the book we are exposed to grandmother's realistic acceptance of her body's infirmities—the need to get up slowly while the dizziness goes away, her inability to walk without a cane, the days when she feels ill. She advises her seventy-five-year-old friend to try to outwit his relatives who are overprotective. Sophia hears the end of the conversation and questions grandmother about whom Verner is going to outwit.

"Relatives," Grandmother said. "Nasty relatives. They tell him what to do without asking him what he wants, and so there's nothing at all he really does want."
  "How awful!" Sophia cried. "That would never happen with us!"
  "No, never!" Grandmother said.

Black poet Sam Cornish writes a story of Grandmother Keyes who lives alone in *Grandmother's Pictures* (Bradbury, 1975). She shows her grandson the old snapshots of his family, and he is enthralled especially with those of his dead father whom he can't remember. The illustrations by Jeanne Johns enhance the revelation of this aged black woman's life and her memories of the past.

The Cay (Doubleday, 1969) by Theodore Taylor is dedicated to "Dr. King's dream, which can only come true if the very young know and understand." This book has been criticized because of the attitude toward blacks that is expressed by Phillip's mother. She tells Phillip, "They are not the same as you. They are different, and they live differently. That's the way it must be." Despite this criticism, however, the book depicts with sensitivity the relationship between young Phillip and Timothy, a black man who is over seventy, when they are marooned on a small island together. As the result of a blow on the head, Phillip becomes blind and is even more dependent on Timothy. Timothy not only cares for Phillip but tries to prepare him for Timothy's own death. Phillip comes to appreciate what the old man is doing for him and asks if he can be Timothy's friend.

James Kruss writes of a fourteen-year-old boy who spends a week with his great-grandfather who has just had a stroke in *My Great-Grandfather, the Heroes and I* (Atheneum, 1973). The two find a common interest in exploring heroes portrayed in literature and both gain insight for themselves through the experience. Here is a moving description of an understanding relationship between a young person and an aged man who is facing death. See this author's earlier book, *My Great-Grandfather and I* (Atheneum, 1964).

An outstanding story of the love between Michael, a little black boy, and Aunt Dew, who is one hundred years old, is *The Hundred Penny Box* (Viking, 1975) by Sharon Bell Mathis. Illustrated in soft brown tones by Leo and Diane Dillon, this picture book is for all ages. Only the child understands the importance of the box, Aunt Dew's treasure, which contains one penny for each year of her life. She tells Michael the stories behind these pennies.

Relationships with old persons are realistically portrayed in many books for young people. Joseph Krumgold writes about an old hobo and his relationship with a young boy in *Onion John* (Thomas Y. Crowell, 1959). He also writes of the warm feelings of a small boy for middle-aged Uncle Mustafa in *The Most Terrible Turk* (Thomas Y. Crowell, 1969). Vera and Bill Cleaver introduce an interesting old man, Ira, in *Ellen Grae* (Lippincott, 1967). Ellen worries about the welfare of Ira, who is strange, but harmless. Many of the books discussed in the section on death in children's literature include the description of a warm, satisfying relationship between a child and an aged person. In *Nonna* (Harvey House, 1975), for

Sharon Bell Mathis

THE HUNDRED PENNY BOX

Illustrated by Leo & Diane Dillon

From The Hundred Penny Box *by Sharon Bell Mathis. Text copyright © 1975 by Sharon Bell Mathis. Illustrations copyright © 1975 by Leo and Diane Dillon. Reprinted by permission of The Viking Press.*

example, Jennifer Bartoli tells of the children's love for their grand-mother. With the adults of the family, they bury Nonna and then share the memories of this person who was an important part of all their lives.

Additional books that portray relationships of children with older people are listed here:

Abrahams, Robert D. *The Bonus of Redonda*. Macmillan, 1969.

Blue, Rose. *Grandma Didn't Wave Back*. Watts, 1972.

Borack, Barbara. *Grandpa*. Harper & Row, 1967.

Bradbury, Bianca. *Andy's Mountain*. Houghton Mifflin, 1969.

Buckley, Helen E. *Grandfather and I*. Lothrop, 1959.

———. *Grandmother and I*. Lothrop, 1961.

DeJong, Meindert. *Puppy Summer*. Harper & Row, 1966.

——— *Journey from Peppermint Street*. Harper & Row, 1968.

Fox, Paula. *A Likely Place*. Macmillan, 1967.

——— *The Stone-Faced Boy*. Bradbury, 1968.

Gauche, Patricia Lee. *Grandpa and Me*. Coward-McCann, 1972.

Kleberger, Ilse. *Grandmother Orna*. Atheneum, 1967.

Lundgren, Max. *Matt's Grandfather*. Putnam, 1972.

Mazer, Norma Fox. *A Figure of Speech*. Delacorte, 1973.

McNeill, Janet. *The Prisoner in the Park*. Little, Brown, 1972.

Roberson, Darrell. *A Boy Called Plum*. Dodd, Mead, 1974.

Shotwell, Louisa R. *Magdalena*. Viking, 1971.

Shura, Mary Francis. *Backwards for Luck*. Knopf, 1967.

Snyder, Zilpha Keatley. *The Witches of Worm*. Atheneum, 1972.

The following story, "The Night of Leonid," gives the reader a new perspective of an older woman, her relationship with her grandson, and subtly, the fact of death, which cannot be ignored. The story comes from the book *Altogether, One at a Time* (Atheneum, 1971) by E. L. Konigsburg. This collection of four short stories portrays with sensitivity some of the personal problems that individuals are encountering today—mental retardation, old age, being fat, and being black in a white world. The stories in this collection would be excellent for use in the classroom.

THE NIGHT OF LEONID

I arrived at Grandmother's house in a taxi. I had my usual three suitcases, one for my pillow and my coin collection. The doorman helped me take the suitcases up, and I helped him; I held the elevator button so that the door wouldn't close on him while he loaded them on and off. Grandmother's new maid let me in. She was younger and fatter than the new maid was the last time. She told me that I should unpack and that Grandmother would be home shortly.

Grandmother doesn't take me everywhere she goes and I don't take her everywhere I go; but we get along pretty well, Grandmother and I.

She doesn't have any pets, and I don't have any other grandmothers, so I stay with her whenever my mother and my father go abroad; they send me post cards. My friend Clarence has the opposite: three Eiffels and two Coliseums. My mother and my father are very touched that I save their post cards. I also think that it is very nice of me.

I had finished unpacking, and I was wondering why Grandmother didn't wait for me. After all, I am her only grandchild, and I am named Lewis. Lewis was the name of one of her husbands, the one who was my grandfather. Grandmother came home as I was on my way to the kitchen to see if the new maid believed in eating between meals better than the last new maid did.

"Hello, Lewis," Grandmother said.

"Hello, Grandmother," I replied. Sometimes we talk like that, plain talk. Grandmother leaned over for me to kiss her cheek. Neither one of us adores slobbering, or even likes it.

"Are you ready?" I asked.

"Just as soon as I get out of this girdle and these high heels," she answered.

"Take off your hat, too, while you're at it," I suggested. "I'll set things up awhile."

Grandmother joined me in the library. I have taught her double solitaire, fish, cheat, and casino. She has taught me gin rummy; we mostly play gin rummy.

The maid served us supper on trays in the library so that we could watch the news on color TV. Grandmother has only one color TV set, so we watch her programs on Mondays, Wednesdays, Fridays and every other Sunday; we watch mine on Tuesdays, Thursdays, Saturdays and the leftover Sundays. I thought that she could have given me *every* Sunday since I am her only grandchild and I am named Lewis, but Grandmother said, "Share and share alike." And we do. And we get along pretty well, Grandmother and I.

After the news and after supper Grandmother decided to read the newspaper; it is delivered before breakfast but she only reads the ads then. Grandmother sat on the sofa, held the newspaper at the end of her arm, then she squinted and then she tilted her head back and farther back so that all you could see were nostrils, and then she called, "Lewis, Lewis, please bring me my glasses."

I knew she would.

I had to look for them. I always have to look for them. They have pale blue frames and are shaped like sideways commas, and they are never where she thinks they are or where I think they should be: *on the nose of her head.* You should see her trying to dial the telephone without her glasses. She practically stands in the next room and points her finger, and she still gets wrong numbers. I only know that in case of fire, I'll make the call.

I found her glasses. Grandmother began reading messages from the paper as if she were sending telegrams. It is one of her habits I wonder about; I wonder if she does it even when I'm not there. "Commissioner of Parks invites everyone to Central Park tonight," she read.

"What for?" I asked. "A mass mugging?"

"No. Something else."

"What else?"

"Something special."

I waited for what was a good pause before I asked, "What special?"

Grandmother waited for a good pause before she answered, "Something spectacular," not even bothering to look up from the newspaper.

I paused. Grandmother paused. I paused. Grandmother paused. I paused, I paused, I paused, and I won. Grandmother spoke first. "A spectacular show of stars," she said.

"Movie stars or rock and roll?" I inquired politely.

"Star stars," she answered.

"You mean like the sky is full of?"

"Yes, I mean like the sky is full of."

"You mean that the Commissioner of Parks has invited everyone out just to enjoy the night environment?" We were studying environment in our school.

"Not any night environment. Tonight there will be a shower of stars."

"Like a rain shower?" I asked.

"More like a thunderstorm."

"Stars falling like rain can be very dangerous and pollute our environment besides." We were also studying pollution of the environment in our school.

"No, they won't pollute our environment," Grandmother said.

"How do you know?" I asked.

"Because they will burn up before they fall all the way down. Surely you must realize that," she added.

I didn't answer.

"You must realize that they always protect astronauts from burning up on their reentry into the earth's atmosphere."

I didn't answer.

"They give the astronauts a heat shield. Otherwise they'd burn up."

I didn't answer.

"The stars don't have one. A heat shield, that is."

I didn't answer.

"That's why the stars burn up. They don't have a shield. Of course, they aren't really stars, either. They are Leonids."

Then I answered.

"Why don't you tell me about the shower of stars that isn't really a shower and isn't really stars?" She wanted to explain about them. I could tell. That's why I asked.

Grandmother likes to be listened to. That's one reason why she explains things. She prefers being listened to when she *tells* things: like get my elbow off the table and pick up my feet when I walk. She would tell me things like that all day if I would listen all day. When she *explains,* I listen. I sit close and listen close, and that makes her feel like a regular grandmother. She likes that, and sometimes so do I. That's one reason why we get along pretty well.

Grandmother explained about the Leonids.

The Leonids are trash that falls from the comet called Temple-Tuttle. Comets go around the sun just as the planet Earth does. But not quite just like the planet Earth. Comets don't make regular circles around the sun. They loop around the sun, and they leak. Loop and leak. Loop and leak. The parts that leak are called the tail. The path that Earth takes around the sun and the path that Temple-Tuttle takes around the sun were about to cross each other. Parts of the tail would get caught in the earth's atmosphere and light up as they burn up as they fall down. Little bits at a time. A hundred little bits at a time. A thousand little bits at a time. A million bits.

The parts that burn up look like falling stars. That is why Grandmother and the Commissioner of Parks called it a Shower of Stars. The falling stars from Temple-Tuttle are called the Leonids. Leonids happen only once every thirty-three and one-third years. The whole sky over the city would light up with them. The reason that everyone was invited to the park was so that we city people could see a big piece of sky instead of just a hallway of sky between the buildings.

It would be an upside-down Grand Canyon of fireworks.

I decided that we ought to go. Grandmother felt the same way I did. Maybe even more so.

Right after we decided to go, Grandmother made me go to bed. She said that I should be rested and that she would wake me in plenty of time to get dressed and walk to Central Park. She promised to wake me at eleven o'clock.

And I believed her.

I believed her.

I really did believe her.

Grandmother said to me, "Do you think that I want to miss something that happens only three times in one century?"

"Didn't you see it last time?" I asked. After all, there was a Shower of Leonids thirty-three and one-third years ago when she was only thirty, and I'll bet there was no one making her go to bed.

"No, I didn't see it last time," she said.

"What was the matter? Didn't the Commissioner of Parks invite you?"

"No, that was not the matter."

"Why didn't you see it then?"

"Because," she explained.

"Because you forgot your glasses and you didn't have Lewis, Lewis to get them for you?"

"I didn't even wear glasses when I was thirty."

"Then why didn't you see it?"

"Because," she said, "because I didn't bother to find out about it, and I lost my chance."

I said, "Oh." I went to bed. I knew about lost chances.

Grandmother woke me. She made me bundle up. She was bundled, too. She looked sixty-three years lumpy. I knew that she wouldn't like it if I expressed an opinion, so I didn't. Somehow.

We left the apartment.

We found the place in the park. The only part that wasn't crowded was up. Which was all right because that was where the action would be.

The shower of stars was to begin in forty-five minutes.

We waited.
And waited.
And saw.

"What are you crying about?" Grandmother asked. Not kindly.

"I have to wait thirty-three and one-third years before I can see a big spectacular Shower of Stars. I'll be forty-three before I can ever see a Leonid."

"Oh, shut up!" Grandmother said. Not kindly.

"I'll be *middle-aged.*"

"What was that for?" I asked. "What did I do?" I asked. "What did I do?" I asked again. I had always thought that we got along pretty well, my grandmother and I.

"You add it up," Grandmother said. Not kindly.

So I did. I added it up. Sixty-three and thirty-three don't add up to another chance.

I held Grandmother's hand on the way back to her apartment. She let me even though neither one of us adores handholding. I held the hand that hit me.

Copyright © 1971 by E. L. Konigsburg. Illustrations by Laurel Schindelman (The Night of Leonid.) From Altogether, One at a Time. *Used by permission of Atheneum Publishers.*

NATIVE AMERICANS

An ethnic group that has largely been ignored in our society until recently is the native American. Today there is even confusion about which terms to use, as noted by members of the Council on Interracial Books for Children.[6] Native Americans have often been stereotyped in children's literature as "noble savages" or threatening killers, so that it is essential that we search for works that present American Indians realisti-

---

[6] "Terminology" in *Guidelines for the Future, Human—and Anti-Human—Values in Children's Books: A Content Rating Instrument for Educators and Concerned Parents* (The Council on Interracial Books for Children, 1976).

cally and sympathetically. Again, we need books for children that actively combat stereotypes.

Scott O'Dell has done just that in *Sing Down the Moon* (Houghton Mifflin, 1970), a short book that middle graders could enjoy. Based on historical fact regarding white men's treatment of the Indians in the last half of the nineteenth century, the story is told from the viewpoint of Bright Morning, a young Navaho girl. Forced from their home in Canyon de Chelly, the Navaho Indians are impoverished and degraded.

O'Dell's Newbery award winner, *Island of the Blue Dolphins* (Houghton Mifflin, 1960), a sensitive portrayal of an Indian girl, Karana, is also historically factual. The well-developed character Karana is a strong young woman who capably handles both the psychological as well as the physical problems of existing alone. The reader is also given a realistic picture of the culture Karana represents.

James Forman's *The Life and Death of Yellow Bird* (Farrar, Straus & Giroux, 1973) tells of Yellow Bird, a young Cheyenne who lived during the battles of Little Big Horn and Wounded Knee. This historical novel also provides an accurate picture of the struggles of the Indians to survive.

Ann Nolan Clark, who taught for many years in schools for Indian children, has written a number of excellent books, such as *Circle of Seasons* (Farrar, Straus & Giroux, 1970), which describes ceremonies of the Pueblo Indians. This nonfiction for middle graders tells of the Indians living in New Mexico on the same sites that their ancestors occupied for hundreds of years, observing the days, the "lawgivers."

A Pueblo Indian lives by his days, and as each day is lived, so shapes his year. A day is not an unplanned happening, not merely a new dawn following the sunset of yesterday. . . . Each day has been determined and patterned by the cumulative wisdom of the Ancients, who walked, uncounted centuries ago, along this same trail of Pueblo living. It has been determined by ritual and patterned by tradition, formed not by man-made laws—arbitrary and artificial—but by natural laws that are in harmony with the Earth Mother who gave them being. (p. 5)

Other books by Ann Nolan Clark include Newbery award winner *Secret of the Andes, In My Mother's House, Paco's Miracle, Medicine Man's Daughter,* and *Summer Is for Growing.*

An excellent book to provide a sympathetic pictorial story of the American Indian tribes is the biography of artist George Catlin, *Indian Gallery* (Four Winds, 1973). Catlin traveled among the Indian tribes and made friends so that he could paint Indian subjects and collect artifacts for an Indian museum. Written by Mary Sayre Haverstock, the book includes hundreds of reproductions.

Patricia Beatty's *The Bad Bell of San Salvador* (Morrow, 1973) is set in the Spanish Southwest of the 1840s. Jacinto, a thirteen-year-old Comanche boy, has been a slave from the age of ten. Throughout his experiences he struggles to keep his Indian identity including his Indian name, Spotted Wild Horse.

Lone Bull's Horse Raid (Bradbury, 1973) is beautifully illustrated by Paul Goble, as shown in the color section. Written by Paul and Dorothy Goble, this book is historically sound. The authors first present information about the Plains Indians and their practice of stealing horses from enemy tribes. As they observe realistically: "Raiding each others' horse herds was the greatest single cause of inter-tribal wars; it gave great excitement and offered rich rewards." Following the factual presentation, the authors tell the story of fourteen-year-old Lone Bull, an Oglala Sioux boy, as he participates in his first raid against the Crow Indians. Although it may be labeled a picture book, this book would be useful through junior high school.

Another fine picture book is the 1975 Caldecott award winner *Arrow to the Sun: A Pueblo Indian Tale* (Viking, 1974). Written and illustrated by Gerald McDermott the story tells of a boy's growing up.

An especially fine writer about American Indians and Eskimos is James Houston. His tale of the Northwest Indians, *Eagle Mask* (Harcourt Brace Jovanovich, 1966), tells of the coming of age of Skemshan. In *Ghost Paddle* (Harcourt Brace Jovanovich, 1972) Houston again writes of an adolescent boy, Hooits, who longs for peace between his people and the Inland River people. In telling these fictional stories Houston is also able to reveal the patterns of living, the beliefs, and practices of the Indian tribes. A distinctive contribution he has made to this literature is *Songs of the Dream People* (Atheneum, 1972), a collection of songs and chants.

Another interesting collection of poetry has been edited by Terry Allen. *The Whispering Wind* (Doubleday, 1972) is poetry written by young Americans from the Institute of American Indian Arts. Contributions are by Eskimo, Aleut, and American Indian students.

Other fine collections of Indian poetry, songs, chants, prayers, and orations include the following:

Bierhorst, John, ed. *In the Trail of the Wind; American Indian Poems and Ritual Orations.* Farrar, Straus & Giroux, 1971.

Hofmann, Charles. *American Indians Sing.* John Day, 1967.

Jones, Hettie, comp. *The Trees Stand Shining; Poetry of the North American Indians*. Dial, 1971.

Wood, Nancy. *Hollering Sun*. Simon and Schuster, 1972.

A very timely book that adds insight into what it means to be both Indian as well as a woman is *American Indian Women* (Hawthorn, 1974) by Marion E. Gridley. The lives of nineteen women are described, ranging over a period of three hundred years and representing widely varied roles.

Several books are now available that feature the folklore of American Indians. Based on Papago and Pima myths is *At the Center of the World* (Macmillan, 1973) by Betty Baker, which includes six myths derived from anthropological findings about the Arizona Indians. *Legends of the Great Chiefs* (Nelson, 1972) is another work that focuses on the Pacific Coastal tribes. Emerson N. Matson describes the lives of such famous Indian chiefs as Sitting Bull and Crazy Horse, but he also provides much information about the general customs and taboos of these tribes. *Coyote Tales* (Holt, 1975), adapted by Hettie Jones and illustrated by Louis Mofsie, is a collection of stories about Coyote, the trickster in Indian lore.

Gradually there is developing a sizable body of literature about American Indians. Listed in the *Children's Catalog* under the heading Nondominant Groups, you will find such titles of fiction as these:

Baker, Betty, *And One Was a Wooden Indian*. Macmillan, 1970.

Bales, Carol Ann. *Kevin Cloud; Chippewa Boy in the City*. Reilly & Lee, 1972.

Baylor, Byrd. *When Clay Sings*. Scribner, 1972.

Benchley, Nathaniel. *Small Wolf*. Harper & Row, 1972.

Clymer, Eleanor. *The Spider, the Cave and the Pottery Bowl*. Atheneum, 1971.

Fife, Dale. *Ride the Crooked Wind*. Coward-McCann, 1973.

Griese, Arnold A. *At the Mouth of the Luckiest River*. Thomas Y. Crowell, 1973.

Harris, Christie. *Raven's Cry*. Atheneum, 1966.

Jones, Weyman. *Edge of Two Worlds*. Dial, 1968.

Lampman, Evelyn Sibley. *The Year of Small Shadow*. Harcourt Brace Jovanovich, 1971.

Peake, Katy. *The Indian Heart of Carrie Hodges*. Viking, 1972.

Sleator, William. *The Angry Moon*. Little, Brown, 1970.

Williams, Barbara. *The Secret Name*. Harcourt Brace Jovanovich, 1972.

Wolf, Bernard. *Tinker and the Medicine Man: The Story of a Navajo Boy of Monument Valley*. Random House, 1973.

In addition to the book about native American women, there are a number of biographies about native Americans, for example:

Geronimo, Apache Chief

Wilson, Charles Morrow. *Geronimo*. Dillon, 1973.

Susette La Flesche

Crary, Margaret. *Susette La Flesche: Voice of the Omaha Indians*. Hawthorn, 1973. (*A chief's daughter who spoke for Indian rights in the nineteenth century.*)

Cochise, Apache Chief

Wyatt, Edgar. *Cochise, Apache Warrior and Statesman*. McGraw-Hill, 1973.

Joseph, Nez Percé Chief

David, Russell and Brent Ashabranner. *Chief Joseph, War Chief of the Nez Percé*. McGraw-Hill, 1962.

Ishi

Kroeber, Theodora. *Ishi: Last of His Tribe*. Parnassus Press, 1964.

Pocahontas

Bulla, Clyde. *Pocahontas and the Strangers*. Thomas Y. Crowell, 1971.

Maria Tallchief

Tobias, Tobi. *Maria Tallchief*. Thomas Y. Crowell, 1970.

Explore other nonfiction about native Americans to discover such titles as these:

D'Amato, Janet. *American Indian Craft Inspirations*. M. Evans, 1972.

Folsom, Franklin. *Red Power on the Rio Grande: The Nature of the American Revolution of 1680*. Follett, 1973.

Glubok, Shirley. *The Art of the Southwest Indians*. Macmillan, 1971.

Hays, Wilma P. *Foods the Indians Gave Us*. Washburn, 1973.

Hofsinde, Robert. *Indian Arts*. Morrow, 1971.

Vlahos, Olivia. *New World Beginnings; Indian Cultures in the Americas*. Viking, 1970.

Robert Hofsinde has written a number of excellent books on Indian culture, in addition to *Indian Arts* listed above. Titles you would find useful include: *The Indian Medicine Man* (Morrow, 1966), *Indian Music Makers* (Morrow, 1967), and *Indians on the Move* (Morrow, 1970).

MEXICAN-AMERICANS OR CHICANOS

Americans whose ancestry is Mexican have been featured in very few books for children until recent efforts gave this group more publicity. There is still confusion in the use of such terms as *Chicano,* which means Mexican-American, and *Spanish,* a term that refers to someone from Spain. Although the more than 400,000 Americans who speak Spanish include persons with Puerto Rican and Latin American origins, we focus in this section on those whose roots are Mexican. Children's literature offers opportunities for a multicultural approach to education that benefits all children. We will examine the following aspects of Mexican-American literature to promote understanding for and about children with this background:

1. Fiction about Mexican-American children in the United States

2. Fiction set in Mexico

3. Mexican folklore

4. Poetry from Mexico

5. Biographies of Mexican-American heroes

6. Nonfiction about Mexican-Americans or Chicanos

Well-written fiction provides one way for all students to gain understanding of the special problems Chicano children face. *Graciela: A Mexican-American Child Tells Her Story* (Watts, 1972), edited by Joe Molnar, is the story of twelve-year-old Graciela's life as a member of a migrant family. Each year the family of ten children moves from Texas to Michigan to pick produce. Graciela describes the prejudice expressed against Mexican-Americans and the family's battle to become better educated. Children with Mexican-American backgrounds can identify with Graciela's problems.

Similar to Graciela's story is that of twelve-year-old Yolanda in *Go Up the Road* (Atheneum, 1972) by Evelyn S. Lampman. Yolanda moved so much as a member of a Chicano migrant family that it was hard to finish the work for fifth grade, even though she tried hard.

Using Spanish words in context is another practice that makes the reader more aware of the knowledge of Spanish as an ability that not everyone has. Barbara Todd uses this technique in a book for primary grade readers, *Juan Patricio* (Putnam, 1972). Juan, who lives in Santa Fe with his family, has a problem that all children can share: he wants a job.

The child who does not speak English at all has special problems functioning in an American neighborhood where most people speak English. Marie Hall Ets writes a sympathetic story, *Bad Boy, Good Boy* (Thomas Y. Crowell, 1967), about young Roberto who is often punished because he simply does not understand. Here is a realistic picture of confused parents who quarrel and a teacher who is human enough to get angry. Roberto is helped to learn skills so that he can function successfully.

Mexicali Soup (Parents' Magazine Press, 1970) is the story of a Chicano family that has moved to the city. Kathryn Hitte and William B. Hayes describe the children's fears that they will be found different from other city dwellers. Mama teaches them a lesson about keeping up with the Joneses. She helps them value their own ways of doing things.

Leo Politi's stories of Mexican-American children in Los Angeles were written some time ago, but they still have much to offer, particularly through the beautiful illustrations. *Pedro, the Angel of Olvera Street* (Scribner, 1946) is the story of Pedro, who was chosen to lead La Posada in the traditional Christmas celebrations. *Juanita* (Scribner, 1948) is also set on atmospheric Olvera Street, where the reader joins in another Mexican celebration, the Blessing of the Animals. Later Politi writes of *Rosa* (Scribner, 1963), a girl who wants a beautiful doll for Christmas but receives instead a tiny baby sister.

Other books that will be helpful in developing understanding of Mexican-Americans are:

Bonham, Frank. *Viva Chicano*. Dutton, 1970.

Colman, Hila. *Chicano Girl*. Morrow, 1973.

Garthwaite, Marian. *Tomás and the Red-Haired Angel*. Messner, 1966.

Krumgold, Joseph. *. . . And Now Miguel*. Thomas Y. Crowell, 1970.

Norman, James. *Charro: Mexican Horseman*. Putnam, 1970.

Ritchie, Barbara. *Ramón Makes a Trade/Los cambios de Ramón*. Parnassus Press, 1959.

Stories set in Mexico may also help develop greater understanding of people with different backgrounds. Told in the first person by Ramón Salazar, *The Black Pearl* (Houghton Mifflin, 1967) is by Scott O'Dell. Ramón dives for pearls in hopes of finding the great Pearl of Heaven. When he does find the beautiful black pearl that weighs more than sixty-two carats, his father gives it to the church as a gift of the House of Salazar, because local dealers will not pay the price he asks. The pearl, however, belongs to the Manta Diablo, the giant shark, which takes its revenge on the family of Salazar.

Another interesting story set in Mexico is *Hill of Fire* (Harper & Row, 1971) by Thomas P. Lewis. Pablo and his father are plowing in the field when the huge volcano Paricutín begins to erupt. Here is the story of the eruption told for primary grades through a young boy's eyes.

Elizabeth Coatsworth also writes of Mexico in *The Place* (Holt, 1966). Ellen, whose father is an archeologist, becomes friends with Jorgé and his sister, Natividad. They show her the Place, a huge limestone cave filled with valuable artifacts. Ellen does not reveal the site of this secret worship place, however, because of loyalty to her Mexican friends who have shared the secret with her.

The humorous story of Chucho is set in a small Mexican village. Written by Francis Kalnay, *It Happened in Chichipica* (Harcourt Brace Jovanovich, 1971) tells of Chucho's efforts to get an education. The characters of the baker, Don Rodolfo, for whom he works, and his uncle, Don Pepe, are both delightful and heart-warming.

Evelyn Lampman developed a historical novel, *The Tilted Sombrero* (Doubleday, 1966), around the Mexican War of Independence in 1810. Thirteen-year-old Nando, proud of his Spanish heritage, is chagrined to find that he has an Indian grandmother. Gradually, however, he comes to identify with the cause of the mestizos and to be proud of this heritage.

Mexican folklore, too, provides an important avenue to understanding a different culture. Explore some of these representative titles:

Brenner, A. *The Boy Who Could Do anything and Other Mexican Folk Tales*. Young Scott Books. Addison-Wesley, 1942.

Campbell, Camilla. *Star Mountain and Other Legends of Mexico*. McGraw-Hill, 1968.

Ross, Patricia F. *In Mexico They Say*. Knopf, 1942.

Traven, B. *The Creation of the Sun and the Moon*. Hill & Wang, 1968.

Poems from Mexico can be included in a class study of poetry. An especially fine collection of poetry is *2-Rabbit, 7-Wind* (Viking, 1971) by Toni de Gerez. The poems reflect ancient Mexico and are adapted from Nahuatl Indian texts. This book is not only informative but also very attractively produced. Richard Lewis has edited *Still Waters of the Air: Poems by Three Modern Spanish Poets* (Dial, 1970). Children will also enjoy *Mother Goose in Spanish/Poesías de la Madre Oca* (Thomas Y. Crowell, 1968) by Alastair Reid and Anthony Kerrigan.

Another important aspect of promoting understanding of the Chicanos is knowledge of Chicano heroes and the problems this minority group has faced. *César Chávez* (Thomas Y. Crowell, 1970), written by Ruth Franchere, is a simple biography that can be read by middle graders and even better primary readers. This biography presents the background of Chávez, how his family came to work as migrant laborers and to experience real poverty. The author follows Chávez' activities until he founds the United Farm Workers Organizing Committee (UFWOC) and participates in the strike and boycott of vineyards at Delano, California.

Twenty Mexican-American biographies are presented by Clarke Newlon in *Famous Mexican-Americans* (Dodd, Mead, 1972). President of Mexico, Benito Pablo Juarez is presented in *Juarez: The Founder of Modern Mexico* (Morrow, 1972) by Ronald Syme. This realistic picture of Juarez is based on accurate primary sources. A contemporary American sports figure, golfer Lee Trevino, is introduced in *Supermex: The Lee Trevino Story* (Walck, 1973) by Robert B. Jackson.

In addition to biographies, we find such nonfiction as Arnold Dobrin's book *The New Life—La Vida Nueva: The Mexican Americans Today* (Dodd, Mead, 1971), which provides an overview of Chicano history. The author effectively uses the interview technique as he presents individual Mexican-Americans. His presentation brings out such typical qualities as family solidarity and the strong role of the Catholic Church in the Chicano's life.

Patricia Miles Martin has written another book that provides historical backgrounds for the Chicano entitled *Chicanos; Mexicans in the United States* (Parents' Magazine Press, 1971). Both historical and contemporary developments are presented.

There is still a great need for good fiction and nonfiction featuring Mexican-Americans in the United States, for they are not adequately portrayed considering the high percentages they represent in many cities today.

❦ *EXPLORING REALISTIC PERSPECTIVES* Choose one of the following activities to extend your knowledge of books about groups within the American culture.

1. Select a group that is present in your community. Collect as much information about this group as possible. Find children's books that would be helpful in promoting intergroup understanding. Set up a learning center that focuses on this group.

2. Research both fiction and nonfiction that features Americans of different religious backgrounds. Compile a list of selected titles that you would recommend for purchase by any elementary school library.

3. Choose one of the groups that are discussed in detail in this chapter. Plan several lessons that you could present to a specific class using the material described. Aim at breaking down stereotypes.

REALISTIC PERSPECTIVES FOR THE CLASSROOM

Through the written word I want to give children a love for the arts that will provoke creative thought and activity. All children are creative. They create music, art, poetry, dances, daydreams and nightmares, fads, myths, and—as I'm sure you know—mischief. A strong love for the arts can enhance and direct their creativity as well as provide satisfying moments throughout their lives.

Thus states Eloise Greenfield, a black writer of realistic books for children, speaking before a large group of teachers attending the International Reading Association Convention in 1975. She says, furthermore: "I want to encourage children to develop positive attitudes toward themselves and their abilities, to love themselves. . . . I want to write stories that will allow children to fall in love with genuine Black heroes and heroines who have proved themselves to be outstanding in ability and in dedication to the cause of Black freedom. . . . I want to be one of those who can choose and order words that children will want to celebrate. I want to make them shout and laugh and blink back tears and care about themselves. They are our future. They are beautiful. They are for loving."

Consider your own role as a teacher of children. What do you want to do for the young people with whom you work? Can any of these aims be met through the use of literature with children? Can you help this author achieve some of the things she wants to do through her writing? In the following pages we will explore possibilities.

IN PRAISE OF AUTHORS

We share stories with children, but we seldom think about sharing authors with our students. Authors are people. Children might be more interested in reading the books these authors have written if they knew more about them as people. As in preceding chapters, we present several authors who have contributed outstanding realistic fiction for children.

VERA AND BILL CLEAVER Vera Cleaver was born in South Dakota, the fifth of eleven children, two of whom were adopted. She was the only one who was totally engrossed with books. Bill Cleaver is a former Air Force sergeant. They had many varied experiences before they began writing children's books. Vera once worked, for example, keeping books for a casket maker, and Bill once took a course in horology. They have lived in Japan and France, but when they were tired of living abroad, they settled in Boone, North Carolina, a tiny mountain community in the Smoky Mountains, where they began writing. They now live in Lutz, Florida. Books by the Cleavers include:

Photograph of Vera and Bill Cleaver by George Flowers

Ellen Grae

Grover

Lady Ellen Grae

Where the Lilies Bloom

Dust of the Earth

I Would Rather Be a Turnip

Vera and Bill Cleaver present realism with great finesse, developing unusually strong characters who are often girls. A good example is *Ellen Grae* (Lippincott, 1967) and the sequel, *Lady Ellen Grae* (Lippincott, 1968). Ellen's parents are divorced, a fact that is handled with equanimity. In the second book Ellen realizes that she can still depend on her parents. Ellen also appears in *Grover* (Lippincott, 1970), the story of a young boy whose mother is dying of cancer. When she kills herself because she cannot bear the pain, Grover and the reader experience grief together.

I Would Rather Be a Turnip (Lippincott, 1971) describes Annie's discomfort when she finds that eight-year-old Calvin, her nephew, is coming to stay with them, for Calvin is illegitimate, and Annie is ashamed. She learns, however, that the thinking of prejudiced people need not affect her and that Calvin is a lovable, bright boy whom she simply cannot hate. Both the father and a black housekeeper are well-developed characters also.

Where the Lilies Bloom (Lippincott, 1969) is a fascinating tale by the Cleavers of fourteen-year-old Mary Call, her brother, and her sisters who struggle to survive in Trails Valley in the Smokies through "wildcrafting," harvesting the medicinal roots and plants that grow in abundance. Assuming responsibility for the family and coping with her father's death is a frightening burden for Mary Call. Protecting her retarded older sister, Devola, is an added concern as is the welfare of Ima Dean and Romey, the younger children.

For Devola I have many fears and I have others, too. Some for our paternal parent, Roy Luther, and some for Ima Dean and Romey and a few for myself also. They are not rash. They are not just things that happened to fritter into my mind because nothing else was there to busy it. They are old fears with me.

Oh, I feel it, this bottomless stomach of fright when I look at Devola and see her so free and innocent, so womanly in form but with a child's heart and a child's mind. I feel it when I watch Ima Dean and Romey at their make-believe games. So carefree they are with never a thought in their little heads as to how they're going to get decently raised. And when I look at Roy Luther who is coughing his life away. (We know now that it isn't just worms that turn him so white and panting weak though we keep doctoring, laying out hope each time along with the salves and other medications.)

Photograph of Norma Klein by Gail Rubin

This book was made into a fine film that has been enjoyed by both young people and adults.

Dust of the Earth (Lippincott, 1975) is set in South Dakota and tells about fourteen-year-old Fern Drawn's life on a sheep ranch that her parents have inherited. This book presents an especially positive image of a young woman who is resourceful and courageous.

NORMA KLEIN Born in New York City on May 13, 1938, Norma Klein is the daughter of a psychoanalyst. She married a biochemist and has two children. She attended Cornell University, received a bachelor's degree from Barnard, and a master's degree from Columbia University.

Norma Klein lives in New York and is a freelance writer who had published more than sixty short stories for adult readers before she began writing for children. Her books for young people include:

If I Had It My Way

It's Not What You Expect

Girls Can Be Anything

Confessions of an Only Child

Mom, the Wolf Man and Me

Taking Sides

What It's All About

Norma Klein is another author who stands out in her ability to handle sensitive subjects. *Confessions of an Only Child* (Pantheon, 1974), the story of two contemporary young girls, includes a premature birth and the subsequent death of a baby. The mother's genuine grief and her daughter's guilt feelings about the baby's death are presented without sentimentality.

The parents, as portrayed by Norma Klein, are open and loving with their young daughter; they are also permitted to have feelings that they accept and share with Toe. Here is a realistic approach to life that reflects contemporary philosophies. Shortly after the baby dies, Toe returns home from school to find her mother crying.

I felt so funny. I didn't know mommies ever cried. When she heard me, Mom looked up and began sniffing and saying, "Oh Ant . . . is it three already?"

I pounced on her and began patting her. It made me so sad to see her cry. I thought I might cry. "Don't cry, Mom."

"I won't, Toe . . . I don't know why I did. It's silly . . . I should get out really."

"Are you still sad about the baby?" I said. "Sometimes if I think about the baby my eyes feel wet at the corners."

She nodded. "I guess. But I know we'll have a baby sometime. So I shouldn't . . . Toe, let's take William and Elvira down, okay? I think I just need some fresh air, that's all." (p. 64)

Frank discussions of sex are part of her *Mom, the Wolf Man and Me* (Pantheon, 1972), which describes an unmarried mother's fine relationship with her eleven-year-old daughter Brett. Brett is horrified when her mother decides to marry.

> A week or two later a horrible thing happened. I was sound asleep, when all of a sudden Mom woke me up. She didn't even click on the light, so I could at least see who it was. She said she and Theo were getting married.
>
> I really felt horribly sick. I can't even describe it. At first, I thought she said they *had* gotten married, without even telling me. But to hear that they were going to do it anyway was more than I could believe. I couldn't believe Theo would do that after I had that long talk with him and told him how bad it would be.
>
> "You'll have a father!" Mom said. She looked really excited and happy.
>
> "I don't want one," I said.

Feminist Norma Klein states that she is "trying to show life as it appears to be, and especially, to try and avoid pernicious moralizing . . . and of course, as I am a feminist, I want freer, more interesting portraits of girls and mothers and aunts."

EMILY CHENEY NEVILLE   The child of an economist, Emily Neville was born on December 28, 1919, in Manchester, Connecticut. She married a newspaperman and they have five children. She has a bachelor's degree from Bryn Mawr, and now lives in Keene Valley, New York. She began her career as a journalist, but soon turned to the writing of books for young people. Books she has written include:

The Seventeenth-Street Gang

Traveler from a Small Kingdom

Old Gumshoe

The Sacred Cow (Fables)

Berries Goodman

It's Like This, Cat

It's Like This, Cat is an excellent story of a boy's efforts to get along with his father. Emily Neville says she was tired of stories about a boy and his dog, so she decided to write one about a boy and a cat for a change.

Berries Goodman by Emily C. Neville (Harper & Row, 1965) is the delightful story of Bertrand, commonly known as "Berries," and his fam-

Photograph of Emily Neville

ily. Emily Neville portrays the problems of a Jewish family moving from comfortable New York City to a suburb where Jews are not accepted. Berries is clearly an outsider until he meets Sidney Fine, who becomes his best friend despite opposition. Realistic handling of interpersonal relations is revealed in this passage:

Dad said, "Listen, Berries, I'm sorry it's like this, but will you promise me not to meet Sidney anymore? Because I pretty much promised Mr. Fine."

"So you already promised." I could feel my lip sticking out, the way it does when I think someone's pushing me into a corner.

"Well, it's just . . . I mean, I don't want to tell Mom she's got to *watch* you every minute. Let's just make a gentlemen's agreement."

I sat staring at the floor and blinking my eyes, because I had that awful feeling again.

"O.K.?" Dad asked.

I jumped out of the car and shouted at him over my shoulder. "You're my father, you can just *tell* me! You don't have to pretend it's any old gentlemen's agreement! It's not!"

I left him sitting there.

This author says, "My writing is probably an outgrowth of my childhood in a large clannish New England family, mingled with my own quite different experiences raising five children in New York City."

PAUL ZINDEL Born on May 15, 1936, in New York City, Paul Zindel is a playwright. His best known play is *The Effect of Gamma Rays on Man-in-the-Moon Marigolds,* first produced in 1965 and later made into an excellent film, which demonstrates the author's understanding of human emotions and his ability to put them into words. A former high school chemistry teacher, he has written several novels for adolescent readers:

I Never Loved Your Mind

My Darling, My Hamburger

The Pigman

Pardon Me, You're Stepping on My Eyeball

The Undertaker Goes Bananas

Photograph of Paul Zindel by Gino

Zindel's work has been criticized because he is more realistic than some people would like. In *My Darling, My Hamburger* (Harper & Row,

1969), for example, he discusses sex and contraception in general, and teenage sexuality with the explicit example of the character Liz becoming pregnant and having an abortion. By contrast, his one picture book, *I Love My Mother* (Harper, 1972), is a beautiful expression of love.

The Pigman (Harper & Row, 1968) is an especially fine novel, and one that is very teachable. Zindel has used an unusual and interesting technique for presenting the story: John Conlan and Lorraine Jensen, two alienated teenagers, take turns writing the chapters, which most fittingly are short and written in teenage idiom. High school sophomores, they write the story as a kind of memorial epic after Mr. Pignati dies.

John and Lorraine meet Angelo Pignati first via the telephone when they are playing the game of dialing someone's number and asking for a contribution to a fictitious charity. Eager to talk, the lonely man agrees to make a contribution, so they go to his home. Both John and Lorraine are glad to get away from homes that are far from congenial, so they visit the Pigman frequently. After one riotous game on roller skates, the Pigman has a heart attack and has to go to the hospital. While he is gone, they continue going to his house. One night friends join them, which results in a party that leaves the house in a mess with Mr. Pignati's collection of china pigs broken. Unfortunately he returns before John and Lorraine can clean up the mess, and he is visibly disillusioned. Later he accepts their offer to go with him again to the zoo and visit his favorite animal, the baboon. When he arrives, however, feeble and ill, he finds that his friend the baboon has died. Mr. Pignati slumps to the floor, dead. The boy and girl look at each other. As John writes in the final chapter:

There was no one else to blame anymore. No Bores or Old Ladies or Nortons, or Assassins waiting at the bridge. And there was no place to hide—no place across any river for a boatman to take us.

Our life would be what we made of it—nothing more, nothing less.

This synopsis cannot do justice, of course, to the sensitive treatment Paul Zindel has accorded this story. He writes with vigor and wit and has produced a story that is a strange mixture of humor and tragedy, a book well worth reading. The same loving sensitivity that characterizes all of his writing appears again in his picture book for young children, *I Love My Mother*.

An important part of any literature program should focus on the authors who have produced the books. As you prepare to teach with a particular book, see what you can discover about the author. Anecdotal information is included, for example, in *More Books by More People* (Citation Press, 1974) by Lee Bennett Hopkins. Factual information is presented in the extensive reference work *Contemporary Authors,* which is in most public libraries.

Celebrate the birthdays of authors occasionally as you casually mention, "Did you know that Norma Klein was born on this date? Let's celebrate her birthday by reading a book she has written." (Many such birth dates are inserted here and there throughout this text.)

As you discuss a book, too, mention the author. Why do you think he chose this setting? What was her intent in making Poll do that? Some times an interesting quotation from the author can lead to a lively discussion. Paul Zindel, for example, moved around a lot. In *Current Biography,* he is quoted as saying:

South Beach was Sicily; Silver Lake was Alexandria; Tottenville was the Congo. . . . By the time I was ten, I had gone nowhere but had seen the world.

What does he mean? What does this statement tell you about this author?

You might also focus attention on realistic books that have received awards, for example:

The Newbery Medal

1951—*Amos Fortune, Free Man* by Elizabeth Yates

1961—*Island of the Blue Dolphins* by Scott O'Dell

1971—*Summer of the Swans* by Betsy Byars

The Hans Christian Andersen Award

1966—Author Tove Jansson from Finland
(See *The Summer Book,* page 177)

The National Book Award

1969—*Journey from Peppermint Street* by Meindert DeJong

Institute your own award in your classroom. Decide on the criteria for selection, and have fun reading as the nominees are decided on. Then hold an election!

TEACHING A NOVEL

Select novels to teach in your classroom as part of the reading or language arts curriculum. As a whole group experience, you can have class sets of a specific book. Or you can depend on reading the chapters aloud to the group and have several copies available for individual student examination. The learning center approach can be used to develop a study based on one novel, the work of one author, or on the novel as a genre. In this section we examine two novels that are worth studying: *The Peppermint Pig* by Nina Bawden and *From the Mixed-Up Files of Mrs. Basil E. Frankweiler* by Elaine Konigsburg. For ideas about planning literature lessons refer to the end of Chapter 3.

The Peppermint Pig by Nina Bawden. Lippincott, 1975.
Born on January 19, 1925, in London, Nina Mary Mabey Bawden Kark was educated at Somerville College at Oxford University and holds both bachelor's and master's degrees. She has three children. Before she began writing books for children, she was known as an author of novels for adults, such as *Change Here for Babylon* and *In Honour Bound*. Her stories for children include:

Photograph of Nina Bawden by Jerry Bauer

The Peppermint Pig

Carrie's War

Three on the Run

The White Horse Gang

The Witch's Daughter

The Runaway Summer

A Handful of Thieves

   The Peppermint Pig is about Poll, a nine-year-old girl, and her brother who is ten, so the story will probably appeal most to children between the ages of eight and eleven. It is a meaty book, however, written by a skilled author, so older students might enjoy it, too. The characters include:

Mother—a strong female character

Father—away from home through most of the story

Poll—likeable, adventurous, with human failings

Theo—sensitive about being small for his age

Annie Dowsett—a poor girl whose family lives nearby

Two aunts—almost direct opposites

Johnny—the Peppermint Pig

As the story begins, Father, James Greengrass, has lost his position because he will not divulge the guilt of his employer's son. The stigma attached to his loss of position makes him decide to go to America. Mother and the children remain in England, but move to the country to live with Aunt Sarah and Aunt Harriet.

The characterization in this book is especially good. Poll is impetuous and full of mischief. Theo is often annoyed because children tease him about being small. Both children love Johnny, the little runt pig that becomes a family pet. The mother is a well-delineated character, a strong woman who manages effectively when she unexpectedly becomes head of the household. Even minor characters are clearly distinctive.

Nina Bawden writes with sensitivity of the relationships within the family. Love and concern are expressed, but there is also anger. When Poll returns after running away from home and frightening the whole family, she is tired and wants only to be cuddled by her mother. The family, in a most normal manner, reacts angrily in their relief: "You naughty girl . . ." Poll's reaction is also consistent:

Poll closed her ears and her mind and let the waves of their anger break over her. When they seemed to have tired themselves out, she said calmly, "I'm all right, what's the fuss about?"

Mother let out her breath in a sigh and sat down. She looked sick and exhausted and Poll wanted to run to her but Aunt Harriet stood in the way. Her eyes glittered and her mouth was down at the corners. "Is that all you can say when your poor mother's been half out of her mind with the worry?"

Confused and hurt, Poll retorts: "Not my fault if she's stupid." Righteously, Aunt Harriet begins another tirade from which Poll retreats shouting, "Damn you, damn the whole blasted lot of you, damn you to hell!"

This book could be read aloud to a group of third or fourth graders, providing a foundation for activities as each chapter is completed. It could also be included as part of a learning center designed to motivate reading and to develop specific understandings about literature. In either case, activities should be varied to provide for different modes of learning and should include speaking and listening as well as reading and writing.

Following are a number of activities that might be incorporated in this study:

1. Write a description of Poll as you imagine her. Use any clues the author gives you. Then draw a picture of her as you have described her. (Prepare a bulletin board for these pictures with the caption "Poll.")

2. Read the first paragraph of this book, which begins: "Old Granny Greengrass had her finger chopped off in the butcher's when she was buying half a leg of lamb." Look at the beginnings of other stories in your library. Compare these story starters, to see how an author tries to get your attention immediately. Which beginnings are best in your opinion? (Arrange for small group discussion about this topic; refer to the information when children are writing original stories.)

3. Select an incident in this story to dramatize for the rest of the class. Work with a small group to develop the action and dialogue. (The whole class can be involved with this activity if each group selects a different incident. These minidramas can be presented in sequence even if the whole story is not presented.)

4. What is your impression of Aunt Harriet? Does your feeling about her change during the story? Discuss this topic in your group. Refer to passages in the book that substantiate your argument. (Multiple copies of the book should be available.)

5. How does Poll feel when Johnny is taken to the butcher's? Have you ever lost a pet? Write about your own feelings when you lost a pet, or describe how you felt when Poll lost hers.

Photograph of Elaine L. Konigsburg used by permission of Atheneum Publishers

From the Mixed-Up Files of Mrs. Basil E. Frankweiler by E. L. Konigsburg. Atheneum, 1967.

Elaine L. Konigsburg was born in New York City but lived much of her early years in Pennsylvania. She obtained a bachelor's degree in chemistry from Carnegie Institute of Technology in Pittsburgh and taught chemistry in a private girls' school in Florida. After her marriage and the birth of three children, she pursued her interest in art, and she began writing. As she stated in her acceptance speech when she received the Newbery Medal for *From the Mixed-up Files of Mrs. Basil E. Frankweiler* in 1968: "I spread words on paper for the same reasons that Cro-Magnon man spread pictures on the walls of caves. I need to see it put down . . . writing it down adds another dimension to reality and satisfies an atavistic need." Books by E. L. Konigsburg include:

From the Mixed-Up Files of Mrs. Basil E. Frankweiler

Jennifer, Hecate, Macbeth, William McKinley, and Me, Elizabeth

About the B'nai Bagels

George

Altogether, One at a Time

207

*REALISTIC
PERSPECTIVES OF
LIFE FOR CHILDREN*

From the Mixed-Up Files of Mrs. Basil E. Frankweiler is set in New York City in general, and in the Metropolitan Museum of Art, in particular. The main character, Claudia, is almost twelve, so the book will probably appeal to students ranging from ten to possibly fourteen, depending on their sophistication. The humor of the situation and the audacity of Claudia Kincaid and her nine-year-old brother, Jamie, serve to broaden the interest span. Imagine the problems of trying to live in an art museum! The characters in this story include:

Claudia Kincaid—an inventive and determined young woman

Jamie Kincaid—the second youngest of her three brothers

Mrs. Frankweiler—narrator of the story, an eighty-two-year-old woman

Claudia, a good organizer, and Jamie, her younger brother, run away from home because Claudia wants to gain some appreciation around home. She and Jamie "complemented each other perfectly. She was cautious (about everything but money) and poor; he was adventurous (about everything but money) and rich." Claudia plans no ordinary running away. She wants to go "to a large place; a comfortable place, an indoor place, and preferably a beautiful place." So she chooses the Metropolitan Museum of Art, a most unlikely but suitable place. This humorous tale is narrated by Mrs. Basil E. Frankweiler, who owns the beautiful statue in the museum that intrigues Claudia. No one is sure who created the sculpture, but the children discover that it may have been Leonardo da Vinci. They find the file about the statue and discover that Mrs. Frankweiler lives in Farmington, so they go to visit her.

Here, again, this book would be excellent for reading aloud because the situation is so humorous. It could also, of course, be part of a learning center focused on literature, or even one developed around the city because the information about New York City and the museum is considerable. The following kinds of activities might add to learnings derived from this book.

1. Describe Jamie's reaction when Claudia tells him she has chosen him to accompany her on this trip. How would you feel if an older brother

or sister invited you to go along on such an escapade? (Arrange time for sharing these reactions, either written or oral, as they will probably be humorous.)

2. Paint a picture of your favorite scene from this story. Tell why you chose that particular happening. (Prepare display space for these pictures.)

3. Discuss the ending of this story with a small group. What does it mean? Do you think it is appropriate? Would you change it in any way? (Provide time for small group discussion about this topic and others you may wish to include.)

4. Choose one of the following:
   a. Enlarge one of the maps on pages 48 and 49 of the book to display on a table in your classroom.
   b. Make a time line of the events that happened to Claudia and Jamie.
   c. Why did Claudia include each of the items on her list on page 145 as they prepared to find information about the statue?

These approaches are representative of the kinds of experiences that can be developed around books that are rich in imagery, characterization, and plot development. As you reread a book, jot down ideas for teaching —interesting words, expressions, sensory images, humor, dialogue. Every book has individual contributions to be considered.

BREAKING DOWN STEREOTYPES

Classroom activities can be designed to aid in changing attitudes and breaking down stereotypes that even young children have already absorbed. Children need to experience what it might be like, for example, to "walk in someone else's moccasins." As Elizabeth Coatsworth wrote in *The Fair American:*

He who has never known hunger
Has never known how good
The taste of bread may be,
The kindliness of food.

Our aim in working with children in this manner is to heighten their awareness. We want them to be thinking, feeling beings. As Natalie Babbitt writes in *The Hornbook* (April 1974):

Why should we not aspire to enhance the awareness of our children? I refuse to believe that we do not have it in us to tell tales that can be works of literature, works of art, and American, and for children—if we are willing to fly in the face of what is, after all, a very young sacred cow. It is necessary to be hopeful to write successfully for children, because children themselves are generically hopeful; but the quality of hopefulness is not something to apologize for. It is not an immature quality. Quite the contrary. If it is something we have abandoned in our adult literature, that is one of the reasons why adult literature remains immature. (p. 185)

Open discussion is an excellent means of bringing up topics that not only interest young people but also make school activities more relevant to the lives of our students. The Glaser circle is one approach that is highly successful for this purpose. All students sit in a circle so they can see each other and speak directly to one another. The teacher, as an equal member of the circle, does not dominate discussion or try to impose ideas on the students. Topics like these might be selected by the group for discussion:

How I feel about death

What I wish school could be like

How it might be not to know English in this classroom

Feelings of loneliness

What makes me really feel good

To help combat sex stereotyping, point out women who are doing things today, such as author Jean Craighead George. Students would be interested in learning about her life. Daughter of an entomologist, she writes:

Our home was always full of pets—falcons, raccoons, owls, opossums, and dozens of sleeping insects that would metamorphose into the most miraculous things—thousands of praying mantises, a trembling luna moth, or a strange beetle that could snap his thorax and abdomen while lying on his back, flip into the air, and come down on all six feet. Hounds and kids ran in and out of the animals as other children run in and out of furniture. It was a rollicking childhood.[7]

A good source of such biographical information are books about winners of Newbery and Caldecott awards published by Horn Book. An example of these titles is *Newbery and Caldecott Medal Books 1966–1975* (Horn Book, 1975). Each volume includes acceptance speeches by the award winners, as well as biographical notes, and excerpts from the award-winning books.

Celebrate the accomplishments of women by observing their birthdays. On January 5, for instance, you might display the poems of Christina Rossetti (1830–1894). Observing Susan B. Anthony's birthday, which was February 15, 1820, might introduce a study of early efforts to gain rights for women. Challenge children to discover additional birthdays.[8]

The biographies and autobiographies of women can be displayed as a part of such birthday celebrations. They also make good reading any day, especially for students who like to know about real people. Maia Wojciechowska, winner of the Newbery award for *Shadow of a Bull* (Harcourt Brace Jovanovich, 1964), wrote an autobiography of her adolescent years. Dominated by World War Two, *Till the Break of Day* (Harcourt Brace Jovanovich, 1972) begins with the family's escape from Poland in 1939 to France. In the foreword, she writes:

Going over your past publicly is somewhat like making a movie. You are its writer and its director and its star. But sooner or later you become its editor. From the patchwork of scenes you begin to discard, splice together sequences. The hardest decision is about what you leave out and what you retain, often at the risk of making yourself seem ridiculous. Is any of it true anymore? Is any of it false?

Writing is by its nature an individualized activity. Keeping a diary offers one way students can write about their feelings without fear of exposure. As students feel more secure in the classroom of an understand-

---

[7] Lee Bennett Hopkins, *More Books by More People: Interviews with 65 Authors of Books for Children* (Citation, 1974), p. 179.

[8] For a more complete list, see Iris M. Tiedt, *Teaching for Liberation* (Contemporary, 1975), pp. 18–21.

ing teacher, they will be able to share their writings about things that are very close to them—a death in the family, being too fat, entering a new school, fears about war. You can come to know your students better as you exchange confidences through both discussion and writing. Small group interaction serves this purpose well.

Student writing has been published in a number of collections that interest students of similar ages. Examples often stimulate writing on the same topic. Collections of student writing that you might find useful in the classroom for this purpose include:

Here I Am! by Virginia Baron. Dutton, 1969.

Stuff by Herbert Kohl and Victor Cruz. World Publishing, 1970.

Male and Female under 18 by Eve Merriam and Nancy Larrick. Avon, 1974.

The Me Nobody Knows by Stephen M. Joseph. Avon, 1969.

Journeys by Richard Lewis. Simon and Schuster, 1969.

Can't You Hear Me Talking to You? by Carolyn Mirthes. Bantam, 1971.

❦ *ACTIVITIES TO EXPLORE* Choose two of these activities that are aimed at teaching understanding of the different groups we have discussed, as well as other groups in our society.

1. Develop a collage celebrating one of the groups presented in this chapter. Clip pictures, words, or articles from magazines or newspapers. Include other items that may seem appropriate to themes such as The Native American; Women in America. Try to make the collage three dimensional by adding real objects. Develop the collage on a piece of cardboard at least 18″ × 24″.

2. Prepare a learning center to teach a specific objective related to developing intergroup understanding in our pluralistic society. Include information and activities for the student, with clear directions about what to do. You can use poetry and prose and have the student engage in activities that involve all of the language arts. Include task cards and a cassette recording.

3. Consider the many different groups in our society today. Make an annotated bibliography of at least ten books or other media that would be helpful in promoting understanding about members of one specific group, for example, Jewish Americans, Puerto Ricans in the United

States, Eskimos. Pass this bibliography out to members of your class and other teachers you know. Include suggestions about how the list might be used.

Use the materials you have prepared in a classroom. Evaluate the effectiveness of your efforts to increase understanding of others among children. Consider how you might improve your presentation.

Broderick, Dorothy M. *Image of Blacks in Children's Fiction*. Bowker, 1973.

Carlson, Ruth Kearney. *Emerging Humanity; Multi-Ethnic Literature for Children and Adolescents*. Wm. C. Brown, 1972.

Council on Interracial Books for Children. *Human-and-Anti-human Values in Children's Books*. The Council, 1976.

Dunfee, Maxine and Claudia Crump. *Teaching for Social Values in Social Studies*. Association for Childhood Education International, 1974.

Fox, Geoff et al., eds. *Writers, Critics and Children*. Agathon, 1976.

Goodykoontz, William, ed. *Prejudice; The Invisible Wall*. Scholastic, 1968.

Harmin, Merrill, Howard Kirschenbaum, and Sidney B. Simon. *Clarifying Values through Subject Matter: Applications for the Classroom*. Winston, 1973.

Hawley, Robert C. and Isabel L. Hawley. *Human Values in the Classroom*. Hart Publishing Co., 1975.

Interracial Books for Children (periodical). Council on Interracial Books for Children, 29 W. 15th St., New York, New York 10011.

Joseph, Stephen M. *Children in Fear*. Holt, 1974.

Keating, Charlotte Matthews. *Building Bridges of Understanding between Cultures*. Palo Verde, 1971.

Reid, Virginia, ed. *Reading Ladders for Human Relations*. National Council of Teachers of English, 1972. (New edition in process.)

Sebesta, Sam and William J. Iverson. *Literature for Thursday's Child*. Science Research Associates, 1975.

Tiedt, Iris M. *Sexism in Education*. General Learning, 1976.

———. *Teaching for Liberation*. Contemporary, 1975.

Tiedt, Pamela L. and Iris M. Tiedt. *Multicultural Teaching: Activities, Information and Resources*. Allyn & Bacon, 1970.

5

*The Sun
Is a Golden
Earring*

The Universal and Traditional in Literature

Title from Natalia M. Belting, *The Sun Is a Golden Earring* (Holt, 1962). Illustration from *Tikki Tikki Tembo* retold by Arlene Mosel. Illustrated by Blair Lent. Copyright © 1968 by Arlene Mosel. Copyright © 1968 by Blair Lent, Jr. Reproduced by permission of Holt, Rinehart & Winston, Publishers.

Children's literature has wild blood in it; its ancestry lies partly in the long ages of storytelling which preceded the novel. Myth, legend, fairytale are alive in their own right, endlessly fertile in their influence. Modern children's fiction is permeated by a sense of story.

John Townsend
A Sense of Story

The folklore of a people takes many forms—fables, fairytales, myths, and legends. Springing from the oral traditions of song and storytelling, folklore is ancient and universal.

At the same time, however, folklore is contemporary and personal, for even young children have already absorbed a store of superstitions, an awareness of the myths that permeate our society. Almost unconsciously we avoid stepping on the crack in the sidewalk; childlike, we stop to wish on the first star at night; and with hope in our hearts we read horoscopes based on the signs of the Zodiac. Our world is filled with the lore that has been passed from age to age, a part of our heritage, very much a part of our lives.

As we explore folklore in this chapter, our focus will be on the following selected topics: the fable, folktales, and mythology. The broad topic of folktales is subdivided into specific categories of tales as well as folktales of two countries, Russia and Japan. Under the study of mythology, we will look at the simple pourquoi tale, Greek and Norse mythology, and two of the great heroes, namely, King Arthur and Robin Hood.

Our intent as we explore the fascinating lore that enriches all of literature will be to:

1. Learn something of the mythology of various groups of people—Roman, Greek, Norse, American Indian—that influences our lives and literature

2. Become acquainted with different forms of folk literature, such as the fable, folktale, and myth

3. Plan strategies for exploring folk literature with students in our classrooms

---

❦ *PREVIEWING THE TOPIC*   These questions give you some idea of how much you know about folklore and suggest areas that will be worth delving into as you pursue the study.

1. What is the difference between a myth and a folktale?

2. Can you match these figures from Greek and Roman mythology?

Roman	*Greek*
____ Cupid	a. Aphrodite
____ Mercury	b. Eros
____ Venus	c. Zeus
____ Minerva	d. Hermes
____ Jupiter	e. Athena

3. How can you distinguish a fable from other kinds of folk literature?

4. Can you tell a story from American Indian mythology?

5. How is the origin of these words related to a study of mythology?

    a. cereal

    b. Thursday

    c. tantalize

    d. lunar

    e. martial

The fable is a very distinctive form of folklore that is designed to point out a moral. Each fable consists of two parts: the narration, which presents a short story, and the moral, the conclusion plainly and briefly stated. The characters are usually animals, although occasionally inanimate or human figures may be included.

Fables are closely related to proverbs, which may actually be the moral statement that accompanies a fable. An example is: "Never count your chickens before they're hatched." In many cases, too, we have proverbial phrases that are derived from fables. When you call someone a "dog in the manger" or jibe someone with "sour grapes," you are calling forth your heritage or literature in the form of a fable.

Fables, as we know them today, have their roots in Oriental and Greek literature. Some of the most famous, attributed to the Greek slave Aesop, date back to the fifth century B.C. Much later, in the seventeenth century, came the poet La Fontaine, who adapted Aesop's fables but also wrote many original ones.

Here is one of Aesop's fables, "The Ant and the Grasshopper," as retold by Joseph Jacobs in *The Fables of Aesop* (Macmillan, 1894).

THE ANT AND THE GRASSHOPPER

In a field one summer's day a grasshopper was hopping about, chirping and singing to its heart's content. An ant passed by, bearing along with great toil an ear of corn he was taking to the nest.

"Why not come and chat with me," said the grasshopper, "instead of toiling and moiling in that way?"

"I am helping to lay up food for the winter," said the ant, "and I recommend that you do the same."

"Why bother about winter?" said the grasshopper. "We have plenty of food at present."

But the ant went on its way and continued its toil. When the winter came the grasshopper had no food, and found itself dying of hunger, while it saw the ants distributing every day corn and grain from the stores they had collected in the summer. Then the grasshopper knew—

It is best to prepare for the days of necessity.

It is interesting to compare this same fable as retold by La Fontaine in *A Hundred Fables* (The Bodley Head, London).

A grasshopper gay
Sang the Summer away,
And found herself poor
By the winter's first roar.

Of meat and of bread,
Not a morsel she had!
So a-begging she went,
To her neighbor the ant
For the loan of some wheat,
Which would serve her to eat
Till the season came round.
"I will pay you," she saith
"On an animal's faith,
Double weight in the pound
Ere the harvest be bound."

The ant is a friend
(And here she might mend)
Little given to lend.

"How spent you the summer?"
Quoth she, looking shame
At the borrowing dame.

"Night and day to each comer
I sang if you please."

"You sang! I'm at ease;
For 'tis plain at a glance,
Now, Ma'am, you must dance."

From India come the *Jatakas,* which describe the stories of Buddha.
Other collections of Indian fables are the *Panchatantra* or the Book of Five
Headings and *The Hitopadesa* or The Book of Good Counsel. An interesting collection of selections from the lore of India has been prepared by
Joseph Gaer in *Fables of India* (Little, Brown, 1955). Dating from the fifth
century B.C., these tales were originally written in Sanskrit, then translated
into Arabic, Hebrew, and finally into Latin. Notice in this example from
the *Panchatantrà* that the story is more developed than in the spare fables
credited to Aesop.

In olden times there lived a King who was so cruel and unjust towards his subjects that he was always called the Tyrant. So heartless was he that his people used to pray night and day that they might have a new king. One day, much to their surprise, he called his people together and said to them,—

"My dear subjects, the days of my tyranny are over. Henceforth you shall live in peace and happiness, for I have decided to try to rule henceforth justly and well."

The King kept his word so well that soon he was known throughout the land as The Just King. By and by one of his favorites came to him and said,—

"Your Majesty, I beg of you to tell me how it was that you had this change of heart towards your people?"

And the King replied,—

"As I was galloping through my forests one afternoon, I caught sight of a hound chasing a fox. The fox escaped into his hole, but not until he had been bitten by the dog so badly that he would be lame for life. The hound, returning home, met a man who threw a stone at him, which broke his leg. The man had not gone far when a horse kicked him and broke his leg. And the horse, starting to run, fell into a hole and broke his leg. Here I came to my senses, and resolved to change my rule. 'For surely,' I said to myself, 'he who doeth evil will sooner or later be overtaken by evil.'"[1]

Here are titles of representative collections of early fables that will appeal to students in the middle grades:

Jack Kent's Fables of Aesop by Jack Kent. Parents' Magazine Press, 1972.

Aesop's Fables by Boris Artzybasheff. Viking, 1933.

Aesop's Fables edited by John Warrington. Dutton, 1961.

Fables from Aesop edited by James Reeves. Walck, 1962.

Jataka Tales edited by Ellen C. Babbitt. Appleton, 1912.

Jataka Tales by Nancy DeRoin. Houghton Mifflin, 1975.

The Fables of La Fontaine adapted by Richard Scarry. Doubleday, 1963.

15 Fables of Krylov translated by David Pascal. Macmillan, 1965.

Many picture books are retellings of a single fable. Marcia Brown, for example, won the Caldecott award for the beautiful woodcuts in *Once a*

---

[1] From Maude Dutton Lynch, *The Tortoise and the Geese and Other Fables of Bidpai* (Houghton Mifflin, 1908, 1936).

Illustration reprinted by permission of Charles Scribner's Sons from Once a Mouse *by Marcia Brown. Copyright © 1961 Marcia Brown.*

Mouse . . . A Fable Cut in Wood (Scribner, 1961), based on an intriguing fable from India. While on the surface this story can be enjoyed by primary grade children, the fable offers more to older students as they observe foreshadowing, symbolism, and the fascinating interweaving of text and illustration, the work of a master storyteller and artist.

Brian Wildsmith has also presented fables enjoyably. With his characteristically flamboyant art, he interprets, for instance, La Fontaine's *The Hare and the Tortoise* (Watts, 1967). You might compare this interpretation with Paul Galdone's picture book of the same story (McGraw-Hill, 1962).

Additional fables by noted illustrators of children's books include:

Barbara Cooney. *Chanticleer and the Fox.* Thomas Y. Crowell, 1958. *(Based on a tale by Chaucer.)*

James Daugherty. *Andy and the Lion*. Viking, 1938.

Ingri and Edgar Parin D'Aulaire. *Don't Count Your Chicks*. Doubleday, 1943.

Roger Duvoisin. *The Miller, His Son, and Their Donkey*. McGraw-Hill, 1962.

Leo Lionni. *Tico and the Golden Wings*. Pantheon, 1964.

Tomi Ungerer. *The Donkey Ride*. Doubleday, 1967.

Mila Lazarevich. *The Fable of the Fig Tree*. Walck, 1975. (*Story by Michael Gross*)

The fable is still used in modified versions as a literary form. Rudyard Kipling's *Jungle Book,* written in 1894, and *Just So Stories,* written in 1902, owe much to earlier fabulists. Walt Disney cartoons are frequently based on well-known fables. *The Cat and the Devil* (Dodd, Mead, 1964) is a modern fable, written by James Joyce in a letter to his grandson Stephen. The form obviously still has appeal.

Because the fable has a strong, visible plot, even young students can understand the meaning. The liveliness of the presentation of the dramatic action also means that these stories provide excellent material for acting out. Children will enjoy writing original fables to fit a known proverb or an original statement. Point out the meaning of the word *fable,* which is related to our word *fabulous.* Discuss the usage of this latter word, which has broadened in meaning as when we say, "Fabulous!"

For further information about the fable, you might consult *Fables from Incunabula to Modern Picture Book,* a selected bibliography prepared by the Library of Congress in 1966. This publication is available from the United States Government Printing Office.

MIRROR, MIRROR ON THE WALL

Children love folktales. From the opening sentence, the listener is involved in the action. The characters are introduced; the setting is announced; and the problem is clearly stated within the first paragraph or two. The story developed in a well-organized framework includes action and suspense and concludes in a logical ending that is satisfying to the audience.

In the section that follows we will discuss the discovery of folktales and some of their characteristics. Then we will explore examples of different categories of tales: the cumulative tale, the fairytale, and drolls or realistic tales. Folktales from specific countries will be introduced, with examples cited in more detail from Russia and Japan.

DISCOVERING THE FOLKTALE

Although we often think of folktales as stories devised to amuse children, in most cases the old folktales were created originally for adults. Much of the lore that is depicted in these tales reflects adult thinking. As a result, the story content is often shocking to adults when they consider the tales as fare for their children. Consider, for example, Red Riding Hood's grandmother, who is eaten by the big bad wolf and then released when the wolf is killed by the hunter's ax. In *The Uses of Enchantment,* psychologist Bruno Bettelheim explains:

Each fairy tale is a magic mirror which reflects some aspects of our inner world, and of the steps required by our evolution from immaturity to maturity.[2]

Folktales are based on universal needs and emotions that people all over the world express—greed, jealousy, love, courage. The same themes, in fact almost identical plots, appear in the literature of different peoples. The tale of Cinderella, the poor girl who is mistreated by her stepmother, helped by a fairy godmother, and discovered by a handsome prince, is an excellent example. This story has been discovered in more than twenty versions,[3] suggesting that early tales were transmitted orally through trade and travel.

The earliest study of folktales, by Jacob and Wilhelm Grimm, was completed at the beginning of the nineteenth century. They began recording German folktales as told to them by such people as Frau Katherina Viehmann, who knew the stories well and told them with effective simplicity. The Grimm brothers retained this simplicity in their writing. Most persons recognize references to *Grimm's Fairy Tales,* but few realize that the collectors of these tales were among the first to study language scientifically.

Thomas Pyles, author of *The Origins and Development of the English Language,* writes of Jacob Grimm's work:

---

[2] Bruno, Bettelheim, *The Uses of Enchantment; The Meaning and Importance of Fairy Tales* (Knopf, 1976), p. 47.
[3] Iona and Peter Opie, *The Classic Fairy Tales* (Oxford, 1973).

It is amusing irony that this great scholar, who never married, should be best known as the "author," with his brother Wilhelm, of a beloved nursery classic—the famous *Grimm's Fairy Tales*. The brothers Grimm, both of them fascinated by folklore, in the scientific study of which they were pioneers, were the collectors of the stories which have delighted generations of children despite the disapproval of modern child psychologists.[4]

Following the work of the Grimm brothers, there was great interest in discovering and recording the folktales of other regions. Such scholars as Elias Lönnrot (Finland), Peter Asbjörnsen (Norway), Jörgen Moe (Norway), Andrew Lang (England), and Joseph Jacobs (England) added their contributions. Soon the collection of folktales in print was sizable.

One of the foremost folklorists of the twentieth century, Stith Thompson, has compiled an impressive index, the *Motif Index of Folk-Literature*.[5] In this work he identifies the significant elements that occur throughout folk literature of all kinds, for example, the fairy godmother, the wicked stepmother, the youngest son or daughter, and three wishes.

Through this type of intensive and extensive study, we can identify a number of categories of folktales. One variety that is familiar to all is the *fairytale,* a story that includes characters with magic powers. The *cumulative tale* represents another often-used type that is distinguished by its structure. A third category is the *droll,* a realistic story based on real people and practical behavior. We will examine these three categories of tales in the sections that follow.

THE CUMULATIVE TALE

A familiar plot structure that has been carefully honed over the years, the cumulative tale is commonly used to tell a series of adventures, as in *Henny Penny,* also known as *Chicken Licken.* This tale is made more interesting by the use of rhyming or alliterative names for the animal characters.

In the version by Joseph Jacobs the story begins quickly, thus:

One day Henny-Penny was picking up corn in the cornyard when—whack!—something hit her upon the head. "Goodness gracious me!" said Henny-Penny; "the sky's a-going to fall; I must go and tell the king."

---

[4] Thomas Pyles, *The Origins and Development of the English Language* (Harcourt Brace Jovanovich, 1964), p. 73.
[5] Stith Thompson, *Motif Index of Folk-Literature* (University of Indiana Press, 1955).

The problem is clear; the main character begins to act. In cumulative style the story develops as each new character is introduced. This story provides suitable material for the beginning storyteller, for the sequence of the story can be learned by simply listing the characters as they appear.

Cocky-Locky

Ducky-Daddles

Goosey-Poosey

Turkey-Lurkey

Foxy-Woxy

Each time the narrative follows the same pattern. "They went along, and they went along, and they went along till they met _____." The new character always asks the same question, "Where are you going to, Henny-Penny, Cocky-Locky and Ducky-Daddles?" and the characters all chorus: "Oh! We're going to tell the king the sky's a-falling." The new character of course asks, "May I come with you?" and all reply, "Oh, certainly, _____." So off they go to tell the king the sky is falling in.

Then comes the denouement! The wily Foxy-Woxy joins the safari, but along the way he suggests a shortcut, which not surprisingly is through his own cave. As the foolish animals enter, "Hrumph," off go their heads, and Foxy-Woxy throws them "over his left shoulder" in a pile. Versions differ, but this time Cocky-Locky calls out to warn Henny-Penny, and "she turned tail and off she ran home; so she never told the king the sky was a-falling." Paul Galdone's *Henny Penny* (Seabury, 1968) is especially attractive with large drawings of each character. Leonard Lubin contributes elaborate costumes in illustrating a version of this old favorite by Veronica Somerville Hutchinson (Little, Brown, 1975).

Each cumulative tale has its own unique details, but the pattern is similar—the beginning, the build-up, the end. The action is quick; the ending is appropriate and satisfying. Young children adore these stories, and so will older students if the stories are presented in such a way that they can be accepted. Preparing stories to share with primary grade children will provide sufficient reason for upper elementary and junior high school students to read and tell these tales, an important part of their heritage.

An attractively illustrated tale by Nonny Hogrogian is *One Fine Day* (Macmillan, 1971), based on an old Armenian folktale. Following the cumulative pattern, we see the problem presented: a fox drinks the milk from an old woman's pail, and she in turn cuts off his bushy tail. She agrees to sew the tail back on if he returns the milk. So, the pattern develops as the fox goes from creature to creature asking for a favor that will eventually lead to his getting milk to return to the old woman.

Other stories that follow this pattern include:

The Gingerbread Boy or Johnny-Cake

The Three Little Pigs

The House That Jack Built

Teeny-Tiny

The Bremen Town Musicians

The Old Woman and Her Pig

The Three Bears

Modern writers have also used the cumulative pattern in developing stories for children. Some of the best include:

Millions of Cats by Wanda Gág

Are You My Mother? by Philip D. Eastman

Ask Mr. Bear by Marjorie Flack

My Mother Is the Most Beautiful Woman in the World by Becky Reyher

Potato Talk by Ennis Rees

The Boy, The Baker, The Miller and More adapted by Harold Berson

THE FAIRYTALE

Albert Einstein was once asked what children should read that would best help them to become scientists. His response was "fairytales." Poet Richard LeGallienne expresses the same feeling for this imaginative literature:

The wonder of the world! Perhaps that is the chief business of the fairy tale,—to remind us that the world is no mere dust-heap pullulating with worms, as some of the old-fashioned scientists tried to make us believe; but that, on the contrary, it is a rendezvous of radiant forces forever engaged in turning its dust into dreams, ever busy with the transmutation of matter into mind, and mind into spirit,—a world, too, so mysterious that anything can happen, or any dream come true. One might set up, and maintain, the paradox that the fairy tale is the most scientific statement of human life; for, of all statements, it insists on the essential magic of living,—the mystery and wonder of being alive, the marvellous happiness, the wondrous sorrow, and the divine expectations.[6]

Remember that the origin of the word *fairy* is the Latin *fatum* (fate), which came to us through French as *feerie* and early English as *faerie*. The fairytale deals with more, therefore, than dainty beings in tinsel and tulle. It deals with the elemental forces of nature, which means that it speaks with a powerful voice and represents a very fundamental form of literature for all peoples.

The earliest fairytales, compiled by Jacob and Wilhelm Grimm, included: *The Elves and the Shoemaker, Little Red Riding Hood, Rapunzel,* and *The Sleeping Beauty.* Following are several attractive editions of tales by the Grimm brothers:

Grimm's Fairy Tales introduced by Frances Clarke Sayers and illustrated by children from around the world. Follett, 1968.

Tales from Grimm adapted and illustrated by Wanda Gág. Coward-McCann, 1936.

About Wise Men and Simpletons; Twelve Tales from Grimm translated by Elizabeth Shub and illustrated by Nonny Hogrogian. Macmillan, 1971.

In addition to the Grimm brothers, a major contributor to the development of the fairytale is Charles Perrault, a prominent French barrister of the seventeenth century. Under his son's name to protect his dignity, he published a collection of eight stories:

Sleeping Beauty

Red Riding Hood

Blue Beard

Puss in Boots

Diamonds and Toads

Cinderella

---

[6] Richard LeGallienne, "Concerning Fairy-Tales," in *Attitudes and Avowals* (John Lane, 1910), pp. 36–37.

Riquet with the Tuft

Hop o' My Thumb

227

THE UNIVERSAL AND
TRADITIONAL IN
LITERATURE

He, too, retained the simplicity of the oral telling of these tales, and has given us several of the finest fairytales that we still enjoy today. Janusz Grabianski illustrated a colorful edition of *Perrault's Classic French Fairy Tales* (Meredith, 1967), which includes several lesser known tales in addition to the favorites above.

In the nineteenth century Hans Christian Andersen wrote such tales as *The Tinderbox, The Emperor's New Clothes,* and *The Princess and the Pea* Born in Odense, Denmark, Hans was steeped in the lore of his country, which he shaped with his own creative mind to produce some of the best of fairytales. A good collection of Andersen's tales is *Seven Trees* (Harper, 1959), translated by Eva Le Gallienne and illustrated by Maurice Sendak.

The tales written by Jacob and Wilhelm Grimm, Charles Perrault, and Hans Christian Andersen are included in many fine anthologies. Several that are worth knowing are the following:

Arbuthnot, May Hill. *Time for Fairy Tales, Old and New.* Scott, Foresman, 1961.

Lang, Andrew. *Fifty Favorite Fairy Tales Chosen from the Color Fairy Books of Andrew Lang* compiled by Kathleen Lines. Watts, 1964.

Provensen, Alice and Martin Provensen, comps. *The Provensen Book of Fairy Tales.* Random House, 1971.

Rackham, Arthur, comp. *Arthur Rackham Fairy Book; A Book of Old Favorites with New Illustrations.* Lippincott, 1950.

As you examine editions of the fairytales, you will find that in general, the collections of tales are suitable for older readers. For primary grade readers it is wise to feature beautiful editions of single stories. Adrienne Adams illustrated, for example, *The Twelve Dancing Princesses* (Holt, 1966), a beautiful book with light romantic paintings. This talented artist also illustrated *Jorinda and Joringel* (Scribner, 1968), *Snow White and Rose Red* (Scribner, 1964), *The Shoemaker and the Elves* (Scribner, 1960), and *Thumbelina* (Scribner, 1961).

Marcia Brown is another fine illustrator who has worked with single fairytales. She did *Cinderella; or The Little Glass Slipper* (Scribner, 1954) in muted pastel colors. Her pictures in *Puss in Boots* (Scribner, 1952) are pen and ink drawings with a touch of color.

What the story does not tell is that it is not at all easy for a cat to stand in boots and to walk on two legs. This he had first to learn. He practiced secretly during the night: first standing up, then walking—until it worked.

Illustrated by Hans Fischer. Reproduced from his volume Puss in Boots *by permission of Harcourt Brace Jovanovich, Inc.*

It is interesting to contrast the interpretations of a single story by different artists. Marcia Brown's version of *Puss in Boots,* for example, can be compared to the humorous interpretation by Hans Fischer (Harcourt Brace Jovanovich, 1959). Janusz Grabianski also illustrated this story in a collection of *Grimm's Fairy Tales.*

Other attractively illustrated versions of single tales have been prepared by the following outstanding artists:

Bernadette. *Little Red Riding Hood.* Watts, 1969.

Joan Walsh Anglund. *Nibble Nibble Mousekin; A Tale of Hansel and Gretel.* Harcourt Brace Jovanovich, 1962.

Felix Hoffman. *Rapunzel.* Harcourt Brace Jovanovich, 1961.

_____. *The Seven Ravens.* Harcourt Brace Jovanovich, 1963.

_____. *The Sleeping Beauty.* Harcourt Brace Jovanovich, 1960.

_____. *The Wolf and the Seven Kids*. Harcourt Brace Jovanovich, 1959.

Nancy Ekholm Burkert. *The Nightingale*. Harper & Row, 1965.

Many writers today adopt the fairytale genre to tell their stories. Isaac Bashevis Singer, for example, tells the story of *The Fearsome Inn* (Scribner, 1967). Told with gusto and humor is this Polish-Jewish tale of Doboshova the witch and her husband who are outwitted by three young men who rescue the three captive maidens—Leitze, Neitze, and Reitze.

Philippa Pearce wrote an original fairytale, *The Squirrel Wife* (Thomas Y. Crowell, 1972). With traditional simplicity this story unfolds with all the usual elements of the fairytale, and good triumphs over evil. The younger brother Jack goes to the rescue of one of the strange little green people. As a reward, he is given a magic ring that must be placed on a squirrel's paw. The squirrel, a transformed human, becomes Jack's wife.

John Ruskin's *King of the Golden River* (World, 1946) is a classic fairytale of three brothers. The youngest, Gluck, discovers the King of the Golden River when he is forced to melt a favorite gold drinking mug that was decorated with the face of a strange little man. Appearing out of the melting gold, the mysterious king agrees to turn the great river into gold for anyone who casts three drops of holy water into the river. Of course the elder brothers try first, but they are mean and unkind, so the water they cast is unholy and they are changed into black stones. Gluck kindly helps the weary and dying en route to the source of the river, so the dwarf king treats him well. "And at the top of the cataract of the Golden River are still to be seen TWO BLACK STONES, round which the waters howl mournfully every day at sunset; and these stones are still called by the people of the valley THE BLACK BROTHERS."

Poet e. e. cummings wrote charming fairytales for his daughter, Nancy. Illustrated by John Eaton, *Fairy Tales* (Harcourt Brace Jovanovich, 1965) includes: "The Old Man Who Said 'Why,'" "The Elephant and the Butterfly," "The House that Ate Mosquito Pie," and "The Little Girl Named I."

When France fell to Hitler in 1940, the famous French aviator-author Antoine de Saint-Exupéry was depressed by the adults around him who were concerned only with material well-being. He searched, therefore, for an audience in tune with his concern for the mysteries of life. He chose the fairytale form for *The Little Prince,* noting. "I have lived a great deal among grown-ups. I have seen them intimately, close at hand. And that hasn't much improved my opinion of them."[7]

_____
[7] Antoine de Saint-Exupéry, *The Little Prince* (Harcourt Brace Jovanovich, 1943), p. 5.

What is it that the child brings to this story that most adults do not?—faith, acceptance of mystery. As James E. Higgins observes:

Saint-Exupéry's little book is not a mystery which excites the rational curiosity of the detective or the scientist. It is a child's mystery—a mystery which excites the awe and wonder of the child when a secret of the heart suddenly explodes in the sunlight of revelation. It is a mystery which has meaning not in the answers it provides, but in the wonder it reveals. It is the mystery of innocence—and therefore it has value and meaning for readers of all ages.[8]

The little prince, the symbol of innocence, searches the planets trying to find love. At last he learns that he has known love all along on his own small planet as he faithfully tended a beautiful rose. Children will find this story beautifully simple, but adults may find it mystically confusing. It is a story, however, that you will find yourself turning to repeatedly.

Other writers choose to rewrite familiar tales. One writer who has done an outstanding job of retelling fairytales as well as folktales from various sources is Ruth Manning-Sanders, whose books provide excellent material for reading aloud or for storytelling. Children in middle and upper grades will enjoy the following collections:

A Choice of Magic. Dutton, 1971.

A Book of Dwarfs. Dutton, 1963.

Gianni and the Ogre. Dutton, 1971.

Peter and the Piskies; Cornish Folk and Fairy Tales. Roy, 1966.

A Book of Monsters. Dutton, 1976.

Especially good collections of stories for primary grade children include:

Told Under the Green Umbrella; Old Stories for New Children. Association for Childhood Education, Literature Committee. Macmillan, 1930.

Golden Goose Book by L. Leslie Brooke. Warne, 1906.

---

[8] James E. Higgins, *Beyond Words: Mystical Fancy in Children's Literature* (Teachers College, 1970), p. 17.

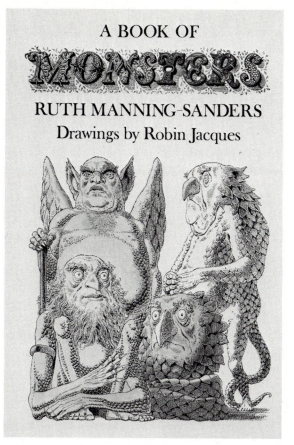

From A Book of Monsters *by*
Ruth Manning Sanders. Copy-
right © 1975 by Ruth Manning
Sanders. Illustrated by Robin
Jacques. Reprinted by permission
of the publishers, E. P. Dutton
and Methuen Children's Book
Ltd.

DROLLS: REALISTIC TALES

The humorous drolls usually describe human characters who, albeit silly
and illogical, are fairly realistic. One such story is "Mr. Vinegar," which
is similar to the Norse variation "Gudbrand on the Hillside." In both
stories the husband makes a series of foolish trades until he ends up with
nothing. In "Mr. Vinegar," however, the story is matter-of-factly told,
with the realistic ending:

At this the bird laughed, and Mr. Vinegar, falling into a violent rage, threw the
stick at its head. The stick lodged in the tree. So Mr. Vinegar returned to his wife
without money, cow, bagpipes, gloves, or stick.

In "Gudbrand on the Hillside," by contrast, the man has a very supportive wife: "No matter what he did, she thought it was always the right thing." He is so sure of this positive attitude toward him, that after making the foolish trades, he bets a hundred dollars with a neighbor that she will not be angry with him. The neighbor pays the hundred dollars when the wife speaks these final words:

"Heaven be praised you did that!" cried the woman. "Whatever you do, you always do the very thing I could have wished. Besides, what did we want with the cock? We are our own masters and can lie as long as we like in the mornings. Heaven be praised! As long as I have got you back again, who manage everything so well, I shall neither want cock, nor goose, nor pig, nor cow."

Gudbrand, therefore, despite his foolishness, manages to come out on top. Perhaps his wife is right!

Another droll that is particularly amusing today is "The Husband Who Was to Mind the House." Wanda Gág presents this tale in *Gone Is Gone* (Coward-McCann, 1935), based on a Bohemian version. Here is the tale as it appears in *Popular Tales from the Norse* by Peter Christen Asbjornsen.

Once upon a time there was a man so surly and cross, he never thought his wife did anything right in the house. So, one evening in hay-making time, he came home, scolding and swearing, and showing his teeth and making a dust.

"Dear love, don't be so angry; there's a good man," said his goody; "tomorrow let's change our work. I'll go out with the mowers and mow, and you shall mind the house at home."

Yes, the husband thought that would do very well. He was quite willing, he said.

So early next morning his goody took a scythe over her neck, and went out into the hayfield with the mowers and began to mow; but the man was to mind the house, and do the work at home.

First of all he wanted to churn the butter; but when he had churned a while, he got thirsty, and went down to the cellar to tap a barrel of ale. So, just when he had knocked in the bung, and was putting the tap into the cask, he heard overhead the pig come into the kitchen. Then off he ran up the cellar steps, with the tap in his hand, as fast as he could, to look after the pig, lest it should upset the churn; but when he got up, and saw that the pig had already knocked the churn over, and stood there, routing and grunting amid the cream which was running all over the floor, he got so wild with rage that he quite forgot his ale barrel and ran at the pig as hard as he could. He caught it, too, just as it ran out of doors, and gave it such a kick that piggy lay for dead on the spot. Then all at once he remembered he had the tap in his hand; but when he got down to the cellar, every drop of ale had run out of the cask.

Then he went into the dairy and found enough cream left to fill the churn again, and so he began to churn, for butter they must have for dinner. When he had churned a bit, he remembered that their milking cow was still shut up in the byre, and hadn't had a bit to eat or a drop to drink all the morning, though the sun was high. Then all at once he thought 'twas too far to take her down to the meadow, so he'd just get her up on the housetop—for the house, you must know, was thatched with sod, and a fine crop of grass was growing there.

Now their house lay close up against a steep down, and he thought if he laid a plank across to the thatch at the back he'd easily get the cow up.

But still he couldn't leave the churn, for there was his little babe crawling about the floor, and "if I leave it," he thought, "the child is sure to upset it!" So he took the churn on his back, and went out with it; but then he thought he'd better first water the cow before he turned her out on the thatch; so he took up a bucket to draw water out of the well; but, as he stooped down at the well's brink, all the cream ran out of the churn over his shoulders, and so down into the well.

Now it was near dinner time, and he hadn't even got the butter yet; so he thought he'd best boil the porridge, and filled the pot with water, and hung it over the fire. When he had done that, he thought the cow might perhaps fall off the thatch and break her legs or her neck. So he got up on the house to tie her up. One end of the rope he made fast to the cow's neck, and the other he slipped down the chimney and tied round his own thigh; and he had to make haste, for the water now began to boil in the pot, and he had still to grind the oatmeal.

So he began to grind away; but while he was hard at it, down fell the cow off the housetop after all, and as she fell, she dragged the man up the chimney by the rope. There he stuck fast; and as for the cow, she hung halfway down the wall, swinging between heaven and earth, for she could neither get down nor up.

And now the goody had waited seven lengths and seven breadths for her husband to come and call them home to dinner; but never a call they had. At last she thought she'd waited long enough, and went home. But when she got there and saw the cow hanging in such an ugly place, she ran up and cut the rope in two with her scythe. But as she did this, down came her husband out of the chimney; and so when his old dame came inside the kitchen, there she found him standing on his head in the porridge pot.

The humorous aspects of the droll make it an excellent choice for storytelling. A very short English tale that you might develop as part of your storytelling repertoire is *Master of All Masters*. This short tale has been illustrated by Marcia Sewall (Little, Brown, 1972) as well as Anne Rockwell (Grosset & Dunlap, 1972). In this tale a country girl is hired by an eccentric old gentleman who has special names for everything around the house. His cat is "white-faced simminy," and he refers to the fire as "hot cockalorum." The obedient girl learns all these names very well. When there is threat of a fire at night, she comes running to her master's room with this message:

Master of all masters, get out of your barnacle and put on your squibs and crackers. White-faced simminy has got a spark of hot cockalorum on her tail, and unless you get some pondalorum, high topper mountain will be all on hot cockalorum!

If you want to know what all that means, you must look for the story. It appears in many anthologies, such as Mary Ann Nelson's *A Comparative Anthology of Children's Literature* (Holt, 1972) and *The Arbuthnot Anthology of Children's Literature* (Scott, Foresman, 1976).

FOLKTALES FROM MANY COUNTRIES

The folktale is an integral part of every culture. A choice selection of representative tales should, therefore, be included in the elementary school curriculum, for this type of literature not only provides exciting and enjoyable reading matter, but it also helps to develop understandings in the social studies, sciences, and language arts. It is an essential part of multicultural education.

A delightful way to introduce children to the varied beliefs of people around the world is through the books created by Natalia Belting. *The Sun Is a Golden Earring* (Holt, 1962), for example, compares ideas that are related to the heavens (see page 214), and might fit nicely with a study of astronomy. *Calendar Moon* (Holt, 1964) relates ideas about the calendar or year. *The Earth Is on a Fish's Back* (Holt, 1965) shows children many explanations of how the earth began. A newer book, *Whirlwind Is a Ghost Dancing* (Dutton, 1974), presents the lore of North American Indian tribes. In each of these books editor, author, and illustrator have worked hard to combine the poetic prose with outstanding art so that the books are truly lovely. Although they are small picture books and young children might enjoy them, these books should be introduced to older children, for they are too good to miss. Included are wonderful examples of metaphors, such as those used in two of the above titles, which would be very useful in a study of poetry.

It would be impossible in this portion of a chapter to discuss in any

The moon is a white cat
that hunts
the gray mice of the night.

—from Hungary

From The Sun Is a Golden
Earring *by Natalia M. Belting.
Illustrated by Bernarda Bryson.
Copyright © 1962 by Natalia
Belting. Copyright © 1962 by
Bernada Bryson. Reproduced by
permission of Holt, Rinehart &
Winston, Publishers.*

great detail the folktales of even the major countries of the world. In this
section, therefore, we will focus on the tales of two countries that are of
special interest today—Russia and Japan. The folktales of the North
American Indians and those of Mexico are discussed under the heading Understanding Others in Chapter 4. A discussion of the folktales and
legends of the United States, including literature about black Americans,
will be found in Chapter 8 in the sections on the history and geography
of the United States.

THE FOLKTALES OF RUSSIA

In a certain kingdom in a certain land there once lived a rich peasant. And the rich
peasant had three sons—Semyon the Soldier, Taras the Big-Belly, and Ivan the
Fool—and one daughter Malanya the Deaf-Mute. Semyon the Soldier went to
war to serve the Tsar, Taras the Big-Belly went to a merchant's in the city to
become a trader, and Ivan the Fool stayed home with his sister to work in the
fields.

Thus begins the familiar Russian tale "Ivan the Fool" by Leo Tolstoy.
This short paragraph includes the "once upon a time" introductory line;
it establishes the magic three; and we immediately identify with Ivan the
Fool, the younger brother who is left at home. Ivan does triumph, of
course, and through hard work. In fact in his realm one custom is sternly

enforced: "If you have calluses on your hands, you're welcome at the table; if you don't, you eat the scraps." This story and six others by Tolstoy are in *Ivan the Fool and Other Tales of Leo Tolstoy* selected and translated by Guy Daniels (Macmillan, 1966).

A very attractive collection of five Russian stories is *Favorite Fairy Tales Told in Russia* retold by Virginia Haviland (Little, Brown, 1961). Included are "To Your Good Health," "Vasilisa the Beautiful," "Snegourka, the Snow Maiden," "The Straw Ox," and "The Flying Ship." Illustrations by Herbert Danska enhance the stories, which are set in large type and could be handled by middle grade students. This volume is part of a set of favorite fairytales told in a number of different countries.

A familiar character in Russian folklore is Baba Yaga, the traditional witch, large and bony and ugly. Here is one story of Baba Yaga and her evil ways.

BABA YAGA AND KIND-HEARTED HILDY
A Russian Fairytale Retold by Iris Tiedt

A poor widower and his little daughter, Hildy, lived in a cottage near the Deep Dark Woods. They were happy together until one day the man decided to marry again so he would have someone to care for his house and his young daughter. When the new wife moved in, however, suddenly everything changed. There were no smiles in the house. There was no strawberry jam on the table. There was no time for playing games.

The stepmother blamed Hildy for everything that went wrong. She said Hildy was naughty, and sent her away from the table with nothing to eat but a crust of bread. Poor Hildy cried as she sat in the woodshed nibbling on the bread. She was alone and unhappy. Then, she heard a squeaking voice, and out popped a tiny gray Mouse Lady with bright twinkling eyes, a soft furry body, and a long, long tail. Hildy stroked the little mouse's fur and gave her bread crumbs to eat. Hildy was happy to find a friend.

"Why are you crying?" asked the Mouse Lady when she had finished the crumbs and wiped her whiskers.

Hildy told her of the stepmother's cruel treatment and how unhappy she and her father were now that this woman ruled the house.

"I would like to help you," squeaked Hildy's new friend, "because you are good and kind. You must be very careful, Hildy, for the stepmother is none other than the sister of the terrible bony-legged witch, Baba Yaga, who lives past the Deep Dark Woods over the hills and far away. If your stepmother sends you to visit Baba Yaga, beware, because that horrible witch would as soon eat you as look at you."

Sure enough, the next day, the stepmother told Hildy to go through the Deep

Dark Woods over the hills and far away to borrow a needle and thread from her sister. Hildy opened a drawer to show her stepmother the needle and thread they already had. "Hush, girl!" the stepmother scolded. "On your way now, so you get home before dark."

Off went Hildy with no time to call the Mouse Lady. Down the road was a wooden bridge, however, and there sat the little mouse waiting for Hildy. "I see you are on your way to visit Baba Yaga," she called. "Don't be afraid, Hildy. Just pick up the things you find in the road, for they will help save you from the wicked witch." And giving Hildy a napkin wrapped around some sandwiches of bread and jam, off scampered the tiny creature.

As Hildy walked along the road, she found first of all a bright blue handkerchief. Remembering the words of the friendly mouse, she put the handkerchief in her pocket. Soon she found a tiny bottle of oil which she also put in her pocket. Next she found a pretty red apple on a tree and then a small amber comb that lay in the road. Farther along the road she caught a tiny fish in a pond.

So on she went and on she went, and soon she came to the fence around Baba Yaga's house. She pushed open the gate, which creaked so loudly that she took out the little bottle of oil to ease its achy hinges. In the yard was a servant girl crying loudly because she was so overworked. Hildy said, "How lucky that I picked up this blue handkerchief." And she gave the handkerchief to the unfortunate girl who smiled with gratitude.

Beside the steps lay a huge black dog that growled at Hildy until she patted its head and gave it the red apple she had picked from the tree. Then Hildy knocked at the door. "Come in," croaked the wicked Baba Yaga, who glared at Hildy from where she sat weaving. "What does my sister want?"

Hildy explained that her stepmother wanted a needle and thread. Baba Yaga smiled widely, showing her big teeth. "All right, my dear. You sit in my place at the loom while I find one."

Baba Yaga hurried to the kitchen where she told the servant to prepare a hot bath to wash the little girl. "I shall have her for dinner," chortled the wicked witch.

When the servant came in for the water pail, Hildy whispered, "Don't be too quick in making the fire, and take your time in filling the bath tub." The servant smiled, but she was clearly afraid of Baba Yaga. She did, however, work very slowly as she prepared Hildy's bath.

Meanwhile, Baba Yaga put her head in the door. "Are you weaving, my dear? Are you weaving, my pretty one?"

"Yes, yes, aunt," replied Hildy. "I am weaving." Then she spoke to the thin gray cat that sat watching the fire. "Poor cat, you are thin and hungry. Here is a little fish for your dinner."

"Thank you," purred the hungry cat as it ate greedily. Then it jumped on Hildy's lap and whispered in her ear. "You are a good girl," the cat said. "You must run away quickly for Baba Yaga plans to eat you. Baba Yaga will chase you for sure, but when she gets close, throw out the napkin you have in your pocket. It will turn into a wide river which should delay the witch. If she gets closer, lay your comb on the ground which will form such a thick fence that she cannot pursue you."

So off ran Hildy while the wise gray cat sat weaving at the loom to fool Baba Yaga. As Hildy ran past the huge dog by the steps, it sprang up ferociously. When it saw who was running by, however, the dog lay down with a gruff, "Run, run." It remembered that Hildy had kindly given it an apple to eat.

As Hildy passed through the gate, it opened easily and soundlessly, for she had oiled the rusty hinges. Oh, how Hildy ran!

Back in the house of the evil witch, Baba Yaga called to Hildy, "Are you weaving, little one?"

"Oh, yes, aunt, I am weaving," answered the wily gray cat who had sent Hildy on her way to safety.

"That isn't my niece!" cried the wary witch as she charged into the room. "What are you doing at the loom?" she shouted at the cat. "Where is my niece? Why didn't you scratch her eyes out?"

"She is far off down the road," purred the insolent cat. "I was glad to help her because she gave me food to eat when I was hungry."

Baba Yaga was furious. She tore madly around the yard gnashing her teeth. "Why didn't you bark?" she cried to the huge dog. "Why didn't you creak?" she demanded of the gate. "Why were you so long preparing the bath?" she berated the servant girl. Each in turn replied that Hildy had been kind, unlike Baba Yaga who had always been cruel and inconsiderate.

Baba Yaga snarled with rage. She was so angry that sparks flew from her wicked eyes. Off she flew down the road after Hildy. Hildy could hear her coming so she threw out the napkin. Sure enough, it spread quickly to form a wide, rushing river. The witch stormed and stamped when she came to the river bank, but she quickly called all her cattle together, commanding them to drink the water. Then on she went after Hildy.

When Hildy could see the big bony shape coming closer, she laid the comb on the ground. Quickly the amber comb formed a thick fence that prevented Baba Yaga from following. Hildy could hear her wailing and lamenting as she hurried on toward home. When she reached the wooden bridge, she heard a small voice calling, "Hildy, Hildy! Here I am waiting for you." There was the little Mouse Lady waiting to greet Hildy and to tell her the good news. "Your stepmother is gone," she cried joyously. "Your father sent her away when he found she had sent you to Baba Yaga's house."

Hildy picked up the little mouse and put it in her pocket. Then Hildy hurried to tell her father that she was safely home. What a happy ending to her visit with Baba Yaga!

The tales of Baba Yaga are many and various. An especially humorous story of another child's encounter with this wicked witch is *Baba Yaga* (Houghton Mifflin, 1966) by Ernest Small. Illustrated by Blair Lent, the story begins as Marusia is on her way to buy turnips for dinner and loses the money her mother had given her. When she wanders in the forest searching for wild turnips, Baba Yaga captures her. The witch depicted by this author is fearsomely funny. At the end she grumbles: "I can't have children around here. Their endless questions make my old bones ache."

Bonnie Carey has translated and adapted an excellent collection of stories entitled *Baba Yaga's Geese and Other Russian Stories* (Indiana University Press, 1973), illustrated handsomely by Guy Fleming. Although the witch herself appears only briefly in "Baba Yaga's Geese," her presence is strong throughout the tale. The author observes that "the mere mention of the witch's name conjures up a storehouse of traditional imagery. Baba Yaga is automatically envisioned as chewing up a forest with her big, sharp teeth or lying in her hut on hen's legs with her nose growing into the ceiling." In this tale young Marya rescues her brother from the witch's flock of geese.

Some authors have taken special interest in Russian folklore. Marie Halun Bloch, for example, has translated a number of tales, such as

From Baba Yaga's Geese *by Bonnie Carey. Reprinted by permission of Indiana University Press.*

Ivanko and the Dragon (Atheneum, 1969). Illustrated by Yaroslava, this old Ukrainian folktale begins with the comfortably familiar words: "There were once an old man and an old woman, and they had no children." The old man makes a cradle of a sapling that turns into a little boy. The boy goes out in his wee boat each day but faithfully returns when his mother calls. An old she-dragon tricks him and nearly eats Ivanko for dinner, but he escapes at the last minute with the help of a gosling. Marie Bloch also translated the stories in *Ukrainian Folk Tales* (Coward-McCann, 1964), illustrated by J. Hnizdovsky. Here are a dozen tales that the author first heard from her own grandmother. Bloch explains that "these animal stories were created by adults purely for their own entertainment and not, as with fables, for the purpose of demonstrating some moral truth or nugget of human wisdom."

Illustrators, too, have often turned to Russian lore. Uri Shulevitz displays his colorful art in *Soldier and Tsar in the Forest* (Farrar, Straus & Giroux, 1972), a story translated humorously by Richard Lourie. A simple soldier, mistreated by his brother, manages to save the Tsar from robbers. The Tsar rewards him handsomely and punishes the brother, which, as the author concludes, "just goes to show what happens when you renounce your very own brother, your own flesh and blood." Shulevitz won the Caldecott award for his illustration of another Russian tale, *The Fool of the World and the Flying Ship* (Farrar, Straus & Giroux, 1968) by Arthur Ransome.

Additional collections of Russian folktales or single stories include the following:

Artzybasheff, Boris. *Seven Simeons; A Russian Tale.* Viking, 1961. (*First published in 1937.*)

*Brown, Marcia. *The Bun; A Tale from Russia.* Harcourt Brace Jovanovich, 1972.

*———. *The Neighbors.* Scribner, 1967.

*Daniels, Guy. *The Tsar's Riddles or The Wise Little Girl.* McGraw-Hill, 1967.

*———. *The Peasant's Pea Patch; A Russian Folktale.* Delacorte Press, 1971.

*Domanska, Janina. *The Turnip.* Macmillan, 1969.

Ginsburg, Mirra, ed. *The Kaha Bird; Tales from the Steppes of Central Asia.* Crown, 1971.

———. *The Lazies; Tales of the Peoples of Russia.* Macmillan, 1973.

Higonnet-Schnopper, Janet. *Tales from Atop a Russian Stove*. Whitman, 1973.

*Jameson, Cynthia. *The Clay Pot Boy*. Coward-McCann, 1973.

Nathan, Dorothy. *The Month Brothers*. Dutton, 1967.

Ransome, Arthur. *Old Peter's Russian Tales*. Nelson, 1917.

*Reesink, Marijke. *The Magic Horse*. McGraw-Hill, 1974.

*Reyher, Becky. *My Mother Is the Most Beautiful Woman in the World*. Lothrop, 1945.

*Robbins, Ruth. *Baboushka and the Three Kings*. Parnassus Press, 1960.

*Tresselt, Alvin. *The Mitten; An Old Ukrainian Folktale*. Lothrop, 1964.

Whitney, Thomas P. *The Story of Prince Ivan, the Firebird, and the Gray Wolf*. Scribner, 1968.

*———. *Vasilisa the Beautiful*. Macmillan, 1970. (*Version of Cinderella*)

*Yaroslava. *Tusya and the Pot of Gold*. Atheneum, 1971.

Yershov, P. *Humpy*. Harcourt Brace Jovanovich, 1966.

Zemach, Harve. *Salt; A Russian Tale*. Follett, 1965.

FOLKTALES OF JAPAN   A celebrated figure in Japanese folklore is Momotaro, Son of a Peach, who is brought, strangely enough, to his foster parents in a giant peach. The story is included in Yoshiko Uchida's collection of Japanese tales, *The Dancing Kettle and Other Japanese Folktales* (Harcourt Brace Jovanovich, 1949). Other collections of Japanese folktales by Yoshiko Uchida are *The Magic Listening Cap; More Folk Tales from Japan* (Harcourt Brace Jovanovich, 1955) and *The Sea of Gold and Other Tales from Japan* (Scribner, 1965).

Virginia Haviland also retells Japanese folktales in *Told in Japan* (Little, Brown, 1967), part of the Favorite Fairy Tales series. Included is the well-known "Momotaro or The Story of the Son of a Peach," as well as "One-Inch Fellow," "The Good Fortune Kettle," "The Tongue-Cut Sparrow," and "The White Hare and the Crocodiles."

Here is a representative tale from Japanese folk literature, which appears in *Folk Tales of Japan* adapted by Shirlee P. Newman (Bobbs-Merrill, 1963).

---

* Suitable for primary grades.

THE MIRROR

Many, many years ago, in a remote part of Japan, lived a family of three—a father, a mother, and a little girl. Nowhere was there a happier family.

One night the father said to his wife, "Tomorrow, dear wife, we must say sayonara (good-by). I must go far away to Tokyo on business. But do not fret, for I shall return as soon as I am able."

"May daughter and I go with you, dear husband?" asked the wife.

"No, it would be better for you to remain here," he said. "The journey is long. You will fare better at home. Be happy here, and keep well, and when I return home, I shall bring you both lovely gifts."

"Very well, dear husband, I shall prepare your belongings." The good wife backed quietly out of the room.

Before long the little girl appeared before the father. "Father," she said, bowing, "mother has told me you must go away." The little girl's eyes looked misty, as if tears were about to fall.

The father smiled gently and held out his arms. "Do not fret, sweet one," he said. "I shall return soon. And I shall bring you a kimono as bright as a flower garden, with a new satin obi to match."

The little girl tried to smile. "Thank you, father," she said, "but I would prefer that you did not go."

The next morning the mother and the little girl accompanied the father to the gate and bade him farewell. Sadly they returned to their house.

"How empty it seems," the mother said. "So lonely and still. It will seem like years until your good father returns."

The little girl's chin quivered as if she were about to cry.

"No, child," said the mother, "no tears. Come, if we busy ourselves, the time will pass more swiftly." And so the mother and daughter wove winter clothing and spun thread and arranged flowers. They missed the father greatly, but the mother was right. Keeping their hands busy did help pass the time. At last the day of the father's return came.

The little girl clapped her hands excitedly. "Father!" she cried. "Thank you for coming home."

The father smiled fondly and took her face between his hands. "Ah, sweet one," he said, looking into her eyes, "it is I who should thank you for being here to welcome me. But see what I have brought you!" Opening his big straw basket, he took out many gifts—a pet cricket in a brass cage, a pair of bright-colored clogs and a pink flowered kimono with an obi to match. The little girl tried on one bit of finery after another, dancing about and chirping as happily as her pet cricket.

Now the father turned to his wife and handed her a square package, tied with red and white ribbons. "For you, dear wife," he said, handing her the gift.

"There was no need. Your return is gift enough," she said. But carefully she untied the bows and removed the paper. Opening the box, she took out an oval piece of metal with a handle attached. She looked at it curiously. One side, she saw, was blue, decorated with birds and trees. Curiously, she turned it over. Why, the other side was as bright as a lake in sunshine. Never had she seen anything like it! She held it up and gazed at the smooth, shiny side. It had a face on it, painted with such detail, it seemed—yes—it seemed alive!

The husband began to laugh. "You look surprised," he said. "Do you not recognize your own lovely face? That is a *mirror,* and whenever you look at it, you will see yourself."

The wife looked puzzled. "Mirror!" she said, holding it higher and turning her face from side to side. "I have never seen such a thing."

"I know," said the husband, "but in the great capital of Tokyo, a mirror is considered necessary for a woman to have. I have heard of a proverb which says, 'The sword is the soul of the samurai (warrior); the mirror is the soul of the woman.'"

"Thank you, dear husband," the wife said, placing the mirror back in its box. "I shall treasure your gift always." And leaving the room, she hid her presents away, lest she and her daughter be tempted to look at themselves too often.

Years passed. The father grew older, though no less good. The wife grew older, though no less beautiful. And the daughter grew to be a gentle young lady, the image of her beautiful mother. Still, the mother kept the mirror hidden, so her daughter would not be tempted to vanity.

One day, the mother fell ill and died. But before she died, she called the daughter to her bedside. "Daughter," she said, "open the cupboard behind you and take out the square box you find on the shelf."

The daughter obeyed. With the box in her hand, she returned to her mother's side.

"Open the box and take out what you find inside," the mother said weakly. The daughter took off the lid and removed the mirror.

"After I die," the mother said, "I want you to look into this mirror every morning and every evening. You will see me there, and you will know I am watching over you."

The daughter never forgot her mother's wish. Every morning and every evening, she gazed at the mirror for a long, long time. On its shiny surface she saw the face of her mother, looking as young and lovely as the day her father had come back from Tokyo. The daughter told her mother her innermost thoughts, her dreams, her troubles, and her joys, and never did she perform an act which would displease her mother.

The father began to wonder at his daughter's habit of gazing into the mirror for long periods of time. Odd, he thought, why does she spend so much time with the mirror? At times, I even think I hear her talking to it. I must ask her why she acts so strange.

"Daughter," he said, when she entered the room, "I did not think you were vain. Why do you spend so much time looking into the mirror?"

"Father," she replied, eyes downcast. "I hope I do not displease you. I look in the mirror to see and talk to my mother." And she told him of her mother's last wish.

The father smiled gently. He could not find it in his heart to tell her that what she saw in the mirror was the reflection of her own lovely face.

A particularly effective version of the Japanese folktale *The Wave* has been adapted by Margaret Hodges (Houghton Mifflin, 1964). Illustrated dramatically by Blair Lent, this book lends itself to reading aloud as a group shares the feelings of Ojiisan, the old man who sets fire to his rice fields in an effort to warn the village of the coming of a tidal wave that would engulf them all. After the great wave passed:

He, their wise old friend, now stood among them almost as poor as the poorest, for his wealth was gone. But he had saved four hundred lives.

The Wave by Margaret Hodges, illustrated by Blair Lent. Copyright © 1964 by Margaret Hodges. Copyright © 1964 by Blair Lent. Reprinted by permission of Houghton Mifflin Company.

Tada ran to him and held his hand. The father of each family knelt before Ojii-san, and all the people after them.

"My home still stands," the old man said. "There is room for many." And he led the way to the house. (p.42)

A fascinating book, *The Possible Impossibles of Ikkyu The Wise* (Macrae Smith, 1971), tells the story of a priest who is a trickster. As I. G. Edmonds explains, "Ikkyu was a real man who lived nearly 600 years ago. He was so famous for the 'impossible' things he did that he has become a folk hero. Stories about him have been told and retold and changed with the years until he has become one of those delightful characters known as the 'tricksters.'" Ikkyu manages to save the neck of the rascally Chobei, the rice merchant, in "Punishment Worse Than Death," for example. Ikkyu helps the Honorable Takamatsu think of a suitable punishment for Chobei who had cheated him three times. The selected punishment makes everyone happy, even Ikkyu, who tricks both men into making substantial contributions to the poor, a punishment worse than death.

The handsome contemporary art of Gerald McDermott now enhances a Japanese folktale, *The Stone Cutter* (Viking, 1975). The story of Tasaku is simply told in boldface oversize print that fits the strength of the collages that dominate every page. Tasaku, a lowly stonecutter, who cuts blocks of stone at the foot of the lofty mountain, wishes he might be wealthy like the prince who passes by. The spirit of the mountain grants his wish, and Tasaku becomes a rich prince. Soon, however, he observes the power of the sun that wilts the flowers he admires, and he wishes to be the sun. Then he wishes to be the cloud that obscures the sun and finally the mountain that withstands the floods. As the immense and powerful mountain, however, he feels the sting of the stonecutter's chisel. "Deep inside, he trembled." *The Stone Cutter* is also available as a film from Weston Woods.

Additional stories that present Japanese folktales to children include the following:

Bang, Garrett. *Men from the Village Deep in the Mountains and Other Japanese Folk Tales*. Macmillan, 1973.

Buck, Pearl S., ed. *Fairy Tales of the Orient*. Simon and Schuster, 1965.

Carpenter, Frances. *People from the Sky; Ainu Tales from Northern Japan*. Doubleday, 1972.

*Ishii, Momoko. *Issun Boshi, the Inchling; An Old Tale of Japan*. Walker, 1967.

*Jameson, Cynthia. *One for the Price of Two*. Parents' Magazine Press, 1972.

*Kijima, Hajime. *Little White Hen*. Harcourt Brace Jovanovich, 1969.

Matsutani, Miyoko. *The Crane Maiden*. Parents' Magazine Press, 1968.

_____. How the Withered Trees Blossomed. Lippincott, 1969. (*Printed and bound in Japanese tradition, it begins at "the back" of the book.*)

*Mosel, Arlene. *The Funny Little Woman*. Dutton, 1972.

Pratt, Davis and Elsa Kula. *Magic Animals of Japan*. Parnassus Press, 1967.

Sakade, Florence, ed. *Japanese Children's Favorite Stories*. Charles E. Tuttle Co., 1958.

Stamm, Claus. *Three Strong Women; A Tall Tale from Japan*. Viking, 1962.

Yamaguchi, Tohr. *The Golden Crane; A Japanese Folktale*. Holt, 1963.

❦ *EXPLORING FOLKTALES*   Select two of the following activities to help you explore folktales of different countries.

1. Choose one country that you would like to know more about. See how many sources you can find that would provide information for children about that country, especially its folklore. Read at least three of the folktales that appear in the books you discover.

2. Tape one folktale that especially appeals to you. Select one that you think would be useful in the classroom. Provide a brief introduction to the story so that listening children will better understand the story and have a clear purpose for listening.

3. Rewrite a folktale for younger children. Try to retain the original flavor of the story while simplifying the language. Illustrate your adaptation with collages, cut paper designs, or another art technique that you enjoy.

---

* Suitable for primary grades.

As Isaac Asimov writes in *Words from the Myths:*

Human beings wouldn't be human if they didn't wonder about the world about them. Many thousands of years ago, when mankind was still primitive, men must have looked out of caves and wondered about what they saw. What makes the lightning flash? Where did the wind come from? Why would winter start soon and why would all the green things die? And then why did they all come to life the next spring?[9]

The myths, then, represent our attempts to explain the world—lightning, stars, the winds, the heat of summer and the cold of winter. These ancient beliefs are akin to religion and yet they have a relationship to science. Above all, we need to remember today that in the times of their origins, these explanations were accepted as truth.

When we think of mythology, we frequently leap immediately to the myths of Greece and Rome. It is important, however, to realize that all cultures have a core of mythology in their early literature. Padraic Colum has prepared an excellent overview, *Orpheus: Myths of the World* (Macmillan, 1930), which presents and discusses myths from seventeen different groups, including myths of Egypt, Persia, Ireland, Iceland, India, China, Japan, Polynesia, Peru, and Mexico.

Full understanding of mythology and the elaborate system developed by the Greeks is not to be expected of elementary school children. We can, on the other hand, introduce children to mythology and to some of the explanations of natural phenomena for example, of how the earth was created or the coming of spring. Children can understand the logic of these early tales, for there is a certain childlike quality in early efforts to explain the mysteries of life.

The study of mythology obviously covers a breadth of knowledge that is impossible to present in one chapter focusing on all of folk literature. We will, therefore, only discuss some aspects of mythology that seem to be useful in the classroom. First of all, we will look at the *pourquoi tale,* which is the least complex of efforts to explain natural events. Then we will examine Greek mythology because of the richness it has to offer and its influence on Roman mythology. The Norse mythology will be included, because it too has influenced our literature and is a stark contrast to Greek mythology. Last, we will examine the literature focusing on

---

[9] Isaac Asimov, *Words from the Myths* (Houghton Mifflin, 1961), p. 9.

two well-known heroes that appear in epics and sagas, King Arthur and Robin Hood.

POURQUOI TALES

Pourquoi is the French word for *why,* and that is exactly what these tales attempt to explain—why the bear has a short tale, why cats and dogs are not friends, why the robin has an orange breast. These tales, which occur in the literature of all cultures, are relatively simple so that young children can understand them. Children accept them as imaginative explanations of natural happenings, and they will enjoy writing original pourquoi tales themselves.

American Indian lore is full of these tales that explain, for example:

Why the woodpecker has a red head.

Why the desert blossoms in the spring.

How butterflies were created.

Why wild roses have thorns.

How the seasons were determined.

The following pourquoi tale explains how the woodpecker was created when the Great Spirit became angry with a selfish woman.

HOW THE WOODPECKER WAS CREATED
An American Indian Tale Retold by Iris M. Tiedt

Listen well, my child, and I will tell you how in ancient times the Great Spirit Who Lives in the Sky came to visit men on Earth. One day in the guise of an old man, he entered the wigwam of a woman who, of course, did not know his true identity.

"Long have I been without food," said the Great Spirit Who Lives in the Sky. "Please share your food with me."

The woman appeared agreeable, for she promptly made a little cake of corn and placed it over the fire to bake. "This cake will be for you," she said. "Just wait until it has baked."

"I will wait," replied the Great Spirit.

When the cake was baked, however, the selfish woman thought to herself, "This cake is bigger than I thought. I will bake a smaller one to give to this stranger." So she put away the first cake and patted out a very small one to put on the fire. "This cake is for you as soon as it has baked," she said again, and again, the man answered, "I will wait."

When the second cake was baked, amazingly, it was twice as big as the first. "This cake is too big," the woman thought. "I will save it for the Feast Day." And so she made an even smaller cake, saying, "This cake will be for you as soon as it has baked." Again the man replied patiently, "I will wait, for I am very hungry."

When the third cake was baked, lo and behold, it was enormous. Poor woman. She did not know that the Great Spirit was testing her. With his magic powers he had made the cakes grow in size. When she saw that the third cake was even bigger than the others, she cried sharply, "There is no food for you here. Search in the woods for berries and bark, if you need food."

At this the Great Spirit Who Lives in the Sky rose up in anger. "You are cruel and selfish," he thundered. "You do not deserve to live the life of a good woman in a comfortable wigwam. Hereafter you shall search in the woods for berries and bugs in the bark of the trees."

As he spoke these words, the woman was transformed into a bird, a bird with black wings and a white breast. The feathers on her head were scarlet. She had become a red-headed woodpecker. And if you look in the woods today, you can still see the woodpecker tap, tapping on the bark of the trees searching for food.

You can find collections of such stories, for example, *Thunderbird and Other Stories* (Pantheon, 1964) by Henry Chafetz. One story in this collection tells how Nasan the giant became Thunderbird, "the maker of the storm clouds and a wanderer of the dark skies. His voice is the noise of thunder and the flash of lightning is the flapping of his wings."

Down from the Lonely Mountain (Harcourt Brace Jovanovich, 1965) is a group of twelve California Indian tales retold by Jane Louise Curry. With animals as the main characters, the Indians tell how the mountains and valleys were made and how the moon and stars were created.

Elphinstone Dayrell tells a pourquoi tale from southern Nigeria in *Why the Sun and the Moon Live in the Sky; An African Folktale* (Houghton Mifflin, 1968). The Water was invited to visit the Sun. At first Water declined because he knew his people would take up a tremendous amount of room. When the Sun persisted, however, he finally went with his entire family. As the Water rose, the Sun's house filled up. The Sun and his wife, the Moon, were soon forced to move up to the Sky to make room for their guest and his people. There they have been since this early beginning.

Pourquoi tales are included in Julius Lester's collection of tales for young children, *The Knee-High Man, and Other Tales* (Dial, 1972). This selection of six animal stories from Negro folk literature provides good material for reading aloud and for storytelling.

The literature of the Polynesians, especially that of Hawaii, includes many pourquoi tales also. One good collection is *Tales of Maui* by W. M.

Hill (Dodd, Mead, 1964). Other pourquoi tales are represented in *Hawaiian Myths of Earth, Sea, and Sky* (Holiday, 1966).

THE MYTHOLOGY OF GREECE

Despite the fact that Greek mythology originated in very early times, Edith Hamilton points out that this body of literature is far from primitive. For the first time "mankind became the center of the universe." In contrast, for example, to Egyptian mythology, the gods were conceived in human form, with all of the human being's imperfections such as jealousy and greed. As she states:

That is the miracle of Greek mythology—a humanized world, men freed from the paralyzing fear of an omnipotent Unknown. The terrifying incomprehensibilities which were worshiped elsewhere, and the fearsome spirits with which earth, air and sea swarmed, were banned from Greece. It may seem odd to say that the men who made the myths disliked the irrational and had a love for facts; but it is true, no matter how wildly fantastic some of the stories are. Anyone who reads them with attention discovers that even the most nonsensical take place in a world which is essentially rational and matter-of-fact.[10]

The following chart of the major Greek gods and goddesses and their Roman counterparts will help you to identify them by name and by the role they played.

The Gods and Goddesses of Greece and Rome

Greek Name	Roman Name	Role
Aphrodite	Venus	Goddess of love and beauty
Apollo	Apollo	God of healing, music, and poetry
Ares	Mars	God of war
Artemis	Diana	Goddess of the hunt and the moon

---

[10] Edith Hamilton, *Mythology* (Little, Brown, 1942), pp. 8–10.

Athena	Minerva	Goddess of weaving and wisdom
Demeter	Ceres	Goddess of the grains and harvest
Dionysus	Bacchus	God of wine
Eos	Aurora	Goddess of the dawn
Eros	Cupid	God of love
Hades	Pluto	God of the underworld
Hebe	Hebe	Goddess of youth
Hephaestus	Vulcan	God of fire and metal
Hera	Juno	Queen of the gods
Hermes	Mercury	God of speed; messenger of the gods
Hestia	Vesta	Goddess of the home
Hypnos	Somnus	God of sleep
Iris	Iris	Goddess of the rainbow
Morpheus	Morpheus	God of dreams
Nemesis	Nemesis	Goddess of vengeance
Pan	Faunus	God of nature
Persephone	Proserpina	Goddess of springtime; Queen of Hades
Poseidon	Neptune	God of the waters
Zeus	Jupiter	King of the gods

"Today the gods of the Greeks and Romans do not have a single temple. They do not have a single worshiper. But they are immortal. They cannot die because the Greeks invented such wonderful myths about them," writes Anne Terry in *The Golden Treasury of Myths and Legends* (Golden Press, 1959). This collection of her adaptations of the familiar myths, illustrated by Alice and Martin Provensen, should help young people become acquainted with the gods and goddesses listed on the chart. Another good overview is provided by the distinguished work of Ingri and Edgar Parin d'Aulaire in *Book of Greek Myths* (Doubleday, 1962).

There are many reminders of Greek and Roman mythology all around us in the twentieth century. Consider, for instance, the following:

Words	*Expressions*
cereal	in the arms of Morpheus
volcano	my nemesis
vulcanized	playing Cupid
somnambulant	

A beautiful edition of stories about the Greek gods is *The God Beneath the Sea* (Longmans, 1970). Illustrated with care and sensitivity by Charles Keeping, the stories are dramatically told by English writers, Leon Garfield and Edward Blishen. This passage accompanies the intriguing horses in Keeping's illustration:

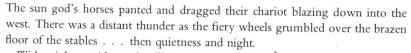

The sun god's horses panted and dragged their chariot blazing down into the west. There was a distant thunder as the fiery wheels grumbled over the brazen floor of the stables . . . then quietness and night.

With mighty strides and still drenched with the golden sweat of his labours, Apollo came. (p. 132).

From Leon Garfield and Edward Blishen: The God Beneath the Sea. *Illustrated by Charles Keeping, p. 133. Illustration copyright © Charles Keeping, 1970.*

"There are no fairytales like these old Greek ones for beauty, wisdom and truth," wrote Charles Kingsley. He prepared for his own children the attractive collection *The Heroes; Greek Fairy Tales* (Macmillan, 1954). Included are stories of Perseus, the Argonauts, and Theseus. Later the oversized book *Theseus* (Macmillan, 1964) was published, retold by Kingsley. This book is particularly interesting in that it includes an afterword by novelist Mary Renault, who is steeped in Greek lore.[11] She tells of the singing storytellers who kept this literature alive. She also relates how scholars such as Heinrich Schliemann discovered elements of truth in the Greek legends.

Recent publications have focused on retelling myths about one god or

---

[11] Among other novels, she has written two about Theseus: *The King Must Die* (Pantheon, 1958) and *The Bull from the Sea* (Pantheon, 1962).

goddess. Sometimes this results in a single story that appeals to younger children, as is true of Sarah F. Tomaino's *Persephone; Bringer of Spring* (Thomas Y. Crowell, 1971), an attractive book illustrated by Ati Forberg. The talented writer and storyteller Doris Gates is developing a series of books that focus on the adventures of one figure in mythology. One volume, *Lord of the Sky: Zeus* (Viking, 1972), includes the tale of Baucis and Philemon, as well as stories about Theseus, Ariadne, Dionysus, and others. To retell the escapades of Zeus for children is no mean feat, considering the amorous nature of many of his pursuits. A second volume is *The Warrior Goddess: Athena* (Viking, 1972), and a third is *The Golden God Apollo* (Viking, 1973).

Other readable books that feature a god or goddess include:

The Twelve Labors of Hercules by Robert Newman. Thomas Y. Crowell, 1972. Illustrated by Charles Keeping.

Daedalus and Icarus by Penelope Farmer. Harcourt Brace Jovanovich, 1971. Illustrated by Chris Conner.

A Fall from the Sky; The Story of Daedalus by Ian Serraillier. Walck, 1966.

The Gorgon's Head; The Story of Perseus by Ian Serraillier. Walck, 1962.

The Way of Danger; The Story of Theseus by Ian Serraillier. Walck, 1963.

NORSE GODS AND GIANTS

When the last ice age came to an end, the great glaciers that capped Northern Europe melted, uncovering a barren and rugged land. On the heels of the withdrawing ice came reindeer, wolves, bears, and foxes. They were pursued by hunters.

These men were forever struggling against Frost Giants, the cold-hearted spirits of the mountains and glaciers. But they found shelter in the valleys, where meadows grew lush and forests grew dense and deep. For thousands of years the beasts and the men who hunted them roamed throughout the north.

Then from the east burst a tribe of fierce horsemen. They stormed westward, settling new lands as they went. Led by a hulking, one-eyed chieftain, they spurred their horses on until at long last they were stopped by the crashing waves of the North Sea. They could go no farther, so they settled and made the land theirs.

Life in the north was hard for these new settlers. The Frost Giants sent bitter storms howling down from the mountains. Wild beasts, trolls and evil spirits lurked in the pathless forests, and cruel mermaids wrecked their ships. But the settlers were tough, and they were protected by their own gods, the Aesir, who had come with them from their faraway lands.

One of the best introductions to Norse mythology for the teacher as well as students is *Norse Gods and Giants* by Ingri and Edgar Parin D'Au-laire (Doubleday, 1967). Beginning with the paragraphs above (pages 9 and 10), these able historians, artists, and authors present the many gods who came from the Northlands, as well as tales of their activities.

The Aesir were the spirits who lived in Asgard watching over the lives of the earth people, and they made the rainbow as a bridge between As-gard and earth. God of War and Wisdom, the one-eyed Odin is the most important of the three original Aesir gods—Odin, Hoenir, and Lodur.

This list of the gods and goddesses will aid you as you examine the literature.

Aegir—god of the sea

Baldur—god of spring and light

Bure—father of the gods

Frey—god of rain, sunshine, and the fruits of the earth

Freya—goddess of love and beauty

Frigga—goddess of earth, marriage, and motherly love; Odin's wife

Heimdall—watchman of the rainbow

Hela—goddess of the dead

Hodur—god of darkness

Hoenir—god of hope

Idun—goddess of youth

Loki—god of fire

Mani—god of the moon

Niord—god of the wind

Odin—king of the gods; god of war and wisdom

Sol—god of the sun

Thor—god of thunder

Tyr—god of truth and battle

Ull—god of skiers

What we know of Norse mythology comes largely from an ancient collection of verse based on the oral tradition, the *Poetic Edda,* and a volume of prose, the *Prose Edda.* All of Germanic mythology is derived from this source. Since English is a Germanic language, there are remnants of this heritage in English, for example, the days of the week. Notice that in German Odin's name is Woden.

Sunday—Sun's Day

Monday—Moon's Day

Tuesday—Tyr's Day

Wednesday—Woden's Day

Thursday—Thor's Day

Friday—Freya's Day

Saturday—Saturn's Day

Of special interest in Norse mythology are the Valkyries, Odin's warrior maidens. They chose the warriors who were to die in battle and then carried them to Valhalla, a great hall in Asgard. There the slain heroes lived, cared for by the Valkyries.

A simple explanation of Norse mythology that would be useful even for upper grades is *The First Book of Norse Legends* (Watts, 1956) written and illustrated by Kathleen Elgin. Beginning with the time when "the world was mist swirling over a vast field of jagged and cavernous ice," the author tells how Audhumla the cow licked at the ice until the first god, Bure, appeared. The grandson of Bure is Odin, who with his brothers created Earth from Ymir the Frost Giant's body.

One of the favorites of the gods is Baldur. Margaret Hodges has retold the story *Baldur and the Mistletoe* (Little, Brown, 1974) in an attractive thirty-two-page book illustrated by Gerry Hoover. Baldur, "brightest and best of all the gods," was loved by everyone except Loki, who managed to destroy him.

Another version that tells of Baldur's dreams of his own death is *In the Morning of Time; The Story of the Norse God Balder* by Cynthia King. His mother, Frigga, tries to save her son by exacting a pledge from the rocks, the wood, and all of the elements, birds and beasts, and all growing things, that they would do no harm to Balder (notice the variant spelling).

The happy news spread like the wind. The feast in Valhalia that night had never been more joyous. Everywhere men and Gods, heroes and Godesses, laughed and kissed and said to each other, "Balder is safe! The Gods are safe! The world is safe! Spring will come again next year."

Only the mistletoe, whom everyone considered too young and weak to swear an oath, had not made a pledge.

The collection of literature for children about Norse mythology is not large. Following are additional selections to explore:

Colum, Padraic. *The Children of Odin; The Book of Northern Myths.* Macmillan, 1962.

Feagles, Anita. *Thor and the Giants; An Old Norse Legend.* Young Scott Books. Addison-Wesley, 1968.

Hosford, Dorothy G. *Thunder of the Gods.* Holt, 1952.

Keary, A. and E. *The Heroes of Asgard; Tales from Scandinavian Mythology.* Macmillan, 1870; Children's edition, 1930.

Synge, Ursula. *Weland; Smith of the Gods.* Illustrated by Charles Keeping. Phillips, 1973.

THE GREAT HEROES

In the literature of any culture there are great heroes, real or imaginary. Like all of folklore, legends about these heroes have been passed down through the oral tradition. We have such well-known folk heroes, therefore, as the following:

Odysseus—Greece

Beowulf—England

Cuchulain—Ireland

King Arthur—England

Roland—France

El Cid—Spain

Siegfried—Germany

Rama—India

Robin Hood—England

Paul Bunyan—United States

These heroes have been extolled in ballads and now appear in a sizable body of literature. Each scholar or teller of tales might reiterate the words of Sir Walter Scott:

I cannot tell how the truth may be;
I say the tale as 'twas said to me.

The Lay of the Last Minstrel

In this section we will explore the literature related to two of these heroes who have appeal for young people, namely, Robin Hood and King Arthur. Although there is not a vast literature about these heroes, what exists is of unusually high quality.

ROBIN HOOD

You who plod amid serious things that you feel it shame to give yourself up even for a few short moments to mirth and joyousness in the language of Fancy; you who think that life hath nought to do with innocent laughter that can harm no one; these pages are not for you. Clap to the leaves and go no farther than this; for I tell you plainly that if you go farther you will be scandalized by seeing good sober folks of real history so frisk and caper in gay colors and motley, that you would not know them but for the names tagged to them.

Thus Howard Pyle challenges the reader who opens the pages of *The Merry Adventures of Robin Hood of Great Renown in Nottinghamshire* (Scribner, 1946). Briefly he introduces Henry II and Queen Eleanor, the Lord Bishop of Hereford, the sour-tempered Sheriff of Nottingham, and the tall, merry King Richard of the Lion's Heart. The reader is invited to enter a land that is not fairyland but "the land of Fancy," which we can enter or leave at will. With sure strokes of an expert pen, Howard Pyle begins the story that involves all of the above-named persons:

In merry England in the time of old, when good King Henry the Second ruled the land, there lived within the green glades of Sherwood Forest, near Nottingham Town, a famous outlaw whose name was Robin Hood. No archer ever lived that would speed a gray goose shaft with such skill and cunning as his, nor were there ever such yeomen as the sevenscore merry men that roamed with him through the greenwood shades. Right merrily they dwelt within the depths of Sherwood Forest, suffering neither care nor want, but passing the time in merry games of archery or bouts of cudgel play, living upon the King's venison, washed down with draughts of ale of October brewing.

Not only Robin himself but all the band were outlaws and dwelt apart from other men, yet they were beloved by the country people round about, for no one ever came to jolly Robin for help in time of need and went away again with an empty fist.

And now I will tell you how it came about that Robin Hood fell afoul of the law.

ROBIN HOOD MEETETH THE TALL STRANGER ON THE BRIDGE

*Reprinted by permission of
Charles Scribner's Sons from
The Merry Adventures of
Robin Hood by Howard Pyle,
text and illustrations by the
author.*

The stories that follow in this classic book make reading aloud a real pleasure with a group of upper grade students. They will be amused, for example, by Robin's meeting with Little John, who tumbles Robin rudely off a log bridge into the creek and yet becomes Robin's most trusted friend. Students will meet Will Scarlet, Allan a Dale, and Guy of Gisbourne, and thrill to the exciting adventures of Robin Hood's band of outlaws.

And they will undoubtedly shed a tear of regret when Howard Pyle tells in the epilogue "as speedily as may be of how that stout fellow, Robin Hood, died . . ." Concluding the final events of the life of Robin Hood, he writes: "And now, dear friend, we also must part, for our merry journeyings have ended, and here, at the grave of Robin Hood, we turn, each going his own way."

This edition of Robin Hood contains twenty-two stories and was published originally in 1883 with Howard Pyle's unique drawings. Later editions of this same work include only twelve stories adapted by Howard Pyle (Scribner; Watts) and are much easier for students to read themselves.

In addition to Howard Pyle's outstanding work, Robin Hood's adventures are featured in these books:

McGovern, Ann. *Robin Hood of Sherwood Forest.* Thomas Y. Crowell, 1968.

McSpadden, J. Walker. *Robin Hood and His Merry Outlaws.* Illustrated by Louis Slobodkin; introduction by May Lamberton Becker. World, 1946.

An interesting collection of eighteen ballads about Robin Hood are presented with words and music in *Songs of Robin Hood,* edited by Anne Malcolmson (Houghton, Mifflin, 1947). Dramatizations of stories from the Robin Hood legend are also available in Bernice Wells Carlson's *Play a Part* (Abingdon, 1970), for example, which includes a play for puppets, "Robin Hood Meets Little John." In Sylvia E. Kamerman's *Dramatized Folk Tales of the World; A Collection of 50 One-Act Plays* (Plays, 1971), we find "Robin Hood Outwits the Sheriff," which children from middle elementary through junior high school would enjoy.

Geoffrey Trease depicts a young boy, Dickon, who joins Robin Hood's band in the novel *Bows Against the Barons* (Meredith, 1967), a rare fictionalized version of Robin Hood's exploits.

A well-known volume for children is *The Boy's King Arthur* (Scribner, 1917), edited by the English poet Sidney Lanier and illustrated with the paintings of N. C. Wyeth. Based on the early narratives of Sir Thomas Malory, Book I begins impressively:

It befell in the days of the noble Utherpendragon, when he was King of England that there was born to him a son who in after time was King Arthur. Howbeit the boy knew not he was the king's son. For when he was but a babe the king commanded two knights and two ladies to take the child bound in rich cloth of gold, "and deliver him to what poor man you meet at the postern gate of the castle." So the child was delivered unto Merlin, and so he bare it forth unto Sir Ector, and made an holy man to christen him, and named him Arthur; and so Sir Ector's wife nourished him. (p.3).

Two years later when King Uther died, the lords began to vie for the position as ruler of the kingdom. Who would be King? The sign came in the form of a massive sword plunged into a stone bearing the words: "Who so pulleth out the sword of this stone and anvil, is rightwise king born of England." The boy Arthur of course is the only one who can draw the sword forth.

Another classic edition is *The Story of King Arthur and His Knights* (Scribner, 1927) written and illustrated by Howard Pyle. He begins his telling of the tale with a description of how Uther-Pendragon became "King of the entire realm" with the help of Merlin and Ulfius. He expresses his pleasure in recounting these legends in the foreword to the book, thus:

After several years of contemplation and of thought upon the matter herein contained, it has at last come about, by the Grace of God, that I have been able to write this work with such pleasure of spirit that, if it gives to you but a part of the joy that it hath afforded me, I shall be very well content with what I have done.

Howard Pyle divides "The Winning of Kinghood" into three chapters or stories as he dramatizes Arthur's first withdrawing of the sword, his repetition of this impossible achievement, and finally the acceptance of Arthur by the lords of the land. The other sections of the book focus on:

The Winning of a Sword

The Winning of a Queen

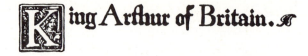

King Arthur of Britain.

The Story of Merlin

The Story of Sir Pellias

The Story of Sir Gawaine

Other editions of the King Arthur stories can be found, although few rival the early work of Howard Pyle. All of the following are appropriate for middle school students:

Hieatt, Constance. *Sir Gawain and the Green Knight*. Thomas Y. Crowell, 1967.

————. *The Joy of the Court*. Thomas Y. Crowell, 1971.

————. *The Sword and the Grail*. Thomas Y. Crowell, 1972.

MacLeod, Mary. *The Book of King Arthur and His Noble Knights*. Various editions; first published in England, 1900.

Picard, Barbara Leonie. *Stories of King Arthur and His Knights*. Walck, 1966.

Robbins, Ruth. *Taliesin and King Arthur*. Parnassus Press, 1970.

White, T. H. *The Sword in the Stone*. Putnam, 1939.

Williams, Jay. *The Sword of King Arthur*. Thomas Y. Crowell, 1968.

Fiction that uses the Arthurian legend as background includes Clyde Robert Bulla's *The Sword in the Tree* (Thomas Y. Crowell, 1956), a story that younger children can enjoy. Eleven-year-old Shan goes to King Arthur's court at Camelot to ask for help in finding his father. Through reading such fiction children gain information about knighthood and chivalry. Another work of fiction that utilizes this background is Andre Norton's *Steel Magic* (World, 1965). In this story three children move through time to the world of King Arthur.

The hero tales provide a sense of greatness, courage, and idealism that is not found in other literature. For this reason all children should have the opportunity to hear the epic tales as they savor the power of these heroic characters.

❦ *EXPLORING MYTHOLOGY* Select two of these activities that will help you explore mythology and prepare materials for teaching.

1. Select one hero from the list on page 256. Read the stories about this person, for example, Roland, so that you know the tales of this hero's adventures.

2. Make a list of all the signs of mythology you can find in contemporary society. Include names of products (Venus pencils), cities (Olympia, Washington), and so on. This is an interesting activity for a group of middle schoolers.

3. Prepare a chart similar to that on page 250 that you could use in a classroom to help children learn the names of the Greek and Roman gods and goddesses. You may use just a few of the main ones, but be sure to make the chart large enough to be seen easily by children.

4. Explore the various stories about one god or goddess (Diana, Neptune), an event (the war between Athens and Sparta), or a topic (the creation of earth). Devise some way of sharing this information with young people—a painting, a diorama, a skit.

STORYTELLING

The ancient art of storytelling is the basis of most folklore, for without the oral sharing of tales, mythology and the great epics could not have developed, spread geographically, and transcended time. Everybody loves a story: young or old, rich or poor, teacher or student.

As Johnson, Sickels, and Sayers comment:

Storytelling offers a direct approach to children. . . . Good storytelling breaks down barriers: differences in age, the fear or awe in which children sometimes hold their elders. Tell a child a story he enjoys, and he looks upon you as an equal, trusts you with revelations he would never have thought of sharing . . .[12]

The teacher who acquires the skills of storytelling will discover a new way of reaching children, for sharing a story is a rich experience in communicating. Children respond eagerly to the intimate warmth. They want to share their own stories with the group. Thus begins a cycle of storytelling that can only result in enthusiastic use of language and eager searching for material.

CHOOSING A STORY

Selection of a story to tell depends largely on the audience to whom you speak. Let us suppose that your audience is a group of children in a classroom. They are a "captive audience," but they represent the most receptive audience you could find.

As a beginning storyteller, select a story that is short and is not familiar to the group. Folktales, fables, and myths provide excellent material. You might, for example, start with one of Aesop's fables, which contains all the elements of a longer story, but is relatively easy to learn.

THE WIND AND THE SUN

Once upon a time when everything could talk, the Wind and the Sun fell into an argument as to which was the stronger. Finally they decided to put the matter to a test; they would see which one could make a certain man, who was walking along

---

[12] Edna Johnson, Evelyn R. Sickels, and Frances Clarke Sayers, *Anthology of Children's Literature* (Houghton Mifflin, 1970), pp. 1141–1142.

the road, throw off his cape. The Wind tried first. He blew and he blew and he blew. The harder and colder he blew, the tighter the traveler wrapped his cape about him. The Wind finally gave up and told the Sun to try. The Sun began to smile and as it grew warmer and warmer, the traveler was comfortable once more. But the Sun shone brighter and brighter until the man grew so hot, the sweat poured out on his face, he became weary, and seating himself on a stone, he quickly threw his cape to the ground. You see, gentleness had accomplished what force could not.

Above all, when you select a story for telling, choose one that you especially like so your enthusiasm will come naturally. Here are sources of additional material for storytelling.

Association for Childhood Education. *Told Under the Magic Umbrella.* Macmillan, 1939.

Belpre, Pura. *The Tiger and the Rabbit, and Other Tales.* Lippincott, 1965.

Carpenter, Frances. *African Wonder Tales.* Doubleday, 1963.

Cothran, Jean. *With a Wig, With a Wag, and Other American Folk Tales.* McKay, 1954.

Felton, Harold W. *Pecos Bill.* Knopf, 1949.

Gruenberg, S. M. *Favorite Stories Old and New.* Doubleday, 1955.

Harmon, Humphrey. *Tales Told Near a Crocodile.* Viking, 1967.

Hitchcock, Patricia. *The King Who Rides a Tiger and Other Tales from Nepal.* Houghton Mifflin, 1967.

Jagendorf, M. A. *Folk Stories of the South.* Vanguard, 1973.

Leach, Maria, ed. *How the People Sang the Mountains Up; How and Why Stories.* Viking, 1967.

Leodhas, S. N. *Gaelic Ghosts.* Holt, 1964.

Macmillan, Cyrus. *Glooskap's Country and Other Indian Tales.* Oxford, 1956.

Manning-Sanders, Ruth. *A Book of Ogres and Trolls.* Dutton, 1973.

Sandburg, Carl. *Rootabaga Stories.* Harcourt Brace Jovanovich, 1922.

Shephard, Esther. *Paul Bunyan.* Harcourt Brace Jovanovich, 1924.

Singer, Isaac. *Zlateh the Goat and Other Stories.* Harper & Row, 1966.

Thompson, Vivian L. *Hawaiian Tales of Heroes and Champions*. Holiday, 1971.

Thorne-Thomsen, G. *East O' the Sun and West O' the Moon*. Roy, 1946.

TELLING THE STORY

The first thing to do, of course, is to learn the story that you have selected. Read the story through carefully, observing especially the beginning lines, the sequence of events, and the ending lines. Note this information on a 4″ × 6″ card, which will be the nucleus of your storyteller's file.

THE WIND AND THE SUN
—*Aesop*

First Line

Once upon a time when everything could talk, the Wind and the Sun fell into an argument as to which was the stronger.

Events

1. Agreed to test
2. Wind tried
3. Wind failed
4. Sun tried
5. Sun succeeded

Last Line

You see, gentleness had accomplished what force could not.

The first and last lines are the most important, so memorize them verbatim. Repeat the first line several times. Can you say it without a cue card? Memorize the last line in the same way.

You also need to memorize the events in order as they happen. Don't try to memorize the lines for the body of the story unless there is an important bit of dialogue or a significant detail that you need to stress. Often there will be a repeated phrase or sentence that is important to maintain the rhythm of the story, such as "He blew and he blew and he blew".

Then read the story again slowly as you concentrate on the essential elements noted on your card. Next, try telling the story aloud using the card as little as possible. Since this is a very short story you will soon have the story elements well in hand.

Then you simply need practice. This is easily handled by telling your story to a cassette recorder. Try to tell the story smoothly without worrying about things you leave out. If you get the essentials—first line, sequence of events, last line—you're well on your way.

To polish the story, listen to the cassette as you note the following:

1. Do you deliver the first line well?

2. Do you introduce all of the events you had listed?

3. Are you speaking clearly?

4. Do you stumble over any words, perhaps tricky names?

5. Is your talking paced well, not too fast or slow?

6. Do you deliver the final line effectively?

STUDENT STORY TELLERS

The whole point of your developing skill as a storyteller is to share literature with children and to help children develop storytelling skills, too. Not only does storytelling extend children's enjoyment of literature, but it also helps them develop poise and linguistic fluency, which are important skills in our verbal society. Have children go through the same steps described for you. They can begin with one of Aesop's fables or a short humorous story such as a droll.

Ask children to work in pairs as they learn stories to tell. They can help each other outline the essential information and practice telling their stories. What an incentive to read, write, speak, and listen!

When a pair of students is ready, they can announce a performance to which everyone in the room is invited. Stress positive reinforcement through appreciative applause. If there are suggestions for improvement to be made, talk to the child or pair of children afterward. As they gain confidence, children can volunteer as storytellers for younger children, and they will enjoy expanding their repertoires.

After children gain some experience, have them generalize about a few things they have learned. Recommendations to storytellers:

1. Face the audience before you begin the story.

2. Speak so you can be heard.

3. Don't make too many gestures; when you do, make them big.

4. Look at the audience as you talk.

✿ *AN EXPERIMENT IN STORYTELLING*   Choose a story that you would like to share with elementary school children. Follow the steps for learning the story so that you can tell it easily. Practice on your friends or use a tape recorder.

   Here are selections from folklore that you might like to try:

Pandora's Box

The Emperor's New Clothes

Rapunzel

The Boy Who Cried Wolf

Arrange to tell your story to an elementary school class.

Broadman, Muriel and Jack Leskoff. *Cinderellas around the World*. McKay, 1976.

Bullfinch, Thomas. *Bullfinch's Mythology: The Age of Fable, The Age of Chivalry, Legends of Charlemagne*. Thomas Y. Crowell, 1947.

Darrell, Margery, ed. *Once upon a Time: The Fairy Tale World of Arthur Rackham*. Viking, 1972.

Frazer, James G. *The New Golden Bough*. Criterion, 1959.

Hamilton, Edith. *Mythology*. Little, Brown, 1942.

Ireland, Norma Olin, comp. *Index to Fairy Tales, 1949–1972*. Faxon, 1973. (*Includes folklore, legends, and myths in collections.*)

Larkin, David, ed. *The Fantastic Kingdom: A Collection of Illustrations from the Golden Days of Storytelling*. Ballantine Books, 1974. (*A paper-bound book that contains many fine reproductions suitable for framing for classroom display.*)

Opie, Iona and Peter Opie. *The Lore and Language of Schoolchildren*. Oxford, 1967.

Wagner, Joseph A. *Children's Literature through Storytelling*. Wm. C. Brown, 1970.

Ziegler, Elsie B. *Folklore: An Annotated Bibliography and Index to Single Editions*. Faxon, 1973. (*Companion to Ireland's work above.*)

6

Be Like
the Bird

Exploring Poetry with Children

From *Winds* copyright © 1971 by Mary O'Neill. Reprinted by permission of Doubleday & Company, Inc.

Wind Colors the World

If wind were not always busy
Moving up, thrusting down,
To the right, to the left,
In whirls, spirals and shafts,
Stirring light like a knife, like a spoon,
To break it into all its colored rays
How dull would be the color of our days.

Mary O'Neill
Winds[1]

Historically, poetry is one of the primary literary forms, for it can be traced to early oral traditions in all cultures. The minstrel singing the stories of Roland, chants of the Indian medicine men, the calls of the shepherds in Grecian fields—all are poetry of the people.

Poetry and children belong together. Children respond naturally to the rhythm and melody, the songs of poetry, and they soon learn to delight in the humorous narrative poems. Gradually young people can also come to appreciate the imagery and wisdom in more sophisticated poems, such as this short one by Victor Hugo:

Be like the bird, who
Halting in his flight

---

[1] Mary O'Neill, *Winds,* illustrated by James Barkley (Doubleday, 1970).

On limb too slight
Feels it give way beneath him,
Yet sings
Knowing he hath wings.

Many teachers are finding that poetry has much to offer in any classroom. Children of all ages enjoy poetry when presented as something vibrant and meaningful, something that evokes a response. As we explore poetry and consider ways to share poetry with children, we will focus on:

1. Becoming acquainted with many poems that children can enjoy—varied topics, moods, and styles

2. Experimenting with many ways of sharing poetry in a classroom

3. Developing an understanding of what poetry is, so that we can convey this attitude and understanding to students

4. Knowing varied forms of poetry

5. Experiencing the writing of poetry and considering ways to motivate children to write poetry

In this chapter we will explore the content of poetry for children under the following categories: (1) What Is Poetry? (2) What Poetry Communicates, (3) The Language of Poetry, (4) Forms of Poetry, and (5) Poets Are People. In the last main section of the chapter, Poetry in Classrooms, we will discuss ways of promoting poetry in the classroom under the topics: (1) Poetry Related to Themes or Topics, (2) Poetry Is Meant to Be Heard, (3) Children Can Read Poems, and (4) Children Can Write Poetry.

🌸 *HOW ABOUT YOU?* Where do you stand in the world of poetry? Do you know poetry and poets? Before beginning this exploration of poetry for children, assess your knowledge of poetry by answering these brief questions.

1. What do you think of when you hear the word *poetry?*

2. Can you name three poets who write especially for children?

3. List three concepts that you would teach children about poetry.

4. Can you describe two forms of the quatrain?

5. Can you repeat several lines of a poem; a whole poem?

EXPLORING POETRY

"You come, too," invites amiable Robert Frost, as he sets out to check the pasture spring. This invitation serves also as the title of an appealing volume of Frost's poetry (Holt, 1959), which you as well as elementary school students will enjoy.

I'm going out to clean the pasture spring;
I'll only stop to rake the leaves away
(And wait to watch the water clear, I may):
I shan't be gone long.—You come too.

I'm going out to fetch the little calf
That's standing by the mother. It's so young
It totters when she licks it with her tongue.
I shan't be gone long.—You come too.

This is the kind of poetry you need to know. You need to know not only Robert Frost and his poetry, but also the writings of Harry Behn, Laura E. Richards, Christina Rossetti, Karla Kuskin, and John Ciardi. You need to be familiar with a variety of poetry written about many subjects, presented in a wide range of forms.

Knowing poetry, you will be able to open doors for children, so that they will also enjoy the language, understand the message communicated, and appreciate the experiments of poets, the music makers of literature. You can then extend the invitation: "You come, too."

In the following section we will consider the question: What is poetry? Then we will discuss what poetry communicates, the language of poetry, forms of poetry, and the poets who write for children.

WHAT IS POETRY?

"Poetry is special," says Karla Kuskin, but "poetry isn't special, to be reserved for deep thoughts and auspicious occasions. It can be as natural a form of expression as shouting or singing. Cultivate poetry and it will provide the shortest distance between an emotion and its articulation, the direct route from saying anything in any way to saying something special."[2]

Many noted scholars have defined poetry, but no definition fits so well as that expressed by Eleanor Farjeon in these lines:

What is poetry? Who knows?
Not the rose, but the scent of the rose;
Not the sky, but the light of the sky;
Not the fly, but the gleam of the fly;
Not the sea, but the sound of the sea;
Not myself, but something that makes me
See, hear and feel something that prose
Cannot; what is it? Who knows?

Poetry is elusive. What is poetry for one person may not be poetry for another, for poetry is personal. Observe the varied subjects, the language styles, and the patterning of these poems.

WIND
Aileen Fisher

The wind has lots of noises:
it sniffs,
it puffs,
it whines;
it rumbles like an ocean
through junipers and pines;
it whispers in the windows,
it howls,
it sings,
it hums;
it tells you VERY PLAINLY
every time it comes.

A MODERN DRAGON
Rowena Bastin Bennett

A train is a dragon that roars through the dark.
He wriggles his tail as he sends up a spark.
He pierces the night with his one yellow eye,
And all the earth trembles when he rushes by.

---

[2] Quoted in *Poetry, Children and Children's Books* (The Children's Book Council, 1976).

SOMETHING TOLD THE WILD GEESE
Rachel Field

Something told the wild geese
  It was time to go.
Though the fields lay golden
  Something whispered, "Snow."
Leaves were green and stirring,
  Berries, luster-glossed,
But beneath warm feathers,
  Something cautioned, "Frost."
All the sagging orchards
  Steamed with amber spice,
But each wild breast stiffened
  At remembered ice.
Something told the wild geese
  It was time to fly—
Summer sun was on their wings,
  Winter in their cry.

HABITS OF THE HIPPOPOTAMUS
Arthur Guiterman

The hippopotamus is strong
  And huge of head and broad of bustle;
The limbs on which he rolls along
  Are big with hippopotomuscle.

He does not greatly care for sweets
  Like ice cream, apple pie, or custard,
But takes to flavor what he eats,
  A little hippopotomustard.

The hippopotamus is true
  To all his principles, and just;
He always tries his best to do
  The things one hippopotomust.

He never rides in trucks or trams,
  In taxicabs or omnibuses,
And so keeps out of traffic jams
  And other hippopotomusses.

   Which poem might appeal to a healthy sixth grade boy or girl who enjoys backpacking? Which poem might appeal to a lively second grader? Which poem appeals to you?

The standards for choosing poetry for children are much the same as those for adults. Children do not respond to insipid, sentimental verse any more eagerly than do adults. Beware, therefore, of such condescending verses as these:

1. A birdie with a yellow bill
   Hopped upon my window sill . . .

2. Blessings on thee, little man,
   Barefoot boy with cheek of tan! . . .

Is poetry all sweetness and light, dainty and refined? Does it necessarily talk of nature, love and happiness? Children today are prepared to enjoy poetry on many subjects—travel, science, self-identity—topics of interest and concern to all of us.

Children can learn to appreciate the fresh images of Carl Sandburg, for example, as he describes the sound of a boat's whistle in the fog, "desolate and lone."

Desolate and lone
All night long on the lake
Where fog trails and mist creeps,
The whistle of a boat
Calls and cries unendingly,
Like some lost child
In tears and trouble
Hunting the harbor's breast
And the harbor's eyes.

They respond to the humorous-serious message of Tom Lehrer on "Pollution."

If you visit American city,
You will find it very pretty.
Just two things of which you must beware;
Don't drink the water and don't breathe the air.

Pollution, pollution,
They got smog and sewage and mud,
Turn on your tap and get hot and cold running crud . . .

Encourage children to react to poetry, to respond in any way that seems natural to them. This reaction may be positive or negative, for as we have already pointed out, poetry is personal. As William Stafford comments:

Poems don't just happen. They are luckily or stealthily related to a readiness within ourselves. When we read or hear them, we react. We aren't just supposed to react—any poem that asks for a dutiful response is masquerading as a poem, not being one. A good rule is—don't respond unless you have to. But when you find you do have a response—trust it. It has a meaning.[3]

Do not expect, therefore, that all children will have the same reaction, nor that they will have the same reaction that you do. As teachers we can develop a classroom climate that is accepting of individuals and their needs, both affective and cognitive. We can provide an environment that includes a rich supply of poetry. Responses will follow and children will discover the poetry that is right for them.

❀ *COLLECTING POETRY* There is "a time for every purpose," and now is the time to explore poetry to discover poems that *you* like. Obtain a collection of poems for children from your college or public library. Every teacher should own a good anthology of poetry, for it is indispensable in a classroom.

1. Examine several of the following books in which the poems in this chapter appear. All are recommended for purchase by individuals or libraries as resource books.

   Arbuthnot, May Hill and Sheldon Root. *Time for Poetry*. Scott, Foresman.

   Austin, Mary C. and Queenie B. Mills. *The Sound of Poetry*. Allyn and Bacon.

   Dunning, Stephen, Hugh Smith and Edward Lueders. *Reflections on a Gift of Watermelon Pickle*. Scott, Foresman.

   Sheldon, William and others. *The Reading of Poetry*. Allyn and Bacon.

---

[3] William Stafford, "Introduction" to *Since Feeling Is First* by James Mecklenburger and Gary Simmons (Scott, Foresman, 1971), p. 7.

Westermark, Tory and Brian Gooch. *Poetry Is for People*. Macmillan of Canada.

When choosing

Examine these books to determine their potential value to you. Consider the following:

a. Variety of poetry included

b. Number of poems; length of book

✓ c. Readability; presentation of poems; format

d. Organization by topic or theme

e. Difficulty level—reading and listening

f. Indexes provided

g. Your personal reaction to the book

2. Designate a section of your notebook for *Poetry*. Begin collecting ideas and materials that will be useful to you, for example:

a. Special poems that you discover (don't copy ones that are in books you own)

b. Notes about using specific poems you like

c. Lessons designed to teach concepts about poetry

WHAT POETRY COMMUNICATES

process of knowing perception

The message of the poet is both emotional and intellectual, affective and cognitive. A poem usually conveys something of both, for it is very difficult to isolate feelings or to be completely objective in presenting an idea expressed in poetic form.

Poets cannot communicate with young children without the assistance of an *interpreter*, someone to read their poetry to young people who cannot yet read it independently. Children's reactions to poetry will be influenced greatly by your presentation as their interpreter of poetry, for attitudes and values are present in your voice as you read, the way you introduce the poem, and your own enthusiasm. Poets are literally dependent on you to facilitate communication.

Eve Merriam describes this dependence of the poet and, indeed, the poem itself, on a reader in *"I," Says the Poem*. The poem ends, thus:

As we serve in this capacity of bringing children and poetry together, it is important that we also recognize the need for selecting the best mode of presenting a poem. Poems that have pronounced rhythms or tell a story are made for reading aloud to children. They are usually easily understood the first time we hear them. Those that are unrhymed and perhaps contain more intricate imagery will require a different approach that may include the study of a written copy, as well as reading aloud followed by discussion. When poems were presented orally without other activities, Ann Terry found that children disliked haiku, free verse, and poems that contained imagery. (Her study is discussed in more detail in Chapter 10.) The way you present a poem, therefore, will obviously affect how well the poet will communicate. Throughout this chapter we will be discussing ways of presenting poetry, of helping children become directly involved with poets and what they have to say.

POETRY PROVIDES INFORMATION AND VOCABULARY   Poetry can communicate even if it is not fully understood. We can share poems we enjoy orally with children who cannot read. Children delight in the rhythm of the language as you read. Their listening vocabularies (much larger than speaking vocabularies) enable them to comprehend new words and ideas when presented in context. They can often get the gist of the meaning through listening although they may not be able to define every word or to read or write these words themselves. Consider "City Pigeons" by Leland Jacobs, for example:

In Herald Square,
In Herald Square,
I saw the pigeons gathered there,

Talking, strutting with an air
As if they owned all Herald Square,
Standing on the hot concrete
Having little snacks to eat.
   And I'd call
   To your attention,
   The pigeons hold
   A huge convention
     There
In Herald Square,
In Herald Square.

The rhythm of the words as they are read aloud carries the listener along, so that young children do not need to know the full meaning of "Herald Square." They get the feeling of *strutting* from your voice, and can picture the flock of pigeons from personal experience without knowledge of a *convention*. A casual explanation or discussion of a few words, however, adds interest to the poem and develops vocabulary in an effective way, thus:

Who knows what *strutting* is? The poet says the pigeons are *strutting*. Can you show us how to *strut*, Dan? That's the way—would you all like to try *strutting*? Strut like a proud pigeon.

The poet says the pigeons were at a convention. I went to a convention last month. Who has some idea what a convention is?—Yes, a meeting of lots of people. Can you picture the pigeons looking like a meeting of people—strutting around, "talking," getting the latest news?

After this type of discussion you might read the poem again. "Listen as I read the poem again. See if you can picture the convention of strutting pigeons in Herald Square." The skillful teacher will make a point of inserting these words in the classroom dialogue later, to reinforce knowledge and to remind children of the enjoyable poetry experience you shared.

POETRY IS HUMOROUS AND FUN-LOVING Many poets have delighted in word play, nonsense, and gentle spoofs. Ogden Nash is a master of audacious plays on words to suit witty observations that tickle the risibilities of both children and adults.

The panther is like a leopard,
Except it hasn't been peppered.
Should you behold a panther crouch,
Prepare to say Ouch.
Better yet, if called by a panther,
Don't anther.

Laura E. Richards, who writes poems especially for children, obviously enjoys her own poems. She often uses a rollicking rhythm, as in "The Umbrella Brigade":

But let it rain
Tree-toads and frogs,
Muskets and pitchforks,
Kittens and dogs!
Dash away! Plash away!
Who is afraid?
Here we go,
The Umbrella Brigade!

Edward Lear's name is almost synonymous with nonsense poetry, especially the limerick. Of his longer works, "The Owl and the Pussy-Cat" is probably best known.

The Owl and the Pussy-Cat went to sea
    In a beautiful pea-green boat,
They took some honey, and plenty of money
    Wrapped up in a five-pound note.
The Owl looked up to the stars above,
    And sang to a small guitar,
"O lovely Pussy, O Pussy, my love,.
    What a beautiful Pussy you are,
                You are,
                You are!
What a beautiful Pussy you are!"

A. A. Milne, creator of Pooh, illustrates his marvelous sense of humor in "Furry Bear." Notice, too, his expert handling of language.

If I were a bear,
    And a big bear too,

I shouldn't much care
    If it froze or snew;
I shouldn't much mind
    If it snowed or friz—
I'd be all fur-lined
    With a coat like his!

For I'd have fur boots and a brown fur wrap,
And brown fur knickers and a big fur cap.
I'd have a fur muffle-ruff to cover my jaws.
And brown fur mittens on my big brown paws.
With a big brown furry-down up to my head,
I'd sleep all the winter in a big fur bed.

    A number of other enjoyable humorous poems you might explore include:

Edward Lear—Limericks, "Calico Pie," "The Jumblies"

Charles Edward Carryl—"The Plaint of the Camel"

Beatrice Curtis Brown—"Jonathan Bing"

Mildred Plew Meigs—"The Pirate Don Durk of Dowdee"

Lewis Carroll—"The Walrus and the Carpenter"

John Ciardi—"The Reason for the Pelican"

William Jay Smith—"Parrot"

POETRY IS SENSUAL   The poet appeals to all of the senses as he or she strives for different effects. Consider which of the senses are required to provide meaning to the imagery in "Down the Rain Falls."

Down the rain falls,
Up crackles the fire,
Tick-tock goes the clock
Neither lower nor higher. . .

Elizabeth Coatsworth

How do you respond to the pushing up of the tulips in this picture of "April"?

The tulips now are pushing up.
Like small green knuckles through the ground.
The grass is young and doubtful yet.
The robin takes a look around
And if you listen you can hear
Spring laughing with a windy sound.

Eunice Tietjens

Christopher Morley's "Smells (Junior)" focuses on a sense that is not as common in poetry as are visual and sound images.

My Daddy smells like tobacco and books,
  Mother, like lavender and listerine;

Uncle John carries a whiff of cigars,
  Nannie smells starchy and soapy and clean.
Shandy, my dog, has a smell of his own
  (When he's been out in the rain he smells most);
But Katie, the cook, is more splendid than all—
  She smells exactly like hot buttered toast!

POETRY DEVELOPS A SENSE OF IDENTITY   Expression of personal feelings and thoughts, typical of poetry, reaches out to the reader. You find yourself sharing the emotion, feeling for and with the speaker, identifying with the poet. We gain inner strength as we become more aware of our emotions, our values. We learn to accept them and even to disclose them to others as poets have done.

   "Keep a poem in your pocket and a picture in your head / and you'll never feel lonely at night when you're in bed," writes Beatrice Schenk de Regniers. Loneliness and aloneness, two quite different feelings, one sad, the other strong, are important feelings to be in touch with. Walt Whitman writes of the feeling of community he feels as he sits alone.

This moment yearning and thoughtful sitting alone,
It seems to me there are other men in other lands yearning and thoughtful,
It seems to me I can look over and behold them in Germany, Italy, France, Spain,
Or far, far away, in China, or in Russia or Japan, talking other dialects,
And it seems to me if I could know those other men I should become attached to
  them as I do to men in my own lands,
O I know we should be brethren and lovers,
  I know I should be happy with them.

   The desire for a private place, a place for hiding precious belongings and one's self, is expressed often, as in "The Secret Cavern" by Margaret Widdemer.

Underneath the boardwalk, way, way back,
There's a splendid cavern, big and black—
If you want to get there, you must crawl
Underneath the posts and steps and all
When I've finished paddling, there I go—
None of all the other children know!

The desire for space and to be closer to nature, as expressed by Richard Hovey in "Spring," is another feeling many of us share.

I said in my heart, "I am sick of four walls and a ceiling.
I have need of the sky.
I have business with the grass.
I will up and get me away where the hawk is wheeling,
Lone and high,
And the snow clouds go by . . . "

"Rudolph Is Tired of the City" by Gwendolyn Brooks states this feeling in another way.

These buildings are too close to me.
I'd like to PUSH away.
I'd like to live in the country,
And spread my arms all day.

I'd like to spread my breath out, too—
As farmers' sons and daughters do.
I'd tend the cows and chickens.
I'd do the other chores.
Then, all the hours left I'd go
A-SPREADING out-of-doors.

Yet another feeling with which children can identify is joy and appreciation of nature's beauty. "O world, I cannot hold thee close enough!" cries Edna St. Vincent Millay, as she glories in the fall beauty of the woods. In "Leisure," William H. Davies says, "What is this life if, full of care, / We have no time to stand and stare?" Bliss Carman's well-known lines share the same joy of beauty in "A Vagabond Song":

There is something in the autumn that is native to my blood—
Touch of manner, hint of mood;
And my heart is like a rhyme,
With the yellow and the purple and the crimson keeping time.

The Chippewa song, "A Song of Greatness," that Mary Austin translated, provides a feeling of strength and self-identity that speaks to many young people.

When I hear the old men
Telling of heroes,
Telling of great deeds
Of ancient days,
When I hear them telling,
Then I think within me
I too am one of these.
When I hear the people
Praising great ones,
Then I know that I too
Shall be esteemed,
I too when my time comes
Shall do mightily.

Children need poetry. They need this chance to share dreams and feelings. They need to hear the poets speaking to them and to realize that poets are people.

✿ *A POETRY EXPERIENCE* Plan a poetry experience that you can use in a classroom to help children understand "what poetry communicates." Your plan might, for example, focus on developing vocabulary, sensory awareness, or self-identity. Here is one idea focusing on sensory awareness.

1. Read the poem "Smells (Junior)" by Christopher Morley aloud.

2. Discuss smells:

   What smells does the child in this poem think of for each person he or she knows? What about the dog's smell?

   Think of the many things you smell each day. What can you learn by using your nose?

3. Work at the board as the group creates a poem, thus:

   Your nose knows—
      that a red rose is fragrant

as you lean over to sniff
the sweet perfume.
Your nose knows—
    that bacon frying in the kitchen
    means "Hurry up! Breakfast is
    ready!"

4. After developing several ideas together, have children write more
   ideas individually. Then let children share these ideas orally.

5. Ask them if they'd like to put their ideas in a book called "Your Nose
   Knows." Encourage them to illustrate the ideas.

THE LANGUAGE OF POETRY

A distinctive attribute of the poet is love of language, for the compact-
ness of poetic forms requires polish. Each word must carry its share of
the impact, its portion of the message. Poets are word merchants who
select words carefully and share their creations. As Robert Frost stated,
"Poetry is a performance in words."

MUSIC Poetry has often been compared to music, and it is easy to substantiate this comparison. You can probably name several terms that are
common to the vocabulary of both music and poetry—rhythm, ballad,
lyric, beat—the list soon becomes rather long. Consider how these concepts fit in the contexts of both music and poetry.

ballad	rhythm	stanza
lyric	measure	tone
beat	line	mood
song	verse	refrain
theme	pattern	chorus
composer		

   Combinations of words are arranged in poetry to create rhythms that
are pleasing to hear, rhythms that convey a foot-tapping beat. David
McCord, for instance, imitates the rhythm of train wheels in "Song of
the Train." Clap your hands as you read this poem aloud.

Clickety-clack,
Wheels on the track,
This is the way
They begin the attack:
Click-ety-clack,
Click-ety-clack,
Click-ety, *clack*-ety,
Click-ety
Clack.

    The traditional meter of formal poetry can be found in many poems that children enjoy. Robert Frost employs the strong beat, which is identified as the *iambic* meter, in "Stopping by Woods on a Snowy Evening." Beat it out as you speak these lines, and you will discover four beats in each line. Each beat consists of an unaccented syllable followed by an accented syllable, for example, "The woods."

The woods are lovely, dark and deep,
But I have promises to keep,
And miles to go before I sleep.
And miles to go before I sleep.

    Eleanor Farjeon also uses the iambic beat in "There Isn't Time."

There isn't time, there isn't time
To do the things I want to do
With all the mountain-tops to climb,
And all the woods to wander through,
And all the seas to sail upon,
And everywhere there is to go,
And all the people, every one
Who lives upon the earth, to know.
There's only time, there's only time
To know a few, and do a few,
And then sit down and make a rhyme
About the rest I want to do.

    In presenting poetry to children, however, we are not concerned about labeling the stylized rhythm that can be found in traditional adult poetry.

Contemporary poets tend to use free verse more frequently, and those who write for children have seldom used the less common meters that earlier poets sometimes chose. Any text on adult poetry will explain the varied meters in detail if you are especially interested in learning about this aspect of poetry composition. Refer for example to:

Ciardi, John. *How Does a Poem Mean?* Houghton Mifflin.

Drew, Elizabeth. *Discovering Poetry*. Norton.

Hillyer, Robert. *In Pursuit of Poetry*. McGraw-Hill.

Untermeyer, Louis and Carter Davidson. *Poetry: Its Appreciation and Enjoyment*. Harcourt Brace Jovanovich.

Walsh, Chad. *Doors into Poetry*. Prentice-Hall.

Gifted students who want to know more about poetry construction might consult *The Poet's Eye: An Introduction to Poetry for Young People* by Arthur Alexander (Prentice-Hall, 1967).

ALLITERATION Part of the music of poetry is achieved through repetition of specific sounds. A classic example, written by Walter de la Mare, repeats the *s* phoneme both at beginnings and ends of words. In his poem "Silver," notice how frequently, too, the word *silver* itself is included. Read this poem aloud to get the full effect.

Slowly, silently, now the moon
Walks the night in her silver shoon;
This way, and that, she peers, and sees
Silver fruit upon silver trees;
One by one the casements catch
Her beams beneath the silvery thatch;
Couched in his kennel, like a log,
With paws of silver, sleeps the dog;
From their shadowy cote the white breasts peep
Of doves in a silver-feathered sleep;
A harvest mouse goes scampering by,
With silver claws, and silver eye;
And moveless fish in the water gleam,
By silver reeds in a silver stream.

The words slide on the tongue to create a feeling of the moonlight's sinuous movements as it silvers everything it touches.

Be sure to notice, too, the unusual *plural* form for shoe, *shoon*. This older form has been largely dropped in modern English, but it appears in *oxen* and *children*. This poem offers a rare opportunity to relate a bit of the history of the English language to children.

Alliteration occurs in many poems that you will have fun using. Rowena Bennett begins a poem with these wonderful lines:

There once was a witch of Willowby Wood,
And a weird wild witch was she,
With hair that was snarled,
And hands that were gnarled,
And a kickety, rickety knee.
She could jump, they say,
To the moon and back
But this, I never did see.

ONOMATOPOEIA Another enjoyable aspect of poetic language is *ono-matopoeia,* which simply means that a word sounds like what it means: such as *bang* for a loud noise. In the poem "Galoshes," for example, Rhoda Bacmeister uses both alliteration and onomatopoeia.

Susie's galoshes
Make splishes and sploshes
And slooshes and sloshes,
As Susie steps slowly
Along in the slush.

They stamp and they tramp
On the ice and concrete,
They get stuck in the muck and the mud;
But Susie likes much best to hear

The slippery slush
As it slooshes and sloshes
And splishes and sploshes,
All round her galoshes!

First, this poet uses splishy, sploshy words that are most appropriate to walking in slush. Then she introduces *stamp* and *tramp,* which certainly sound like what they mean, and "stuck in the muck and the mud," which through alliteration and onomatopoeia reminds us of experiences we've had. Onomatopoeia is an interesting way of adding to the sensuous effect of poetry.

WORD PLAY Many poets, in addition to Ogden Nash whom we already mentioned, enjoy playing with words. Children will have fun with the playful poem "Eletelephony" by Laura E. Richards. You'll need to practice this verse several times before reading it aloud to children. Make the title sound like *telepathy,* a word the poet adapted for her own humorous purposes.

Once there was an elephant,
Who tried to use the telephant—
No! no! I mean an elephone
Who tried to use the telephone—
(Dear me! I am not certain quite
That even now I've got it right.)

Howe'er it was, he got his trunk
Entangled in the telephunk;
The more he tried to get it free,
The louder buzzed the telephee—
(I fear I'd better drop the song
Of elephop and telephong!)

Introduce children to such word play, which occurs in both poetry and prose. Children love Mary Poppins' use of words, which have now been presented in song lyrics that add to the enjoyment of language. Ask children if they know the word *Supercalifragilisticexpialidocious,* which as Mary Poppins says, sounds "most atrocious!"

Hilaire Belloc makes a plea for being kind to frogs in "The Frog." Could you have thought of such names?

Be kind and tender to the Frog,
  And do not call him names,
As "Slimy-skin," or "Polly-wog,"
  Or likewise, "Ugly James,"

Or "Gape-a-grin," or "Toad-gone-wrong,"
  Or "Billy-Bandy-knees";
The Frog is justly sensitive
  To epithets like these.

Guy Wetmore Carryl parodies the words and ideas of "Little Miss Muffet" when he expands it into "The Embarrassing Episode of Little Miss Muffet." This is a great poem to read aloud to older students.

Little Miss Muffet discovered a tuffet,
  (Which never occurred to the rest of us)
And, as 'twas a June day, and just about noonday,
  She wanted to eat—like the best of us;
Her diet was whey, and I hasten to say
  It is wholesome and people grow fat on it.
The spot being lonely, the lady not only
  Discovered the tuffet, but sat on it . . . .

Three more stanzas follow to describe Miss Muffet's exciting encounter with the spider. The poet adds this sagacious moral:

And the MORAL is this: Be it madam or miss
  To whom you have something to say,
You are only absurd when you get in the curd,
  But you're rude when you get in the whey!

Humorous poetry like these examples will often serve to introduce children to poetry that they can respond to readily with enjoyment. Once they have a positive feeling for poetry, you can gradually introduce them to poems that may require a more sophisticated palate; for example, poetry that contains subtle imagery.

IMAGERY Fresh, vivid images distinguish good poetry from the mediocre. Begin a search for these pictures in words.

Houses are faces
(haven't you found?)
with their hats in the air,
and their necks in the ground.[4]

From "Houses" by Aileen Fisher

---

[4] Reprinted by permission of the author.

Myra Cohn Livingstone shares images of "Whispers," which is the title poem of her book of poetry *Whispers and Other Poems*.

Whispers
  tickle through your ear
  telling things you like to hear.
Whispers
  are as soft as skin
  letting little words curl in.
Whispers
  come so they can blow
  secrets others never know.

Children can learn about the simile and metaphor, which are fascinating to use. The *simile* is easy to recognize because the comparison is very clear with the words *as* or *like* pointing it out to you. Maude E. Uschold develops a simile in "Moonlight":

Like a white cat
Moonlight peers through windows,
Listening, watching.
Like a white cat it moves
Across the threshold
And stretches itself on the floor;
It sits on a chair
And puts white paws on the table.
Moonlight crouches among shadows,
  Watching, waiting
  The slow passing of night.

Tennyson's well-known poem "The Eagle" develops a powerful image that ends with a simile.

He clasps the crag with crooked hands;
Close to the sun in lonely lands,
Ringed with the azure world, he stands.

The wrinkled sea beneath him crawls;
He watches from his mountain walls,
And like a thunderbolt he falls.

The *metaphor* achieves a similar effect, but is more subtle because it is a direct comparison of two things; one thing *is* another.

Night gathers itself into a ball of yarn.
Night loosens the ball and it spreads . . .

From "Night" by Carl Sandburg

In the morning the city
Spreads its wings . . .

From "City" by Langston Hughes

Skins of lemons are waterproof slickers . . .

From "Skins" by Aileen Fisher

A metaphor can be extensive, as in Emily Dickinson's "I Like to See It Lap the Miles." This poet describes a train in terms of a horse that "feeds itself," "neighs," and finally stops "at its own stable door." Kaye Starbird compares December and breakfast cereal in the following poem "December Leaves":

The fallen leaves are cornflakes
That fill the lawn's wide dish,—
And night and noon
The wind's a spoon
That stirs them with a swish.—

The sky's a silver sifter
A-sifting white and slow,
That gently shakes
On crisp brown flakes
The sugar known as snow.

Aileen Fisher develops an image of spring in "Pussy Willows":

Close your eyes
and do not peek
and I'll rub Spring
across your cheek—

smooth as satin,
soft and sleek—
close your eyes
and do not peek.[5]

FORMS OF POETRY

Poetry is first distinguished from prose by its form. The short lines set in stanzas or other groupings make it truly distinctive. The forms of poetry, however, are numerous, and this is something interesting to discuss with children. Forms typically found in collections of poetry for children range from rhymed varieties to unrhymed patterns to free verse.

Rhymed Forms

Couplet

Triplet

Quatrain

Limerick

Patterned Poems

Cinquain

Haiku

Free Verse

All of these forms are easily understood by children who can also try writing the varied forms. Patterned poems and free verse provide good models for writing, but they are not always the best selections for reading aloud. Choose poems with rhythm and humor for first experiences in listening to poetry read aloud.

COUPLET The couplet is a two-line poem that rhymes, as in this example by an unknown author.

A big turtle sat on the end of the log
Watching a tadpole turn into a frog.

---

[5] Acknowledgment for permission to reprint is made to Aileen Fisher for "Pussy Willows" from *In the Woods, in the Meadow, in the Sky,* Charles Scribner's Sons, N.Y., 1965.

Couplets can be extended into a longer poem, of course, simply by adding stanzas as desired. "Jump or Jiggle" by Evelyn Beyer is a good example for young children.

Frogs jump
Caterpillars hump

Worms wiggle
Bugs jiggle

Rabbits hop
Horses clop

Snakes slide
Seagulls glide

Mice creep
Deer leap

Puppies bounce
Kittens pounce

Lions stalk—
But—
I walk!

In "Little Charlie Chipmunk," by Helen C. LeCron, couplets are used in a slightly different way to form a six-line poem or sextet.

Little Charlie Chipmunk was a talker. Mercy me!
He chattered after breakfast and he chattered after tea!
He chattered to his father and he chattered to his mother!
He chattered to his sister and he chattered to his brother!
He chattered till his family was almost driven wild!
Oh, little Charlie Chipmunk was a very tiresome child!

TRIPLET The triplet is not so widely used as are couplets and quatrains. This old familiar jingle, with all three lines rhyming, is a good example of a triplet.

Rain, rain, go away,
Come again another day;
Little Johnny wants to play.

Joseph Auslander's poem "A Blackbird Suddenly" combines three triplets, thus

Heaven is in my hand, and I
Touched a heartbeat of the sky,
Hearing a blackbird cry.

Strange, beautiful, unquiet thing,
Lone flute of God, how can you sing
Winter to spring?

You have outdistanced every voice and word,
And given my spirit wings until it stirred
Like you—a bird.

Another variation forms stanzas for Lew Sarett's sensitive description of "Four Little Foxes."

Speak gently, Spring, and make no sudden sound;
For in my windy valley, yesterday, I found
New-born foxes squirming on the ground—
       Speak gently.

Walk softly, March, forbear the bitter blow;
Her feet within a trap, her blood upon the snow,
The four little foxes saw their mother go—
       Walk softly.

Go lightly, Spring, oh, give them no alarm;
When I covered them with boughs to shelter them from harm,
The thin blue foxes suckled at my arm—
       Go lightly.

Step softly, March, with your rampant hurricane;
Nuzzling one another, and whimpering with pain,
The new little foxes are shivering in the rain—
       Step softly.

Other examples of triplets are found in these poems:

"Sonic Boom" by John Updike

"Dinky" by Theodore Roethke

"People Buy a Lot of Things" by Annette Wynne

"Tulip"; "Butterfly" by William Jay Smith

"Peepers" by Melville Cane

LIMERICK   The limerick contains both a couplet and a triplet and is usually humorous. Frequently, limericks begin with the words "There once was . . . " or "There was . . . ," as in these examples:

There once was a lady from Niger
Who smiled as she rode on a tiger
  They came back from the ride
  With the lady inside
And the smile on the face of the tiger.

Cosmo Monkhouse

There was an old man of Blackheath,
Who sat on his set of false teeth.

  Said he, with a start,
  "Oh, Lord, bless my heart!

I've bitten myself underneath!

Unknown

At times poets use the limerick form for stanzas in longer poems. Laura E. Richards uses limericks in "Antonio" and "Some Fishy Nonsense," as well as other poems. Read "Antonio" aloud just for fun!

Antonio, Antonio,
Was tired of living alonio.
  He thought he would woo
  Miss Lissamy Lu,
Miss Lissamy Lucy Molonio.

Antonio, Antonio,
Rode off on his polo-ponio.
  He found the fair maid
  In a bowery shade,
A-sitting and knitting alonio.

Antonio, Antonio,
Said, "If you will be my ownio,

I'll love you true,
  And I'll buy for you,
An icery creamery conio!"

"Oh, nonio, Antonio!
You're far too bleak and bonio!
  And all that I wish
  You singular fish,
Is that you will quickly begonio."

Antonio, Antonio,
He uttered a dismal moanio;
  Then ran off and hid
  (Or I'm told that he did)
In the Antarctical Zonio.

"The Animal Fair" is composed of two comical limericks that delight
children.

I went to the animal fair,
The birds and the beasts were there.
  The big baboon,
  By the light of the moon,
Was combing his auburn hair!

The monkey, he got drunk,
And sat on the elephant's trunk.
  The elephant sneezed
  And fell on his knees,
And what became of the monk, the monk?
And what became of the monk?

QUATRAIN Quatrains are combinations of four rhymed lines in various patterns. One rhyme pattern is *abab*, which means that lines 1 and 3
rhyme while 2 and 4 have a different rhyme. This verse is an example:

I eat my peas with honey;
I've done it all my life.
It makes the peas taste funny
But it keeps them on my knife.

A second pattern is *aabb*, in which the lines comprise two couplets.
Lines 1 and 2 rhyme while 3 and 4 have a different pair of rhymes. "The

Octopussycat'' by Kenyon Cox is an example of this pattern. This poem is a parody of another familiar poem. Do you recognize it?

I love Octopussy, his arms are so long;
There's nothing in nature so sweet as his song.
Tis true I'd not touch him—no, not for a farm!
If I keep at a distance, he'll do me no harm.[6]

The third common rhyme scheme for a quatrain is *abcb,* in which only two lines rhyme. This short poem by Lord Bowen illustrates the quatrain form, as well as humorous word play.

The rain it raineth on the just
    And also on the unjust fella;
But chiefly on the just, because
    The unjust steals the just's umbrella.

The quatrain is frequently used for longer poems, as in "When Mummy Slept Late and Daddy Cooked Breakfast" by John Ciardi. Another favorite is "The Jabberwocky" by Lewis Carroll, who uses nonsense words in a narrative poem.

'Twas brillig, and the slithy toves
    Did gyre and gimble in the wabe:
All mimsy were the borogoves,
    And the mome raths outgrabe.

"Beware the Jabberwock, my son!
    The jaws that bite, the claws that catch!

---

[6] The poem that this one parodies is "I Love Little Pussy" by Jane Taylor.

I love little Pussy,
Her coat is so warm.
And if I don't hurt her,
She'll do me no harm.
So I'll not pull her tail
Nor drive her away,
But Pussy and I
Very gently will play.

Beware the Jubjub bird, and shun
    The Frumious Bandersnatch!"

He took his vorpal sword in hand:
    Long time and manxome foe he sought—
So rested he by the Tumtum tree,
    And stood awhile in thought.

And, as in uffish thought he stood,
    The Jabberwock, with eyes of flame,
Came whiffling through the tulgey wood,
    And burbled as it came!

One, two! One, two! And through and through
    The vorpal blade went snicker-snack!
He left it dead, and with its head
    He went galumphing back.

"And hast thou slain the Jabberwock?
    Come to my arms, my beamish boy!
O frabjous day! Callooh! Callay!"
    He chortled in his joy.

'Twas brillig, and the slithy toves
    Did gyre and gimble in the wabe:
All mimsy were the borogoves,
    And the mome raths outgrabe.

CINQUAIN This word is pronounced variously, but preferring to emphasize the French word *cinq* and the meaning *five-line poem,* I pronounce it *sánkĕn.* A cinquain can take various forms. As written by Adelaide Crapsey, author of a small volume titled *Verse,* it follows this form:

These be—
Three silent things—
The falling snow, the hour
Before the dawn, the mouth of one
Just dead.

    Count the syllables in each line. Can you see the pattern of this unrhymed poem?

    Children can write cinquains readily. You can have them count the syllables, but for young children it is simpler to have them count whole words, so that the pattern is 1, 2, 3, 4, 1 in terms of words, rather than 2,

4, 6, 8, 2 when counting syllables. To guide children in developing a cohesive poem, teachers have often used these specifications:

Line 1: One word (subject of the poem)

Line 2: Two words (describes the subject)

Line 3: Three words (an action or actions)

Line 4: Four words (a feeling or feelings)

Line 5: One word (synonym for subject)

Sunshine—
Warming, yellow;
Swimming, running, playing,
Enjoying the summer day—
August.

HAIKU   A three-line verse form that originated in Japan, the haiku consists of only seventeen syllables arranged in three lines, thus:

Line 1: 5 syllables

Line 2: 7 syllables

Line 3: 5 syllables

Haiku were written by ancient philosopher-poets such as Bashō, Buson, Boncho, Sōkan, and others. A good source of information about this form and its characteristics is *An Introduction to Haiku* by Harold G. Henderson (Doubleday, 1967). An excellent collection for young people is *Cricket Songs* (Harcourt Brace Jovanovich, 1964) by Harry Behn, a poet who writes poetry for children and has also translated many haiku from the Japanese. See also *More Cricket Songs* (Harcourt Brace Jovanovich, 1971).

Authentic haiku include references to nature and the time of year, as in this example:

From Cricket Songs: Japanese Haiku, *translated and © 1964 by Harry Behn. Reprinted by permission of Harcourt Brace Jovanovich, Inc.*

All sky disappears
The earth's land has gone away;
Still the snowflakes fall.

Hashin

There has been a real question about the presentations of haiku to children in elementary school as a simplistic pattern to emulate. Ann Atwood tries to remedy this situation in *My Own Rhythm* (Scribners, 1973). "We all think, we all feel, we all aspire," she writes. "Through imagining, through feeling, through intuition, we may enter that state of mind which is the haiku moment . . . to become increasingly conscious . . . to feel joy and compassion . . . and listen with quiet attention until we move to the poetry and music of the universe, each in his own rhythm."

A fine presentation of authentic haiku is *In a Spring Garden,* edited by Richard Lewis and illustrated tastefully by Ezra Jack Keats (Dial, 1965); see the color section. This book is now available as a film from Weston Woods. Modern haiku written especially for young children are presented in an attractive book, *Fat Polka-dot Cat and Other Haiku,* by Betsy Maestro and illustrated by Giulio Maestro (Dutton, 1976).

Haiku offers an unusual addition to the understanding of other cultures. As part of a social studies unit on Japan, this form of literature could be studied extensively. After they understand the intent of the haiku masters, children could then try to write their own haiku.

FREE VERSE As the name implies, free verse does not follow a set pattern nor does it rhyme. The writer of free verse, however, uses many of the devices employed by those who choose to write more structured types of poetry. The writer of free verse is very much concerned, for example, with rhythm and imagery. Freed from set patterns and the need to rhyme, the poet is able to experiment.

An excellent example of free verse for children is the poetry of Hilda Conkling, which was written when she was eight. Her simple, direct style includes vivid imagery, as in "Dandelion":

O little soldier with the golden helmet,
What are you guarding on my lawn?
You with your green gun
And your yellow beard,
Why do you stand so stiff?
There is only the grass to fight!

Other poets who write free verse that can often be enjoyed by children are Carl Sandburg, Walt Whitman, and e. e. cummings. One of Cummings' most delightful poems is "In Just-Spring."

BE LIKE THE BIRD

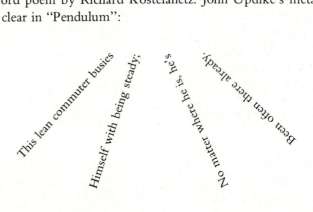

in Just-
spring   when the world is mud-
luscious the little
lame balloonman

whistles   far   and wee

and eddieandbill come
running from marbles and
piracies and it's
spring

when the world is puddle-wonderful

the queer
old balloonman whistles
far   and   wee
and bettyandisbel come dancing

from hop-scotch and jump-rope and

it's
spring
and
     the
          goat-footed

balloonMan   whistles
far
and
wee

EXPERIMENTS WITH FORM   Many poets have experimented with
form and content as they present ideas.
     The *concrete* poem takes the shape of the subject, as in "The Lollypop,"
a one-word poem by Richard Kostelanetz. John Updike's metaphor is
visually clear in "Pendulum":

L
O
L
L
Y
P
O
P

This lean commuter busies
Himself with being steady;
No matter where he is, he's
Been often there already.

"How pleasant to know Mr. Lear!" begins this engaging poem as the poet paints a picture of himself. How do you feel about a man who can present himself in such a comical light?

How pleasant to know Mr. Lear!
    Who has written such volumes of stuff!
Some think him ill-tempered and queer,
    But a few think him pleasant enough.

His mind is concrete and fastidious,
    His nose is remarkably big;
His visage is more or less hideous,
    His beard it resembles a wig.

He has ears, and two eyes, and ten fingers,
    Leastways if you reckon two thumbs;
Long ago he was one of the singers,
    But now he is one of the dumbs.

He sits in a beautiful parlour,
    With hundreds of books on the wall;
He drinks a great deal of Marsala,
    But never gets tipsy at all.

He has many friends, laymen and clerical;
    Old Foss is the name of his cat;
His body is perfectly spherical,
    He weareth a runcible hat.

When he walks in a waterproof white,
    The children run after him so!
Calling out, 'He's come out in his night-
    Gown, that crazy old Englishman, oh!'

He weeps by the side of the ocean,
    He weeps on the top of the hill;
He purchases pancakes and lotion,
    And chocolate shrimps from the mill.

He reads but he cannot speak Spanish,
    He cannot abide ginger-beer:
Ere the days of his pilgrimage vanish,
    How pleasant to know Mr. Lear!

Children will enjoy hearing you read these humorous stanzas. Suggest that they draw a picture based on the images presented. Then read some of Lear's limericks.

We seldom think of poets as real people who live much as we do. They have children who go to school; they must deal with such mundane matters as laundry and income tax; they are human beings like the man next door or the woman driving that car down the freeway. Let's get acquainted with poets as people so that we can introduce them to children.

Who are the poets who write for children? First of all, we need to recognize that many poets whose poems children enjoy are not primarily children's poets. Included in most collections for children are poems by poets whose names you probably already know, such poets as:

Stephen Vincent Benét	Vachel Lindsay
William Blake	Henry Wadsworth Longfellow
Gwendolyn Brooks	Edna St. Vincent Millay
Lewis Carroll	Ogden Nash
John Ciardi	Theodore Roethke
e. e. cummings	Carl Sandburg
Emily Dickinson	William Shakespeare
T. S. Eliot	Robert Louis Stevenson
Langston Hughes	Alfred Tennyson
John Keats	Walt Whitman
Rudyard Kipling	William Wordsworth
Edward Lear	

Kenneth Koch, author of *Wishes, Lies, and Dreams,* develops ideas for teaching great poetry to children in *Rose, where did you get that red?* (Random House, 1973). He uses the poetry of William Carlos Williams, Federico García Lorca, William Shakespeare, John Donne, and other known adult poets to serve as models for children's writing.

In contrast we can compile a list of other poets who are known *chiefly* for the poems they write for children. How many of these names do you recognize?

Dorothy Aldis	Dorothy Baruch
Mary Austin	Harry Behn
Rhoda Bacmeister	Rowena Bennett

Elizabeth Coatsworth

Hilda Conkling

Eleanor Farjeon

Rachel Field

Aileen Fisher

Rose Fyleman

Kate Greenaway

Karla Kushkin

Myra Cohn Livingstone

David McCord

Eve Merriam

A. A. Milne

Mary O'Neill

Laura E. Richards

Christina Georgina Rossetti

William Jay Smith

James S. Tippett

Do you know, for example, Mary O'Neill? When she was over sixty, she began teaching creative writing as a Peace Corps Volunteer in Costa Rica and Ghana. She tells of her experiences in ". . . fresh from Africa, to speak about Children's Literature" in *Elementary English* (October 1973, pp. 1011–1018). Included is a full-page picture of Mary O'Neill, who has written many fine books for children, such as *Words, Words, Words; What Is That Sound?* (Doubleday). The best loved, however, is the first, *Hailstones and Halibut Bones* (Doubleday), in which she talks about colors.

What is orange?
  Orange is a tiger lily,
  A carrot,
  A feather from
  A parrot,
  A flame,
  The wildest color
  You can name.

She delights in children's reactions as they write her: "Please tell me what poetry really is. I like the way you write. Makes me think I can do it, too." And they do. Poetry from *Hailstones and Halibut Bones* is presented on film (Sterling), read by Celeste Holmes, and interpreted through colorful shapes, figures, and music.

Do you know Eve Merriam? Her poems for children are published in three delightful volumes: *Catch a Little Rhyme, It Doesn't Always Have to Rhyme,* and *There Is No Rhyme for Silver* (Atheneum). She gives sage advice, for example, "How to Eat a Poem":

Don't be polite.
Bite in.
Pick it up with your fingers and lick the juice that may run down your chin.
It is ready and ripe now, whenever you are.

You do not need a knife or fork or spoon
or plate or napkin or tablecloth.

For there is no core
or stem
or rind
or pit
or seed
or skin
to throw away.

But Eve Merriam also has other interests, as shown in her *Inner City Mother Goose* (Simon and Schuster, 1969). She translates these familiar poems into contemporary commentary, thus:

There was a crooked man
And he did very well.

With Nancy Larrick, Eve Merriam compiled a collection of original verse by young people titled *Male and Female Under 18* (Avon, 1973). In these poems students express their feelings about sex roles and stereotyped behavior.

More than just a list of poems or books published, each poet is a human being with varied interests, some reflected in their poetry for children, others discovered only by the adult who searches further.

❦ *EXPLORING* Complete two of these activities as you explore further.

1. After exploring in collections of children's poetry, discover as much information as possible about three poets whose poetry you especially like. Prepare short informative sketches that you can use in a poetry study with children. What interesting tidbits would children like to know?

2. Write to one of the poets who is writing today. Write in care of a publisher who has published the poet's work. What questions do you have about poetry? About poems written by this specific poet?

3. Begin a collection of articles about poetry and poets. Include pictures of poets in your collection. *Language Arts* often includes such articles as well as full-page photographs. e. e. cummings (who doesn't care for capital letters) is featured in the November/December issue, 1973.

POETRY IN CLASSROOMS

If our purpose is to promote poetry for and with children, we will make poetry an integral part of the elementary school curriculum. We can explore with children as we discover new perspectives of poetry together.

There are many opportunities to share poetry and varied strategies for introducing it. Holidays and the changing seasons suggest obvious possibilities, as do topics being studied in subject areas such as the social studies. Poetry is a natural part of the oral language development experiences planned for any classroom, as children speak poetry together, sing it, and tape their favorites. Children can read poetry, and above all, children can write poetry. As Kenneth Koch comments in *Wishes, Lies and Dreams* (Vintage, 1970):

Children have a natural talent for writing poetry and anyone who teaches them should know that. Teaching really is not the right word for what takes place: it is more like permitting the children to discover something they already have. (p. 25)

Bringing poetry and children together adds excitement to the classroom. In this section we will discuss specific ideas for working with children and poetry as we make sure that they have a chance to know poetry and to create poetry themselves. As Ann Terry points out in summarizing her study of children's poetry preferences: "The majority of teachers pay little attention to poetry in class, seldom reading it to children or encouraging them to write their own poems."[7] Certainly we have a responsibility to develop a classroom in which poetry plays an important part.

POETRY RELATED TO THEMES

Children's poetry is often grouped in anthologies according to selected themes or topics. This is helpful to the teacher or librarian who needs poetry to fit a season, a holiday, or a topic of interest to a specific child. Some of the themes we often use are:

Can you remember the substance of a poem your teacher read on any of these subjects?

Seasons	*Holidays*	*Weather*
Fall	Christmas	Rain
Winter	New Year's Day	Snow
Spring	Washington's Birthday	Wind
Summer	Fourth of July	
	Columbus Day	
	Thanksgiving	

---

[7] Ann Terry, *Children's Poetry Preferences: A National Survey of Upper Elementary Grades* (National Council of Teachers of English, 1974), inside front cover. See Chapter 10 for further discussion of this study.

Animals	Traveling	Social Studies	
Cats	Trains	City living	
Dogs	Airplanes	Outdoor life	
Birds	Boats	People	
Mice		The farm	

An interesting topic you might explore in March, for example, is *wind*. Christina Rossetti questions, "Who has seen the wind? Neither I nor you . . ." In "The Wind" Robert Louis Stevenson addresses the wind accusingly, "I saw you toss the kites on high and blow the birds about the sky . . ."

The wind is often considered fearsome and threatening. Harry Behn likens the wind to an owl in "Windy Morning," while William D. Sar-

Windy Nights

Whenever the moon and stars are set,
    Whenever the wind is high,
All night long in the dark and wet,
    A man goes riding by.
Late in the night when the fires are out,
Why does he gallop and gallop about?

Whenever the trees are crying aloud,
    And ships are tossed at sea,
By, on the highway, low and loud,
    By at the gallop goes he:
By at the gallop he goes, and then
By he comes back at the gallop again.
                    —Robert Louis Stevenson

gent talks of "wind-wolves hunting across the sky" in his poem "Wind-Wolves." In yet another poem, "Windy Nights," Stevenson associates the wind with a mysterious night-rider. Children can interpret such a poem through varied media. For example, see the pen and ink drawing by Dana Rewak.

A fascinating image of the wind as a fussy old woman appears in "Wind Weather" by Virginia Brasier.

The wind's an old woman in front of the rain
Picking up papers and laying them again;
Muttering, fussing, and slamming a door
That only comes back to be slammed at some more.

The wind's an old woman indignantly trying
To gather her goods from the rain's hasty prying.
She frightens the trees till they circle and flail,
But the sensible cows turn their back to her wail.

Yet, when the rain starts its imperative fall,
The old-woman-wind doesn't mind it at all.
She chuckles and puffs, unconcerned as you please
At the terrible scare she has given the trees.

Another metaphor is developed in "Wind Is a Cat" by Ethel Romig Fuller:

Wind is a cat
    That prowls at night,
Now in a valley,
    Now on a height,

Pouncing on houses
    Till folks in their beds
Draw all the covers
    Over their heads.

It sings to the moon
    It scratches at doors;
It lashes its tail
    Around chimneys and roars.

It claws at the clouds
    Till it fringes their silk,

It laps up the dawn
  Like a saucer of milk;

Then, chasing the stars
  To the tops of the firs,
Curls down for a nap
  And purrs and purrs.

    Encourage children to collect their own poetry as they create an individual anthology. Poet William Jay Smith describes making such a collection as a child:

I once prepared as a school project a notebook on poetry and on the cover I pasted the picture of a majestic carved gate that I had cut from a magazine and to the top of the gate I attached a bright feather; inside my notebook I copied out my favorite poems and the definitions of poetry by a number of great poets. I realize now that my cover was itself my own definition, for poetry is indeed a splendid gateway to intense and rewarding experience, offering, throughout one's life, "magnificence within a frame."[8]

SPEAKING POETRY

Read poetry aloud to children or learn favorites together. Poetry can fill the air of a classroom in many different ways. Try the "voice choir," set poetry to music, or tape poetry collections.

THE VOICE CHOIR An exciting way to enjoy poetry in the classroom is through speaking together. Children can soon learn to supply the lines that are repeated in such poems as "Poor Old Woman." First, read or recite the poem to the group so that they hear the funny ending. Then encourage children to join in as you go through the poem again.

There was an old woman who swallowed a fly.

Class: Oh, my! Swallowed a fly?
     Poor old woman, I think she'll die!

cumulative poem

---

[8] Quoted in Children's Book Council, *Poetry, Children and Children's Books* (The Children's Book Council, 1976).

There was an old woman who swallowed a bird;
That's what I heard; she swallowed a bird!

Class: She swallowed the bird to kill the fly;
Oh, my! Swallowed a fly?
Poor old woman, I think she'll die!

There was an old woman who swallowed a cat;
Think of that, she swallowed a cat!

Class: She swallowed the cat to kill the bird;
She swallowed the bird to kill the fly;
Oh, my! Swallowed a fly?
Poor old woman, I think she'll die!

There was an old woman who swallowed a dog;
Jiggety, jog, she swallowed a dog!

Class: She swallowed the dog to kill the cat;
She swallowed the cat to kill the bird;
She swallowed the bird to kill the fly;
Oh, my! Swallowed a fly?
Poor old woman, I think she'll die!

(Other verses may be invented.)

There was an old woman who swallowed a horse!

Class (quickly): She died, of course!

Look through collections of poetry to select poems that are appropriate for speaking together. Choose poems that appeal to you first of all; then try them with the group to see if the poems hold their interest. Repetition, rhythm, and humor add to the possibilities of a poem for oral interpretation by a group. Some poems that you might examine for this purpose are:

"The Monkeys and the Crocodile" by Laura E. Richards

"Puppy and I" by A. A. Milne

"The Pirate Don Durk of Dowdee" by Mildred Plew Meigs

One that is especially enjoyable is "Fire, Fire!" Divide the children into groups that speak the lines about each person in rapid succession. All join in patiently and slowly with the last two lines.

"Fire! Fire!"
Cried Mrs. McGuire.
"Where? Where?"
Asked Mrs. Blair.
"All over town!"
Said Mrs. Brown.
"Get some water!"
Said her daughter.
"We'd better jump!"
Said Mrs. Grump.
"That would be silly!"
Said Mrs. Minelli.
"What'll we do?"
Asked Mrs. LaRue.
"Turn in the alarm!"
Said Mrs. Parm.
"Save us! Save us!"
Cried Mrs. Davis.

The fire department got the call
And the firemen saved them, one and all.

"The Noble Duke of York" permits the use of movement as the words are spoken. Consider how children might fit motions to the words of this nursery rhyme.

The grand Old Duke of York
   He had ten thousand men,
He marched them up a very high hill
   And he marched them down again.
And when he was up he was up,
   And when he was down he was down,
And when he was only halfway up,
   He was neither up nor down.

TAPING POETRY   Tape or cassette recorders can be used to advantage when children record their favorite poems. Selections can be made after a study of poetry in which children have been reading various poems, exploring and developing a collection of their own favorite poems. Selections might, on the other hand, be made from those the class has heard or spoken together.

Set up the recorder so that children can go to it whenever they are ready to record. Have one child introduce the tape by recording Eve Merriam's "How to Eat a Poem" or Beatrice Schenk de Regniers' "Keep a Poem in Your Pocket." The other poems can follow then without concern for order: A Potpourri of Poetry.

Taping the voice choir is also effective. Have the children select from their repertoire as they prepare a poetry "Pops" concert, which can be delivered live or taped. Discuss the need for variety, an appropriate length for the presentation, as well as the specific poems to be spoken.

SINGING POETRY Many poems have been set to music. In any comprehensive poetry collection you will find ballads and folksongs that children may recognize: "Erie Canal," "Puff, the Magic Dragon," "The Fox Went Out on a Chilly Night," and "Sweet Betsy of Pike." Mother Goose rhymes have often been set to music, too. Students may be introduced to poetry through the lyrics of songs they like. Singing these songs is certainly a way of increasing children's exposure to poetry.

A number of contemporary books present the words and music of a single song, for example:

Desmond Digby. *Waltzing Matilda*. Holt, 1976.

Robert Quackenbush. *Go Tell Aunt Rhody*. Lippincott, 1975.

Glen Rounds. *Sweet Betsy from Pike*. Golden Gate, 1975.

Another creative way of enjoying poetry is to set a poem to music yourself. Choose a short lyrical poem or one that contains interesting rhythm or repetition. Then try singing a line or two. Repeat the lines to see if they feel comfortable; adjust them any way you like because it's your song. Then do the same for the other lines until you have the whole poem set to music you created yourself.

Share the song with children. Then encourage them to create melodies for poems they like, too. You can do this as a group project first, which is a successful way to start. Some of these poems have potential as songs:

"The Wind Has Such a Rainy Sound" by Christina Rossetti

"Rain" by Robert Louis Stevenson

"Firefly" by Elizabeth Madox Roberts

"Sea Shell, Sea Shell" by Amy Lowell

"I Never Saw a Moor" by Emily Dickinson

The Fog

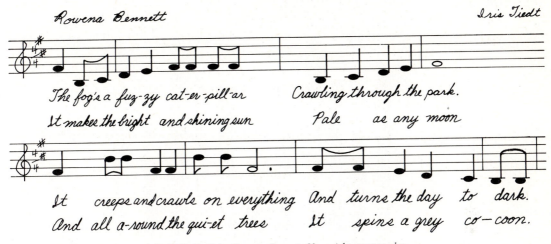

Rowena Bennett

Iris Tiedt

The fog's a fuz-zy cat-er-pill-ar   Crawling through the park.
It makes the bright and shining sun   Pale   as any moon

It   creeps and crawls on everything   And   turns the day   to   dark.
And   all a-round the qui-et   trees   It   spins a grey   co—coon.

Here is a melody that was created for "The Fog" by Rowena Bennett. You might want to play this song on the piano or melody bells and share it with children. Words copyright by Rowena Bennett; reprinted by permission.

CHILDREN CAN READ POEMS

Today there are many books of poetry written especially for children to use themselves. Visit the children's section of your public library to see what they have on the poetry shelves. Look especially for some of the newer titles, such as:

Mary Ann Hoberman. *A Little Book of Beasts.* Simon and Schuster, 1973. (*Eighteen funny little verses about small animals.*)

Millicent Brower. *I Am Going Nowhere.* Putnam, 1973. (*Seventeen nonsense rhymes.*)

Lee Bennett Hopkins, and Misha Arenstein. *Thread One to a Star.* Four Winds Press, 1976. (*An attractive collection of fresh poems.*)

Karla Kuskin. *Any Me I Want to Be.* Harper & Row, 1972. (*Intriguing poems in which familiar creatures and objects speak.*)

Cara Lockhart Smith. *Riding to Canonbie.* Bradbury, 1972. (*Imaginative poems based on children's names.*)

Valerie Worth. *Small Poems.* Farrar, Straus & Giroux, 1972. (*Easy poems for young children about varied common topics.*)

315

Jacket cover from Zero Makes Me Hungry: A Collection of Poems for Today *by Edward Lueders and Primus St. John. Copyright © 1976 by Scott, Foresman and Company. Reprinted by permission.*

Relate poetry to other subjects. Many poems add interest to units of study in history or science. Recent books worth looking for are:

James Houston, ed. *Songs of the Dream People; Chants and Images from the Indians and Eskimos of North America.* Atheneum, 1972. (*Beautiful, comprehensive collection.*)

Robert Mezey, ed. *Poems from the Hebrew.* Thomas Y. Crowell, 1973. (*Variety of Hebrew poems for the advanced student.*)

Stephen Benét, and Rosemary Carr Benét. *Book of Americans.* Rinehart, 1933. (*Good poems about noted persons in history.*)

We talk more about using poetry in the social studies and other subject areas in Chapters 8 and 9.

More and more teachers are discovering that children at all levels can write poetry, usually unrhymed verse or patterned verse forms, such as the cinquain or haiku. In addition to the suggestions already made, here are other ideas for involving children with poetry.

INVENTED FORMS If your students enjoy writing poetry, you may wish that you could find other patterns to challenge them. It was this need that led me to create several new poetry patterns that students could use. The patterns lend structure, but the structure is not limiting.

The *diamante* (dee ah mahn' tay), for example, is a seven-line diamond-shaped poem that contrasts two ideas and follows this pattern:

_____

_____

_____

_____

_____

_____

_____

The poem can be developed according to the following specifications, which aid the student in composing a successful poem.

Line 1: subject noun (1 word)

Line 2: adjectives (2 words)

Line 3: participles (3 words)

Line 4: nouns (4 words)

Line 3: participles (3 words)

Line 2: adjectives (2 words)

Line 1: noun-opposite of subject (1 word)

Notice that this poem creates a contrast between two opposite concepts, with the middle line serving as the transition. The following example is by a sixth grade student, Diana Hu:[9]

Country

Beautiful, peaceful,

Calming, resting, flowering

Shade,   trees,   dust,   smog,

Rushing, hurrying, working,

Busy,   ugly,

City.

A second innovated form is the *septolet,* which consists of seven lines (fourteen words) with a break in the pattern, as indicated below:

Students can also experiment with creating new verse patterns. They can invite others in the class to try using their poetry forms.

POETRY MODELS   Another way of facilitating the writing of poetry is by pointing out the possibilities of writing a poem like one the children

---

[9] Iris M. Tiedt, "A New Poetry Form: The Diamante," *Elementary English* (May 1969), p. 589.

have read. A simple, but effective type of poem is a listing poem like "Poem of Praise" by Elizabeth Coatsworth.

Swift things are beautiful:
Swallows and deer,
And lightning that falls
Bright-veined and clear,
Rivers and meteors,
Wind in the wheat,
The strong-withered horse,
The runner's sure feet.

And slow things are beautiful:
The closing of day,
The pause of the wave
That curves downward to spray,
The ember that crumbles,
The opening flower,
And the ox that moves on
In the quiet of power.

As a beginning exercise, use only the first stanza as a model. Children can write about "swift things," as this poet did, or they can begin with a line that introduces a different category, for example, sweet things, strong things, or soft things. They will write more effectively, too, if they don't try rhyming the lines.

Carl Sandburg's "Arithmetic" offers a second model that children will enjoy emulating.

Arithmetic is where numbers fly like pigeons in and out of your head.
Arithmetic tells you how many you lose or win if you know how many you had before you lost or won.
Arithmetic is seven eleven all good children go to heaven—or five six bundle of sticks.
Arithmetic is numbers you squeeze from your head to your hand to your pencil to your paper till you get the answer.
Arithmetic is where the answer is right and everything is nice and you can look out of the window and see the blue sky—or the answer is wrong and you have to start all over and try again and see how it comes out this time.
If you take a number and double it and double it again and then double it a few more times, the number gets bigger and bigger and goes higher and higher and

only arithmetic can tell you what the number is when you decide to quit doubling.

Arithmetic is where you have to multiply—and you carry the multiplication table in your head and hope you won't lose it.

If you have two animal crackers, one good and one bad, and you eat one and a striped zebra with streaks all over him eats the other, how many animal crackers will you have if somebody offers you five six seven and you say No no no and you say Nay nay nay and you say Nix nix nix?

If you ask your mother for one fried egg for breakfast and she gives you two fried eggs and you eat both of them, who is better in arithmetic, you or your mother?

Encourage children to write about a different school subject, a season or month, an animal, or a topic that interests them, for example, space, ecology, the night sky, clouds, the woods, sleeping, singing.

Sara Teasdale's "The Falling Star" demonstrates another structure for a poem. Children can begin their poem, too, with the words, "I saw . . ." Again, rhyming should be avoided.

I saw a star slide down the sky,
Blinding the north as it went by,
Too burning and too quick to hold,
Too lovely to be bought or sold,
Good only to make wishes on
And then forever to be gone.

Another poem that begins in the same way is Rachel Field's "A Summer Morning."

Children can also follow the pattern established by Hilda Conkling in "Mouse," as she asks a question, makes a comment, and then asks other questions.

Little Mouse in gray velvet,
Have you had a cheese-breakfast?
There are no crumbs on your coat,
Did you use a napkin?
I wonder what you had to eat,
And who dresses you in gray velvet?

In using poetry as models for writing, the teacher does need to discuss with children the fact that poetry written in this fashion is not totally original. You might encourage them to title such work: Poetry in the style of _____, or My Version of Carl Sandburg's "Arithmetic."

PUBLISHED POETRY BY CHILDREN Children will be interested in seeing the published collections of poetry written by other young people, for example:

Here I Am! Edited by Virginia O. Baron. Dutton, 1969.

Stuff. Edited by Herbert Kohl and Victor H. Cruz. World, 1970.

Miracles. Edited by Richard Lewis. Simon and Schuster, 1966.

Have You Seen a Comet? Children's Art and Writing from around the World. Edited by Anne Pellowski et al. John Day, 1971.

These books may inspire them to publish their own classroom collections, a highly stimulating activity!

The publication of children's writing should not be an end in itself, but it can be motivating. Patricia Dombrink has compiled a good list of periodicals that welcome children's contributions in "Kids in Print," which appeared in *Teacher* (April 1976).

❀ *FINAL ACTIVITIES WITH POETRY* Choose two of these activities to culminate your study of poetry.

1. Write a paragraph or two explaining what poetry is, as you might explain it to a third grader who has asked you that question.

2. Write original examples of three verse forms described in this chapter.

3. Prepare a quiz about poetry on a task card to use with children, for example: Can you match at least three of these poets with the poems they wrote?

   a. Robert Frost _____ "In Herald Square"

   b. Leland Jacobs _____ "The Owl and the Pussy-cat"

   c. Walter de la Mare _____ "Eletelephony"

d. Edward Lear   ____ "Silver"

e. Laura E. Richards   ____ "The Pasture"

4. Prepare a poster that teaches one concept about poetry.

5. Prepare three task cards that direct children to read a specific poem and follow it up with a creative activity.

Anderson, Douglas. *My Sister Looks Like a Pear; Awakening the Poetry in Young People*. Hart, 1974.

Arnstein, Flora J. *Poetry and the Young Child*. Dover, 1970.

Behn, Harry. *Chrysalis*. Harcourt Brace Jovanovich, 1968.

Elementary English. "Experiencing *Poetry*" (a collection of articles) (January 1975), pp. 103–50.

Hopkins, Lee Bennett. *Pass the Poetry, Please*. Citation, 1972.

Koch, Kenneth. *Wishes, Lies and Dreams: Teaching Children to Write Poetry*. Vintage, 1970.

Larrick, Nancy, ed. *Somebody Turned on a Tap in These Kids; Poetry and Young People Today*. Delta, 1971.

Perrine, Laurence. *Sound and Sense; An Introduction to Poetry*. Harcourt Brace Jovanovich, 1971.

Poets in the Schools: A Handbook. Distributed by National Council of Teachers of English.

Sandburg, Carl. "Short Talk on Poetry" in *Early Moon*. Harcourt Brace Jovanovich, 1950.

Terry, Ann. *Children's Poetry Preferences: A National Survey of Upper Elementary Grades*. National Council of Teachers of English, 1974.

Tiedt, Iris M. and Sidney W. Tiedt. "Exploring Poetry" in *Contemporary English in the Elementary School*. 2nd ed. Prentice-Hall, 1975.

Walter, Nina. *Let Them Write Poetry*. Holt, 1962.

7

Come
Read with Me

Teaching Reading with Trade Books

★ Illustration from *A Bedtime Story* by Joan Levine, illustrated by Gail Owens. Copyright © 1975 by Joan Goldman Levine & Gail Owens. Reprinted by permission of the publishers, E. P. Dutton.

Except a living man, there is nothing more wonderful than a book! a message to us from human souls we never saw. And yet these arouse us, terrify us, teach us, comfort us, open their hearts to us as brothers.

Charles Kingsley

Literature enriches a child's experiential background, develops knowledge of language, and provides something exciting to talk about. Concurrently with learning the decoding skills of reading, therefore, children need a rich diet of literature with which to grow. As they move beyond beginning reading skills, the emphasis on reading trade books should increase as children learn that books have much to offer them personally. We need to aim at getting young people literally "hooked on books." Selma Fraiberg notes:

The long years spent by our children in mastery of the mechanics of reading rob them of pleasure and discoveries in literature, and also rob them of the possibility of *addiction,* which is one of the characteristics of the good reader. The addiction to reading is acquired at an early age—usually, I believe, under eight or nine.[1]

As we endeavor to promote the integration of literature into the reading program, we are trying to:

1. Develop a curriculum aimed at teaching literature concepts to elementary school children

---

[1] Selma Fraiberg, "The American Reading Problem," *Commentary,* (June 1965).

2. Help children learn developmental reading skills through reading trade books

3. Discover ways of stimulating children to read widely with enjoyment and for many purposes

Children's literature offers the resourceful classroom teacher a wealth of materials that can make teaching reading an exciting experience. Although there is no denying that it does require some effort to find the books most appropriate to your immediate needs, this search is a treasure hunt that promises to yield great riches.

In this chapter we will first discuss developing a kind of literature program that usually does not exist in elementary schools. Then we will explore ways of motivating children of all ages and abilities to read more as they learn what books have to offer.

❀ *PREVIEWING THE TOPIC*   You probably already know much about incorporating trade books in the reading program. These questions are designed to open up topics for further consideration.

1. Name three literature concepts that you would teach children in the primary grades.

   _____

   _____

   _____

2. How would you develop a reading learning center?

3. Why should group work be part of an individualized reading program?

4. Describe three methods of sharing books that you might suggest to students in a fourth grade room.

5. How does teaching *literature* differ from teaching *reading?*

DEVELOPING A LITERATURE PROGRAM

In considering the development of an elementary school literature program, there are basic questions that should be explored. The answers to these questions will serve to guide the planning of a scope and sequence, the selection of appropriate materials for use in the program, and the determination of methodology to be utilized.

It should be noted, first of all, that the questions posed here are not ones to which there are simple answers or even questions to which there are clear-cut "right" answers. They are questions, however, that require careful consideration as we conceive of an ideal, yet feasible, literature program:

1. Why should literature be included in the elementary school program?
2. How does teaching *literature* differ from teaching *reading?*
3. Where does literature fit into the present curriculum?
4. Is there a need for a planned scope and sequence in literature?
5. How will literature be selected for this program?

WHY INCLUDE LITERATURE?

Why should literature be included in the elementary school curriculum? Few would deny the wisdom or the desirability of including literature in the elementary school curriculum. In general, the reasons given include the following:

To increase the child's self-awareness

To transmit the cultural heritage

To help children understand other people

To expose children to excellent writing

To stimulate the child's enjoyment of reading

To teach children concepts about literature

In a literature-oriented reading program, we can teach literary concepts such as: (1) plot or story line, (2) theme, (3) characterization, (4) setting, and (5) imagery. These concepts are important as students observe the style of authors in using the English language and how they organize ideas to achieve a desired effect. As students write original stories themselves and as they discuss books they are reading, they can learn to identify the elements of a story:

Story Development Chart

When?

Where?   Setting (time and place)

Who?	Protagonist(s) (characters)
	Antagonist(s)
What?	Problem (plot; theme)
Why?	
How?	Solution
	Dénouement (conclusion)

We should also consider, however, another type of concept that we might better term *understandings,* for literature presents values; it teaches attitudes. E. B. White not only tells an adventure story about Charlotte and Wilbur, but he also conveys mature concepts of friendship, loneliness, and death. We can only begin a list of the many understandings to be gained from literature, for example:

1. Everybody has problems.

2. Problems are to be solved.

3. Appearances may be deceiving.

4. People are not all "good" or all "bad."

5. People are much the same all over the world.

As you can see, this list is inexhaustible and will need constant revision. Many books that are helpful in developing these kinds of understandings are discussed in Chapter 4. Eve Merriam's *Mommies at Work* teaches young children, for instance, that it's all right to have a mother who works and that many mothers work outside the home.

A Penny a Look (Farrar, Straus & Giroux, 1971), written by Harve Zemach and illustrated by Margot Zemach, clearly teaches the fact that difference is relative. A greedy, insensitive man persuades his brother to go with him to the land of the one-eyed people to capture a one-eyed person to display in a sideshow so the greedy man can become rich. The one-eyed people are so amazed to see a two-eyed person, however, that they put the greedy man himself on display and collect a penny for each look at this rarity.

Another important reason for including literature in the elementary school curriculum is to ensure that all children know their literary heritage. Children who do not have early experiences with the literature of childhood will probably never again have the opportunity to know Mother Goose rhymes, the nursery tales that delight children. All children should meet such characters as Thidwick the Moose, Curious

George, and Madeline, and enjoy the many other rich experiences that come with reading good books. We have a responsibility, therefore, to ascertain if children know "Jack and Jill" or *The Three Little Pigs,* and to see that this literature saturates the kindergarten and first grade classroom.

Teachers of older children should survey their students' knowledge of this literature, too, because it is not too late to introduce children to Mother Goose in fifth grade or even eighth. It may take a little ingenuity, however, as you ask students to develop creative presentations to share with young children, make posters of Mother Goose poems to place in a children's hospital, or study children's books as a basis for creating original ones.

Children need a knowledge of literature to live comfortably in a literate world. The references to this body of literature permeate even our everyday speech in such expressions as:

Dog in the manger

Sour grapes

Rain, rain, go away

Star, light; star, bright; first star I see tonight

Sleeping beauty

Don't count your chickens

Look before you leap

The golden touch

Ugly duckling

If this literature is familiar to you, it is easy to take it for granted. We should not assume, however, that all children have been exposed to these poems and stories in their homes. We need to ensure that they know children's literature by incorporating this literature in the elementary school curriculum.

TEACHING LITERATURE AND READING

How does teaching literature differ from teaching reading? The teaching of reading focuses on developing a skill. It involves teaching the phoneme-grapheme relationship, for example, the development of word attack skills, the knowledge of words. It moves into the study of morphology or word forms and the use of syntax to gain meaning. *The teaching of literature, on the other hand, remains focused on ideas, varied genres, and appreciation of the writer's performance with words.* Through literature children experience the heritage of the past and discover meaning for their own lives. Children are led to express original ideas and to manipulate words as they, too, create literature.

Any literature program must be sufficiently flexible to permit growth of all students at all levels. It must satisfy the voracious appetites of bright students as well as encourage development by slower learners. Provision must be made, too, for additional enrichment for children who need to build a background of literature experiences, for example, children who live in non-English–speaking homes. Building around a core of materials that all children will experience, the ideal program will suggest activities to extend the learning of able students. It will also suggest enrichment activities for those who need to develop a richer background before moving on. It will include multicultural literature to benefit all students.

In order to present well-organized, effective literature lessons, prepare exciting learning experiences that children will respond to. Focus objectives on important concepts and take advantage of the offerings of each selection, for example, the contrast of British and American English in Lucy Boston's series of books about Green Knowe. An integrated language arts approach focusing on language and literature opens the door to a dramatic interpretation of *The Fools of Chelm,* choric speaking of Zindel's *I Love My Mother,* or painting a mural featuring native Americans. Teaching such a program can be joyful.

The most useful organization for studying literature will probably be a combination of individual study and the seminar approach, for work in large groups does not promote student involvement. Discard such methods as the traditional book report, which is still being used in many classrooms, for this limited approach to literature serves only to stifle interest in reading. Try creative approaches to sharing books such as the following:

The *diorama* is an excellent medium for depicting a scene from a story. Homer Price (cardboard or papier-mâché figure) could be shown with Aroma, his pet skunk, as they creep up on the robbers who are camping in the woods. The diorama also can be used to portray a scene from historical fiction or from the life of a figure in American history.

A *mobile* can present a book by displaying the characters as well as objects or ideas essential to the story. *The 500 Hats of Bartholomew Cubbins* might, for instance, be interpreted through a mobile which features many unusual hats created in three dimensions.

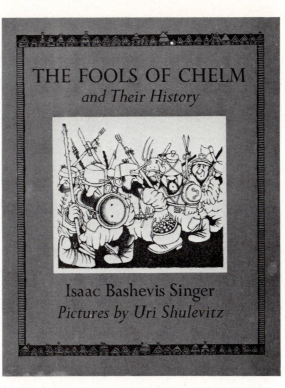

Music can be related to book sharing as a student or a small group of students composes a ballad about *Mary Poppins*. Older students might write a calypso or a folk song about the adventures of Huckleberry Finn or a real person about whom they have read.

A *collage* is an intriguing method of combining art with literature. *Chitty-Chitty-Bang-Bang,* for example, might be depicted on a large poster which includes a cut-out drawing of this distinctive green car, the faces of Man-Mountain Fink, Joe, the Monster, and the twins. Portions of a map of England, the English Channel and northern France might be worked into the background as would be other illustrative ideas from the story. Words can also be incorporated in the collage—*Paris, transmogrifications, Paragon Panther, Ian Fleming,* and so on.[2]

In developing an elementary school literature program strive to achieve an exciting, stimulating curriculum that will truly involve children in their literature. The teaching of literature at this level will open

---

[2] Iris M. Tiedt and Sidney W. Tiedt, *Contemporary English in the Elementary School* (Prentice-Hall, 1975), pp. 368–369.

the door to an extended and expanded literature program at the secondary school level. Most important, however, let us stimulate children's love of reading, their enjoyment of books, for the child who acquires this feeling for books at an early age will never lose it. What a rich legacy you are in a position to pass on to children!

PLACING LITERATURE IN THE CURRICULUM

Where does literature fit into the present curriculum? The elementary school curriculum is already suffering from overexpansion, so that it is no idle question to consider just where literature is to be placed. Several possibilities exist: (1) in a period of time labeled *literature;* (2) in an English program; (3) as part of a reading program; or (4) as an essential component of an integrated language arts program.

Ideally language arts in the elementary school consists of a well-integrated program focused directly on the English language. English is thus studied through the skills of reading, writing, speaking, and listening. The content to be studied is language and literature. Certainly the interrelationship between encoding and decoding should be taught, and children should perceive themselves as both readers and writers. Not only can they appreciate the writing of others but, as young authors, they can produce "literature." The literature they read should be pointed to as a model for their own creative efforts.

The encoding-decoding process is a unified approach to the teaching of linguistic skills basic to reading and spelling, both of which are essential to developing skills of composition and to the independent study of literature. While linguistic abilities are developing, a large amount of language time is devoted to oral language activities, for children learn language through listening and speaking. One of the most important of the learning experiences planned for these early years is listening to literature read aloud by the teacher. Children need to hear the language of literature

A well-organized, integrated language program has the emphasis expressed in this schema.

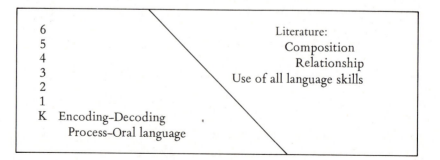

before they try to read it, for this language is much different from that which they speak. Formal literature instruction is supplemented by exciting incidental experiences that occur when the teacher reads such books as Evelyn Lampman's *A City Under the Back Steps* aloud or shares a poem like "Velvet Shoes" by Elinor Wylie when the first flakes of winter suddenly appear. These experiences are enriching and stimulating, but their very spontaneity means that they are irregular and unplanned. We do need a fully developed literature program as discussed in the next section.

PLANNING A SCOPE AND SEQUENCE FOR LITERATURE

For each subject taught in the elementary school curriculum we have a carefully delineated scope and sequence. Many educators, however, hesitate to submit literature to this type of structure. They state: "We must feel free to present the 'right' book at the exact moment it is appropriate." Whether teachers take full advantage of this idealized approach remains questionable. Literature continues to be presented incidentally and may be just as often *ex*cluded as *in*cluded.

The advantages of a planned scope and sequence for literature lie not in the elimination of incidental, enriching experiences with literature, but rather in ensuring a planned presentation of excellent literature selected to teach specific concepts. The planned literature program is directed at providing instruction about literature, the teaching of concepts that young children can absorb at their individual levels of understanding.

The carefully developed program, furthermore, avoids the unfortunate repetition that occurs as every teacher "discovers" haiku with his or her students or shares *Johnny Tremain*. Even the best of literature becomes distasteful when repeated in this unorganized manner. One could anticipate the result that children would dislike writing haiku or resent hearing Johnny's adventures for the third time.

The planned program not only eliminates this repetition but it also ensures continuity. Developed both vertically and horizontally, it includes selections designed to instruct as well as to please. A number of contemporary reading texts now include literature by known authors. English and even spelling texts are also including literature as part of the learning experiences presented. What they lack, however, in most cases, is the planned scope and sequence of literature concepts and the close interrelationship with other language learnings, such as the reading of poetry that results in the composition of poetry. Little effort is made to teach literature concepts in these texts, and the child is never provided with the rich experience of studying a whole book—such as Madeline L'Engle's *A Wrinkle in Time* with its introduction to symbolism.

As you begin developing a scope and sequence for a literature program, consider first the goals and objectives you wish to achieve. What concepts would you have students learn? What competencies do you want them to develop? The goals and objectives selected will determine what literature is studied, the methods used, the activities planned for students, and the resulting performance by the student.

If we are chiefly concerned about readers responding to literature, then we must plan a student-centered approach such as has been emphasized in activities throughout this book. Goals and objectives will reflect both cognitive and affective aspects of learning, for how can they be separated? As Piaget noted: "Affective life, like intellectual life, is a continuous adaptation, and the two are not only parallel but interdependent, since feelings express the interest and values given to actions of which intelligence provides the structure.[3]

As teachers, how can we bring students and literature together with the best effect? As you plan a literature program, keep in mind that our task is:

1. To serve as resource persons who make available a wide variety of reading materials and related media with attention to individual needs and interests

2. To capitalize on the "reading readiness" generated by such media as television and films; to recognize through the students' talking and reading that, in Daniel Fader's terms, they can be "hooked on"

3. To deal with specific individuals and small groups, recognizing the wide range of tastes, abilities, and deficiencies they represent

4. To introduce students to the people in literature, the qualities of human excellence, real heroes and phonies, and to encourage students who question values

5. To help students discover relationships between literature and life, particularly their own experiences

6. To encourage each student to discover, partly through reading, his or her own identity

7. To involve students in open, informal talking related to their reading and to encourage them to judge and react to what they have read

8. To encourage students to read regularly and with enthusiasm

----

[3] John H. Flavell, *The Developmental Psychology of Jean Piaget* (Van Nostrand, n.d.), p. 80.

A student-centered approach to literature cannot be genre-oriented. We will not focus, therefore, on literature itself, but rather on the student who is experiencing life, of which literature is a part. Students learn inductively, and they develop competencies through responding to literature, thus:

Valuing	Students state what they like or admire and what they reject in the literature they experience.
Describing	Students identify and describe elements of literature, such as characters, setting, behavior.
Relating	Students make connections, see similarities, relate literature to life.
Discriminating	Students identify differences.
Generalizing	Students state ideas abstracted from literature.
Judging	Students criticize literature read or experienced.[4]

Goals and performance objectives can be specified to develop each of these competencies. Activities that allow for different levels of reading ability can be planned for each objective to be developed. Sufficient activities should be planned so students have choices. These activities can be assigned to a full group or they can be presented on task cards (see p. 356). Books can be read aloud by the teacher, recorded on tape, or read independently by individuals or small groups. You will want to expand or modify the objectives provided here and the representative activities to develop a full scope and sequence that meets your needs.

A. Valuing

Goal A1: The student finds reading a satisfying activity.

Objective A1.1: The student browses and reads when exposed to books and magazines.

Activity: Discuss something you discovered in a magazine or newspaper recently.

Objective A1.2: The student obtains a library card.

Activity: Explain how you can get a library card.

---

[4] J. N. Hook, and others, *Representative Performance Objectives for High School English: A Guide for Teaching, Evaluating, and Curriculum Planning* (Ronald, 1971).

Objective A1.3: The student develops a personal library.
Activity: Tell about a book you have at home.

Objective A1.4: The student participates in literature-related activities.
Activity: "Sell" a book you have just read to the class.

Objective A1.5: The student reads for his or her own purpose.
Activity: Keep a reading log of everything you read for two weeks.

Goal A2: The student talks about books read.
Objective A2.1: The student develops preferences that are reflected in choice of books.
Activity: Make a list of books about your favorite topic.

Objective A2.2: The student is open to new experiences through reading.
Activity: Read a book about something you know nothing about.

Objective A2.3: The student develops a sense of humor.
Activity: Write a riddle to put in a book of riddles.

Objective A2.4: The student recognizes the rights of others to react differently.
Activity: Participate in a panel discussion about a book that other students have read.

B. Describing

Goal B1: The student describes a literature selection.
Objective B1.1: The student defines words in context.
Activity: Define three interesting words that appear in *Sam, Bangs & Moonshine*.

Objective B1.2: The student retells the plot of a story.
Activity: Write a blurb for the jacket cover of your favorite book.

Objective B1.3: The student talks about the characters in a story.
Activity: Identify the characters in *Charlotte's Web*.

Objective B1.4: The student recognizes different forms of literature.
Activity: Explain the difference between fiction and nonfiction.

Goal B2: The student understands the literal meaning of what is read.
Objective B2.1: The student states the main idea or theme of a story.
Activity: Describe the main idea of *I Love My Mother* by Paul Zindel.

Objective B2.2 The student locates specific information.
Activity: Locate a definition of *mammals*.

Objective B2.3: The student identifies the narrator, point of view.

Activity: Identify the speakers in Marie Lawson's poem "Halloween."

Objective B2.4: The student answers questions about the meaning of a poem.

Activity: List the words that tell you what Emily Dickinson is describing in "I Like to See It Lap the Miles."

C. Relating

Goal Cl: The student relates the story line to his or her own experience or archetypal experiences.

Objective C1.1: The student recognizes archetypal characters such as the villain, the scapegoat, the nonconformist.

Activity: Name several villains you have met in stories.

Objective C1.2: The student identifies archetypal experiences such as alienation, love, initiation, or fear.

Activity: Discuss Irving's feelings as he waited in *Gladys Told Me to Meet Her Here* by Marjorie Sharmat.

Goal C2: The student recognizes relationships between characters in a story.

Objective C2.1: The student recognizes the source of conflict between two characters.

Activity: Explain how Poll felt toward her mother in *Peppermint Pig* when Johnny, her pig, was taken to the butcher.

Objective C2.2: The student identifies problems of relating with others in real life.

Activity: Tell about a problem you had to solve as John Henry did in *John Henry McCoy* by Lillie Chaffin.

Goal C3: The student compares features of different cultures, countries, or ethnic groups.

Objective C3.1: The student points out similarities of human behavior across cultures.

Activity: Compare Hooits' desire for peace in *Ghost Paddle* with your desire for peace in the same land.

Objective C3.2: The student identifies differences in beliefs of the past compared to contemporary thinking.

Activity: Compare the life of Abigail Adams with that of the President's wife today.

Goal C4: The student recognizes the relationship of language and meaning.

Objective C4.1: The student identifies the use of literary conventions such as: "Once upon a time . . . " and "So they lived happily ever after," the refrain of a poem, use of flashbacks.

Activity: Read *Puss in Boots* aloud.

Objective C4.2: The student discusses the imagery in poetry and prose.

Activity: Read "Southbound on the Freeway" by May Swenson or "Fog" by Rowena Bennett.

Objective C4.3: The student recognizes the tone or mood of a story or poem.

Activity: Discuss the poem "Someone" by Walter de la Mare.

Goal C5: The student recognizes the relationship of form and meaning.

Objective C5.1: The student identifies differences between poetry and prose.

Activity: Rewrite "The Squirrel" in prose.

Activity: Tap out the rhythm of "Hippity Hop to the Barber Shop."

Objective C5.2: The student identifies differences between fiction and nonfiction.

Activity: Identify the outline in one chapter of your science textbook.

Objective C5.3: The student recognizes chapters, the acts of a play, or stanzas of poetry.

Activity: Compose music for the poem "Who Has Seen the Wind?" by Christina Rossetti.

Activity: Read the stanzas of "America the Beautiful."

D. Discriminating

Goal D1: The student identifies different forms of literature.

Objective D1.1: The student uses the terms poetry, fiction, nonfiction, drama, film appropriately.

Activity: Compare *The Door in the Wall* by Marguerite de Angeli in play and story form.

Objective D1.2: The student compares the content of fact and fiction or fantasy and science fiction.

Activity: Discuss why *The Children of Green Knowe* is fantasy rather than science fiction.

Goal D2: The student identifies the narrator or person speaking (point of view).

Objective D2.1: The student uses different points of view in personal writing.

Activity: Write a description of the funniest thing that ever happened to you.

Objective D2.2: The student discusses the effect of using different viewpoints.

Activity: Discuss the meaning and tone of "Puppy and I" by A. A. Milne.

Goal D3: The student notes the effect of language on meaning.

Objective D3.1: The student experiments with intonation in reading aloud.

Activity: Recite the ABC's as a question, as a reply, in a happy mood, in an angry mood.

Objective D3.2: The student recognizes language that is imaginative or figurative compared to factual language.

Activity: Discuss the picture of a train as a dragon in "A Modern Dragon" by Rowena Bennett.

Goal D4: The student identifies representative features of forms of writing.

Objective D4.1: The student reads the dialogue of a character in a story.

Activity: Present *The Three Little Pigs* as Readers' Theater.

Objective D4.2: The student tells which lines rhyme in a poem.

Activity: Write limericks after reading examples by Lear and others.

Objective D4.3: The student lists the facts presented in nonfiction.

Activity: Make a time line for the life of Louisa May Alcott based on *Invincible Louisa.*

Objective D4.4: The student identifies a character description.

Activity: Paint a picture of Petronella.

Goal D5: The student identifies the character traits of people in fiction.

Objective D5.1: The student observes both good and bad traits in one character.

Activity: List three good traits and three bad traits of Pippi Longstocking.

Objective D5.2: The student compares the self-image of a character with the perception of others.

Activity: Describe Aunt Polly's reaction to Tom Sawyer's behavior with Tom's way of looking at it.

E. Generalizing

Goal E1: The student recognizes the difference between the literal meaning of a passage and the underlying assumptions or meaning.

Objective E1.1: The student identifies satire, parody, or irony.
Activity: Compare "The Octopussy Cat" by Kenyon Cox with "I Love Little Pussy."

Objective E1.2: The student identifies the assumptions of the author who is writing a story.
Activity: Discuss the way John Christopher views society after reading *The Prince in Waiting* and others of his books.

Goal E2: The student follows the logical development of a literary work.
Objective E2.1: The student predicts what will happen next in a sequence of events.
Activity: Predict how the film *The Loon's Necklace* will end after viewing the first half.

Objective E2.2: The student states how a story might continue.
Activity: Write another chapter or adventure for Homer Price.

Goal E3: The student understands what is humorous.
Objective E3.1: The student uses word play orally or in writing.
Activity: Write Tom Swifties such as:
"I hurt my leg," said Tom lamely.

Objective E3.2: The student recognizes exaggeration as a humorous device.
Activity: Write a tall tale after reading about Paul Bunyan or Pecos Bill.

Goal E4: The student recognizes what behavior reveals about character.
Objective E4.1: The student describes a character in a story.
Activity: Discuss the characteristics of the father in *And To Think That I Saw It on Mulberry Street* by Dr. Seuss.

Objective E4.2: The student states how a character might behave.
Activity: Describe what Curious George might say or do if he were to visit your classroom.

F. Judging

Goal F1: The student identifies strengths and weaknesses in a literary work.
Objective F1.1: The student compares different versions of a story.
Activity: Discuss what television has added to *The Little House* stories.

Objective F1.2: The student compares two books on the same subject.
Activity: Compare Jean George's discussion of the ways of wolves in *Julie and the Wolves* and that presented by Charles Ripper in *Foxes and Wolves*.

Goal F2: The student assesses the accuracy of nonfiction.
Objective F2.1: The student researches the qualifications of an author.
Activity: Analyze the qualifications of Herbert Zim to write about science topics.

Objective F2.2: The student checks statements presented as fact.
Activity: Support or refute the accuracy of this statement: The cheetah is the fastest animal in the world.

Goal F3: The student develops criteria for excellent writing.
Objective F3.1: The student compares realistic fiction to real life.
Activity: Discuss what you and Queenie Peavy have in common.

Objective F3.2: The student recognizes fresh, appropriate imagery.
Activity: Explain the theme of Walt Whitman's poem "I Hear America Singing."
Activity: Compare the way the wind is described in "The Kite" by Harry Behn and "Wind-Wolves" by William Sargent.

Objective F3.3: The student observes effective use of language.
Activity: Examine the sentences in Paula Fox's *The Slave Dancer* to see how the author uses varied kinds of sentences.

Objective F3.4: The student pictures characters, setting, or action described.
Activity: Paint a picture of the setting for *Stranger at Green Knowe*.

SELECTING BOOKS FOR A LITERATURE PROGRAM

How will literature be selected for this program? Teachers and librarians share the responsibility for ordering trade books for school libraries and for the literature program. Children can also contribute to this selection process. Utilizing the opinions of children may assist you in choosing books that children really enjoy.

Clarify the criteria you will use in making the selection of individual titles. These criteria will reflect your objectives for a literature program and the concepts you wish to teach. The criteria should include quality of writing, recommendation by experts, and enjoyment by children.

Published aids for book selection are helpful, especially those which are kept up-to-date. The following are especially useful:

The Booklist and Subscription Books Bulletin, A Guide to Current Books, American Library Association, 60 E. Huron St., Chicago, Ill.

Children's Catalog, New York: H. W. Wilson Company. 950 University Avenue, Bronx, N.Y. 10452. (*With regular supplements.*)

When we think of literature for the elementary school, we usually mean books. Within the broad category of books, however, there are subclassifications to be examined, for example, the various genres listed here with examples given for each:

Contemporary novels: *And Now, Miguel; Stoneflight; Dragonwing*

Nonfiction: *From Drumbeat to Tickertape; The Presidency*

Poetry: *Cricket Songs; You Come, Too*

Short stories: *Homer Price; Jahdu Tales*

Drama: *Peter Pan; Door in the Wall* (play version)

Biography: *Invincible Louisa; American Indian Women; Ray Charles*

Remember also that literature includes more than books. Excellent films and filmstrips have much to offer a literature program. *The Red Balloon* (Albert LaMorrisse), *Hailstones and Halibut Bones* (Sterling Films), and *Rainshower* (Churchill Films) are three excellent films that present the

Public domain in U.S. For outside U.S.: From The Red Balloon *copyright © 1956 by Albert La Morrisse. Reprinted by permission of Doubleday & Company, Inc.*

same fine qualities found in books. In addition, films offer the visual imagery contributed by outstanding photography and imagination. In *The Red Balloon,* for example, children can observe the same elements that a printed story would offer in a literature program: characterization, foreshadowing, and plot structure.

Recordings present literature through yet another sense. *Ruth Sawyer, Story Teller* (Weston Woods Studios) and *The Just So Stories* (Caedmon) are recordings by skilled storytellers, who share fine literature with young children. Recordings, as well as films, can stretch children to learn as they are exposed to new vocabulary and interesting ideas.

In the next section we will consider how we can implement some of these ideas for introducing children to literature. The focus is on motivating children to read.

INVITING CHILDREN TO READ

Children learn to read by reading. Studies in psycholinguistics tell us that children learn reading skills most effectively through reading words that are set in the context of stories. They read (gain meaning) by working with the syntax of the sentence and the surrounding context of sentences that precede or follow.[5] Our purpose, therefore, in a reading program is to encourage students to open books, to get involved with characters, to be lured by illustrations so they will want to read; for as they read, they will develop the ability to read.

We need to consider how we can increase the child's desire to read, for true motivation comes from within. In this section we will consider ways of inviting children to read, for example:

1. Planning experiences so children hear language

2. Creating a climate conducive to reading

3. Scheduling time for reading and sharing books

4. Displaying books in the classroom

ORAL FOUNDATION FOR READING

Oral language provides the foundation for learning to read. Children who have well-developed language abilities before entering school tend

---

[5] Frank Smith, *Understanding Reading: A Psycholinguistic Analysis of Reading and Learning to Read* (Holt, 1971).

to become fluent readers with little problem. Anastasiow describes a not uncommon experience in a middle class home where books abound:

> A three-year-old sat on the floor, his legs stretched straight in front of him as only the very young can manage. He held a large book in his lap and "read," "The horsie said, 'Come and I'll give you a ride.' I ride horsie far away until I'm all gone. I'm all gone, gone away." The mother smiled proudly even though the child was holding the brightly colored book with a picture of a horse on the cover upside down.[6]

For those children who do not have this enriched background with language, particularly with book language, we need to make special efforts to provide a variety of language and literature experiences. The listening center is an effective way of seeing that children have many opportunities to hear stories, to hear the language of literature that they will later be expected to read. Book language is much different from the language learned orally by children. Children are not accustomed, for example, to hearing the third person in ordinary speech and certainly not the formal sentence structure that is used in writing. Through listening, children continue to learn language abilities—vocabulary, new concepts, more complicated syntax. At the same time, furthermore, they are being exposed to more of their literary heritage—folktales, poetry, fantasy. This is a happy combination for learning.

For too long the classroom was a silent place in which children were "to be seen and not heard." Studies show that children are literally afraid to ask questions in school. Why would this be true when young children are so full of questions as they go busily about their work of discovering the world? We need to consider how we can correct this attitude, for children learn by questioning.

Oral language lends a liveliness to a classroom, furthermore, that is enriching and involving. Children who are discussing "matters of consequence," as the Little Prince calls it, are happily engaged in learning. But then "on matters of consequence, the little prince had ideas that were very different from the grown-ups."[7]

---

[6] Nicholas Anastasiow, *Oral Language: Expression of Thought* (International Reading Association, 1971).
[7] Antoine de Saint-Exupéry, *The Little Prince* (Harcourt Brace Jovanovich, 1943), pp. 56–57.

Read aloud to students of all ages. Nothing can substitute for the personal contact between a teacher and the class members who are sharing a good book—*The Hobbit, May I Cross Your Golden River?* or *Baba Yaga's Geese.* The selection to be shared can be very short—short stories, jokes, items from the newspaper, an appropriate poem. You extend the invitation and students will follow by bringing things to share. Children need to hear language, for strong oral language skills lead to fluent reading.

If we want to encourage oral language development, we need to provide the opportunity for children to talk, as well as ideas to talk about. We can provide such exciting stimuli as *The Giving Tree* by Shel Silverstein (Harper & Row, 1964). This very small picture book presents big ideas about love for students to ponder. The tree delights in the small boy who climbs in its branches. It gladly gives him apples to sell and wood to build a house. As the boy grows up, the tree continues to give him what he needs, until there is nothing left but an old stump. Here the elderly man comes at last to rest.

Another provocative stimulus is *The Chairy Tale,* a charming filmed presentation of an improvisation with only two actors, a young man and a chair. Filmed by the National Film Board of Canada, the film depicts a man's attempts to sit on a chair to read his book—a simple act, but not when the chair doesn't want to be "sat upon"! This film can be enjoyed on several levels, from a factual representation of exactly what happens

He would climb up her trunk

to a more sophisticated consideration of a relationship between two people. The chair symbolizes a person who is taken for granted and suddenly rebels.

Even older students can discuss the message of a picture book story, such as . . . *And to Think That I Saw It on Mulberry Street* (Random House, 1937) by Dr. Seuss. Here is a sample from the book:

AND TO THINK THAT I SAW IT ON MULBERRY STREET
By Dr. Seuss

That's nothing to tell of,
That won't do, of course . . .
Just a broken-down wagon
That's drawn by a horse.

That *can't* be my story. That's only a *start*.
I'll say that a ZEBRA was pulling that cart!
And that is a story that no one can beat,
When I say that I saw it on Mulberry Street.

Other books that will stimulate children's use of language in the class-room include the following:

No Ducks in "Our" Bathtub by Martha Alexander. Dial, 1973.
How do you think David felt when he returned to find that his "fish eggs" had turned into 103 frogs? How do you think his mother felt?

Georgie Goes West by Robert Bright. Doubleday, 1973.
Would you like to know a ghost named Georgie? What kinds of adventures might you have?

Bubble Bubble by Mercer Mayer. Parents' Magazine Press, 1973.
Tell the story of this bubble maker as you look at the pictures by Mr. Mayer.

The Secret Name by Barbara Williams. Harcourt Brace Jovanovich, 1972.
Can you imagine how Betsy felt when she came from the Indian reservation to live with Laurie's family?

Emil and Piggy Beast by Astrid Lindgren. Follett, 1973.
How would you feel if you had a brother like Emil? How do you get along with your brother or sister?

Olga da Polga by Michael Bond. Macmillan, 1971.
Make up another adventure for this adventurous guinea pig.

Students can tell their stories to classmates in small groups or they might record them on the cassette recorder. Large group discussion can follow the reading aloud of books the group has experienced together. These kinds of activities can be explained on task cards that students draw from a file after reading a specific book, a good way of handling individualized reading.

DEVELOPING A READING ENVIRONMENT

The classroom in which children are busily exploring books has a happy atmosphere. The teacher always has a good story going that the group can enjoy together. Not only are they learning through listening, but the shared experience lends a feeling of camaraderie in which everyone is included. Many learning activities are initiated by reading while others lead children to reading, and children are the ones who plan these experiences

---

* For younger children.

and select the books that best serve their purposes. This kind of active, purposeful, yet enjoyable learning is a goal worth working toward.

The warm, friendly climate of a classroom reflects the thinking of a teacher who cares about children. This teacher knows how to share decision making with young people, who need many opportunities to grow. This teacher knows also that even such things as the way the desks are arranged in the room affect the children's attitudes and determine to a large extent the kinds of activities that will take place there.

ORGANIZING THE CLASSROOM TO PROMOTE READING The way furniture is arranged in a classroom immediately indicates our expectation of what kind of learning experiences will occur in that room. Very structured, teacher-dominated activities will probably take place in a classroom that is organized in the traditional way with the teacher's desk at the front of the classroom.

Literature-centered activities fit well in a more open classroom arrangement. Small groups of children gather to talk about Shirley Arora's "What Then, Raman?" which they have just read. A pair of children put their desks together as they read Laura Ingalls Wilder's *Little House in the Big Woods* together. A group sits around a table as they share the results of their research on life in the tide pools near their homes; of course, they have Holling C. Holling's book *Pagoo*. Several others pore over the colored illustrations by Nicolás in Rudyard Kipling's *Just So Stories* (Watts, 1952), as they plan to dramatize "The Elephant's Child."

Working in pairs or small groups of five or six is an effective organiza-

Two floor plans showing (left) a structured, teacher-dominated classroom and (right) an open classroom designed to promote reading activities.

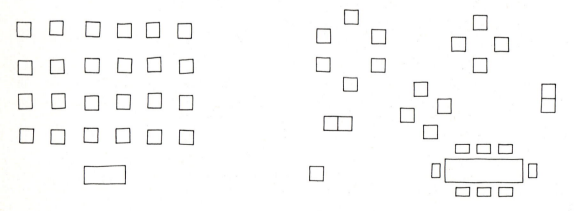

tion for reading activities, for children have the need, even when working in individualized programs, to work in group situations. A Great
Books Club lends itself to such seminar grouping, as children meet with
or without the teacher to talk about books. Students reading the same
book, for example, *Miss Bianca in the Salt Mines* by Margery Sharp (Little,
Brown, 1967), can think of a number of ways to share this funny book
with the larger group, for instance:

Enlarge drawings of the characters in the story to display on the classroom walls. Include famous words for each character in a balloon shape
attached to the appropriate character with black yarn.

Prepare a bulletin board display with the caption: MICE WE HAVE
KNOWN. Here they could display poems about mice, as well as drawings of Miss Bianca and her friends, Anatole, and Amos, and the mouse
in *Ben and Me*.

A group of students can read various books on the same general topic,
for example, the contributions of blacks to our society. To share their
findings with the larger group they could, for example, plan a twenty-to-
thirty-minute program entitled Black Is Beautiful:

Music by Duke Ellington played while pictures of black musicians are
shown on record albums.

Readers' Theater presentation of *I Wish I Had an Afro* by John Shearer
(Cowles).

Reading of several poems by Langston Hughes, perhaps using choral
reading. (See *Don't You Turn Back; Poems of Langston Hughes,* comp. by
Lee Bennett Hopkins, Knopf.)

Presentation of facts about other black people who have made notable
contributions, for example: Martin Luther King, Marian Anderson,
George Washington Carver.

Discussion of some of the stories written about black people, especially
those written by black authors, for instance, Lorenz Graham.

Music by one of the fine black women vocalists, for example, Mahalia
Jackson or Carmen Macrae. (See *Big Star Fallin' Mama; Five Women in
Black Music* by Hettie Jones, Viking, 1974.)

Sharing books in various ways not only encourages oral language development but also motivates children to read the books their classmates

recommend. Suggest different ways children can share a book, for example, book surprises, presents to the class. These surprises may incorporate art, music, or special interests of an individual student, thus:

Dress a doll to represent Dorothy in *The Wizard of Oz*. Prepare a three-dimensional scene in which the doll is placed to enact a scene from the story.

Show a set of original pictures about the adventures of *Danny Dunn and the Homework Machine*. Students could talk about the ways this machine might help them, or how it might get them in trouble as it did Danny and his friends.

Share a butterfly collection and tell the class about various butterflies that are common in your local area. Bring in several books about butterflies, such as *Butterflies and Moths* by Robert Mitchell and Herbert S. Zim or *Butterflies* by Dorothy Hogner, who tells how to raise butterflies from a caterpillar.

Ask the class some riddles that the student knows and let others share ones they know. Show riddle books, such as *Black Within and Red Without* compiled by Lillian Morrison.

Write a song based on *Henry Huggins*. Make up words about Ribsy, Henry's comical dog, for example, to be sung to the tune, "Oh where, oh where, has my little dog gone?"

Work with a group of students who have read the same book on preparing a mural. Scenes from *Where the Lilies Bloom* can be prepared in the irregular spaces of a collage-mural.

Example of a collage-mural showing scenes from Where the Lilies Bloom.

Eliminate book reports as you think of other ways of having children let you know what they're reading. The book talk offers an interesting way of combining the use of oral language skills as well as letting you and the class know about the book a student has just read.

Book talks are great for presentations to younger children also. Children can make figures for the flannel board to accompany their talk. They can also sketch on the board as they present a chalk talk, to illustrate it as they tell the story. A poster can be created that is aimed at "selling" classmates on reading a specific book.

Give a chalk talk based on *The Hobbit.* The student might draw Bilbo Baggins or describe his neat little house. A chalk talk also lends itself to describing the overall adventures in a kind of time line across the board. Several students could participate in this presentation.

Prepare an oversize magazine ad for *Mom, The Wolfman, and Me.* Use clippings from magazines, perhaps emulating an ad seen in a magazine or on television.

THE READING/LANGUAGE CENTER   Children enjoy having a special center that encourages reading in a cozy setting that is comfortable and private. A reading retreat can take varied forms, for example, a carpeted corner of the room set off by screens the children have made themselves. Books are available on shelves that are readily accessible. Lots of browsing material, such as magazines for children, make the reading center an appealing place for even the reluctant reader.

How can you develop a reading retreat without special funds? Enlist the help of students in the classroom. It's their classroom, and they will certainly be more involved in using the reading center if they help to plan and to create it. Talk with students about things they might be able to contribute, for example:

1. Books no longer needed at home

2. Daily newspapers brought in the following day

3. Magazines their families may subscribe to

4. A piece of carpeting that is available

5. Pillows, stools, or a rocking chair

You really never know what possibilities there are until you begin talking with a group. If funds are available, you might make several large pillows. Children can decorate the covers and actually sew them by hand or with a portable machine. Children can also paint bookshelves with bright colors. There are endless ways of developing the center to make it functional and appealing.

You might also consider combining a reading area with facilities for writing or for making original books, a publishing house. The supplies needed for such a center are readily available in most classrooms. Collect writing materials:

Small notebooks	Colored construction paper
Composition paper	File folders
Newsprint	Tagboard; other cardboard
White typing paper	Stapler
Pens and pencils	Glue, paste
Colored felt pens	Ruler
Typewriter	Paper punch
Printing letters; stamp pad	Scissors

Books that children make can be displayed in the reading center, too. Children enjoy reading what their classmates have written.

A reading/language center motivates students to read more and to react to their reading through writing. Do away with the sterile report form as you ask students to write about books they read in a log that each one keeps individually. More than just a synopsis of the story, this kind of reaction essay encourages even young children to consider how they feel about what they are reading, to become involved with a character, to jot down questions that occur as they read.

Using the read/write approach makes both reading and writing more stimulating. Although students should certainly have time to read with no expectation of having to complete any follow-up activity, you may at times read a story aloud with the specific intent of having students write in response. Many of the stories already mentioned in this chapter lend themselves to this strategy. In addition you might read:

Rain Rain Rivers by Uri Shulevitz (Farrar, Straus & Giroux,)
How do you feel about rain? Has there ever been a time when you had more rain than you wanted?

Sam, Bangs & Moonshine by Evaline Ness (Holt)
How did Sam's moonshine get her into real trouble? Have you ever told a lie that got you into trouble?

Dragon Stew by Tom McGowen (Follett)
What would you put in dragon stew if you were the king's cook?

Books often provide models that children can follow. Try some of these with a class:

Supposing by Alastair Reid (Little, Brown)
This book can be used in two ways. Students can write to complete the story introduced on each page. Students can also create short supposing stories themselves, perhaps to make a Supposing Book authored by the students in the class. (See illustration, page 354.)

Happiness Is a Warm Puppy by Charles Schulz (Determined Press)
Even young children can write books with a similar structure. They may choose to write more happiness ideas or to focus on a different topic, for example: sadness, freedom, a boy is . . . , a girl is . . . , the future.

What Do You Say, Dear? by Sesyle Joslin (Harcourt Brace Jovanovich)
These humorous letters will motivate upper grade students to write letters as they envision themselves in the unlikely situations pictured by this author.

Stories that are based on the adventures of a central character are often useful in motivating students to write further adventures of the same character. There are many possibilities, for example:

SUPPOSING I read a book about
how to change into animals and said a spell and changed
myself into a cat and when I climbed on the book to change
myself back I found I couldn't read...

From Supposing, *copyright Alastair Reid, by permission of the author.*

Henry Huggins by Beverly Cleary. Morrow.

Pippi Longstocking by Astrid Lindgren. Viking.

Henry Reed's Baby-Sitting Service by Keith Robertson. Viking.

Ellen Grae by Vera and Bill Cleaver. Lippincott.

Students who are busily interacting in a lively classroom will find many reasons for reading and writing. Their writing experiences will naturally evolve out of reading activities that excite them. It will be very common for them to make posters to advertise books, write reports, compose letters to authors, and to write their own books as they develop individual and group projects. Books that children write and publish should be displayed in the school library. This publicity is highly motivating to student authors and to other students who might like to create a book too.

❦ *LANGUAGES OTHER THAN ENGLISH* In most classrooms today there are children who speak a language other than English. Support these students by providing books in their language. English-speaking children will enjoy examining these books, too, as they try to read the Spanish language, for example, in such books as:

Jorge el Curioso. H. A. Rey. Houghton Mifflin, 1961. (*Éste es Jorge. Vivía en África.*)

Babar y el pícaro Arturo. Laurent de Brunhoff. Librairie Hachette, 1971.

There are many selections available in Spanish as well as French. You can find some books in almost any language; just ask the librarian.

SCHEDULING TIME FOR READING

Children learn to read by reading. If we keep this in mind, we will schedule more time for reading and talking about books and less time for completing workbook pages. There is nothing more motivating than the story itself, for as the adventures unfold before a young reader, he or she can scarcely put the book down. What will happen next?

Several promising practices have appeared on the reading scene that are designed to promote reading. One that stands out is USSR or Uninterrupted Sustained Silent Reading, a new approach to doing something we have known about for a long time. A second method of seeing that children actually read is the planned literature lesson. Another way of promoting reading is Readers' Theater, which provides yet another reason for reading as well as a way of sharing reading.

USSR—WHAT A TRIP![8] When people first hear about USSR, they are mystified. An explanation of the meaning of this acronym as it pertains to reading, however, begins to clarify the mystery:

U—Uninterrupted

S—Sustained

S—Silent

R—Reading

---

[8] From *Reading Ideas* (October 1975), p. 1.

This approach to reading simply means that a specific time is set aside for reading. At 11:30 every day the principal, the janitor, the secretary, the teachers, and the children sit down to read. If everybody takes time to read, naturally children get the message that reading is important.

During the reading session, everyone reads. There is no talking or other activity. Children may read anything they choose, but they must read (or at least pretend to read). Even reluctant readers soon get bored with pretending when everybody else is busy. Sooner or later something catches their eyes, and they really begin to read; they become involved.

To take full advantage of USSR you do need to have a large selection of reading material available—books, magazines, newspapers. This is a good time to encourage children to bring books they would like to share or magazines they may get at home. You can arrange to trade reading materials with another room and get books from the local library.

You don't have to wait until you can convince the whole school to join you in this adventure either. You can talk about USSR with your own class, and you can begin tomorrow!

PLANNED LITERATURE LESSONS Planning lessons based on good books is another way of emphasizing the actual reading of stories. Books can provide models for children's writing, and we can help young people observe the way authors handle language—dialogue, imagery, beginnings and endings of stories.

Following is a lesson that focuses on characterization in fiction. Planned for children in a third grade classroom, it fits under two goals listed earlier in this chapter: (1) Goal D4: The student identifies representative features of forms of writing, and (2) Goal F3: The student develops criteria for excellent writing. The two activities aid students in developing the competencies of discrimination and judging or evaluation as they use the skills of speaking, reading, and writing.

The first activity might be introduced by reading the book *Honk, the Moose* aloud to the class. The students will thus already know Ivar, who is described at the beginning of this activity.

❁ *PEOPLE IN STORIES* The people in a story are called characters. Here is a short description of one character in the book *Honk, the Moose*.

Ivar's hair was so light that it was almost white. He had smiled so much in the ten years of his life that two small smile wrinkles had set up business at the corners of his eyes to make it easier for him.

How many sentences are used to describe Ivar? How many facts about Ivar has the author, Phil Stong, told you in only two sentences? List the facts you know about this character, for instance:

The character's name is Ivar.

Here is a description of another character, written by Henry Lent in his book *Tony, the Steam Shovel Man:*

Tony is the man who runs the steam shovel. He wears a bright red handkerchief about his neck. He twirls his shiny black mustache and smiles.

In one hand he carries his lunch box, full of good things to eat when the twelve o'clock whistle blows. It is a hard job to run a steam shovel, but Tony is very strong.

List the facts you know about Tony after reading these two paragraphs.

Could you paint a picture of Ivar or Tony based on the word pictures written by these authors?

Beginning the activity orally works well if a group of students are to complete the same exercise. Have children state sentences orally that they will later write describing Ivar, as follows:

Ivar's hair is very light (blonde).

It is almost white.

He smiles a lot.

He is ten years old.

He has little wrinkles in the corners of his eyes.

This activity demonstrates to students the way a skillful writer combines short sentences into longer, more interesting sentences. It also illustrates a good description of a character, a model for the writing students will do in the second activity.

The transition to writing descriptions of people is natural because it builds directly on the first activity. Again, you might find that an oral discussion is an excellent method of introducing the task to be accomplished.

WRITING DESCRIPTIONS OF PEOPLE When you write stories, you need to paint pictures, too. Suppose you wanted to write a story about a little boy. You can imagine what the little boy is like. Then you can write sentences to describe the boy in your mind so that other people can see him too.

Imagine a small boy. Can you answer some of these questions about him?

How tall is he?

What is his name?

What color is his hair?

What kind of clothes is he wearing?

How is he behaving?

Where is he?

How old is he?

Now that you have decided on the answers to these questions, see how many of them you can include in a paragraph that describes this boy. Can you make your friends see him clearly?

Exchange your description with another person in the classroom, and then see if you can paint a picture of the boy based on the description you receive.

These are the kinds of lessons that you can develop to help children become more aware of various literature concepts—an author's style, the way stories are begun, the handling of dialogue, how an author tells the reader about such character. This kind of study and provocative discussion can enhance the student's enjoyment of a good book. Certainly it helps the student develop more sophisticated reading skills that involve critical reading, making judgments and evaluation, and substantiating an argument.

READERS' THEATER Here again is a way of promoting reading that is simple, but also effective. The teacher needs no training in drama, because the participants do not "act out" the story; they read it. Almost any story can be adapted as described on the following pages.

The first step is to prepare a script. Select something relatively short to present, for example, a short story or scene from a book. The story must be "cut" in preparation for reading. During this process you eliminate all writing that does not move the story along, information that is not important. You eliminate, of course, all phrases indicating the speaker: "he said", "she remarked," "they cried," because the dialogue is read directly by the students.

Examine a familiar story, *The Three Little Pigs,* as we decide how to present it through Readers' Theater. To prepare this story for a Readers' Theater presentation, we need to determine first how many different readers we need. There is always a Narrator who sets the story spinning, plus one person for each character who speaks, so for this story we need:

The Narrator

Pig 1

Pig 2

Pig 3

The Wolf

We need a copy of the story, a script, for each reader. Although multiple copies of a book can be used, there are distinct advantages to duplicating copies. These copies can be cut literally and marked for sound effects or intonation. Here is one version of *The Three Little Pigs,* published in 1892, that you can duplicate for your first experiment with Readers' Theater.

THE THREE LITTLE PIGS[9]

Once upon a time when pigs spoke rhyme
And monkeys chewed tobacco,
And hens took snuff to make them tough,
And ducks went quack, quack, quack, O!

There was an old sow with three little pigs, and as she had not enough to keep them, she sent them out to seek their fortune. The first that went off met a man

---

[9] From *English Fairy Tales* by Joseph Jacobs (Putnam, 1892).

with a bundle of straw, and said to him,

"Please, man, give me that straw to build me a house."

Which the man did, and the little pig built a house with it. Presently came along a wolf, and knocked at the door, and said,

"Little pig, little pig, let me come in."

To which the pig answered,

"No, no, by the hair of my chiny chin chin."

The wolf then answered to that,

"Then I'll huff, and I'll puff, and I'll blow your house in."

So he huffed, and he puffed, and he blew his house in, and ate up the little pig.

The second little pig met a man with a bundle of furze and said,

"Please, man, give me that furze to build a house."

Which the man did, and the pig built his house. Then along came the wolf, and said,

"Little pig, little pig, let me come in."

"No, no, by the hair of my chiny chin chin."

"Then I'll puff, and I'll huff, and I'll blow your house in."

So he huffed, and he puffed, and he puffed and he huffed, and at last he blew the house down, and he ate up the little pig.

The third little pig met a man with a load of bricks, and said,

"Please, man, give me those bricks to build a house with."

So the man gave him the bricks, and he built his house with them. So the wolf came, as he did to the other little pigs, and said,

"Little pig, little pig, let me come in."

"No, no, by the hair of my chiny chin chin."

"Then I'll huff, and I'll puff, and I'll blow your house in."

Well, he huffed, and he puffed, and he huffed and he puffed, and he puffed and huffed; but he could *not* get the house down. When he found that he could not, with all his huffing and puffing, blow the house down, he said,

"Little pig, I know where there is a nice field of turnips."

"Where?" said the little pig.

"Oh, in Mr. Smith's home-field, and if you will be ready tomorrow morning I will call for you, and we will go together, and get some for dinner."

"Very well," said the little pig, "I will be ready. What time do you mean to go?"

"Oh, at six o'clock."

Well, the little pig got up at five and got the turnips before the wolf came (which he did about six), who said,

"Little pig, are you ready?"

The little pig said, "Ready! I have been and come back again and got a nice potful for dinner."

The wolf felt very angry at this, but thought that he would be up to the little pig somehow or other, so he said,

"Little pig, I know where there is a nice apple-tree."

"Where?" said the pig.

"Down at Merry-Garden," replied the wolf, "and if you will not deceive me, I will come for you at five o'clock tomorrow and get some apples."

Well, the little pig bustled up the next morning at four o'clock, and went off for the apples, hoping to get back before the wolf came; but he had farther to go and had to climb the tree, so that just as he was coming down from it, he saw the wolf coming, which, as you may suppose, frightened him very much. When the wolf came up he said:

"Little pig, what! are you here before me? Are they nice apples?"

"Yes, very," said the little pig. "I will throw you down one."

And he threw it so far, that, while the wolf was gone to pick it up, the little pig jumped down and ran home. The next day the wolf came again and said to the little pig,

"Little pig, there is a fair at Shanklin this afternoon; will you go?"

"Oh, yes," said the pig, "I will go; what time shall you be ready?"

"At three," said the wolf. So the little pig went off before the time as usual and got to the fair and bought a butter-churn, which he was going home with, when he saw the wolf coming. Then he could not tell what to do. So he got into the churn to hide, and by so doing turned it round, and it rolled down the hill with the pig in it, which frightened the wolf so much, that he ran home without going to the fair. He went to the little pig's house and told him how frightened he had been by a great round thing which came down the hill past him. Then the little pig said,

"Hah, I frightened you then. I had been to the fair and bought a butter-churn; and when I saw you, I got into it, and rolled down the hill."

Then the wolf was very angry indeed and declared he *would* eat up the little pig, and that he would get down the chimney after him. When the little pig saw what he was about, he hung on the pot full of water and made up a blazing fire and, just as the wolf was coming down, took off the cover and in fell the wolf; so the little pig put on the cover again in an instant, boiled him up, and ate him for supper and lived happy ever afterwards.

What words would you immediately eliminate? How would you want the Narrator to begin this story? One advantage of using selections for which there is no known author is that you can find many versions, one of which may be more pleasing to you than another. Your own version is equally valid, so you can change the wording as you like.

A duplicated script, then, is cut and adapted as desired. After making additions, inserting the speakers' names, and marking the script for effects such as *pause, knock on the door,* or *speak slowly,* duplicate the completed script again so that each participant has a marked copy.

Narrator

The Three Little Pigs

Pause

Once upon a time when pigs spoke rhyme
And monkeys chewed tobacco,
Narrator
And hens took snuff to make them tough,
And ducks went quack, quack, quack, O! — *More quickly*

There was an old sow with three little pigs, and as she had
not enough to keep them, she sent them out to seek their
n. fortune. *Pause* The first that went off met a man
with a bundle of straw.

Pig 1 . "Please man, give me that straw to build me a house."

Which the man did, and the little pig built a house with
n. it. *Pause* Presently came along a wolf, and
knocked at the door.

Wolf "Little pig, little pig, let me come in."

Pig 1. "No, no, by the hair of my chiny chin chin."

Wolf "Then I'll huff, and I'll puff, and I'll blow your house in."

So he huffed and he puffed, and he blew the house in, and
n. ate up the little pig.

n. The second little pig met a man with a bundle of furze.

Mount the script on stiff paper or cardboard so that students can handle it easily and the script is not distracting to the audience. A short selection might be mounted on a single sheet of colored construction paper so
the audience sees only the sheets of paper. A selection about the length of
this folktale can be mounted within a folded sheet of 12″ × 18″ construction paper to resemble a book. Selections can also be mounted within
standard file folders, which are easily stored for later use by other students.

Traditionally in the Readers' Theater presentation each participant sits
on a tall stool. These are fun and do provide a certain distinctive way of
operating that students enjoy. You can, however, achieve equally satisfactory results by using varied types of seating or standing. In presenting
The Three Little Pigs, for instance, you might have only the Narrator
seated at one side, since that person speaks frequently throughout the

performance. The three pigs might be grouped in the center with the wolf toward the right, like this:

$$P_3 \quad P_2 \quad P_1$$

$$n \qquad\qquad\qquad w$$

As the presentation begins, all participants walk to their places. The Narrator sits down facing the audience, but all other readers take their places with backs to the audience. As each one is introduced by the Narrator's words, that reader turns quickly, ready to read the lines indicated. As their roles are completed, these readers turn with backs to the audience again until the story is finished. Then all bow simply and walk off as they came in.

Students do need to practice reading their parts. They also need to go through the whole performance a number of times as they decide how they will read, perhaps changing words or phrases as they work with the story. Students learn to read fluently and to come in on cue. To add interest, the group can also include taped music or sound effects. Very simple costumes or props may be added, for example, hats or a distinctive piece of clothing such as shoes for an elf or overalls for a workman. None of these effects should intrude on the story because the story is the primary concern of the readers.

In working with Readers' Theater, many kinds of material are possible —short stories, plays, adapted long stories, and poetry. It is best to choose material that is:

Fast-moving with lots of action

Full of dialogue

Exciting or humorous

Familiar stories such as folktales are fun, but there is also much to be gained if groups select stories that the others don't know. Folktales from other lands provide good material that may fit with topics in the social studies. Short books for younger children can be used, particularly by less able readers, providing an acceptable reason for reading easy books. Here are two sources to explore as you select possible stories.

Arbuthnot, May Hill and Zena Sutherland. *The Arbuthnot Anthology*. 3rd ed. Scott, Foresman, 1971.

Johnson, Edna, Evelyn R. Sickels, Frances Clarke Sayers. *Anthology of Children's Literature*. 5th ed. Houghton Mifflin, 1976.

Both of these well-known anthologies include excellent material for Readers' Theater. The collections of stories listed under the section on storytelling will supply more possibilities.

DISPLAYING BOOKS

Invite children to read by displaying books in the classroom. Displays can be on bulletin boards, walls, tables, and bookshelves. The books themselves offer the best means of enticing children, and an open book is more effective than a closed one. Our aim, therefore, is to open books for children in as many ways as possible.

CAPTIONS   Whether the display is on the bulletin board or the wall, you will usually want a phrase, a single word, or perhaps a whole sentence that draws attention. A good caption is the secret to an effective display. Our focus is on books, on reading books, and on relating books to other concerns and interests of children. The caption will reflect this focus. What display possibilities come to your mind as you read these captions?

Pathway to Good Reading

Horse Tales

Corral Good Books

Sea Fever

F Is for France

2001

Key to Kenya

   Usually there is some picture element that you can develop, for example, a curving pathway, as suggested by the first caption, along which book covers are displayed to feature new books in the library. The last caption could be developed with a large key shape cut from black construction paper. Captions are often based on word play, for example, "Horse Tales" could also be thought of as "Horse Tails." "Corral Good Books" suggests the fence of a corral or a rope mounted on the bulletin board in the shape of a lasso.

Many useful captions are adaptable for varied topics. The idea suggested by "F Is for France" could be adapted to fit any topic you wanted to present: A Is for Adventure, B Is for Bears, M Is for Mexico, P Is for Poetry. Another good caption is a date printed in large figures; "2001" suggests books on the future or space travel. What do these dates suggest? 1492, 1776, 1865?

Additional ideas for creating lively bulletin boards that invite students to read are described here.

Brand New Books. Let students who are interested in the West and cowboy stories prepare a display that features brands used by cattle owners. Print the brands on ragged pieces of brown paper and scatter them over the board with jackets of suitable books.

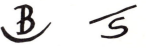

Ghastly Ghouls. This caption is a good one for October as Halloween approaches. Include torn-paper ghosts floating among the book jackets. A black background might be effective for this display. With this caption you are probably exposing children to new words and also interesting spellings.

Lining Up. Use clothespins to attach book jackets to a piece of clothesline that can be stretched across a long bulletin board or the wall. Here's

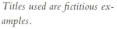

Titles used are fictitious examples.

an opportunity to include all kinds of books that have proved to be favorites.

I Recommend. Invite students to write short letters recommending specific books. The students sign their names so others will know that one of their friends has read the book and enjoyed it, a powerful recommendation. Design attractive notepaper that can be used by students, who then mount their recommendations on the display area.

Swing into Spring. Students will enjoy making a real rope swing to place on this display. Feature new books that have general appeal to different groups, or you might feature ideas associated with spring such as baseball, camping, bicycling, making kites, and planning for vacations.

LETTERING Good lettering is an essential component of a display, but it does not have to require great artistic ability. Consider what effect you want to create. If the caption is short, lettering or figures can be larger. The size also depends on the total area of the display. A short caption printed in tiny letters would be lost on a huge wall display. Some of the things to be considered about lettering are:

1. Is the lettering appropriate to the size of the display?

2. Can lettering be read at a distance?

3. Does the lettering add to the effect of the display?

A simple kind of lettering that anyone can make is the block style. By using graph paper that has larger blocks you can create a set of larger letters. For smaller posters children can copy the letters they need on graph paper with smaller blocks. Developing these letters on graph paper is a good learning experience, as children not only follow a model but also have a beginning experience in enlarging and reducing. For a few even bigger letters enlarge the ones you need by projecting them on the wall with an opaque projector.

Have children cut a set of these letters in several basic colors that you use frequently—black, white, red. Prepare tagboard patterns if children will be copying the letters. For one set of letters you need approximately the following numbers of each letter:

10 E I A O S T R

6 B C D L M N P U

4 F G H K W Y

2 J Q V X Z

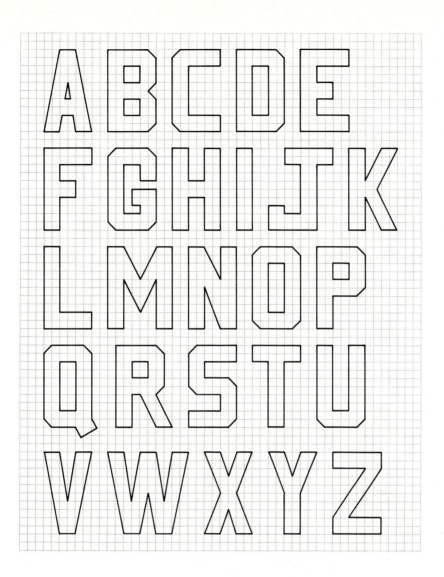

You can have fun by devising lettering out of varied materials that fit the mood or the meaning of a display. A display featuring, for example, the outdoors or trees might be enhanced by a short caption made of twigs. If you feature yarns (stories), why not "write" the caption with heavy yarn? Try some of these less common materials for letters:

Wire (covered with plastic)

Pipe cleaners (colored)

Crepe paper streamers

Newspaper or pages of magazines

Twisted foil

Wrapping papers

Brown paper bags

Rope or twine

Burlap; other cloth

Ribbon; braid

Cardboard cartons; other corrugated paper

Also try different styles of printing or writing. Some materials lend themselves to cursive writing, which is not difficult if you have a supply of straight pins handy to secure the yarn or twine each time you change direction. Lettering doesn't have to be formally correct; in fact, these varied materials demand less formal approaches to lettering. Collect a number of full-page magazine advertisements, for instance. From each page cut one large letter freehand. If you use the whole sheet for each letter, the size will be in proportion, but don't worry about straight lines and exact shapes. Scatter the letters unevenly across the display.

BACKGROUND MATERIALS   Another aspect of a display that is interesting is the background. The typical brown corkboard is attractive for some purposes, but do try varied materials for different effects. Buy yard

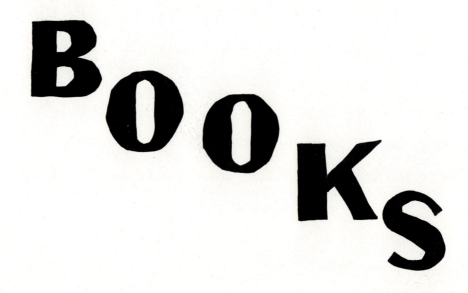

goods, for example, to fit your display area. Experiment with some of the following:

Burlap (natural and bright colors)

Homespun or other rough woven cloth

Corduroy

Various cotton prints, stripes

A red, white, and blue print would be effective background for a display about the early days of the United States. Bright yellow burlap provides an attractive background for a spring display about birds in books. Cloth is especially useful because it can be stored easily.

Various papers and cardboards are good backgrounds. Buy them in large rolls or sheets so that one piece covers the whole area. Here are materials you might try:

Corrugated cardboard (lightweight; bright colors)

Christmas wrapping foil in bright colors

Colored tissue paper

Crepe paper in many colors; can be stretched

Use your imagination as you consider the possibilities of chicken wire and other mesh fencing. Bamboo curtains or beach mats are attractive and easy to manage. Tablecloths and old draperies may offer further possible backgrounds.

DISPLAY MATERIALS What will you display? Here, too, you can use your imagination. How can you add interest to the display? How can you achieve a three-dimensional effect? Small realia (real items) can be fastened directly to the display—a doll's dress can be stapled to the background; feathers can be mounted with circles of masking tape; small items can be suspended from covered thumbtacks.

Book jackets are useful for developing displays about books. Don't hesitate to cut them up for varied focuses. In February, for example, cut the jackets into heart shapes. Cut a large heart pattern that covers most of the illustration as well as the title and author. Hang the heart shapes on a tree that spreads across the bulletin board or a classroom wall.

Posters or other large pictures provide interest and help develop a theme. Travel posters are often available free from travel agencies or for-

Titles used are fictitious examples.

eign embassy offices in large cities. Encourage children to suggest ideas for what should be displayed and, of course, include the pictures they have drawn to illustrate stories. Students might create attractive poetry posters (like that on page 371) that can be displayed with information about poets or books of poetry.

MORNING

by Emily Dickinson

Will there really be a morning?
Is there such a thing as day?
Could I see it from the mountains
If I were tall as they?

Has it feet like water lilies?
Has it feathers like a bird?
Is it brought from famous countries
Of which I've never heard?

Calligraphy by Cit

*Reprinted by permission from
Reading Ideas, Box 1524, San
Jose, California 95109.*

The following activities will involve you in experimenting with some of the ideas discussed in this chapter.

1. Prepare a display based on one book. This could be a poster or a bulletin board display. Consider the caption you will use; you might select a phrase from the book. Arrange this display in a classroom. Discuss it with the class and read at least a portion of the book to the children to motivate their interest in reading the book themselves.

2. Begin outlining a literature program for grades 1–6. Choose three books that you think are worth including for each grade level. Note the special attributes of each book. What literature concept is it teaching? How would you present the book to a group of children? Consider the activities that might precede their hearing or reading the story as well as follow-up activities.

3. Prepare two lessons based on one of the books you have selected. You could follow the examples given on characterization. Try to include a variety of language skills and different methods of presentation. Art and music can add interest to the presentation also.

4. Develop a three-dimensional way of sharing a book. Try to create something that no one else will think of doing, for example:

Diorama

Peek box

Scroll theater

Your creation will serve to demonstrate this kind of sharing of books to children.

5. Select a story that you would like to develop for Readers' Theater with a small group. Work with this small group to prepare the presentation as described in this chapter. Let the small group present the story to the full class. This presentation will serve to demonstrate Readers' Theater to the class.

   Then divide the class into small groups of five or six students each. Help each group select something to present. This first effort will probably include a potpourri of stories. Later the class could focus on a varied presentation around a single theme, perhaps, The Future or Our Country's Beginnings.

ADDITIONAL SOURCES TO INVESTIGATE

Carlson, Ruth Kearney. *Speaking Aids through the Grades.* Teachers College Press, 1975.

Daniels, Steven. *How 2 Gerbils, 20 Goldfish, 200 Games, 2,000 Books and I Taught Them How to Read.* Westminster, 1971.

Dunning, Stephen. *Teaching Literature to Adolescents, Short Stories.* Scott, Foresman, 1968.

Moffett, James. *A Student-Centered Language Arts Curriculum, Grades K–6.* 2nd ed. Houghton Mifflin, 1973.

Purdy, Susan. *Books for You to Make.* Lippincott, 1973.

Reading Ideas; A Newsletter for Teachers of all Levels. Contemporary Press, 1975. (*Published monthly.*)

Smith, James. *Creative Teaching of Reading in the Elementary School.* 2nd ed. Allyn and Bacon, 1975.

Spache, Evelyn B. *Reading Activities for Child Involvement.* Allyn and Bacon, 1975.

Tiedt, Iris M., ed. *Drama in Your Classroom*. National Council of Teachers of English, 1974.

Tiedt, Iris M. *Reading Strategies*. Contemporary Press, 1976.

Tiedt, Iris M., ed. *What's New in Reading?* National Council of Teachers of English, 1974.

Tiedt, Sidney W. and Iris M. Tiedt, *Language Arts Activities for the Classroom*. Allyn & Bacon, 1978.

8

The Many Ways
of Seeing

Reading for Information

From *The Way of an Ant* by Kazue Mizumura. Copyright © 1970 by Kazue Mizumura. Used with the permission of the Thomas Y. Crowell Company.

Learning has always been fun in the sense of exciting, invigorating, stimulating and en-
tertaining, but it has never offered to be effortless. The delight in discovery goes far
deeper than "fun." A title that uses the word "quest" or "discover" or "look at" picks
up and uses the energy which boys and girls are ready to exercise if they are helped to
do so. The writer who respects readers will call upon them to exercise their minds as
well as their hands; no better exercise-machine for the intellect has yet been devised than
a book.

Margery Fisher
Matters of Fact[1]

Reading is an essential element of teaching and learning in any classroom. Teachers of every subject, therefore, need to be very much aware of the kinds of books that are available to add interest and information to topics that are being explored. For some readers, nonfiction is fascinating, and they find the statistics of the *Guinness Book of Records* or information presented in Jean George's *All Upon a Sidewalk* as absorbing as any fiction. If we are concerned with "matters of fact"—discovering, inquiring, exploring—however, we will also extend our quest into fiction as well, for nonfiction and fiction can be complementary. Fiction can open the door to student-initiated research, so an informed teacher may use a story or even a poem to generate interest in a topic. How does an airplane fly? What causes a hurricane? Or, the question posed by Hilda Conkling:

---

[1] Margery Fisher, *Matters of Fact* (Thomas Y. Crowell, 1972).

WATER

The world turns softly
Not to spill its lakes and rivers.
The water is held in its arms.
And the sky is held in the water.
What is water,
That pours silver,
And can hold the sky?

There are many exciting informational books for children today on a wide variety of subjects—ecology, death, space travel, sex, cooking, oceanography. We can expect these trade books to be not only accurate, but also readable and pleasing in format. In addition, a good work of nonfiction should:

Distinguish clearly between facts and theories

Include all significant facts

Support generalizations with facts

Present differing views on controversial subjects

Observe basic principles prohibiting racism and sexism

The following objectives will guide our investigation of literature as it relates to various studies in the elementary school curriculum.

1. To know a number of books on topics in science, the study of language, and those related to calendar events, including the holidays

2. To identify the contributions of various authors who have specialized in writing nonfiction for young people

3. To develop a module focused on one specific topic as a useful method of teaching

4. To learn how to integrate nonfiction with poetry and fiction in meaningful ways

In this chapter we begin with children's books that supply information about language. The second section focuses on several representative topics in the broad field of science—oceanography, metrics, animals, ecology, and how-to books. Then comes a section on books related to calendar events. The final part of this chapter contains a learning module focused on living in the city. The emphasis on informational books continues in Chapter 9, on the literature of the social studies.

❦ See how many of these questions you can answer as you begin this study.

1. Name three books that will add to elementary school children's understanding of the history of the English language.

   _____

   _____

   _____

2. Can you list three informational books that would add interest to a study of ecology?

   _____

   _____

   _____

3. What special contributions have each of the following authors made to provide information for young readers?

   Holling C. Holling _____

   Jean Craighead George _____

   Isaac Asimov _____

   Jeanne Bendick _____

   Charles Ferguson _____

4. Can you describe works of nonfiction, fiction, and poetry about one specific animal that would be useful in science instruction?

5. Discuss three books that would help children learn more about cities in America today.

STUDYING THE ENGLISH LANGUAGE

What is this creation we call the English language? This rich resource that we use daily is largely taken for granted, but the study of the history of English—the way words are created, how language changes through time, the vast vocabulary—constitutes an exciting subject to investigate.

Many books have been written to introduce children to the enjoyment of English words and their ways. As Alastair Reid writes in the introduction to *Ounce, Dice, Trice,* (Little, Brown, 1958):

. . . if you grow to love words for their own sake, you will begin to collect words for yourself, and you will be grateful, as I am, to all the people who collect odd words and edit odd dictionaries, out of sheer astonishment and affection.

The title of Jessica Davidson's book *Is That Mother in the Bottle?* (Watts, 1972) is meant, of course, to catch your attention. The subtitle clarifies the intent of this work, however: *Where Language Came from and Where It Is Going.* Appropriate for upper elementary and junior high school students, the book deals with the nature of language and how it changes through use. The author notes:

We think nothing of the term "shoulder of the road"—at least not until we come to a sign "SOFT SHOULDERS" and find it amusing. We don't think about the "eye of a potato" until a young child asks why a potato has more eyes than he does and whether it can see behind it. We *pinpoint* a problem or we *highlight* it, we *spearhead* a campaign and we build a strong *framework* for an argument, and all without thinking of pins or lights, or spears or the construction of a building. (p. 97)

The study of words is a never-ending source of pleasure, amusement, and surprise. As Lewis Carroll says: "Alice had not the slightest idea of what latitude was, or longitude either, but she thought they were nice grand words to say." Young children already enjoy language as they repeat jingles and nonsense syllables. We can continue this savoring of language as we introduce them to *Sparkle and Spin* (Harcourt Brace Jovanovich, 1957), a delightful book about words for young children by Ann and Paul Rand. Older students will enjoy *The Magic and Mystery of Words* (Holt, 1963) by J. Donald Adams, author of "Speaking of Books" in the *New York Times Book Review.* Written for adults, his discussion of language offers much information that can be shared with students. Essays are included on such topics as "The Dawn of Language," "Clichés and Curious Expressions," "Notes on Slang," and "Words of Tomorrow."

"Abecedarian is a real word three hundred years old to describe a person who is either learning or teaching the ABC's." Thus begins *The Abe-*

cedarian Book (Little, Brown, 1964), in which Charles W. Ferguson presents strong and wonderful words. The first paragraph gives the flavor of Ferguson's writing in this unusual ABC book.

A is for ANTEDILUVIAN

Of course you could just say "before the Flood," because that is what antediluvian means. But antediluvian, besides being a beautiful word with little bells ringing in it, is also a comical word. And if you learn the life story of the word and see how men have used it for its humor as well as for its loveliness, you will understand a great deal more than the word itself. (p. 3)

Another author who writes of word origins is Margaret S. Ernst in *More about Words* (Knopf, 1951). A sequel to *In a Word* (Knopf, 1939), this book is described as "a kind of random dictionary of some thousand bits of the English language," which the author hopes will be a "stimulus to students of words."

BONFIRE

From *bone fire,* a fire of bones. We usually think of a bonfire as the brightest outdoor part in some celebration such as the Fourth of July; but its origin was less lively. In the Middle Ages, a *bone-fire* (it was so spelled till 1760) was a funeral pyre for burning the bodies of plague victims; a fire for burning witches, heretics, proscribed books. Johnson, in 1755 in his *Dictionary,* decided the word was "bonfire" and derived it "from, *bon,* good (French) and fire." The original charnel meaning was forgotten. (p. 37)

Here is a group of books about language that will be useful with primary grade children:

Alexander, Arthur. *The Magic Words*. Prentice-Hall, 1962.

Hymes, Lucia and James M. Hymes. *Oodles of Noodles*. Scott, Foresman, 1964.

Merriam, Eve. *A Gaggle of Geese*. Knopf, 1960.

Provensen, Alice and Martin Provensen. *Karen's Opposites*. Golden Press, 1963.

Rossner, Judith. *What Kind of Feet Does a Bear Have?* Bobbs-Merrill, 1963.

Vasiliu. *The Most Beautiful Word*. John Day, 1970.

Waller, Leslie. *Our American Language*. Holt, 1960.

There are far more books about word play and interesting ideas about language for the middle school. Isaac Asimov, the renowned writer of both science fiction and scholarly nonfiction, has also produced several books about words: *Words from the Myths, Words in Genesis, Words of Science and the History Behind Them,* and *Words on the Map* (Houghton Mifflin, 1961, 1962, 1959, 1962). These books are available in paperback and are very helpful in working with varied content areas. Other books that are highly recommended include:

Briggs, F. Allen. *The Play of Words*. Harcourt Brace Jovanovich, 1972.

Cataldo, John W. *Words and Calligraphy for Children*. Van Nostrand, 1969.

Dugan, William. *How Our Alphabet Grew*. Golden Press, 1972.

Fadiman, Clifton. *Wally the Wordworm*. Macmillan, 1964. *(Rather easy)*

Foster, G. Allen. *Communication; From Primitive Tom-toms to Telstar*. Criterion, 1965.

Helfman, Elizabeth. *Signs and Symbols Around the World*. Lothrop, 1967.

Laird, Charlton and Helene Laird. *Tree of Language*. World, 1957.

Lambert, Eloise and Mario Pei. *Our Names: Where They Came from and What They Mean*. Lothrop, 1960.

O'Neill, Mary. *Words Words Words*. Doubleday, 1966. *(Poems)*

A person who presents language as enjoyable and informative is Alvin

Schwartz. His books feature Americanisms relating to folklore and American history, such as the Tom Swifties which were popular in the 1960s: "I'll have a hotdog," said Tom frankly. Illustrated by Glen Rounds, Schwartz's attractive books are available in both hardback and softcover. His titles reflect this quote from Josh Billings: "When you . . . laugh open your mouth wide enough for the noise to get out without squealing, throw your head back as though you was going to get shaved, hold on to your false hair with both hands and then laugh until your soul gets thoroughly rested," which introduces *Witcracks.*

A Twister of Twists, A Tangler of Tongues. Lippincott, 1972.

Witcracks; Jokes and Jests from American Folklore. Lippincott, 1973.

Tomfoolery; Trickery and Foolery with Words. Lippincott, 1973.

A sample from *Tomfoolery:*

Would you like to join a secret society?
  OK.
Good! It's called the Royal Order of Siam. Just bow five times and repeat these Siamese words:
  OWAH TAGOO SIAM!

Sometimes an author uses word play as an essential part of fiction. *The Phantom Tollbooth* (Random House, 1961) by Norton Juster is built around word play completely, as the main character visits Dictionopolis and Digitopolis. It takes a rather sophisticated student to appreciate the complexities of references to the Land of the Doldrums and so forth, but an enthusiastic teacher can develop an exciting study around this book. *The Phantom Tollbooth* can be appreciated on different levels.

A word puzzle is incorporated in the plot of *The Mysterious Disappearance of Leon (I Mean Noel)* (Dutton, 1971) by Ellen Raskin. *Alvin Steadfast on Vernacular Island* (Dial, 1965) by Frank Jacobs and Tomie De Paola's *Andy (that's my name)* (Prentice-Hall, 1973), an easy book, also include word play in the plot. These kinds of books promote a positive feeling toward language. They help develop a greater appreciation and awareness of the words we use and of the richness of our language that may lead to further exploration of the history of English, the origins of words, and new vocabulary.

Copyright © 1961 by Jules Feiffer. Reprinted from The Phantom Tollbooth, *by Norton Juster, Illustrated by Jules Feiffer, by permission of Random House, Inc.*

THE MANY WAYS
OF SEEING

The broad field of science offers much information that is inherently fascinating to young children who are eagerly exploring new concepts. To get a flavor of the variety of topics available in this field for children, browse through the 500 section in the children's department of your local library. Notice the writers who specialize in science writing: Paul Showers, Irving and Ruth Adler, Isaac Asimov, Jeanne Bendick, Jean Craighead George, Millicent Selsam, Franklyn M. Branley, Herbert S. Zim, and many others.

Learn the names of authors who present scientific information in a fictional framework that is also very useful in the classroom. An outstanding example of this kind of writer is Holling C. Holling, who wrote *Pagoo* (Houghton Mifflin, 1957), the story of a hermit crab. The reader becomes involved with Pagoo's struggle for existence. Information about tide pool life is included both in the text, the exceptional full-page

From the book Animal Disguises *by Aileen Fisher, illustrated by Tim and Gred Hildebrandt, handlettering by Paul Taylor. Copyright © 1973 by Aileen Fisher illustrations © 1973 Bowmar. Reprinted by permission of Bowmar Publishing Corporation.*

colored illustrations by the author, and the detailed black and white sketches by Lucille W. Holling that surround the text.

A writer known chiefly as a poet, Aileen Fisher, combines poetic presentation and narrative style with information for young children. *Valley of the Smallest* (Thomas Y. Crowell, 1966) tells the life cycle of a shrew, developing a background in ecology. *Animal Disguises* (Bowmar, 1973) shows children how animals are protected by their coloring and shape.

Other authors write both nonfiction and fiction for young people. Isaac Asimov is unusual in that he writes both science, science fiction, and other books, such as those about words mentioned in the last section. Jean Craighead George is another fine writer whose ability to write informational science books lends a rich quality to the fiction she writes as well.

In this section we will focus attention on selected topics in the field of science, recognizing the fact that we can offer only a sampling of the many possibilities. The topics selected reflect current interests of society as well as long-standing interests of children, such as the study of animals:

Down to the Sea

Think Metric!

Animal Life

Ecology: Struggle for Survival

The How-to Book

DOWN TO THE SEA

Some of the most attractive information books for children reflect the current interest in oceanography and developing new uses for the ocean. In *Come with Me to the Edge of the Sea* (Messner, 1972), William Stephens invites children to explore:

Have you ever really looked at sand? How would you describe it? Is it like sugar? Like salt? Like dirt or mud? Like tiny rocks or pieces of glass? (p. 12)

And beyond that sand is the vast ocean, mysterious and foreboding, but also inviting. A special edition of Rachel Carson's *The Sea Around Us* was adapted by Anne Terry White (Golden Press, 1958). This oversize book

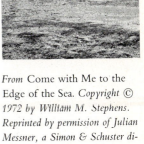

From Come with Me to the Edge of the Sea. *Copyright © 1972 by William M. Stephens. Reprinted by permission of Julian Messner, a Simon & Schuster division of Gulf & Western Corporation.*

contains many fine colored photographs and drawings. Jerome Williams'
Oceanography (Watts, 1972) provides an overview of topics such as the
ocean floor, tides, waves, sea monsters, water pollution, and answers
questions that children might have. Another similar book is *Deep-sea
World; The Story of Oceanography* (Morrow, 1966) by Charles Coombs.
Julian May describes *The Land Beneath the Sea* (Holiday, 1971), a topic of
increasing interest. Additional books that discuss the ocean, its formation, and the action of the waters include:

Berger, Melvin. *Oceanography Lab*. John Day, 1973.

Bergaust, Erik and William O. Foss. *Oceanographers in Action*. Putnam,
1968.

Brindze, Ruth. *The Rise and Fall of the Seas; The Story of the Tides*. Harcourt Brace Jovanovich, 1964.

Clemons, Elizabeth. *Waves, Tides, and Currents*. Knopf, 1967.

Coggins, Jack. *Hydrospace; Frontier beneath the Sea*. Dodd, Mead, 1966.

Engel, Leonard. *The Sea*. Time, 1967.

Fisher, James. *The Wonderful World of the Sea*. Doubleday, 1970.

*Goldin, Augusta. *The Bottom of the Sea*. Thomas Y. Crowell, 1966.

Greenhood, David. *Watch the Tides*. Holiday, 1961.

*Holsaert, Eunice and Faith Holsaert. *A Book to Begin On: Ocean Won-
ders*. Holt, 1965.

Shannon, Terry and Charles Payzant. *Project Sealab; The Story of the
United States Navy's Man In The Sea Program*. Golden Gate, 1966.

Telfer, Dorothy. *Exploring the World of Oceanography*. Childrens Press,
1968.

Weiss, Malcolm E. *Man Explores the Sea*. Messner, 1969.

Zim, Herbert. *Waves*. Morrow, 1967.

Marine biology is an equally fascinating topic that leads us to books
such as *Tide Pools and Beaches* (Knopf, 1964) by Elizabeth Clemons or, for
primary grades, *The Sunlit Sea* (Thomas Y. Crowell, 1968) by Augusta
Goldin. Children are introduced to animals that live in the ocean. Sea animals have a special attraction, perhaps because they are less familiar. Just

* For younger children.

listing them demonstrates the intriguing variety—seal, walrus, whale, shark, octopus, oyster, porpoise, eel, tuna.

Since we can't explore each of these animals in detail, we will focus on one, the whale, just to see what we can discover. We can investigate non-fiction about different varieties of whales, stories about the part whaling played in the history of the United States, and a number of stories about whales as fictional characters, either fearsome or lovable according to the author's desires.

Joseph J. Cook and William L. Wisner have written *Killer Whale!* (Dodd, Mead, 1963), a short book for middle graders that is exciting nonfiction. An especially well-written book that explains the life cycle of the whale and describes the many varieties is *Whales: Their Life in the Sea* by Faith McNulty (Harper & Row, 1975), handsomely illustrated by John Schoenherr. The final chapter "To Save Whales" concludes:

To people who love animals it seems terribly wrong to kill these great, sensitive, intelligent creatures for any purpose. As more and more people learn more about whales they realize that they are also precious to us alive in the sea. If enough people protest against the killing of whales it is possible that it can be stopped. Already there are many, many of us who pray that day will come soon. (p. 85)

Whales includes a one-page list of books "For Further Reading" and a short, helpful index. An exciting record to use with such books is *Songs of the Humpback Whales,* available from CRM Books (*Psychology Today*).

Other books about whales and their habits are:

Cook, Joseph J. and William L. Wisner. *Blue Whale; Vanishing Leviathan.* Dodd, Mead, 1973.

Hoke, Helen and Valerie Pitt. *Whales.* Watts, 1973.

McClung, Robert M. *Thor, Last of the Sperm Whales.* Morrow, 1971.

*McGovern, Ann. *Sharks.* Four Winds, 1976.

*Mizumura, Kazue. *The Blue Whale.* Thomas Y. Crowell, 1971.

A number of authors have written stories that center around whales and whaling. Few can compete with the most famous of all, *Moby Dick,* but children can wait for that hair-raising tale. Typical of the stories for

---

* For younger children.

older children is *Whaler 'Round the Horn* (Harcourt Brace Jovanovich, 1950) by Stephen W. Meader. This book not only tells of the early days of whaling and a thrilling trip around Cape Horn, but it also describes life in Hawaii, where the main character, Rodney Glenn, is shipwrecked. Another tale of whaling in early New England is *The Death of Evening Star; The Diary of a Young New England Whaler* (Doubleday, 1972), written by Leonard Everett Fisher. This well-researched documentary is based on the diary of a cabin boy, but it has the added appeal of a well-written tale about the power of supernatural forces. Roderick Haig-Brown writes of the pre-Columbian Nootka Indian tribe and the boy whale chief Atlin in *The Whale People* (Morrow, 1963). Holling C. Holling writes of an ivory gull that brought good luck to the whaling family of Ezra Brown in *Seabird* (Houghton Mifflin, 1948). Ongoing interest in this enormous mammal is evident in that new books continue to appear about whales. *Hunters of the Whale: An Adventure of Northwest Coast Archaeology* (Morrow, 1974) is Richard Doughtery's account of excavating the site of an Indian village near Ozette, Washington. More specific to the life of the whale is *Journey of the Gray Whales* (Holiday House, 1974) by Gladys Conklin, a short book for middle school that describes the migration habits of the California gray whale.

One of the best known stories for primary children is Robert McCloskey's *Burt Dow, Deep-water Man* (Viking, 1963), a charming whale story for primary grades. A salty seaman, Burt, goes out each day in his dory, the Tidely-Idely, and one day he catches a whale by the tail. McCloskey's humorous presentation of this "tale of the sea in the classic tradition" and his beautiful illustrations make this an enchanting book that is helpful in developing concepts for young children. Another playful story of a whale for little children is *The Deep Dives of Stanley Whale* (Harper & Row, 1973) by Nathaniel Benchley, in which Uncle Moby appears. William Steig combines a whale, Boris, and a mouse, Amos, "a devoted pair of friends with nothing at all in common, except good hearts and a willingness to help their fellow mammal," in *Amos & Boris* (Farrar, Straus & Giroux, 1971). *When the Whale Came to My Town* (Knopf, 1974) is an unusual story for primary grades by Jim Young about a young child's reaction to the beaching of a whale on a Cape Cod beach, a true incident.

Many aspects of the ocean can be explored with children. In addition to those already mentioned, keep in mind such topics as:

Ocean Plant Life

Wonders of a Kelp Forest by Joseph E. Brown. Dodd, Mead, 1974.

Amphibians

Loggerhead Turtle: Survivor from the Sea by Jack D. Scott. Putnam, 1974.

Skin Diving and Scuba Diving

The U.S. Frogmen of World War II by Wyatt Blassingame. Random House, 1964.

The First Five Fathoms by Mike Wilson (photographs) and Arthur C. Clarke. Introduction by Jacques-Yves Cousteau. Harper, 1960.

Seashells

Houses from the Sea by Alice E. Goudey. Scribner, 1959.

Sea Shells of the World by R. Tucker Abbott. Golden Press, 1962.

Submarines

From the Turtle to the Nautilus by Edwin P. Hoyt. Little, Brown, 1963.

The Big Book of Submarines by Jack McCoy. Grosset & Dunlap, 1966.

❀ *THINK METRIC! A SPECIAL TOPIC* Although there has been no sudden decree that the United States will change to the metric system in all respects by a specific date, most of us have become aware of certain strange words entering our environment. What is this?—The temperature is 23° Celsius!

Our monetary system based on the decimal system is so sensible that few can deny the wisdom of changing other measurements to the same kind of base. Admittedly, however, we all need explanation. This need in children's literature is beginning to be met by such books as *Think Metric!* (Thomas Y. Crowell, 1972) by Franklyn M. Branley. This overview explains the advantages of the metric system and shows intermediate grade children how to translate from one system to the other. A similar treatment that is perhaps a little more advanced is *Meter Means Measure* (Viking, 1973) by S. Carl Hirsch. The latter book also discusses the politics involved, both historically and at present, which account for the United States having resisted making this change for so long.

---

* For younger children.

Look for a surge of new titles designed to inform children about different aspects of the metric system.

ANIMAL LIFE

Both tame and wild animals have always been of interest to humans. Cats, dogs, and horses; elephants, wolves, and snakes—there is a vast literature focusing on animal life. Combine poetry, fiction, and nonfiction as you help children learn about animals.

Consider, for example, the wolf, an animal often pictured as a threat to humans. The wolf is described sympathetically in Jean Craighead George's Newbery award–winning book, *Julie and the Wolves* (G. K. Hall, 1973). We share this young Eskimo girl's knowledge of the ways of wolves that saves her life. *Mowgli and His Brothers* is Rudyard Kipling's story of a young boy who lives happily with the wolves. This haunting story, read effectively on a Caedmon recording by Basil Rathbone, serves further to break down the stereotype of a wolf as evil, an enemy.

A number of authors have tried to give young people insight into the ways of the wolf. Farley Mowat has written an informative story of wolves in *Never Cry Wolf* (Little, Brown, 1963); included is a map of where wolves live. *Sasha, My Friend* (Atheneum, 1969) presents another picture of a wolf by Barbara Corcoran. Hallie, who is lonesome after moving from California to Montana, makes friends with a wolf as well as an old Indian and a crippled girl, and suddenly realizes she is no longer lonesome. *The Jezebel Wolf* (Simon and Schuster, 1971) is F. N. Monjo's short version of a true story from the Revolutionary War. Israel Putnam tells his son how he tracked down a marauding wolf that was terrorizing the colonial farmers in this book illustrated by John Schoenherr.

Nonfictional studies of wolves include:

Dixon, Paige. *Silver Wolf*. Atheneum, 1973.

Fox, Michael. *The Wolf*. Coward, McCann & Geoghegan, 1973.

Ripper, Charles L. *Foxes and Wolves*. Morrow, 1961.

Steiner, Barbara A. *Biography of a Wolf*. Putnam, 1973.

After the wolf, we might consider quite a different kind of animal, the ant. *The City under the Back Steps* (Doubleday, 1960) is a fictional but informational explanation of ant life written by Evelyn Sibley Lampman. Craig and Jill are taken prisoner by the ants as punishment for stepping on one of the members of the ant colony. Through their participation in the work of the ants, the reader comes to know the structure of a colony with a queen ant as ruler over the worker ants. The children's reward for helping the ants is to be returned to their normal size.

"It couldn't have been a dream," said Craig, as though he might have been reading her mind. "We couldn't both have had the same dream at the same time. And besides, we weren't asleep. But it is funny about those shadows. They were nearly like that when I came around the house and found you sitting here feeding cookies to the ants." (p. 209)

After children have read this fictional account of ant life, they could be directed to such nonfiction as *The Fantastic World of Ants; A Microview of Earth's Most Ingenious Insect* (McKay, 1974) by Herbert Molloy Mason, Jr. Written in a clear readable style, the text is accompanied by good diagrams and photographs. A comparison of the two books might focus on the accuracy of the information presented in the fictional presentation. You might point out, for example, the painstaking research that a writer of fiction must often undertake in order to provide a credible background for an imaginative story. *The Way of an Ant* (Thomas Y. Crowell, 1970) is a story for beginning readers by Kazue Mizumura (see the illustration at the beginning of this chapter).

There appears to be a general fascination about life in the anthill. We find, therefore, a number of books about ants that describe their anatomy, the variety of their habits, and the structure of communal life in the ant colony.

Bartlett, Ruth. *Insect Engineers; The Story of Ants.* Morrow, 1957.

*Brenner, Barbara. *If You Were an Ant* . . . Harper & Row, 1973.

Doering, Harald and Mary Jo McCormick. *An Ant Is Born.* Sterling, 1964. (*Excellent large photographs*)

Selsam, Millicent E. *Questions and Answers about Ants.* Four Winds Press, 1967.

Shuttlesworth, Dorothy E. *The Story of Ants.* Doubleday, 1964.

Vevers, Gwynne. *Ants and Termites.* McGraw-Hill, 1966.

----

* For younger children.

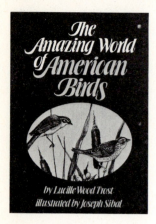

Another interesting group of animals presented in many children's books is the bird. One of the most beautiful of these books is *Brian Wildsmith's Birds* (Watts, 1967), which not only contains spectacular large paintings of birds, but also uses the proper terms for a group of the same kind, such as a *nye* of pheasants or a *watch* of nightingales. A very useful guidebook is *Birds; A Guide to the Most Familiar American Birds* (Golden Press, 1956) by Herbert S. Zim and Ira N. Gabrielson. Helpful, too, is *Birds on Your Street* (Holiday, 1974) by Barbara Brenner.

Many authors have focused on specific ideas about birds, for example, *Wingspread; A World of Birds* (Four Winds Press, 1972) by George Laycock, which describes such large birds as the albatross. Roma Gans describes *Bird Talk* (Thomas Y. Crowell, 1971) in an attractive book for primary grades, while Robert G. Hudson talks of nests and baby birds in *Nature's Nursery; Baby Birds* (John Day, 1971). Adrien Stoutenburg writes of vanishing species in *A Vanishing Thunder; Extinct and Threatened American Birds* (Natural History Press, 1967).

Books have been prepared for young people about a surprisingly wide

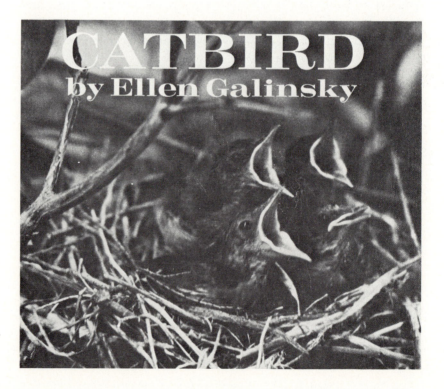

variety of individual birds from the bald eagle to the vulture. Here is just a sampling:

Catbird

Galinsky, Ellen. *Catbird.* Coward, McCann & Geoghegan, 1971.

Crow

*Hazelton, Elizabeth Baldwin. *Sammy, The Crow Who Remembered.* Scribner, 1969.

Eagle

Turner, John F. *The Magnificent Bald Eagle: America's National Bird.* Random House, 1971.

Geese

*Mannheim, Grete. *The Geese Are Back.* Parents' Magazine Press, 1969.

Gulls

Eimerl, Sarel. *Gulls.* Simon and Schuster, 1969.

Hummingbird

Gans, Roma. *Hummingbirds in the Garden.* Thomas Y. Crowell, 1969.
Simon, Hilda. *Wonders of Hummingbirds.* Dodd, Mead, 1964.

Oriole

Brenner, Barbara. *Baltimore Orioles.* Harper & Row, 1974.

Owl

Freschet, Berniece. *The Owl and the Prairie Dog.* Scribner, 1969.
Hoke, Helen L. and Valerie Pitt. *Owls.* Watts, 1975.

---

* For younger children.

Pelican

Laycock, George. *The Pelicans*. Natural History Press, 1970.

Penguin

Mizumura, Kazue. *The Emperor Penguins*. Thomas Y. Crowell, 1969.

Rau, Margaret. *The Penguin Book*. Hawthorn, 1968.

Redbird

McClung, Robert M. *Redbird: The Story of a Cardinal*. Morrow, 1968.

Robin

*Eberle, Irmengarde. *Robins on the Window Sill*. Thomas Y. Crowell. 1968.

Sandpiper

Hurd, Edith Thacher. *Sandpipers*. Thomas Y. Crowell, 1961.

Sparrow

McCoy, J. J. *House Sparrows; Ragamuffins of the City*. Seabury, 1968.

Swan

Hutchins, Ross E. *The Last Trumpeters*. Rand McNally, 1967.

McCoy, J. J. *Swans*. Lothrop, 1967.

Vulture

Turner, Ann Warren. *Vultures*. McKay, 1973.

Interest in animals seems to be almost universal. Certainly children find them intriguing, whether they are small and cunning like chipmunks and hamsters or such large, fearsome animals as the grizzly bear or the giant python.

---

* For younger children.

❦ *EXPLORING ANIMAL THEMES* Explore one of these activities as you develop ideas for teaching related to animals.

1. Choose an animal that is of special interest to the class. Decide on a variety of ways to share information about, for example, owls. You might begin by showing the group the film *The Happy Owls* (Weston Woods), which presents a book by Celestino Piatti and illustrated by Blair Lent (Atheneum, 1964). Obtain a copy or two of this attractive book, because many children will be motivated to read the book after seeing the film.

   Another book about owls that might inspire children to paint their versions of these fascinating birds is *The Owl Book* (Warne, 1970), which was compiled by Richard Shaw. In addition to beautiful illustrations, it includes both prose and poetry about owls, for example, fables by both Aesop and La Fontaine. Other owl books that provide interesting information are Edith Thacher Hurd's *The Mother Owl* (Little, Brown, 1974) for primary grades, while *Owlet, The Great Horned Owl* (Houghton Mifflin, 1974) by Irene Brady is for middle school.

2. Provide a long list of animals to members of your class. Have each person select one animal to investigate. Encourage each one to try to find nonfiction, fiction, and poetry about the chosen animal. Each person then shares the animal—tiger, bear, snake, raccoon, mole, elk, crab—with the group in some way.

   Books that a student might find about that unusual bird the crane, for example, include:

Byars, Betsy. *The House of Wings*. Viking, 1972.

Matsutani, Miyoko. *The Crane Maiden*. Parents' Magazine Press, 1968.

Robertson, Keith. *In Search of a Sandhill Crane*. Viking, 1973.

Yamaguchi, Tohr. *The Golden Crane; A Japanese Folktale*. Holt, 1963.

And, Mary Austin wrote the lovely poem "The Sandhill Crane," which pictures the long-legged bird "slowly, solemnly stalking."

ECOLOGY: STRUGGLE FOR SURVIVAL

Another contemporary problem represented in children's literature is ecology, with all its ramifications. We find such topics as air pollution, water pollution, refuse disposal, and conservation of natural resources, for children's books mirror adult literature in reflecting concerns of the times.

Laurence Pringle's *Ecology: Science of Survival* (Macmillan, 1971) is a good example of an overview of the problems involved. Another is *Ecology; The Circle of Life* (Childrens Press, 1971) by Harold R. Hungerford. Basic conservation practices are emphasized in *The Community of Living Things* (Creative Education, 1960), which was produced in cooperation with the National Audubon Society. The five-volume work, edited by Etta Schneider Ress, covers these broad areas: Field and Meadow, Fresh and Salt Water, Parks and Gardens, Forest and Woodland, and The Desert.

Water pollution is one specific concern that has received close attention. Helen Bauer discusses *Water: Riches or Ruin* (Doubleday, 1959) in an early appeal for conservation of our resources. Sigmund Kalina presents water pollution in a lucid book for younger children, *Three Drops of Water* (Lothrop, 1974), which traces the water cycle for three different drops of water. Another good explanation of the part water plays in our lives is *The New Water Book* (Thomas Y. Crowell, 1973) by Melvin Berger. An unusual treatment is *The Town That Launders Its Water; How a California Town Learned to Reclaim and Reuse Its Water* (Coward, McCann, 1971) by Leonard A. Stevens, who tells of Santee, California's efforts to recycle sewage water.

Recycling has received increasing publicity, and children are conscious of the need to put our refuse back into the cycle again. Helen Ross Russell tells of the ecological interrelationships on the earth in *Earth, the Great Recycler* (Nelson, 1973). She particularly stresses the human role in the ecosystem.

Other books that provide pertinent information for the young researcher include:

Beame, Rona. *What Happens to Garbage?* Messner, 1975.

Elliott, Sarah M. *Our Dirty Air.* Messner, 1971.

Hyde, Margaret E. *For Pollution Fighters Only.* McGraw-Hill, 1971.

Israel, Elaine. *The Great Energy Search.* Messner, 1974.

*Leaf, Munro. *Who Cares? I Do.* Lippincott, 1971.

Lefkowitz, R. J. *Fuel for Today and Tomorrow.* Parents' Magazine Press, 1974.

———

* For younger children.

Marshall, James. *Going to Waste; Where Will All the Garbage Go?* Coward, McCann & Geoghegan, 1972.

Perera, Thomas and Gretchen Perera. *Louder and Louder; The Dangers of Noise Pollution.* Watts, 1973.

Shuttlesworth, Dorothy E. *Litter—The Ugly Enemy; An Ecology Story.* Doubleday, 1973.

Tannenbaum, Beulah and Myra Stillman. *Clean Air.* McGraw-Hill, 1974.

The study of ecology encompasses almost everything when we recognize the interdependencies of all living matter. We might, therefore, develop a study of our human dependence on natural resources, for example, trees. Such a study could include information about the life cycle of trees, ways of identifying various species, and how we depend on trees for food and lumber. Anne Dowden has authored and illustrated with great precision *The Blossom on the Bough: A Book of Trees* (Thomas Y. Crowell, 1975), highly informative as well as beautiful. This botany book for grades five, six, and up supplies much information about the

From The Blossom on the Bough *by Anne Ophelia Dowden. Copyright © 1975 by Anne Ophelia Dowden. Used with the permission of the Thomas Y. Crowell Company.*

usefulness of trees, as well as their ecological relationships with other living things, and describes the different kinds of trees that thrive in the United States.

Oil is another natural resource of contemporary concern, and for primary grade children we find *Oil: The Buried Treasure* (Thomas Y. Crowell, 1975) by Roma Gans. Here are the answers to a young child's questions, whether they focus on obtaining oil or the use of petroleum to produce other things.

Contemporary awareness of ecology has brought about renewed interest in the out-of-doors, and with it has come information about hiking, camping, and backpacking. Tony Gibbs describes equipment and offers suggestions in *Backpacking* (Watts, 1975) for upper elementary school students. Richard B. Lyttle has created a slightly more advanced book, *The Complete Beginner's Guide to Backpacking* (Doubleday, 1975), designed to give the information a novice needs.

Others of the vast number and variety of books pertinent to the broad topic of ecology include:

Primary Grades

The Cave: What Lives There by Andrew Bronin. Coward, McCann & Geoghegan, 1972.

Twist, Wiggle, and Squirm; A Book about Earthworms by Laurence Pringle. Thomas Y. Crowell, 1973.

Adaptation by Jeanne Bendick. Watts, 1971.

Middle School

The Kingdom of the Forest by Ann Atwood. Scribner, 1972.

Animal Movers; A Collection of Ecological Surprises by George Laycock. Natural History Press, 1971.

What Good Is a Weed? Ecology in Action by Robert H. Wright. Lothrop, 1972.

Path of Hunters; Animal Struggle in a Meadow by Robert N. Peck. Knopf, 1973.

Our Six-legged Friends and Allies; Ecology in Your Back Yard by Hilda Simon. Vanguard, 1972.

This is the age of the "how-to" book. Adults and children alike want to know how to make things as well as how to do things, and so you find such titles as *How to Eat Fried Worms, How to Write Codes and Send Secret Messages,* and *How to Play Better Football.* Few children will be interested in eating worms themselves, although reading this story about somebody else's endeavors is humorous and fascinating. Potentially, however, many students would be drawn by a title about writing codes and secret messages, and a number of aspiring athletes would like to improve their football game. Whatever the interest, there is a book to explain just how to go about it, or at least there should be. Here is a representative sampling:

How to Bring Up Your Pet Dog by Kurt Unkelbach. Dodd, Mead, 1972.

How to Be a Nature Detective by Millicent E. Selsam. Harper & Row, 1966.

How to Build a Body by Julian May. Creative Education, 1970.

How to Care for Your Dog by Jean Bethell. Four Winds Press, 1967.

How to Explore the Secret Worlds of Nature by Vinson Brown. Little, Brown, 1962.

How to Grow House Plants by Millicent W. Selsam. Morrow, 1960.

How to Improve Your Model Railroad by Raymond F. Yates. Harper, 1953.

How to Know the Birds by Roger T. Peterson. Houghton Mifflin, 1962.

How to Make a Home Nature Museum by Vinson Brown. Little, Brown, 1954.

How to Make a Miniature Zoo by Vinson Brown. Little, Brown, 1957.

How to Make & Fly Paper Airplanes by Ralph S. Barnaby. Four Winds Press, 1968.

How to Understand Animal Talk by Vinson Brown. Little, Brown, 1958.

How to Write a Report by Sue R. Brandt. Watts, 1968.

We need to recognize, of course, that not all books that explain how to do something, use this obvious title. Titles may begin with such words as make or making, discovering, creating, or the name of the skill itself as in these examples:

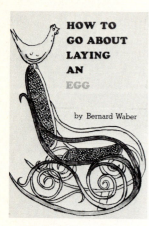

HOW TO
GO ABOUT
LAYING
AN
EGG

by Bernard Waber

How To Go About Laying an Egg by Bernard Waber. Copyright © 1963 by Bernard Waber. Reprinted by permission of Houghton Mifflin Publishers.

Making Things; The Hand Book of Creative Discoveries by Ann Wiseman. Little, Brown, 1973.

Make Your Own Animated Movies by Yvonne Andersen. Little, Brown, 1970.

Creating with Papier-mâché by James E. Seidelman/Grace Mintonye. Crowell-Collier, 1971.

Skiing for Beginners by Bruce Gavett and Conrad Brown. Scribner, 1971.

Bernard Waber has written a delightful spoof of how-to books called *How To Go About Laying an Egg* (Houghton Mifflin, 1963). The information is only useful if you're a hen, but the book is great for motivating children to write simple explanatory books of their own.

It is important to make these informative books available, for they can serve to open new doors as children discover their own potential.

❦ *EXPLORING SCIENCE BOOKS* Choose one problem or topic related to science that you think middle graders would consider important. See what books you can find that you could recommend to students who want to begin investigating that topic. You might choose, for instance:

Cancer

Drugs

Natural foods

Space travel

Extrasensory perception

Electronics

Fingerprints

Cyclones

The titles themselves of such books as *Tricks of Eye and Mind: The Story of Optical Illusion* by Larry Kettelkamp (Morrow, 1974) or *How Did We Find Out about Vitamins?* by Isaac Asimov (Walker, 1974) would appeal to many students. Just displaying such books might lead a group of students to undertake a study of an exciting topic. Exchange the lists prepared by members of your group so that you have a set of bibliographies on science topics.

In any classroom the seasonal events and holidays add interest to the sub-
ject-oriented curriculum. Much learning and pleasure can be derived
from reading about, doing research on, and developing activities related
to the calendar, as suggested by this poem.

THE GARDEN YEAR

Sara Coleridge

January brings the snow,
Makes our feet and fingers glow.

February brings the rain,
Thaws the frozen lake again.

March brings breezes, loud and shrill,
To stir the dancing daffodil.

April brings the primrose sweet,
Scatters daisies at our feet.

May brings flocks of pretty lambs
Skipping by their fleecy dams.

June brings tulips, lilies, roses,
Fills the children's hands with posies.

Hot July brings cooling showers,
Apricots, and gillyflowers.

August brings the sheaves of corn,
Then the harvest home is borne.

Warm September brings the fruit;
Sportsmen then begin to shoot.

Fresh October brings the pheasant;
Then to gather nuts is pleasant.

Dull November brings the blast;
Then the leaves are whirling fast.

Chill December brings the sleet,
Blazing fire, and Christmas treat.

It is natural to display books and other materials that relate to a specific
person whose birthday you are celebrating, or information about other

holidays and special events. Have students search out materials that are in your library as well as the nearest public library. Following are a few books and teaching ideas that have been published for the major holidays celebrated in school.

COLUMBUS DAY   Many books have been written for young people about Christopher Columbus. Here is a sampling:

*D'Aulaire, Ingri and Edgar P. *Columbus*. Doubleday, 1955.

DeKay, James. *Meet Christopher Columbus*. Random House, 1968.

Foster, Genevieve. *Year of Columbus*. Scribner, 1969.

Hodges, Walter. *Columbus Sails*. Coward-McCann, 1950.

*Kaufman, Mervyn. *Christopher Columbus*. Garrard, 1963.

*Norman, Gertrude. *A Man Named Columbus*. Putnam, 1960.

Sperry, Armstrong. *The Voyages of Christopher Columbus*. Random House, 1950.

As you make plans to feature Columbus Day (October 12), use the saturation approach. For the week preceding the holiday, saturate your classroom with everything you can find that relates to Columbus Day. Talk with the students about this plan so they are involved from the beginning in collecting books, finding poems, writing informative flyers to distribute, making posters, painting a mural, preparing skits, obtaining a film, making a papier mâché figure of Columbus, drawing a map, and so on.

On October 12, invite other classes to visit your classroom. As they enter, they will know that it is Columbus Day! This is an effective way to integrate reading, the language arts, social studies, and art in an outstanding learning experience. Try this saturation approach also for Halloween and other holidays.

HALLOWEEN   Most of the books about Halloween (October 31) are fiction and are written for young children, for example:

*Beim, Jerrold. *Sir Halloween*. Morrow, 1959.

Borten, Helen. *Halloween*. Thomas Y. Crowell, 1965.

———
* For younger children.

*From Mr. McFadden's Hal-
lowe'en by Rumer Godden.
Copyright © 1975 by Anthony
and Jennifer Jane Murray-
Flutter. Reprinted by permission
of The Viking Press.*

*Coombs, Patricia. *Dorrie and the Haunted House*. Lothrop, 1970.

*Freeman, Don. *Tilly Witch*. Viking, 1969.

Manning-Sanders, Ruth. *A Book of Witches*. Dutton, 1966.

Schauffler, Robert. *Halloween (Our American Holidays)*. Dodd, Mead,
1933.

*Schulz, Charles. *It's the Great Pumpkin, Charlie Brown*. World, 1967.

*Slobodkin, Louis. *Trick or Treat*. Macmillan, 1959.

*Tudor, Tasha. *Pumpkin Moonshine*. Walck, 1962.

*Yolen, Jane. *The Witch Who Wasn't*. Macmillan, 1964.

*Zolotow, Charlotte. *A Tiger Called Thomas*. Lothrop, 1963.

---

* For younger children.

Many Halloween tales will suggest creative drama, as children enact stories they have read together. Many of them will know, for example, *It's the Great Pumpkin, Charlie Brown,* which has been well publicized. They can move from this story to less familiar ones by skilled authors, such as Jane Yolen's *The Witch Who Wasn't.* Add characters freely so that a number of children can be included in playing out the story.

The following poem is arranged naturally for two voices—the child and Granny. This would be fun for upper grade students to prepare as a presentation for younger children. It is also very effective for a large group that is divided in two parts.

HALLOWEEN

Marie A. Lawson

"Granny, I saw a witch go by,
I saw two, I saw three!
I heard their skirts go swish, swish, swish—"

"Child, 'twas leaves against the sky,
And the autumn wind in the tree."

"Granny, broomsticks they bestrode,
Their hats were black as tar,
And buckles twinkled on their shoes—"

"You saw but shadows on the road,
The sparkle of a star."

"Granny, all their heels were red,
Their cats were big as sheep.
I heard a bat say to an owl—"

"Child, you must go straight to bed,
'Tis time you were asleep."

"Granny, I saw men in green,
Their eyes shone fiery red,
Their heads were yellow pumpkins—"

"Now you've told me what you've seen,
WILL you go to bed?"

"Granny?"

"Well?"

"Don't you believe—?"

"What?"

"What I've seen?
Don't you know it's Halloween?"

THANKSGIVING DAY In celebrating Thanksgiving (the last Thursday in November), it is important to place the emphasis on giving thanks, and to recognize the origins of the holiday. Be especially aware also of harmful stereotyping in the traditional depiction of the Indian. These topics can be discussed with children as they prepare to celebrate Thanksgiving.

Here is a selection of books that might be helpful to have available as students begin saturating the classroom for Thanksgiving:

Barksdale, Lena. *The First Thanksgiving*. Knopf, 1942.

*Bartlett, Robert M. *Thanksgiving Day*. Thomas Y. Crowell, 1965.

*Dalgliesh, Alice. *The Thanksgiving Story*. Scribner, 1954.

*Embry, Margaret. *Peg-leg Willy*. Holiday, 1966.

Luckhardt, Mildred C., comp. *Thanksgiving; Feast and Festival*. Abingdon, 1966.

Sechrist, Elizabeth H. and Janette Woolsey. *It's Time for Thanksgiving*. Macrae, 1957.

Weisgard, Leonard. *The Plymouth Thanksgiving*. Doubleday, 1967.

An interesting activity to include as you prepare for the celebration is to list all the symbols associated with the holiday. With Thanksgiving you might list such symbols as the *Mayflower,* shocks of corn, turkey, pumpkins, Pilgrims, a cornucopia, Indians, and so on. Why each of these symbols is appropriate for Thanksgiving provides a good discussion topic for the classroom.

CHRISTMAS Of all the holidays we celebrate, Christmas (December 25) has the richest supply of lore surrounding it. Just consider the symbols that we associate with this holiday:

Christmas tree: candles, ornaments, lights, tinsel

Nativity: Christ child, manger, stable, animals, star, Wise Men, Mary and Joseph

---

* For younger children.

Santa Claus: reindeer, presents, elves, sleigh, stockings

Joy: bells, carols, caroling

Love: cards, mistletoe, giving gifts

Winter: snowflakes, snow figures, sleigh bells

This sampling of the books about Christmas includes nonfiction that will provide background information, as well as collections of stories and poems.

Anglund, Joan Walsh. *Christmas Is a Time of Giving*. Harcourt Brace Jovanovich, 1961.

Cooney, Barbara. *Christmas*. Thomas Y. Crowell, 1967.

Foley, Daniel J. *Christmas the World Over . . .* Chilton, 1963.

Harper, Wilhelmina, comp. *Merry Christmas to You; Stories for Christmas*. Dutton, 1965.

Luckhardt, Mildred C., ed. *Christmas Comes Once More; Stories and Poems for the Holiday Season*. Abingdon, 1962.

Patterson, Lillie. *Christmas Feasts and Festivals*. Garrard, 1968.

Reeves, James, comp. *The Christmas Book*. Dutton, 1970.

Rollins, Charlemae, comp. *Christmas gif' . . .* Follett, 1963.

Sawyer, Ruth. *Joy to the World; Christmas Legends*. Little, Brown, 1966.

Sechrist, Elizabeth H., ed. *Christmas Everywhere; A Book of Christmas Customs of Many Lands*. Macrae, 1962.

Spicer, Dorothy Gladys. *46 Days of Christmas; A Cycle of Old World Songs, Legends and Customs*. Coward, McCann & Geoghegan, 1960.

Tudor, Tasha, ed. *Take Joy! The Tasha Tudor Christmas Book*. World, 1966.

Wernecke, Herbert H., ed. *Celebrating Christmas Around the World*. Westminster, 1962.

In addition to these books, there is a varied selection of fiction. Again, however, most of these stories are for preschool and primary levels. One story, *Nine Days to Christmas* (Viking, 1959) by Marie Hall Ets and Aurora Labastida, was awarded the Caldecott Medal in 1960. This book tells of a five-year-old girl, Ceci, who lives in Mexico City, and depicts the Christmas Celebration *la posada* and the parties that precede it. Other stories for young children are:

Baker, Laura N. *The Friendly Beasts*. Parnassus Press, 1957.

Balet, Jan. *The Gift; A Portuguese Christmas Tale*. Delacorte, 1967.

Brown, Margaret W. *On Christmas Eve*. Young Scott Books, 1961.

Brown, Palmer. *Something for Christmas*. Harper, 1958.

Duvoisin, Roger. *Petunia's Christmas*. Knopf, 1952.

Hoban, Lillian. *Arthur's Christmas Cookies*. Harper & Row, 1972.

Hoban, Russell. *Emmet Otter's Jug-Band Christmas*. Parents' Magazine Press, 1971.

Joslin, Sesyle. *Baby Elephant and the Secret Wishes*. Harcourt Brace Jovanovich, 1962.

Kahl, Virginia. *Plum Pudding for Christmas*. Scribner, 1957.

Kroeber, Theodora and Ilon Wikland. *A Green Christmas*. Parnassus Press, 1967.

Lindgren, Astrid. *Christmas in the Stable*. Coward, McCann & Geoghegan, 1962.

Mariana. *Miss Flora McFlimsey's Christmas Eve*. Lothrop, 1949.

Politi, Leo. *Pedro, The Angel of Olvera Street*. Scribner, 1946.

Seuss, Dr. *How the Grinch Stole Christmas*. Random House, 1957.

Thayer, Jane. *The Puppy Who Wanted a Boy*. Morrow, 1958.

Tudor, Tasha. *The Doll's Christmas*. Walck, 1950.

Uchida, Yoshiko. *The Forever Christmas*. Scribner, 1963.

Stories for older children that have a Christmas theme include *The Best Christmas Pageant Ever* (Harper & Row, 1972) by Barbara Robinson. This hilarious tale of "the worst kids in the history of the world," the Herdmans, will amuse you and your students. These bullies manage to get the leading roles in the local church pageant, which features, naturally enough, the Nativity. The experience does help these youngsters derive a feeling for the meaning of Christmas, but this moral does not detract from the high good humor of the description.

A very different kind of book is Gian-Carlo Menotti's *Amahl and the Night Visitors* (McGraw-Hill, 1952), adapted by Frances Frost from the opera and illustrated by Roger Duvoisin. This classic story of the crippled shepherd boy who entertained the three Wise Men as they passed enroute to Bethlehem is a beautiful work to share. Both the music and a filmed version could add to the enjoyment of the experience.

Another excellent work that middle school children will respond to is Dylan Thomas' *A Child's Christmas in Wales* (New Directions), beautiful poetic prose read by Dylan Thomas himself on a Caedmon record. His deep resonant voice is a joy to hear as he rolls out the rich images of his boyhood remembrances. This is the kind of work that needs to be heard more than once and to be talked about. A filmed version uses this same recording and still photographs that add much to the humor and enjoyment, and will help younger students understand the words more readily. Just talking about this talented human being, who also had serious personal problems, would be interesting to older students. A good source of information is the paperback pictorial biography *The Days of Dylan Thomas* (McGraw-Hill, 1964) by Bill Read.

Another favorite story that is part of the heritage of us all is *A Christmas Carol in Prose* by Charles Dickens. This story of the miserly Scrooge who finally is touched by the Christmas spirit has been published in several attractive editions. Everyone should know this tale, the source of the familiar quotation, "God bless us everyone!"

Additional Christmas stories for older students include:

Andersen, Hans Christian. *Hans Christian Andersen's The Fir Tree*. Harper & Row, 1970.

Bemelmans, Ludwig. *Hansi*. Viking, 1934.

Burch, Robert. *Renfroe's Christmas*. Viking, 1968.

Butler, Suzanne. *Starlight in Tourrone*. Little, Brown, 1965.

Carlson, Natalie Savage. *Befana's Gift*. Harper & Row, 1969.

Hays, Wilma Pitchford. *Christmas on the Mayflower*. Coward, McCann & Geoghegan, 1956.

Kingman, Lee. *The Best Christmas*. Doubleday, 1949.

Sauer, Julia L. *The Light at Tern Rock*. Viking, 1951.

Sawyer, Ruth. *The Christmas Anna Angel*. Viking, 1944.

_____. *Maggie Rose; Her Birthday Christmas*. Harper, 1952.

_____. *This Way to Christmas*. Harper, 1952.

Schulz, Charles M. *A Charlie Brown Christmas*. World, 1965.

Tudor, Tasha. *Becky's Christmas*. Viking, 1961.

Wiggin, Kate Douglas. *The Birds' Christmas Carol*. Houghton Mifflin, 1941. (*First published in 1888.*)

Encourage children to use the holiday symbols in various ways, as part of their classroom celebration. Book reviews can be written on bell-shaped paper. Christmas poems can be written on holly leaves or a large star. Puzzles can be arranged in the shape of the Christmas tree, as shown here.

OTHER RELIGIOUS HOLIDAYS

Whenever we celebrate a holiday that has religious origins, we need to remember that not all families observe these holidays. This is something that can be discussed with children, for our beliefs represent yet another way in which people differ. Children will be the richer and better informed if you make a point of observing the holidays of other countries and those representing different religions. Children may be surprised to find that not all religions have holidays such as Christmas and Easter, which have been heavily commercialized.

For Jewish people, for example, an important holiday is Passover, which is observed in the spring. Such a book as *Passover* (Thomas Y. Crowell, 1955) by Norma Simon might be shared at this time. A good explanation of the various Jewish holidays is *Jewish Holidays; Facts, Activities, and Crafts* (Lippincott, 1969) by Susan Gold Purdy.

Other religions are explained in these books:

Elgin, Kathleen. *The Mormons; The Church of Jesus Christ of Latter-Day Saints.* McKay, 1969.

————. *The Quakers; The Religious Society of Friends.* McKay, 1968.

Fitch, Florence Mary. *Their Search for God; Ways of Worship in the Orient.* Lothrop, 1947.

————. *Allah, The God of Islam; Moslem Life and Worship.* Lothrop, 1950.

Floethe, Louise Lee. *A Thousand and One Buddhas.* Farrar, Straus & Giroux, 1967.

Roy, Cal. *The Serpent and the Sun; Myths of the Mexican World.* Farrar, Straus & Giroux, 1972.

Seeger, Elizabeth. *Eastern Religions.* Thomas Y. Crowell, 1973.

SOURCES OF GENERAL INFORMATION

Check your library to see what references are available to provide information about calendar activities. Students will enjoy poring over the holidays described, which will perhaps suggest dramatizations or art activities. These representative titles are useful to have in a school library.

Cavannah, Frances. *Holiday Roundup*. Macrae, 1968.

Dupuy, Trevor. *Holidays: Days of Significance for All Americans*. Watts, 1965.

Hopkins, Lee B. and Misha Arenstein. *Do You Know What Day Tomorrow Is?* Citation Press, 1975.

Krythe, M. R. *All about the Months*. Harper & Row, 1966.

Purdy, Susan. *Festivals for You to Celebrate*. Lippincott, 1969.

Sechrist, Elizabeth. *Red Letter Days; A Book of Holiday Customs*. Macrae, 1965.

Highly motivating is the use of a calendar that lists a variety of information of interest to young people. One of the best is up-dated monthly in *The Elementary Teacher's Ideas and Materials Workshop* (Parker Publishing Co., Inc., West Nyack, New York 10994; request a sample copy). Included on the calendar are such listings as:

Birthdays of well-known people, for example, Robert Frost's birthday

Holidays such as Easter, Passover, St. Patrick's Day

Important events: the first man on the moon; end of World War II

❧ *TEACHING WITH THE CALENDAR* Developing activities related to calendar events can be exciting. Select two of these ideas to develop for use in the classroom.

1. Choose one of the lesser-known holidays to explore, for example:

   St. Patrick's Day, March 17

   Constitution Day, September 17

   Admission Day for your state

   Search for poetry, books (nonfiction and fiction), films, records, and any other material related to the topic you choose. Then list as many learning experiences as possible that you might develop around this theme. St. Patrick's Day offers a great opportunity to feature the Irish, while Constitution Day would be a good chance to focus on American history. Focusing on your state's admission day gives you a chance to explore local history.

2. Examine the sample calendar on this page. Select one event or person that suggests an interesting study to you, for example, the publishing of the first newspaper (September 21) or Balboa's discovery of the Pacific Ocean (September 25). Plan a way of featuring that event or person in the classroom.

3. Enlarge a calendar for one month other than September on which you can place events and persons' birth dates. If you plan to cover an entire

	SUN	MON	TUE	WED	THUR	FRI	SAT
S E P T E M B E R		**1** Commerical T.V. authorized, 1940 Child Labor Act, 1916 World War II began, 1939 LABOR DAY	**2** U.S. Treasury Dept. established 1789 V-J Day, 1945 Eugene Field 1850-1895	**3** Henry Hudson discovered Manhattan, 1609 Treaty of Paris ended Revolutionary War, 1783	**4** First transcontinental television, 1951	**5** Continental Congress Convened in Philadelphia, 1774	**6** Jane Adams 1860-1935 Marquis de Lafayette 1757-1834 Rosh Hashanah
	7 Elizabeth I 1533-1603 Elinor Wylie 1885-1928 Brazilian Independence from Portugal 1822	**8** Antonin Dvorak 1841-1904 Richard the Lion-Hearted 1157-1199	**9** California (31st state) 1850 Admission Day (in California)	**10** Elias Howe invented sewing machine, 1846 Battle of Lake Erie, 1813	**11** William Sydney Porter (O. Henry) 1862-1910 Jenny Lind's first concert in U.S., 1850	**12** Defender's Day (in Maryland)	**13** Dr. Walter Reed 1851-1902 First Rocket hits moon—Lunik II, U.S.S.R., 1959
	14 Francis Scott Key wrote "The Star-Spangled Banner," 1814 Ivan Pavlov 1849-1936	**15** Yom Kippur James Fenimore Cooper 1789-1851 William Howard Taft (27th Pres.) 1857-1930	**16** Alfred Noyes 1880-1958 *Mayflower* set sail 1620 Commemoration of Mexican Independence, 1810	**17** Constitution Day; adoption of Constitution, 1787 (Citizenship Day) Steuben Day	**18** Capitol cornerstone laid by George Washington, 1793	**19** Washington's "Farewell Address" 1796 Rachel Field 1894-	**20** Alexander the Great 356-323 B.C. U.S.S. *Constitution* (Old Ironsides) launched, 1797
	21 H.G. Wells 1866-1946 First daily newspaper published in U.S., 1784	**22** George Gershwin 1898-1937 First French Republic est., 1792	**23** First day of fall	**24** Supreme Court created, 1789 "Black Friday" 1869 Zachary Taylor (12th Pres.) 1784-1850	**25** Columbus began second trip to America, 1493 Balboa discovered Pacific Ocean 1513 First American newspaper published 1690	**26** T.S. Eliot 1888-1965	**27** American Indian Day First railroad with a steam locomotive (England), 1825 Samuel Adams 1722-1803
	28 William the Conqueror invaded England, 1066	**29** Michaelmas (Old English Holiday) Enrico Fermi 1901-1954	**30** First use of ether as anesthetic, 1846 Munich Pact 1938	Flower: Aster or Morning Glory	Birthstone: Sapphire	From second Sunday: National Hispanic Heritage Week From Sept. 17: Constitution Week	Fourth week: National 4-H Club Week Last full week: National Dog Week

From The Elementary Teacher's Ideas and Materials Workshop, *September 1975 by Parker Publishing Co., Inc. © 1975 by Parker Publishing Company, Inc. Published by Parker Publishing Co., Inc., West Nyack, New York.*

bulletin board, dividing lines can be strips of colored paper. Make the letters and numbers that you will need for the month you choose. See how many listings you can find for that month, particularly birthdays of authors or poets.

CREATING A LEARNING MODULE

An interesting kind of teaching material that teachers can create is the *learning module,* designed for individualized work at learning centers. The term *module* comes to us from electronics: a module is one element in an extensive, complex system. In this case the module is one element in the total curriculum. Although modules can be developed in varied ways, one type that teachers find useful has the following characteristics:

1. It is a softbound book, 9″ × 12″, of varied length (5–20 pages usually), and nonconsumable.

2. It speaks directly to the student who will use it and provides information and activities related to a specific topic; for example, Unrhymed Poetry Forms, Folklore of Mexico, or Writers of Oklahoma.

3. It directs the student to perform certain activities that involve listening, speaking, reading or writing, and may also include art, music or information related to other subject areas such as social studies or science.

4. The module may begin with a pretest so that students who already know the information do not waste their time; the pretest may also be used to introduce the study as it indicates what kinds of things will be presented in the module. A posttest concludes the module, serving to assess the students' understanding of the topic presented.

Modules can be developed on a number of topics that relate to literature, for few studies do not lead to the exploration of books. Topics presented in any of the chapters of this book, for instance, could be developed into useful modules for teaching literature. Following is a short module developed as a sample of what can be done with a topic that deals with science and social studies as well as reading: Living in the City. The module is prepared for upper elementary school, but it can easily be adapted for both younger and older students. If you were to reproduce this module, you might prepare a simple cover of colored construction paper with an outline of a city skyline.

TEACHER'S GUIDELINES This module is designed to develop under-standings about life in the city. It should be useful for both children who live in cities as well as those living in rural areas. The module is written as though the reader does live in a sizable city (since a high percentage of Americans do, indeed, live in cities), so that you should adapt the material accordingly if you teach in a rural area.

These are the kinds of understandings that we hope to teach or rein-force through the activities included:

1. There are many exciting things to do in a city.

2. Cities have certain common characteristics.

3. Each city has distinctive features that make it unique.

4. A great variety of people live in a city. They differ in color, race, religion, beliefs, and the way they live.

5. When thousands, and even millions, of people live close together, there are problems to be solved.

Before presenting the module to your students (either individually or in a group), saturate your classroom with books of all kinds about city living. Here are suggested titles:

Nonfiction

A Crack in the Pavement by Ruth Rea Howell. Atheneum, 1970.

State Capital Cities by Delia Goetz. Morrow, 1971.

How the World's First Cities Began by Arthur S. Gregor. Dutton, 1967.

The City in Art by Chase and Sue Cornelius. Lerner, 1966.

It's Time Now by Alvin Tresselt. Lothrop, 1969.

Let's Find Out about the City by Valerie Pitt. Watts, 1968.

Cities and Metropolitan Areas in Today's World by Samuel L. Arbital. Creative Education, 1968.

Build Your Own Moon Settlement by Forrest Wilson. Pantheon, 1973.

---

* For younger children.

Central City/Spread City: The Metropolitan Regions Where More and More of Us Spend Our Lives by Alvin Schwartz. Macmillan, 1973.

Cities in the March of Civilization by Barbara Habenstreit. Watts, 1973.

*Have You Seen Houses? by Joanne Oppenheim. Young Scott Books, 1973.

Housing in Tomorrow's World by David Reuben Michelsohn. Messner, 1973.

New Towns: Building Cities from Scratch by Martha Munzer and John Vogel, Jr. Knopf, 1974.

The Ugly Palaces: Housing in America by Robert A. Liston. Watts, 1974.

A Piece of the Power; Four Black Mayors by James Haskins. Dial, 1972.

How Will We Move All the People? by Sterling McLeod. Messner, 1971.

An excellent bibliography, which might be helpful, is *What Is a City? A Multi-media Guide on Urban Living,* edited by Rose Moorachian and published by the Boston Public Library in 1969.

An especially fine collection of books about cities has been done by Miroslav Sasek, who provides brief information about specific cities and many colored drawings to show exactly what each city is like. Some of his titles are *This Is Paris, This Is New York, This Is London,* and *This Is San Francisco* (Macmillan, varied dates).

Fiction

*Round about the City, Child Study Association of America.

*Noisy Nancy Norris by LouAnn Gaeddert. Doubleday, 1965.

*Tiny Toosey's Birthday by Mabel G. LaRue. Houghton Mifflin, 1950.

*Big Cowboy Western by Ann H. Scott. Lothrop, 1965.

What's New, Lincoln? by Dale Fife. Coward, McCann & Geoghegan, 1970.

*On the Other Side of the River by Joanne Oppenheim. Watts, 1972.

*Apt. 3 by Ezra Jack Keats. Macmillan, 1971.

*Adams A B C by Dale Fife. Coward, McCann & Geoghegan, 1971.

---

* For younger children.

In addition, there are numerous books that are set in one city, for instance, New York, Chicago, or San Francisco. Representative titles are:

Chicago

The Green Ginger Jar; A Chinatown Mystery by Clara Ingram Judson. Houghton Mifflin, 1949.

The Story of the Great Chicago Fire, 1871 by Mary Kay Phelan. Thomas Y. Crowell, 1971.

New York

The Mysterious Disappearance of Leon (I Mean Noel) by Ellen Raskin. Dutton, 1971.

*Ladder Company 108 by Rona Beame. Messner, 1973.

A Month of Sundays by Rose Blue. Watts, 1972.

Luke Was There by Eleanor Clymer. Holt, 1973.

The Carp in the Bathtub by Barbara Cohen. Lothrop, 1972.

The Witch of Fourth Street and Other Stories by Myron Levoy. Harper & Row, 1972.

Train Ride by John Steptoe. Harper & Row, 1971.

All-of-a-kind Family Downtown by Sidney Taylor. Follett, 1972.

*I Wrote My Name on the Wall by Ronni Solbert. Little, Brown, 1971.

There are many more fictional stories set in New York City than we can list here. Check the *Children's Catalog* for additional titles.

San Francisco

The Cable Car and the Dragon (Doubleday, 1972) is a zany tale by Herb Caen, a newspaper columnist who knows San Francisco well. A young cable car (only sixty years old) named Charlie gets tired of his rut, so off he goes to join the Chinese New Year parade. He offers a friendly dragon, Chu Chin Chow, a ride down Russian Hill. They almost end up in San Francisco Bay, but Chu is able to stop the cable car just in time.

---

* For younger children.

In addition, try these titles:

Maybelle, the Cable Car by Virginia Lee Burton. Houghton Mifflin, 1952.

Fly High, Fly Low by Don Freeman, Viking, 1957.

The Rice Bowl Pet by Patricia Miles Martin. Thomas Y. Crowell, 1962.

Black and Blue Magic by Zilpha K. Snyder. Atheneum, 1966.

STUDENT PRESENTATION This module can be as long or as short as you want it to be. It includes reading for students to do, but it also is interspersed with varied activities that permit children to think and to express their ideas in different ways. Develop the module, page by page, something like this:

---

* For younger children.

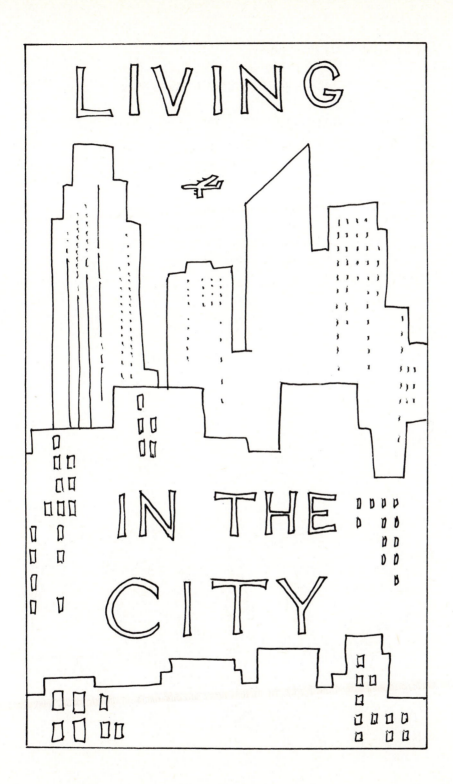

LIVING IN THE CITY

Do you live in a city? How big is it? What do you like about life in the city?

Here is a poem that describes the things that we see in a city—your city, my city, any city.

A TRIP

James S. Tippett

We went about the city,
We walked along the street,
We saw the stores and houses,
We saw the people meet.

We saw the railroad station,
We saw the fire hall,
We saw the post office,
And people in them all.

We saw the trucks and street cars,
We saw the green park,
And street lamps at the corners
To be lighted after dark.

What things do you see on the street where you live? Write a paragraph describing your block. What is it like? How do you feel about it?

Page 2: DRIVING IN THE CITY

417

*READING FOR
INFORMATION*

SIGNS
Ilo Orleans

When I went riding
　Yesterday,
I watched the signs
　Along the way.

"No Parking"; "Exit";
　"To the Zoo";
"Traffic Circle";
　"Fifth Avenue";

"Stay in Line";
　And "Stop" and "Go";
"Tunnel"; Bridge";
　"Steep Hill"; "Go Slow";

"No Trucks"; "One Way";
　"No Turns"; "Keep Right";
The signs are everywhere
　In sight!

I read out loud
　Each sign I saw,
So daddy should
　Obey the law!

TRAFFIC SOUNDS
James S. Tippett

Taxis are honking,
Great trucks are bumping,
Autos are wheezing,
Street cars are thumping,

Whistles are screaming,
Airplanes are zooming,
Wheel brakes are screeching,
Fast trains are booming.

Sounds of the traffic
Come rushing and pouring
Loud as the winds
When a great storm
　is roaring.

MOTOR CARS
Rowena Bennett

From a city window, 'way up high,
I like to watch the cars go by.
They look like burnished beetles, black,
That leave a little muddy track
Behind them as they slowly crawl.
Sometimes they do not move at all
But huddle close with hum and drone
As though they feared to be alone.
They grope their way through fog and night
With the golden feelers of their light.

　Imagine that you are riding in a car along a city street. Make a list of the things that you might see. Make another list of things you might hear.

Page 3: SKYSCRAPERS

Tip your head back. Look way up to the top of that tall building. It's a skyscraper! Why do you think this word was invented?

BUILDING A SKYSCRAPER
James S. Tippett

They're building a skyscraper
Near our street.
It's height will be nearly
One thousand feet.

It covers completely
A city block.
They drilled its foundation
Through solid rock.

They made its framework
Of great steel beams
With riveted joints
And welded seams.

A swarm of workmen
Strain and strive
Like busy bees
In a honeyed hive.

Building the skyscraper
Into the air
While crowds of people
Stand and stare.

SKYSCRAPERS
Rachel Field

Do skyscrapers ever grow tired
Of holding themselves up high?
Do they ever shiver on frosty nights
With their tops against the sky?
Do they feel lonely sometimes
Because they have grown so tall?
Do they ever wish they could lie
  right down
And never get up at all?

What is the tallest building that you have been in? Describe what you could see from the windows of the building or from the rooftop.

As you think about the city, what words do you think of? List all the words on a sheet of paper.

Share your list with classmates. Some words might be—

traffic	skyscrapers
bus	automobile
sidewalk	museum
park	police Officer

As you read the list, consider how you can group the words. Are there groups of words that fit these categories, for instance?

> Vehicles
> Buildings
> People

List as many categories as you need. You may also find that you need to change some categories as you sort the words into groups. Make a chart like this.

CITY WORDS		
Places	People	Buildings
park	policeman	skyscraper
		museum

THE MANY WAYS
OF SEEING

Lois Lenski

Sing a song of people
Walking fast or slow;
People in the city
Up and down they go.

People on the sidewalk,
People on the bus;
People passing, passing,
In front and back of us.

People on the subway
Underneath the ground;
People riding taxis
Round and round and round.

People with their hats on
Going in the doors;
People with umbrellas
When it rains and pours.

People in tall buildings
And in stores below;
Riding elevators
Up and down they go!

People walking singly
People in a crowd;
People saying nothing
People talking loud.

People laughing, smiling,
Grumpy people too.
People who just hurry
And never look at you.

Sing a song of people
Who like to come and go;
Sing of city people
You see but never know.

Think about the people the poet describes. Paint a picture of CITY
PEOPLE. What kind of people will be in your picture?

Many books describe life in big cities such as New York, San Francisco, and Chicago. Choose one that you would like to read. Here are a few suggestions, but there are many others.

A funny book that takes place in New York City is *The Carp in the Bathtub* by Barbara Cohen. This author tells about two Jewish children who try to save Joe, a carp, from being made into gefilte fish. A very different kind of story that also takes place in New York is *Luke Was There* by Eleanor Clymer. Julius and his brother, Danny, meet Luke, a young black man, in the children's shelter to which they are assigned. When Luke, a conscientious objector, has to serve time in a military hospital, Julius is so upset that he runs away only to encounter danger on the city streets.

Perhaps you'd be interested in a story set in a city in another country, for example, London. Leon Garfield has written two stories set in eighteenth-century London. *Mister Corbett's Ghost* tells of Benjamin's encounter with the Devil, while *Smith* is the story of a twelve-year-old pickpocket. A book that is set in Paris is *The Family under the Bridge* written by Natalie Savage Carlson. This is a fascinating story of a tramp, Armand, who discovers three children hidden under a bridge by their mother who has to work to earn food for them. The old man takes the children to a gypsy camp and soon finds himself acting as a grandfather to the children.

After you have read the story you chose, share your book with the members of the class. On one sheet you can tell enough about the book so that others can decide whether they would like to read that book, too. The following book review manages to include information about the title, author, and publisher as well as to tell what the story is about. Do you think you would enjoy reading this story?

❦ *The Pushcart War* by Jean Merrill (Scott, 1964) is a humorous story set in New York City. As the author explains:

The Pushcart War started on the afternoon of March 15, 1976, when a truck ran down a pushcart belonging to a flower peddler. Daffodils were scattered all over the street. The pushcart was flattened, and the owner of the pushcart was pitched headfirst into a pickle barrel.

The owner of that pushcart, Morris the Florist, takes an active part in the fight between the trucks that created traffic problems and the pushcart owners, who attack the trucks with peashooters. They use peas, of course, with pins stuck in them that can quickly deflate a huge truck tire. You can imagine the mess the city is in when traffic can't move at all!

The war is finally settled by the Pushcart Peace Conference and the formulation of the Flower Formula for Peace with which "every high school student in New York is now familiar." Do you think this is really true?

Page 7: STUDYING ONE CITY

Choose one city that you would like to know more about. Try to choose a city that no one else is studying. Look in the *World Almanac* to find a list of big cities, for example:

United States	*Other Countries*
New York	Tokyo
Los Angeles	London
Chicago	Paris
Seattle	Rome
San Diego	Berlin
New Orleans	Buenos Aires
Philadelphia	Rio de Janeiro
Boston	Sydney
San Francisco	Cairo
Your city	Montreal

Make a book about the city you have chosen. Include as much information as you can find. Include pictures that you might find in magazines or ones that you draw. Here are other suggestions:

1. Make a sheet with the title: All About _____. List general information such as the area, population, origin of the name, important landmarks, and so on.

2. Draw a map of the country showing where this city is located. Show any rivers, lakes, or oceans. Mark other land features such as mountains.

3. Draw a map of the city itself showing some of the major streets or the location of important places in the city. Perhaps you can get a city street map that shows the location of all streets and interesting places.

4. List any books you can find about this city. Include fiction set in that city.

5. Write a poem about this city. Incorporate the information you discovered through reading about your city.

6. Draw pictures of things of special interest in this city.

Write a commentary about this city. Why did it become an important city? Why would you recommend that people visit it? What are some of the problems this city has?

Page 8: POSTTEST FOR LIVING IN THE CITY

Here are several questions that you should be able to answer after studying what it is like to live in a city. Discuss your answers with other students who have completed this study.

1. Name three big cities in the United States.

   a. _____

   b. _____

   c. _____

2. Name three big cities located in other countries of the world.

   a. _____

   b. _____

   c. _____

3. List three characteristics of a big city.

a. _____

b. _____

c. _____

4. Describe one city that you would like to visit. What attracts you about this city?

5. Discuss one problem that all big cities have to handle.

❦ *CREATING A LEARNING MODULE* Choose a topic that you would like to teach in a specific classroom. Use Living in the City as a model as you develop a module that you could present in a learning center. Include both information and activities throughout the module. Reference books that will help you include:

Children's Catalog or *Junior High School Catalog.*
Browsing through the subject index of these catalogues will suggest topics that might interest you. You will get some idea, in addition, of the number of books that will be available for this topic.

Encyclopedias, especially those written for young people.
Look under the specific topic you choose as well as related subjects.

Education Index or *Reader's Guide to Periodical Literature.*
These indexes will suggest articles that discuss specific topics or even teaching ideas related to the topics. *Education Index* and the periodicals indexed will be found only in college or university libraries.

Nonfiction written for adults as well as that prepared for young people. These works may also include bibliographies of additional material. They may offer maps, graphs, diagrams, and other drawings that you can enlarge or reproduce in the module.

American Association for the Advancement of Science. *Science Books: A Quarterly Review.* Published in May, Sept., Dec., and March. Also, *Science Film Catalog.* (1515 Massachusetts Ave., NW. Washington, D.C. 20005).

Eakin, Mary K. "The Changing World of Science and the Social Sciences," in *Children and Literature; Views and Reviews* edited by Virginia Haviland. Scott, Foresman, 1973, pp. 316–322.

Fisher, Margery. *Matters of Fact.* Thomas Y. Crowell, 1972.

Hardgrove, Clarence Ethel and Herbert F. Miller. *Mathematics Library: Elementary and Junior High School.* National Council of Teachers of Mathematics, 1973.

Reading Ideas; A Newsletter for Teachers of All Levels. Contemporary Press (monthly).

Root, Shelton L., Jr., ed. with a Committee of the National Council of Teachers of English. *Adventuring with Books.* NCTE, 1973, pp. 236–344.

Science and Children, a journal published by the National Science Teachers Association, Washington, D.C.

Selsam, Millicent E. "Writing about Science for Children," in *A Critical Approach to Children's Literature* edited by Sara Innis Fenwick. University of Chicago, 1967, pp. 96–99.

Tiedt, Iris M. and Sidney W. Tiedt. "Language Study" and "Future Imperfect," in *Contemporary English in the Elementary School.* 2nd ed. Prentice-Hall, 1975.

9

*They Were
Strong
and Good*

Literature for the Social Studies

Title from Walter D. Edmonds, *They Were Strong and Good* (Dodd, 1944). Illustration copyright 1953 by Robert Lawson.
From *Mr. Revere and I* by Robert Lawson, by permission of Little, Brown and Co.

What I want to show are the qualities of plain ordinary people, who after all carry the burden of human progress. I want to know about people, how they lived, what they hoped for, what they feared. I want to know what it was like to be born into this time or that, and what a man left behind when he died.

Walter D. Edmonds
The Matchlock Gun

Reading about real people, times, and places can be fascinating if the books are well written. Biographies, historical fiction, and fiction set in specific various regions of the United States and other countries add much to students' understanding of history and geography. Good books can serve to make the people who lived in earlier times seem real, to come alive for children reading about them today. A combination of nonfiction and fiction can be the nucleus of an exciting approach to the social studies.

Quality historical fiction or an excellent biography is not a facile production, for even the simplest of these books is based on extensive research. An additional requirement is that the author write with sensitivity, style, and authority if the reader is to be convinced. In the words of Geoffrey Trease, historical characters must be "alive and warm and tangible, as if they are in the room with him," and we must feel "that they are not modern people . . . but in another time and place whose atmosphere they have thrown around him and ourselves, like some modern pavilion." He notes the difficulties encountered when he writes a story in a specific historical time and place:

Stop and imagine the simplest things—the significance of nightfall when there was no good artificial light; the misery of winter for the same reason, as well as many others; conversely the tremendous liberation of May Day and the lengthening days. Imagine the bodily sensation of cluttering clothes; wet weather before the invention of rubber and plastics. Think of the different sense of time before we had watches with minute hands.[1]

The authors of regional and historical fiction, biography, and other nonfiction for children command our respect, therefore. Such authors as Robert Lawson, Lois Lenski, Walter D. Edmonds, and Laura Ingalls Wilder are steeped in the lore of the times and places of which they write. Their people are "warm and tangible."

It is important to be aware of authors who have delighted in writing, for example, of American history.

Cornelia Meigs	*Swift Rivers*
Rachel Field	*Hitty, Her First Hundred Years*
Elizabeth Coatsworth	*Away Goes Sally*
Alice Dalgliesh	*The Courage of Sarah Noble*
Rebecca Caudill	*Tree of Freedom*
Robert Lawson	*Ben and Me*
Elizabeth Speare	*The Witch of Blackbird Pond*
Esther Forbes	*Johnny Tremain*
Ann Petry	*Tituba of Salem Village*
Leonard Wibberley	*The Treegate* series
Stephen Meader	*Boy with a Pack*
Walter D. Edmonds	*Wilderness Clearing*
Lois Lenski	*Indian Captive*
Laura Ingalls Wilder	*Little House on the Prairie* series

The objectives of this study of books for children that portray real people, times, and places can be stated thus:

---

[1] Geoffrey, Trease. "The Historical Novelist at Work," *Children's Literature in Education* (March 1972), p. 12.

1. To know a number of autobiographies and biographies of great Americans

2. To read books representing different historical periods including both historical fiction as well as nonfiction

3. To know books that present various regional settings in the United States as well as settings in other countries

4. To develop ways of presenting this kind of literature to elementary school children as part of the social studies curriculum

---

❧ This assessment will not only help you evaluate your knowledge of this aspect of children's literature but will also suggest topics to explore.

1. Can you match the titles and authors of these books?

   ——— *Little House on the Prairie*   a. Robert Lawson

   ——— *Abe Lincoln Grows Up*   b. Carol Ryrie Brink

   ——— *Strawberry Girl*   c. Carl Sandburg

   ——— *Caddie Woodlawn*   d. Laura Ingalls Wilder

   ——— *Mr. Revere and I*   e. Lois Lenski

   ——— *Ishi*   f. Theodora Kroeber

2. In which country are these stories located?

   The Children of Green Knowe   ———————————————

   Wheel on the School   ———————————————

   The Red Balloon   ———————————————

3. Who wrote these titles?

   Johnny Tremain   ———————————————

   Blue Willow   ———————————————

   Brady   ———————————————

4. What books would help you integrate a study of the life of George Washington with the times and places in which he lived?

THE GROWTH OF OUR COUNTRY

The year 1976 marked the Bicentennial of the United States of America. As our country enters its third century, it is appropriate that we stimulate children to relive the history that represents their heritage through examining the fine tradebooks now available.

Rosemary Carr Benét and Stephen Vincent Benét set the stage for this study with their poem "U.S.A.," from *Book of Americans* (Holt, 1952):

So we march into the present,
And it's always rather pleasant
To speculate on what the years ahead of us will see,
For our words and thoughts and attitudes,
All our novelties and platitudes,
Will be Rather Ancient History in 2033.

They conclude with the sage observation, "And we shan't know all the answers till we're history, ourselves."[2]

An investigation of children's literature related to the development of the United States could take many directions—historical, geographical, political, social—and it might focus on a wide variety of specific topics. Of necessity, therefore, we need to select representative topics to discuss that will perhaps suggest other studies you might undertake independently. We will explore: (1) a period of history, the American Revolution; (2) a geographic area, the Mississippi River; (3) an important group in our society, black Americans; and (4) a literary subgenre, the historical novel.

THE AMERICAN REVOLUTION

As you develop a study of American history before and after the Revolution, consider titles from fiction, nonfiction, poetry, and drama. You and your students can create a learning center with activities focused on the American Revolution. Display a map of the United States, as well as pictures of people and events to add interest to the study. Help the students find books that discuss the Revolutionary War directly, or stories that provide much incidental information as a setting for adventures of people living at that time.

---

[2] Rosemary Carr Benét and Stephen Vincent Benét, *Book of Americans* (Rinehart, 1952), p. 114.

Many excellent resources have been developed to aid teachers in celebrating the beginnings of our country. As one compiler wrote:

Young people have always had an appetite for adventure, romance, and idealism in their reading fare. Fiction can stir their imaginations, but stories based on fact are equally enjoyable when the facts are as lively as those a writer can find in the story of the American Revolution.[3]

The title *1776: Year of Independence* (Scribner, 1970) is appropriate for Genevieve Foster's presentation of the events and people who were particularly influential at the time of the American Revolution. Because the book is divided into short focused segments, such as "The Boston Tea Party," "The First Flag," and "President George Washington," as well as concurrent happenings around the world: "The Montgolfier Brothers," and "Captain Cook's Voyages," it lends itself to reading aloud to students of all ages. Filled with illustrations of events, portraits, and maps, such a presentation of the facts could form the basis for a more extensive study.

Following this examination of factual information about the times and people, children from third grade through sixth would be well prepared to enjoy Robert Lawson's humorous fictional biographies. *Ben and Me,* which is narrated by Ben Franklin's friend, Amos the mouse, is discussed on page 107. *Mr. Revere and I* (Little, Brown, 1953) is narrated by his horse, Sherry, who started out as "Scheherazade, once the most admired mount of the Queen's Own Household Cavalry." At first when Sherry becomes Paul Revere's mount, she looks askance at his activities with the Sons of Liberty, but during an encounter with her former master, Sir Cedric Barnstable, and his horse, Ajax, Sherry writes:

In a great blinding flash I knew that I would die rather than exchange my new-found liberty for that old prisonlike existence I had once thought so glorious. I was a free horse! I was a Colonial! I was a Patriot, my life dedicated to the ideals of Liberty and Freedom! (p. 103)

---

[3] John H. Pell, Chairman, The New York State American Revolution Bicentennial Commission, *The American Revolution for Young Readers; A Bibliography* (Office of State History, Albany, New York, 1971), p. iii.

Both British and American men who figured in the Revolution are included as characters in this lighthearted but factual account. Sam Adams is developed, for example, as a humorous character who is always interrupting Paul Revere's meals, sending Paul off on an important mission, while he eats the good cooking prepared by Paul's wife. Children who are familiar with the historical facts of this period will be better able to appreciate the humor of this version. See also *Where Was Patrick Henry on the 29th of May?* (Coward, McCann & Geoghegan, 1975) by Jean Fritz.

Historical novels also provide this kind of information about the times as the reader follows a particular character's involvement. A good example to follow the preceding books is *Johnny Tremain* (Houghton Mifflin, 1943), which won the Newberry award for Esther Forbes. More advanced readers will enjoy this tale of fourteen-year-old Johnny who is apprenticed to a silversmith. When Johnny's hand is hurt so that he can no longer work with his trade, he becomes a rider for the Committee of Public Safety. Through these activities he meets such important figures as John Hancock and Samuel Adams and is involved in the activities of the rebellious patriots. Esther Forbes, who is steeped in the history of this period, won the Pulitzer Prize for her adult work *Paul Revere and the World He Lived In.*

There are many such books to be explored. Following is a sampling of the selections from nonfiction, biography, fiction, and poetry that would add to a study of the American Revolution.

Johnny Tremain *by Esther Forbes, illustrated by Lynd Ward. Copyright 1943 by Esther Forbes Hoskins. Copyright © renewed 1971 by Linwood M. Erskine, Jr. Reprinted by permission of Houghton Mifflin Company.*

Nonfiction

Bliven, Bruce. *The American Revolution, 1760–1783.* Random House, 1958.

Colby, C. B. *Revolutionary War Weapons: Pole Arms, Hand Guns, Shoulder Arms and Artillery.* Coward, McCann & Geoghegan, 1963.

*Haley, Gail E. *Jack Jouett's Ride.* Viking, 1973.

Hall-Quest, Olga W. *The Bell That Rang for Freedom: The Liberty Bell and Its Place in American History.* Dutton, 1965.

Lancaster, Bruce. *The American Revolution.* Garden City Books, 1957.

Mason, F. Van Wyck. *The Winter at Valley Forge.* Random House, 1953.

Penner, Lucille. *The Colonial Cookbook.* Hastings House, 1976.

Phelan, Mary Kay. *Midnight Alarm: The Story of Paul Revere's Ride.* Thomas Y. Crowell, 1968.

---

* For younger children.

*D'Aulaire, Ingri and Edgar Parin. *Benjamin Franklin*. Doubleday, 1950. (*Illustrated attractively*)

Brown, Slater. *Ethan Allen and the Green Mountain Boys*. Random House, 1956.

Davis, Burke. *Heroes of the American Revolution*. Random House, 1971.

DeLeeuw, Adele. *George Rogers Clark: Frontier Fighter*. Garrard, 1967.

Fritz, Jean. *And Then What Happened, Paul Revere?* Coward, McCann & Geoghegan, 1973.

Graham, Alberta P. *Lafayette: Friend of America*. Abingdon, 1952.

Jacobs, William Jay. *Roger Williams*. Watts, 1975.

Holbrook, Stewart. *America's Ethan Allen*. Houghton Mifflin, 1949.

Kelly, Regina Z. *Paul Revere: Colonial Craftsman*. Houghton Mifflin, 1963.

Sutton, Felix. *Sons of Liberty*. Messner, 1969.

Fiction

Finlayson, Ann. *Rebecca's War*. Warne, 1972.

*Fritz, Jean. *The Cabin Faced West*. Coward, McCann & Geoghegan, 1958.

*Gauch, Patricia L. *Aaron and the Green Mountain Boys*. Coward, McCann & Geoghegan, 1972.

Hays, Wilma P. *The Scarlet Badge*. Holt, 1963.

*Lowrey, Janette S. *Six Silver Spoons*. Harper & Row, 1971.

Savery, Constance. *The Reb and the Redcoats*. Longmans, 1961.

Poetry

Brand, Oscar. *Songs of '76: A Folksinger's History of the Revolution*. M. Evans, 1973.

Carmer, Carl. *The Boy Drummer of Vincennes*. Harvey House, 1972.

Longfellow, Henry Wadsworth. *Paul Revere's Ride*. Illustrated by Paul Galdone. Thomas Y. Crowell, 1963.

---

* For younger children.

*Reprinted by permission of Cow-
ard, McCann & Geoghegan, Inc.
from* The Cabin Faced West *by
Jean Fritz. Copyright © 1958
by Jean Fritz.*

As you pursue this study, refer to some of the bibliographies and teaching materials that were published in 1975–1976 for the Bicentennial, for example:

Arlene Pillar. "Revolutionary Reading: An Annotated Bibliography." *Language Arts.* 52 (September 1975): 902–912.

Bicentennial Reading, Viewing, Listening. American Library Association, 50 E. Huron St., Chicago, Illinois 61611.

Belshaw, Sharon and Candy Carter. *Celebrating America.* Contemporary Press, Box 1524, San Jose, California 95109 ($3.50).

Maring, Gerald. "Bicentennial Reading." *Reading Ideas.* 1:4 (January 1976).

THE MISSISSIPPI RIVER

Another emphasis for a unit of study might be on a specific area or region, for example, the area touched by the great Mississippi River. Few rivers have had as great an impact as the Mississippi, wending its ponderous way through Missouri to Louisiana. Up the Father of Waters from the Gulf of Mexico came early explorers, and down the river came the developing commerce. A study that focuses on the Mississippi will obviously touch on a number of topics:

Early explorers

Indians along the Mississippi

New Orleans

Trade on the Mississippi

Mark Twain

An excellent introduction to the early explorers of the Mississippi is *Exploring the Great River* (Little, Brown, 1969) edited by Robert Meredith and E. Brooks Smith. Although others knew of the river, it was Spaniard Hernando de Soto who explored it extensively. A good biography for middle graders about this explorer is *De Soto, Finder of the Mississippi* (Morrow, 1957), written by Ronald Syme. Another noted explorer of the Mississippi was Frenchman Robert Cavelier de la Salle who came from Canada through the Great Lakes in the 1680s and finally down the river to claim Louisiana for France. Ronald Syme has also written a biography of this explorer, *La Salle of the Mississippi* (Morrow, 1953).

Fiction set on or along the Mississippi serves to add interest to a study of the great river. Clyde Bulla, for example, wrote *Down the Mississippi* (Thomas Y. Crowell, 1954), a book for middle graders. Born in Minnesota, Erik Lind is fascinated by the river. Despite his father's obvious hope that he will stay on the family farm, Erik is even more convinced that life on the river is for him after his trip with his cousin Gunder as a cook's helper on a log raft.

Swift Rivers (Little, Brown, 1932) is an exciting story of life on the Mississippi River written by Cornelia Meigs for older students. Eighteen-year-old Chris Dahlberg, concerned about his grandfather's welfare, conceives of a plan for floating logs from Minnesota down the river to connect with the Mississippi. A good adventure story, this book holds the reader's interest and provides excellent historical background.

Holling C. Holling writes fiction that is as informational as any nonfiction. *Minn of the Mississippi* (Houghton Mifflin, 1951) depicts the whole Mississippi River Valley through the adventures of a snapping turtle that was gradually pushed along the river from Canada to the Gulf of Mexico. Beautiful colorful illustrations plus many black and white sketches provide the reader with further information as we follow Minn's travels.

Other similar informative fiction by Holling C. Holling includes *Paddle-to-the Sea, Tree in the Trail, Pagoo,* and *Seabird*.

Fiction could be supplemented with such nonfiction as Louis Solomon's *The Mississippi; America's Mainstream* (McGraw-Hill, 1971). This factual presentation describes the history of the great river from the early explorations to its present polluted state.

No study of the Mississippi would be complete without presenting Samuel Langhorne Clemens, who chose his pseudonym Mark Twain from experiences as a steamboat pilot. Middle grade students will enjoy May McNeer's *America's Mark Twain* (Houghton Mifflin, 1962), which tells of Mark Twain's travels on the Mississippi and is illustrated handsomely by Lynd Ward. Sterling North's *Mark Twain and the River* (Houghton Mifflin, 1961) and Catherine Owens Peare's *Mark Twain; His Life* (Holt, 1954) add additional interesting facts about this noted author's life on the river.

The stories of Tom Sawyer and Huck Finn, of course, must be part of this focus on Mississippi River country. One good edition of *The Adventures of Tom Sawyer* was published by Macmillan in 1962, with an afterword by Clifton Fadiman. A play, "Tom Sawyer, Pirate," based on this book is included in Adele Thane's collection of *Plays from Famous Stories and Fairy Tales* (Plays, Inc., 1967).

Reprinted by permission of the William Collins & World Publishing Co., from The Adventures of Tom Sawyer, *by Mark Twain, illustrated by Louis Slobodkin.*

BLACK AMERICANS

One of the most satisfactory approaches to presenting members of any group is to treat them as individuals not particularly different because of their membership in that group. Today a number of authors are depicting black Americans realistically. Ezra Jack Keats, for example, writes and illustrates stories about black children. His stories are, however, primarily about children who just happen to be black, a fact that is revealed only through the illustrations. In *The Snowy Day* (Viking, 1962), for example, Peter plays in the snow, interacts with his mother, and tries to save a snowball in his pocket; he could be any little boy.

Lucille Clifton provides a lively, sensitive introduction to a six-year-old black boy through poetry in *Some of the Days of Everett Anderson* (Holt, 1970).

Being six
Is full of tricks
And Everett Anderson knows it.

Being a boy
  is full of joy
  and Everett Anderson shows it.

Her book, *The Times They Used to Be,* is discussed on page 160.

I Wish I Had an Afro (Cowles, 1970) is an especially fine presentation of a black family by John Shearer, a talented young black photographer. The story is told mainly in the words of Little John, an eleven-year-old boy, who expresses his thinking about many concerns:

It's really boss when some of my sister's friends come over. Dad an' them start fightin' about what the white man is doin' wrong. They always be sayin', "Things are different now, old man!" They say what they want, wear what they want, an' do what they want. They don't let nobody push them around. Sometimes I think, deep inside Dad he really agrees with them. I wonder, though, if he agrees with them, why don't he go along with them an' why don't he let me grow my hair like theirs. They sure do dig bein' black. I which I could be like them. I wish I had an Afro.

Little John

Sounder, written by William H. Armstrong and illustrated by James Barkley (Harper & Row, 1969), is perhaps one of the most touching portrayals of the troubles encountered by a family that has been written for children. The tragedy of a poor black sharecropper who steals food to keep his wife and children from starving is presented realistically. So also are the boy's sensitivity to his mother's feelings and his awareness of his own sense of loneliness.

His mother always hummed when she was worried. When she held a well child on her lap and rocked back and forth, she sang. But when she held a sick child close in her arms and the rocker moved just enough to squeak a little, she would hum. Sometimes she hummed so softly that the child heard the deep concerned breathing of terror above the sound of the humming.

Sounder has been highly criticized because of the dominance of whites in the story; white people are the villains, but they are also the problem solvers and they hold the power. While it is not likely that the sympathies of any reader will be with the white people portrayed, this point should certainly be discussed.

John Steptoe is a young black illustrator and author who focuses on portraying black children realistically. His first book, *Stevie* (Harper & Row, 1969), was very well received. It was followed by such titles as *Uptown* (Harper & Row, 1970) and *Train Ride* (Harper & Row, 1971). Born in 1950, John Steptoe presents the dialect and the ideas of young black boys who live in the city. In *Uptown* John and Dennis talk about what they will be when they grow up. John narrates the story.

Dennis is my main man; we hang out together. Almost every day me and him go play in Mt. Morris Park after school. We go play up on the hill, around the big bell tower. It's kinda boss jumpin' off the rocks, climbin' stone walls, playin' fort. It could be Soldiers or Cowboys and Indians, but most of the time it's Cops and Junkies. And there's always a real junkie around to mess with.

The boys conclude that they don't know what they will be, so "Guess we'll just hang out together for a while and just dig on everythin' that's goin'." Steptoe's *Marcia* (Viking, 1976) describes the intimate details of two young girls who are growing up. At fourteen, sex and boyfriends realistically dominate the girls' lives. John Steptoe also illustrated an attractive picture book by Eloise Greenfield, *She Come Bringing Me That Little Baby Girl* (Lippincott, 1974), which describes a young black boy's reaction to a new baby sister.

Steptoe's effort to present dialect realistically brings up an important question to consider. Is the dialect accurate? If it is not, is an author's attempt to reproduce a semblance of the character's black English helpful? As members of the Council on Interracial Books for Children point out, "the richness of black English rarely comes across" and the final impression may be "inferiority."[4] It is really difficult to depict a dialect accurately. The effect is almost always demeaning.

Virginia Hamilton is another black author who presents strong black characters. In *Zeely* (Macmillan, 1967), illustrated by Symeon Shimin, she deals realistically with the feelings of young black people. Geeder and Toeboy, alias Elizabeth and John, are portrayed sensitively as they cope with new experiences during a summer on their uncle's farm. They encounter Zeely, a statuesque young black woman of Watusi origins, who is more than six and one-half feet tall. She particularly influences Geeder, an eleven-year-old girl in the process of maturing, who sees her as a queen. Virginia Hamilton's *M. C. Higgins the Great* (Macmillan, 1974), which won the 1975 Newbery award, is a beautiful story of a family and a boy growing up.

Paula Fox won the Newbery award for her fine historical novel *The Slave Dancer* (Bradbury, 1973). Thirteen-year-old Jessie Bollier, a white boy living in New Orleans in 1840, is kidnapped by Captain Cawthorne's crew to play his fife aboard a slave ship. Jessie plays to make the slaves dance during their brief exercise periods enroute from Africa back to the United States. *The Moonlight* is a ship of horror as the food and water supply diminishes until finally a storm ends it all. Jessie and a young black boy, Ras, manage to get ashore where they are rescued by Daniel, an escaped slave. Ras is passed through the Underground to freedom in the North, while Jessie returns home, very much changed by his experiences. He states:

When I passed a black man, I often turned to look at him, trying to see in his walk the man he had once been before he'd been driven through the dangerous heaving surf to a long boat, toppled into it, chained, brought to a waiting ship all nar-

---

[4] The Council on Interracial Books for Children, *Human- and Anti-human-Values in Children's Books* (The Council, 1976), p. 8.

rowed and stripped for speed, carried through storms, and the bitter brightness of sun-filled days to a place, where if he had survived, he would be sold like cloth. (p. 174)

Another fascinating historical novel is *Tituba of Salem Village* (Thomas Y. Crowell, 1964). Ann Petry describes the Salem witch trials in 1692 and tells in detail the story of the slave Tituba, one of the first to be condemned. Although people tried to defend this intelligent black woman, she was placed in the Boston jail with many others as a result of the prevailing hysteria. A kind weaver paid her fees and bought both Tituba and her husband. Ann Petry has also written a biography of Harriet Tubman, a black slave who escaped and managed to assist hundreds of other slaves in their flight to freedom—*Harriet Tubman: Conductor on the Underground Railroad* (Thomas Y. Crowell, 1955).

Thirteen-year-old Benjie Johnson is a contemporary disillusioned black adolescent in *A Hero Ain't Nothin' But a Sandwich* (Coward, McCann & Geoghegan, 1973) by black author Alice Childress. At times tense and dramatic, this story for older students has yet a touch of humor as Benjie describes life in the language of the streets he knows.

Other stories that feature black characters include:

Agle, Nana Hayde. *Maple Street*. Seabury, 1970.

Cone, Molly. *The Other Side of the Fence*. Houghton Mifflin, 1967.

Devereaux, Alexis. *Na-ni*. Harper & Row, 1973.

Graham, Lorenz. *I, Momolu*. Thomas Y. Crowell, 1966.

Hamilton, Virginia. *The House of Dies Drear*. Macmillan, 1968.

Justus, May. *A New Home for Billy*. Hastings House, 1966.

Konigsburg, E. L. *Jennifer, Hecate, Macbeth, William McKinley, and Me, Elizabeth*. Atheneum, 1967.

Krementz, Jill. *Sweet Pea: A Black Girl Growing Up in the Rural South*. Harcourt Brace Jovanovitch, 1969.

Wilkinson, Brenda. *Ludell*. Harper & Row, 1975.

Many other fine books about black Americans are recommended for school libraries, for example, these biographies:

Berg, Jean Horton. *I Cry When the Sun Goes Down: The Story of Herman Wrice*. Westminster, 1975. (*Philadelphia youth organizer*)

Chittenden, Elizabeth F. *Profiles in Black and White: Stories of Men and Women Who Fought Against Slavery*. Scribner, 1973.

Douty, Esther Morris. *Charlotte Forten: Free Black Teacher*. Garrard, 1971.

Folsom, Franklin. *The Life and Legends of George McJunkin, Black Cowboy*. Nelson, 1973.

Greenfield, Eloise. *Rosa Parks*. Thomas Y. Crowell, 1973. (*She refused to give up a seat on the bus.*)

————. *Paul Robeson*. Thomas Y. Crowell, 1975. (*Artist*)

Hardwich, Richard. *Charles Richard Drew: Pioneer in Blood Research*. Scribner, 1967.

Haskins, James. *From Lew Alcindor to Kareem Abdul Jabbar*. Lothrop, 1972. (*Sports*)

Jones, Hettie. *Big Star Fallin' Mama; Five Women in Black Music*. Viking, 1974.

Kaufman, Mervyn. *Jesse Owens*. Thomas Y. Crowell, 1973. (*Sports*)

Mathis, Sharon Bell. *Ray Charles*. Thomas Y. Crowell, 1973. (*Musician*)

McGovern, Ann. *Runaway Slave: The Story of Harriet Tubman*. Four Winds Press, 1965.

Meltzer, Milton. *Langston Hughes: A Biography*. Thomas Y. Crowell, 1968. (*Poet*)

Meyer, Howard. *Colonel of the Black Regiment: The Life of Thomas Wentworth Higginson*. Norton, 1967.

Montgomery, Elizabeth. *William C. Handy: Father of the Blues*. Garrard, 1968.

Newman, Shirlee P. *Marian Anderson: Lady from Philadelphia*. Westminster, 1966. (*Singer*)

Rollins, Charlemae Hill. *They Showed the Way: Forty American Negro Leaders*. Thomas Y. Crowell, 1964.

Rowe, Jeanne. *An Album of Martin Luther King, Jr.* Watts, 1970.

Rubin, Robert. *Satchel Paige: All-time Baseball Great*. Putnam, 1974.

Tobias, Tobi. *Arthur Mitchell*. Thomas Y. Crowell, 1975. (*Dancer*)

Turk, Midge. *Gordon Parks*. Thomas Y. Crowell, 1971. (*Author*)

Williams, John A. *The Most Native of Sons*. Doubleday, 1970. (*Richard Wright, author*)

Yates, Elizabeth. *Amos Fortune: Free Man*. Dutton, 1950.

In addition to fiction and biography about blacks, we need to examine the poetry and folklore of blacks, which are part of our American heritage. The poetry of black writers such as Langston Hughes, Countee Cullens, and Gwendolyn Brooks is presented in *The Magic of Black Poetry* (Dodd, Mead, 1972) edited by Raoul Abdul. An anthology for older students, *Kaleidoscope; Poems by American Negro Poets* (Harcourt Brace Jovanovich, 1967), features more than forty poets, and editor Robert Hayden comments on the poems from a literary viewpoint. An attractive collection of poems by Langston Hughes is *Don't You Turn Back* (Knopf, 1969), which Lee Bennett Hopkins compiled. The woodcuts by Ann Grifalconi make this a handsome edition.

Folklore is another essential aspect of black culture, which even young children can enjoy. Virginia Hamilton, for example, writes of *The Time-Ago Tales of Jahdu* (Macmillan, 1969). Mama Luka, with whom Lee Edward stays while his mother works, tells the spellbound boy stories of the clever boy who was both wise and powerful. Set in Harlem, the book is enhanced by black and white illustrations by Nonny Hogrogian. Lorenz Graham tells Bible stories for primary grade children in *David He No Fear* (Thomas Y. Crowell, 1971) and *Every Man Heart Lay Down* (Thomas Y. Crowell, 1970). The charm of these poetic stories is that they are told by an African who knows only a little English. *A Road Down in the Sea* (Thomas Y. Crowell, 1970) is another tale in Liberian dialect told for middle school students. All of these stories are from the author's collection *How God Fix Jonah*. Diane Wolkstein has developed another tale from black American folklore for primary grades in *The Cool Ride in the Sky* (Knopf, 1973), which is illustrated by Paul Galdone.

A number of books present historical documentation of blacks in the United States—in the areas of civil rights, protest, and legislation, as well as personal contributions. Arnold Adoff, for example, has compiled a collection of commentaries by black Americans, *Black on Black* (Macmillan, 1968), which older students will find useful. Bernice E. Young tells of "America's most notorious ghetto" in *Harlem: The Story of a Changing Community* (Messner, 1972). Bradford Chambers documents the history of black power with the texts of forty-two documents significant to the history of the black movement in *Chronicles of Negro Protest* (Parents' Magazine Press, 1968). An impressive book is author-illustrator Tom Feelings' *Black Pilgrimage* (Lothrop, 1972), in which he tells of his personal experiences as a black man living with his family here and in Africa. A history of the fight for civil liberties for blacks in America is described in *The Long Freedom Road* (McGraw-Hill, 1968) by Janet Harris.

Poet June Jordan portrays the history of black Americans through poetry and American paintings in an especially fine book for older students, *Who Look at Me?* (Thomas Y. Crowell, 1969). She describes the intent of this beautiful book in these words:

We do not see those we do not know. And, in a nation suffering fierce hatred the question race to race, man to man, is "Who look at me." *We answer with our lives.* Let the human eye begin unlimited embrace of human life. (p. 98)

HISTORICAL NOVELS

Authors frequently use events in history as background for an adventure story. Whether presented as part of a developed study or just a good book, students will learn much about American history through reading these books. *The Terrible Wave* (Coward, McCann & Geoghegan, 1972) by Marden Dahlstedt, for instance, focuses on the famous Johnstown Flood, a well-known event that occurred in Pennsylvania in 1889. Brian O'Meara and Megan Maxwell are involved in helping people cope with this diaster as they search for their own families and seek temporary shelter.

In *Stout-hearted Seven* (Houghton Mifflin, 1973), Neta Lohnes Frazier writes of the Sager children who were adopted by Marcus and Narcissa Whitman when the children's own parents were killed en route to Oregon. Based on historical documents, this novel describes with accurate detail the problems encountered by early settlers who traveled the Oregon Trail.

Sid Fleischman writes of the Gold Rush in California in *By the Great Horn Spoon!* (Little, Brown, 1963). Jack and a butler named Praiseworthy stow away on a boat in order to get to California. Their adventures aboard the ship and involved with the forty-niners in California are hilarious. The pen and ink drawings of Eric von Schmidt add to the appeal of the book.

One of the earlier positive images of a strong young woman appears in *Caddie Woodlawn* (Macmillan, 1935) by Carl Ryrie Brink. Based on the lives of real people, this Newbery award winner tells of Caddie Woodlawn who was eleven in 1864. The "despair of her mother and of her elder sister Clara," Caddie was accepted as an equal by her brothers, Tom and Warren. It was at her father's insistence that red-headed Caddie was permitted to run freely with her brothers, but her mother still insisted that she wear long dresses with buttons up the back. This exciting adventure story is set in the early days of Wisconsin, at a time when women played a strong and highly visible role in the work of the family.

An exciting historical novel that contributes to children's understanding of the Underground Railroad is *The House of Dies Drear* by Virginia Hamilton (Macmillan, 1968). Set in the Miami Valley in southern Ohio, an area noted for its active participation in helping slaves escape to freedom in Canada, this mystery centers around a house filled with secret passages and hiding places. Thirteen-year-old Thomas Small moves from North Carolina to Ohio where his father is to be a college professor, and the family has rented the haunted house that once belonged to Dies Drear, an active abolitionist.

Additional historical novels that will give readers a better understanding of what living in America was like in those earlier days include:

Elizabeth Coatsworth. *The Golden Horseshoe*. Macmillan, 1963. *(Colonial)*

Marguerite De Angeli. *Elin's Amerika*. Doubleday, 1941. *(Colonial Delaware)*

Jean Fritz. *Brady*. Coward, McCann & Geoghegan, 1960. *(Slavery, Pennsylvania)*

Walter D. Edmonds. *Cadmus Henry*. Dodd, 1949. *(Civil War)*

Enid L. Meadowcroft. *The First Year*. Thomas Y. Crowell, 1946. *(Pilgrims)*

————. *By Secret Railway*. Crowell, 1948. *(Underground Railroad)*

Erick Berry. *Hay-foot, Straw-foot*. Viking, 1954. *(French and Indian War)*

Armstrong Sperry. *Storm Canvas*. Winston, 1944. *(War of 1812)*.

William O. Steele. *Perilous Road*. Harcourt Brace Jovanovich, 1958. *(Civil War, Tennessee)*

An extensive bibliography of such books, prepared by Jeanette Hotchkiss, is *American Historical Fiction and Biography for Children and Young People* (Scarecrow Press, 1973).

❦ *EXPLORING FURTHER* Choose one of these activities to help you explore literature related to the social studies that might help children understand the development of the United States both historically and geographically.

1. Begin a study of fiction set in different states. List the names of the fifty states and see if you can find at least one book for each state, for example:

Kansas: *The Sod House* by Elizabeth Coatsworth (Macmillan, 1954).

Pennsylvania: *Beneath the Hill* by Jane Louise Curry (Harcourt Brace Jovanovich, 1967).

California: *Blue Willow* by Doris Gates (Viking, 1940).

Utah: *The Great Brain* by John D. Fitzgerald (Dial, 1967).

Vermont: *The Blue Cat of Castle Town* by Catherine C. Coblentz (Longmans, 1949).

2. See how many books and other materials you can locate that would help children know more about the state you live in. Include both fiction and nonfiction, films, records, poems, plays. Search under the name of the state as well as names of cities, rivers, people, or significant events. If you live in the state of Florida, for example, you might find listed under Florida:

Nonfiction

Florida; From Its Glorious Past to the Present by Allan Carpenter (Childrens Press, 1965).

Fiction

Strawberry Girl by Lois Lenski (Lippincott, 1945).

The Secret River by Marjorie K. Rawlings (Scribner, 1955).

Under the Everglades you might find:

Alligator Hole by Julian May (Follett, 1969).

The Moon of the Alligators by Jean Craighead George (Thomas Y. Crowell, 1969).

GREAT AMERICANS

As we explore the lives of great Americans, it is natural to turn first to biographies as a source of information. The biography has come into its own today in both adult and children's literature as a form of writing that is realistic and exciting. As Arbuthnot and Broderick note in *Time for Biography:*

One theme runs through most of the selections: to achieve greatness, men and women must have perseverance in the face of obstacles, patience with a world that often initially rejects them, and above all, courage.

Biography is not, however, the only source of information about a person's life. We will find ourselves investigating the life and times of a person through other nonfiction as well as poetry and folklore. Fiction written about or by the person or about others who lived in the same time provides further insight. Children should be encouraged to engage in this type of library research, which can be informative and satisfying.

Much information has already been provided about great Americans as attention was focused on specific groups, such as native Americans, Mexican-Americans, and American blacks, and also in the discussions of authors throughout the book. In each of these sections exemplary biographies were cited. Here, therefore, specific approaches that can be used in the social studies curriculum will be discussed. The first section will describe the in-depth study of one person's life through a search of the literature. The second section focuses on studying different groups of people who are important in our contemporary society, such as women, sports figures, and musicians.

FOCUSING ON ONE PERSON

A valid approach to the study of history focuses on the life and times of a single person. Certainly there are many influential Americans around whom a study could be organized. For this purpose we have chosen to present first Abraham Lincoln, a president who is exceptionally interesting and about whom there is a great body of literature for young people. Then, we will focus on Louisa May Alcott, a favorite author around whom an innovative study could be developed.

THE LIFE AND TIMES OF ABRAHAM LINCOLN   A study focusing on Lincoln might begin with the question: What kind of person was the famous Abraham Lincoln? In *Life in Lincoln's America* (Random House, 1964) Helen Reeder Cross describes Lincoln, for example, as an indulgent parent who did not punish his sons for playing tricks on him, a fact that caused many to shake their heads. This author begins her book, thus: "Have you ever wondered what daily life was like in America a century and a half ago?" Of particular interest to student readers are the comments about the lives of children at that time.

Related to this approach is *Me and Willie and Pa* (Simon and Schuster,

1973) by F. N. Monjo. Told through the eyes of Tad Lincoln, this biography provides unusual personal insights into the family life of the Lincolns. Children will be interested in Tad's problems as a child, for instance, the fact that he was poor in school and that he had a speech defect.

Rosemary Carr Benét and Stephen Vincent Benét wrote of Lincoln in their *Book of Americans* (Rinehart, 1952), thus:

ABRAHAM LINCOLN

1809–1865

Lincoln was a long man.
He liked out of doors.
He liked the wind blowing
And the talk in country stores. (p. 83)

A study of Lincoln's time in history should certainly include Mary Kay Phelan's *Mr. Lincoln's Inaugural Journey* (Thomas Y. Crowell, 1972). This unusual biography of Lincoln tells of the trip through seven states from Illinois to Washington.

A variety of biographies have been written for children about this great American folk hero. An outstanding book for younger children is *Abraham Lincoln* (Doubleday, 1957) by Ingri and Edgar Parin d'Aulaire, an oversized book that is handsomely illustrated. An exceptional biography of Lincoln that older students should know is Carl Sandburg's classic work, *Abe Lincoln Grows Up* (Harcourt, 1928), the first volume of seven.

Like something out of a picture book for children he was.

Carl Sandburg

Other biographies of Abraham Lincoln that could add much to this approach to history are:

Abraham Lincoln by Genevieve Foster. Scribner, 1950.

Abraham Lincoln; Friend of the People by Clara Ingram Judson. Follett, 1950. (*Includes reproductions of fine Kodachromes*)

America's Abraham Lincoln by May McNeer. Houghton Mifflin, 1957.

That Lincoln Boy by Earl Schenck Miers. World, 1968.

Lincoln: A Big Man by Helen Kay. Hastings House, 1958.

Abe Lincoln: Log Cabin to White House by Sterling North. Random House, 1956.

THE LIFE AND TIMES OF LOUISA MAY ALCOTT The rich lore that has grown up around such a person as Lincoln is not available for most of the other Americans we might study. We will need to search a little harder, therefore, and also to recognize the limitations as we begin a study of the life and times of Louisa May Alcott.

Born in 1832 on November 29th, Louisa May Alcott grew up in the warmth of a loving family created by Abba May and Bronson Alcott, a philosopher-educator with ideas ahead of his time. It is this family life about which Louisa wrote effectively that gained her fame in her own time and has caused her books to retain interest for contemporary young people.

A natural place to begin a study of this talented writer is the fine biography *Invincible Louisa* (Little, Brown, 1933) by Cornelia Meigs, who won the Newbery award for this book in 1934. Throughout the biography we have a picture of Louisa as a strong, independent person, an excellent model for young women today. Louisa fought for the right of young people to earn their living as they chose, for well she knew the painful struggles required for a woman to succeed as a writer at a time when "nice women" didn't work. Louisa never married, and aside from her adolescent crush on Ralph Waldo Emerson, a family friend, there is no indication that she was ever interested in marrying. When her sister Anna married, she wrote: "Very sweet and pretty; but I would rather be a free spinster and paddle my own canoe."

An interesting contrast can be made between this outstanding biography and another well-written book about the Alcott family "as seen through the eyes of 'Marmee,' mother of *Little Women*." Told in the first person, *We Alcotts* (Atheneum, 1968) was written by Aileen Fisher and Olive Rabe who also wrote *We Dickinsons*. "Since most of the responsibility for keeping the Alcott household together rested on the shoulders of Abba May Alcott . . . it seemed to us appropriate to tell the story of the family from her point of view," wrote the authors of this book. The story they tell is highly readable:

---

* For younger children.

I shall never forget the 8th of August, 1827, the day I first met Mr. Alcott. I was visiting my brother, the Reverend Samuel May, at his parsonage in Connecticut, as an escape from the strangeness of my old home in Boston after my father's second marriage. Things had not been going too well for me. I no longer felt needed by my father. My two sisters had married and established homes of their own, and my brother Sam, upon whom I depended for intellectual companionship, no longer lived in Boston. I had no occupation. Though I could play the piano and sing, in the tradition of the May family, I was not accomplished enough to think of making music a career.

The facts are the same, but the style of writing, the use of dialogue, the greater development of character as the fictionalized biography progresses, lends more of a story element that will appeal to young readers. It is enlightening also to compare the recounting of specific incidents, for example, Abby's hostility toward Mr. Lane, who tried to interest her husband in joining a community that advocated celibacy, and would, therefore, mean a separation of the family. In *We Alcotts,* Abba is seen taking the initiative in calling a family council, which included Anna and Louisa, to decide if they would continue following Mr. Lane's "disruptive theories"; they decide together "that about all we had of any value was each other." In *Invincible Louisa,* "Bronson called a family council and laid the matter before them all." Abba, as usual, does not venture an opinion for herself or the children. There are many such instances that can be compared in these two books. Children can discuss how biographers work and on what they base their writing.

Although Louisa wrote during her earlier years, *Little Women* did not appear until 1868 when she was thirty-four. One of her first stories was shown to a well-known publisher who said, "Tell Louisa to stick to her teaching. She is never going to be a writer." Undaunted, Louisa declared, "I will *not* stick to my teaching; I will be a writer. And I will write for his magazine too." The books she wrote were received with great acclaim, for young people had little of this kind of literature available to them. Selected editions of *Eight Cousins, Little Men,* and *Little Women* that are still enjoyed by young people today include:

Eight Cousins (first published in 1874)

Little, Brown (Orchard House edition). Illustrated in color by Hattie Longstreet Price.

World (Rainbow Classics). Illustrated by C. B. Falls; introduction by May Lamberton Becker.

Little Men (first published in 1871)

Grosset & Dunlap (Illustrated Junior Library). Illustrated by Douglas W. Gorsline; subtitle: *Life at Plumfield with Jo's Boys.*

Macmillan (The Macmillan Classics). Illustrated by Paul Hogarth; afterword by Clifton Fadiman.

Little Women (first published in 1868)

Thomas Y. Crowell. Illustrated by Barbara Cooney.

Little, Brown (Centennial edition). Illustrated in color by Jessie Wilcox Smith; new introduction by Cornelia Meigs.

For more information about Louisa and the time in which she lived, students will need to search out books about other people who lived at the same time. Catherine Owens Peare, for example, has written a biography of Louisa, *Louisa May Alcott, Her Life* (Holt, 1954), for younger children, and also *Henry Wadsworth Longfellow* (Holt, 1935), a biography of one of the Alcotts' family friends. Emerson, Thoreau, the Peabody sisters, and Emily Dickinson are other noted people living at that time about whom information is available. A particularly good discussion of the history of this period is provided by Suzanne Hilton in *The Way It Was—1876* (Westminster, 1975), well-researched history written with verve and spontaneity for young people.

FOCUSING ON A THEME

Another interesting approach to use in the social studies is a study focused on a theme, such as Sports in America or American Music. This approach offers an opportunity to feature the historical development and the contributions of specific groups important in our society, such as native Americans, Mexican-Americans, or American women. For literature to support such studies we naturally turn to biography. Some of the finest of contemporary writing is in the category of biography or autobiography. Biography as a genre for young people has also grown as publishing companies have produced biographies for even the youngest readers. Often these books are part of a publisher's series produced to meet the demand for biographies about famous people of current interest or to meet a recognized societal need such as biographies about black Americans. The writing in most cases is adequate, but not outstanding in the books thus produced. Few children's biographies equal the quality, for example, of *Invincible Louisa*.

One biography that does stand out is *Fighting Shirley Chisholm* (Dial, 1975) by James Haskins, an excellent choice for junior high school readers. Shirley Chisholm—honest, courageous, outspoken—stands out herself, of course, as the first black woman to serve in the United States Congress, and the first black woman, the first *woman,* to try for the nomination as President of the United States. Included in this biography is much information about the work of a member of the House, the problems a woman must cope with, and decisions about controversial issues.

In selecting books for young people we can often borrow good adult literature. *Blackberry Winter; My Earlier Years* (Morrow, 1972), anthropologist Margaret Mead's exciting autobiography, can be enjoyed by good readers in the middle and junior school. Here is a fascinating story of a contemporary woman who defied conventions long before there was much support for women. She serves today as a model of a person who has made distinctive contributions to the field of anthropology. Writing clearly and vividly, Margaret Mead has many stories to tell about her work as an anthropologist and her own growth as a woman.

Another such book is novelist and teacher Sylvia Ashton-Warner's autobiography, *Myself* (Simon and Schuster, 1967). Students might also enjoy her earlier work, *Teacher* (Simon and Schuster, 1963), which tells of her teaching experiences with Maori children in New Zealand. In both books the classroom plays a major part, well described by an able author and an exciting teacher.

These biographies of women who have made distinctive contributions could be used in a study focused on contributions of American women. Many outstanding women—Mary McLeod Bethune, Jane Addams, Rachel Carson—are the subjects of biographies for young people. In addition to the titles already discussed, look for the following titles (suitable for fourth grade and up):

Clara Barton

Boylston, Helen Dore. *Clara Barton, Founder of the American Red Cross.* Random House, 1955.

Mary McLeod Bethune

Sterne, Emma Gelders, *Mary McLeod Bethune.* Knopf, 1957.

Rachel Carson

Sterling, Philip. *Sea and Earth; The Life of Rachel Carson.* Thomas Y. Crowell, 1970.

Mary Cassatt

Wilson, Ellen. *American Painter in Paris: A Life of Mary Cassatt.* Farrar, Straus & Giroux, 1971.

Willa Sibert Cather

Franchere, Ruth. *Willa.* Thomas Y. Crowell, 1958.

Lydia Maria Child

Meltzer, Milton. *Tongue of Flame: The Life of Lydia Maria Child.* Thomas Y. Crowell, 1965.

Shirley Chisholm

Brownmiller, Susan. *Shirley Chisholm.* Doubleday, 1970.

Charlotte Forten

Douty, Esther M. *Charlotte Forten: Free Black Teacher.* Garrard, 1971.

Elizabeth Freeman

Felton, Harold W. *Mumbet: The Story of Elizabeth Freeman.* Dodd, Mead, 1970.

Dr. Connie Guion

Campion, Nardi Reeder. *Look to This Day!* Little, Brown, 1965.

Frances Anne Kemble

Scott, John Anthony. *Fanny Kemble's America.* Thomas Y. Crowell, 1973.

Mary Todd Lincoln

Randall, Ruth Painter. *I Mary.* Little, Brown, 1959.

Juliette Low

Pace, Mildred. *Juliette Low.* Scribner, 1947.

Davidson, Margaret. *The Story of Eleanor Roosevelt.* Four Winds Press, 1969.

Bessie Smith

Moore, Carman. *Somebody's Angel Child; The Story of Bessie Smith.* Thomas Y. Crowell, 1970.

Ellen Alicia Terry

Fecher, Constance. *Bright Star; A Portrait of Ellen Terry.* Farrar, Straus & Giroux, 1970.

Sojourner Truth

Bernard, Jacqueline. *Journey toward Freedom: The Story of Sojourner Truth.* Norton, 1967.

Harriet Tubman

Lawrence, Jacob. *Harriet and the Promised Land.* Windmill, 1968.

Martha Washington

Vance, Marguerite. *Martha, Daughter of Virginia; The Story of Martha Washington.* Dutton, 1947.

Narcissa Prentiss Whitman

Eaton, Jeanette. *Narcissa Whitman: Pioneer of Oregon.* Harcourt, 1941.

Frances Willard

Judson, Clara Ingram. *Pioneer Girl.* Rand McNally, 1939.

If you plan a similar study in the field of sports, you will also find a rich offering. Football players currently starring on major teams are featured in such biographies as *Roger Staubach: A Special Kind of Quarterback* (Putnam, 1974) by George Sullivan. Included is much of the excitement of the game and an introduction to many players of renown as the readers follow the exploits of this Dallas Cowboy star. A similar title in this series is *O. J.: The Story of Football's Fabulous O. J. Simpson* (Putnam, 1974) by Bill Libby, which relates the story of this football hero who played for USC's Trojans and the Buffalo Bills.

Baseball, too, has its heroes who are eulogized in such biographies as *Jackie Robinson: Baseball's Giant Fighter* (Garrard, 1974), a very easy book to read by Sam and Beryl Epstein. *The Leo Durocher Story* (Messner, 1955) is by Gene Schoor, who has written more than ten sports biographies. *Satchel Paige: All-Time Baseball Great* (Putnam, 1974), by Robert Rubin, describes this pitcher's fastball: "It starts out like a baseball, but when it gets to the plate, it looks like a marble."

The Olympics followed by millions of viewers on television have inspired whole series of biographies for young readers. One series, published by Creative Education, includes such titles as *Mark Spitz; The Shark* (1974) by James Tolsen, a natural follow-up to this swimmer's winning of seven gold medals. A book featuring a woman swimmer is *Shane Gould: Olympic Swimmer* (EMC, 1974) by Linda Jacobs, part of another extensive series of easy biographies, called Women Who Win. Women in sports is a new interest exemplified by *Billie Jean King* (Grossett, 1974) by Jim Baker, an easy-to-read biography for young readers.

Music and musicians are featured in biographies for children, for example, Woody Guthrie, in *A Mighty Hard Road: The Woody Guthrie Story* (McGraw-Hill, 1970) by Henrietta Yurchenco assisted by Marjorie Guthrie. An interesting publisher's note appears at the front of this book:

Woody Guthrie had his own way of seeing things and talking about them. His language was informal, his spelling often unorthodox, but there was always a reason behind his seeming casualness. In quoting various selections from Woody's writings, the publisher has thought it best to print them exactly as they appeared, without changes.

An excellent collection of the biographies of five singers is *Big Star Fallin' Mama; Five Women in Black Music* by Hettie Jones (Viking, 1974). Included are short biographies of Ma Rainey, Bessie Smith, Mahalia Jackson, Billie Holiday, and Aretha Franklin. There are photographs of each singer as well as pictures of incidents in their lives. An excellent annotated list of "Other Notable Women in Black Music" is at the end of the book. Aretha Franklin expresses the feeling achieved by this collection: "Everybody who's livin' has problems and desires just as I do. When the fellow on the corner has something bothering him, he feels the same way I do. When we cry, we all gonna cry tears, and when we laugh, we have to smile."

We need more good biographies about contemporary Americans for young people. Obviously those about contemporary figures are harder to write because there is no extensive literature from which to draw. The author does, however, have the advantage of being able to interview the subject. Additional useful biographies of twentieth-century Americans include:

Angel of Appalachia: Martha Berry by Elisabeth P. Myers. Messner, 1968.

Roberto Clemente: Batting King by Arnold Hano. Putnam, 1973.

The Picture Life of Ralph J. Bunche by Margaret B. Young. Watts, 1968.

Amelia Earhart: First Lady of the Air by Jerry Seibert. Houghton Mifflin, 1960.

Walt Disney: Master of Make-believe by Elizabeth Rider Montgomery. Garrard, 1971.

Harry Truman by Doris Faber. Abelard, 1973.

The Mayo Brothers by Jane Goodsell. Thomas Y. Crowell, 1972.

Leonard Bernstein by Molly Cone. Thomas Y. Crowell, 1970.

Wilt Chamberlain by Kenneth Rudeen. Thomas Y. Crowell, 1970.

Genius with a Scalpel: Harvey Cushing by Justin F. Denzel. Messner, 1971.

Malcolm X by Arnold Adoff. Thomas Y. Crowell, 1970.

The Life and Words of John F. Kennedy by James Playsted Wood. Doubleday, 1964.

Martin Luther King: The Peaceful Warrior by Ed Clayton. Prentice-Hall, 1968.

Annie Sullivan by Mary Malone. Putnam, 1971.

Joe Namath, Maverick Quarterback by Phil Berger. Cowles, 1969.

❦ *ACTIVITIES TO HELP YOU EXPLORE* Choose one of these activities as you probe into biographies written for young people.

1. Write five Who Am I? cards based on specific biographies that you could use with children in upper elementary grades. You might write something like this:

I was the last member of the Yahi Indian Tribe. We managed to survive in California undiscovered until the twentieth century. Can you imagine how we hid to avoid hunters who came close to our homes? Theodora Kroeber wrote my story. WHO AM I?

Ishi.   *Ishi, Last of His Tribe*
          Theodora Kroeber. Parnassus Press, 1964.

2. Compare two biographies about the same person. Note similarities and differences in how each author handled the subject. Compare the writing style and devices used to make the presentation more interesting. How is illustration helpful in presenting information?

TEACHING THE SOCIAL STUDIES WITH TRADE BOOKS

Frequently teachers decry the fact that social science textbooks are too difficult for most of the children to read. One solution to this problem seems obvious: use the many fine library books, both nonfiction and fiction, that have been prepared for children. Begin by consulting a booklist such as *Children's Books to Enrich the Social Studies; For the Elementary Grades* prepared by Helen Huus for the National Council for the Social Studies, 1966. *The Children's Catalog,* with its annual supplements, is an excellent source of more up-to-date material than can usually be found in any other published lists.

Not only does children's literature provide information, but children experience the enjoyment of an attractive book. Usually, also, the writing in these books is better than in a textbook. It is wise to select books that are up-to-date in order to avoid stereotyping and to provide accurate information.

Experiences aimed at promoting social studies understandings might be organized in various ways. A class might decide to develop an area study to find out as much as possible about one area, a country perhaps, with everyone focusing attention on that country. The problems approach is a second way of organizing a study. A third interesting approach is to read fiction set in different countries that gives insight into how children live around the world and provides information about geography and history, too. Helen Huus recommends the "saturation technique," in which you saturate the classroom environment with so many excellent books that children cannot possibly avoid finding a suitable book on the topic or area being explored.

THE AREA STUDY

A useful kind of classroom study focuses on one area—a country, a region, a state, or even a whole continent. Each group of students selects one segment of the total study to investigate. Books can serve to develop understanding of the peoples of different parts of the world. Children can read, for example, both fiction and nonfiction, poetry and prose, picture books and more advanced books as they explore a single country. Children's books provide information about all aspects of life, for instance:

People—Origins, customs, relationships

Language—Writing, borrowed words

Geography—Cities, rivers, mountains

History—Early beginnings, wars, contemporary events

Folklore—Stories, beliefs, myths

Two resources that will aid you in exploring books about other countries have been prepared by Virginia Haviland, Children's Librarian with the Library of Congress.

Haviland, Virginia, ed. *Children's Books of International Interest; A Selection from Four Decades of American Publishing.* American Library Association, 1972.

Haviland, Virginia, comp. *The Wide World of Children's Books; An Exhibition for International Book Year.* Library of Congress, 1972. (From Sup. of Documents, U.S. Gov't., 50¢)

In this section we present the possibilities for a study focused on a whole continent, Africa, and a single country, China.

EXPLORING A CONTINENT: AFRICA If the class is studying Africa, each group might focus on one country—Algeria, Nigeria, Tanzania, Kenya, Rhodesia. Saturate the classroom with material about Africa. Sources of information about Africa include:

Africa: An Annotated List of Printed Materials Suitable for Children. Information Center on Children's Cultures, UNICEF, 1968.
Selected and annotated by a joint committee of the American Library Association's Children's Services Division and the African-American Institute; lists recommended materials as well as that categorized as "Not Recommended or Special"; gives grade levels; organized by countries.

Studying Africa in Elementary and Secondary Schools by Leonard Kenworthy. Teachers College, 1965.
Includes suggestions for curricula at varied grade levels; discusses stereotypes; provides activities and experiences.

For additional up-to-date information write to: Africa Agency, 639 Massachusetts Avenue, Suite 335, Cambridge, Massachusetts 02139. Following is a list one interaction group compiled of materials about the African country Ghana:

Fiction

Courlander, Harold and Albert Prempah. *The Hat-Shaking Dance and Other Tales from Ghana.* Harcourt Brace Jovanovich, 1957. *(Folklore)*

McDermott, Gerald. *Anansi the Spider.* Holt, 1972.

Nonfiction

Gidal, Sonia and Tim. *My Village in Ghana.* Pantheon, 1969.

Hutchinson, Alfred. *Road to Ghana.* John Day, 1960.

Lobsenz, Norman M. *The First Book of Ghana.* Watts, 1960 *(Somewhat dated)*

Sale, J. Kirk. *The Land and People of Ghana.* Lippincott, 1972.

Schloat, G. Warren, Jr. *Kwaku; A Boy of Ghana.* Knopf, 1962.

*Sutherland, Efua. *Playtime in Africa.* Atheneum, 1966.

Zemba, Lydia Verona. *Ghana in Pictures.* Sterling, 1966.

EXPLORING ONE COUNTRY: CHINA   A class that decided to study China could set out on a discovery trip to locate as many sources of information about China as possible. Some will discover facts about the

---

* For younger children.

country's development, while others read stories set in China that reveal information about family life. Still others might search out stories of Chinese people living in the United States.

Each student, thus, contributes to the class study and to the body of information to be shared. Discovery of a book such as *You Can Write Chinese* (Viking, 1945) by Kurt Wiese leads students to try writing a few of these graceful characters. Perhaps a local parent can be invited to demonstrate Chinese writing and to help students in their efforts.

An effective way to share Chinese folklore is to read the charming picture book (even to older students) *Tikki Tikki Tembo* (Holt, 1968). After reading this retelling of an ancient pourquoi tale by Arlene Mosel, share the film (Weston Woods), which features the splendid illustrations by Blair Lent and explains why "from that day to this the Chinese have always thought it wise to give all their children little, short names instead of great long names." (See the illustration at the beginning of Chapter 5.)

Other sources of Chinese folklore include the following:

Tales of a Chinese Grandmother by Frances Carpenter. Doubleday, 1937.

The Black Heart of Indri adapted by Dorothy Hoge. Scribner, 1966.

Favorite Children's Stories from China and Tibet by Lotta C. Hume. Tuttle, 1962.

The Milky Way and Other Chinese Folk Tales by Adet Lin. Harcourt Brace Jovanovich, 1961.

*The Emperor and the Kite by Jane Yolen. World, 1957.

Chinese poetry is another aspect of the culture of China that young people can explore. Robert Wyndham has edited *Chinese Mother Goose Rhymes* (World, 1968), an attractive volume of authentic verses that are read vertically in the Chinese custom. *The Moment of Wonder* (Dial, 1964), which includes poetry of both China and Japan, is a beautiful book encompassing the ancient as well as contemporary poets compiled by Richard Lewis.

As part of this exploration of China, the teacher can select a story to read aloud that will add interest and information for the whole class. Suggested titles are the following:

Chrisman, Arthur. *Shen of the Sea.* Dutton, 1953. *(Short stories)*

---

* For younger children.

DeJong, Meindert. *The House of Sixty Fathers*. Illustrated by Maurice Sendak. Harper, 1956.

*Flack, Marjorie. *The Story about Ping*. Viking, 1933.

*Handforth, Thomas. *Mei Li*. Doubleday, 1938.

Jones, Adrienne. *Ride the Far Wind*. Little, Brown, 1964.

*Lattimore, Eleanor. *Peachblossom*. Harcourt Brace Jovanovich, 1943.

*Liang. Yen. *Happy New Year*. Lippincott, 1961.

Merrill, Jean. *The Superlative Horse*. Scott, 1961.

Ritchie, Alice. *The Treasure of Li-Po*. Harcourt Brace Jovanovich, 1949. (*Short stories*)

Treffinger, Carolyn. *Li Lun, Lad of Courage*. Abingdon, 1947.

*Wiese, Kurt. *Fish in the Air*. Viking, 1948.

Older students will be interested in such nonfiction as *The Chinese in America* (Macmillan, 1972), in which Betty Lee Sung gives an excellent overview of the contributions of the Chinese in settling the West as well as pictures of contemporary Chinese-Americans. This approach may lead children to discover other books about Chinese in the United States, for example:

Judson, Clara. *The Green Ginger Jar; A Chinatown Mystery*. Houghton Mifflin, 1949.

*Martin, Patricia Miles. *The Rice Bowl Pet*. Illustrated by Ezra Jack Keats. Thomas Y. Crowell, 1962.

*Politi, Leo. *Moy Moy*. Scribner, 1960.

Robertson, Keith. *The Year of the Jeep*. Viking, 1968.

Informative nonfiction is also available.

Archer, Jules. *The Chinese and the Americans*. Hawthorn Books, 1976

Buell, Hal. *The World of Red China*. Dodd, Mead, 1967.

Caldwell, John C. *Let's Visit China Today*. John Day, 1973.

Hall, Elvajean. *Hong Kong,* Rand McNally, 1967.

Herrmanns, Ralph. *Lee Lan Flies the Dragon Kite*. Harcourt Brace Jovanovich, 1962.

———
* For younger children.

Sasek, Miroslav. *This Is Hong Kong*. Macmillan, 1965.

Schloat, G. Warren. *Fay Gow: A Boy of Hong Kong*. Knopf, 1964.

Spencer, Cornelia. *The Yangtze, China's River Highway*. Garrard, 1963.

Spencer, Cornelia. *The Land and People of China*. Lippincott, 1972.

What else can a class do as a way of exploring China? The possibilities are endless.

1. Put on a Chinese puppet play.
   "Chop-Chin and the Golden Dragon" in *7 Plays & How to Produce Them* by Moyne Rice Smith. Walck, 1968.
2. Read a Chinese version of *Cinderella*.
   "A Chinese Cinderella" in *Favorite Children's Stories from China and Tibet* by Lotta Carswell Hume. Tuttle, 1962.
3. Cook fried rice or other Chinese favorites.
   Eating and Cooking Around the World; Fingers before Forks by Erick Berry. John Day, 1963.
4. Celebrate Chinese New Year.
   Holidays Around the World by Joseph Gaer. Little, Brown, 1953.

A CONTEMPORARY PROBLEMS APPROACH

The social studies offer rich topics of study that are not always geographic or historical in focus. The contemporary problems approach touches on topics that are intensely interesting to young people growing up—unemployment and poverty, ecology, changing lifestyles, the urban environment.

Incorporating materials that treat such topics in the reading program will help children learn to read nonfiction that involves skills that are sometimes ignored. Although we expect children to gain an increasing amount of knowledge from textbooks that carry a heavy concept load, we need to teach the new skills involved in reading nonfiction such as scanning or using an index.

For a problems approach have children form small groups based on a common interest rather than their abilities to read. Members of each group should agree on a statement of the question they want to investigate and then begin searching for material that will provide the information they need. They can share their findings in various ways—a play, panel discussion, bulletin board display, exhibit, a book, and so on. Here are a number of sample questions that groups might choose to research with examples of books that would be available for each topic:

1. How can cities be made better places to live?

    Association for Childhood Education. *Told under the City Umbrella.* Macmillan, 1972. *(Stories by children)*

    Corcos, Lucille. *The City Book.* Golden Press, 1972.

    Hiller, Carl. *Babylon to Brasilia: The Challenge of City Planning.* Little, Brown, 1972.

    *Pitts, Valerie. *Let's Find out about the City.* Watts, 1968.

    Tannenbaum, Beulah and Myra Stillman. *City Traffic.* McGraw-Hill, 1972.

2. Why can't women do some of the things men do?

    Gauber, Ruth. *Felisa Rincón de Gautier: The Mayor of San José.* Thomas Y. Crowell, 1972.

    Ingraham, Claire and Leonard. *An Album of Women in American History.* Watts, 1972.

    Noble, Iris. *Israel's Golda Meir: Pioneer to Prime Minister.* Messner, 1972.

    Ross, Pat. *Young and Female.* Random House, 1972.

3. What is Vietnam like?

    Buell, Hal. *Viet Nam; Land of Many Dragons.* Dodd, Mead, 1968.

    Cooke, David D. *Vietnam; The Country, the People.* Norton, 1968.

    Graham, Gail. *Cross-Fire: A Vietnam Novel.* Pantheon, 1972.

    Lifton, Betty Jean and Thomas Fox. *Children of Vietnam.* Atheneum, 1972.

    Nielsen, Jon, with Kay Nielsen. *Artist in South Vietnam.* Messner, 1969.

4. Are we really in danger of running out of important resources?

    Hungerford, Harold R. *Ecology; The Circle of Life.* Childrens Press, 1971.

    Massini, Giancario. *S. O. S. Save Our Earth.* Grosset & Dunlap, 1972.

    Millard, Reed. *Natural Resources: Will We Have Enough for Tomorrow's World?* Messner, 1972.

---

* For younger children.

Remember that children learn to read by reading, so our task is to provide situations that encourage reading. Exploring self-selected research topics can lead young people to the joys of discovering new information through books.

❦ *ACTIVITIES TO EXPLORE* Choose one of these activities as you prepare teaching materials you can use in the classroom.

1. Investigate stories of American children living abroad in different countries, for example:

   France

   Brink, Carol Ryrie. *Family Sabbatical*. Viking, 1956.

   Italy

   *Politi, Leo. *Little Leo*. Scribner, 1951.

   Lebanon

   Rugh, Belle D. *Crystal Mountain*. Houghton Mifflin, 1955.

   Scotland

   Willard, Barbara. *Storm from the West*. Harcourt Brace Jovanovich, 1963.

   Plan a classroom study around such books.

2. Focus on Childhood in Different Lands as you search out children's books that describe children's lives in different countries. Use such books as these:

   Greece

   Mayne, William. *The Glass Ball*. Dutton, 1962.

---

* For younger children.

Spain

Wojciechowska, Maia. *Shadow of a Bull*. Atheneum, 1964.

Egypt

Byars, Betsy. *The 18th Emergency*. Viking, 1973.

England

Boston, Lucy. *The Children of Green Knowe*. Harcourt, 1955.

Netherlands

DeJong, Meindert. *The Wheel on the School*. Harper, 1954.
*Williams, Jay, *The Youngest Captain*. Parents' Magazine Press, 1972.

Russia

Korinetz, Yuri. *There, Far Beyond the River*. O'Hara, 1973.

3. Search for filmed materials that could be used in conjunction with books in studies of other countries. *Red Balloon* (Lamorisse) and *Clown* (Learning), for example, are excellent films about children living in Paris.

---

* For younger children.

Arbuthnot, May Hill and Dorothy M. Broderick, comps. *Time for Stories of the Past and Present*. Scott, Foresman, 1968.

———. *Time for Biography*. Scott, Foresman, 1969.

Hotchkiss, Jeanette. *American Historical Fiction and Geography for Children and Young People*. Scarecrow Press, 1973.

Jarolimek, John. *Social Studies in Elementary Education*. Macmillan, 1974.

Metzner, Seymour. *World History in Juvenile Books; A Geographical and Chronological Guide*. Wilson, 1973.

Michaelis, John U. *Social Studies for Children in a Democracy*. Prentice-Hall, 1974.

Tiedt, Pamela L. and Iris M. Tiedt. *Multicultural Teaching: Activities, Information, and Resources*. Allyn and Bacon, 1979.

Welton, David A. and John T. Mallan. *Children and Their World*. Rand McNally, 1976.

Wise, William. *American Freedom and the Bill of Rights*. Parents' Magazine Press, 1975.

10

Nobody
Is Perfick

New and Old Directions in
Children's Literature

Title and illustration from Bernard Waber, *Nobody Is Perfick* (Houghton Mifflin, 1971). Copyright
© 1971 by Bernard Waber. Reprinted by permission of Houghton Mifflin Publishers.

Today we have a real literature for children which is continuously evolving and changing, partly in response to its own dynamism. It is a literature with distinct antecedents, which has developed its own characteristic features, its particular identity, both from its past and its correspondence to changing social conditions.

Isabelle Jan
On Children's Literature[1]

Following strict chronological development, it is more common to present the history of children's literature at the beginning of a text. The author of this book, however, has chosen to present an overview of the field after you, the reader, have become acquainted with a sufficient amount of the literature to provide you with an informed perspective. You will be better able to understand the issues involved, the need for further research, and to view trends in light of history.

The objectives in this chapter reflect the purpose of an overview of the field, thus:

1. To examine some of the controversial issues and new directions in the field of children's literature

2. To summarize the findings of research related to literature for young people and to consider the implications of these findings for classroom instruction

3. To review the development of children's literature from the earliest years through the latest multimedia contributions, with emphasis on the twentieth century

---

[1] Isabelle Jan, *On Children's Literature* (Schocken, 1974), p. 13.

As we examine the field, we will first look at new directions and controversial issues in the field of children's literature—the increasing development of varied media, the kinds of books produced, and the handling of stereotyping in children's literature. We will then review the research that has been done of reading interests, the effect of instructional practices, and the teaching of poetry. In the brief history of literature for children, a comparison of the development during the early years with growth during the twentieth century is made, and also the development of children's literature in the future is considered.

ISSUES AND DIRECTIONS IN CHILDREN'S LITERATURE

In the twentieth century the world of children's books has extended immeasurably. Books and other reading matter for children constitute "big business." New directions in children's literature reflect many of the same directions that can be observed in all of contemporary society, but at the same time we find ourselves looking again at some of the issues that have been discussed and questioned repeatedly in the past.

One direction that clearly appears in society is a greater freedom and frankness about topics that once were shunned by most people and certainly were not discussed openly in the media. Today we can read detailed discussions of sex, death, divorce, and the use of drugs in any newspaper. These topics are also being treated more realistically in books for children, and therein lies controversy.

Discussion of realism in children's books leads naturally to another issue that is not totally new, the role of the adult in children's literature. Should adults censor or control the content of children's books? Who decides what children should read? And, which books receive the coveted awards? Here, again, there is mixed opinion (of adults, of course).

Another societal concern that has greatly influenced publication of books for children is the pressure for equal rights that comes from racial and ethnic groups as well as from feminists. Publishers and authors have been criticized in terms of both racism and sexism, as researchers examine illustrations, subjects treated, and language used, making all of us more conscious of the discrimination that has existed in children's literature.

Mass media, an influence on all of society, is also part of the children's literature field. Despite the purist's attempts to consider children's literature as consisting only of printed matter, few can deny the importance of films and recordings for children, and we know that children spend more time watching television than they do reading books. A definition of *literature,* therefore, may include nonprint media as well as print.

These issues and directions are worth discussing here as we look at the field of children's literature. If we are stimulated by changes that are going on in society, we will appreciate that same sense of excitement in literature for young people.

REALISM IN CHILDREN'S BOOKS

One of the trends in children's literature that is causing some people literally to squirm is the frank treatment of such topics as sex, drugs, death, and divorce. This trend, as we have noted, follows a generally more open attitude in all aspects of society. Some persons obviously feel uncomfortable with this trend in society and, therefore, question presenting such topics to children.

Children today, however, are living in a very real world. They are much more aware of personal relationships in the home, for example, and certainly become directly involved in problems that may lead to divorce. Pretending that such problems do not exist, therefore, is scarcely helpful to a child who needs support and understanding. Just realizing that other people, who may be book characters, have similar problems is supportive.

It does take a skillful author to handle a topic like death without strain, but good writers are able to meet the challenge. In *The Peppermint Pig* (Lippincott, 1975), for instance, Nina Bawden provides a fine story that depicts human relationships realistically and sensitively. When Johnny, the little runt pig, becomes a huge animal that gets into trouble, Mother decides rationally to send him to the butcher. Naturally, nine-year-old Poll is upset and finds it difficult to accept this decision. Here is an experience that children can understand, for many have known the death of a pet.

Another realistic treatment of death is Doris Buchanan Smith's *A Taste of Blackberries* (Thomas Y. Crowell, 1973), which was awarded the Georgia Children's Book Award in 1974. This author describes the death of a young boy that might have been averted if his friend had run for help. When Jamie reacts violently to a bee sting, the unnamed friend thinks he is just clowning and runs away. Only later does the child learn that Jamie was dying. How would you feel if you were the character in this story? Guilty and unhappy, of course, but life does go on, much as Doris Smith describes it.

Realism becomes increasingly noticeable as we move into material for adolescent students. Such books as Maia Wojciechowska's *Tuned Out* (Harper & Row, 1968) may be a little difficult for adults to accept, probably because we don't want to acknowledge the fact that young people are really using marijuana and LSD as Kevin is in this book. Sixteen-year-old Jim also finds it hard to believe that his older brother is into drugs, and he reveals his feelings in a journal, simply and effectively. The journal begins with the line, "One day I ought to find out how it is with other kids," which is exactly the purpose the book may serve.

Mia Alone by Gunnel Beckman (Viking, 1975), which was translated from the Swedish book *Tre Veckor över Tiden* by Joan Tate, deals with yet another contemporary problem, adolescent pregnancy and abortion. Although Mia is a high school student, adolescents of all ages share this concern. This book also treats, less directly, other important societal problems, including divorce and the life of aged people in an old people's home.

Again, we adults who do control the literature that children read, need to think seriously about our attitudes toward realism for young people. How are our own values revealed by our objections? If we object to certain books, just what specifically are we objecting to? Is it poor writing? Is it language that we have been taught "nice" people don't use? Before we censure or censor books for children, we might consider these matters.

ADULT DOMINANCE OF CHILDREN'S LITERATURE

The field of children's literature is dominated by adults. Most children's books are written by adults, and the books are edited and produced by grownups. Teachers, parents, and librarians select books for children, and it is chiefly the adult who buys children's books. Public school teachers and professors study children's literature; they comment on books and evaluate them. They are involved in giving awards to authors and illustrators who develop books for children. Seldom are the children in evidence, however, except as consumers. This in itself might work out all right for children, but there are certain pitfalls that we should examine.

AWARD BOOKS Many book awards are given each year. An interesting publication initiated by the Children's Book Council is *Children's Books: Awards & Prizes,* which is revised biennially. This compilation of honors awarded in the children's book field by organizations, schools, universities, publishers, and newspapers includes international and for-

*Reproduced by permission of Jan
Adkins*

eign awards in English-speaking countries. In general, the awards are decided upon by adults; an exception is the Georgia Children's Book
Award established in 1969. A number of questions can be discussed regarding award books, for example:

1. Aren't some of the honor books each year just as good as the ones
    selected for top honors?

2. Ought all children to read these award books?

3. Should librarians use these lists as buying guides?

4. Are award books the books children choose to read?

Buying from award lists exclusively is, of course, an uninspired way of
selecting books for any purpose. Certainly these lists can serve as guides,

but to buy every book on the list of Newbery or Caldecott winners, for example, is far from advisable. Consider that books selected in the 1930s for these particular lists were written in a different time, reflecting the society, education, and the needs and interests of children at that time. Before being purchased, these books must be evaluated in terms of how well they speak to children today, how well they have transcended time.

In many instances award books appear to represent what adults think children ought to like, books that will be good for them. All of us appreciate quality in children's books, but there is a real question about how many children will choose voluntarily to read Paula Fox's fine historical novel *Slave Dancer,* which won the Newbery award in 1974. On the other hand, I would guess that many will discover and enjoy *Julie of the Wolves* by Jean Craighead George, which won the award in 1973. Certainly we adults made a mistake, in my opinion, when we overlooked *Charlotte's Web* in 1953, which was listed as an Honor Book for the Newbery award, while Ann Nolan Clark's *Secret of the Andes* was given the award. Perhaps the time has come to reexamine the intent of such awards, as they were originally established years ago, and to make some adjustment in light of current needs.

We should be aware, too, of certain characteristics of specific award lists. Both the Newbery list and the National Book Award (extended in 1969 to include juveniles) tend to be given to books for older children. Because the Caldecott award is for illustrations, quite naturally it is a list more suitable for primary grade readers, as are other awards established for excellence in graphics, such as the Brooklyn Art Books for Children Citations or the Printing Industries of America Graphic Arts awards. Some groups cite books that achieve specified purposes, such as promoting human relations—the Coretta Scott King Award or the Council on Interracial Books for Children awards. Other awards focus on authors from certain geographic areas, for example, Australian Books of the Year awards or Commonwealth Club of California awards.

A list of many of the awards now being given to books for children is included in the Appendix. The list grows each year, however, as there is a trend toward establishing new awards that recognize good books for children. For example, an award was initiated in 1976 by the California Association of Teachers of English, who honored Theodor Seuss Geisel with a student-made statue of Thidwick.

THE CLASSICS The question of books we term *classic* is another aspect of children's literature that we need to rethink. We need to consider, for example, who labels books as *classics* and why. Who is examining these books in light of the needs of children today? As Alice Jordan noted, there seems to be a perpetual dilemma:

Until a book has weathered at least one generation and is accepted in the next, it can hardly be given the rank of classic and no two people are likely to be in full agreement as to what should be included in a list of them.[2]

Following is a list of twenty-five titles that are frequently referred to as *classics:*[3]

Pinocchio by Carlo Lorenzini (Collodi, pseud.)

Hans Brinker or the Silver Skates by Mary Mapes Dodge

Robinson Crusoe by Daniel Defoe

Household Tales by Jacob and Wilhelm Grimm

Heidi by Johanna Spyri

Treasure Island by Robert Louis Stevenson

Tales by Hans Christian Andersen

Alice in Wonderland by Lewis Carroll

Gulliver's Travels by Jonathan Swift

Huckleberry Finn by Samuel L. Clemens (Mark Twain, pseud.)

Little Women by Louisa May Alcott

Swiss Family Robinson by Johann Wyss

Black Beauty by Anna Sewell

Kidnapped by Robert Louis Stevenson

Tom Sawyer by Samuel L. Clemens (Mark Twain, pseud.)

Arabian Nights, author unknown

Two Years Before the Mast by Richard Henry Dana

---

[2] Alice M. Jordan, "Children's Classics," *Horn Book Magazine* 23 (February 1947): 4.
[3] Adapted from such sources as James S. Smith, *A Critical Approach to Children's Literature* (McGraw-Hill, 1967), pp. 117–18.

The Water Babies by Charles Kingsley

Jungle Books by Rudyard Kipling

Tales from Shakespeare by Charles and Mary Lamb

At the Back of the North Wind by George MacDonald

The Odyssey by Homer

Toby Tyler by James Otis

A Child's Garden of Verses by Robert Louis Stevenson

Twenty Thousand Leagues under the Sea by Jules Verne[3]

Which of these twenty-five books have you read? Are there some titles that do not sound at all familiar? As we examine such a list, the question that immediately comes to mind is: Are these books that every child will enjoy or gain some benefit from?

The books are all old, written in a different time. Only a few were written expressly for children. In listing classics, only those books that advanced readers could handle are usually included, so that books for young children are automatically excluded except for tales such as *The Ugly Duckling* by Hans Christian Andersen or *How the Elephant Got a Trunk* by Rudyard Kipling.

Certainly some students still read *Heidi* and *Little Women* with enjoyment. Others are entranced with such adventures as *Robinson Crusoe* and *Swiss Family Robinson*. Included on this list, however, are titles that are of questionable quality. *Black Beauty,* for example, is a very sentimental horse story, a "period piece" that horse lovers still enjoy. Should we recommend, however, that all students read this book?

Labeling is always a dangerous practice, for once a label is applied, it is seldom removed. Once placed on a list of classics, therefore, a title may remain forever without reevaluation. No person can possibly read all of the books that are available today, so that we constantly make choices. Surely some of the fine contemporary titles have as much right to claim a child's attention as do *The Water-Babies, Hans Brinker,* or *Toby Tyler.* You might refer to Ann Terry's study of children's poetry preferences, which has something to say about "classics" in poetry (discussed later in this chapter).

Do we need such a list? My feeling is that we could do without the concept of classic as applied to books. It is a term and a way of thinking that has outlived its usefulness and should now be discarded. The books included in this list that deserve to be recognized will continue to delight children and to remain an active part of children's literature. The award given to "books that deserve to sit on the shelf with Alice in Wonderland," the Lewis Carroll Shelf Award, given at the University of Wisconsin, reflects this attitude.

COMBATING STEREOTYPING IN CHILDREN'S BOOKS

Never has there been so much discussion of the stereotyped images of human beings in children's books—blacks, women, American Indians, Chinese-Americans. Even to name individuals as belonging to these groups is to lose a sense of their individuality.

Maureen Mansell deals with that very point in her article "Seeing the Other Point of View."[4] She points out that stereotyping is a natural result of the thinking process that necessarily involves categorizing or classification. She writes: "Every teacher and parent knows to some extent the implication of limited understanding between groups, whether at the national or the neighborhood level." Human perception, she adds, "works to achieve well-ordered categories" in which we place all objects in our universe including people. Classification is an essential skill that we teach children as a way of comprehending, but stereotyping may result as a natural consequence of "narrow category systems and limited experience." Because it is quite literally impossible to know each individual as a discrete entity, it may be impossible to eliminate stereotyping entirely.

Assuming that we can accept this rational explanation of stereotyping, then our concern is combating the kind of categorizing that results in negative attitudes and values that are harmful to certain groups of people. The solution is not "to ban all books that present a stereotyped image." We need instead to take some positive action; we need to teach children to recognize stereotypes themselves, for there are important understandings to be developed from the earliest years. Education and increased knowledge have always been the best way to combat prejudice.

Discussion of what is presented in a book is the most effective means of helping children develop insight into feelings and needs, the similarities among people. We need to emphasize the human experience as well, as, for example, the black experience. Questions that we ask should elicit responses that demonstrate the universality of human emotions—fear, anger, hope, love—that have nothing to do with the color of a person's eyes or skin, the shape of their feet or nose, their way of speaking.

---

[4] Maureen Mansell, "Seeing the Other Point of View," *Elementary English* 52, 4 (April 1975): 505–507.

How do you think Mark felt when he had to give up his pet bear? (*Gentle Ben* by Walter Morey)

How would you feel if you had to move to a new city as the La Rosa family did? (*The Sun Train* by Renee Reggiani)

Have you ever been hurt by losing a friend? (*The New Friend* by Charlotte Zolotow)

Are there times when you can't have everything you want? (*Striped Ice Cream* by Joan M. Lexau)

Reading stories aloud is an excellent way to enable a group to talk about such important concepts. Primary grade children would enjoy, for example, *My Mother Is the Most Beautiful Woman in the World* (Lothrop, 1969), in which Becky Reyher points up the differences in individual points of view. A little lost girl is looking for her mother, but no one can help her, for none of the villagers would have described the simple peasant woman as beautiful. Young children can easily understand why the child thinks her mother is beautiful, but we can help children make this understanding explicit. The concept will be more powerful as children apply the insight to other situations. We should help them, therefore, make the generalization: People see things in different ways.

An observed stereotype might lead to a rewarding study designed to destroy the stereotype. Children who become aware of the stereotyped black characters in *Hitty, Her First Hundred Years* or *Doctor Dolittle* might discuss the question: Why are many people concerned about how the characters in these books are portrayed? The students might then search out books that present more realistic images such as *The Snowy Day, Lily of Watts,* or *The Egypt Game*.

Today we are especially concerned with investigating images of women in children's books as we realize the socializing effect such materials have. The usual depiction of women in subordinate roles behaving passively, while men are authoritive figures who behave strongly and assertively has recently been questioned. Gradually the protests have had effect as many publishers have issued directives to their editors. Today we see such new books as *The Real Me* by Betty Miles (Knopf, 1974), in which a girl fights to get a newspaper route, and her mother begins a new career—both supported by the men in the family. New biographies of women, particularly noted contemporary women, are appearing in quantity. Girls today can find new models, and they can learn to question the limitations placed on girls in books written before we became conscious of the need for freeing women from these psychological bonds. *Caddie Woodlawn* is an excellent example of a fine story that girls could enjoy today, while discussing the active role of women at that time.

The first step in combating stereotypes is to recognize their existence. We help students develop more advanced reading skills as they criticize what they read, question facts and ideas, and appreciate realistic portrayals of people who don't fit a stereotypic mold.

FILMS AND RECORDINGS OF CHILDREN'S LITERATURE

The major question regarding multimedia and literature for children seems to be: Is *literature* limited to books? If we define the word literally, of course, we will conclude that literature consists of printed matter that we read. There are those, however, who extend the interpretation of literature to include other visual, nonprint media in general, and expand the concept of *reading* to include gaining meaning from varied kinds of sensory input. They might even refer to "reading the world."

Certainly it is easy to extend the term *literature* to include filmed and recorded presentations of stories that first appeared in books. Weston Woods' filmstrip of *Arrow to the Sun,* an adaptation of Gerald McDermott's Caldecott award–winning work, would then be considered literature, as would their live-action color motion picture of *Zlateh the Goat,* written by Isaac Bashevis Singer. Television's production based on the Laura Ingalls Wilder *Little House* books would also fall into this category.

A more difficult question is whether films or other media are to be considered literature if they have no relationship to something in print, for example, a film such as *Clown* or *Rainshower.* There have been cases, indeed, when a fine film such as *The Red Balloon* has been the basis for a book, reversing the more common procedure. Admittedly, there is no right or wrong answer to this whole question. Attitudes, philosophy, and opinion affect our thinking.

Although we have not focused directly on films and recordings as literature in this text because of space limitations, there is no reason to exclude these genres from literature. Good films, records, or television programs serve to reinforce and augment the child's interest in printed matter. Listening to and viewing good stories will never replace reading them, for the delight in stories is a universal that will not be sated. We need stories presented through all kinds of media, from storytelling to videotape.

One criticism that is frequently heard is that a filmed version of a book is "not the same as the book." Perhaps the film does not follow the plot exactly; something may be omitted or the ending may be changed. We do need to recognize that filming requires different techniques, and at the same time also produces varied results. Because film is a different medium it has different limitations, but on the other hand film has outstanding contributions to make through the visual effects of fine photography. To expect a film to be identical to a book is inappropriate, therefore. Rather than dwelling on a comparison between the two, we should view each production as a valuable entity in itself and consider the qualities of each in light of the medium represented.

It is interesting to consider the reasoning behind objections to including films and records as literature. Is this mode of learning perhaps too easy? If we focus clearly on our objectives in working with children, then the medium, the means, may not be as important as the ends. Films and records can present things that books cannot. Certainly they should be accorded a place in the field of literature for children.

❦ *PROBING THE ISSUES*   Consider the following problems that you might have to deal with as you work with children's literature. Note your reactions and ideas as you prepare to discuss these issues. What would you do in each of these situations?

1. A parent demands that you remove Norma Klein's book *Mom, the Wolfman and Me* from the school library.

2. Your school district decides to establish an annual award for children's literature. You are asked to serve on the committee that will develop criteria and specify what the award will be as well as how it will be given.

3. One of your friends complains that the film of *Sounder* is not well done because it does not follow the plot in the book.

RESEARCH IN THE FIELD OF CHILDREN'S LITERATURE

What does research tell us in the field of children's literature? As teachers, it is important that we be aware of current research findings in order to consider the implications of these findings for instruction. Following is a summary of recent research related to children's literature under the topics: Reading Interests, Language and Reading Abilities, Teaching Literature, Poetry Instruction, and Effect of Mass Media. A bibliography of studies referred to in the discussion appears at the end of this section of the chapter.

READING INTERESTS

One of the most widely researched aspects of literature for any level is what do people like to read. Researching reading interests involves the immediate problem of methodology, however, for most methods have inherent fallacies or biases. Does checking books out of the library, for example, really indicate the reader's interests? What if the books are never read? The most commonly used method, the questionnaire, may skew the results through the wording of questions. The answers are always limited, too, by the reader's ability to recall books read. Keeping these hazards in mind, we will try to make a few generalizations about reading interests of elementary school children.

One of the most comprehensive statements on children's reading interests is included in the study by Purves and Beach (1972), who discuss both personal and institutional determinants of reading interests. Personal determinants such as age, sex, intelligence, reading ability, attitude, and psychological needs are the influences that we more commonly consider. We need to be aware, on the other hand, that interests can be influenced just as strongly by such practical matters as availability of books, socioeconomic and ethnic factors, peer, parent and teacher influences, and mass media.

Tibbetts (1975) summarizes studies showing the influence of teachers, peers, and home environment on the reading interests of children. Teachers can have negative or limiting influences through book selection and curriculum development, but the influence can be very positive if the teacher is enthusiastic and knowledgeable (Odland, 1970). Young children are particularly influenced by the teacher and the stories presented in the classroom. Zimet (1966) and other researchers report that peer recommendations are more influential, however, than those of adults. The home environment and parental attitudes toward reading represent another strong influence on children's reading interests (Buzzing, 1963).

Purves and Beach summarize the developmental patterns of school children's reading interests, thus:

Primary Grades

Animals, nature, fantasy (fairytales), children

Middle Grades

Adventure, daily life, familiar experiences, nature, animals

Upper Elementary

Adventure, heroes and heroines

Boys: War, travel, mystery

Girls: Love stories

Junior High School

Nonfiction, historical and mystical romance, adolescents

Boys: Science fiction, mystery, adventure, biography, history, animals, sports

Girls: Mystery, romance, animals, religion, careers, comedy, biography

A number of studies substantiate the finding that boys and girls have different reading preferences. Schulte (1967), for example, found that in grades four, five, and six, boys preferred history, historical fiction, social studies, science, and health. Girls preferred realistic fiction, biography, poetry, fanciful tales, and recreational interests.

During the elementary school years interests develop rapidly, a change that tends to take place more quickly for brighter, more sophisticated students who move toward greater realism and more mature interests. Although studies show that in general children's interests have remained similar over the years, several interests today reflect current cultural concerns, namely, stories about space travel and sports heroes. In general, we can observe the following based on research studies:

1. Children prefer fiction to nonfiction or informational material.

2. From the earliest years, children like stories, narration, action plots.

3. Children seem to have a need for both fantasy and realism.

Perhaps the most valid generalization we could make is that if we want to know about reading interests, we should consult the individual child. While it is probably true that many young children like stories about animals, they will not respond with equal enthusiasm to every animal story. Summaries of reading interests, therefore, will be useful to a librarian who is ordering two thousand books for an elementary school, but the teacher conducting an individualized reading program must be able to help Mildred, Karen, and Thomas find books that fit their individual tastes or needs today.

LANGUAGE AND READING ABILITIES

How does literature used in the classroom affect the development of basic language abilities? Does, for example, extensive oral reading affect children's reading, speaking, or writing abilities?

Children who listen extensively to stories read by a teacher or other adult show marked superiority in making inferences compared to children who read independently, according to Burgdorf's study (1966). Participants in a read-aloud program comprised of high school students reading to students in grades four, five, and six gained in reading achievement. The high school students involved, moreover, developed more positive self-concepts (Porter, 1969).

Studies indicate that 40 percent of teachers in middle grades do not read aloud to children in their classrooms (Tom, 1969). Reasons for not reading aloud by teachers included:

1. Lack of time

2. Other subjects more important

3. Lack of knowledge about children's books

Teachers might reconsider the importance of taking time for reading aloud if they knew more of such findings as those by Dorothy Cohen, who studied the effect of an extensive program of listening to stories by inner city second graders. Fifty books were read aloud during the school year to the experimental group, which improved significantly on a reading test and a vocabulary test. Sirota (1971) also found that a planned oral reading program increased the total number of books students in the experimental group read, and their reading scores increased correspondingly. Clearly hearing the "language of literature" is an essential aspect of learning to read, for book language differs greatly from the oral language that children learn to speak. They need to hear stories told in the third person, the reporting of dialogue, and the more formal syntax of the written sentence before they try to read this different kind of language.

Evertts, Sebesta, and Thompson (1967) found, furthermore, that use of the Nebraska Curriculum for English, a literature-based English curriculum, increased children's composition abilities.

The National Assessment of Reading showed that children in general were not skilled in critical and interpretive reading exercises. A number of studies relate to the teaching of these more advanced skills. Wolf, Huck, and King (1967) studied the critical reading ability of elementary school children and found children could be taught critical reading skills. This longitudinal study of children in all elementary grades also showed that children with all levels of intelligence could benefit from such instruction.

This study relates to those of questioning as a method of instruction in the classroom, which teachers could use with greater effect. Guzak (1969), studying teacher questioning at second, fourth, and sixth grade levels, concluded:

The most frequent kind of quesition requires a literal, factual answer.

Incorrect answers are often accepted as correct.

The pattern of interaction tends to be a teacher question answered by a single congruent response.

Floyd (1968) investigated questioning in the classrooms of forty teachers identified as the "best teachers" in a large city district. He found:

Teachers asked 96 percent of the questions while 802 students asked only 4 percent.

Questions seldom required problem solving; 85 percent demanded recall of factual information.

Effective use of questions by the teacher could teach more advanced skills such as comparison, analysis, and synthesis.

Such representative studies indicate that teaching does make a difference. Oral reading by the teacher can yield results; children can learn advanced reading skills appropriate to the reading of literature; and teachers do need instruction in how to use questioning techniques more effectively as they guide children toward more advanced reading skills.

TEACHING LITERATURE

There are a number of variables related to literature instruction that bear investigation. What, for example, is the effect of teaching practices? Are teachers teaching literature concepts? Are teachers prepared to teach children's literature?

Research indicates that planned instruction in literary analysis does not lead children to an understanding of literature more effectively than does unguided exploration. Morris (1970) studied the effects of planned literature instruction on a group of sixth graders. Although the control groups were given only incidental literature experiences, they performed equally well on the Literature Appreciation Test.

Teacher enthusiasm is the single most influential factor in developing student interest in reading (Sirota, 1971). Other important teacher competencies identified by Miller (1969) include:

1. Knowledge of children's books

2. Knowledge of children's interests

3. Ability to create a favorable reading climate

4. Sensitivity to literary quality

These findings are supported by Ashley (1970), who studied the likes and dislikes of children in grades four through seven and concluded that a course in children's literature was a necessity for any teacher who worked with individualized instruction. Tom's study (1969) revealed that only half the elementary teachers have had a course in children's literature within the past eight years. Only a small number of teachers participate in conferences or in-service training in children's literature.

Few teachers have implemented literature curricula in the elementary school. It is perhaps not too surprising, therefore, to find that the overwhelming majority of research related to literature instruction deals with instruction in the high school. For the most part literature appears in elementary schools as a part of the reading program or is used in conjunction with social studies instruction (Odland).

POETRY IN THE ELEMENTARY SCHOOL

That poetry is a neglected form of literature in most elementary school classrooms is the conclusion of a comprehensive study of poetry preferences in grades four through six. Conducted by Ann Terry and published in 1974 by the National Council of Teachers of English, the report includes interesting findings regarding teachers' knowledge of poetry and their attitudes toward poetry. Also enlightening is the finding that teachers' tastes do not coincide with those of children.

An early study by Mackintosh (1924) found that teachers tended to choose traditional poems. This finding is corroborated by a more recent study by Tom (1969), who identified such choices as "Paul Revere's Ride," "Stopping by Woods on a Snowy Evening," "A Visit from St. Nicholas," "Casey at the Bat," "Little Orphan Annie," "Shadow," and "Hiawatha." Represented are the poets Longfellow, Frost, Moore, Thayer, Riley, Stevenson. Notice that no contemporary poets are included, nor are the poets listed those who write especially for children.

Terry found that teachers' choices of poems to share with children are not among the most popular poems as selected by the children themselves. Eight of twenty poems were in fact unpopular with children. Such traditional poems as "Paul Revere's Ride" and "The Village Blacksmith" were among those selected by teachers, although children do not respond enthusiastically to either of these poems.

This study clearly indicates that teachers are not enthusiastic about poetry since few teachers read poetry aloud frequently. The majority of the teachers questioned also noted that children seldom write poetry in their classrooms. In general, teachers show a lack of knowledge of poetry, which no doubt affects their enthusiasm and their hesitation about using poetry with children. This in turn certainly affects children's knowledge of poetry and their attitude toward it as well.

Terry's detailed study reveals thst children in the sample showed a clear preference for poems that are funny, have a story element, and tend to be contemporary in flavor. The poem received most enthusiastically by the sample of 422 fourth, fifth, and sixth graders was "Mummy Slept Late and Daddy Fixed Breakfast" from *You Read to Me, I'll Read to You* by John Ciardi (Lippincott, 1962).

The next ten poems ranked high in appeal by these students were the following:

"Fire! Fire!" (Anonymous)

"There was an old man of Blackheath" (Anonymous)

"Little Miss Muffet" by Paul Dehn

"There once was an old kangaroo" by Edward Mullim

"There once was a young lady of Niger" (Anonymous)

"Hughbert and the Glue" by Karla Kushkin

"Betty Barter" (Anonymous)

"Lone Dog" by Irene R. McLeod

"Eletelephony" by Laura E. Richards

"Questions" by Marci Ridlow

Supporting again the finding that children like humor is the fact that they placed three limericks in this top group.

By contrast children disliked listening to haiku, although many teachers find that students enjoy writing haiku. Children tended to dislike any poetry that did not rhyme so that free verse ranked low. Imagery, too, was difficult to understand and caused students to dislike a poem. Children failed to understand the following poem, for example, although a teacher might consider it an excellent example of imagery.

SHADOWS
Patricia Hubbell

Chunks of night
Melt
In the morning sun.
One lonely one
Grows legs
And follows me
To school.

In addition to "Shadows" and various haiku, the following were among the most disliked poems:

"The Red Wheelbarrow" by William Carlos Williams

"April Rain Song" by Langston Hughes

"The Forecast" by Dan Jaffe

"Dreams" by Langston Hughes

"The Base Stealer" by Robert Francis

"December" by Sanderson Vanderbilt

"A Song of Greatness" (Chippewa Indian Song)

"Catalogue" by Carl Sandburg

"Fog" by Carl Sandburg

"This Is My Rock" by David McCord

What do these findings mean? Certainly we will not avoid exposing children to Carl Sandburg or selections by Langston Hughes that perhaps require more careful presentation. If we want to turn children on to poetry, however, we may find it wise to begin with poems that have the natural appeal of humor or rhyme, as we gradually help children learn to understand imagery. One avenue to appreciation is poetry composition, for children who are writing images or trying free verse may prove to be more interested in reading this kind of poetry written by other poets. This does entail, moreover, better preparation for teachers, for only an informed, enthusiastic teacher can successfully present poetry in the classroom.

The method of presentation is important, too, for Terry relied solely on poetry taped by a single reader for the sake of providing the same experience for all children. They listened, furthermore, to ten to twelve poems each day, hearing each poem twice; the children listened to one hundred and thirteen poems in ten days. This method of sharing poetry can scarcely compete with an enthusiastic, timely reading of, for example, "A Song of Greatness" as part of a well-developed study of native Americans.

EFFECT OF TELEVISION

"Book people" are naturally concerned about the effects that such media as television might have on children's reading. Does watching television, which children certainly do, cut down on the time spent reading? Do they prefer watching television to reading a book? What kinds of shows do they prefer? What is the effect of stereotyping in television shows that children watch? These are the questions that people who work with children's literature are asking today.

Schramm et al. (1961) analyzed various aspects of television in the lives of children. Clearly children spend more time watching television than they spend using any other form of mass media, although the use of radio increased to almost 37 percent for high school seniors. One of the most comprehensive studies of television-viewing patterns has been conducted over a period of years by Paul Witty. In 1965 he reported that first grade children view television fifteen hours per week; fifth grade children, twenty-five hours; high school students, twelve to fourteen hours. By comparison Witty found that children who view television three hours per day read only about one hour. This does not mean, however, that children are substituting television viewing for reading, because Witty also noted that children read more than they did previously. This indicates that television may be stimulating reading.

Feeley (1973), summarizing studies on television and children's reading, notes that children view television from twenty to twenty-eight hours per week. The uses children make of television are influenced by age, sex, intelligence, emotional needs, and socioeconomic status of the family. There is some evidence that vocabulary is increased through language experience viewed on television, but other studies have found a negative correlation between long hours of viewing and scholastic achievement. In another study, Feeley (1974) states that teachers should "be aware of middlegraders' consistent preference to watch rather than to read content of all types." Teachers should use, therefore, visual means of education such as films, filmstrips, pictures and educational television more frequently in all areas of the curriculum. Women on Words and Images (1975) conducted an extensive study of sex stereotyping in prime time television shows, indicating concern for the effect on children of another aspect of televised content.

Before we can draw any real conclusions regarding the effect of television viewing on children's reading of books, we need more extensive, up-to-date studies that investigate such matters as:

The effect of viewing on development of tastes and attitudes

The relationship between amount of viewing time and children's achievement in school

Ways that television is being used to stimulate learning

The long term effect of the content in shows children watch—violence, sex, stereotyping

Meanwhile, we need to be aware of television and the need for visual education that includes filmed materials and television as well as printed matter. It may be, as David Sansom points out, that we adults have a new role to play:

Children no longer have to read to combat boredom. When their legs refuse to join in any more football or skipping, they feed their souls at the television set. The love of reading must now be taught to children who, thirty years ago, would have turned naturally into booklovers.[5]

SELECTED RESEARCH REFERENCES

Buzzing, R. S. "Influences on Primary School Children's Reading." *The School Librarian and School Library Review* 2 (December 1963): 584–586.

---

[5] David Sansom, "Read This: You'll Love It," *Children's Literature in Education* (March 1971), p. 55.

Cooper, Bernice and Doyne M. Smith. "Reactions of Sixth-Grade Students to Remembered Favorite Books of Elementary School Teachers." *Elementary English* 49, 7 (November 1972): 1010–1014.

Cullinan, Beatrice, ed. "Teaching Literature to Children, 1966–1972." *Elementary English.* 49 (November 1972): 1028–1037.

Feeley, Joan T. "Television and Children's Reading." *Elementary English.* 50 (January 1973): 141–148.

_____. "Interest Patterns and Media Preferences of Middle-Grade Children" in Research Report, *Elementary English* 51 (October 1974): 1006–1008.

Floyd, William D. "Do Teachers Talk Too Much?" *Instructor* 78 (October 1968): 61–63.

Guzak, Frank J. "Teacher Questioning and Reading." *The Reading Teacher,* 21 (October 1969): 227–234.

King, Ethel M. "Critical Appraisal of Research on Children's Reading Interests, Preferences and Habits." *Canadian Education and Research Digest* 7 (December 1967): 312–326.

Kujoth, Jean S., comp. *Reading Interests of Children and Young Adults.* Scarecrow Press, 1970.

Luckenbill, W. Bernard. "American Doctoral Dissertations in Children's and Adolescents' Literature; A Working Bibliography of Dissertations Recorded in Selected Bibliographical Sources from 1930 through 1970." University of Illinois Graduate Library School. *Occasional Papers.*

Monson, Dianne L. and Bette J. Peltola, comps. *Research in Children's Literature; An Annotated Bibliography.* International Reading Association, 1976.

National Assessment of Educational Progress. *Newsletter.* (June–July 1972).

Nist, Joan S. "Media for Children: Cornucopia for Language Learning." *Elementary English* 52, 4 (April 1975): 513–514.

Norvell, George W. *The Reading Interests of Young People.* Heath, 1950.

_____. *The Reading Interests of Young People.* Michigan State University Press, 1973.

Odland, Norine. "Discovering What Children Have Learned about Literature." *Elementary English* 47, 7 (November 1970): 1072–1076.

Purves, Alan C. and Richard Beach. *Literature and the Reader: Research in*

Response to Literature, Reading Interests, and the Teaching of Literature. National Council of Teachers of English, 1972.

Schramm, Wilbur, Jack Lyle, and Edwin B. Parker. *Television in the Lives of Our Children.* Stanford University, 1961.

Terry, Ann. *Children's Poetry Preferences: A National Survey of Upper Elementary Grades.* Research Report No. 16. National Council of Teachers of English, 1974.

Tibbetts, Sylvia-Lee. "The Influence of Teachers, Peers, and Home Environment on the Reading Interests of Children" in "Research Report." *Language Arts* 52, 7 (October 1975).

Wiberg, J. Lawrence and Marion Trost. "What Children Choose to Read and What They Have to Read." *Elementary English* 48 (1970): 792–798.

Witty, Paul. "Children of the Television Era." *Elementary English* 44 (May 1967): 528–535.

──────. "Studies of the Mass Media." *Science Education* 50 (March 1966): 119–126.

Wolf, Willovene, Charlotte S. Huck, Martha L. King and Bernice D. Ellinger. *Critical Reading Ability of Elementary School Children.* Report of Project No. 5-1040. U.S. Office of Education, 1967.

Women on Words and Images. *Channeling Children: Sex Stereotyping in Prime-Time TV.* The Assn., 1975.

Zimet, Sara F. "Children's Interest and Story Preferences: A Critical Review of the Literature." *The Elementary School Journal* 67, 3 (December 1966): 122–130.

──────, ed. *What Children Read in School: Critical Analysis of Primary Reading Textbooks.* Grune & Stratton, 1972.

❧ CONSIDERING RESEARCH   Now that you have read about some of the kinds of research that are being done in the field of children's literature, complete the following:

1. List five to ten questions that you would like to know the answers to related to children's literature.

2. Select one of the questions that most interests you. Write a paragraph or two about how you might find out information to answer your question.

Would you design a questionnaire to give to children?

Could you interview students?

Could you read something to groups of children to compare the results of different presentations?

3. If you would like to carry out this study, ask your instructor for help in designing the study and in handling the data you collect.

THE DEVELOPMENT OF CHILDREN'S LITERATURE

Books read by children can be traced back to the seventh century, when such scholars as Aldhelm and Bede prepared lesson books written in Latin. Our primary interest, however, is in the books that came later, particularly the books that were written especially for young children. We shall discuss in more detail, therefore, books written in the nineteenth and twentieth centuries, literature that is still relevant to children today. We will also attempt to make some predictions about the future of children's literature.

EARLY ANTECEDENTS

The following outline provides a quick overview of the significant events in the development of children's literature prior to the eighteenth century. It is interesting to observe how meager the list is although it spans several hundred years. Until the advent of the printing press, children, like adults, had to rely on oral literature—folktales, myths, and legends.

1450   Johann Gutenberg invented the earliest form of printing press, movable type set in a mold, which was used to print the Gutenberg Bible.

1484   William Caxton's version of *Aesop's Fables* printed.

1495   Wynken de Worde's *Properties of Things,* an early science book.

1497   William Caxton's *Book of Courtesye.*

1463   Thomas Newbery's *A Booke in Englysh Metre, of the great Marchante Man called Dives Pregnaticus, very preaty for children to reade.*

1657   *Orbis Pictus (World in Pictures)* written by John Amos Comenius, the first picture book.

1671   *A Token for Children: Being an Exact Account of the Conversion, Holy and Exemplary Lives and Joyful Deaths of Several Young Children to Which Is Added: A Token for the Children of New England.*

1678   John Bunyan's *Pilgrim's Progress*, moral and religious instruction.

1696   John Bunyan's *A Book for Boys and Girls or Country Rhymes for Children*, lessons in verse.

EIGHTEENTH-CENTURY DEVELOPMENTS

During the 1800s we see the development of what can truly be called children's literature with the work of John Newbery. The production is still slight, of course, and emphasis is on moral instruction, but Newbery did add a touch of humor and entertainment for children. The following events are noteworthy during this century:

1719   Publication of Daniel Defoe's *Robinson Crusoe,* written for adults but greatly appreciated by young readers.

1726   Daniel Defoe's *Gulliver's Travels,* also written for adults.

1729   The English translation of Charles Perrault's *Contes de Ma Mère L'Oye* (Tales of Mother Goose; published in France in 1697. This is the first mention of Mother Goose.)

1744   John Newbery's *A Little Pretty Pocketbook; Intended for the Instruction and Amusement of Little Master Tommy and Pretty Miss Polly, with an Agreeable Letter to read from Jack the Giant Killer, as also a Ball and a Pincushion, the use of which will infallibly make Tommy a good Boy, and Polly a good Girl.*

1766   *The History of Little Goody Two Shoes* published by John Newbery; may have been written by Oliver Goldsmith.

1783–89   *The History of Sandford and Merton,* the story of two six-year-old boys, by Thomas Day; three parts.

1789   *Songs of Innocence* by William Blake, poetry for adults that children enjoyed.

    During this century, in addition to the above publications, there was an even larger production of textbooks. Noah Webster, for example, prepared the famous *Blue Backed Speller* in 1783, which bore the subtitle: *Simplified and Standardized American Spelling.* The *New England Primer* cautioned the young reader: "He that ne'er learns his A, B, C, For ever

THE LITTLE LIBRARY

GOODY TWO SHOES

ILLUSTRATED BY ALICE WOODWARD

POSSIBLY BY **OLIVER GOLDSMITH**

Reprinted with permission of Macmillan Publishing Co., Inc. from Goody Two Shoes illustrated by Alice Woodward. Copyright 1924 by Macmillan Publishing Co., Inc., renewed 1952 by Macmillan Publishing Co., Inc.

will a Blockhead be." Books appeared on geography, history, and arithmetic. One of the first science books, written by Isaac Watts, bore the impressive title: *The Knowledge of the Heavens and the Earth Made Easy, or the First Principles of Geography and Astronomy Explained* (1726). The textbooks produced at this time represent the beginnings of a vast publication enterprise that developed as schooling grew into the complex educational system we have today.

THE NINETEENTH CENTURY

Reflecting the industrial development that made vast changes in ways of living and thinking, children's literature burgeoned in the nineteenth century. At the beginning we see the heavy emphasis on moral teachings, but toward the end of the century there were critical changes in attitudes toward children that influenced the kinds of books produced. Such

Used with permission of The Horn Book, Inc.

philosopher-educators as John Dewey and John Locke, for example, advocated an open type of education based on experience, which no doubt helped to move authors of children's books away from the predominantly didactic approach. Literature for children reflected such societal trends as nationalism, individualism, and secularism.

During this century the body of literature written expressly for children flourished. This is the time when Mark Twain, Lewis Carroll, and Louisa May Alcott created books that have lasting appeal, a welcome addition to the literature of the day. The variety of content expanded to include not only instructional subject matter but also adventure, fantasy, poetry, animal stories, folktales, and stories about real people. Here is a brief chronology of some of the major events in the field of children's literature during the nineteenth century:

1804 *Original Poems for Infant Minds* by Ann and Jane Taylor; included "Twinkle, Twinkle, Little Star."

1806 *Tales from Shakespeare,* Charles and Mary Lamb, published in England.

1814 *Swiss Family Robinson* by J. H. Wyss translated into English.

1819 *The Sketch Book* by Washington Irving; included "Rip Van Winkle."

1822 *A Visit from St. Nicholas* by Clement Moore (*The Night before Christmas*)

1824 *Household Stories,* fairytales by Jacob and Wilhelm Grimm, appeared in English.

1826 *The Last of the Mohicans,* adult adventure, by James Fenimore Cooper.

1829 *Adventures of a Naval Officer,* first adventure story for boys, by Captain Frederick Marryat.

1846 *The Heroes* by Charles Kingsley, stories from the Greek myths; followed by *The Water-Babies* in 1863.

Midcentury

1856 *The Young Fur Trader* adventure series by Robert Ballantyne.

1865 *Alice's Adventures in Wonderland* by Lewis Carroll; *Through the Looking Glass* followed in 1871.

1867 *Elsie Dinsmore,* adventure series for girls, by Martha Finley.

1868   *Little Women* by Louisa May Alcott, first story of family life without heavy didacticism.

1871   *At the Back of the North Wind* by George MacDonald, an influential fantasy.

1871   *Child Life, A Collection of Poems* by American poet John Greenleaf Whittier.

1872   *More Nonsense* by Edward Lear; included "The Owl and the Pussy Cat."

1872   *Sing Song* by Christina Rossetti, poetry for children.

1876   *The Adventures of Tom Sawyer* by Mark Twain; *Huckleberry Finn* followed in 1884; pure entertainment.

1877   *Black Beauty* by Anna Sewell; written to publicize poor treatment of animals.

1880   *The Five Little Peppers,* series of family stories, by Margaret Sidney, pseudonym of Harriet Lathrop.

1881   *Uncle Remus, His Songs and Sayings* by Joel Chandler Harris; used black dialect.

1882   *Treasure Island* by Robert Louis Stevenson; *A Child's Garden of Verses* followed in 1885.

1884   *Heidi* by Johanna Spyri.

1886   *Little Lord Fauntleroy* by Frances Hodgson Burnett, who later wrote *The Secret Garden* (1910).

1889   *The Blue Fairy Book* by Andrew Lang; followed by his other fairy-tale collections.

1891   *Rhymes of Childhood* by James Whitcomb Riley; introduced dialect in poetry.

1892   *Pinocchio* by C. Collodi, pseudonym of Carlo Lorenzini.

1894   *The Jungle Book* by Rudyard Kipling.

1896   *Poems of Childhood* by Eugene Field; included "The Sugar Plum Tree."

1898   *Wild Animals I Have Known* by Ernest Thompson Seton.

1899   *Little Black Sambo* by Helen Bannerman; a first picture book, now controversial.[6]

---

[6] See *Little Black Sambo; A Closer Look* by Phyllis J. Yuill (The Council on Interracial Books for Children, 1976).

*Reproduced with the permission
of Farrar, Straus & Giroux, Inc.
From* The Light Princess *by
George MacDonald with pictures
by Maurice Sendak. Pictures
Copyright © 1969 by Maurice
Sendak.*

The fact that we are able to list the titles of all the major publications during the entire century shows clearly that the publication of children's books is still relatively young. Examining this list of publications during the nineteenth century is especially interesting to us in the twentieth century. For one thing, considering the wealth of published works today, it would be impossible to present a comparable list for the twentieth century in this chapter. The list would be far too long despite the fact that the century is not yet over.

A comparison of the books published prior to 1850 and those published during the last half of the century is also enlightening. You can quickly notice the fact that production leaped tremendously after 1850. This was facilitated by improved methods of making paper from wood pulp around 1840. In addition, the development of the Linotype machine, patented in 1884, increased the ease of publication, as did the availability of steam power.

As you read through the book titles published during the nineteenth century, you will find many books that are listed as "classics" today. These early books had an impact that could scarcely be equaled by any book published today. It is interesting to consider how some of the nineteenth-century titles would be received today if they were to appear as newly published books. We know, for example, that modern children still enjoy *Tom Sawyer* and *Swiss Family Robinson,* but would these titles receive the same wide acclaim as new books in today's highly competitive market?

Of one thing we can be certain, however; the books created at this time marked the beginning of fiction for children and young people. You can easily imagine how young readers eagerly devoured the Horatio Alger books, the Elsie Dinsmore series, *The Five Little Peppers,* and *Little Lord Fauntleroy,* as well as the titles that have had more lasting effect.

CHILDREN'S BOOKS IN THE TWENTIETH CENTURY

From the publication of L. Frank Baum's *The Wizard of Oz* in 1900 and Beatrix Potter's *The Tale of Peter Rabbit* in 1901, the field of children's literature expanded, blossoming forth with an incredible array of books

Reproduced by kind permission of F. Warne & Co., Ltd. from The Tale of Peter Rabbit *by Beatrix Potter. © Copyright F. Warne & Co., Ltd., London & New York.*

for children. Childhood at last was recognized as an important stage of development when children need to play and to grow in their own unique ways. Books are accorded an essential role in this process of growth.

Consider the happenings in this century that have had some effect directly or indirectly on books for children. A review of contemporary history is overwhelming—world wars, mass media, fast transportation, space travel. Included, too, in this fast pace are such problems as the struggle for individual rights, ecology, effects of urbanization, and changing attitudes toward such institutions as marriage. Children's literature reflects these events and problems, and provides information about them. Books also continue to convey a sense of joy and beauty. Children today can select from a virtual treasure trove of fine books on every imaginable subject.

Libraries, schools, and organizations have promoted children's book publication. Numerous book awards have been established that serve to add stimulus to the field. Such journals as the Horn Book Magazine (1924) and more recently *Children's Literature in Education* (1970) were created for the express purpose of talking about books for children. And, of course, the increase in the number of publishers who produce juveniles has grown correspondingly with the demand.

Although the lists of Caldecott and Newbery award winners provide a chronological perspective, many significant publications are omitted from those listings. The following chronology of highlights in the field of children's literature during the twentieth century summarizes much of what we have been discussing in the preceding chapters. You will recognize most of the titles listed because they have been presented as outstanding examples of books for children throughout this text.

1900   *The Wizard of Oz* by L. Frank Baum.

1901   *The Tale of Peter Rabbit* by Beatrix Potter.

1902   *Just So Stories* by Rudyard Kipling.

1902   *Songs for Childhood* by Walter de la Mare.

1904   *Peter Pan* by James Barrie.

1908   *Wind in the Willows* by Kenneth Grahame.

1912   *East o' the Sun and West o' the Moon* by Gudrun Thorne-Thomsen.

1920   *The Story of Doctor Doolittle* by Hugh Lofting.

1922   Establishment of the Newbery Medal.

Reprinted by permission of Coward, McCann & Geoghegan, Inc. from The ABC Bunny *by Wanda Gág. Copyright 1933 by Wanda Gág; renewed* Millions of Cats *by Wanda Gág. Copyright 1928 by Coward-McCann, Inc.; renewed.*

1924 Beginning of *The Horn Book Magazine.*

1926 *Winnie-the-Pooh* by A. A. Milne.

1928 *Millions of Cats* by Wanda Gág.

1932 *Little House in the Big Woods* by Laura Ingalls Wilder.

1934 *Mary Poppins* by Pamela Travers.

1936 *George Washington* by Ingri and Edgar Parin d'Aulaire.

1937 *And to Think That I Saw It on Mulberry Street* by Theodor Seuss Geisel.

1937 *The Hobbit* by J. R. R. Tolkien.

1938 Establishment of the Caldecott Medal.

1939 *Madeline* by Ludwig Bemelmans.

1941 *Paddle-to-the-Sea* by Holling C. Holling.

1943 *Homer Price* by Robert McCloskey.

1944 *Rabbit Hill* by Robert Lawson.

1945 *Strawberry Girl* by Lois Lenski.

1947 *Children and Books* by May Hill Arbuthnot.

1947 *Stone Soup* by Marcia Brown.

1950 *Pippi Longstocking* by Astrid Lindgren, translated from the Swedish.

1952 *Charlotte's Web* by E. B. White.

1961 *Island of the Blue Dolphins* by Scott O'Dell.

1962 *A Wrinkle in Time* by Madeleine L'Engle.

1963 *Where the Wild Things Are* by Maurice Sendak.

1967 *The Outsiders* by Susan Hinton

1968 *Brian Wildsmith's Fishes* by Brian Wildsmith.

1969 *Where the Lilies Bloom* by Vera and Bill Cleaver.

1969 *Stevie* by John Steptoe.

1972 *Julie of the Wolves* by Jean Craighead George.

1974 *Frog Goes to Dinner* by Mercer Mayer.

The above list and the following discussion about it serve as a summary of all that has been presented in this text. Realizing that we can include only a few representative titles on such a list, there are certain observations that we can make. In examining the list, for example, it may surprise readers to discover how long ago some great favorites were written. Books that today's children love such as *Mary Poppins* and *The Hobbit* were published decades ago. We can see, too, that there has been a steady stream of books for children, a stream that has gradually widened into a river, as the number of books published has increased.

Books today are beautifully illustrated. Young children, and adults, too, are treated to some of the finest artistic talent. Illustrations range from the bold colors of the d'Aulaires, Brian Wildsmith, and John Steptoe to the black and white line drawings of Robert McCloskey and Robert Lawson. Picture books of the twentieth century can be thrilling, as we noted in Chapter 2 with many examples of art in children's books.

Outstanding writers are producing books for children. E. B. White, author of *Charlotte's Web* and other enjoyable books, is a noted example of a skilled writer recognized in the adult literary world also. All of the writers on this highly selective list stand out in the crowd—Milne, Wilder, Holling, McCloskey, O'Dell, L'Engle, the Cleavers. Those who write for children obviously love their work; they write carefully in the full sense of the word.

On this list you will notice a large number of fantasies for young people. A fantasy for young children that proved to be controversial is Maurice Sendak's *Where the Wild Things Are*. For older children *The Hobbit* has probably been the most influential, and may lead many advanced readers to *The Lord of the Rings* trilogy that follows. A great variety of fantasy has developed, ranging from the creation of other worlds (Tolkien's work) to transportation in time (*A Wrinkle in Time*) and imaginary happenings (*Pippi Longstocking*). Fantasy for children has developed to such an extent that it deserves equal footing with realism.

Throughout children's literature of the twentieth century, we see a growing concern for the person. Reflecting society's increasing awareness of human needs, children's literature can express a black child's hurt at being called "nigger," a child's fear about entering a new school, or a young girl's desire to be an individual. Children's books can include a character who is mentally retarded or physically disabled, and characters can have honest emotions—anger, love, fear, depression, grief, joy. Children's literature is realistic.

An overriding characteristic of children's literature today is its great variety. In addition to fantasy and realistic fiction, there are historical fiction, humor, poetry, folktales. Perhaps one of the most amazing developments of this century, although it doesn't show up on this list, are the tremendous numbers of information books, nonfiction for young people. A very current development, for instance, is the biographical writing for young people, which began with the work of the d'Aulaires in the 1930s but has increased in the 1970s as the concern for recognizing the contributions of women and members of ethnic groups has grown.

During this century we have seen many new developments in the field of children's literature. The tremendous production of paperbacks for adults has gradually trickled down to children's literature. There are even children's book clubs of inexpensive books. The creation of children's literature as a field of study has resulted in new publications, college courses, and the writing of articles criticizing and analyzing writing for young people. Children's literature may be seen as an integral part of the whole field of literature with much overlapping of authors and illustrators and the reading of adult literature by adolescents. Children's literature has come of age!

Probing the future has always been a fascinating diversion. No one can be judged either "right" or "wrong," because we literally do not know the answers, but we can certainly make predictions. We can even make predictions that have some validity, as past development provides clues, for the past is prologue to the future.

We can predict, for example, that at least for some time, the production of books for children will continue to be "big business," and the number of books produced annually will remain in the thousands. Around 1975, there was a noticeable retrenching in the publishing world as paper prices rose and the economy suffered from inflation and at the same time unemployment. The full effect of these economic conditions is certainly a matter to be determined in the future. One result may be more careful selection of which books are to be published.

As we move into the last quarter of the twentieth century, there are other influences that may curb the fantastic increases in book publication. The dropping birthrate, for instance, means that the market for children's books will be smaller. Both economic conditions and the birthrate are also having direct effects on school budgets. As schools have to consider ways of curtailing expenditures, they will probably spend less for library budgets.

Children's books today are, on the other hand, better than ever. With the development of new methods of printing and better reproduction of colored illustrations, this high quality will continue. Cheap, unattractive books just won't sell. There is no reason, however, to think that books will be less expensive as all prices continue to rise.

The content of these books will reflect new interests, knowledge, and concerns of society. Many books will focus on the person, including understanding of the self and the needs of other individuals. Books will continue to focus on multicultural and ethnic concerns as we try to present more realistic pictures of different groups such as native Americans. New groups will be recognized, for example, the Vietnamese. The trend toward presenting positive, realistic images of women will increase, and the contributions of women will be featured in biography and other nonfiction. Children's literature will reflect new discoveries in the future, perhaps developments in oceanography, interpersonal communication, or living in space.

Many book lovers are concerned about the influence of mass media on the future of books. Will the book as a format be replaced by new viewing or listening devices? There seems little doubt that both adults and children are turning to television for information and entertainment; on the other hand, there continues to be a demand for newspapers, magazines, and books. As information retrieval systems are more effective, there may be less need for books as storehouses of knowledge, and we will have access to instant information. Obviously libraries are already having trouble storing the volume of printed material that promises to multiply at increasing rates. We need new ways of dealing with the information explosion.

At the same time, however, the book has something to offer that nonprint media do not have. At present it is hard to envision a day when we would have no books as we know them today, for the book is something we can physically handle, possess. The reader has more control over input from the book than is possible with screened material. A person can read a passage over again for sheer enjoyment or turn back several pages to check on something confusing. With the book, furthermore, the reader can exercise his or her imaginative powers. No one can tell the reader of a book exactly how a character reacted or the feeling of the atmosphere of a setting. All this, the reader provides; it is a vital part of the interaction between author and audience. As Oliver Goldsmith once wrote: "The first time I read an excellent book, it is to me just as if I had gained a new friend." It is this feeling for books that will ensure their continuance, for we want to have our friends around us, to be able to see them and to touch them. And this is the feeling we can continue to instill in young people as a part of their heritage.

☙ *GAINING A PERSPECTIVE OF THE FIELD* As you think about the development of children's literature during the past three hundred years, complete these activities:

1. See if you can find, in any of the libraries available to you, three of the books published prior to 1900. Examine these books to compare them with books of the present.

2. Read one of the popular books of the nineteenth century. Why is this book still popular today? If it is not one that endured, what are its shortcomings?

3. As you examine the list of twentieth-century developments in children's literature, what additions or deletions would you make. Discuss the reasons for your suggestions.

4. What do you think the future of children's literature will be? Discuss your ideas with other members of the class.

ADDITIONAL SOURCES TO INVESTIGATE

503

*NEW AND OLD
DIRECTIONS IN
CHILDREN'S
LITERATURE*

Anderson, William and Patrick Groff. *A New Look for Children's Literature*. Wadsworth, 1972.

Crouch, Marcus. *The Nesbit Tradition; The Children's Novel in England 1945–1970*. Rowman and Littlefield, 1972. See also his *Treasure Seekers and Borrowers; Children's Books in Britain, 1900–1960*. The London Library Association, 1962.

Gillespie, Margaret C. *Literature for Children: History and Trends*. Wm. C. Brown, 1970.

Haviland, Virginia, and Margaret N. Coughlan, comps. *Yankee Doodle's Literary Sampler of Prose, Poetry & Pictures; Being an Anthology of Diverse Works Published for the Edification and/or Entertainment of Young Readers in America before 1900*. Thomas Y. Crowell, 1974.

Isabelle Jan. *On Children's Literature*. Schocken, 1974.

Jordan, Alice M. *From Rollo to Tom Sawyer*. Horn Book, 1948.

Kingston, Carolyn T. *The Tragic Mode in Children's Literature*. Teachers College, 1974.

Meigs, Cornelia, Anne Eaton, Elizabeth Nesbitt, and Ruth Hill Viguers. *A Critical History of Children's Literature*. Macmillan, 1969.

Monson, Dianne L. and Bette J. Peltola, comps. *Research in Children's Literature; An Annotated Bibliography*. International Reading Association, 1976.

Sheldon, William D. "A Summary of Research Studies Related to Reading Instruction in Elementary Education." *Elementary English* 50 (February 1973): 281–320; also *Language Arts* 53 (January 1976): 85–110.

Smith, James Steel. *A Critical Approach to Children's Literature*. McGraw-Hill, 1967.

Townsend, John Rowe. *Written for Children: An Outline of English Children's Literature*. Lothrop, 1967.

AWARDS GIVEN TO CHILDREN'S BOOKS

Following is a list of a number of awards given for the content and illustration of children's books. A brief description of each award is included as well as the address of the sponsoring organization.

Jane Addams Book Award
Established in 1953 by the Women's International League for Peace and Freedom and the Jane Addams Peace Association (345 E. 46th St., New York, N.Y. 10017).

American Institute of Graphic Arts Children's Books Show
Held since 1941, the exhibit is displayed first at the AIGA gallery, then travels throughout the United States. AIGA, 1059 Third Avenue, New York, N.Y. 10021.

American Institute of Graphic Arts Fifty Books of the Year
Established in 1923 by the American Institute of Graphic Arts (AIGA, 1059 Third Avenue, New York, N.Y. 10021).

Hans Christian Andersen Awards
Established in 1956 by the International Board on Books for Young People; Children's Book Council, 67 Irving Place, New York, N.Y. 10003.

Australian Books of the Year Awards
Established in 1946, the award was administered by a number of Australian state agencies until the formation of the Australian Children's Book Council in 1959 made it possible to establish an all-Australian Book of the Year Award. In 1956, the Picture Books of the Year Award was established. In 1974, an award for the Best Illustrated Children's Book of the Year was added. This award, administered by the Australian Children's Book Council, is sponsored and selected by the Visual Art Board of the Australian Council for the Arts.

Mildred L. Batchelder Award
Established in 1966, the award is donated and administered by ALA Children's Services Division (50 East Huron Street, Chicago, Ill. 60611).

Irma Simonton Black Award
First presented in 1973, this award is given by the Bank Street College of Education (610 West 112th Street, New York, N.Y. 10025).

Boston Globe–Horn Book Awards
Established in 1967 by *The Boston Globe* and *The Horn Book* (585 Boylston Street, Boston, Mass. 02116).

Brooklyn Art Books for Children Citations
Established in 1972 and given jointly by the Brooklyn Museum (188 Eastern Parkway, Brooklyn, N.Y. 11238) and the Brooklyn Public Library (Grand Army Plaza, Brooklyn, N.Y. 11238).

California Association of Teachers of English Award
Established in 1975 by CATE (Box 4427, Whittier, Calif. 90607) and awarded to a California author.

Randolph J. Caldecott Medal
Awarded annually since 1938 under the supervision of the American Library Association Children's Services Division (50 E. Huron St., Chicago, Ill. 60611).

Canadian Library Association Awards Books of the Year for Children
Given annually since 1947 by the Canadian Library Association (151 Sparks St., Ottawa K1P 5E3, Canada).

Carnegie Medal
Given annually since 1937 by the British Library Association (7 Ridgmount St., Store St., London W.C. 1, England).

Lewis Carroll Shelf Awards
Given annually since 1958 by the University of Wisconsin (Wisconsin Book Conference, School of Education, Madison, Wis. 53706).

Children's Book Showcase
Initiated in 1972 by the Children's Book Council (67 Irving Place, New York, N.Y. 10003).

Children's Reading Round Table Award
Given annually since 1953 by the Chicago chapter of the Children's Reading Round Table (Caroline Rubin, ed., 1321 E. 56th St., Chicago, Ill. 60637).

Child Study Association of America/Wel-Met Children's Book Award
Given annually by the Child Study Association (50 Madison Ave., New York, N.Y. 10010).

Christopher Awards—Children's Book Category
Established in 1949, the award is given by the Christophers (12 E. 48th St., New York, N.Y. 10017).

Commonwealth Club of California Awards—Children's Book Category
Given annually since 1939 by the Commonwealth Club of California (Monadnock Arcade, 681 Market St., San Francisco, Calif. 94105).

Council on Interracial Books for Children Awards
Established in 1968, the award is given annually by the Council on Interracial Books for Children (1841 Broadway, New York, N.Y. 10023).

Eleanor Farjeon Award
Established in 1966, the award is presented by the Children's Book Circle, (England).

Dorothy Canfield Fisher Children's Book Award
First given in 1956, the award is cosponsored by Vermont State PTA and State Department of Libraries. For further information write Janice J. Byington (Dorothy Canfield Fisher Children's Book Award, Craftsbury Common, Vt. 05827).

Charles W. Follett Award
Established in 1950 by the four sons of Charles W. Follett. Presently, the award is for an unpublished manuscript, subsequently published by Follett Publishing Co. (1010 W. Washington Blvd., Chicago, Ill. 60607).

Georgia Children's Book Award
Established in 1969, the award is sponsored by the College of Education of the University of Georgia (Athens, Ga. 30602).

Esther Glen Award
Established in 1945, the award is administered by the New Zealand Library Association (10 Park St., Wellington 1, New Zealand).

Golden Kite Award
Begun in 1973, this award is sponsored and administered by the Society of Children's Book Writers (SCBW), P.O. Box 827, Laguna Beach, Calif. 92652.

Kate Greenaway Medal
Given annually by the British Library Association (7 Ridgmount St., Store St., London W.C. 1, England).

Guardian Award for Children's Fiction
Given annually by *The Guardian* (164 Deansgate, Manchester, England).

Sue Hefley Award
Introduced in 1972, the award is sponsored by the Louisiana Association of School Librarians (P.O. Box 131, Baton Rouge, La. 70821).

Amelia Frances Howard-Gibbon Medal
Given annually since 1971 by the Canadian Library Association (151 Sparks St., Ottawa, Canada K1P 5E3) for outstanding illustrations in a children's book.

International Board on Books for Young People (IBBY) Honor List
Chosen every two years since 1956, each National Section of IBBY selects two books (one for text and one for illustration) published in a two-year period before the year in which they are selected for an IBBY biennial Congress. In the United States, the books are selected by a committee of the Children's Services Division

of the American Library Association. For a listing including all titles, write Children's Book Council (67 Irving Place, New York, N.Y. 10003).

International Reading Association Children's Book Award
Given for the first time in 1975, the award is sponsored by the Institute for Reading Research and administered by the International Reading Association (800 Barksdale Rd., Newark, Del. 19711).

Coretta Scott King Award
First presented in 1970, this award is sponsored by the Atlanta University School of Library Service, Encyclopaedia Britannica, Johnson Publishing Company, World Book Encyclopedia and Xerox Corporation. (Awards Chairwoman: Ms. Glyndon Flynt Greer, 1236 Oakcrest Dr. S.W., Atlanta, Ga. 30311).

Lucky Four-Leaf Clover Award
Presented annually since 1971 by the Lucky Book Club (Scholastic Magazines, Inc., 50 W. 44th St., New York, N.Y. 10036).

Media & Methods Maxi Awards
Established in 1973. Nomination ballots for materials in all media are solicited from *Media & Methods* subscribers. For complete lists of award winners write *Media & Methods* (North American Publishing Co., 134 N. 13th St., Philadelphia, Pa. 19107).

National Book Awards—Children's Book Category
Established in 1969, the award was administered by the National Book Committee until 1974. In 1975, the award was administered by the National Book Awards Advisory Committee. Future sponsorship has not yet been announced.

National Jewish Book Awards—Charles and Bertie G. Schwartz Juvenile Award
Given annually in May by the Jewish Book Council of the National Jewish Welfare Board (15 E. 26th St., New York, N.Y. 10010).

Nene Award
Given annually in the spring since 1964 and sponsored by the Children's Section of the Hawaii Library Association and Hawaii Association of School Librarians.

John Newbery Medal
Donated by the Frederic G. Melcher family, the Newbery Medal has been awarded annually since 1922 under the supervision of the American Library Association Children's Services Division (50 E. Huron St., Chicago, Ill. 60611).

New England Round Table of Children's Librarians Award
Initiated in 1972. Direct requests concerning the award to Mary D. Porter (Supervisor, Work with Children, Lynn Public Library, Lynn, Mass. 01902).

New Jersey Institute of Technology New Jersey Author Citations
Given annually since 1959, this award was under the auspices of the New Jersey Council of Teachers of English. Since 1972, the New Jersey Institute of Technology has presented citations to writers who are either natives or residents of New

Jersey. For information on current and past winners, write Dr. Herman A. Estrin (Department of Humanities, New Jersey Institute of Technology, 323 High St., Newark, N.J. 07102).

New York Academy of Sciences Children's Science Book Awards
Established in 1972 by the New York Academy of Sciences (2 East 63rd St., New York, N.Y. 10021).

New York Times Choice of Best Illustrated Children's Books of the Year
Initiated in 1952 and sponsored annually by *The New York Times* (229 W. 43rd St., New York, N.Y. 10036).

North Carolina Division American Association of University Women's Award in Juvenile Literature
Given annually in November through the North Carolina Literary and Historical Association (109 E. Jones St., Raleigh, N.C. 27611).

Ohioana Book Awards—Juvenile Book Category
Awarded annually in October by the Ohioana Library Association (1109 Ohio Departments Building, Columbus, Ohio 43215).

Pacific Northwest Library Association Young Readers' Choice Award
Given annually since 1940 by the Pacific Northwest Library Association. Selection is done by the children from Washington, Oregon, Montana, Idaho and British Columbia in grades 4–8, who vote at their public or school library from a list of 15 titles prepared by the children's librarians.

Edgar Allen Poe Awards—Best Juvenile Mystery Category
First awarded in 1961 and given by the Mystery Writers of America (105 E. 19th St., New York, N.Y. 10003).

Printing Industries of America Graphic Arts Awards.
Given annually since 1951 and selected by a panel of judges. An annual Awards Catalog is available free from Printing Industries of America (Dept. of Public Relations, 1730 N. Lynn St., Arlington, Va. 22209).

Regina Medal
Given annually since 1959 by the Catholic Library Association (461 W. Lancaster Ave., Haverford, Pa. 19041).

Rutgers Award
Given since 1966 at irregular intervals to New Jersey residents at the discretion of the award administrators, the Graduate School of Library Service (Rutgers University, New Brunswick, N.J. 08903).

Sequoyah Children's Book Award
Given annually since 1959 by the Sequoyah Children's Book Award Committee. Oklahoma School children in grades 3–6 vote for the best book from a master list.

Charlie May Simon Children's Book Award

Presented annually by the Elementary School Council (Department of Education, Little Rock, Ark. 72201) and fifteen cooperating sponsors. Arkansas school children in grades 4–6 vote from a master list selected by specialists.

Southern California Council on Literature for Children and Young People Awards

Given each November since 1961 to authors, illustrators, and other contributors living in Southern California by the Southern California Council on Literature for Children and Young People (Founder: Dorothy McKenzie. President, 1974–1975: Betty L. Ryder, Coordinator of Extension, Pasadena Public Library, Pasadena, Calif. 91101).

George G. Stone Center for Children's Books Recognition of Merit Award

Given annually since 1965 by the Claremont Reading Conference (Claremont Graduate School, Claremont, Calif. 91711).

Times Educational Supplement Information Book Awards

Established in 1972 by the *Times Educational Supplement* (Times Newspaper Ltd., Printing House Sq., London E.C. 4, England).

Mark Twain Award

Given annually since 1972, the winner is chosen by Missouri school children, grades 3–8, from a master list assembled by an awards committee. Cosponsored by the Missouri Library Association (403 South Sixth St., Columbia, Mo. 65201).

University of Southern Mississippi Children's Collection Medallion

Established in 1969, the award is given annually at the University of Southern Mississippi Children's Book Festival (Library, Hattiesburg, Miss. 39401).

Western Heritage Awards—Juvenile Book Category

Given annually in April since 1961 by the National Cowboy Hall of Fame and Western Heritage Center (1700 N.E. 63rd St., Oklahoma City, Okla. 73111).

Western Writers of America Spur Awards—Best Western Juvenile Categories

Awarded annually by the Western Writers of America, Inc. (Nellie Yost, Exec. Sec'y., 1505 W. D St., North Platte, Neb. 69101).

Whitbread Awards—Children's Book Category

Initiated in 1971 and given to a British author or one who has been settled in the United Kingdom or the Republic of Ireland for five years. Sponsored by Whitbread's and administered by the Booksellers Association of Great Britain and Ireland (154 Buckingham Palace Road, London S.W. 1W 9TZ, England).

William Allen White Children's Book Award

Given annually since 1953 by the William Allen White Memorial Library at Emporia Kansas State College (Emporia, Kans. 66801). Kansas school children in grades 4–8 vote from a list chosen by specialists.

Laura Ingalls Wilder Award
Established in 1954 and given every five years since 1960. Administered by American Library Association Children's Services Division (50 E. Huron St., Chicago, Ill. 60611).

Carter G. Woodson Book Award
First presented in 1974 and sponsored by the National Council for the Social Studies (Suite 405, 1200 17th St., N.W., Washington, D.C. 20036).

Woodward School Annual Book Award
Given since 1958 by the Woodward School (321 Clinton Ave., Brooklyn, N.Y. 11205).

Young Reader Medal
First presented in 1974 by the California Reading Association (3400 Irvine Avenue, Suite 211, New Port, Cal. 92660), the California Library Association (717 K Street, Sacramento, Cal. 95814), and the California Association of School Librarians (Box 1277, Burlingame, Cal. 94010). Awarded to any fiction written in English by a living author published within the previous five years falling in three specified categories: primary, intermediate, and young adult.

THE CALDECOTT MEDAL

The following books have been awarded the Caldecott Medal for outstanding illustration. Included also are the books named as Honor Books. For more information about this award see Chapter 2.

Notice that for this award, the illustrator winning the award is listed first, followed by the title and author of the book in which the illustrations appear. If only one name is listed, the illustrator is also the author of the book.

1938
Dorothy P. Lathrop, illus. *Animals of the Bible* by Helen Dean Fish. Lippincott.

Honor Books:
Boris Artzybasheff. *Seven Simeons*. Viking.
Robert Lawson, illus. *Four and Twenty Blackbirds* by Helen Dean Fish. Stokes.

1939
Thomas Handforth. *Mei Lei*. Doubleday.

Honor Books:
Laura Adams Armer. *The Forest Pool*. Longmans.
Robert Lawson, illus. *Wee Gillis* by Munro Leaf. Viking.

Wanda Gág. *Snow White and the Seven Dwarfs*. Coward-McCann.
Clare Newberry. *Barkis*. Harper & Row.
James Daugherty. *Andy and the Lion*. Viking.

1940
Ingri and Edgar d'Aulaire. *Abraham Lincoln*. Doubleday.

Honor Books:
Berta and Elmer Hader. *Cock-A-Doodle Doo*. Macmillan.
Ludwig Bemelmans. *Madeline*. Viking.
Lauren Ford. *The Ageless Story*. Dodd, Mead.

1941
Robert Lawson. *They Were Strong and Good*. Viking.

Honor Books:
Clare Newberry. *April's Kittens*. Harper & Row.

1942
Robert McCloskey. *Make Way For Ducklings*. Viking.

Honor Books:
Maud and Miska Petersham. *An American ABC*. Macmillan.
Velino Herrera, illus. *In My Mother's House* by Ann Nolan Clark. Viking.
Holling C. Holling. *Paddle-To-The-Sea*. Houghton Mifflin.
Wanda Gág. *Nothing At All*. Coward-McCann.

1943
Virginia Lee Burton. *The Little House*. Houghton Mifflin.

Honor Books:
Mary and Conrad Buff. *Dash and Dart*. Viking.
Clare Newberry. *Marshmallow*. Harper & Row.

1944
Louis Slobodkin, illus. *Many Moons* by James Thurber. Harcourt Brace Jovanovich.

Honor Books:
Elizabeth Orton Jones, illus. *Small Rain: Verses From the Bible* selected by Jessie Orton Jones. Viking.
Arnold E. Bare, illus. *Pierre Pigeon* by Lee Kingman. Houghton Mifflin.
Berta and Elmer Hader. *The Mighty Hunter*. Macmillan.
Jean Charlot, illus. *A Child's Good Night Book* by Margaret Wise Brown. W. R. Scott.
Plao Chan, illus. *Good Luck Horse* by Chin-Yi Chan. Whittlesey.

1945

Elizabeth Orton Jones, illus. *Prayer For A Child* by Rachel Field. Macmillan.

Honor Books:
Tasha Tudor. *Mother Goose*. Walck.
Marie Hall Ets. *In The Forest*. Viking.
Marguerite de Angeli. *Yonie Wondernose*. Doubleday.
Kate Seredy, illus. *The Christmas Anna Angel* by Ruth Sawyer. Viking.

1946

Maud and Miska Petersham. *The Rooster Crows*. Macmillan.

Honor Books:
Leonard Weisgard, illus. *Little Lost Lamb* by Golden MacDonald. Doubleday.
Marjorie Torrey, illus. *Sing Mother Goose* by Opal Wheeler. Dutton.
Ruth Gannett. *My Mother Is the Most Beautiful Woman in the World* by Becky
    Reyher. Lothrop.
Kurt Wiese. *You Can Write Chinese*. Viking.

1947

Leonard Weisgard, illus. *The Little Island* by Golden MacDonald. Doubleday.

Honor Books:
Leonard Weisgard, illus. *Rain Drop Splash* by Alvin Tresselt. Lothrop.
Jay Hyde Barnum, illus. *Boats on the River* by Marjorie Flack. Viking.
Tony Palazzo, illus. *Timothy Turtle* by Al Graham. Welch.
Leo Politi, *Pedro, The Angel of Olvera Street*. Scribner.
Marjorie Torrey, illus. *Sing In Praise: A Collection of the Best Loved Hymns* by Opal
    Wheeler. Dutton.

1948

Roger Duvoisin, illus. *White Snow, Bright Snow* by Alvin Tresselt. Lothrop.

Honor Books:
Marcia Brown. *Stone Soup*. Scribner.
Dr. Seuss. *McElligott's Pool*. Random House.
George Schreiber. *Bambino the Clown*. Viking.
Hildegard Woodward, illus. *Roger and the Fox* by Lavinia Davis. Doubleday.
Virginia Lee Burton, illus. *Song of Robin Hood* edited by Anne Malcolmson.
    Houghton Mifflin.

1949

Berta and Elmer Hader. *The Big Snow*. Macmillan.

Honor Books:
Robert McCloskey. *Blueberries for Sal*. Viking.
Helen Stone, illus. *All Around the Town* by Phyllis McGinley. Lippincott.

Leo Politi. *Juanita*. Scribner.
Kurt Wiese. *Fish in the Air*. Viking.

1950

Leo Politi. *Song of the Swallows*. Scribner.

Honor Books:
Lynd Ward, illus. *America's Ethan Allen* by Stewart Holbrook. Houghton Mifflin.
Hildegard Woodward, illus. *The Wild Birthday Cake* by Lavinia Davis. Double-
day.
Marc Simont, illus. *The Happy Day* by Ruth Krauss. Harper & Row.
Dr. Seuss. *Bartholomew and the Oobleck*. Random House.
Marcia Brown. *Henry Fisherman*. Scribner.

1951

Katherine Milhous. *The Egg Tree*. Scribner.

Honor Books:
Marcia Brown. *Dick Whittington and His Cat*. Scribner.
Nicolas, illus. *The Two Reds* by William Lipkind. Harcourt Brace Jovanovich.
Dr. Seuss. *If I Ran the Zoo*. Random House.
Helen Stone, illus. *The Most Wonderful Doll in the World* by Phyllis McGinley. Lip-
pincott.
Clare Newberry. *T-Bone, The Baby Sitter*. Harper & Row.

1952

Nicolas, illus. *Finders Keepers* by William Lipkind. Harcourt Brace Jovanovich.

Honor Books:
Marie Hall Ets. *Mr. T. W. Anthony Woo*. Viking.
Marcia Brown. *Skipper John's Cook*. Scribner.
Margaret Bloy, illus. *All Falling Down* by Gene Zion. Harper.
William Pène du Bois. *Bear Party*. Viking.
Elizabeth Olds. *Feather Mountain*. Houghton Mifflin.

1953

Lynd Ward. *The Biggest Bear*. Houghton Mifflin.

Honor Books:
Marcia Brown, illus. and trans. *Puss In Boots* by Charles Perrault. Scribner.
Robert McCloskey. *One Morning in Maine*. Viking.
Fritz Eichenberg. *Ape In A Cape*. Harcourt Brace Jovanovich.
Margaret Bloy Graham, illus. *The Storm Book* by Charlotte Zolotow. Harper &
Row.
Juliet Kepes. *Five Little Monkeys*. Houghton Mifflin.

1954
Ludwig Bemelmans. *Madeline's Rescue*. Viking.

Honor Books:
Robert McCloskey, illus. *Journey Cake, Ho!* by Ruth Sawyer. Viking.
Jean Charlot, illus. *When Will the World Be Mine?* by Miriam Schlein. Scott.
Marcia Brown, illus. *The Steadfast Tin Soldier* by Hans Christian Andersen.
  Scribner.
Maurice Sendak, illus. *A Very Special House* by Ruth Krauss. Harper & Row.
A. Birnbaum. *Green Eyes*. Capitol.

1955

Marcia Brown, illus. and trans. *Cinderella, Or the Little Glass Slipper* by Charles
  Perrault. Scribner.

Honor Books:
Marguerite de Angeli, illus. *Book of Nursery and Mother Goose Rhymes*. Doubleday.
Tibor Gergely, illus. *Wheel on the Chimney* by Margaret Wise Brown. Lippincott.
Helen Sewell, illus. *The Thanksgiving Story* by Alice Dalgliesh. Scribner.

1956
Feodor Rojankovsky, illus. *Frog Went A-Courtin'* edited by John Langstaff. Harcourt Brace Jovanovich.

Honor Books:
Marie Hall Ets. *Play With Me*. Viking.
Taro Yashima. *Crow Boy*. Viking.

1957
Marc Simont, illus. *A Tree Is Nice* by Janice May Udry. Harper & Row.

Honor Books:
Marie Hall Ets. *Mr. Penny's Race Horse*. Viking.
Tasha Tudor. *1 Is One*. Walck.
Paul Galdone, illus. *Anatole* by Eve Titus. McGraw-Hill.
James Daugherty, illus. *Gillespie and the Guards* by Benjamin Elkin. Viking.
William Pène du Bois. *Lion*. Viking.

1958
Robert McCloskey. *Time of Wonder*. Viking.

Honor Books:
Don Freeman. *Fly High, Fly Low*. Viking.
Paul Galdone, illus. *Anatole and the Cat* by Eve Titus. McGraw-Hill.

1959
Barbara Cooney, illus. *Chanticleer and the Fox* adapted from Chaucer. Crowell.

Honor Books:
Antonio Frasconi. *The House That Jack Built*. Harcourt Brace Jovanovich.
Maurice Sendak, illus. *What Do You Say, Dear?* by Sesyle Joslin. Scott.
Taro Yashima. *Umbrella*. Viking.

1960
Marie Hall Ets, illus. *Nine Days to Christmas* by Marie Hall Ets and Aurora Labastida. Viking.

Honor Books:
Adrienne Adams, illus. *Houses From the Sea* by Alice E. Goudey. Scribner.
Maurice Sendak. *The Moon Jumpers* by Janice May Udry. Harper & Row.

1961
Nicholas Sidjakov, illus. *Baboushka and the Three Kings* by Ruth Robbins. Parnassus Press.

Honor Books:
Leo Lionni. *Inch by Inch*. Astor-Honor.

1962
Marcia Brown. *Once a mouse* . . . Scribner.

Honor Books:
Peter Spier. *The Fox Went Out on a Chilly Night*. Doubleday.
Maurice Sendak. *Little Bear's Visit* by Else Holmelund Minarik. Harper & Row.
Adrienne Adams, illus. *The Day We Saw the Sun Come Up* by Alice E. Goudey. Scribner.

1963
Ezra Jack Keats. *The Snowy Day*. Viking.

Honor Books:
Bernarda Bryson, illus. *The Sun Is a Golden Earring* by Natalia M. Belting. Holt.
Maurice Sendak, illus. *Mr. Rabbit and the Lovely Present* by Charlotte Zolotow. Harper & Row.

1964
Maurice Sendak. *Where the Wild Things Are*. Harper & Row.

Honor Books:
Leo Lionni. *Swimmy*. Pantheon.
Evaline Ness, illus. *All in the Morning Early* by Sorche Nic Leodhas. Holt.
Philip Reed. *Mother Goose and Nursery Rhymes*. Atheneum.

1965
Beni Montresor, illus. *May I Bring a Friend?* by Beatrice Schenk de Regniers. Atheneum.

Honor Books:
Marvin Bileck, illus. *Rain Makes Applesauce* by Julian Scheer. Holiday.
Blair Lent, illus. *The Wave* by Margaret Hodges. Houghton Mifflin.
Evaline Ness, illus. *A Pocketful of Cricket* by Rebecca Caudill. Holt.

1966

Nonny Hogrogian, illus. *Always Room for One More* by Sorche Nic Leodhas. Holt.

Honor Books:
Roger Duvoisin, illus. *Hide and Seek Fog* by Alvin Tresselt. Lothrop.
Marie Hall Ets. *Just Me*. Viking.
Evaline Ness. *Tom Tit Tot*. Scribner.

1967

Evaline Ness. *Sam, Bangs & Moonshine*. Holt.

Honor Book:
Ed Emberley, illus. *One Wide River to Cross* by Barbara Emberley, Prentice-Hall.

1968

Ed Emberley, illus. *Drummer Hoff* by Barbara Emberley. Prentice-Hall.

Honor Books:
Leo Lionni. *Frederick*. Pantheon.
Taro Yashima. *Seashore Story*. Viking.
Ed Young, illus. *The Emperor and the Kite* by Jane Yolen. World.

1969

Uri Shulevitz, illus. *The Fool of the World and the Flying Ship* by Arthur Ransome. Farrar, Straus & Giroux.

Honor Book:
Blair Lent, illus. *Why the Sun and the Moon Live in the Sky* by Elphinstone Dayrell. Houghton Mifflin.

1970

William Steig. *Sylvester and the Magic Pebble*. Windmill/Simon & Schuster.

Honor Books:
Ezra Jack Keats. *Goggles*. Macmillan.
Leo Lionni. *Alexander and the Wind-Up Mouse*. Pantheon.
Robert Andrew Parker, illus. *Pop Corn & Ma Goodness* by Edna Mitchell Preston. Viking.
Brinton Turkle. *Thy Friend, Obadiah*. Viking.
Margot Zemach, illus. *The Judge* by Harve Zemach. Farrar, Straus & Giroux.

1971

Gail E. Haley. *A Story, A Story*. Atheneum.

Honor Books:
Blair Lent, illus. *The Angry Moon* by William Sleator. Atlantic–Little, Brown.
Arnold Lobel. *Frog and Toad Are Friends*. Harper & Row.
Maurice Sendak. *In the Night Kitchen*. Harper & Row.

1972

Nonny Hogrogian. *One Fine Day*. Macmillan.

Honor Books:
Arnold Lobel, illus. *Hildilid's Night* by Cheli Duran Ryan. Macmillan.
Janina Domanska. *If All the Seas Were One Sea*. Macmillan.
Tom Feelings, illus. *Moja Means One* by Muriel Feelings. Dial.

1973

Blair Lent, illus. *The Funny Little Woman* retold by Arlene Mosel. Dutton.

Honor Books:
Gerald McDermott. *Anansi the Spider*. Holt.
Leonard Baskin, illus. *Hosie's Alphabet* by Hosea, Tobias and Lisa Baskin. Viking.
Nancy Ekholm Burkert, illus. *Snow White and the Seven Dwarfs,* translated by
     Randall Jarrell. Farrar, Straus & Giroux.
Tom Bahti. *When Clay Sings* by Byrd Baylor. Scribner.

1974

Margot Zemach, illus. *Duffy and the Devil* retold by Harve Zemach. Farrar, Straus
     & Giroux.

Honor Books:
Susan Jeffers. *Three Jovial Huntsmen: A Mother Goose Rhyme*. Bradbury.
David Macaulay. *Cathedral: The Story of Its Construction*. Houghton Mifflin.

1975

Gerald McDermott. *Arrow to the Sun*. Viking.

Honor Book:
Tom Feelings. *Jambo Means Hello: A Swahili Alphabet Book* written by Muriel
     Feelings. Dial.

1976

Leo and Diane Dillon, illus. *Why Mosquitoes Buzz in People's Ears* retold by Verna
     Ardema. Dial.
Honor Books:
Peter Parnall. *The Desert Is Theirs* by Byrd Baylor. Scribner.
Tomie de Paola. *Strega Nona*. Prentice-Hall.

THE NEWBERY MEDAL

The following books have been named as winners of the Newbery Medal since its inception in 1922. Included in the list also are those books that were named as Honor Books. For more information about this award, see Chapters 3 and 4.

1922

Hendrik Willem van Loon. *The Story of Mankind*. Liveright.

Honor Books:
Charles Hawes. *The Great Quest*. Little, Brown.
Bernard Marshall. *Cedric The Forester*. Appleton Century Crofts.
William Bowen. *The Old Tobacco Shop*. Macmillan.
Padraic Colum. *The Golden Fleece and the Heroes Who Lived Before Achilles*. Macmillan.
Cornelia Meigs. *Windy Hill*. Macmillan.

1923

Hugh Lofting. *The Voyages of Doctor Dolittle*. Lippincott.

Honor Book: No record

1924

Charles Hawes. *The Dark Frigate*. Atlantic–Little, Brown.

Honor Book: No record

1925

Charles Finger. *Tales From Silver Lands*. Doubleday.

Honor Books:
Anne Carroll Moore. *Nicholas*. Putnam.
Anne Parrish. *Dream Coach*. Macmillan.

1926

Arthur Bowie Chrisman. *Shen of the Sea*. Dutton.

Honor Book:
Padraic Colum. *Voyagers*. Macmillan.

1927

Will James. *Smoky, The Cowhorse*. Scribner.

Honor Book: No record

1928

Dhan Gopal Mukerji. *Gayneck, The Story of a Pigeon*. Dutton.

Honor Books:
Ella Young. *The Wonder Smith and His Son*. Longmans.
Caroline Snedeker. *Downright Dencey*. Doubleday.

1929
Eric P. Kelly. *The Trumpeter of Krakow*. Macmillan.

Honor Books:
John Bennett. *Pigtail of Ah Lee Ben Loo*. Longmans.
Wanda Gág. *Millions of Cats*. Coward-McCann.
Grace Hallock. *The Boy Who Was*. Dutton.
Cornelia Meigs. *Clearing Weather*. Little, Brown.
Grace Moon. *Runaway Papoose*. Doubleday.
Elinor Whitney. *Tod of the Fens*. Macmillan.

1930
Rachel Field. *Hitty, Her First Hundred Years*. Macmillan.

Honor Books:
Jeanette Eaton. *Daughter of the Seine*. Harper & Row.
Elizabeth Miller. *Pran of Albania*. Doubleday.
Marian Hurd McNeely. *Jumping-Off Place*. Longmans.
Ella Young. *Tangle-Coated Horse and Other Tales*. Longmans.
Julia Davis Adams. *Vaino*. Dutton.
Hildegarde Swift. *Little Blacknose*. Harcourt Brace Jovanovich.

1931
Elizabeth Coatsworth. *The Cat Who Went to Heaven*. Macmillan.

Honor Books:
Anne Parrish. *Floating Island*. Harper & Row.
Alida Malkus. *The Dark Star of Itza*. Harcourt Brace Jovanovich.
Ralph Hubbard. *Queer Person*. Doubleday.
Julia Davis Adams. *Mountains Are Free*. Dutton.
Agnes Hewes. *Spice and the Devil's Cave*. Knopf.
Elizabeth Janet Gray. *Meggy MacIntosh*. Doubleday.
Herbert Best. *Garram the Hunter*. Doubleday.
Alice Lide and Margaret Johansen. *Ood-Le-Uk the Wanderer,* Little, Brown.

1932
Laura Adams Armer. *Waterless Mountain*. Longmans.

Honor Books:
Dorothy P. Lathrop. *The Fairy Circus*. Macmillan.
Rachel Field. *Calico Bush*. Macmillan.
Eunice Tietjens. *Boy of the South Seas*. Coward-McCann.
Eloise Lownsbery. *Out of the Flame*. Longmans.
Marjorie Alee. *Jane's Island*. Houghton Mifflin.

Mary Gould Davis. *Truce of the Wolf and Other Tales of Old Italy*. Harcourt Brace Jovanovich.

1933
Elizabeth Lewis. *Young Fu of the Upper Yangtze*. Winston.

Honor Books:
Cornelia Meigs. *Swift Rivers*. Little, Brown.
Hildegarde Swift. *The Railroad to Freedom*. Harcourt Brace Jovanovich.
Nora Burglon. *Children of the Soil*. Doubleday.

1934
Cornelia Meigs. *Invincible Louisa*. Little, Brown.

Honor Books:
Caroline Snedeker. *The Forgotten Daughter*. Doubleday.
Elsie Singmaster. *Swords of Steel*. Houghton Mifflin.
Wanda Gág. *ABC Bunny*. Coward-McCann.
Erick Berry. *Winged Girl of Knossos*. Appleton.
Sarah Schmidt. *New Land*. McBridge.
Padraic Colum. *Big Tree of Bunlahy*. Macmillan.
Agnes Hewes. *Glory of the Seas*. Knopf.
Anne Kyle. *Apprentice of Florence*. Houghton Mifflin.

1935
Monica Shannon. *Dobry*. Viking.

Honor Books:
Elizabeth Seeger. *Pageant of Chinese History*. Longmans.
Constance Rourke. *Davy Crockett*. Harcourt Brace Jovanovich.
Hilda Van Stockum. *Day on Skates*. Harper & Row.

1936
Carol Brink. *Caddie Woodlawn*. Macmillan.

Honor Books:
Phil Strong. *Honk, The Moose*. Dodd, Mead.
Kate Seredy. *The Good Master*. Viking.
Elizabeth Janet Gray. *Young Walter Scott*. Viking.
Armstrong Sperry. *All Sail Set*. Winston.

1937
Ruth Sawyer. *Roller Skates*. Viking.

Honor Books:
Lois Lenski. *Phebe Fairchild: Her Book*. Stokes.
Idwal Jones. *Whistler's Van*. Viking.

Ludwig Bemelmans. *Golden Basket*. Viking.
Margery Bianco. *Winterbound*. Viking.
Constance Rourke. *Audubon*. Harcourt Brace Jovanovich.
Agnes Hewes. *The Codfish Musket*. Doubleday.

1938
Kate Seredy. *The White Stag*. Viking.

Honor Books:
James Cloyd Bowman. *Pecos Bill*. Little, Brown.
Mabel Robinson. *Bright Island*. Random House.
Laura Ingalls. *On the Banks of Plum Creek*. Harper & Row.

1939
Elizabeth Enright. *Thimble Summer*. Rinehart.

Honor Books:
Valenti Angelo. *Nino*. Viking.
Richard and Florence Atwater. *Mr. Popper's Penguins*. Little, Brown.
Phyllis Crawford. *Hello The Boat!* Holt.
Jeanette Eaton. *Leader by Destiny: George Washington, Man and Patriot*. Harcourt
    Brace Jovanovich.

1940
James Daugherty. *Daniel Boone*. Viking.

Honor Books:
Kate Seredy. *The Singing Tree*. Viking.
Mabel Robinson. *Runner of the Mountain Tops*. Random House.
Laura Ingalls Wilder. *By the Shores of Silver Lake*. Harper & Row.
Stephen W. Meader. *Boy With a Pack*. Harcourt Brace Jovanovich.

1941
Armstrong Sperry. *Call It Courage*. Macmillan.

Honor Books:
Doris Gates. *Blue Willow*. Viking.
Mary Jane Carr. *Young Mac of Fort Vancouver*. Crowell.
Laura Ingalls Wilder. *The Long Winter*. Harper & Row.
Anna Gertrude Hall. *Nansen*. Viking.

1942
Walter D. Edmonds. *The Matchlock Gun*. Dodd, Mead.

Honor Books:
Laura Ingalls Wilder. *Little Town on the Prairie*. Harper & Row.
Genevieve Foster. *George Washington's World*. Scribner.

Lois Lenski. *Indian Captive: The Story of Mary Jemison*. Lippincott.
Eva Roe Gaggin. *Down Ryton Water*. Viking.

1943
Elizabeth Janet Gray. *Adam of the Road*. Viking.

Honor Books:
Eleanor Estes. *The Middle Moffat*. Harcourt Brace Jovanovich.
Mabel Leigh. *Have You Seen Tom Thumb?* Lippincott.

1944
Esther Forbes. *Johnny Tremain*. Houghton Mifflin.

Honor Books:
Laura Ingalls Wilder. *These Happy Golden Years*. Harper & Row.
Julia Sauer. *Fog Magic*. Viking.
Eleanor Estes. *Rufus M*. Harcourt Brace Jovanovich.
Elizabeth Yates. *Mountain Born*. Coward-McCann.

1945
Robert Lawson. *Rabbit Hill*. Viking.

Honor Books:
Eleanor Estes. *The Hundred Dresses*. Harcourt Brace Jovanovich.
Alice Dalgliesh. *The Silver Pencil*. Scribner.
Genevieve Foster. *Abraham Lincoln's World*. Scribner.
Jeanette Eaton. *Lone Journey: The Life of Roger Williams*. Harcourt Brace Jovano-
    vich.

1946
Lois Lenski. *Strawberry Girl*. Lippincott.

Honor Books:
Marguerite Henry. *Justin Morgan Had a Horse*. Rand McNally.
Florence Crannell Means. *The Moved-Outers*. Houghton Mifflin.
Christine Weston. *Bhimsa, The Dancing Bear*. Scribner.
Katherine Shippen. *New Found World*. Viking.

1947
Carolyn Sherwin Bailey. *Miss Hickory*. Viking.

Honor Books:
Nancy Barnes. *Wonderful Year*. Messner.
Mary and Conrad Buff. *Big Tree*. Viking.
William Maxwell. *The Heavenly Tenants*. Harper & Row.
Cyrus Fisher. *The Avion My Uncle Flew*. Appleton.
Eleanore Jewett. *The Hidden Treasure of Glaston*. Viking.

1948
William Pène du Bois. *The Twenty-One Balloons*. Viking.

Honor Books:
Claire Huchet Bishop. *Pancakes-Paris*. Viking.
Carolyn Treffinger. *Li Lun, Lad of Courage*. Abingdon.
Catherine Besterman. *The Quaint and Curious Quest of Johnny Longfoot*. Bobbs-
    Merrill.
Harold Courlander. *The Cow-Tail Switch, and Other West African Stories*. Holt.
Marguerite Henry. *Misty of Chincoteague*. Rand McNally.

1949
Marguerite Henry. *King of the Wind*. Rand McNally.

Honor Books:
Holling C. Holling. *Seabird*. Houghton Mifflin.
Louise Rankin. *Daughter of the Mountains*. Viking.
Ruth S. Gannett. *My Father's Dragon*. Random House.
Arna Bontemps. *Story of the Negro*. Knopf.

1950
Marguerite de Angeli. *The Door in the Wall*. Doubleday.

Honor Books:
Rebecca Caudill. *Tree of Freedom*. Viking.
Catherine Coblentz. *The Blue Cat of Castle Town*. Longmans.
Rutherford Montgomery. *Kildee House*. Doubleday.
Genevieve Foster. *George Washington*. Scribner.
Walter and Marion Havighurst. *Song of the Pines*. Winston.

1951
Elizabeth Yates. *Amos Fortune, Free Man*. Aladdin.

Honor Books:
Mabel Leigh Hunt. *Better Known as Johnny Appleseed*. Lippincott.
Jeanette Eaton. *Gandhi, Fighter Without a Sword*. Morrow.
Clara Ingram Judson. *Abraham Lincoln, Friend of the People*. Follett.
Anne Parrish. *The Story of Appleby Capple*. Harper & Row.

1952
Eleanor Estes. *Ginger Pye*. Harcourt Brace Jovanovich.

Honor Books:
Elizabeth Baity. *Americans Before Columbus*. Viking.
Holling C. Holling. *Minn of the Mississippi*. Houghton Mifflin.
Nicholas Kalashnikoff. *The Defender*. Scribner.
Julia Sauer. *The Light at Tern Rocks*. Viking.
Mary and Conrad Buff. *The Apple and the Arrow*. Houghton Mifflin.

1953

Ann Nolan Clark. *Secret of the Andes*. Viking.

Honor Books:
E. B. White. *Charlotte's Web*. Harper & Row.
Eloise McGraw. *Moccasin Trail*. Coward-McCann.
Ann Weil. *Red Sails to Capri*. Viking.
Alice Dalgliesh. *The Bears on Hemlock Mountain*. Scribner.
Genevieve Foster. *Birthdays Of Freedom*. Vol. 1. Scribner.

1954

Joseph Krumgold, . . . *And Now Miguel*. Crowell.

Honor Books:
Claire Huchet Bishop. *All Alone*. Viking.
Meindert DeJong. *Shadrach*. Harper & Row.
Meindert DeJong. *Hurry Home Candy*. Harper & Row.
Clara Ingram Judson. *Theodore Roosevelt, Fighting Patriot*. Follett.
Mary and Conrad Buff. *Magic Maize*. Houghton Mifflin.

1955

Meindert DeJong. *The Wheel on the School*. Harper & Row.

Honor Books:
Alice Dalgliesh. *Courage of Sarah Noble*. Scribner.
James Ullman. *Banner in the Sky*. Lippincott.

1956

Jean Lee Latham. *Carry On, Mr. Bowditch*. Houghton Mifflin.

Honor Books:
Marjorie Kinnan Rawlings. *The Secret River*. Scribner.
Jennie Lindquist. *The Golden Name Day*. Harper & Row.
Katherine Shippen. *Men, Microscopes, and Living Things*. Viking.

1957

Virginia Sorensen. *Miracles on Maple Hill*. Harcourt Brace Jovanovich.

Honor Books:
Fred Gipson. *Old Yeller*. Harper & Row
Meindert DeJong. *The House of Sixty Fathers*. Harper & Row.
Clara Ingram Judson. *Mr. Justice Holmes*. Follett.
Dorothy Rhoads. *The Corn Grows Ripe*. Viking.
Marguerite de Angeli. *Black Fox of Lorne*. Doubleday.

1958

Harold Keith. *Rifles for Watie*. Thomas Y. Crowell.

Honor Books:
Mari Sandoz. *The Horsecatcher*. Westminster.
Elizabeth Enright. *Gone-Away Lake*. Harcourt Brace Jovanovich.
Robert Lawson. *The Great Wheel*. Viking.
Leo Gurko. *Tom Paine, Freedom's Apostle*. Thomas Y. Crowell.

1959
Elizabeth George Speare. *The Witch of Blackbird Pond*. Houghton Mifflin.

Honor Books:
Natalie S. Carlson. *The Family Under the Bridge*. Harper & Row.
Meindert DeJong. *Along Came a Dog*. Harper & Row.
Francis Kalnay. *Chucaro: Wild Pony of the Pampa*. Harcourt Brace Jovanovich.
William O. Steele. *The Perilous Road*. Harcourt Brace Jovanovich.

1960
Joseph Krumgold. *Onion John*. Thomas Y. Crowell.

Honor Books:
Jean George. *My Side of the Mountain*. Dutton.
Gerald W. Johnson. *America Is Born*. Morrow.
Carol Kendall. *The Gammage Cup*. Harcourt Brace Jovanovich.

1961
Scott O'Dell. *Island of the Blue Dolphins*. Houghton Mifflin.

Honor Books:
Gerald W. Johnson. *America Moves Forward*. Morrow.
Jack Schaefer. *Old Ramon*. Houghton Mifflin.
George Selden. *The Cricket in Times Square*. Farrar, Straus & Giroux.

1962
Elizabeth George Speare. *The Bronze Bow*. Houghton Mifflin.

Honor Books:
Edwin Tunis. *Frontier Living*. World.
Eloise McGraw. *The Golden Goblet*. Coward-McCann.
Mary Stolz. *Belling the Tiger*. Harper & Row.

1963
Madeleine L'Engle. *A Wrinkle in Time*. Farrar, Straus & Giroux.

Honor Books:
Sorche Nic Leodhas. *Thistle and Thyme*. Holt.
Olivia Coolidge. *Men of Athens*. Houghton Mifflin.

1964
Emily Cheney Neville. *It's Like This, Cat*. Harper & Row.

Honor Books:
Sterling North. *Rascal*. Dutton.
Ester Wier. *The Loner*. McKay.

1965
Maia Wojciechowska. *Shadow of a Bull*. Atheneum.

Honor Book:
Irene Hunt. *Across Five Aprils*. Follett.

1966
Elizabeth Borten de Treviño. *I, Juan De Pareja*. Farrar, Straus & Giroux.

Honor Books:
Lloyd Alexander. *The Black Cauldron*. Holt.
Randall Jarrell. *The Animal Family*. Pantheon.
Mary Stolz. *The Noonday Friends*. Harper & Row.

1967
Irene Hunt. *Up a Road Slowly*. Collett.

Honor Books:
Scott O'Dell. *The King's Fifth*. Houghton Mifflin.
Isaac Bashevis Singer. *Zlateh the Goat and Other Stories*. Harper & Row.
Mary K. Weik. *The Jazz Man*. Atheneum.

1968
E. L. Konigsburg. *From the Mixed-Up Files of Mrs. Basil E. Frankweiler*. Atheneum.

Honor Books:
E. L. Konigsburg. *Jennifer, Hecate, MacBeth, William McKinley, and Me, Elizabeth*. Atheneum.
Scott O'Dell. *The Black Pearl*. Houghton Mifflin.
Isaac Bashevis Singer. *The Fearsome Inn*. Scribner.
Zilpha Keatley Snyder. *The Egypt Game*. Atheneum.

1969
Lloyd Alexander. *The High King*. Holt.

Honor Books:
Julius Lester. *To Be a Slave*. Dial.
Isaac Bashevis Singer. *When Shlemiel Went to Warsaw & Other Stories*. Farrar, Straus & Giroux.

1970
William H. Armstrong. *Sounder*. Harper & Row.

Honor Books:
Sulamith Ish-Kishor. *Our Eddie*. Pantheon.
Janet Gaylord Moore. *The Many Ways of Seeing: An Introduction to the Pleasures of Art*. World.
Mary Q. Steele. *Journey Outside*. Viking.

1971
Betsy Byars. *Summer of the Swans*. Viking.

Honor Books:
Natalie Babbitt. *Knee-Knock Rise*. Farrar, Straus & Giroux.
Sylvia Louise Engdahl. *Enchantress from the Stars*. Atheneum.
Scott O'Dell. *Sing Down the Moon*. Houghton Mifflin.

1972
Robert C. O'Brien. *Mrs. Frisby and the Rats of NIMH*. Atheneum.

Honor Books:
Miska Miles. *Annie and the Old One*. Atlantic–Little, Brown.
Zilpha Keatley Snyder. *The Headless Cupid*. Atheneum.
Allan W. Eckert. *Incident at Hawk's Hill*. Little, Brown.
Virginia Hamilton. *The Planet of Junior Brown*. Macmillan.
Ursula K. Le Guin. *The Tombs of Atuan*. Atheneum.

1973
Jean Craighead George. *Julie of the Wolves*. Harper & Row.

Honor Books:
Arnold Lobel. *Frog and Toad Together*. Harper & Row.
Johanna Reiss. *The Upstairs Room*. Thomas Y. Crowell.
Zilpha Keatley Snyder. *The Witches of Worm*. Atheneum.

1974
Paula Fox. *The Slave Dancer*. Bradbury.

Honor Book:
Susan Cooper. *The Dark Is Rising*. Atheneum.

1975
Virginia Hamilton. *M. C. Higgins the Great*. Macmillan.

Honor Books:
Ellen Raskin. *Figgs & Phantoms*. Dutton.
James Lincoln Collier and Christopher Collier. *My Brother Sam Is Dead*. Four Winds Press.
Elizabeth Marie Pope. *The Perilous Gard*. Houghton Mifflin.
Bette Green. *Phillip Hall Likes Me, I Reckon Maybe*. Dial.

1976
Susan Cooper. *The Grey King*. Atheneum.

Honor Books:
Sharon Bell Mathis. *The Hundred Penny Box*. Viking.
Lawrence Yep. *Dragonwings*. Harper & Row.

THE CARNEGIE MEDAL

Sponsored by the British Library Association, the Carnegie Medal was established in 1937. It is awarded annually to an outstanding book published in the United Kingdom and written in English.

1936 *Pigeon Post* by Arthur Ransome. Cape.

1937 *The Family from One End Street* by Eve Garnett. Muller.

1938 *The Circus Is Coming* by Noel Streatfeild. Dent.

1939 *Radium Woman* by Eleanor Doorly. Heinemann.

1940 *Visitors from London* by Kitty Barne. Dent.

1941 *We Couldn't Leave Dinah* by Mary Treadgold. Penguin.

1942 *The Little Grey Men* by B. B. Eyre & Spottiswoode.

1943 No Award

1944 *The Wind on the Moon* by Eric Linklater. Macmillan.

1945 No Award

1946 *The Little White Horse* by Elizabeth Goudge. Brockhampton Press.

1947 *Collected Stories for Children* by Walter de la Mare. Faber.

1948 *Sea Change* by Richard Armstrong. Dent.

1949 *The Story of Your Home* by Agnes Allen. Transatlantic.

1950 *The Lark on the Wing* by Elfrida Vipont Foulds. Oxford.

1951 *The Wool-Pack* by Cynthia Harnett. Methuen.

1952 *The Borrowers* by Mary Norton. Dent.

1953 *A Valley Grows Up* by Edward Osmond. Oxford.

1954 *Knight Crusader* by Ronald Welch. Oxford.

1955 *The Little Bookroom* by Eleanor Farjeon. Oxford.

1956 *The Last Battle* by C. S. Lewis. Bodley Head.

1957 *A Grass Rope* by William Mayne. Oxford.

1958 *Tom's Midnight Garden* by Phillippa Pearce. Oxford.

1959 *The Lantern Bearers* by Rosemary Sutcliff. Oxford.

1960 *The Making of Man* by I. W. Cornwall. Phoenix.

1961 *A Stranger at Green Knowe* by Lucy Boston. Faber.

1962 *The Twelve and the Genii* by Pauline Clarke. Faber.

1963 *Time of Trial* by Hester Burton. Oxford.

1964   *Nordy Banks* by Sheena Porter. Oxford.

1965   *The Grange at High Force* by Philip Turner. Oxford.

1966   No Award

1967   *The Owl Service* by Alan Garner. Collins.

1968   *The Moon in the Cloud* by Rosemary Harris. Faber.

1969   *The Edge of the Cloud* by K. M. Peyton. Oxford.

1970   *The God Beneath the Sea* by Leon Garfield and Edward Blishen. Kestrel.

1971   *Josh* by Ivan Southall. Angus & Robertson.

1972   *Watership Down* by Richard Adams. Rex Collings.

1973   *The Ghost of Thomas Kempe* by Penelope Lively. Heinemann.

1974   *The Stronghold* by Mollie Hunter. Hamilton.

1975   *The Machine-Gunners* by Robert Westall. Macmillan.

DIRECTORY OF SOURCES

Abelard, Schuman, Ltd., 666 Fifth Avenue, New York, NY 10019

Abingdon Press, 201 Eighth Avenue South, Nashville, TN 37202

ACI Films, 35 West 45 Street, New York, NY 10036

Addison-Wesley Publishing Co., Reading, MA 01867

Aims Instructional Media Services, P.O. Box 1010, Hollywood, CA 90028

Allyn & Bacon, Rockleigh, NJ 07647

American Heritage Press, 1221 Avenue of the Americas, New York, NY 10020

American Library Association, Publishing Services, 50 E. Huron St., Chicago, IL 60611

Association for Childhood Education International, 3615 Wisconsin Ave., NW, Washington, D.C. 20016

Atheneum Publishers, 122 East 42d Street, New York, NY 10017

Avon Books, 959 Eighth Avenue, New York, NY 10019.

Barr Films, P.O. Box 7-C, Pasadena, CA 91104

Beacon Press, 25 Beacon St., Boston, MA 02108

Bell & Howell, 2201 West Howard, Evanston, IL 60202

Bobbs-Merrill Company, 4300 W. 62d Street, Indianapolis, IN 46268

Stephen Bosustow Productions, 1649 11th Street, Santa Monica, CA 90404

The R. R. Bowker Company, Xerox Education Group, 1180 Avenue of the Americas, New York, NY 10036

Bowmar Publishing Corporation, 622 Rodier Drive, Glendale, CA 91201

Bradbury Press, 2 Overhill Road, Scarsdale, NY 10583

Brigham Young University, Motion Picture Dept., M.P.S., Provo, UT 84602

Centron Educational Films, 1621 West Ninth, Lawrence, KS 66044

Changing Times Education Service, 1729 H Street, N.W., Washington, DC 20006

Children's Book Council, Inc., 67 Irving Place, New York, NY 10003.

Childrens Press, 1224 W. Van Buren Street, Chicago, IL 60607

Churchill Films, 662 North Robertson Blvd., Los Angeles, CA 90069

Citation Press, 50 W. 44th Street, New York, NY 10036

Clearvue, 6666 North Oliphant Avenue, Chicago, IL 60631

William Collins & World Publishing Co., 2080 West 117th Street, Cleveland, OH 44111

Columbia University Press, 562 W. 113th Street, New York, NY 10025

Contemporary Press, Box 1524, San Jose, CA 95109

Coronet Instructional Media, 65 East South Water Street, Chicago, IL 60601

Council on Interracial Books for Children, 1841 Broadway, New York, NY 10023

Coward, McCann & Geoghegan, 200 Madison Avenue, New York, NY 10016

Thomas Y. Crowell Co., 666 Fifth Avenue, New York, NY 10019

Crowell-Collier Press, 640 5th Ave., New York, NY 10019

Crown Publishers, 419 Park Avenue South, New York, NY 10016

The John Day Co., 666 Fifth Avenue, New York, NY 10019

Delacorte Press, 1 Dag Hammarskjold Plaza, 245 East 47th Street, New York, NY 10017

The Dial Press, 1 Dag Hammarskjold Plaza, 245 East 47th Street, New York, NY 10017

Dilton Press, 106 Washington Ave. N. Minneapolis, MN 55401

Disney, Walt, Educational Materials, 800 Sonora Avenue, Glendale, CA 91201

Dodd, Mead & Co., 79 Madison Avenue, New York, NY 10016

Doubleday & Co., 245 Park Avenue, New York, NY 10017

Doubleday Multimedia, 1371 Reynolds Avenue, Santa Ana, CA 92705

E. P. Dutton & Co., 201 Park Avenue South, New York, NY 10003

Educational Development Corporation, 202 Lake Miriam Drive, Lakeland, FL 33803

EMC Corporation, 180 East Sixth Street, St. Paul, MN 55101

Encyclopaedia Britannica Educational Corporation, 425 North Michigan Avenue, Chicago, IL 60611

M. Evans & Co., 216 East 49th Street, New York, NY 10017

Farrar, Straus & Giroux, 19 Union Square West, New York, NY 10003

F. W. Faxon Company, 15 Southwest Park, Westwood, MA 02090

The Feminist Press, Box 334, Old Westbury, NY 11568

Follett Publishing Co., 1010 West Washington Blvd., Chicago, IL 60607

Four Winds Press, 50 West 44th Street, New York, NY 10036

Funk & Wagnalls, Inc., 53 E. 77th St., New York, NY 10021

Garrard Publishing Company, 1607 N. Market St., Champaign, IL 61820

General Educational Media, 350 Northern Blvd., Great Neck, NY 10021

Golden Gate Junior Books, 1247½ North Vista Street, Hollywood, CA 90046

Golden Press, (Western Publishing Co.), 850 Third Avenue, New York, NY 10022

Goldsholl Associates, 420 Frontage Road, Northfield, IL 60093

Grant, Allan, Productions, 808 Lockearn Street, Los Angeles, CA 90049

Grosset & Dunlap, 51 Madison Avenue, New York, NY 10010

Guidance Associates, 41 Washington Avenue, Pleasantville, NY 10570

G. K. Hall & Company, 70 Lincoln St., Boston, MA 02111

Harcourt Brace Jovanovich, 757 Third Avenue, New York, NY 10017

Harper & Row, Publishers, 10 East 53rd Street, New York, NY 10022

Harvey House, 20 Waterside Plaza, New York, NY 10010

Hastings House Publishers, 10 East 40th Street, New York, NY 10016

Hawthorn Books, 260 Madison Avenue, New York, NY 10016

Holiday House, 18 East 56th Street, New York, NY 10022

Holt, Rinehart & Winston, 383 Madison Avenue, New York, NY 10017

Horn Book, Inc., 585 Boylston St., Boston, MA 02116

Houghton Mifflin Co., 2 Park Street, Boston, MA 02107

International Reading Association, 800 Barksdale Rd., Newark, DE 19711

Alfred A. Knopf, 201 East 50th Street, New York, NY 10022

Learning Corporation of America, 711 Fifth Avenue, New York, NY 10022

Learning Resources Company, P.O. Box 3709, 202 Lake Mirian Dr., Lakeland, FL 33803

Learning Tree Filmstrips, 934 Pearl Street, P.O. Box 1590, Dept. 105, Boulder, CO 80302

Lerner Publications Company, 241 First Avenue North, Minneapolis, MN 55401

Libraries Unlimited, Box 263, Littleton, CO 80120

J. B. Lippincott Company, 521 Fifth Avenue, New York, NY 10017

Little, Brown & Co., 34 Beacon Street, Boston, MA 02106

Lothrop, Lee & Shepard Company, 105 Madison Avenue, New York, NY 10016

Macrae Smith Company, Lewis Tower Bldg., 225 S. 15th St., Philadelphia, PA 19102

Macmillan Publishing Co., 866 Third Avenue, New York, NY 10022

McGraw-Hill Book Co., 1221 Avenue of the Americas, New York, NY 10020

David McKay Company, Publishers, 750 3d Avenue, New York, NY 10017

Merrill, Charles E., Publishing Co., 1300 Alum Creek Dr., Columbus, OH 43216

Julian Messner (A Division of Simon & Schuster), 1 West 39th Street, New York, NY 10018

Miller-Brody Productions, 711 Fifth Avenue, New York, NY 10022

William Morrow & Co., 105 Madison Avenue, New York, NY 10016

National Council for the Social Studies, 1201 Sixteenth St. NW, Washington, DC 20036

National Council of Teachers of English, 1111 Kenyon Rd., Urbana, IL 61801

National Council of Teachers of Mathematics, 1906 Assoc. Dr., Reston, VA 22091

National Instructional Television, Box A, Bloomington, IN 47401

Thomas Nelson, 407 7th Ave. S., Nashville, TN 37203

Newsweek, 444 Madison Avenue, New York, NY 10022

New York Library Association, Children and Young Adult Services Section 230 W. 41st Street, Suite 1800, New York, NY 10036

New York Office of State History, State Education Dept., 99 Washington Ave., Albany, NY 12210

J. Philip O'Hara, 20 E. Huron Street, Chicago, IL 60611

Oxford Films, 1136 North Las Palmas Avenue, Los Angeles, CA 90036

Oxford University Press, 200 Madison Avenue, New York, NY 10016

Pantheon Books, 201 East 50th Street, New York, NY 10022

Parents' Magazine Press, 52 Vanderbilt Avenue, New York, NY 10017

Parnassus Press, 4080 Halleck Street, Emeryville, CA 94608

Pathescope Educational Films, 71 Weyman Avenue, New Rochelle, NY 10802

S. G. Phillips, 305 West 86th Street, New York, NY 10024

Pied Piper Productions, P.O. Box 320, Verdugo City, CA 91046

Plays, 8 Arlington Street, Boston, MA 02116

Platt & Munk, Publishers, 1055 Bronx River Avenue, Bronx, NY 10572

Prentice-Hall, Englewood Cliffs, NJ 07632

Psychology Today, De Mar, CA 92014

G. P. Putnam's Sons, 200 Madison Avenue, New York, NY 10016

Pyramid Films Corporation, P.O. Box 1048, Santa Monica, CA 90406

Q-ED Productions, P.O. Box 1608, Burbank, CA 91507

Rand McNally & Co., P.O. Box 7600, Chicago, IL 60680

Random House Educational Media, Order Entry Department-Y, 400 Hahn Road, Westminster, MD 21157

The Reilly & Lee Co., 114 W. Illinois Street, Chicago, IL 60610

The Ronald Press Co., 79 Madison Ave., New York, NY 10016

St. Martin's Press, 175 Fifth Avenue, New York, NY 10010

Salinger Educational Media, 1635 12th Street, Santa Monica, CA 90404

Scarecrow Press, 52 Liberty St. Box 656, Metuchen, NJ 08840

Schloat Productions, 150 White Plains Road, Tarrytown, NY 10591

Schmitt, Hall & McCreary Co., 110 N. Fifth Street, Minneapolis, MN 55403

Scholastic Magazines, Audio Visual and Media Dept., 50 West 44th St., New York, NY 10036

Scott, Foresman & Co., Educational Publishers, 1900 E. Lake Ave., Glenview, IL 60025

Screen Education Enterprises, 3220 16th Avenue West, Seattle, WA 98119

Charles Scribner's Sons, 597 Fifth Street, New York, NY 10017

Scroll Press, Publishers, 129 East 94th Street, New York, NY 10028

The Seabury Press, 815 Second Avenue, New York, NY 10017

See Hear Now! Ltd., 49 Wellington Street East, Toronto M5E 1C9 Canada

Simon & Schuster, Publishers, 630 5th Avenue, New York, NY 10020

Steck-Vaughn Co., Division of Intext Publishers Group, Box 2028, Austin, TX 78767

Sterling Publishing Co., 419 Park Ave. S., New York, NY 10016

Teaching Resources Films, Station Plaza, Bedford Hills, NY 10507

Technicolor, 299 Kalmus Drive, Costa Mesa, CA 92626

Troll Associates, 320 Route 17, Mahwah, NJ 07430

University of Chicago Press, 5801 Ellis Ave., Chicago, IL 60637

University of Pittsburgh Press, 127 N. Bellefield Ave., Pittsburgh, PA 15213

The Vanguard Press, 424 Madison Ave., New York, NY 10017

Van Nostrand-Reinhold Co., 450 W. 33rd Street, New York, NY 10001

The Viking Press, 625 Madison Ave., New York, NY 10022

Henry Z. Walck, Publishers, 19 Union Square W., New York, NY 10003

Walker & Co., 720 5th Ave., New York, NY 10019

The Ward Ritchie Press (Anderson, Ritchie & Simon), 3044 Riverside Dr., Los Angeles, CA 90039

Frederick Warne & Co., 101 5th Ave., New York, NY 10003

Ives Washburn, 750 3d Ave., New York, NY 10017

Franklin Watts, 730 5th Ave., New York, NY 10019

Westminster Press, Witherspoon Bldg., Philadelphia, PA 19107

Weston Woods, Weston, CT 06880

Albert Whitman & Co., 560 West Lake Street, Chicago, IL 60606

The H. W. Wilson Co., 950 University Ave., New York, NY 10452

Windmill Books, 201 Park Ave. S., New York, NY 10003

William Collins & World Publishing Co., 2080 W. 117th St., Cleveland, OH 44111

Xerox Films, 245 Long Hill Rd., Middletown, CT 0647

Young Scott Books, Reading, MA 01867

Index

Aardema, Verna, 59
Aaron and the Green Mountain Boys, 433
Abbott, R. T., 387
ABC, 42
ABC Alphabet Cookbook, 41
ABC An Alphabet Book, 42
ABC Bunny, The, 42, 520
ABC of Buses, 42
ABC of Cars and Trucks, 41
Abecedarian Book, The, 378–379
Abortion, 470
About the B'nai Bagels, 207
*About Wise Men and Simpletons; Twelve
    Tales from Grimm,* 226
Abraham Lincoln, 511
Abraham Lincoln Friend of the People, 523
Abraham Lincoln's World, 522
Abrahams, Robert D., 180
Abrashkin, Raymond, 128
Across Five Aprils, 526
Acrostics, 25
Acting out, 221
Adam of the Road, 522
Adams, Abigail, 337
Adams, Adrienne, 60, 66, 227, 515
Adams, J. Donald, 378
Adams, Julia D., 519
Adams, Richard, 49
Adams ABC, 412
Adaptation, 396
Addams, Charles, 35
Adler, Irving, 382
Adler, Ruth, 382
Adoff, Arnold, 156
Adolescents, 470
Adoption, 55
Adult roles, 468, 470–474
Adults, 16–19
Adventures of a Naval Officer, 493
Adventures of Obadiah, The, 152
Adventures of Paddy Pork, The, 75
Adventures of Pinocchio, The, 87
Adventures of Tom Sawyer, The, 436,
    473, 494, 496
Adventures with a Cardboard Tube, 57

Adventuring with Books, 425
*Adventuring with Books: Twenty-four
    Hundred Titles for Preschool —Grade
    8,* 28
Aesop, 217, 262–263, 264, 393
Aesop's Fables, 219, 490
A for the Ark, 41
Africa, 52
African folklore, 249
African Wonder Tales, 263
Aged, 55, 177–186
Ageless Story, The, 511
Agle, Nana H., 440
Aiken, Joan, 130, 134–135
A Is for Annabelle, 42
Alain *see* Chartier, Emile
Album of Martin Luther King, An, 441
*Album of Women in American History,
    An,* 175
Alcoholism, 153
Alcott, Louisa May, 69, 339, 473, 474
    493, 494
Aldis, Dorothy, 50, 304
Alee, Marjorie, 519
Alexander, Anne, 41
Alexander, Arthur, 287, 380
Alexander, Lloyd, 11, 53, 86, 130, 131,
    135–136, 143, 526
Alexander, Martha, 54, 74, 347
Alexander and the Wind-Up Mouse, 516
Alger, Horatio, 496
Alice in Wonderland, 86, 473, 475, 493
Alice's Adventures in Wonderland, 87
Aliki, 35
All about the Months, 408
*Allah, The God of Islam; Moslem Life and
    Worship,* 407
All Alone, 524
All Around the Town, 41, 512
Allen, Terry, 188
All Falling Down, 513
All in a Suitcase, 42
All in the Morning Early, 68, 515
Alliteration, 287–288
All Kinds of Mothers, 173

All-of-a-kind Family Downtown, 413
All Sail Set, 520
"All Sky Disappears," 300
All Upon a Sidewalk, 375
Allusions, 329
Along Came a Dog, 67, 525
Alphabet books, 41–43
Alphabet Tale, The, 42
Altogether, One at a Time, 167, 180, 207
Alvin Steadfast on Vernacular Island, 381
Always Room for One More, 59, 516
Amahl and the Night Visitors, 405
Ambrus, Victor G., 52
America Is Born, 525
America Moves Forward, 525
American ABC, An, 511
American Association for the
    Advancement of Science, 425
American Birds, 390
"American Doctoral Dissertations in
    Children's and Adolescents'
    Literature," 488
American history, 428
American Indian, 14
American Indian Craft Inspirations, 191
American Indians Sing, 188
American Indian Women, 189, 342
American Institute of Graphic Arts, 60
American Library Association, 58
American Revolution, 430–434
American Revolution, The, 432
*American Revolution for Young Readers;
    A Bibliography, The,* 431
American Revolution, 1760–1783, The,
    432
Americans Before Columbus, 523
America's Ethan Allen, 433, 513
America's Mark Twain, 436
"America the Beautiful," 338
Amos & Boris, 386
Amos Fortune, Free Man, 203, 441, 523
Amphibians, 387
Amy and Laura, 152
Anansi, the Spider, 517
Anastasiow, Nicholas, 344

Anatole, 514
Anatole and the Cat, 50, 64, 107, 514
Anatole and the Thirty Thieves, 25
Andersen, Hans Christian, 65, 66, 227, 406, 473, 474, 514
Andersen, Yvonne, 398
Anderson, C. W., 49
Anderson, Douglas, 322
Anderson, Lonzo, 109
Anderson, Marian, 349
Anderson, William, 503
And I Must Hurry for the Sea Is Coming In, 149
. . . And Now Miguel, 194, 342, 524
And One Was a Wooden Indian, 190
And Then What Happened, Paul Revere?, 433
And to Think That I Saw It on Mulberry Street, 50, 72, 340, 346, 498
Andy and the Lion, 221, 511
Andy's Mountain, 180
Andy (that's my name), 381
Angel of Olvera Street, The, 512
Angels, Valenti, 521
Anglund, Joan W., 35, 161, 228, 404
Angry Moon, The, 190, 517
Animal Disguises, 382, 383
"Animal Fair, The," 297
Animal Family, The, 67, 526
Animal Homes, 57
Animal Land: The Creatures of Children's Fiction, 49, 83
Animal Movers; A Collection of Ecological Surprises, 396
Animals, stories about, 45–50, 88–109, 308–311, 388–393
Animals of the Bible, 510
Anker, Charlotte, 157
Ann Aurelia and Dorothy, 174
Ann Can Fly, 174
Annie and the Old One, 160, 527
Annie Annie, 152
Ant and the Grasshopper, The, 217–218
Anthology of Children's Literature, 262, 364
Anthony, Susan B., 210
Ant Is Born, An, 389
"Antonio," 167, 296
Ants and Termites, 389
Any Me I Want to Be, 315
Apt. 3, 11, 412
Ape in a Cape, 42, 513
Apple and the Arrow, The, 523
Apprentice of Florence, 520
"April," 281
"April Rain Song," 485
April's Kittens, 511
Arabia, 66
Arabian Nights, 473
Arbital, Samuel L., 411

Arbuthnot Anthology of Children's Literature, The, 234, 363
Arbuthnot, May H., 22, 143, 227, 275, 363, 499
Archetypes, 337
Ardema, Verna, 517
Ardizzone, Edward, 51, 173
Arenstein, Misha, 315, 408
Are You My Mother?, 225
"Arithmetic," 319
Armenia, 52
Armer, Laura A., 510, 519
Armstrong, William H., 438, 526
Arnstein, Flora J., 322
Arora, Shirley, 348
Around and Around Love, 149
Arrow to the Sun, 59, 188, 477, 517
Art, 10–11, 20, 77, 211, 330–331
Arthur Mitchell, 441
Arthur Rackham Fairy Books; A Book of Old Favorites with New Illustrations, 227
Arthur's Christmas Cookies, 405
Art of the Plains Indians, The, 14
Art of the Southwest Indians, The, 192
Artzybasheff, Boris, 219, 240, 510
Aruego, José, 74
Asbjörnsen, Peter, 223, 232
Ashabranner, Brent, 191
Asimov, Isaac, 246–247, 380, 382, 383, 398
Ask Mr. Bear, 225
Assessing books, 13
Association for Childhood Education, 230, 263
At the Back of the North Wind, 87, 474, 494
At the Center of the World, 189
At the Mouth of the Luckiest River, 190
Attitudes and Avowals, 226
Atwater, Florence, 108, 521
Atwater, Richard, 108, 521
Atwood, Ann, 301, 396
Audubon, 521
Auslander, Joseph, 295
Austin, Mary C., 275, 304, 393
Authors, 10, 50–51, 58–70, 197–202, 341, 499–500
Avion My Uncle Flew, The, 522
Awards, 470–474, 504–510
Away Goes Sally, 428
Away Is So Far, 160
Ayme, Marcel, 108

Babar y el picaro Arturo, 355
Baba Yaga, 238
Baba Yaga and Kind-Hearted Hildy, 236–238
"Baba Yaga's Geese," 239, 345

Baba Yaga's Geese and Other Russian Stories, 239
Babbitt, Ellen C., 219
Babbitt, Natalie, 12, 21, 115, 174, 209, 527
Baboushka and the Three Kings, 241, 515
Baby Elephant and the Secret Wishes, 405
Baby Starts to Grow, A, 82
Bach, Alice, 150
Backpacking, 396
Backwards for Luck, 180
Bacmeister, Rhoda, 288, 304
Bad Bell of San Salvador, The, 188
Bad Boy, Good Boy, 193
Bahti, Tom, 517
Bailey, Carolyn S., 522
Baity, Elizabeth, 523
Baker, Betty, 189, 190
Baker, Laura N., 405
Baldur and the Mistletoe, 255
Baldwin, Anne N., 153
Bales, Carol A., 190
Balet, Jan, 405
Ballantyne, Robert, 493
Baltimore Orioles, 391
Bambi, 69
Bambino the Clown, 512
Bang, Garrett, 245
Bannerman, Helen, 494
Banner in the Sky, 524
Bare, Arnold, 511
Barkis, 511
Barkley, James, 269, 438
Barksdale, Lena, 403
Barnaby, Ralph S., 397
Barnes, Nancy, 522
Barnum, Jay H., 512
Barnwell, Robinson, 158
Baron, Virginia, 211, 321
Barrie, Sir James, 87, 143, 497
Bartholomew and the Oobleck, 513
Bartlett, Robert M., 403
Bartlett, Ruth, 389
Bartoli, Jennifer, 55, 160
Barton, Byron, 74
Baruch, Dorothy, 305
"Base Stealer, The," 485
Baskin, Hosea, 41, 517
Baskin, Leonard, 41, 517
Baskin, Lisa, 517
Baskin, Tobias, 517
Bat-Poet, The, 67
Bauer, Helen, 394
Baum, L. Frank, 87, 496, 497
Baum, Willi, 74
Bawden, Nina, 151, 168, 204–206, 469
Baylor, Byrd, 190, 517
Baynes, Pauline, 37
Beach, Richard, 479–480, 488–489
Beame, Rona, 394, 413

Bear Called Paddington, A, 89
Bear Party, 513
Bears on Hemlock Mountain, The, 524
Beatty, Patricia, 188
Beckman, Gunnel, 470
Becky's Christmas, 406
Bedtime for Frances, 47
Bedtime Story, A, 324
Bee-Man of Orn, The, 115
Befana's Gift, 406
Behn, Harry, 171, 300, 305, 309, 322, 341
Beim, Jerrold, 400
Being Afraid, 168
Being Small, 168
Being Overweight, 168
"Be like the bird," 269–270
Belling the Tiger, 108, 525
Belloc, Hilaire, 289
Bell That Rang for Freedom: The Liberty Bell and Its Place in American History, The, 432
Belov, Ruth, 57
Belpré, Pura, 52, 263
Belshaw, Sharon, 434
Belting, Natalie M., 214, 515
Bemelmans, Ludwig, 6, 60, 171, 173, 406, 498, 511, 514, 521
Ben and Me, 107, 349, 428, 431
Benchley, Nathaniel, 107, 190, 386
Bendick, Jeanne, 382, 396
Benét, Rosemary C., 316, 430
Benét, Stephen V., 304, 316, 430
Benjamin Franklin, 433
Benjie, 64
Bennett, John, 519
Bennett, Rowena B., 272, 305, 338, 339, 417
Beowulf, 256
Berg, Jean H., 440
Bergaust, Erik, 384
Berger, Melvin, 384, 394
Bernadette, 228
Berries Goodman, 200
Berry, Erick, 520
Berson, Harold, 52, 225
Best, Herbert, 519
Best Christmas, The, 406
Best Christmas Pageant Ever, The, 405
Besterman, Catherine, 523
Best Friends, 163
Best in Children's Books: The University of Chicago Guide to Children's Literature, 1966–72, The, 28
Bethell, Jean, 397
Bettelheim, Bruno, 222
Better Known as Johnny Appleseed, 523
"Betty Botter," 40, 484
Beyer, Evelyn, 294
Beyond the Burning Lands, 127

Beyond Words, 87, 230
Bhimsa, The Dancing Bear, 522
Bianco, Margery, 108, 521
Bicentennial, 430
"Bicentennial Reading," 434
Bicentennial Reading, Viewing, Listening, 434
Bierhorst, John, 188
Big Book of Submarines, The, 387
Big City, A, 42
Big Cowboy Western, 412
Biggest Bear, The, 48, 50, 513
Biggest Fish in the Sea, The, 52
Big Sister and Little Sister, 53, 54
Big Snow, The, 512
Big Star Fallin' Mama, 349, 441
Big Tree, 522
Big Tree of Bunlahy, 520
Big Wave, The, 159
Bileck, Marvin, 516
Billings, Josh, 381
Billy and Blaze, 49
Biographies, 50, 187, 195, 210, 342, 433, 440–441, 476, 500
Biography of a Wolf, 388
Bird of Time, The, 53
Birds, 390
Birds; A Guide to the Most Familiar American Birds, 390
Birds' Christmas Carol, The, 406
Birds of a Feather, 74
Birds on Your Street, 390
Bird Talk 390
Birnbaum, A., 514
Birth, 32
Birthdays, 210
Birthdays of Freedom, 524
Bishop, Claire H., 523, 524
Bissett, Donald J., 76
Black, Algernon, 68
Black Americans, 54, 150, 162–163, 164–165, 175, 178, 179, 349, 421, 436–445, 476
Black and Blue Magic, 414
Black authors, 196
Black Beauty, 473, 474, 494
"Blackbird Suddenly, A," 295
Black Cauldron, The, 122, 526
Black English, 438–439, 494
Black folklore, 249
Black Fox of Lorne, 524
Black Hearts of Battersea, 135
Black Is Brown Is Tan, 156
Black Pearl, The, 194, 526
Blacks, see Black Americans
Bladerunner, The, 126
Blaine, Marge, 153
Blake, William, 304, 491
Blassingame, Wyatt, 387
Bleeker, Sonia, 161

Blegvad, Erik, 14
Blindness, 164, 165, 178
Blishen, Edward, 252
Bliven, Bruce, 432
Bloch, Marie H., 239–240
Blossom on the Bough: A Book of Trees, The, 395
Blount, Margaret, 49, 83
Blowfish Live in the Sea, 152
Bloy, Margaret, 513
Blue Backed Speller, 491
Blue Beard, 226
Blueberries for Sal, 512
Blue Cat of Castle Town, The, 523
Blue Fairy Book, The, 494
Blue, Rose, 55, 156, 180, 413
Blue Rose, The, 165
Blue Whale, The, 385
Blue Whale; Vanishing Leviathan, 385
Blue Willow, 521
Blume, Judy, 12, 13, 156, 167, 168
Boats on the River, 512
Bobo's Dream, 74
Bodies, 57
Bollinger-Savelli, Antonella, 74
Bond, Michael, 49, 89, 347
Bond, Nancy, 115
Bonham, Frank, 193
Bonsall, Crosby, 52
Bontemps, Arna, 523
Bonus of Redonda, The, 180
Book about Pandas, A, 57
Book awards, 58–60, 470, 478, 504–510
Booke in Englysh Metre, A, 490
Book file, 15
Book for Boys and Girls, A, 491
Book language, 138, 344
Booklist and Subscription Books Bulletin, The, 341
Book of Americans, 316, 430
Book of Courtesye, 490
Book of Dwarfs, A, 230
Book of Greek Myths, 251
Book of King Arthur and His Noble Knights, The, 260
Book of Monsters, A, 21, 230–231
Book of Nursery and Mother Goose Rhymes, 514
Book of Ogres and Trolls, A, 263
Book of Scottish Nursery Rhymes, A, 37
Book of Three, The, 121, 122
Book of Witches, A, 401
Book production, 501
Book reports, 138–139, 351
Books Are by People, 12
Book selection, 20, 33–34, 42, 147, 341–343, 471
Books, evaluating, 13–15, 18
Books for You to Make, 372

Book talks, 351
Book to Begin On: Ocean Wonders, A, 384
Book Week, 24
Borack, Barbara, 180
Borrowers, The, 4, 5, 109
Borten, Helen, 400
Boston, Lucy, 16, 111, 130, 143, 330
Boston Globe, The, 60
Botany, 395
Bottom of the Sea, The, 384
Bova, Benjamin, 128
Bowen, Lord, 298
Bowen, William, 518
Bowman, James C., 521
Bows Against the Barons, 258
Boy, A Dog, A Frog and a Friend, A, 73
Boy, A Dog and A Frog, A, 73
Boy Called Plum, A, 180
Boy Drummer of Vincennes, The, 433
Boy of the South Seas, 519
Boys and Girls Book About Divorce, The, 158
Boys and Girls; Girls and Boys, 172
Boy's King Arthur, The, 258
Boy, The Baker, The Miller and More, The, 52, 225
Boy Who Could Do Anything and Other Mexican Folk Tales, The, 194
Boy Who Cried Wolf, The, 266
Boy Who Was, The, 519
Boy with a Pack, 428, 521
Bradbury, Bianca, 152, 180
Bradbury, Ray, 128
Brady, Irene, 393
Braille, Louis, 167
Brand, Oscar, 433
Brandenberg, Aliki, 46
Brandenberg, Franz, 46
Brandt, Sue R., 397
Branley, Franklyn M., 382, 387
Brasier, Virginia, 310
Bremen Town Musicians, The, 225
Brenner, A., 194
Brenner, Barbara, 57, 389, 390, 391
Brian Wildsmith's ABC, 41
Brian Wildsmith's Birds, 390
Brian Wildsmith's Fishes, 499
Brian Wildsmith's Mother Goose, 37
Brian Wildsmith's 1, 2, 3, 44
Bridgman, Laura D., 167
Briggs, F. Allen, 380
Briggs, Raymond, 35
Bright, Robert, 51, 347
Bright Island, 521
Brighty of the Grand Canyon, 11
Brindze, Ruth, 384
Brink, Carol, 520
British books, 20
British English, 20, 330

British Library Association, 130
British writers, 130
Broadman, Muriel, 267
Brock, Emma, 55
Broderick, Dorothy M., 213
Bronin, Andrew, 57, 396
Bronze Bow, The, 525
Brooke, Leslie, 35, 230
Brooks, Gwendolyn, 283, 304
Brooks, Jerome, 160
Brooks, Walter, 108, 128
Brower, Millicent, 315
Brown, Beatrice C., 281
Brown, Conrad, 398
Brown, Joseph E., 386
Brown, Marc, 43, 45
Brown, Marcia, 3, 13, 33, 59, 64, 66–67, 68, 219–220, 227, 240, 499, 512, 513, 514, 515
Brown, Margaret W., 64, 69, 82, 158, 405, 511, 514
Brown, Palmer, 405
Brown, Slater, 433
Brown, Vinson, 397
Brown Cow Farm, 44
Brownstone, Cecily, 173
Bruno Munari's ABC, 42
Bryson, Bernarda, 515
Bubble Bubble, 347
Buckley, Helen E., 180
Buck, Pearl, 152, 245
Buff, Conrad, 49, 65, 511, 522, 523, 524
Buff, Mary, 49, 65, 511, 522, 523, 524
"Building a Skyscraper," 418
Building Bridges of Understanding Between Cultures, 213
Build Your Own Moon Settlement, 411
Bulla, Clyde R., 14, 152, 191, 261, 435
Bulletin board captions, 364–366
Bulletin of the Center of Children's Books, 14, 21
Bullfinch, Thomas, 267
Bullfinch's Mythology, 267
Bull from the Sea, The, 252
Bun; A Tale from Russia, The, 240
Bunyan, John, 491
Burch, Robert, 162, 172, 406
Burglon, Nora, 520
Burkert, Nancy E., 66, 229, 517
Burnett, Frances H., 109, 494
Burton, Virginia L., 414, 511, 512
Burton and Dudley, 46
Butler, Suzanne, 406
Butterflies, 350
Butterflies and Moths, 350
"Butterfly," 296
Buzzing, R. S., 479, 487

Byars, Betsy, 165, 173, 177, 203, 393, 527
By the Shores of Silver Lake, 521

Cabin Faced West, The, 433, 434
Cable Car and the Dragon, The, 413
Caddie Woodlawn, 477, 520
Caen, Herb, 413
Caldecott, Randolph, 35, 58
Caldecott award, 10, 66, 68, 70, 80–81, 129, 170, 188, 219–220, 240, 404, 470–474, 477, 497, 505, 510–517
Caldecott Medal, 32, 48, 58–60, 63, 64, 498
Caldecott Medal Books: 1938–1957, 83
Calendar, The, 24
Calendars, 408–410
Calibrated Alligator; And Other Science Fiction Stories, The, 128
Calico Bush, 519
"Calico Pie," 281
California, 394
California Indian Tales, 249
Call It Courage, 521
Cameron, Eleanor, 128, 143
Campbell, Camilla, 194
Cane, Melville, 296
Canterbury Tales, The, 68
Can't You Hear Me Talking to You?, 211
Carbonel: The King of the Cats, 108
Careers, 174
Carey, Bonnie, 239
Carle, Eric, 44, 74
Carlson, Bernice W., 258
Carlson, Natalie S., 174, 406, 421, 525
Carlson, Ruth K., 28, 83, 213, 372
Carman, Bliss, 283
Carmer, Carl, 433
Carnegie Medal, 112, 130, 505, 528–529
Carpenter, Frances, 245, 263
Carp in the Bathtub, The, 413, 421
Carr, Mary Jane, 521
Carrick, Donald, 49
Carrie's War, 151, 159, 204
Carroll, Lewis, 87, 130, 143, 281, 298–299, 304, 378, 473, 475, 493
Carroll, Ruth, 73, 74
Carryl, Charles E., 281
Carryl, Guy W., 290
Carry On, Mr. Bowditch, 524
Carson, Rachel, 176, 383
Carter, Candy, 434
Cartwright, Sally, 57
Carver, George W., 349
Case of the Cat's Meow, The, 52
Castle of Llyr, The, 122
Cataldo, John W., 380

"Catalogue," 485
Cat and the Devil, The, 221
Cat and the Hat, The, 50
Catbird, 390, 391
Catch a Little Rhyme, 305
Categories, 27–28, 419
Cathedral: The Story of Its Construction, 517
Cat in the Mirror, 115
Catlin, George, 187
Cat Who Went to Heaven, The, 108, 519
Cat Who Wished to Be a Man, The, 25, 136
Caudill, Rebecca, 68, 152, 428, 516
Cavannah, Frances, 408
Cave: What Lives There, The, 396
Caxton, William, 490
Cay, The, 178
Cedric the Forester, 518
Celebrate the Morning, 156
Celebrating America, 434
Celebrating Christmas Around the World, 404
Celestino Piatti's Animal ABC, 42
Censorship, 478
Centerburg Tales, 109
Central City/Spread City: The Metropolitan Regions Where More and More of Us Spend Our Lives, 412
César Chávez, 195
Chafetz, Henry, 249
Chaffin, Lillie, 337
Chairy Tale, The, 345
Chan, Chin-Yi, 511
Chan, Plao, 511
Change Here for Babylon, 204
Changeling, The, 175
Changes, 156
Changes, Changes, 75
"Changing World of Science and the Social Sciences, The," 425
Channeling Children: Sex Stereotyping in Prime-Time TV, 489
Chanticleer and the Fox, 68, 220, 514
Characterization, 356–358, 427
Charades, 25–27, 28
Charles Addams Mother Goose, The, 35
Charles Richard Drew, 441
Charlie and the Chocolate Factory, 115
Charlie Brown Christmas, A, 406
Charlip, Remy, 43
Charlot, Jean, 511, 514
Charlotte Forten: Free Black Teacher, 452
Charlotte Sometimes, 126
Charlotte's Web, 4, 5, 86, 133, 159, 328, 336, 472, 500, 524
Charro: Mexican Horseman, 194
Chartier, Emile, 44
Chase, Mary Ellen, 3
Chaucer, 514

Cheney, Cora, 174
Chicago, 413
Chicano Girl, 193
Chicanos, *see* Mexican-Americans
Chicanos; Mexicans in the United States, 195
Chicken Licken, 223–224
Chief Joseph, War Chief of the Nez Percé, 191
Child Life, A Collection of Poems, 494
Child of the Silent Night, 167
Children and Books, 22, 143, 499
Children and Literature; Views and Reviews, 425
Children in Fear, 158, 213
Children of Green Knowe, The, 16, 111, 338
Children of Odin; The Book of Northern Myths, The, 256
Children of the Soil, 520
"Children of the Television Era," 489
Children's Book Council, The, 24, 60, 311, 470
Children's Books: Awards & Prizes, 470
Children's Book Showcase, 60
Children's Catalog, 21–22, 23, 57, 60, 161, 341, 424
"Children's Classics," 473
"Children's Interest and Story Preferences: A Critical Review of the Literature," 489
Children's Letters to God, 175
Children's literature
   definition, 16, 17
   future, 501–502
   history, 466–503
   issues, 467, 468–478
   research, 467, 478–490
Children's Literature in Education, 497
Children's Literature in the Elementary School, 28
Children's Literature Through Storytelling, 267
Children's Poetry Preferences: A National Survey of Upper Elementary Grades, 308, 322, 489
Childress, Alice, 440
Child's Christmas in Wales, A, 406
Child's First Books: A Critical Study of Pictures and Text, The, 83
Child's Garden of Verses, A, 34, 474, 494
Child's Good Night Book, A, 511
Child Study Association of America, 54–55, 412
Chile, 52
Chippewa Indians, 284, 485
Chittenden, Elizabeth F., 441
Chitty-Chitty-Bang-Bang; The Magical Car, 87, 331
Choice of Magic, A, 230

Choric speaking, 311–312, 330, 402–403
Chrisman, Arthur B., 518
Christmas, 403–404
Christmas, 404
Christmas Anna Angel, The, 406, 512
Christmas Book, The, 404
Christmas Carol in Prose, A, 406
Christmas Comes Once More; Stories and Poems for the Holiday Season, 404
Christmas Everywhere; A Book of Christmas Customs of Many Lands, 404
Christmas Feasts and Festivals, 404
Christmas gif' . . . , 404
Christmas in the Barn, 69
Christmas in the Stable, 405
Christmas Is a Time of Giving, 404
Christmas Kitten, The, 74
Christmas on the Mayflower, 406
Christmas the World Over . . . , 404
Christopher, John, 127, 130, 340
Chrysalis, 322
Chucaro: Wild Pony of the Pampa, 525
Chukovsky, Kornei, 31
Church Cat Abroad, The, 48
Church Mice and the Moon, The, 48
Church Mice Spread Their Wings, The, 48, 85
Church Mouse, The, 48
Chwast, Jacqueline, 161
Cianciolo, Patricia J., 83
Ciardi, John, 281, 287, 298, 304, 484
Cinderella, 59, 222, 226
Cinderella, or The Little Glass Slipper, 66, 227, 514
Cinderellas Around the World, 267
Cinquain, 299–300
Circle of Seasons, 187
Circus, 3
Cities and Metropolitan Areas in Today's World, 411
Cities in the March of Civilization, 412
"City," 292
City-Country ABC, 42
City in Art, The, 411
City life, 410–424
City Noisy Book, The, 64
"City Pigeons," 277–278
City Under the Back Steps, A, 333, 388
City Under the Ground, The, 128
Clarifying Values through Subject Matter: Applications for the Classroom, 213
Clark, Ann N., 187, 472, 511, 524
Clarke, Arthur C., 128, 387
Clarke, Pauline, 115
Classic Fairy Tales, The, 222
Classics, 472–475
Classroom climate, 347–355
Clay Pot Boy, The, 52, 241

Clean Air, 395
Clearing Weather, 519
Cleary, Beverly, 2, 108, 354
Cleaver, Bill, 158, 160, 166, 172, 179, 197–198, 354, 499
Cleaver, Vera, 158, 160, 166, 172, 179, 197–198, 354, 499
Clemens, Samuel L., 436, 473, 493, 494
Clemons, Elizabeth, 384
Clever Kate, 52
Clifton, Lucille, 68, 146, 160, 162, 436
Clown, 477
Clymer, Eleanor, 152, 156, 174, 190, 413, 421
Coatsworth, Elizabeth, 108, 154, 194, 281, 305, 319, 428, 519
Coblentz, Catherine, 523
Cochise, Apache Warrior and Statesman, 191
Cock-A-Doodle Doo, 511
Coconis, Red, 165
Codfish Market, The, 521
Coggins, Jack, 384
Cohen, Barbara, 413, 421
Cohen, Miriam, 163
Colby, C. B., 432
Cole, Dana Rewak, 309–310
Coleridge, Sara, 399
Coles, Robert, 164
Collage, 10–11, 331
Collier, Christopher, 527
Collier, James L., 527
Collodi, Carlo, *see* Lorenzini, Carlo
Colman, Hila, 193
Colonel of the Black Regiment, 441
Colonial Cookbook, The, 432
Colors, 306–307
Columbus, 400
Columbus, Christopher, 400
Columbus Day, 400
Columbus Sails, 400
Colum, Padraic, 256, 518, 520
Come Back, Amelia Bedelia, 52
Comenius, John A., 490
Come with Me to the Edge of the Sea, 383
Commanche Indians, 188
Communication; From Primitive Tom-toms to Telstar, 380
Community of Living Things, The, 394
Comparative Anthology of Children's Literature, A, 234
Complete Beginner's Guide to Backpacking, The, 396
Complo, Sr. Jannita Marie, 78
Concrete poetry, 302
Cone, Molly, 152, 440
Confessions of an Only Child, 172, 199
Conford, Ellen, 64
Congo, 53
Conklin, Gladys, 386

Conkling, Hilda, 301, 305, 320, 375–376
Constant Alberta, 174
Constitution Day, 408
Contemporary Authors, 69, 135, 143, 203
Contemporary English in the Elementary School, 28, 322, 331, 425
Contes de Ma Mère l'Oye, 34–35, 491
Controversial issues, 467
Cook, Joseph J., 385
Coolidge, Olivia E., 175, 525
Cool Ride in the Sky, The, 53
Coombs, Charles, 384
Coombs, Patricia, 115, 401
Cooney, Barbara, 35, 42, 46, 60, 66, 68–69, 220, 404, 514
Cooper, Bernice, 488
Cooper, James F., 493
Cooper, Susan, 88, 130, 131–132, 527, 528
Corcoran, Barbara, 164, 388
Cornelius, Chase, 411
Cornelius, Sue, 411
Corn Grows Ripe, The, 524
Cornish, Sam, 178
Cothran, Jean, 263
Coughlan, Margaret, 503
Council on Interracial Books for Children, 186, 213, 439
Couplet, 293–294
Courage of Sarah Noble, The, 428, 524
Courlander, Harold, 458, 523
Courtship, Merry Marriage, and Feast of Cock Robin and Jenny Wren, to Which Is Added the Doleful Death of Cock Robin, The, 35, 69
Cowles, Fleur, 71
Cow-Tail Switch and Other West African Stories, The, 523
Cox, Kenyon, 298, 340
Coyote, 189
Coyote Tales, 189
Crack in the Pavement, A, 411
Crane, Caroline, 167
Crane Maiden, The, 246, 393
Cranes, 393
Crapsey, Adelaide, 299
Crary, Margaret, 191
Crawford, Phyllis, 521
Creating with Papier-mâché, 398
Creation of the Sun and the Moon, The, 195
Creative Dramatics for All Children, 78
Creative Dramatics Handbook, 78
Creative Teaching of Reading in the Elementary School, 372
Creativity, 71–73
Cricket and the Emperor's Son, 108
Cricket in Times Square, The, 106–107, 140, 525

Crickets and Frogs, 52
Cricket Songs: Japanese Haiku, 300, 342
Criteria, 147, 376, 427
Criterion-referenced instruction, 138
"Critical Appraisal of Research on Children's Reading Interests, Preferences and Habits," 488
Critical Approach to Children's Literature, A, 425, 474, 503
Critical History of Children's Literature, 503
Critical Reading Ability of Elementary School Children, 489
Committee on the Role and Image of Women of NCTE, 171
Crocodile in the Tree, The, 58
Crouch, Marcus, 503
Crow Boy, 61, 514
Crow Indians, 188
Crows, 391
Cruise of the Happy-Go-Gay, The, 175
Crump, Claudia, 213
Cruz, Victor, 211, 321
Cuchulain, 256
Cullinan, Beatrice, 488
Cummings, E. E., 229, 301, 304, 307
Cumulative tale, 223–225
Cunningham, Julia, 105, 115
Curious George, 3, 25, 340
Current Biography, 203
Curry, Jane L., 249
Cutler, Ivor, 173

Daedalus and Icarus, 253
Dahl, Roald, 66, 115
Dalgliesh, Alice, 403, 428, 514, 522, 524
Dalrymple, De Wayne, 149
D'Amato, Janet, 191
Damp and Daffy Doings of a Daring Pirate Ship, The, 76
Dana, Richard H., 473
Dance of the Animals, 52
Dancing in the Moon, 44
Dancing Kettle and Other Japanese Folktales, The, 241
"Dandelion," 301
Daniel Boone, 521
Daniels, Guy, 236, 240
Daniels, Steven, 372
Danish, Barbara, 173
Danny Dunn and the Homework Machine, 350
Danny Dunn and the Smallifying Machine, 128
Danska, Herbert, 236
Dark Frigate, The, 518
Dark Is Rising, The, 88, 131, 527
Dark Star of Itza, The, 519

Darling, Louis, 2
Darrell, Margery, 267
Dash and Dart, 49, 511
Daugherty, James, 60, 221, 511, 514, 521
Daughter of the Mountains, 523
Daughter of the Seine, 519
d'Aulaire Edgar P., 221, 251, 253, 400, 433, 498, 499, 511
d'Aulaire, Ingri, 221, 251, 253, 400, 433, 498, 499, 511
David, Russell, 191
Davidson, Carter, 287
Davidson, Jessica, 378
Davies, William H., 283
Davis, Burke, 433
Davis, Lavinia, 512, 513
Davis, Mary G., 520
Davy Crockett, 520
Dawn, 69
Day, Thomas, 491
Day on Skates, 520
Dayrell, Elphinstone, 249, 516
Days of Dylan Thomas, The, 406
Day We Saw the Sun Come Up, The, 515
Dead Bird, The, 64, 82, 158
Dead End School, 164
Dead Tree, The, 56
Deafness, 165, 166
De Angeli, Marguerite, 35, 167, 338, 512, 514, 523, 524
Dear Rat, 105–106
Death, 32, 54, 55, 158–161, 197, 469–470
Death of Evening Star, The, 386
De Brunhoff, Jean, 47
De Brunhoff, Laurent, 355
"December," 485
"December Leaves," 292
De Crow, Karen, 175
Deenie, 167
Deep Dives of Stanley Whale, The, 386
Deep-sea World; The Story of Oceanography, 384
Deer in the Pasture, The, 49
Deers, Dorothy S., 41
Defender, The, 523
Defoe, Daniel, 16, 473, 474, 491
De Gerez, Toni, 167, 195
Dehn, Paul, 484
De Jong, Meindert, 67, 180, 203, 524, 525
DeKay, James, 400
de la Mare, Walter, 69, 287, 338, 497
de la Salle, Robert C., 435
Delaunay, Sonia, 41
DeLeeuw, Adele, 433
Denmark, 227
DePaola, Tomie, 381, 517

deRegniers, Beatrice S., 59, 64, 67, 282, 515
DeRoin, Nancy, 219
de Saint-Exupéry, Antoine, 229, 344
Describing, 335, 336–337
Desert Is Theirs, The, 517
Desert: What Lives There, The, 57
"Desolate and lone," 274
deSoto, Hernando, 435
DeSoto, Finder of the Mississippi, 435
de Treviño, Elizabeth B., 526
Developmental Psychology of Jean Piaget, The, 334
Devereaux, Alexis, 440
Devil's Children, The, 127
Devil's Storybook, The, 21
Dewey, John, 493
deWorde, Wynken, 490
Dialect, 438–439
Diamante, 317
Diamonds and Toads, 226
Diana and Her Rhinoceros, 173
Dick Foote and the Shark, 115
Dickens, Charles, 406
Dickinson, Emily, 292, 304, 314, 337
Dickinson, Peter, 127, 130
Dick Whittington and His Cat, 66, 513
Did You Carry the Flag Today, Charlie?, 152
Digby, Desmond, 314
Dillon, Diane, 59, 517
Dillon, Leo, 59, 517
"Dinky," 295
Diorama, 330
Director of Sources, 529–533
Discovering Poetry, 287
"Discovering What Children Have Learned about Literature," 488
Discriminating, 335, 338–339
Discussing Death, 161
Disney, Walt, 221
Displaying books, 364–372
Display materials, 368–371
Ditties for the Nursery, 37
Diving, 387
Divorce, 54, 153, 156, 197, 469–470
Dixon, Paige, 160, 388
D. J.'s Worst Enemy, 162
Dobrin, Arnold, 160, 195
Dobry, 520
Doctor to the Galaxy, 128
Dodge, Mary M., 473, 474
Dodgson, Charles L., 87
Doering, Harold, 389
Dog Who Could Swim under Water, The, 140
Dollhouse Caper, The, 14
Doll's Christmas, The, 405
Dolphin Island, 128
Domanska, Janina, 240, 517

Dombrink, Patricia, 321
Donkey Ride, The, 221
Donne, John, 304
Donovan, John, 83
Don't Count Your Chicks, 221
Don't Feel Sorry for Paul, 146, 165–166
Don't Take Teddy, 167
Don't You Turn Back; Poems of Langston Hughes, 349
Door in the Wall, 167, 338, 342, 523
Doors into Poetry, 287
Drop Dead, 115
Dorrie and the Haunted House, 401
"Do Teachers Talk Too Much," 488
"Doughnut Machine, The," 109
Doughtery, Richard, 386
Douty, Esther, 441
Dowden, Anne, 395
Down from the Lonely Mountain, 249
Downright Dency, 519
Down Ryton Water, 522
Down the Mississippi, 435
"Down the Rain Falls," 281
Do You Have the Time, Lydia?, 68
Do You Know What Day Tomorrow Is?, 408
Do You Know What I'll Do?, 53
Do You Love Me?, 55
Do You Want to Be My Friend?, 74
Drag, Denise, 41
Dragon and the Doctor, The, 173
Dragonsong, 26, 88
Dragon Stew, 353
Dragonwings, 342, 528
Drama, 221, 330, 342
Drama in Your Classroom, 78, 373
Dramakinetics in the Classroom, 78
Dramatization, 77–78
Dramatized Folk Tales of the World, 258
Dream Coach, 518
Dream Days, 90
"Dreams," 485
Drew, Elizabeth, 287
Droll tales, 223, 231–234
Drowning Boy, The, 156
Drugs, 469–470
Drummer Hoff, 59, 65, 516
duBois, William P., 60, 86, 112, 130, 137, 513, 514, 523
Duffy and the Devil, 59, 517
Dugan, William, 380
Dumas, Gerald, 46
Dunfee, Maxine, 213
Dunning, Stephen, 275, 372
Dupuy, Trevor, 408
Dust of the Earth, 197, 198
Duvoisin, Roger, 41, 44, 50, 58, 64, 65, 221, 405, 512, 516

"Eagle, The," 291
Eagle Mask, 188
Eagles, 391
Eakin, Mary K., 425
Early childhood education, 6, 10–11, 19–21, 30–83, 288, 291, 292–294
Early Moon, 322
Earth, the Great Recycler, 394
Eastern Religions, 407
Eastman, Philip D., 225
East O' the Sun and West O' the Moon, 264, 497
Eaton, Anne, 503, 519, 521, 522, 523
Ebbie, 150
Eberle, Irmengarde, 392
Eckert, Allan W., 527
Ecology, 393–396
Ecology: Science of Survival, 394
Ecology: The Circle of Life, 394
Eddie's Bear, 50, 64
Edge of Two Worlds, 190
"Editors Write about Authors," 83
Edmonds, I. G., 245
Edmonds, Walter D., 426, 427, 428, 521
Education Index, 424
Effect of Gamma Rays on Man-in-the-Moon Marigolds, The, 201
Egg Tree, The, 513
Egoff, Sheila, 28
Egypt Game, The, 476, 526
Ehrlich, Harriet, 78
Eichenberg, Fritz, 42, 44, 513
Eighteenth-century books, 421, 491–492
Eimerl, Sarel, 391
Einstein, Albert, 19, 225
El Cid, 256
Elementary English, 12, 22, 76, 322
Elementary Teacher's Ideas and Materials Workshop, The, 408
Elephant, 74
"Elephant and the Butterfly, The," 229
"Elephant's Child, The," 348
"Eletelephony," 289, 484
Elgin, Kathleen, 255, 407
Eliot, T. S., 304
Elkin, Benjamin, 44, 514
Ellen Grae, 158, 179, 197, 354
Ellinger, Bernice D., 489
Ellington, Duke, 349
Elliott, Sarah M., 394
Ellis, Ella T., 156
Elsie Dinsmore, 493, 496
Elves and the Shoemaker, The, 226
"Embarrassing Episode of Little Miss Muffet, The," 290
Emberley, Barbara, 59, 65, 516
Emberley, Ed, 35, 59, 65, 516

Embry, Margaret, 403
Emerging Humanity; Multi-Ethnic Literature for Children and Adolescents, 213
Emil and Piggy Beast, 347
Emily and the Klunky Baby and the Next-door Dog, 54
Emma in Winter, 126
Emmet Otter's Jug-Band Christmas, 405
Emperor and the Kite, The, 64, 516
Emperor Penguins, The, 392
Emperor's New Clothes, The, 227, 266
Enchantress from the Stars, 527
Encoding-decoding, 332
Engdahl, Sylvia, 128, 527
Engel, Leonard, 384
England, 66, 223
English Fairy Tales, 359
English folklore, 68, 141–142, 256
English language, 377–382
Enrichment Ideas: Sparkling Fireflies, 28
Enright, Elizabeth, 521, 525
Environment, 347–351
"Erie Canal," 314
Erie Canal, The, 13
Ernst, Margaret S., 379
Erwin, John, 108
Eskimos, 52, 173, 188, 316, 388
Estes, Eleanor, 522, 523
Ethan Allen and the Green Mountain Boys, 433
Ets, Marie H., 60, 193, 404, 512, 513, 514, 515, 516
Evans, Katherine, 44
Exactly Alike, 68
"Experiencing Poetry," 322
"Exploring Poetry," 322
Exploring the Great River, 435
Exploring the World of Oceanography, 384

Fable of the Fig Tree, The, 221
Fables, 52, 217–221, 262–263
Fables from Aesop, 219
Fables from Incunabula to Modern Picture Book, 221
Fables of Aesop, The, 217
Fables of India, 218
Fables of La Fontaine, The, 219
Fader, Daniel, 334
Fadiman, Clifton, 380, 436
Fairy Circus, The, 519
Fairytales, 222, 223, 225–231
Fairy Tales, 229
Fairy Tales of Grimm, The, 65
Fairy Tales of the Orient, 245
Fall from the Sky; The Story of Daedalus, A, 253
"Falling Star, The," 320

Families Are Like That!, 54
Family Book of Nursery Rhymes, A, 37
Family life, 152–161
Family Tree, The, 154
Family under the Bridge, The, 421, 525
Famous Mexican-Americans, 195
Fantastic Kingdom: A Collection of Illustrations from the Golden Days of Storytelling, The, 267
Fantastic World of Ants; A Microview of Earth's Most Ingenious Insect, The, 389
Fantasy, 14, 50–52, 84–143, 500
Faraway Lurs, The, 171
Farber, Norma, 43
Farjeon, Eleanor, 272, 286, 305
Farley, Carol, 152
Farmer, Penelope, 126, 253
Farthest Shore, The, 132
Fassler, Joan, 161
Father Like That, A, 53, 152
Father role, 153–154, 155, 157
Fatio, Louise, 65
Fatness, 180
Fat Polka-dot Cat and Other Haiku, 301
Favorite Fairy Tales Told in Russia, 236
Favorite Stories Old and New, 263
Feagles, Anita, 256
Fearsome Inn, The, 229, 526
Feather Mountain, 513
Feeley, Joan T., 486, 487, 488
Feelings, Muriel, 517
Feelings, Tom, 60, 517
Feiffer, Jules, 381
Feldman Fieldmouse, 107
Felton, Harold W., 263
Feminism, 175–176
Feminist Press, The, 173
Fenner, Carol, 57
Fenwick, Sara, 425
Ferguson, Charles W., 379
Festivals for You to Celebrate, 408
Field, Elinor W., 83
Field, Eugene, 494
Field, Rachel, 273, 305, 320, 418, 428, 512, 519
Fife, Dale, 190, 412
Fifteen Fables of Krylov, 219
Fifty Favorite Fairy Tales Chosen from the Color Fairy Books of Andrew Lang, 227
Figgs and Phantoms, 527
Figure of Speech, A, 180
Films, 310, 312, 315, 393, 468, 477–478
Filmstrips, 477
Finders Keepers, 513
Finger, Charles, 518
Finland, 203, 223
Finlayson, Ann, 433

Finley, Martha, 493
Finn Family Moomintroll, 89
"Fire, Fire!," 312–313, 484
"Firefly," 314
Firegirl, 173
First Book of Norse Legends, The, 255
First Five Fathoms, The, 387
First Four Years, The, 176
First Thanksgiving, The, 403
Fir Tree, The, 66
Fischer, Hans, 228
Fish, Helen D., 510
Fisher, Aileen, 12, 46, 272, 290, 292, 305, 382, 383
Fisher, Cyrus, 522
Fisher, James, 384
Fisher, Leonard E., 386
Fisher, Margery, 375, 425
Fish in the Air, 513
Fisk, Nicholas, 126
Fitch, Florence M., 407
Fitzhugh, Louise, 174
Five Children and It, 111
Five Hundred Hats of Bartholomew Cubbins, The, 50, 330
Five Little Monkeys, 513
Five Little Peppers, The, 494, 496
Flack, Marjorie, 49, 107, 225, 512
Flavell, John H., 334
Fleischhauer-Hardt, Helga, 82
Fleming, Alice, 176
Fleming, Guy, 239
Fleming, Ian, 87
Floating Island, 519
Floethe, Louise L., 407
Floyd, William D., 482, 488
Fly High, Fly Low, 414, 514
Flying Carpet, The, 66
Flying Saucer Full of Spaghetti, A, 75
Flying Ship, The, 236
"Fog," 338, 485
Fog Magic, 113–114, 522
Foley, Daniel J., 404
Folklore, 214–267
Folklore: An Annotated Bibliography and Index to Single Editions, 267
Folk Stories of the South, 263
Folktales, 221–246
Folk Tales of Japan, 241–245
Folsom, Franklin, 192, 441
Foods the Indians Gave Us, 192
Fool of the World and the Flying Ship, The, 59, 70, 240, 516
Fools of Chelm and Their History, The, 70, 331
Forberg, Ati, 46, 252
Forbes, Esther, 428, 432, 522
Ford, Lauren, 511
"Forecast, The," 485
Forest Pool, The, 510

Forever Christmas, The, 405
Forgotten Daughter, The, 520
Forman, James, 187
For Pollution Fighters Only, 394
Forty-six Days of Christmas; A Cycle of Old World Songs, Legends and Customs, 404
Foss, William O., 384
Foster, G. Allen, 380
Foster, Genevieve, 400, 431, 521, 522, 523, 524
Four and Twenty Blackbirds, 510
"Four Little Foxes," 295
Fox, Geoff, 213
Fox, Michael, 388
Fox, Paula, 145, 152, 164, 180, 341, 439, 472, 527
Fox and the Fire, 64
Foxes and Wolves, 340, 388
Fox Went Out on a Chilly Night, The, 13, 314, 515
Fraiberg, Selma, 325
France, 52, 66
Francés, Esteban, 72
Franchere, Ruth, 195
Francis, Robert, 485
Francoise, (Pseud. of Francoise Seignobosc), 44
Frasconi, Antonio, 35, 515
Frazer, James G., 267
Freddy and the Men from Mars, 128
Freddy Goes to Florida, 108
Frederick, 108, 516
Freeman, Don, 414, 514
Free to Be . . . You and Me, 176
Free verse, 301–302, 485
French folklore, 256
Freschet, Berniece, 391
Friday Night Is Papa Night, 55
Friend Is Someone Who Likes You, A, 161
Friendly Beasts, The, 405
Friendly Wolf, The, 14
Friendship, 161–164
Friis-Baastad, Babbis, 167
Fritz, Jean, 432, 433, 434
"Frog, The," 289
Frog and Toad Are Friends, 517
Frog and Toad Together, 527
Frog Goes to Dinner, 73, 499
Frog on His Own, 73
Frog Went A-Courtin', The, 65, 514
Frog, Where Are You?, 33, 73
From Anna, 167
From Drumbeat to Tickertape, 342
From Lew Alcindor to Kareem Abdul Jabbar, 441
From Rollo to Tom Sawyer, 503
From the Mixed-Up Files of Mrs. Basil E. Frankweiler, 206–208. 526

From the Turtle to the Nautilus, 387
From Two to Five, 31
Frontier Living, 525
Frost, Frances, 405
Frost, Robert, 271, 285, 286
Fuel for Today and Tomorrow, 394
Fuller, Ethel R., 310
Funny Little Woman, The, 59, 246, 517
"Furry Bear," 279
Future development, 501–502
"Future Imperfect," 425
Fyleman, Rose, 305

Gabrielson, Ira N., 390
Gaeddert, LouAnn, 173, 412
Gaelic Ghosts, 263
Gaer, Joseph, 218
Gág, Wanda, 42, 49, 60, 225, 226, 232, 498, 511, 519
Gaggin, Eva R., 522
Gaggle of Geese, A, 380
Galdone, Paul, 35, 52, 60, 220, 224, 433, 514
Galinsky, Ellen, 390, 391
"Galoshes," 288
Games, 24–28, 39
Gammage Cup, The, 525
Gandhi, Fighter without a Sword, 523
Gannett, Ruth, 512, 523
Gans, Roma, 390, 391, 396
Garden of Broken Glass, 153
"Garden Year, The," 399
Gardner, Richard, 158
Garfield, Leon, 252, 421
Garner, Alan, 114, 130
Garran the Hunter, 519
Garten, Jan, 42
Garthwaite, Marian, 193
Gasiorowicz, Cathy, 43
Gasiorowicz, Nina, 43
Gates, Doris, 252, 521
Gauche, Patricia L., 180, 433
Gaudenzia, 11
Gavett, Bruce, 398
Gayneck, The Story of a Pigeon, 518
Geese, 391
Geese Are Back, The, 391
Geisel, Theodore S., 50, 60
Generalizing, 335, 339–340
Genie of Sulton Place, The, 136, 137, 138, 139–141
Genre, literary, 335, 342
Gentle Ben, 476
George, 207
George, Jean C., 12, 146, 173, 209, 340, 375, 382, 383, 388, 472, 499, 527
George Rogers Clark: Frontier Fighter, 433
George Washington, 498, 523

George Washington's World, 521
Georgia, 162
Georgia and the Dragon, 174
Georgia Children's Book Award, 469, 471, 506
Georgie, 51
Georgie Goes West, 51, 347
Georgie to the Rescue, 51
Gergely, Tibor, 514
German folklore, 254–256
Germany, 52
Geronimo, Apache Chief, 191
Getting Something on Maggie Marmelstein, 164
Ghost Paddle, 188, 337
Gianni and the Ogre, 230
Gibbs, Tony, 396
Gibson, Rich, 173
Gift; A Portuguese Christmas Tale, The, 405
Gillespie, Margaret C., 503
Gillespie and the Guards, 514
Gillies, Emily, 78
Gingerbread Boy or Johnny-Cake, The, 225
Ginger Pye, 523
Ginsburg, Mirra, 72, 240
Gipson, Fred, 524
Girl and the Goatherd, The, 53
Girl Called Al, A, 157, 174
Girl Like Tracy, A, 167
Girls Can Be Anything, 56, 172, 199
"Girls Can Too!," 176–177
Girl Who Would Rather Climb Trees, The, 151
Giving Tree, The, 345
Glad Man, The, 151
Gladys Told Me to Meet Her Here, 337
Glooskaps Country and Other Indian Tales, 263
Glory of the Seas, 520
Glubok, Shirley, 14, 192
Goals, 137, 334–341
Goble, Dorothy, 14, 188
Goble, Paul, 14, 188
God Beneath the Sea, The, 252
Godden, Rumer, 401
Gods and goddesses, 254
Goetz, Delia, 411
Goff, Beth, 157
Goffstein, M. B., 174
Goggles!, 11, 32, 516
Going to Waste; Where Will All the Garbage Go?, 395
Golden Age, The, 90
Golden Basket, 520
Golden Crane; A Japanese Folktale, The, 246, 393
Golden Fleece and the Heroes Who Lived Before Achilles, The, 518

Golden Goblet, The, 525
Golden God Apollo, The, 253
Golden Goose Book, 230
Golden Name Day, The, 524
Golden Treasury of Myths and Legends, The, 251
Goldin, Augusta, 384
Goldreich, Esther, 57, 174
Goldreich, Gloria, 57, 174
Goldsmith, Oliver, 491
Gone-Away Lake, 525
Gone Is Gone, 232
Gonzalez, Gloria, 151
Gooch, Brian, 276
Goodall, John, 75
Good Bird, The, 76
"Good Fortune Kettle, The," 241
Good Greenwood, The, 160
Good Luck Horse, 511
Good Master, The, 520
Good Times, 146, 160
Goodykoontz, William, 213
Gordon Parks, 441
Gorey, Edward, 79
Gorgon's Head; The Story of Perseus, The, 253
Gorilla Gorilla, 57
Goshorn, Elizabeth, 75
Go Tell Aunt Rhody, 314
Goudey, Alice E., 387, 515
Go Up the Road, 193
Grabianski, Janusz, 227–228
Graciela: A Mexican-American Child Tells Her Story, 192
Grade levels, 139
Graham, Al, 512
Graham, Alberta P., 433
Graham, Lorenz, 349, 440
Graham, Margaret B., see Bloy, Margaret
Grahame, Kenneth, 89, 90–105, 130, 143, 497
Grandfather and I, 180
Grandma Didn't Wave Back, 180
Grandmother and I, 180
Grandmother Orna, 180
Grandmother's Pictures, 178
Grandpa, 180
Grandpa and Me, 180
Grandparents, 55, 159, 177–186
Granny's Fish Story, 177
Gray, Elizabeth G., 519
Gray, Elizabeth J., 520, 522
Great Books Club, 349
Great Energy Search, The, 394
Great Geppy, The, 137
Great Quest, The, 518
Great Rebellion, The, 108
Great Wheel, The, 525
Greek folklore, 256

Greek mythology, 250–253
Green, Bette, 527
Green and Burning Tree; On the Writing and Enjoyment of Children's Books, The, 143
Greenaway, Kate, 37, 304
Green Christmas, A, 405
Greene, Constance, 157, 174
Green Eyes, 514
Greenfield, Eloise, 196, 439, 441
Green Ginger Jar; A Chinatown Mystery, The, 413
Greenhood, David, 384
Gregor, Arthur S., 411
Grey King, The, 528
Grey Wolf, The, 130, 132
Gridley, Marion E., 189
Griese, Arnold A., 190
Griffin and the Minor Canon, The, 115
Grimm, Jacob, 222–223, 473, 493
Grimm, Wilhelm, 222–223, 473, 493
Grimm's Fairy Tales, 226, 228
Grinny, 126
Gripe, Maria, 174
Groff, Patrick, 503
Gropper, Nancy B., 81
Gross, Michael, 221
Grossbart, Francine, 42
Grover, 197
Grover, Eulalie O., 37
Growing Time, 158
Growing Up Female in America; Ten Lives, 172
Gruenberg, Sidonie M., 82, 263
"Gudbrand on the Hillside," 231
"Guidelines for Women's Studies, Grades 1–12," 171
Guiliano, Edward, 143
Guiness Book of World Records, 375
Gulliver's Travels, 16, 473, 491
Gulls, 391
Gunderson, Doris V., 81
Gurko, Leo, 525
Gutenberg, Johann, 490
Guzak, Frank J., 482, 488

Habenstreit, Barbara, 412
Hader, Berta, 60, 511, 512
Hader, Elmer, 60, 511, 512
Haig-Brown, Roderick, 386
Haiku, 11, 300–301, 333, 485
Hailstones and Halibut Bones, 306–307, 342
Haiti, 68
Hale, Lucretia P., 110
Haley, Gail E., 52, 56, 59, 432, 517
Hall, Anna G., 521
Hall, Lucretia, 86
Hallock, Grace, 519

"Halloween," 337, 402
Halloween, 400–403
Halloween (Our American Holidays), 401
Hall-Quest, Olga W., 432
Hamilton, Edith, 250, 267
Hamilton, Virginia, 439, 440, 527
Hample, Stuart, 175
Handforth, Thomas, 510
Handful of Surprises, A, 72
Handful of Thieves, A, 204
Handicapped children, 164–167
Handtalk: An ABC of Finger Spelling & Sign Language, 43
Hang Tough, Paul Mather, 159
Hans Brinker or the Silver Skates, 473, 474
Hans Christian Andersen Award, 67, 203
Hans Christian Andersen's The Fir Tree 406
Hansi, 406
Happiness Is a Sad Song, 162
Happiness Is a Warm Puppy, 162, 353
Happy Day, The, 513
Happy Lion, The, 65
Happy Owls, The, 62, 393
Hardgrove, Clarence E., 425
Hardwich, Richard, 441
Hare and the Tortoise, The, 220
Harmin, Merrill, 213
Harmon, Humphrey, 263
Harold and the Purple Crayon, 51
Harper, Wilhelmina, 404
Harriet the Spy, 174
Harriet Tubman, 440
Harris, Audrey, 161
Harris, Christie, 128, 190
Harris, Joel C., 494
Harris, Rosemary, 115
Hashin, 300
Haskins, James, 412, 441
Hassall, Joan, 37
Haverstock, Mary S., 188
Have Space Suit—Will Travel, 125
Have You Seen a Comet? Children's Art and Writing from around the World, 321
Have You Seen Houses?, 412
Have You Seen Tom Thumb?, 522
Havighurst, Marion, 523
Havighurst, Walter, 523
Haviland, Virginia, 236, 241, 425, 503
Having a Younger Brother or Sister, 168
Hawaii, 249, 386
Hawaiian folklore, 249
Hawaiian Myths of Earth, Sea, and Sky, 249
Hawaiian Tales of Heroes and Champions, 264
Hawes, Charles, 518

Hawkstone, The, 114
Hawley, Isabel L., 213
Hawley, Robert C., 213
Hayes, William B., 193
Hays, Wilma P., 192, 406, 433
Haywood, Carolyn, 55
Hazelton, Elizabeth B., 391
Headless Cupid, The, 527
Heartsease, 127
Heathers, Anne, 72
Heavenly Tenants, The, 522
Hebrew poems, 316
Hector Protector, and As I Went Over the Water, 37
Heide, Florence P., 144, 157, 164
Heidi, 473, 474, 494
Heimdall, 254
Heinlein, Robert, 123–125
Helfman, Elizabeth, 380
Hello the Boat!, 521
Henderson, Harold G., 300
Henny Penny, 223–224
Henrietta, the Wild Woman of Borneo, 55
Henry, Marguerite, 11, 522–523
Henry Fisherman, 513
Henry Huggins, 2, 3, 350, 354
Henry Reed's Baby-Sitting Service, 354
Here I Am!, 211, 321
Hero Ain't Nothin' But a Sandwich, A, 440
Heroes, The, 493
Heroes; Greek Fairy Tales, The, 252
Heroes of Asgard; Tales from Scandinavian Mythology, The, 256
Heroes of the American Revolution, 433
Hero from Otherwhere, The, 114
Herrera, Velino, 511
Hewes, Agnes, 519, 520, 521
Hey Diddle Diddle Picture Book, 35
Hi, Cat!, 11
Hickok, Lorena, 165
Hidden Treasure of Glaston, The, 522
Hide-and-Seek, 75
Hide and Seek Fog, 78, 516
Hieatt, Constance, 260
Higgins, James, 87, 230
Higginson, Thomas W., 441
High King, The, 121, 122, 130, 526
Higonnet-Schnopper, Janet, 241
Hildebrandt, Gred, 382
Hildebrandt, Tim, 382
Hildilid's Night, 517
Hill, W. M., 249
Hill of Fire, 194
Hillyer, Robert, 287
Hinton, Susan, 499
"Hippity Hop to the Barber Shop," 338
Hirsch, S. Carl, 387
Historical novel, 439, 440, 472

History, 56, 330
History of children's literature, 466–503
History of Little Goody Two Shoes, The, 491
History of Sandford and Merton, The, 491
History of Simple Simon, The, 35
Hitchcock, Patricia, 263
Hitopadesa, The, 218
Hitte, Kathryn, 193
Hitty, Her First Hundred Years, 428, 476, 519
Hnizdovsky, J., 240
Ho, Minfong, 151
Hoban, Lillian, 58, 65, 174, 405
Hoban, Russell C., 44, 47, 65, 405
Hoban, Tina, 75
Hobbit, The, 119, 345, 351, 498, 499, 500
Hoberman, Mary A., 315
Hodges, Margaret, 244, 255, 516
Hodges, Walter, 400
Hoffman, Felix, 228
Hofmann, Charles, 188
Hofsinde, Robert, 192
Hogner, Dorothy, 350
Hogrogian, Nonny, 52, 59, 224, 226, 516, 517
Hoke, Helen, 385, 391
Holbrook, Stewart, 433
Hole, The, 71
Hole Is to Dig, A, 64, 67, 71
Holiday Roundup, 408
Holidays, 308, 399
Holidays: Days of Significance for All Americans, 408
Holl, Adelaide, 72
Holland, Marion, 55
Hollering Son, 189
Holling, Holling C., 25, 348, 382, 386, 435, 499, 511, 523
Holling, Lucille W., 383
Holsaert, Eunice, 384
Holsaert, Faith, 384
Holt, Norma, 165
Homer, 474
Homer Price, 3, 6, 109, 330, 342, 499
Honk, the Moose, 356–358, 520
Hook, J. N., 335
Hooray for Us, 161
Hoover, Gerry, 255
Hopkins, Lee B., 12, 136, 176, 210, 315, 322, 349, 408
Horn Book, 60, 209, 492, 497, 498
Horse and His Boy, The, 117
Horsecatcher, The, 525
Horton Hears a Who, 49
Hosford, Dorothy G., 256
Hosie's Alphabet, 41, 517
Houseboat Summer, 154

Household Tales, 473, 493
House of Dies Driers, The, 440
House of Sixty Fathers, The, 524
House of Wings, The, 177, 393
"Houses," 290
Houses from the Sea, 387, 515
House Sparrows; Ragamuffins of the City, 392
"House That Ate Mosquito Pie, The," 229
House That Jack Built, The, 35, 225, 515
Housing in Tomorrow's World, 412
Houston, James, 52, 188, 316
Hovey, Richard, 283
How Did We Find Out about Vitamins?, 398
How Does a Poem Mean?, 287
Howell, Ruth R., 411
How I Went Shopping and What I Got, 156
How Our Alphabet Grew, 380
"How Pleasant to Know Mr. Lear!," 303
"How the Elephant Got a Long Trunk," 3
How the Elephant Got a Trunk, 474
How the Grinch Stole Christmas, 405
How the People Sang the Mountains Up; How and Why Stories, 263
How the Sun Was Brought Back to the Sky, 72
How the Withered Trees Blossomed, 246
How the Woodpecker Was Created, 248–249
How the World's First Cities Began, 411
How to Be a Nature Detective, 397
How-to books, 397–398
How to Bring Up Your Pet Dog, 397
How to Build a Body, 397
How to Care for Your Dog, 397
"How to Eat a Poem," 305–306
How to Eat Fried Worms, 162, 397
How to Explore the Secret Worlds of Nature, 397
How to Go About Laying an Egg, 398
How to Grow House Plants, 397
How to Improve Your Model Railroad, 397
How to Know the Birds, 397
How to Make a Home Nature Museum, 397
How to Make a Miniature Zoo, 397
How to Make & Fly Paper Airplanes, 397
How to Play Better Football, 397
How to Understand Animal Talk, 397
How to Write a Report, 397
How to Write Codes and Send Secret Messages, 397
How 2 Gerbils, 20 Goldfish, 200 Games, 2,000 Books and I Taught Them How to Read, 372

How Will We Move All the People?, 412
Hoyt, Edwin P., 387
Hu, Diana, 318
Hubbard, Ralph, 519
Hubbell, Patricia, 485
Huck, Charlotte, 28, 482, 489
Huckleberry Finn, 331, 436, 473, 494
Hudson, Robert G., 390
"Hughbert and the Glue," 484
Hughes, Langston, 292, 304, 349, 485
Hughes, Ted, 79
Hugo, Victor, 269
Human-and-Anti-human Values in Children's Books, 213, 439
Human Values in the Classroom, 213
Hummingbirds in the Garden, 391
Humor, 139–141, 162, 231–234, 340, 485
Humpy, 241
Hundred Dresses, The, 522
Hundred Fables, A, 217
Hundred Penny Box, The, 179
Hungary, 52
Hungerford, Harold R., 394
Hunt, Irene, 526
Hunt, Mabel L., 523
Hunter, Edith F., 167
Hunter, Mollie, 28, 115
Hunters of the Whale: An Adventure of Northwest Coast Archaeology, 386
Hurd, Edith T., 392, 393
Hurray for Captain Jane!, 174
Hurry Home, Candy, 67, 524
Hurry, Skurry, and Flurry, 65
"Husband Who Was to Mind the House, The," 232
Hush Little Baby, 35
Hutchins, Pat, 75
Hutchins, Ross E., 392
Hutchinson, Veronica S., 224
Hyde, Margaret E., 394
Hydrospace; Frontier beneath the Sea, 384
Hymes, James M., 380
Hymes, Lucia, 380

I Am Adopted, 55
I Am Going Nowhere, 315
I Cry When the Sun Goes Down, 440
Ida Tarbell; First of the Muckrakers, 176
Identity, 282–284, 334
I Do Not Like It When My Friend Comes to Visit, 164
"I Eat My Peas with Honey," 297
If All the Seas Were One Sea, 517
If I Had It My Way, 199
If I Ran the Zoo, 513
If It Weren't for You, 168
I Found Them in the Yellow Pages, 43
If You Were an Ant . . . , 389

"I had a little nut-tree," 36
I Have Four Names for My Grandfather, 33
"I Hear America Singing," 341
I, Juan De Pareja, 526
I Know You, Al, 157
"I Like to See It Lap the Miles," 292, 337
I Like You, 161
Illegitimacy, 198
Illustrations in Children's Books, 83
Illustrators, 10, 13–14, 58–70
Illustrators of Books for Young People, 83
Illustrators of Children's Books, 67, 83
"I Love Little Pussy," 298, 340
I Love My Mother, 149, 153, 173, 202, 336
Image of Blacks in Children's Fiction, 213
Imagery, 277, 281–282, 290–293, 301–302, 338, 339, 485
Imagination, 3
I, Momolu, 440
Improvising the Image of Women in Textbooks, 170
In a Spring Garden, 11, 301
In a Word, 379
Inch by Inch, 515
Incident at Hawk's Hill, 527
Incredible Deborah, The, 174
Independent Voices, 172
Index to Fairy Tales, 1949–1972, 267
India, 218–219
Indian Arts, 192
Indian Captive, 428
Indian Captive: The Story of Mary Jemison, 522
Indian folklore, 256
Indian Gallery, 187
Indian Heart of Carrie Hodges, The, 190
Indians, see Native Americans
Individualized instruction, 136–142, 326, 347–355
I Need All the Friends I Can Get, 162
I Never Loved Your Mind, 21
"I Never Saw a Moor," 314
Inferences, 138
"Influence of Teachers, Peers, and Home Environment on the Reading Interests of Children, The," 489
"Influences on Primary School Children's Reading," 487
Information, reading for, 374–425
Informational books, 55–57
Ingalls, Laura, see Wilder, Laura Ingalls
Ingraham, Claire R., 175
Ingraham, Leonard W., 175
In Honour Bound, 204
"In Just-Spring," 301–302
In My Mother's House, 187, 511

Inner City Mother Goose, 306
In Pursuit of Poetry, 287
In Search of a Sandhill Crane, 393
Insect Engineers; The Story of Ants, 389
"Interest Patterns and Media
    Preferences of Middle-Grade
    Children," 488
International Board on Books for
    Young People, 67
Interpersonal relations, 148–168
Interracial Books for Children, 213
In the Forest, 512
"In the Hall of the Mountain Kings,"
    137
In the Morning of Time; The Story of the
    Norse God Balder, 255
In the Night Kitchen, 79, 80, 517
In the Trail of the Wind; American Indian
    Poems and Ritual Orations, 188
In the Woods, in the Meadow, in the Sky,
    293
Intonation, 339
Introduction to Haiku, An, 300
Invincible Louisa, 339, 342, 520
"Inviting Jason," 167
Ipcar, Dahlov, 44, 52
Ireland, Norma O., 267
Irish folklore, 256
Irving, Washington, 493
I Saw a Ship A-Sailing, 37
"I," Says the Poem, 276
Ishi, 191
Ishii, Momoko, 245
Ishi, Last of His Tribe, 132, 191
Ish-Kishor, Sulamith, 527
I Should Have Stayed in Bed, 54
Island of the Blue Dolphins, 25, 146, 173,
    187, 203, 499, 525
Israel, Elaine, 394
Israel, 69
Issun Boshi, the Inchling; An Old Tale of
    Japan, 245
Is That Mother in the Bottle?, 378
It Doesn't Always Have to Rhyme, 305
It Happened in Chichipica, 194
It's Like This, Cat, 155, 200, 525
It's Not the End of the World, 156–158
It's Not What You Expect, 199
It's the Great Pumpkin, Charlie Brown,
    401, 402
It's Time for Thanksgiving, 403
It's Time Now, 411
Ivanko and the Dragon, 240
"Ivan the Fool," 235–236
Ivan the Fool and Other Tales of Leo
    Tolstoy, 236
Iverson, William, 28, 213
Iwasaki, Chihiro, 55
I Wish I Had an Afro, 349, 437
"I Woke Up This Morning," 154–155

I Wonder If Herbie's Home Yet, 164
I Would Rather Be a Turnip, 197
I Wrote My Name on the Wall, 413

"Jabberwocky, The," 298–299
Jack Jouett's Ride, 56, 432
Jack Kent's Fables of Aesop, 219
Jackson, Jacqueline, 107
Jackson, Mahalia, 349
Jacobs, Frank, 381
Jacobs, Joseph, 217, 223, 359
Jacobs, Leland, 277
Jacobs, William J., 433
Jaffe, Dan, 485
Jagendorf, M. A., 263
Jahdu Tales, 342
Jambo Means Hello; A Swahili Alphabet
    Book, 517
James Will, 518
James and the Giant Peach, 66, 115
Jameson, Cynthia, 52, 241, 246
Jan, Isabelle, 467, 503
Jane's Island, 159
Janey, 53
Janine Is French, 135
Jansson, Tove, 89, 177, 203
Japan, 300–301
Japanese Children's Favorite Stories, 246
Japanese folklore, 241–246
Japanese Children's Favorite Stories, 246
Jarrell, Mary, 149
Jarrell, Randall, 67, 517, 526
Jasmine, 50
Jatakas, 218
Jataka Tales, 219
Jazz Man, The, 167
Jeanne-Marie Counts Her Sheep, 44
Jeffers, Susan, 37, 517
Jellybeans for Breakfast, 174
Jennifer, Hecate, Macbeth, William
    McKinley, and Me, Elizabeth, 207,
    440, 526
Jenny's Revenge, 153
Jeschke, Susan, 162
Jessie Owens, 441
Jewett, Eleanore, 522
Jewish Americans, 421
Jewish holidays, 407
Jewish Holidays; Facts, Activities, and
    Crafts, 407
Jews, 200–201, 421
Jezebel Wolf, The, 388
Johansen, Margaret, 519
John Henry McCoy, 337
Johnny Tremain, 333, 428, 432, 522
Johns, Jeanne, 178
Johnson, Crockett, 51
Johnson, Doris, 55
Johnson, Edna, 262, 364
Johnson, Gerald W., 525

John Tabor's Ride, 66
"Jonathan Bing," 281
Jones, Elizabeth O., 60, 511, 512
Jones, Harold, 37
Jones, Helen L., 83
Jones, Hettie, 189, 349, 441
Jones, Idwal, 520
Jones, Weyman, 190
Jordan, Alice, 473, 503
Jordan, June, 55
Jorge el Curioso, 355
Jorinda and Joringel, 227
Josefina February, 68
Joseph, Nez Percé Chief, 191
Joseph, Stephen M., 158, 211, 213
Joseph's Yard, 33
Joslin, Sesyle, 64, 67, 353, 405, 515
Journey Between Two Worlds, 128
Journey Cake, Ho!, 514
Journey from Peppermint Street, 180, 203
Journey of the Grey Whales, 386
Journey Outside, 527
Journeys, 211
Journeys of Sebastian, 75
Joyce, James, 221
Joy of the Court, The, 260
Joy to the World; Christmas Legends, 404
Juanita, 193, 513
Juan Patricio, 193
Juarez: The Founder of Modern Mexico,
    195
Judge, The, 516
Judge: An Untrue Tale, The, 65
Judging, 335, 340–341
Judson, Clara I., 413, 523, 524
Julie of the Wolves, 146, 173, 340, 388,
    472, 499, 527
"Jumblies, The," 281
Jumping-off Place, 519
"Jump or Jiggle," 294
Jungle Book, 221, 473, 494
Junior high school, 40, 43, 63, 480
Junior High School Catalog 424
Juster, Norton, 18, 115, 381
Justin Morgan Had a Horse, 11, 522
Just Me, 516
Just So Stories, 221, 343, 348, 497
Just the Thing for Geraldine, 64
Justus, May, 440

Kaha Bird; Tales from the Steppes of
    Central Asia, The, 240
Kahl, Virginia, 405
Kalashnikoff, Nicholas, 523
Kalina, Sigmund, 394
Kalnay, Francis, 194, 525
Kamerman, Sylvia E., 258
Kantrowitz, Mildred, 164
Karen's Opposites, 380

Kate, 152
Kaufman, Mervyn, 400, 441
Keary, A., 256
Keary, E., 256
Keating, Charlotte M., 213
Keats, Ezra J., 4, 10, 32, 53, 60, 301, 412, 436, 515, 516
Keats, John, 304
"Keep a poem in your pocket," 282
Keeping, Charles, 33, 252, 256
Keith, Harold, 524
Kelly, Eric P., 519
Kelly, Regina Z., 433
Kelpie's Pearls, The, 115
Kendall, Carol, 525
Kent, Jack, 219
Kepes, Juliet, 37, 513
Kerrigan, Anthony, 195
Kesselman, Wendy, 46
Kettelkamp, Larry, 398
Kevin Cloud; Chippewa Boy in the City, 190
Kevin's Grandma, 55
Key, Mary R., 81
Kidnapped, 473
"Kids in Print," 321
Kijima, Hajime, 246
Kildee House, 523
Killer Whale!, 385
King, Cynthia, 255
King, Ethel M., 488
King, Martha L., 482, 489
King, Martin Luther, 349
King Arthur, 256, 258–261
Kingdom of the Forest, The, 396
Kingman, Lee, 67, 69, 83, 174, 406, 511
King Must Die, The, 252
King of the Golden River, 229
King of the Wind, 11, 523
King's Fifth, The, 526
King's Fountain, The, 11, 53
Kingsley, Charles, 87, 252, 325, 473, 474, 493
Kingston, Carolyn T., 503
King Who Rides a Tiger and Other Tales from Nepal, The, 263
Kipling, Rudyard, 3, 221, 304, 348, 388, 473, 474, 494, 497
Kirn, Ann, 44
Kirschenbaum, Howard, 213
"Kite, The," 341
Kiviok's Magic Journey, 52
Kleberger, Ilse, 180
Klein, Gerda, 165
Klein, Norma, 56, 172, 198–200, 478
Knee-Baby, The, 149
Knee-High Man, and Other Tales, The, 249
Kneeknock Rise, 115, 527
Knight, Damon, 128

Knitted Cat, The, 74
Knowledge of the Heavens and the Earth Made Easy, or the First Principles of Geography and Astronomy Explained, The, 492
Koch, Kenneth, 304, 308, 322
Kohl, Herbert, 211, 321
Komisar, Lucy, 175
Konigsburg, Elaine L., 167, 180, 206–208, 440, 526
Kostelanetz, Richard, 302
Krahn, Fernando, 75
Krasilovsky, Phyllis, 69
Krauss, Ruth, 64, 67, 71, 513, 514
Krementz, Jill, 440
Kroeber, Alfred, 132
Kroeber, Theodora, 132, 191, 405
Krumgold, Joseph, 179, 194, 524, 525
Kruss, James, 44, 178
Krythe, M. R., 408
Kuhn, Doris, 28
Kujoth, Jean S., 488
Kula, Elsa, 246
Kuskin, Karla, 154, 271, 304, 315, 484
"Kwakiutl Indian Chant," 149
Kyle, Anne, 520

Labastida, Aurora, 404, 515
Ladder Company, 108, 413
Lady Bird, Quickly, 37
Lady Ellen Grae, 197
La Farge, Phyllis, 177
Lafayette: Friend of America, 433
La Flesche, Susette, 191
La Fontaine, 217–218, 220, 393
Laird, Charlton, 380
Laird, Helene, 380
Lakoff, Robin, 81
Lamb, Charles, 474, 493
Lamb, Mary, 474, 493
Lambert, Eloise, 380
LaMorrisse, Albert, 342
Lampman, Evelyn S., 190, 193, 194, 333, 388
Lancaster, Bruce, 432
Land Beneath the Sea, The, 384
Lanes, Selma G., 143
Lang, Andrew, 223, 227, 494
Langstaff, John, 44, 514
Langston Hughes, 441
Language, 6–10, 20, 40, 43, 140–141, 252, 254–255, 285–293
Language and reading abilities, 481–482
Language Arts, 22, 307, 434
Language Arts Activities for the Classroom, 373
Language arts instruction, 136–142
"Language Study," 425

Lanier, Sidney, 258
Lapsley, Susan, 55
Larkin, David, 267
Larrick, Nancy, 211, 306, 322
LaRue, Mabel G., 412
La Salle of the Mississippi, 435
Lasky, Kathryn, 33
Last Battle, The, 117
Last Night I Saw Andromeda, 157
Last of the Mohicans, The, 493
Last Trumpeters, The, 392
Latham, Jean L., 176, 524
Lathrop, Dorothy P., 49, 510, 519
Lathrop, Harriet, 494
Lavender's Blue, 37
Lawson, Marie A., 337, 402
Lawson, Robert, 60, 61, 107, 108, 130, 154, 426, 428, 431, 499, 510, 511, 522, 525
Laycock, George, 390, 392, 396
Lay of the Last Minstrel, The, 256
Lazarevich, Mila, 221
Lazies; Tales of the Peoples of Russia, The, 240
Leach, Maria, 263
Leader by Destiny: George Washington, Man and Patriot, 521
Leaf, Munro, 61, 394, 510
Lear, Edward, 42, 279, 281, 303–304, 494
Learning centers, 138, 430
Learning disabilities, 164–167
Learning module, 410–424
Learning to Say Good-by, 161
LeCron, Helen C., 294
Lee, Mildred, 174
Lee, Patrick G., 81
Lee, Virginia, 160
Lefkowitz, R. J., 394
LeGallienne, Eva, 227
LeGallienne, Richard, 225–226
Legends of the Great Chiefs, 189
LeGuin, Ursula, 88, 123, 132–133, 527
Lehrer, Tom, 274
Leigh, Mabel, 522
"Leisure," 283
L'Engle, Madeleine, 125, 130, 333, 499, 525
Lenski, Lois, 420, 428, 499, 520, 522
Lent, Blair, 59, 66, 214, 238, 244–245, 393, 516, 517
Lent, Henry, 357
Lentil, 6
Leodhas, Sorche N., 59, 68, 263, 515, 516, 525
LeShan, Eda, 161
Leskoff, Jack, 267
Lester, Julius, 249, 526
Let's Be Enemies, 67
Let's Find Out about the City, 411

Letter for Amy, A, 11
Lettering, 366–369
Letters, 353, 366
*Letters to Horseface: Being the Story of
Wolfgang Amadeus Mozart's Journey
to Italy 1769–1770 When He Was a
Boy of Fourteen,* 15
Let the Balloon Go, 167
Let Them Write Poetry, 322
Levine, Joan, 324
Levoy, Myron, 413
Levy, Elizabeth, 150
Lewis, Clive S., 116, 117, 130, 143
Lewis, Elizabeth, 520
Lewis, Richard, 11, 195, 211, 301, 321
Lewis, Thomas P., 194
Lewis Carroll Observed, 143
Lewis Carroll Shelf Award, 475
Lexau, Joan, 54, 55, 64, 158, 476
Library, 16, 24
Library of Congress, 221
Lide, Alice, 519
Life and Death, 161
Life and Death of Yellow Bird, The, 187
*Life and Legends of George McJunkin,
The,* 441
Light at Tern Rock, The, 406, 523
Lightner, Alice M., 128
Light Princess, The, 495
Likely Place, A, 180
Lillie of Watts, 156, 476
Li Lun, Lad of Courage, 523
Limericks, 281, 296–297, 339
Lindgren, Astrid, 5, 171, 347, 354, 405,
499
Lindquist, Jennie, 524
Lindsay, Vachel, 304
Lines, Kathleen, 37, 143, 227
Lion, 514
Lionni, Leo, 60, 62, 108, 116, 221,
513
Lipkind, William, 513
Lisa and the Grompet, 115
Listening, 277
Listening center, 344
Liston, Robert A., 412
Literary concepts, 327–329
Literary Market Place, 45
Literature
learning, 76
lessons, 357–358
program, 326–343
study, 136–142
*Literature and the Reader: Research in
Response to Literature, Reading
Interests, and the Teaching of
Literature,* 489–490
*Literature for Children: History and
Trends,* 503
Literature for Thursday's Child, 28, 213

*Litter – The Ugly Enemy; An Ecology
Story,* 395
Little, Jean, 152, 156, 164, 167
Little Bear, 50
Little Bear's Visit, 515
Little Blacknose, 519
Little Black Sambo, 494
Little Book of Beasts, A, 315
"Little Charlie Chipmunk," 294
"Little Girl Named I, The," 229
Little House, The, 340, 477, 511
Little House in the Big Woods, 348, 498
Little House on the Prairie, 428
Little Island, The, 64, 512
Little Lord Fauntleroy, 494, 496
Little Lost Lamb, 512
"Little Miss Muffet," 40, 290, 484
Little Pretty Pocketbook, A, 491
Little Prince, The, 229, 344
Little Red Riding Hood, 226, 228
Little Tim and the Brave Sea Captain, 51
Little Town on the Prairie, 521
Little White Hen, 246
Little Women, 69, 159, 473, 474, 494
Lively Art of Picture Books, The, 68
Living in the city, 415–424
Livingstone, Myra C., 291, 304
Lizzie Lies a Lot, 150
Lobel, Anita, 52
Lobel, Arnold, 47, 52, 60, 517, 527
Locke, John, 493
Lofting, Hugh, 87, 130, 497, 518
Loggerhead Turtle: Survivor from the Sea,
387
"Lollypop, The," 302
London Bridge Is Falling Down!, 37
*London Bridge Is Falling Down; The
Song and Game,* 35
Lone Bull's Horse Raid, 188
"Lone Dog," 484
*Lone Journey: The Life of Roger
Williams,* 522
Loneliness, 282
Loner, The, 152, 526
Longfellow, Henry W., 304, 433
Longtemps, Kenneth, 144, 164
Long Winter, The, 521
Lönnrot, Elias, 223
Look Again!, 75
Look What I Can Do, 74
Loon's Necklace, The, 340
Lorca, Federico G., 304
Lord of the Rings, The, 119, 500
Lord of the Sky: Zeus, 252
*Lore and Language of School-children,
The,* 267
Lorenzini, Carlo, 87, 473, 494
Lorraine, Walter, 44
*Louder and Louder; The Dangers of Noise
Pollution,* 395

Lourie, Richard, 68, 240
Love, 149, 345
Lowell, Amy, 314
Lownsbery, Eloise, 519
Lowrey, Janette S., 433
Lubin, Leonard, 224
Luckenbill, W. Bernard, 488
Luckhardt, Mildred C., 403, 404
Ludell, 150, 153, 440
Lueders, Edward, 275
Luke Was There, 413, 421
Lundgren, Max, 180
Lyle, Jack, 489
Lyle, Lyle Crocodile, 47
Lynch, Maude D., 219
Lyttle, Richard B., 396

McCaffrey, Anne, 88
MacCann, Donnarae, 83
McCloskey, Robert, 6, 13, 46, 59, 109,
386, 488, 511, 512, 513, 514
McClung, Robert M., 385, 392
McCord, David, 285, 305, 485
McCormick, Mary Jo, 389
McCoy, J. J., 392
McCoy, Jack, 387
McDermott, Gerald, 53, 59, 245, 477,
517
MacDonald, George, 18, 64, 86, 87,
130, 474, 494, 495
MacDonald, Golden, 512
McElligott's Pool, 50, 77, 512
McGinley, Phyllis, 41, 512, 513
McGovern, Ann, 258, 385, 441
McGowen, Tom, 353
McGraw, Eloise, 524, 525
MacGregor, Ellen, 128
McLeod, Emilie W., 44
McLeod, Irene R., 484
MacLeod, Mary, 260
McLeod, Sterling, 412
Macmillan, Cyrus, 263
McNeely, Marian H., 519
McNeer, May, 436
McNeill, Janet, 180
McNulty, Faith, 385
Macrae, Carmen, 349
McSpadden, J. Walker, 258
Madeline, 6, 33, 171, 173, 498, 511
Madeline's Rescue, 514
Maestro, Betsy, 301
Maestro, Guilio, 301
Magdalena, 180
Maggie Rose; Her Birthday Christmas 406
Magic and Mystery of Words, The, 378
Magic Animals of Japan, 246
Magic Finger, The, 115
Magic Horse, The, 241
Magician, The, 70

Magician of Cracow, The, 52
Magician's Nephew, The, 117
Magic Listening Cap; More Folk Tales
  from Japan, The, 241
Magic Maize, 524
Magic Moth, The, 160
Magic Tree, The, 53
Magic Words, The, 380
Magnificent Bald Eagle: America's
  National Bird, The, 391
Make Way for Ducklings, 6, 33, 46–47,
  59, 78, 511
Make Your Own Animated Movies, 398
Making Friends, 76
Making Things; The Hand Book of
  Creative Discoveries, 398
Malcolmson, Anne, 258, 512
Male and Female Under 18, 172, 211, 306
Malkus, Alida, 519
Man Explores the Sea, 384
Man Named Columbus, A, 400
Mannheim, Grete, 391
Manning-Sanders, Ruth, 21, 230–231,
  263, 401
Mansell, Maureen, 475
Man Who Didn't Wash His Dishes, The,
  69
Many Moons, 511
Many Ways of Seeing: An Introduction to
  the Pleasures of Art, The, 527
Maple Street, 440
Marcia, 438
Marguerite de Angeli's Book of Nursery
  and Mother Goose Rhymes, 35
Mariana, 405
Marian Anderson, 441
Maria Tallchief, 191
Marine life, 385–387
Maring, Gerald, 434
Mark Twain and the River, 436
Mark Twain: His Life, 436
Marquardt, Dorothy A., 83
Marryat, Captain F., 493
Marshall, Bernard, 518
Marshall, James, 395
Marshmallow, 511
Martel, Suzanne, 128
Martin, Patricia M., 55, 64, 195, 414
Marvelous Misadventures of Sebastian,
  The, 136
Mary Poppins, 18, 86, 116, 289, 331,
  498, 499
Mason, F. Van Wyck, 432
Mass media, 468, 477–478, 486–487,
  501
Master of All Masters, 233–234
Matchlock Gun, The, 427, 521
Mathematics Library: Elementary and
  Junior High School, 425
Mathis, Sharon B., 179, 441, 528

Matson, Emerson N., 189
Matsutani, Miyoko, 246, 393
Matters of Fact, 375, 425
Matthew, Mark, Luke and John, 152
Matthiesen, Thomas, 42
Matt's Grandfather, 180
Maximilian's World, 108
Maxwell, William, 522
May, Julian, 82, 384, 397
Maybelle, the Cable Car, 414
Mayer, Marianna, 73
Mayer, Mercer, 12, 33, 53, 73, 79, 347,
  499
May I Bring a Friend?, 59, 64, 515
May I Cross Your Golden River?, 160,
  345
Mazer, Norma F., 180
M. C. Higgins the Great, 439, 527
Meader, Stephen W., 386, 428, 521
Meal One, 173
Mean Mouse and Other Mean Stories,
  The, 72
Means, Florence C., 152, 522
Meat in the Sandwich, The, 150
Mecklenburger, James, 275
Me Day, 54, 64, 158
"Media for Children: Cornucopia for
  Language Learning," 488
Medicine Man's Daughter, 187
Meet Christopher Columbus, 400
Meggy MacIntosh, 519
Meigs, Cornelia, 428, 435, 503, 518,
  519, 520
Meigs, Mildred P., 281, 312
Mei Lei, 510
Melcher, Frederic J., 58
Melo, John, 149
Meltzer, Milton, 441
Mendoza, George, 149
Men from the Village Deep in the
  Mountains and Other Japanese Folk
  Tales, 245
Men, Microscopes, and Living Things,
  524
Mennonites, 151
Men of Athens, 525
Menotti, Gian-Carlo, 405
Menuhin, Yehudi, 71
Meredith, Robert, 435
Merriam, Eve, 12, 172, 211, 276,
  305–306, 328, 380
Merrill, Jean, 421
Merry Adventures of Robin Hood of Great
  Renown in Nottinghamshire, The,
  257
Merry Christmas to You; Stories for
  Christmas, 404
Merryman, Mildred P., 281
Metaphor, 292–293, 310–311
Meter, 286

Meter Means Measure, 387
Me Too, 166
Metrics, 387–388
Mexicali Soup, 193
Mexican-Americans, 192–196
Mexican folklore, 194
Mexico, 404, 407
Meyer, Howard, 441
Meyer, Renate, 75, 76
Mezey, Robert, 316
Mia Alone, 470
Mice, 349
Michelsohn, David R., 412
Middle Earth, 119–121
Middle grades, 480
Middle Moffat, The, 522
Midnight Alarm: The Story of Paul
  Revere's Ride, 432
Mighty Hunter, The, 511
Miles, Betty, 149, 476
Miles, Miska (Patricia), 48, 50, 64, 160,
  527
Milgrom, Harry, 57
Milhous, Katherine, 513
Millay, Edna St. Vincent, 283, 304
Miller, Bertha M., 83
Miller, Elizabeth, 519
Miller, Herbert F., 425
Miller, His Son, and Their Donkey, The,
  221
Millions of Cats, 49, 225, 498, 519
Mills, Gretchen, 161
Mills, Queenie B., 275
Milne, A. A., 30, 88, 279, 305, 312,
  339, 498
Mime Alphabet Book, The, 43
Minarik, Else, 50, 67, 515
Minn of the Mississippi, 435, 523
Mintonye, Grace, 398
Miracles, 321
Miracles on Maple Hill, 524
Mirthes, Carolyn, 211
Miss Bianca in the Orient, 107
Miss Bianca in the Salt Mines, 107, 349
Miss Flora McFlimsey's Christmas Eve,
  405
Miss Hickory, 522
Mississippi; America's Mainstream, The,
  436
Mississippi Possum, 64
Mississippi River, 434–436
Miss Pickerell Goes to Mars, 128
Mister Corbett's Ghost, 421
Mistletoe, 255
Mistral, Gabriela, 52
Misty of Chincoteague, 11, 523
Mitchell, Robert, 350
Mitten; An Old Ukrainian Folktale, The,
  241
Mr. Justice Holmes, 524

Mr. McFadden's Halloween, 401
Mr. Penny's Race Horse, 514
Mr. Popper's Penguin's, 108, 521
Mr. Rabbit and the Lovely Present, 515
Mr. Revere and I, 108, 426, 431
Mr. T. W. Anthony Woo, 513
"Mr. Vinegar," 231
Mrs. Fox, 108
Mrs. Frisby and the Rats of NIMH, 86, 130, 527
Multicultural Teaching: Activities, Information and Resources, 213
"Mummy Slept Late and Daddy Fixed Breakfast," 484
Munari, Bruno, 2, 42
Munzer, Martha, 412
Mural, 330
Music, 314–315, 331
Music and poetry, 285–289
My Brother Sam Is Dead, 527
My Brother Stevie, 152, 174
My Darling, My Hamburger, 201
My Father's Dragon, 523
My First Counting Book, 44
My Granpa Died Today, 161
My Grandson Lew, 54, 159
My Great-Grandfather and I, 179
My Great Grandfather, the Heroes and I, 178
My Mother Is the Most Beautiful Woman in the World, 225, 241, 476, 512
My Own Rhythm, 301
My Side of the Mountain, 525
My Sister Looks Like a Pear; Awakening the Poetry in Young People, 322
Mizumura, Kazue, 374, 385, 389, 392
Mobile, 330
Moby Dick, 385
Moccasin Trail, 524
"Modern Dragon, A," 272, 339
Moe, Jörgen, 223
Moffett, James, 372
Mofsie, Louis, 189
Moja Means One, 517
Mole Family's Christmas, The, 65
Molly Patch and Her Animal Friends, 46
Molnar, Joe, 192
Mommies at Work, 172, 328
"Momotaro or The Story of the Son of a Peach," 241
Mom, the Wolf Man and Me, 172, 199, 351, 478
Monjo, Ferdinand N., 15, 388
"Monkeys and the Crocodile, The," 312
Monkhouse, Cosmos, 296
Monson, Dianne L., 488, 503
Monsters, 79–80
Montana, 388
Montgomery, Norah, 37

Montgomerie, William, 37
Montgomery, Elizabeth, 441
Montgomery, Rutherford, 523
Month Brothers, The, 241
Month of Sundays, A, 156, 413
Months, 399–410
Montresor, Beni, 37, 59, 64, 515
Moon, Grace, 519
"Moonlight," 291
Moon in the Cloud, The, 115
Moon Jumpers, The, 67, 515
Moon Man, 52
Moon of Gomrath, The, 114
Moorachian, Rose, 412
Moore, Anne C., 518
Moore, Clement, 493
Moore, Janet G., 527
Moore, Lilian, 44
Mordillo, Guillermo, 76
More About Words, 379
More Books by More People, 12, 136, 203
More Books by More People: Interviews with 65 Authors of Books for Children, 210
More Cricket Songs, 300
More Nonsense, 494
Morey, Walter, 476
Morgan, Alison, 153
Morley, Christopher, 281, 284
Mormons; The Church of Jesus Christ of Latter-Day Saints, The, 407
Morrison, Lillian, 350
Morse, Samuel F., 42
Mosel, Arlene, 59, 214, 246, 517
Most Beautiful Word, The, 380
Most Native of Sons, The, 441
Most Terrible Turk, The, 179
Most Wonderful Doll in the World, The, 513
Mother Goose, 18, 32, 34–41, 35, 329, 512
Mother Goose ABC; In a Pumpkin Shell, A, 35
Mother Goose and Nursery Rhymes, 37, 515
Mother Goose in Hieroglyphics, 37
Mother Goose in Spanish/Poesías de la Madre Oca, 195
Mother Goose Lost, 37
Mother Goose; or, The Old Nursery Rhymes, 37
Mother Goose rhymes, 314
Mother Goose; The Old Nursery Rhymes, 37
Mother Goose; The Volland Edition, 37
Mother Goose Treasury, The, 35
Mother Owl, The, 393
Mother role, 153
Mother Tree, The, 160
Motif Index of Folk-Literature, 223

Motivation, 343–372
"Motor Cars," 417
Motoring Millers, The, 174
Mountain Born, 522
Mountains Are Free, 519
"Mouse," 320
Mouse and the Motorcycle, The, 108
Moved-Outers, The, 522
Movement, 313
Mowat, Farley, 388
Mowgli and His Brothers, 388
Mud Pies and Other Recipes, 72
Mukerji, Dhan G., 518
Mulberry Music, The, 160
Multicultural concerns, 501
Multicultural teaching, 24, 146–147, 192–196, 234–246
Mysterious Disappearance of Leon (I Mean Noel), The, 381, 413
Mystery of the Fog Man, 152
Mythology, 246–256, 261, 267
Myths, 189

Nahuatl Indians, 195
Names, 315
Nana Upstairs and Nana Downstairs, 159
Na-ni, 440
Nansen, 521
Narnia, 116–118
Nash, Ogden, 278, 304
Nathan, Dorothy, 241
National Assessment of Educational Progress, 488
National Assessment of Reading, 481–482
National Audubon Society, 394
National Book Award, 203
National Council of Teachers of English, 22, 28, 425
National Science Teachers Association, 425
Native American folklore, 249
Native Americans, 14, 148–149, 150, 186–192, 316, 330, 386, 403
Natural resources, 395–396
Nature, 283–284
Nature's Nursery; Baby Birds, 390
Navaho Indians, 150, 187
Nebraska Curriculum for English, 481
Neighbors, The, 240
Nelson, Mary A., 234
Nesbit, E., 111
Nesbitt, Elizabeth, 503
Nesbit Tradition; The Children's Novel in England 1945–1970, The 503
Ness, Evaline, 30, 53, 59, 66, 68, 353, 515, 516
Never Cry Wolf, 388
Neville, Emily C., 153, 155, 200, 525

New baby, 55, 149, 439
New Baby Comes, A, 82
Newberry, Clare, 60, 511
Newbery, John, 491
Newbery, Thomas, 490
Newbery and Caldecott Medal Books 1966–1975, 210
Newbery award, 11, 125, 129–130, 132, 140, 142, 145, 155, 165, 187, 203, 210, 388, 432, 439, 470–474, 497, 507, 518–528
Newbery Medal, 107, 122, 173, 497
New England Primer, 491
New Feminism, The, 175
New Found World, 522
New Friend, The, 476
New Golden Bough, The, 267
New Home for Billy, A, 440
New Land, 520
New Life—La Vida Nueva: The Mexican Americans Today, The, 195
New Life: New Room, 55
Newlon, Clarke, 195
New Look for Children's Literature, A, 503
Newman, Robert, 253
Newman, Shirlee P., 241–245, 441
New Mexico, 187
Newsletter, 488
New Towns: Building Cities from Scratch, 412
New Water Book, The, 394
New World Beginnings; Indian Cultures in the Americas, 192
New York, 413
New York City, 207, 421–422
New York *Times,* 60
Next Door to Xanadu, 175
Nibble Nibble Mousekin; A Tale of Hansel and Gretel, 228
Nice Little Girls, 151
Nicholas, 518
Nicolás, 348, 513
"Night," 292
Nightbirds on Nantucket, 135
Night Daddy, The, 174
"Night of the Leonid, The," 181–186
Nilsen, Alleen P., 170
Nine Days to Christmas, 404, 515
Nine in a Line, 44
Nineteenth century, 492–496
Nino, 521
Ninon, 41
Nist, Joan S., 488
"Noble Duke of York, The," 313
Nobody Is Perfick, 466
Nobody's Cat, 48
No Ducks in "Our" Bathtub, 347
Noisy Nancy Norris, 173, 412
Nonfiction, 56–57, 342

Nonna, 55, 160, 179
Nook, Gerard, 14
Noonday Friends, The, 162, 526
Norman, Gertrude, 400
Norman, James, 194
Norse Gods and Giants, 253
Norse mythology, 253
North, Sterling, 436, 526
Northwest Indians, 188
Norton, Alice M., 125
Norton, Andre, 123, 125, 261
Norton, Mary, 5, 86, 109
Norvell, George W., 488
Norway, 53, 223, 232–233
Not Bad for a Girl, 175
Nothing at All, 511
Nothing Is Impossible: The Story of Beatrix Potter, 50
Nothing Place, The, 166
Nourse, Alan, 126
Novels, 136–142, 342
Number concepts, 45
"Nun's Priest's Tale, The," 68
Nursery rhymes, 32, 34–41
Nutcracker Suite, The, 137

Oakley, Graham, 48, 84
Objectives, 137, 146, 334–341, 376, 429
O'Brien, Robert C., 127, 130, 527
Ocean, 383–387
Oceanographers in Action, 384
Oceanography, 384
Oceanography Lab, 384
O'Connell, Jean S., 14
"Octopussycat, The," 298, 340
O'Dell, Scott, 12, 25, 146, 173, 187, 194, 203, 499, 525, 526, 527
Odland, Norine, 479, 483, 488
Odyssey, The, 474
Of Other Worlds: Essays and Stories, 143
Ohlsson, Ib, 42, 56
Oil, 396
Oil: The Buried Treasure, 396
Old Gumshoe, 200
Old Man Is Always Right, The, 65
"Old Man Who Said 'Why,' The," 229
Old Mother Hubbard and Her Dog, 35
Old Peter's Russian Tales, 241
Old Ramón, 525
Olds, Elizabeth, 513
Old Tobacco Shop, The, 518
Old Woman and Her Pig, The, 35, 225
Old Yeller, 524
Olga da Polga, 347
Olga Meets Her Match, 89
Once a Mouse, 3, 33, 59, 64, 66, 219–220

Once Upon a Time: The Fairy Tale World of Arthur Rackham, 267
On Children's Literature, 467, 503
On Christmas Eve, 405
One Fine Day, 52, 59, 224, 517
One for the Price of Two, 246
100 Hamburgers: The Getting Thin Book, 168
O'Neill, Mary, 268, 269, 305, 306–307, 380
"One-Inch Fellow," 241
1 Is One, 44, 514
One Monday Morning, 70
One Morning in Maine, 513
One Snail and Me: A Book of Numbers and Animals and a Bathtub, 44
One's None; Old Rhymes for New Tongues, 37
One Step, Two . . . , 44
One to Grow On, 156, 164
One Two Three: An Animal Counting Book, 45
One, Two, Three Going to Sea, 44
One Way Johnny, 44
One Wide River to Cross, 516
Onion John, 179, 525
Only Connect: Readings on Children's Literature, 28
Onomatopoeia, 288–289
On the Banks of Plum Creek, 521
On the Other Side of the River, 412
Oodles of Noodles, 380
Ood-Le-Uk the Wanderer, 519
Opie, Iona, 37, 222, 267
Opie, Peter, 37, 222, 267
Oppenheim, Joanne, 412
Oral language, 343–347
Oral Language: Expression of Thought, 344
Orbis Pictus, 490
Orchestra Mice, The, 107
Orgel, Doris, 160, 175
Oriental religions, 407
Original Poems for Infant Minds, 493
Origins and Development of the English Language, The, 222–223
Orioles, 391
Orleans, Ilo, 417
Ormondroyd, Edward, 128
Orphan, 154
Orpheus: Myths of the World, 247
Oscar Lobster's Fair Exchange, 140
Other Side of the Fence, The, 440
Otherwise Known as Sheila the Great, 168
Otis, James, 474
Ounce, Dice, Trice, 6, 378
Our American Language, 380
Our Dirty Air, 394
Our Eddie, 527

Our Names: Where They Came From and What They Mean, 380
Our Six-legged Friends and Allies; Ecology in Your Back Yard, 396
Out of the Flame, 519
Out! Out! Out!, 74
Outsiders, The, 499
Over in the Meadow, 44
Over Sea, Under Stone, 131
Owens, Gail, 324
Owl and the Prairie Dog, The, 391
"Owl and the Pussy-Cat, The," 279, 494
Owl at Home, 47
Owl Book, The, 393
Owlet, The Great Horned Owl, 393
Owls, 391
Owl Service, The, 114
Oxford Nursery Rhyme Book, The, 37

Paco's Miracle, 187
Paddle-to-the-Sea, 25, 436, 499, 511
Padraic Colum, 247
Pageant of Chinese America, 520
Pagoo, 348, 382, 436
Painting the Moon, 66
Palazzo, Tony, 512
Pancakes-Paris, 523
Panchatantra, 218–219
Pandora's Box, 266
"Panther, The," 279
Papago Indians, 189
Paperback books, 500
Parade, The, 72
Pardon Me, You're Stepping on My Eyeball, 201
Paris, 421
Parish, Peggy, 52
Parker, Edwin B., 489
Parker, Robert A., 516
Parnall, Peter, 517
Parrish, Anne, 518, 519, 523
"Parrot," 281
Pascal, David, 219
Passover, 407
Pass the Poetry, Please, 322
"Pasture Spring, The," 271
Path of Hunters; Animal Struggle in a Meadow, 396
Patterson, Lillie, 404
Paul Bunyan, 256, 263, 340
Paul Revere and the World He Lived In, 432
Paul Revere: Colonial Craftsman, 433
"Paul Revere's Ride," 433
Paul Robeson, 441
Pavo and the Princess, 68
Payzant, Charles, 384
Peacock Pie, 69

Peake, Katy, 190
Pearce, Philippa, 112
Peare, Catherine O., 436
Peasant's Pea Patch; A Russian Folktale, The, 240
"Peas Porridge Hot," 39
Peck, Robert N., 396
Pecos Bill, 263, 340, 521
Pedro, the Angel of Olvera Street, 193, 405
"Peepers," 296
Peg-leg Willy, 403
Pei, Mario, 380
Pelicans, The, 392
Pell, John H., 431
Pellowski, Anne, 321
Peltola, Bette, 488, 503
"Pendulum," 302
Penguin Book, The, 392
Penner, Lucille, 432
Penny a Look, A, 328
"People Buy a Lot of Things," 296
People from the Sky; Ainu Tales from Northern Japan, 245
People of the Ax, The, 114
People Lobby, The, 151
Peppermint Pig, The, 168, 204–206, 337, 469
Perera, Gretchen, 395
Perera, Thomas, 395
Performance criteria, 138
Perilous Gard, The, 131, 136, 137, 141–142, 527
Perilous Road, The, 525
Perrault, Charles, 35, 66, 226, 491, 513, 514
Perrault's Classic French Fairy Tales, 227
Perrine, Laurence, 322
Persephone; Bringer of Spring, 252
Peter, 153
Peter and the Piskies; Cornish Folk and Fairy Tales, 230
Peter and Veronica, 164
Peterkin Papers, The, 86, 110
Peter Pan, 87, 342, 497
Peter Rabbit, 50
Peter's Chair, 11
Petersham, Maud, 60, 511, 512
Petersham, Miska, 60, 511, 512
Peter's Long Walk, 69
Peterson, Roger T., 397
Petronella, 62, 339
Petry, Ann, 428
Petunia's Christmas, 405
Phantom Tollbooth, The, 18, 115, 381
Phebe Fairchild: Her Book, 520
Phelan, Mary K., 413, 432
Phillippine folklore, 74
Phillip Hall Likes Me, I Reckon Maybe, 527

Phlëger, Fred, 174
Phoebe's Revolt, 174
Phoenix and the Carpet, The, 111
Photography, 343, 478
Piaget, 334
Piatti, Celestino, 42, 62, 393
Picture books, 6, 10–11, 12, 20, 30–83, 219–221, 227, 240–241, 261
Picture Books for Children, 83
Picture for Harold's Room; A Purple Crayon Adventure, A, 51
Piece of the Power; Four Black Mayors, A, 412
Pierre Pigeon, 511
Pigeon Flight, 108
Pigman, The, 160, 201, 202
Pigtail of Ah Lee Ben Loo, 519
Pilgrim's Progress, 491
Pillar, Arlene, 434
Pima Indians, 189
Pinocchio, 473, 494
Pippi Longstocking, 4, 5, 171, 339, 354, 499, 500
"Pirate Don Durk of Dowdee, The," 281, 312
Pitt, Valerie, 385, 391, 411
Place, The, 194
Plains Indians, 14, 188
"Plaint of the Camel, The," 281
Planet of Junior Brown, The, 527
Plascencia, Peter, 42
Play a Part, 258
Play of Words, The, 380
Plays from Famous Stories and Fairy Tales, 436
Play with Me, 514
Plum Pudding for Christmas, 405
Plymouth Thanksgiving, The, 403
Pocahontas and the Strangers, 191
Pocketful of Cricket, A, 68, 516
Podkayne of Mars, 124
"Poem of Praise," 319
Poems from the Hebrew, 316
Poems of Childhood, 494
Poetic Edda, 254
Poetry, 34–41, 188–189, 195, 268–322, 342, 376, 399, 402–403, 416, 417, 418, 420, 433–434, 483–486
  anthology, 311
  by children, 318, 321
  definition, 271–272
  forms, 293–302, 317–318
  instruction, 302–322
  models, 318–321
  oral, 311–315
  singing, 314–315
  themes, 308–311
Poetry and the Young Child, 322

Poetry, Children and Children's Books, 272, 311
Poetry Is for People, 276
Poetry: Its Appreciation and Enjoyment, 287
Poets, 303–307
Poet's Eye: An Introduction to Poetry for Young People, The, 287
Poets in the Schools: A Handbook, 322
Point of view, 338
Poland, 52
Polish folklore, 229
Politi, Leo, 32, 60, 193, 405, 512, 513
"Pollution," 274
"Poor Old Woman," 311–312
Pope, Elizabeth M., 131, 137, 141–142, 527
Popular Tales from the Norse, 232
Portrait of Ivan, 164
Positive reinforcement, 18
Possible Impossibles of Ikkyu the Wise, The, 245
Potato Talk, 225
Potter, Beatrix, 46, 50, 143, 496, 497
Potter, Bronson, 167
Porquoi tales, 72, 248–249
Poverty, 162
Pran of Albania, 519
Pratt, Davis, 246
Prayer for a Child, 512
Pregnancy, 470
Prejudice; The Invisible Wall, 213
Preschool children, 6, 10–11, 19–21, 30–83, 288, 291, 292–294
Presenting literature, 137
Presidency, The, 342
Preston, Edna M., 516
Primary children, 479–480
Prince Caspian, 117
Prince in Waiting, The, 127, 340
Princess and Curdie, The, 18
Princess and the Pea, The, 227
Pringle, Laurence, 57, 394, 396
Printing press, 490
Prisoner in the Park, The, 180
Profiles in Black and White, 441
Project Sealab; The Story of the United States Navy's Man in the Sea Program, 384
Promised Year, The, 25
Properties of Things, 490
Prose Edda, 254
Provensen, Alice, 227, 380
Provensen, Martin, 227, 380
Provensen Book of Fairy Tales, The, 227
Proverbs, 217
Prydain, 121–122
Psychology, 222
Publication of student writing, 321
Publishers' addresses, 529–533

Pueblo Indians, 187
Puerto Ricans, 149, 163
Puerto Rico, 52
"Puff, the Magic Dragon," 314
Pumpkin Moonshine, 401
"Punishment Worse Than Death," 245
Puppetry, 72
"Puppy and I," 312, 339
Puppy Summer, 180
Puppy Who Wanted a Boy, The, 405
Puptents and Pebbles, 41
Purchasing books, 18
Purdy, Susan, 372, 408
Purves, Alan C., 479–480, 488–489
Pushcart War, The, 421
Puss in Boots, 66, 226, 227–228, 338, 513
"Pussy Willows," 292–293
Putnam, Peter, 167
Pyle, Howard, 31, 257, 259
Pyles, Thomas, 222–223

Quackenbush, Robert, 314
Quaint and Curious Quest of Johnny Longfoot, The, 523
Quakers; The Religious Society of Friends, The, 407
Quatrain, 297–299
Queenie Peavy, 162, 172, 341
Queer Person, 519
Questioning, 344, 475–476, 482
Questions, 138
"Questions," 484
Questions and Answers about Ants, 389
Quiet on Account of Dinosaur, 174
Quitting Deal, The, 55

Rabbit Hill, 108, 130, 499, 522
Rabin, Gil, 156
Racecourse for Andy, A, 167
Rachel Carson: Who Loved the Sea, 176
Rackham, Arthur, 37, 65, 89, 227
Railroad to Freedom, The, 520
"Rain," 314
Rain Drop Splash, 512
"Rain It Raineth on the Just, The," 298
Rain Makes Applesauce, 516
"Rain, Rain, Go Away," 294
Rain, Rain, Rivers, 70, 353
Rainshower, 342, 477
Rama, 256
Ramón Makes a Trade/Los Cámbios de Ramón, 194
Rand, Paul, 378
Rankin, Louise, 523
Ransome, Arthur, 59, 70, 240, 241, 516
Rapunzel, 226, 228, 266
Rascal, 526

Raskin, Ellen, 381, 413, 527
Rathbone, Basil, 388
Rau, Margaret, 392
Raven's Cry, 190
Rawlings, Marjorie K., 524
Ray Charles, 342, 441
"Reactions of Sixth-Grade Students to Remembered Favorite Books of Elementary School Teachers," 488
Reader's Guide to Periodical Literature, 424
Reader's Theatre, 339, 358–364
Reading, 42–43, 76, 315–316
Reading Activities for Child Involvement, 372
Reading aloud, 19–21, 28, 77, 344–345, 476, 481–482
Reading Ideas; A Newsletter for Teachers of All Levels, 372, 425, 434
Reading instruction, 324–373
Reading interests, 479–481
Reading Interests of Children and Young Adults, 488
Reading Interests of Young People, The, 488
Reading/language center, 351–355
Reading of Poetry, The, 275
Reading instructions, 136–142
Reading Ladders for Human Relations, 22, 213
Reading readiness, 334
Reading Strategies, 373
"Read This: You'll Love It," 487
Read/write approach, 353–354
Realism, 53–55, 144–213, 468, 469–470, 500
Real Me, The, 476
Real Mother Goose, The, 37
"Reason for the Pelican, The," 281
Reavin, Sam, 174
Reb and the Redcoats, The, 433
Rebecca's War, 433
Recipe for a Magic Childhood, 3
Recordings, 343, 468, 417–418
Recycling, 394
Red Balloon, The, 342–343, 477
Redbird: The Story of a Cardinal, 392
Red Letter Days; A Book of Holiday Customs, 408
Red Power on the Rio Grande: The Nature of the American Revolution of 1680, 192
Red Riding Hood, 222
Red Sails to Capri, 524
"Red Wheelbarrow, The," 485
Reed, Philip, 37, 515
Rees, Ennis, 225
Reesink, Marijke, 241
Reeves, James, 37, 219, 404

Reflections on a Gift of Watermelon Pickle, 275
Reggiani, Renee, 476
Reid, Alastair, 6–10, 195, 353, 354, 378
Reid, Virginia M., 22, 213
Reiss, Johanna, 527
Relating, 335, 337–338
Religions, 407
Reluctant Dragon, The, 65, 90–105
Renault, Mary, 252
Renfroe's Christmas, 406
Representative Performance Objectives for High School English, 335
Research in Children's Literature, 488, 503.
Responding to literature, 335
Ress, Etta S., 394
Retardation, 165, 166, 167, 180, 198
Return of the Twelves, The, 115
Revolution, 56
"Revolutionary Reading: An Annotated Bibliography," 434
Revolutionary War, 174, 388
Revolutionary War Weapons: Pole Arms, Hand Guns, Shoulder Arms and Artillery, 432
Rey, H. A., 25, 355
Reyher, Becky, 225, 241, 476, 512
Rhoads, Dorothy, 524
Rhodin, Eric, 160
Rhyme scheme, 297–298
Rhymes of Childhood, 494
Rice, Eve, 150
Rice Bowl Pet, The, 414
Richard, Olga, 83
Richards, Laura E., 279, 289, 296, 305, 312, 484
Ride the Crooked Wind, 190
Riding to Canonbie, 315
Ridlow, Marci, 484
Rifles of Watie, 524
Riley, James W., 494
Ring-a Ring o' Roses, 35
Ring O'Roses: A Nursery Rhyme Picture Book, 35
Rinkoff, Barbara, 167
Ripper, Charles, 340, 388
Rip Van Winkle, 137
"Rip Van Winkle," 493
Riquet with the Tuft, 227
Rise and Fall of the Seas; The Story of the Tides, The, 384
Ritchie, Barbara, 194
Ritchie, T., 37
River at Green Knowe, The, 112
"Roads go ever ever on," 120
Robber! A Robber!, A, 46
Robbins, Ruth, 241, 261, 515

Robert Lawson, Illustrator: A Selection of His Characteristic Illustrations, 83
Roberts, Elizabeth M., 314
Robertson, Cliff, 71
Robertson, Darrell, 180
Robertson, Keith, 12, 354, 393
Robin Hood, 256–258
Robin Hood and His Merry Outlaws, 258
Robin Hood of Sherwood Forest, 258
"Robin Hood Meets Little John," 258
"Robin Hood Outwits the Sheriff," 258
Robinson, Barbara, 405
Robinson, Mabel, 521
Robinson Crusoe, 16, 473, 474, 491
Robins on the Window Sill, 392
Rock and the Willow, The, 174
Rocket Ship Galileo, 125
Rockwell, Anne, 233–234
Rockwell, Thomas, 162
Roethke, Theodore, 295, 304
Roger and the Fox, 512
Roger Williams, 433
Rojankovsky, Feodor, 35, 44, 63, 65, 514
Roland, 256
Roller Skates, 520
Rollins, Charlemae, 404, 441
Roman mythology, 250–253
Rooster Crows, The, 512
Rooster Who Set Out to See the World, The, 44
Root, Shelton L., Jr., 28, 275, 425
Rootabaga Stories, 263
Rosa, 193
Rosa Parks, 441
Rosen, Winfred, 5
Rose on My Cake, The, 154
Rose, where did you get that red?, 304
Ross, Patricia F., 176, 195
Rossetti, Christina, 210, 305, 309, 314, 338, 494
Rossner, Judith, 380
Round about the City, 412
Rounds, Glen, 314, 381
Rourke, Constance, 520, 521
Rowe, Jeanne, 441
Roy, Cal, 407
Rubin, Johanna, 44
Rubin, Robert, 441
"Rudolph Is Tired of the City," 283
Rufus M., 522
Runaway Papoose, 519
Runaway Ralph, 108
Runaway Slave, 441
Runaway Summer, The, 204
Runner of the Mountain Tops, 521
Ruskin, John, 229
Russell, Helen R., 394
Russia, 52

Russian folklore, 69, 70, 235–241
Ruth Sawyer, Story Teller, 343
Ryan, Cheli D., 517

Sachs, Marilyn, 152, 156, 158, 164, 175
Sacred Cow, The, 200
St. Patrick's Day, 408
Sakade, Florence, 246
Salt; A Russian Tale, 241
Salten, Felix, 69
San, 149, 164
Sam, Bangs, and Moonshine, 30, 59, 68, 336, 353, 516
Sammy, the Crow Who Remembered, 391
Sandburg, Carl, 263, 274, 292, 301, 304, 319, 322, 485
"Sandhill Crane, The," 393
Sandoz, Mari, 525
Sandpipers, 392
San Francisco, 413–414
Sansom, David, 487
Sarett, Lew, 295
Sargent, William D., 309–310, 341
Sasek, Miroslav, 412
Sasha, My Friend, 388
Satchel Paige, 441
Saturation approach, 400, 441
Sauer, Julia, 113, 406, 522, 523
Savery, Constance, 433
Sawyer, Ruth, 404, 406, 512, 514, 520
Sayers, Frances C., 226, 262, 364
Scarlet Badge, The, 433
Scarry, Richard, 219
Scat, 160
Schaefer, Jack, 525
Schauffler, Robert, 401
Schecter, Ben, 46
Scheer, Julian, 516
Schick, Eleanor, 76
Schindelman, Laurel, 181
Schlein, Miriam, 151, 514
Schmidt, Sarah, 520
Schoenherr, John, 385
Schramm, Wilbur, 486, 489
Schreiber, George, 512
Schultz, Charles, 162, 353, 401, 406
Schwartz, Alvin, 380–381, 412
Science, 57, 225, 382–398
Science and Children, 425
Science Books: A Quarterly Review, 425
Science fiction, 123–129
Scope and sequence, 333–343
Scott, Ann, 149, 412
Scott, Jack D., 387
Scott, Sir Walter, 256
Sea, The, 384
Sea Around Us, The, 383
Seabird, 386, 436, 523
Seal-Singing, The, 115

Sea of Gold and Other Tales from Japan, The, 241
Search for Delicious, The, 115
Seashells, 387
"Sea Shell, Sea Shell," 314
Sea Shells of the World, 387
Seashore Story, 516
Seasons, 308–311
Sea Star, Orphan of Chincoteaque, 11
Sebesta, Sam, 28, 213
Sechrist, Elizabeth H., 403, 404, 408
"Secret Cavern, The," 282
Secret Garden, The, 109–110, 494
Secret Name, The, 150, 191, 347
Secret of the Andes, 187, 472, 524
Secret River, The, 524
Seeger, Elizabeth, 520, 407
Seeing Fingers: The Story of Louis Braille, 167
"Seeing the Other Point of View," 475
"Seeing with The Third Eye," 143
Segal, Lore, 72, 78
Seidelman, James E., 398
Selden, George, 86, 106, 136, 139, 525
Self-awareness, 148–152
Self-esteem, 22
Selig, Sylvie, 44
Selsam, Millicent, 382, 389, 397, 425
Sendak, Maurice, 37, 44, 60, 64, 66, 67, 71, 72, 79, 80, 227, 495, 499, 500, 514, 515
Sense of Story, A, 16, 28, 215
Sensory imagery, 281
Seredy, Kate, 512, 520, 521
Serpent and the Sun: Myths of the Mexican World, The, 407
Serraillier, Ian, 253
Seton, Ernest T., 494
Seuss, Dr. (Theodore S. Geisel), 12, 49, 50, 60, 340, 346, 405, 472, 498, 512, 513
Seven Ravens, The, 228
Seven Simeons; A Russian Tale, 240, 510
1776: Year of Independence, 431
Seventeenth-Street Gang, The, 200
Seven Trees, 227
Sewall, Marcia, 233–234
Sewell, Anna, 473, 474, 494
Sewell, Helen, 514
Sex, 199–200, 202, 469–470
Sex education, 82
Sex fair books, 171–177
Sexism, 169–171
Sexism in Education, 213
Sexism in Textbooks Committee of Women at Scott, Foresman, 170
Sex roles, 172
Sex stereotyping, 487
Shadow of a Bull, 152, 159, 210, 526
Shadow on the Sun, The, 115

Shadow on the Water, 158
"Shadows," 485
Shadrach, 524
Shahn, Ben, 6
Shakespeare, William, 85, 304
Shannon, Monica, 520
Shannon, Terry, 384
Sharing books, 18, 20, 76, 350–351
Sharks, 385
Sharmat, Majorie W., 46, 164, 337
Sharp, Margery, 107, 349
Shaw, Richard, 393
Shearer, John, 349, 437
She Come Bringing Me That Little Baby Girl, 439
Sheffield, Margaret, 82
Sheldon, William, 275, 503
Shen of the Sea, 518
Shepard, Ernest H., 65, 88, 89
Shephard, Esther, 263
Sherman, Ivan, 164
Sherwood Ring, The, 142
Shimin, Symeon, 439
Shippen, Katherine, 522, 524
Shoemaker and the Elves, The, 227
Shoeshine Girl, 14
Shoestrings, 75
Shortall, Leonard, 42
Short stories, 342
"Short Talk on Poetry," 322
Shotwell, Louisa R., 180
Showers, Paul, 82, 382
Show Me!, 82
Shrewbettina's Birthday, 75
Shub, Elizabeth, 52, 226
Shulevitz, Uri, 12, 33, 59, 66, 69–70, 240, 353, 516
Shura, Mary F., 180
Shuttlesworth, Dorothy, 42, 395
Sickels, Evelyn R., 262, 364
Sidjakov, Nicholas, 515
Sidney, Margaret, *see* Lathrop, Harriet
Siegfried, 256
Sign, 43
"Signs," 417
Signs and Symbols Around the World, 380
"Silver," 287
Silverberg, Robert, 128
Silver Chair, The, 117
Silver Pencil, The, 522
Silverstein, Shel, 345
Silver Wolf, 388
Simile, 291
Simmons, Gary, 275
Simon, Hilda, 391, 396
Simon, Norma, 149, 407
Simon, Sidney B., 213
Simont, Marc, 60, 513, 514
"Simple Simon," 36
Since Feeling Is First, 275

"Sing a Song of People," 420
Sing Down the Moon, 187, 527
Singer, Isaac, B., 70, 229, 263, 331, 477, 526
Singing Tree, The, 521
Sing in Praise: A Collection of the Best Loved Hymns, 512
Single parent families, 153
Singmaster, Elsie, 520
Sing Mother Goose, 512
Sing Song, 494
Sing to the Dawn, 151
Sioux Indians, 188
Sir Gawain and the Green Knight, 260
Sir Halloween, 400
S Is for Space, 128
Six Foolish Fishermen, 44
Six Silver Spoons, 433
Sketch Book, The, 493
Skiing for Beginners, 398
"Skins," 292
Skin Spinners, The, 135
Skipper John's Cook, 513
Sky Man on the Totem Pole, 128
"Skyscrapers," 418
Slave Dancer, The, 341, 439, 472, 527
Sleator, William, 190, 517
Sleeping Beauty, 35, 226, 228
Sleigh, Barbara, 108
Slobodkin, Louis, 128, 401, 436, 511
Slote, Alfred, 159
Small, Ernest, 238
Small Poems, 315
Small Rain: Verses from the Bible, 511
Small Wolf, 190
"Smells (Junior)," 281, 284
Smith, Carla L., 315
Smith, Doris B., 156, 159, 164, 469
Smith, Doyne M., 488
Smith, E. Brooks, 435
Smith, Hugh, 275
Smith, James S., 372, 474, 503
Smith, William J., 41, 281, 296, 305, 311
Smith, 421
Smoke, 56
Smoke from Cromwell's Time, 135
Smoky, the Cowhorse, 518
Snedeker, Caroline, 519, 520
"Snegourka, the Snow Maiden," 236
Snow White and Rose Red, 227
Snow White and the Seven Dwarfs, 511, 517
Snowy Day, The, 10, 32, 436, 476, 515
Snyder, Zilpha K., 12, 155, 175, 180, 414, 526, 527
Social studies, 308–311
Social studies instruction, 426–465
Solbert, Ronni, 413
Soldier and Tsar in the Forest, 69, 240

Solomon, Louis, 436
Solot, Mary L., 168
Somebody Turned on a Tap in These Kids; Poetry and Young People Today, 322
"Some Fishy Nonsense," 296
Some of the Days of Everett Anderson, 68, 463
"Someone," 338
Something, The, 115
Something for Christmas, 405
Something Queer at the Ball Park, 151
Something Queer Is Going On, 150–151
"Something Told the Wild Geese," 273
"Song of Greatness, A," 284, 485
Song of Robin Hood, 512
Song of the Pines, 523
Song of the Swallows, 513
"Song of the Train," 285–286
Songs for Childhood, 497
Songs of Innocence, 491
Songs of Robin Hood, 258
Songs of '76: A Folksinger's History of the Revolution, 433
Songs of the Dream People, 188, 316
Songs of the Humpback Whales, 385
Sonia Delaunay's Alphabet, 41
"Sonic Boom," 295
Sonneborn, Ruth, 55
Sons of Liberty, 433
Sorenson, Virginia, 524
Sound and Sense; An Introduction to Poetry, 322
Sounder, 159, 438, 478, 526
Sound of Poetry, The, 275
Sound of Sunshine, Sound of Rain, 144, 164
Southall, Ivan, 167
"Southbound on the Freeway," 338
South Dakota, 198
Space Alphabet, 42
Space Cadet, 125
Space Cat, 128
Space Ship under the Apple Tree, 128
Spache, Evelyn B., 372
Spain, 61, 160
Spanish, 52, 193
Spanish folklore, 256
Spanish language, 355
Sparkle and Spin, 378
Sparrows, 392
Speaking, 345–347
Speaking Aids through the Grades, 83, 372
Speare, Elizabeth, 175, 428, 525
Special Trick, A, 79
Sperry, Armstrong, 400, 520, 521
Spice and the Devil's Cave, 519
Spicer, Dorothy G., 404
Spider, the Cave and the Pottery Bowl, The, 190

Spier, Peter, 13, 37, 515
"Spring," 283
Spyri, Johann, 473, 474, 494
"Squirrel, The," 338
Squirrel Wife, The, 229
SST Story, The, 151
Stafford, William, 275
Stamm, Claus, 246
Starbird, Kaye, 292
Star Born, 125
Starlight in Tourrone, 406
Star Mountain and Other Legends of Mexico, 194
Stars Are Ours, The, 125
Star-Spangled Banner, The, 13
State Capital Cities, 411
Steadfast Tin Soldier, The, 514
Steele, Mary Q., 527
Steele, William O., 525
Steel Magic, 261
Steig, William, 59, 81, 170, 386, 516
Steigs, Walter, 45
Steiner, Barbara A., 388
Stephens, William, 383
Steptoe, John, 33, 62, 413, 438, 499
Stereotypes, 80–82, 186–192, 388, 403, 468, 475–477
    combating, 208–211
Stereotyping, 168–177
Stevens, Leonard A., 394
Stevenson, Janet, 176
Stevenson, Robert L., 34, 304, 309–310, 314, 473, 474, 494
Stevie, 33, 62, 438, 499
Stillman, Myra, 395
Still Waters of the Air: Poems by Three Modern Spanish Poets, 195
Stockton, Frank R., 115
Stolz, Mary, 108, 115, 162, 164, 175, 525, 526
Stone, Helen, 512, 513
Stone Cutter, The, 245
Stone-Faced Boy, The, 180
Stoneflight, 342
Stone Soup, 66, 499, 512
Stong, Philip, 49, 520
"Stopping by Woods on a Snowy Evening," 286
Storey, Margaret, 154
Stories, 477
Stories of King Arthur and His Knights, 261
Storm Book, The, 513
Story, A Story, A, 52, 59, 517
Story elements, 327–328
Story of Appleby Capple, The, 523
Story of Babar, The, 47
Story of Dr. Dolittle, The, 87, 476, 497
Story of Ferdinand, The, 61
Story of Helen Keller, The, 165

Story of King Arthur and His Knights, The, 259
Story of Mankind, The, 129, 518
Story of Ping, The, 49
Story of Prince Ivan, the Firebird, and the Gray Wolf, The, 241
Story of the Amulet, The, 111
Story of the Great Chicago Fire, The, 413
Story of the Negro, 523
Storytelling, 233–234, 262–266
Stoutenburg, Adrien, 390
Stranger at Green Knowe, A, 112, 341
Stranger Came Ashore, A, 115
Strawberry Girl, 499, 522
"Straw Ox, The," 236
Strega Nona, 517
String in the Harp, A, 115
Striped Ice Cream, 64, 476
Stuart Little, 133, 134
Stubley, Trevor, 37
Student-centered instruction, 334–341
Student-Centered Language Arts Curriculum, Grades K–6, A, 372
Student involvement, 137
"Studies of the Mass Media," 489
Stuff, 211, 321
Submarines, 387
Suffrage, 174, 175
"Sugar Plum Fairy, The," 494
Sugar Snow Spring, The, 58
Sultan's Bath, The, 52
"Summary of Research Studies Related to Reading Instruction in Elementary Education," 503
Summer Birds, The, 126
Summer Book, The, 177, 203
Summer Is for Growing, 187
"Summer Morning, A," 320
Summer of the Swans, The, 165, 173, 203, 527
Sun Is a Golden Earring, The, 214
Sunlit Sea, The, 384
"Sunshine," 300
Sun Train, The, 476
Supermex: The Lee Trevino Story, 195
Supernatural forces, 386
Supposing, 353, 354
Susette La Flesche: Voice of the Omaha Indians, 191
Sustained Silent Reading, 355–356
Sutherland, Zena, 14, 22, 28, 143, 363
Sutton, Feliz, 433
Swans, 392
Sweet Betsy from Pike, 314
"Sweet Betsy of Pike," 314
Sweet Pea, 440
Swenson, May, 338
Swift, Hildegarde, 519, 520
Swift, Jonathan, 16, 473
Swift Rivers, 428, 435, 520

Swimmy, 62, 78, 515
Swiss Family Robinson, 473, 474, 493, 496
Sword and the Grail, The, 260
Sword in the Stone, The, 261
Sword in the Tree, The, 261
Sword of King Arthur, The, 261
Sword of the Spirits, The, 127
Swords of Steel, 520
Sylvester and the Magic Pebble, 45, 59, 81, 170, 516
Symbolism, 220, 333, 345–346
Symbols, 403–404
Syme, Ronald, 195, 435
Synge, Ursula, 256

Take Joy! The Tasha Tudor Christmas Book, 404
Take Wing, 167
Taking Sides, 199
Talent Is Not Enough, 28
Tale of a Black Cat, The, 72
Tale of Peter Rabbit, The, 46, 496, 497
Tales, 473
Tales from Atop a Russian Stove, 241
Tales from Grimm, 226
Tales from Shakespeare, 474, 493
Tales from Silver Lands, 518
Tales of a Fourth Grade Nothing, 156
Tales of Maui, 249
Tales Told Near a Crocodile, 263
Taliesin and King Arthur, 261
Tall Book of Mother Goose, 35, 63
Tallchief, Maria, 191
Tallow, Robert, 42
Tamarack Tree, The, 175
Tamarin, Alfred, 14
Tangle-Coated Horse and Other Tales, 519
Tannenbaum, Beulah, 395
Taping, 313–314, 347
Taran Wanderer, 122
Tarbell, Ida, 176
Tashima, Taro, 60
Taste of Blackberries, A, 159, 469
Tate, Joan, 470
Taves, Isabella, 175
Taylor, Ann, 493
Taylor, Jane, 298, 493
Taylor, Sidney, 413
Taylor, Theodore, 178
T-Bone, the Baby Sitter, 513
Teacher, 321
Teacher enthusiasm, 483
Teacher preparation, 482–483, 486
"Teacher Questioning and Reading," 488
Teacher's role, 334–335
Teaching, 19–28, 482–483

Teaching for Liberation, 210, 213
Teaching for Social Values in Social Studies, 213
Teaching Literature to Adolescents, Short Stories, 372
"Teaching Literature to Children, 1966–1972," 488
Teasdale, Sara, 320
Teeny-Tiny, 225
Telfer, Dorothy, 384
Tell Me a Mitzi, 72, 78
Ten Big Farms, 44
Tenggren, Gustaf, 37
Tenggren Mother Goose, The, 37
Tennyson, Alfred, 291, 304
Tenth Good Thing about Barney, The, 159
Ten What? A Mystery Counting Book, 44
Terrible Thing That Happened at Our House, The, 153
Terris, Susan, 156
Terry, Ann, 251, 308, 322, 483–486, 489
Thailand, 151
Thane, Adele, 436
Thanksgiving Day, 403
Thanksgiving; Feast and Festival, 403
Thanksgiving Story, The, 403, 514
Thayer, Jane, 174, 405
Their Search for God; Ways of Worship in the Orient, 407
The Me Nobody Knows, 211
Theodore Roosevelt, Fighting Patriot, 524
There Is No Rhyme for Silver, 305
"There Isn't Time," 286
"There once was an old kangaroo," 484
"There once was a witch of Willowby Wood," 288
There's a Nightmare in My Closet, 79
"There was a crooked man," 36, 307
"There was an old man of Blackheath," 296, 484
"These Be — ," 299
These Happy Golden Years, 522
Theseus, 252
They Showed the Way, 441
They Were Strong and Good, 154, 426, 511
Thimble Summer, 521
Think Metric!, 387
This and That and Thus and So, 53
This Is London, 412
"This Is My Rock," 485
This Is New York, 412

This Is Paris, 412
This Is San Francisco, 412
Thistle and Thyme, 525
This Way to Christmas, 406
Thomas, Dylan, 406
Thomas, Marlo, 176
Thompson, Stith, 223
Thompson, Vivian L., 264
Thor and the Giants; An Old Norse Legend, 256
Thor, Last of the Sperm Whales, 385
Thorne-Thomsen, Gudrun, 264, 497
Thousand and One Buddhas, A, 407
Thread One to a Star, 315
Three Bears, The, 225
3 X 3 Three by Three, 44
Three Drops of Water, 394
Three Jovial Huntsmen, 37, 38, 517
Three Little Pigs, The, 225, 339, 359–364
Three on the Run, 204
Three Strong Women; A Tall Tale from Japan, 246
Through the Looking Glass, 87, 493
Thumbelina, 66, 277
Thunderbird and Other Stories, 249
Thunder of the Gods, 256
Thurber, James, 511
Thy Friend, Obadiah, 516
Tibbetts, Sylvia-Lee, 479, 489
Tico and the Golden Wings, 221
Tide Pools and Beaches, 384
Tiedt, Iris M., 28, 78, 210, 213, 236–238, 248, 317–318, 331, 373, 425
Tiedt, Pamela L., 213
Tiedt, Sidney W., 28, 322, 331, 373, 425
Tietjens, Eunice, 281, 519
Tiger and the Rabbit, and Other Tales, The, 263
Tiger Called Thomas, A, 401
Tiger Flower, 71
Tikki Tikki Tembo, 214
Till the Break of Day, 210
Tilted Sombrero, The, 194
Tim All Alone, 51
Time at the Top, 128
Time for Fairy Tales, Old and New, 227
Time for Jody, 46
Time for Poetry, 275
Time of Wonder, 59, 514
Times They Used to Be, The, 162, 437
Timothy Turtle, 512
Tim's Last Voyage, 51
Tinderbox, The, 227
Tinker and the Medicine Man: The Story of a Navajo Boy of Monument Valley, 191
Tin Lizzie, 13

Tiny Toosey's Birthday, 412
Tiost, Lucille W., 390
Tippett, James S., 305, 416, 417, 418
Tituba of Salem Village, 428, 440
Titus, Eve, 25, 50, 64, 107, 514
To Be a Slave, 526
Tobias, Tobi, 191, 441
Toby Tyler, 474
Todd, Barbara, 193
Todd, Ruthven, 128
Tod of the Fens; 519
Token for Children, A, 491
Told in Japan, 241
*Told Under the Green Umbrella; Old
    Stories for New Children,* 230
Told Under the Magic Umbrella, 263
Tolkien, J. R. R., 119, 130, 498, 500
Tolstoy, Leo, 235-6
Tomaino, Sarah F., 252
Tomás and the Red-Haired Angel, 193
Tombs of Atuan, The, 88, 527
*Tomfoolery; Trickery and Foolery with
    Words,* 381
Tom Paine, Freedom's Apostle, 525
Tom Sawyer, 28, 339, 436
"Tom Sawyer, Pirate," 436
Tom's Midnight Garden, 112
Tom Swifties, 340, 381
Tomten and the Fox, 68
Tom Tit Tot, 516
Tom, Tom the Piper's Son, 35
"Tongue-Cut Sparrow, The," 241
Tony, the Steam Shovel Man, 357
Torry, Marjorie, 512
*Tortoise and the Geese and Other Fables of
    Bidpai, The,* 219
Tough Chauncey, 156, 164
Townsend, John R., 16, 28, 215, 503
*Town That Launders Its Water; How a
    California Town Learned to Reclaim
    and Reuse Its Water, The,* 394
"To Your Good Health," 236
"Traffic Sounds," 417
*Tragic Mode in Children's Literature,
    The,* 503
Train Ride, 413, 438
Traveler from a Small Kingdom, 200
Traveling, 308-311
Traven, B., 195
Travers, Pamela, 18, 116, 489
Trease, Geoffrey, 258, 427
Treasure Island, 473, 494
Treasure of Green Knowe, 112
Treasure Seekers. The, 111
*Treasure Seekers and Borrowers;
    Children's Books in Britain,* 503
Treegate, The, 428
Tree in the Trail, 436
Tree Is Nice, A, 514
Tree of Freedom, 428, 523

Tree of Language, 380
Trees, 395-396
*Trees Stand Shining; Poetry of the North
    American Indians, The,* 189
Treffinger, Carolyn, 523
Tresselt, Alvin, 56, 64, 78, 241, 411,
    512, 516
Trevino, Lee, 195
Trick or Treat, 401
*Tricks of Eye and Hand; The Story of
    Optical Illusion,* 398
"Trip, A", 416
Triplet, 294-296
Tripp, Wallace, 24
Triumph of the Seeing Eye, The, 167
Trost, Marion, 489
Trouble with Terry, The, 64
*Truce of the Wolf and Other Tales of Old
    Italy,* 520
Trumpeter of Krakow, The, 519
Trumpet of the Swan, The, 133
Truth about Mary Rose, The, 156
*Tsar's Riddles or The Wise Little Girl,
    The,* 240
Tucker, Nicholas, 37
Tudor, Tasha, 37, 42, 44, 401, 404,
    405, 406, 512, 514
"Tulips," 296
Tuned Out, 470
Tunis, Edwin, 525
Tunnel in the Sky, 123
Turk, Midge, 441
Turkle, Brinton, 152, 516
Turnabout, 53
Turner, Ann W., 392
Turner, John F., 391
Turnip, The, 240
Turska, Krystyna, 52
Tusya and the Pot of Gold, 241
Twain, Mark, see Clemens, Samuel L.
Twelve Dancing Princesses, The, 227
Twelve Labors of Hercules, The, 253
Twenty-One Balloons, The, 112-113,
    130, 523
Twenty Thousand Leagues Under the Sea,
    474
Twins, 166
*Twister of Twists, A Tangler of Tongues,
    A,* 381
Twist, Wiggle and Squirm, 57, 396
Two Hundred Rabbits, 109
Two Lonely Ducks, 44
Two Piano Tuners, 174
2-Rabbit, 7 Wind, 195
Two Reeds, The, 513
Two Years before the Mast, 473
Tyrant Who Became a Just Ruler, The,
    219

Uchida, Yoshiko, 25, 241, 405

Udry, Janice, 55, 72, 67, 514, 515
Ugly Duckling, The, 474
Ugly Palaces: Housing in America, The,
    412
Ukrainian folklore, 240
Ukrainian Folk Tales, 240
Ullman, James, 524
"Umbrella Brigade, The," 279
Uncle Mike's Boy, 160
Uncle Remus, His Songs and Sayings, 494
Understandings, 328
Undertaker Goes Bananas, The, 201
Underwood, Betty, 175
Ungerer, Tomi, 52, 221
United States folklore, 256
"U.S.A.," 430
Universals, 222
Unkelback, Kurt, 397
Unmarried mother, 199-200
Untermeyer, Louis, 287
Unwin, Nora, 87
Up a Road Slowly, 526
Updike, John, 295, 302
Upstairs Room, The, 527
Uptown, 438
Uschold, Maude E., 291
Uses of Enchantment, The, 222
U.S. Frogmen of World War II, The, 387
Us Maltbys, 152
USSR, 355-356

"Vagabond Song, A," 283
Vaisso, 519
Valley of the Smallest, 383
Valuing, 335-336
Vanderbilt, Sanderson, 485
*Vanishing Thunder; Extinct and
    Threatened American Birds, The,*
    390
Van Loon, Hendrick W., 129, 519
Van Stockum, Hilda, 520
"Vasilisa the Beautiful," 236, 241
Vasiliu, 380
Vavara, Robert, 71
Veckor över Tiden, The, 470
Velveteen Rabbit, The, 108, 145
"Velvet Shoes," 333
Verne, Jules, 474
Veronica Ganz, 158, 175
Verse, 299
Very Special House, A, 514
Vevers, Gwynne, 389
Vicki, 76
Victoria, 164
Viguers, Ruth H., 503
Viollet, 115
Viorst, Judith, 159
Visit from St. Nicholas, A, 493
Viva Chicano, 193

Vlahos, Olivia, 192
Vogel, John, Jr., 412
Voice choir, 311–312
Voyage of the "Dawn Treader," The, 117
Voyagers, 518
Voyages of Christopher Columbus, The, 400
Voyages of Doctor Dolittle, The, 130, 518
Vulcan, 251
Vultures, 392

Waber, Bernard, 47, 398, 466
Wagner, Joseph A., 267
Wales, 151
Walking Stones, The, 115
Waller, Leslie, 380
Wallner, John C., 153, 164
Wally the Wordworm, 380
"Walrus and the Carpenter, The," 281
Walsh, Chad, 287
Walter, Mildred, 156
Walter, Nina, 322
Walters, Marguerite, 42
Walter the Lazy Mouse, 107
Waltzing Matilda, 314
Warburg, Sandol S., 158, 161
Ward, Lynd, 48, 50, 60, 432, 436, 513
Ward, Martha E., 83
Warrior Goddess: Athena, The, 253
Watchers, The, 167
Watch the Tides, 384
Water, 376
Waterbabies, The, 87, 473, 474, 493
Waterless Mountain, 519
Water pollution, 394
Water: Riches or Ruin, 394
Watership Down, 49
Watts, Isaac, 492
Wave, The, 244–245, 516
Waves, 384
Waves, Tides, and Currents, 384
Way of an Ant, The, 374, 389
Way of Danger; The Story of Theseus, The, 253
Weather, 308
Weathermakers, The, 128
Weathermonger, The, 127
Webster, Noah, 491
Wee Gillis, 510
Weik, Mary H., 167, 526
Weil, Ann, 524
Weirdstone of Brisingamen, The, 114
Weisgard, Leonard, 60, 64, 403, 512
Weiss, Malcomb E., 384
Weitzman, Lenore J., 81
Weland; Smith of the Gods, 256
Welsh folklore, 151
Wernecke, Herbert H., 404
Westermark, Tory, 276

Weston, Christine, 522
Wezel, Peter, 76
Whale People, The, 386
Whaler 'Round the Horn, 386
Whales, 385
Whales: Their Life in the Sea, 385
Whaling, 385–386
What Can I Do?, 149
What Can She Be? A Lawyer, 56, 174
What Can You Do With a Shoe?, 67
"What Children Choose to Read and What They Have to Read," 489
What Children Read in School: Critical Analysis of Primary Reading Textbooks, 489
What Do You Do, Dear?, 67
What Do You Say, Dear?, 64, 67, 353, 515
What Good Is a Weed? Ecology in Action, 396
What Happens to Garbage?, 394
What Is a City? A Multi-media Guide on Urban Living, 412
"What Is a Hamburgler?," 6–10
"What is orange?," 306–307
"What is poetry?," 272
What It's All About, 199
What Kind of Feet Does a Bear Have?, 380
What's Fun without a Friend?, 55
What's New in Reading?, 373
What's New, Lincoln?, 412
"What Then, Raman?," 348
What Whiskers Did, 73
Wheeler, Opal, 512
Wheel on the Chimney, 514
Wheel on the School, The, 524
When Clay Sings, 190, 517
"When Mummy Slept Late and Daddy Cooked Breakfast," 298
When Schemiel Went to Warsaw and Other Stories, 526
When the Sad One Comes to Stay, 157
When the Whale Came to My Town, 386
When We Were Very Young, 30
When Will the World Be Mine?, 514
Where Do Babies Come From?, 82
Where Language Came from and Where It Is Going, 378
Where's Daddy?, 157
Where the Lilies Bloom, 160, 197, 350, 499
Where the Wild Things Are, 67, 79, 499, 500, 515
Where Was Patrick Henry on the 29th of May?, 432
Whispering Mountain, The, 135
Whispering Wind, The, 188
"Whispers," 291
Whispers and Other Poems, 291

Whistle for Willie, 11, 32
Whistler's Van, 520
White, Anne T., 383
White, E. B., 5, 133, 328, 499, 524
White, T. H., 261
White Bird, 152
"White Hare and the Crocodiles, The," 241
Whitehead, Ruth, 160
White Horse Gang, The, 204
White Land, The, 35
White Snow, Bright Snow, 64, 512
White Stag, The, 521
White Stallion of Lipizza, 11
Whitman, Walt, 282, 301, 304, 341
Whitney, Elinor, 519
Whitney, Thomas P., 241
Whittier, John G., 494
Who Cares? I Do, 394
Who Goes There?, 49
"Who has seen the wind?," 309, 338
Who's There, Open the Door, 2
Who's Who in the Animal World?, 47
Why Did He Die?, 161
Why Mosquitoes Buzz in People's Ears, 59, 517
Why the Sun and the Moon Live in the Sky; An African Folktale, 249, 516
Wibberly, Leonard, 428
Wiberg, J. Lawrence, 489
Widdemer, Margaret, 282
Wier, Ester, 526
Wiese, Kurt, 60, 512, 513
Wiesner, William, 53
Wiggin, Kate D., 406
Wikland, Ilon, 405
Wild Animals I Have Known, 494
Wild Birthday Cake, The, 513
Wilder, Laura I., 176, 348, 428, 477, 498, 521, 522
Wilderness Clearing, 428
Wildsmith, Brian, 3, 32, 33, 37, 44, 220, 499
Wilkinson, Brenda, 150, 440
William C. Handy, 441
Williams, Barbara, 55, 150, 191, 347
Williams, Garth, 44, 47, 106, 107, 133–134
Williams, Jay, 62, 114, 128, 261
Williams, Jeanne, 151
Williams, Jerome, 384
Williams, John A., 441
Williams, Margery, 145
Williams, Ursula M., 175
Williams, William C., 304, 485
William's Doll, 53
Will I Have a Friend?, 163
Wilson, Charles M., 191
Wilson, Forrest, 411
Wilson, Mike, 387

"Wind," 272
"Wind, The," 309
"Wind Colors the World," 269
"Wind Has Such a Rainy Sound, The," 314
Wind in the Willows, The, 49, 65, 89, 497
Winds, 268, 269
"Wind Weather," 310
"Wind-Wolves," 310, 341
Windy Hill, 518
"Windy Morning," 309
"Windy Nights," 309–310
Winged Girl of Knossos, 520
Wingspread; A World of Birds, 390
Winnie-the-Pooh, 65, 86, 88, 498
Winslow, Marjorie, 72
Winter at Valley Forge, The, 432
Winterbound, 521
Winter Wheat, 151
Wiseman, Ann, 398
Wishes, Lies and Dreams, 304, 308, 322
Wisner, William, L., 385
Witches of Worm, The, 155–156, 180, 527
Witch of Blackbird Pond, The, 175, 428, 525
Witch of Fourth Street and Other Stories, The, 413
Witch's Daughter, The, 204
Witch trials, 440
Witch Who Wasn't, The, 401, 402
Witcracks; Jokes and Jests from American Folklore, 381
With a Wig, With a Wag, and Other American Folk Tales, 263
Withers, Carl, 66, 72
Witty, Paul, 486, 489
Wizard of Oz, The, 87, 350, 496, 497
Wojciechowsha, Maia, 152, 210, 470, 526
Wolf, Bernard, 146, 166, 191
Wolf, Willovene, 482, 489
Wolf, The, 388
Wolf and the Seven Kids, The, 229
Wolf of My Own, A, 174
Wolkstein, Diane, 53
Wolves, 388
Wolves of Willoughby, The, 135
Woman of the Wood, The, 68
Women, 80–82, 169–177, 189
Women, positive images, 476–477
Women on Words and Images, 487, 489

Women's Rights, 176
Women's Rights
careers, 56–57
Women's Rights: The Suffrage Movement in America 1848–1920, 175
Wonderful Farm, The, 108
Wonderful Flight to the Mushroom Planet, 128
Wonderful Story of How You Were Born, The, 82
Wonderful, Terrible Time, A, 164, 175
Wonderful World of the Sea, The, 384
Wonderful Year, 522
Wonder-Smith and His Son, The, 519
Wonders of a Kelp Forest, 386
Wonders of Hummingbirds, 391
Wood, Nancy, 189
Woodward, Hildegard, 512
Woolsey, Janette, 403
Wordless books, 73–76
Word play, 289–290
Words, 6–10, 419
Words and Calligraphy for Children, 380
Words from the Myths, 246–247, 380
Words in Genesis, 380
Words of Science and the History Behind Them, 380
Words on the Map, 380
Word study, 378–381
Words Words Words, 307, 380
Wordsworth, William, 304
World Almanac, 422
Worlds to Come, 128
Worth, Valerie, 315
Wrice, Herman, 440
Wright, Blanche F., 37
Wright, Richard, 396, 441
Wrightson, Patricia, 167
Wrinkle in Time, A, 125, 130, 333, 499, 500, 525
Writers, Critics and Children, 213
Writer's Market, 45
Writing, 11–12, 317, 352–354, 356–358
"Writing about Science for Children," 425
Writing competencies, 138
Written for Children: An Outline of English Children's Literature, 503
Wiggly Ump, The, 79
Wyatt, Edgar, 191
Wyeth, N. C., 259
Wylie, Elinor, 333

Wynne, Annette, 296
Wyss, Johann, 473, 474, 493

Yamaguchi, Tobr, 246, 393
Yankee Doodle's Literary Sampler of Prose, Poetry & Pictures, 503
Yaroslava, 240, 241
Yashima, Taro, 61, 514, 515, 516
Yates, Elizabeth, 203, 441, 516
Yates, Raymond F., 397
Year of Columbus, 400
Year of Small Shadow, The, 190
Yep, Lawrence, 528
Yershov, P., 241
Yiddish folklore, 70
Yolen, Jane, 53, 64, 401, 402, 516
Yonie Wondernose, 512
You Can Write Chinese, 512
You Come, Too, 342
You Don't Look Like Your Mother, 46
Young and Female, 176
Young, Ed, 516
Young, Ella, 519
Young Fu of the Upper Yangtze, 520
Young Fur Trader, The, 493
Young, Jim, 386
Young Mac of Fort Vancouver, 521
Young, Miriam, 174
Young Walter Scott, 520
Young Women's Guide to Liberation, 175
You Read to Me, I'll Read to You, 484

Zacks, Irene, 42
Zeely, 439
Zemach, Harve, 59, 64–65, 241, 328, 516, 517
Zemach, Margot, 59, 64–65, 241, 328, 516, 517
Zeus, 251, 253
Z for Zachariah, 127
Ziegler, Elsie B., 267
Zim, Herbert, 161, 341, 350, 382, 384, 390
Zimet, Sara F., 479, 489
Zindel, Paul, 149, 160, 173, 201–202, 336
Zion, Gene, 513
Zlateh the Goat and Other Stories, 263, 526
Zolotow, Charlotte, 12, 44, 53–54, 152, 159, 164, 168, 401, 476, 513, 515
Zoophabets, 42

ABCDEFGHIJ–H–798